PATHWAYS

SCENARIOS FOR SENTENCE AND PARAGRAPH WRITING

PATHWAYS

SCENARIOS FOR SENTENCE AND PARAGRAPH WRITING

Fourth Edition

KATHLEEN T. McWHORTER

Niagara County Community College

PEARSON

Boston   Columbus   Hoboken   Indianapolis   New York   San Francisco
Amsterdam   Cape Town   Dubai   London   Madrid   Milan   Munich   Paris   Montreal   Toronto
Delhi   Mexico City   São Paulo   Sydney   Hong Kong   Seoul   Singapore   Taipei   Tokyo

Executive Acquisitions Editor: Matthew Wright
Program Manager: Anne Shure
Senior Development Editors: Gillian Cook and Janice Wiggins
Product Marketing Manager: Jennifer Edwards
Senior Field Marketing Manager: John Meyers
Executive Digital Producer: Stefanie Snajder
Content Specialist: Erin E. Jenkins
Project Manager: Donna Campion

Project Coordination, Text Design, and Electronic Page Makeup: Lumina Datamatics, Inc.
Program Design Lead: Heather Scott
Cover Designer: Studio Montage
Cover Photo: Jiraphoto/Shutterstock
Senior Manufacturing Buyer: Roy L. Pickering, Jr.
Printer/Binder: Courier/Kendallville
Cover Printer: Courier/Kendallville

Acknowledgments of third-party content appear on pages **583–587**, which constitute an extension of this copyright page.

PEARSON, ALWAYS LEARNING, and MYWRITINGLAB are exclusive trademarks owned by Pearson Education Inc. or its affiliates in the United States and/or other countries.

Unless otherwise indicated herein, any third-party trademarks that may appear in this work are the property of their respective owners and any references to third-party trademarks, logos, or other trade dress are for demonstrative or descriptive purposes only. Such references are not intended to imply any sponsorship, endorsement, authorization, or promotion of Pearson's products by the owners of such marks, or any relationship between the owner and Pearson Education, Inc., or its affiliates, authors, licensees, or distributors.

Library of Congress Cataloging-in-Publication Data
McWhorter, Kathleen T.
  Pathways : scenarios for sentence and paragraph writing / Kathleen T. Mcwhorter, Niagara County Community College.—Fourth Edition.
    pages cm
  ISBN 978-0-321-97416-7
1. English language—Rhetoric—Problems, exercises etc. 2. English language—Sentences—Problems, exercises etc. 3. English language—Paragraphs—Problems, exercises etc. 4. Report writing—Problems, exercises, etc. 5. Critical thinking. 6. College readers. I. Title.
  PE1417.M4565 2015
  808'.0427—dc23   2014045815

www.pearsonhighered.com

Student Edition ISBN 10: 0-321-97416-6
Student Edition ISBN 13: 978-0-321-97416-7
A la Carte ISBN 10: 0-321-98480-3
A la Carte ISBN 13: 978-0-321-98480-7

Brief Contents

Detailed Contents

PART V ESSAY BASICS, DEVELOPMENT, AND COMMON PROBLEMS 438

Preface

Pathways: Scenarios for Sentence and Paragraph Writing teaches fundamental sentence, paragraph, and essay writing skills by engaging student interest, stressing the interconnection of the reading and writing processes, and maintaining a focus on expressing ideas rather than on following rules.

OVERVIEW OF THE TEXT

This book focuses on presenting the study of grammar and the study of the "whole paper" as inseparable. Seven of *Pathways'* 17 chapters deal with grammar topics; in these chapters, students examine student essays, read and respond to ideas, and write and revise paragraphs. In Parts II through IV, students are encouraged to apply what they have learned about sentence-level correctness to their own writing as they explore logical paragraph development and organization of ideas. The last two chapters of the book provide an introduction to essay writing, enabling students to make the transition from paragraphs to essays. This lively, integrated approach leads to greater student interest and better, more fully assimilated writing skills.

Chapters 2–17 of *Pathways* each contain a brief, high-interest professional reading that sets up opportunities for writing and relates the chapter's lesson to the student's own work. These readings encourage students to think about, discuss, and consider their own experiences, and to respond to what they read by writing, strengthening their confidence in the value and worth of their ideas. Many chapters also include sample student essays that serve as realistic models of student writing. "A Thematic Reader," Part VI, provides extra opportunities to explore the reading-writing connection. Through the readings and the accompanying apparatus, the text stresses that effective writing must evolve from student interest and experience.

NEW TO THE FOURTH EDITION

The goals of this revision were to strengthen the reading-writing connection by including an interactive thinking guide with each professional reading, a new Thematic Reader, and two new workshops that focus on visual and digital literacy as applied to writing essays, as well as new and engaging in-chapter professional and student essays. The fourth edition offers the following new features.

■ **NEW Think as You Read** Many students fail to interact with text as they read. Instead, they allow ideas to pass in front of them—without engaging with them, without taking them from the page or screen and subjecting them to examination and analysis. This edition offers a unique Think as You Read feature that demonstrates to students the thought processes that should occur while reading. Marginal questions interspersed throughout each professional reading model the thinking that should occur during reading. These questions may encourage students to connect the reading to their own experience, examine the flow of ideas, recognize connections between and among ideas and images, or analyze the writer's technique, for example.

Questions guide students in the areas listed below.

- ***Activating Prior Knowledge*** *questions ask students to discover what they already know about the topic of the reading.*
- ***Previewing*** *questions ask students what they have learned about the content and organization of the reading based on their preview.*
- ***Predicting*** *questions ask students to follow the author's train of thought and anticipate what is to follow.*
- ***Examining Features of Writing*** *questions ask students to consider the impact and usefulness of such writing features as the introduction, thesis, and conclusion of the reading.*
- ***Factual Recall*** *questions ask students specific facts about the reading to strengthen their understanding.*
- ***Critical Analysis*** *questions ask students to interpret and evaluate the author's ideas.*
- ***Word Meaning and Choice*** *questions ask students to consider the choice of words used in a reading and/or the positive or negative connotations of those words.*
- ***Visual and Image*** *questions ask students to consider the meaning of the visual or image that accompanies the reading and consider other appropriate choices.*

Thinking while reading strengthens factual recall, promotes critical thinking, and enables students to generate ideas to write about. This guide, by modeling the types of thinking that should occur while reading, will enable students to develop their own questions and become active readers, prepared to write in response to reading.

■ ***NEW Part VI: A Thematic Reader.*** The previous multicultural reader has been replaced with three pairs of themed readings that offer students interesting topics to write about and provide instructors with alternative reading and writing assignments. The themes include dating and relationships, surveillance and the right to privacy, and bullying. Each theme concludes with a section, "Critical Reading and Writing: Integrating Ideas," which encourages students to analyze and synthesize ideas.

■ ***NEW Writers' Workshops on Using Visuals in Student Writing.*** Print and electronic sources, including textbooks, are becoming increasingly visual, and writing instructors are encouraging students to incorporate visuals into their own writing. In response to these trends, this set of workshops emphasizes

- the function of visuals in text.
- the use of visuals to support student writing.
- methods for finding effective visuals.
- ethical use of visuals.
- context and captions to accompany visuals.

■ ***NEW Writers' Workshops on Digital Literacy.*** Because digital literacy is now expected of all college students, a new set of workshops equip beginning college writers with skills, strategies, and resources for online writing and research. The workshops include

- basic need-to-know information and sources of help with computer literacy.
- strategies for evaluating online sources.

- advice for effective online communication and self-presentation.
- useful Web sites for college writers.

■ **_NEW Professional Readings._** Eight new professional readings have been added. Topics include the allocation of donor kidneys, arranged marriages in Afghanistan, the ethics of killing in war, parenthood, sports, food waste in America, going off the technology grid, and lying.

■ **_NEW Student Essays._** Eight new student essays demonstrate the skills taught in the relevant chapters and present good models of academic writing. The essays engage students with current issues such as reality TV, professional athletes as role models, social media, and post-graduation employment.

■ **_NEW Online Mastery Tests in MyWritingLab._** For each chapter, an online mastery test is available to use for additional practice or assessment.

■ **_NEW Handbook Exercises in MyWritingLab._** These exercises link the handbook to supplemental online exercises for numerous topics within Part VII, "Reviewing the Basics."

■ **_NEW!_** The *Pathways 4e MyWritingLab/etext* course now includes a book-specific module where students can complete activities, practice sets, and writing assignments from the print book right in MyWritingLab! Just look for the MyWritingLab icon throughout all the chapters!

MyWritingLab™

■ **_NEW! Accelerate to Essays!_** The *Pathways 4e MyWritingLab/etext* course now offers access to *Expressways: Scenarios for Paragraph and Essay Writing* 3e essays chapters enabling students to accelerate to higher order content at any point in time!

FEATURES

The following features further distinguish *Pathways* from other developmental writing texts and make its approach unique:

■ **_Emphasis on Reading Skills._** Chapter 2 presents strategies for active reading that include previewing, connecting to prior knowledge, reading to learn, using idea maps to understand a reading, understanding difficult readings, and responding to readings using highlighting and annotating. Chapter 3 focuses on vocabulary development including using a dictionary, using context and word parts to figure out unfamiliar words, and developing a system for learning new words. Reading skills are emphasized throughout the text using professional readings in every chapter. Each professional reading includes an interactive thinking guide ("Think As You Read"), which models thinking and interacting with ideas while reading.

■ **_Visual Approach to Writing._** Many students are visual learners and respond well to diagrams, charts, and maps. In *Pathways*, students learn to draw idea maps—visual representations of the content and organization of a paragraph or essay—in order to examine ideas as well as revision maps of their own writing as a way to evaluate the effectiveness of the content and organization and to help them make any necessary changes. Sections that feature idea or revision maps are labeled "Visualize It!"

■ **_Focus on Critical Thinking._** The text emphasizes the role and benefits of critical thinking in the writing process. Chapter 2 addresses specific skills. Then each full-length reading offers opportunities for application and practice.

■ **_Paragraph Writing Scenarios._** Each of Chapters 4–17 contains a set of writing assignments grouped into four categories—friends and family, classes and campus life, working students, and communities and cultures—that give students the opportunity to apply chapter content while exploring a relevant theme.

■ ***Emphasis on Grammar and Correctness.*** Seven chapters are devoted to grammar topics. Part VII, "Reviewing the Basics," is a handbook that provides a simple, clear presentation of the forms and rules of grammar, plentifully illustrated with examples, and includes ample exercises for review of skills.

■ ***Writers' Workshops.*** Two sets of workshops, "Using Words Effectively" and "Using Language Effectively" offer opportunities for immediate skill improvement. Two new sets of workshops, "Digital Literacy in the Wired Classroom" and "Using Visuals in Your Writing," offer students skills and strategies for improving digital and visual literacy.

■ ***Interconnected Writing in Progress Exercises.*** These exercises build on each other throughout the course of each chapter, walking students through the different steps of the writing process from prewriting through drafting, writing using different modes, and revision.

■ ***"Working Together" Exercises.*** Throughout the text, these collaborative exercises provide opportunities for students to learn and practice skills together and to learn from one another.

■ ***Student Essays.*** Chapter 1 and all the chapters in Parts IV and V each contain a sample student essay that provides a model of the writing process and sets realistic, attainable expectations for students. Each essay is annotated and is followed by questions that guide students in evaluating the essay.

■ ***High-Interest, Engaging Readings.*** Beginning with Chapter 2, each chapter includes a professional reading around which prewriting, critical thinking, and writing assignments are structured. Readings are on topics such as image and the media, genetic testing, biomechanics, sweatshops at sea, and electronic waste. Each reading offers students a model for the writing skills taught in the particular chapter, as well as a source of ideas and a base for discussion and collaborative learning activities.

MyWritingLab™ Resources for Students and Instructors

MyWritingLab

Where practice, application, and demonstration meet to improve writing.

MyWritingLab, a complete online learning program, provides additional resources and effective practice exercises for developing writers. MyWritingLab accelerates learning through layered assessment and a personalized learning path utilizing the Knewton Adaptive Learning Platform™, which customizes standardized educational content to piece together the perfect personalized bundle of content for each student. With over eight thousand exercises and immediate feedback to answers, the integrated learning aids of MyWritingLab reinforce learning throughout the semester.

What makes MyWritingLab more effective?

Diagnostic Testing: MyWritingLab's diagnostic Path Builder test comprehensively assesses students' skills in grammar. Students are provided with an individualized learning path based on the diagnostic's results, identifying the areas where they most need help.

Progressive Learning: The heart of MyWritingLab is the progressive learning that takes place as students complete the Overview, Animation, Recall, Apply, and Write exercises along with the Post-test within each topic. Students move from preparation (Overview, Animation) to literal comprehension (Recall) to critical understanding (Apply) to the ability to demonstrate a skill in their own writing (Write) to total mastery (Post-test). This progression of critical thinking enables students to truly master the skills and concepts they need to become successful writers.

Online Gradebook: All student work in MyWritingLab is captured in the Online Gradebook. Instructors can see what and how many topics their students have mastered. They can also view students' individual scores on all assignments throughout MyWritingLab, as well as overviews by student, and class performance by module. Students can monitor their progress in new Completed Work pages, which show them their totals, scores, time on task, and the date and time of their work by module.

MyWritingLab™

A Deeper Connection between Print and Media: The MyWritingLab logo (show logo) is used throughout the book to indicate exercises and writing activities that can be completed and submitted through MyWritingLab (appropriate results flow directly to the Instructor Gradebook).

Professional Development

Pearson offers a variety of professional development programs and resources to support full- and part-time instructors. These include Pedagogy & Practice, an open-access digital resource gallery [http://pedagogyandpractice.pearsonhighered.com/], and our Speaking About English online conference series, featuring scholar/educators addressing pedagogical topics via web-based presentations. These conferences are held twice a year and are free of cost to attend. Information about future conferences, as well as archives of past sessions, can be found on the conference website [http://www.pearsonhighered.com/speakingabout/english/]. Updated information about any and all of these Partnership Programs can always be found on our catalog page [http://www.pearsonhighered.com/english/].

Annotated Instructor's Edition for *Pathways: Scenarios for Sentence and Paragraph Writing* (ISBN 0321984765/9780321984760)

The Annotated Instructor's Edition for *Pathways* is identical to the student edition except that it includes the answers to all the exercises.

Instructor's Resource Manual & Test Bank for *Pathways: Scenarios for Sentence and Paragraph Writing* (ISBN 0321984757/9780321984753)

This supplement, written by Joanna Chrzanowski, is full of useful teaching suggestions and includes an introduction to the textbook, activities to engage students' interest, advice to new instructors, and additional writing assignments. The manual also offers suggestions for handling the professional readings, sample syllabi, overhead transparencies, and a full bank of test questions.

PowerPoint Presentation for *Pathways: Scenarios for Sentence and Paragraph Writing* (ISBN 0321984609/9780321984609)

Joanna Chrzanowski has created PowerPoint presentations to accompany each chapter of Pathways and consists of classroom ready lecture outline slides, lecture tips, classroom activities, and review questions.

Answer Key for *Pathways: Scenarios for Sentence and Paragraph Writing* (ISBN 0321984676/9780321984678)

The Answer Key contains the solutions to the exercises in the student edition of the text.

The Pearson Writing Package

Pearson is pleased to offer a variety of support materials to help make teaching writing easier for teachers and to help students excel in their coursework. Many of our student supplements are available free or at a greatly reduced price when packaged with *Pathways: Scenarios for Sentence and Paragraph Writing*. Visit http://www.pearsonhighereducation.com, contact your local Pearson sales representative, or review a detailed listing of the full supplements package in the *Instructor's Manual* for more information.

ACKNOWLEDGMENTS

I appreciate the excellent ideas, suggestions, and advice of my colleagues who served as reviewers:

Julie Armbrecht, Truckee Meadows Community College; Andrew Ball, Malcolm X College; Craig Barthalomaus, Metropolitan Community College–Penn Valley; Sharon Bone, Ivy Tech Community College–Central Indiana; Cheyenne Bonnell, Copper Mountain College; Frieda Campbell-Peltier, Portland Community College; Elissa Caruth, Oxnard College; Irene Caswell, Lander University; Kristyn Clark, Ridgewater College; Jennie Donovan, Full Sail University; Laura Foster-Eason, Collin County Community College; Susan Fuchs, Kellogg Community College; Jean Garrett, Mt. San Antonio College; Joanne Giordano, University of Wisconsin; Marcia Glasgow, Ranger College; Karen Glass, Aiken Technical College; Joan Grimes, East Central Community College; John Grosskopf, North Florida Community College; Janet Harclerode, Santa Monica College; Eric Hibbison, J. Sargeant Reynolds Community College; Catheryn Jennings, Virginia College Tulsa; Cheryta Jones, Southwest Tennessee Community College; Mark Knockemus, Northeastern Technical College; Kathryn Lane, Northwestern Oklahoma State University; Anne Mattrella, Naugatuck Valley Community College; Elise McKenna, Full Sail University; Melissa Michelson, Santa Monica College; Elizabeth Mills, Central

Piedmont Community College; Jan Tolar Modisette, Jacksonville College; Lisa Moreno, LA Trade Technical College; Mary Nielsen, Dalton State College; Maria Palazzolo, City Colleges of Chicago; Carmen Parks, Chesapeake College; Jody Ragsdale, Northeast Alabama Community College; Tim Reding, Morehead State University; Samuel Rush, Malcolm X College; Karin Russell, Keiser University; Jim Schwartz, Wright State University; Marcea K. Seible, Hawkeye Community College; Hayley Sogren, Keiser University; Shari Waldrop, Navarro College; Heather Weiss, Technical County of the Lowcountry; Eleanor Welsh, Chesapeake College; Elizabeth White, Itawamba Community College; and Audrey Wick, Blinn College.

The entire editorial staff with whom I have worked deserves praise and credit for its assistance throughout the writing and revision of this text. In particular, I wish to thank Matthew Wright, executive editor, for his enthusiastic support throughout the project and Gillian Cook and Janice Wiggins, development editors, whose knowledge of the field, creative energy, and organizational abilities kept me on target throughout the revision. I also thank Kathy Tyndall for her professional advice and support and Phoebe Mathews for her assistance with manuscript preparation. I also appreciate the willingness of the following students to provide samples of their writing for the paragraph samples and student essays:

Claire Stroupe, Jessica Nantka, Jacob Frey, Jessica Beebe, Sarah Frey, Aurora Gilbert, Amanda Keithley, Chase Beauclair, and Catherine Lee.

I also value the professional and creative efforts of Lindsay Bethoney and her team at Lumina Datamatics. Finally, I thank my students, who have made teaching a challenging and rewarding profession.

KATHLEEN T. MCWHORTER

PATHWAYS

SCENARIOS FOR SENTENCE AND PARAGRAPH WRITING

1

An Introduction to Writing

WRITE ABOUT IT!

In the photo above, the student at the computer is writing an assigned essay. Write a few sentences describing what that student might be feeling, using your own experiences with writing as a guide. What problems might she be facing? What things can she do well? What are her trouble spots?

For problems and trouble spots, did you identify problems such as not knowing what to write about, not knowing what to say, or problems catching and correcting spelling and grammar errors?

This book will address common writing problems and help you improve your writing. It will concentrate on writing as a means of expressing ideas. You will learn to plan, organize, and develop your ideas. You will learn to write sentences and paragraphs that express your ideas clearly and effectively. You will also learn how to avoid common problems writing paragraphs and sentences. Finally, after you have expressed your ideas, you will discover that grammar, punctuation, and spelling do have an important function in writing.

WRITING

UNDERSTANDING WHAT WRITING IS AND IS NOT

GOAL 1 Use the writing process

The following list explains some correct and incorrect notions about writing:

Writing is . . .

- following a step-by-step process of planning, drafting, and revising.
- thinking through and organizing ideas.
- explaining *your* ideas or experiences clearly and correctly.
- using precise, descriptive, and accurate vocabulary.
- constructing clear, understandable sentences.
- a skill that can be learned.

Writing is not . . .

- being able to pick up a pen (or sit at a computer) and write something wonderful on your first try.
- developing new, earthshaking ideas no one has ever thought of before.
- being primarily concerned with grammatical correctness.
- showing off a large vocabulary.
- constructing long, complicated sentences.

EXERCISE 1-1   Describing the Writing Process

Directions: Suppose you are writing a letter to a toy manufacturer about a defective toy you purchased for your niece or nephew. You feel the toy is unsafe for toddlers. Describe, step by step, how you would go about writing this letter. (What is the first thing you would do? What would you do after that? And so forth.) You are not actually writing the letter in this exercise or listing what you would say. You are describing your writing *process*. ■

The Writing Process: An Overview

Writing, like many other skills, is not a single-step process. Think of the game of football, for instance. Football players spend a great deal of time planning and developing offensive and defensive strategies, trying out new plays, improving existing plays, and practicing. Writing involves similar planning and preparation. It also involves testing ideas and working out the best way to express them. Writers often explore how their ideas might "play out" in several ways before settling upon one plan of action.

People have many individual techniques for writing, but all writing involves five basic steps, as shown in Table 1-1.

TABLE 1-1

Steps in the Writing Process	Description of Steps
1. **Generating ideas**	Finding ideas to write about
2. **Organizing your ideas**	Discovering ways to arrange your ideas logically
3. **Writing a first draft**	Expressing your ideas in sentence and paragraph form without worrying about spelling, punctuation, capitalization, and grammar
4. **Revising**	Rethinking your ideas and finding ways to make your writing clearer, more complete, and more interesting. Revising involves changing, adding, deleting, and rearranging your ideas and words to make your writing better
5. **Proofreading**	Checking for errors in grammar, spelling, punctuation, and capitalization

NEED TO KNOW
The Writing Process

- Writing is a step-by-step process of explaining your ideas and experiences.
- Writing involves five basic steps: generating ideas, organizing your ideas, writing a first draft, revising, and proofreading.

Tip for Writers

A *draft* is a piece of writing that is not finished.

Revising is the process of rethinking your ideas. It involves adding ideas, deleting ideas, rearranging ideas, and changing the way you have expressed your thoughts.

BEGINNING TIPS FOR GENERATING IDEAS

GOAL 2 Generate ideas

Before you can write about a topic, you have to collect ideas to write about. Because many students need help with this right away, three helpful techniques are described here: (1) freewriting, (2) brainstorming, and (3) branching. These techniques are discussed in detail in Chapter 11. Here is a brief introduction to each.

Freewriting

What is freewriting? Freewriting is writing nonstop about a topic for a specified period of time.

How does freewriting work? You write whatever comes into your mind, and you do not stop to be concerned about correctness. After you have finished, you go back through your writing and pick out ideas that you might be able to use.

What does it look like? Here is a sample of freewriting done on the topic of owning a dog.

Sample Freewriting

I really wish I had a dog. I need some what's it called . . . oh, yeah, unconditional love. Something that never gets mad at me, no matter what I do. Jumping up and happy whenever it sees me. Definitely loves me best. I could teach it tricks, like roll over and speak or dance with me. Maybe I could get on TV, like Letterman's Stupid Pet Tricks or Those Amazing Animals. What breeds are the smartest? I don't want one that's so big I can't lift it by myself. But I hate those yappy little ones that shiver all the time. I saw a woman walking one once in the winter. It had a little coat on that matched the woman's coat. I wouldn't do something that lame. How do you get them to be good guard dogs? Guess I'd have to pay for training. Ow. What else would I have to pay for; shots, neutering, bed, collar, vet bills? I can't afford that stuff, even if I get a mutt from the shelter. Can I take it to work? Ha! I can just see my boss's face when I walk in with a giant, slobbering Newfoundland! There goes that job. And how could I get home to walk it in between work and class? I only have half an hour. Guess I'd better wait.

Brainstorming

What is brainstorming? Brainstorming is making a list of everything you can think of that has to do with your topic.

How does brainstorming work? Try to stretch your imagination and think of everything related to your topic. Include facts, ideas, examples, questions, and feelings. When you have finished, read through what you have written and highlight usable ideas.

What does brainstorming look like? Here is a sample of brainstorming on the topic of reality TV:

Sample Brainstorming on Reality TV

Shows: COPS, American Idol, The Bachelor, Jon and Kate Plus 8, Wedding Island, Toddlers and Tiaras, Celebrity Apprentice

Many to choose from	Topic of discussion at work
On TV every day and night	Why are they popular?
Huge fan base	Celebrity shows
Real or unreal?	Not a new concept
Provide escape for viewers	Sometimes ridiculous situations
Addictive	Do people like this really exist?
Not professional actors	Effects of watching
Exotic locations	Messy lives
Make-overs	
More men or women viewers?	
Pretty people	

Branching

What is branching? Branching is a way of using diagrams or drawings to generate ideas.

How does branching work? Begin by drawing a 2-inch oval in the middle of a page. Write your topic in that oval. Think of the oval as a tree trunk. Next, draw lines radiating out from the trunk, as branches would. Write an idea related to your topic at the end of each branch. When you have finished, highlight the ideas you find most useful.

What does branching look like? Here is a sample of branching done on the topic of religious holidays:

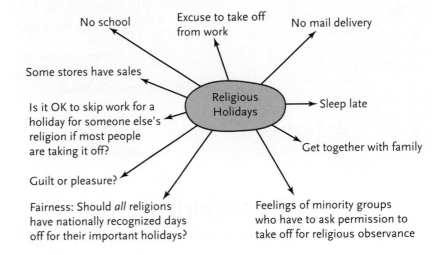

EXERCISE 1-2   Practicing Generating Ideas

Writing in Progress

Directions: Choose one of the following topics. Then try out two of the techniques described for generating ideas.

1. Identity theft

2. Internet communication

3. Telemarketing

4. Advertising ploys and gimmicks

5. Airport security ■

BEGINNING TIPS FOR ORGANIZING YOUR IDEAS

GOAL 3 Organize ideas

Two common methods of organizing ideas are outlining and idea mapping. Understanding each of them will help you decide how to arrange the ideas that you have identified as useful.

Outlining

What is outlining? Outlining is a method of listing the main points you will cover and their subpoints (details) in the order in which you will present them.

How does outlining work? To make an outline, you list the most import-ant ideas on separate lines at the left margin of a sheet of paper, leaving space underneath each idea. In the space under each main idea, list the details that you will include to explain that main idea. Indent the list of details that fits un-der each of your most important ideas.

What does outlining look like? Here is a sample outline for a brief essay on the topic of a vacation in San Francisco:

Sample Outline for Paragraph on Favorite Places

I. Chinatown
   A. Restaurants and markets
      1. Fortune cookie factory
      2. Dim sum restaurants
   B. Museums
      1. Chinese Culture Center
      2. Pacific Heritage Museum
II. Fisherman's Wharf
   A. Pier 39
      1. Street performers
      2. Sea lions sunning themselves on the docks
   B. Ghirardelli Square

Idea Mapping

What is idea mapping? An idea map is a drawing that shows the content and organization of a piece of writing.

How does idea mapping work? An idea map shows you how ideas are con-nected and can help you see which ideas are not relevant to the topic of your essay.

What does an idea map look like? Here is a sample idea map drawn for a paragraph on the topic of choosing an Internet password:

 Visualize It!

Idea Map

It is important to choose Internet passwords carefully.

Do not use common words or names.

Do not use the same password in many places.

Use both numbers and letters.

Change your password frequently.

Tell no one your password.

EXERCISE 1-3   Using Outlining or Mapping

Writing in Progress

Directions: For the topic you chose in Exercise 1-2, use outlining or idea mapping to organize your ideas. ■

WRITING PARAGRAPHS

GOAL 4 Write a paragraph

A **paragraph** is a group of sentences, usually at least three or four, that expresses one main idea. Paragraphs may stand alone to express one thought, or they may be combined into essays. Paragraphs are one of the basic building blocks of writing, so it is important to learn to write them effectively.

A paragraph's one main idea is expressed in a single sentence called the **topic sentence**. The other sentences in the paragraph, called **supporting details**, explain or support the main idea. You can visualize a paragraph as follows:

 Visualize It!

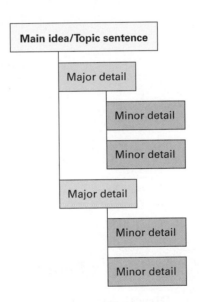

Here is a sample paragraph; its idea map appears on the following page.

The Abkhasians (an agricultural people who live in a mountainous region of Georgia, a republic of the former Soviet Union) may be the longest-lived people on earth. Many claim to live past 100—some beyond 120 and even 130. Although it is difficult to document the accuracy of these claims, government records indicate that an extraordinary number of Abkhasians do live to a very old age. Three main factors appear to account for their long lives. The first is their diet, which consists of little meat, much fresh fruit, vegetables, garlic, goat cheese, cornmeal, buttermilk and wine. The second is their lifelong physical activity. They do slow down after age 80, but even after the age of 100 they still work about four hours a day. The third factor—a highly developed sense of community—goes to the very heart of the Abkhasian culture. From childhood, each individual is integrated into a primary group, and remains so throughout life. There is no such thing as a nursing home, nor do the elderly live alone.

—adapted from Henslin, *Sociology*, pp. 380–381.

 Visualize It!

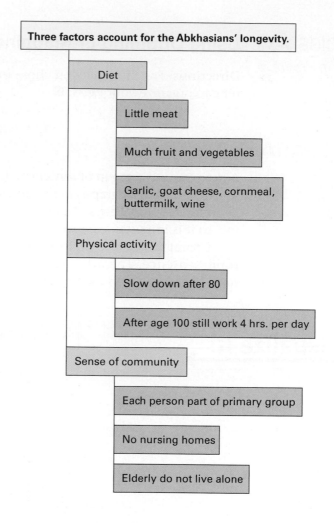

Three factors account for the Abkhasians' longevity.

- Diet
  - Little meat
  - Much fruit and vegetables
  - Garlic, goat cheese, cornmeal, buttermilk, wine
- Physical activity
  - Slow down after 80
  - After age 100 still work 4 hrs. per day
- Sense of community
  - Each person part of primary group
  - No nursing homes
  - Elderly do not live alone

EXERCISE 1-4
Writing in Progress

Writing a Paragraph

Directions: Using one or more of the ideas you generated and organized in Exercises 1-2 and 1-3, write a paragraph about the topic you chose. ■

EXERCISE 1-5
Working Together

Writing a Paragraph

Directions: Write a paragraph on one of the following topics. Be sure to begin with a sentence that states the one idea your paragraph is about.

TOPIC 1.   Describe a space alien's fear or surprise when stepping out of a spaceship onto Earth. Explain what the alien sees or hears and how it reacts to what it sees.

TOPIC 2.   Describe your reaction to your first day of college classes. Include specific examples to support your description.

Working with a classmate, compare and evaluate each other's paragraphs. Is the opening sentence clear? Is that idea explained in the remainder of the paragraph? ■

WRITING ESSAYS

An essay, which consists of three or more paragraphs, expresses and explains a series of related ideas, all of which support a larger, broader idea.

The emphasis of this text is on writing effective sentences and paragraphs. However, in some of your courses your instructors may ask you to write essays or take essay exams. Some writing instructors prefer that their students write essays right away. Other instructors prefer that their students begin by writing single paragraphs and then progress to essay writing. Regardless of when you begin writing essays, the following introduction to essay techniques will be useful to you. It will show you why good paragraph-writing skills are absolutely necessary for writing good essays.

What Is an Essay?

An **essay** is a group of paragraphs about one subject. It contains one key idea about the subject that is called the **thesis statement**. Each paragraph in the essay supports or explains some aspect of the thesis statement.

How Is an Essay Organized?

An essay follows a logical and direct plan: it introduces an idea (the thesis statement), explains it, and draws a conclusion. Therefore, an essay usually has at least three paragraphs:

1. Introductory paragraph
2. Body (one or more paragraphs)
3. Concluding paragraph

The Introductory Paragraph

Your **introductory paragraph** should accomplish three things:

1. It should establish the topic of the essay.
2. It should present the thesis statement of your essay in an appropriate way for your intended audience.
3. It should interest your audience in your essay.

The Body

The **body** of your essay should accomplish three things:

1. It should provide information that supports and explains your thesis statement.
2. It should present each main supporting point in a separate paragraph.
3. It should contain enough detailed information to make the main point of each paragraph understandable and believable.

The Concluding Paragraph

Your **concluding paragraph** should accomplish two things:

1. It should reemphasize but not restate your thesis statement.
2. It should draw your essay to a close.

You can visualize the organization of an essay using the following idea map:

 Visualize It!

Idea Map

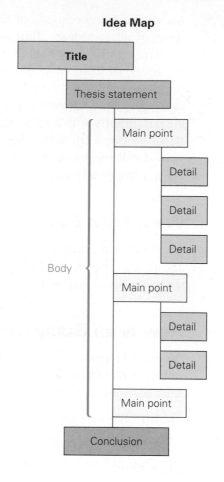

Title

Thesis statement

Body

Main point

Detail

Detail

Detail

Main point

Detail

Detail

Main point

Conclusion

The following sample student essay by Claire Stroup was written in response to an assignment by her writing instructor. She was asked to select a form of media entertainment and write an analysis of it. In her essay, the marginal notes indicate the function of each paragraph. Read the essay and study the idea map that follows it.

A SAMPLE STUDENT ESSAY

The Allure of Reality TV

Title: identifies the topic

Introduction: topic is introduced

1   *Real Housewives, Jersey Shore, America's Next Top Model*, and *Shahs of Sunset* surface in every-day conversations in college, high school, and even middle school classrooms. Reality television shows have become completely ingrained in American society and culture; they influence fashion, food, and frolicking. Why is it that Americans have become so obsessed with the day-to-day lives of people they have never met? Why have Americans become so content with staying home and watching someone else's life rather than living their own? Reality TV is not so real, so America's

obsession with it stems from a desire to escape the mundane nine-to-five, dinner, shower, bedtime routine. Because of reality TV's unusual and unrealistic premises, entertaining and humorous characters, and beautiful people, American TV-watchers have become completely and totally addicted to this mindless escape.

Thesis statement

Description of exciting settings

2   Reality TV viewers find themselves completely entranced with the glamorous Hollywood Hills, rugged Western terrain, or even a suspicious trailer park. People tend to become bored with their daily routine and lifestyle, whether it be in a clean and safe neighborhood, a rural cow farm, or a drug-filled urban apartment complex. When a person grows up and lives one way for his/her whole life, he/she often harbors a deep desire to escape to some exotic location. So, reality TV provides that escape. A person can "experience" a faraway place with completely different people and animals and music without leaving the responsibility of kids, work, and mortgages behind.

Description of interesting characters

3   Images of bustling cities or ancient ruins are beautiful, of course, but what fun are they without a friend to experience them with? In this way, reality TV provides its viewers with a cast of characters who are interesting, vivacious, and unusually quirky. Experiencing someone else's drama and life story can be exciting for a viewer who lives quietly with her many cats. Seeing a bodybuilder's journey from a scrawny young kid to a gigantic muscleman can be inspiring to a young bully victim. The characters shown on reality TV more often than not are hardly real at all, but their stories throughout a season are compelling all the same.

Description of physically attractive characters

4   In order to make the reality shows even more addictive, producers have tapped into Americans' desires to escape with someone attractive. These characters may be interesting, but no one wants to watch Quasimodo take a trip around the world in twenty-four hours. Supermodels hanging out in their bikinis are much more interesting than pasty, middle-aged men playing videogames in their mothers' basements. Attractiveness has become so incredibly important to American culture and society that those who do not fit the mold are deemed uninteresting or unworthy of being seen on TV. Thus, reality TV does not show many average-looking people doing average-looking things.

Description of viewer issues

5   Because of this emphasis on attractiveness and being "interesting," reality TV contributes to a larger, more serious problem: the viewers want to be considered attractive and interesting. This often leads to the glamorization of teen pregnancy, creation of eating disorders, use of harmful tanning beds, and/or objectification of the opposite sex. Women are more often viewed as sexual objects in reality shows, but men can be as well. Regardless, people on reality TV are considered valued or worthwhile if they are desirable, and this translates into people in the real world being considered valued if they are desirable. Physical attractiveness has become such a desirable trait that other factors of a person's worth, like education, intelligence, work ethic, and moral compass, are swept under the rug or just viewed as add-ons.

Conclusion: draws essay to a close and suggests options   6   While the idea of having an at-home escape is wonderful and fun, the realities of reality TV are not wonderful at all. Viewers confuse reality TV with the real world and alter their lives in order to become thinner, funnier, and prettier. Rather than encouraging individuals to love themselves as they are, reality TV encourages its viewers to be more like the characters on the screen. Perhaps if networks had shows like, "John Goes to College," or "Mary Got a Job that Makes Her Happy," the effects would be different. The unfortunate reality of the situation is that America's obsession with train-wreck reality shows creates train-wrecks in reality. It is a confusing paradox but a real one that affects Americans in more ways than they know.

To review the organization of "The Allure of Reality TV" see the Visualize It! idea map on page 13.

EXERCISE 1-6
Writing in Progress

Writing an Essay

Directions: Using the ideas you generated in Exercise 1-2 but did not use to write a paragraph in Exercise 1-4, write a short essay. You may need to do additional brainstorming, freewriting, or branching to come up with enough ideas to write about. ■

PRACTICAL ADVICE FOR GETTING STARTED

GOAL 6 Prepare to write

Writing is a skill that you can learn with the help of this book, your instructor, and your classmates. Like any other skill, such as basketball, accounting, or cooking, writing takes practice. Be sure to focus your attention on new techniques suggested by your instructor as well as the ones given in each chapter of this book. To improve, you often need to be open to doing things differently. Expect success; don't hesitate to experiment.

Get the Most out of Your Writing Class

Attend all classes. Do not miss any classes and be sure to come prepared to class with readings and writing assignments complete. Take notes during class, and ask questions about things you do not understand. Be sure to participate in class discussions and attend all writing conferences offered by your instructor.

Take a Positive Approach to Writing

Use the following tips to achieve success:

Think First, Then Write

Writing is a thinking process: it is an expression of your thoughts. Don't expect to be able to pick up a pen or sit down at a computer and immediately produce a well-written paragraph or essay. Plan to spend time generating ideas and deciding how to organize them before you write your first draft.

 Visualize It!

Title	**The Allure of Reality TV**
Thesis statement	People have become addicted to reality TV because of many factors.
Main point	Viewers are drawn to reality TV because of its settings.
Details	1. People are bored
	2. People desire escape
	3. Reality TV provides escape
Main point	Reality TV offers interesting characters.
Details	1. Viewers "live" through the characters
	2. Bodybuilder's story
	3. Unrealistic characters
Main point	Viewers prefer attractive characters.
Details	1. Quasimodo
	2. Supermodels
	3. Importance of attractiveness
Main point	The focus on attractiveness leads to problems.
Details	1. Glamorization of teenage issues.
	2. Women viewed as sex objects.
	3. Less focus on more important traits.
Conclusion	Reality TV has a negative effect on its viewers. Shows should focus on more positive aspects of humanity.

Plan on Making Changes

Most writers revise (rethink, rewrite, change, add, and delete) numerous times before they are pleased with their work. For example, I revised this chapter of *Pathways* five times before I was satisfied with it.

Give Yourself Enough Time to Write

For most of us, writing does not come easily. It takes time to think, select a topic, generate ideas, organize them, draft a piece of writing, revise it, and proofread it. Reserve a block of time each day for writing. Use the time to read this book and to work on its writing exercises and assignments. Begin by reserving an hour per day. This may seem like a lot of time. However, most instructors expect you to spend at least two hours outside of class for every hour you spend in class. If your writing class meets for a total of three hours per week, then you should spend at least six hours per week working on writing.

Develop a Routine

Try to work at the same time each day. You will develop a routine that will be easy to follow. Be sure to work at peak periods of concentration. Don't write when you are tired, hungry, or likely to be interrupted.

Take Breaks

If you get stuck and cannot think or write, take a break. Clear your mind by going for a walk, talking to a friend, or having a snack. Set a time limit for your break, though, so you return to work in a reasonable time. When you begin again, start by rereading what you have already written. If you still cannot make progress, use freewriting, brainstorming, and branching techniques (see pp. 3–5) to generate more ideas about your topic.

Keep a Journal

A writing journal is an excellent way to improve your writing and keep track of your thoughts and ideas. A **writing journal** is a collection of your writing and reflections.

How to Keep a Writing Journal

1. Buy an 8.5-by-11-inch spiral-bound notebook. Use it exclusively for journal writing. Alternatively, you can use a computer file.

2. Reserve ten to 15 minutes a day to write in your journal. Write every day, not just on days when a good idea strikes.

3. Write about whatever comes to mind. You might write about events that happened and your reactions to them, or describe feelings, impressions, or worries.

If you have trouble getting started, ask yourself some questions:

- What happened at school, work, or home?
- What world, national, or local events occurred?
- What am I worried about?
- What positive experience have I had lately? Maybe it was eating a good meal, making a new friend, or finding time to wash your car.
- What did I see today? Practice writing descriptions of beautiful, funny, interesting, or disturbing things you've noticed.

- What is the best or worst thing that happened today?
- Who did I talk to? What did I talk about? Record conversations as fully as you can.

Sample Journal Entries

The following student journal entries will give you a better picture of journal writing. They have been edited for easy reading. However, as you write, do not be concerned with neatness or correctness.

Jeffrey

The best thing that happened today happened as soon as I got home from work. My cell phone rang. At first, I wasn't going to answer it because I was tired and in one of those moods when I wanted to be by myself. It rang so many times I decided to answer it. Am I glad I did! It was Alexis, a long-lost girlfriend whom I'd always regretted losing touch with. She said she had just moved back into the neighborhood, and . . . I took it from there.

Malcolm

This morning while walking across campus to my math class, I stopped for a few minutes under a chestnut tree. Perfect timing! I've always loved collecting chestnuts, and they were just beginning to fall. When I was a kid, I used to pick up lunch bags full of them. I never knew what to do with them once I had them. I just liked picking them up, I guess. I remember liking their cold, sleek, shiny smoothness and how good they felt in my hand. So I picked up a few, rubbed them together in my hand, and went off to class, happy that some things never change.

Benefits of Journal Writing

When you write in your journal, you are practicing writing and becoming better at expressing your thoughts in writing. You can practice without pressure or fear of criticism. Besides practice, journal writing has other benefits:

1. Your journals will become a good source of ideas. When you have a paper assigned and must select your own topic, review your journal for ideas.
2. You may find that journal writing becomes a way to think through problems, release pent-up feelings, or keep an enjoyable record of life experiences. Journal writing is writing *for yourself*.

Use Peer Review

Not everything you write in a college writing class needs to be graded by your instructor. Instead, you can get valuable *peer review*, or feedback, from other members of your class. Peers (classmates) can tell you what they like and what they think you need to do to improve your writing. You can also learn a lot from reading and commenting on the work of other students.

Here are suggestions for making peer reviewing as valuable as possible:

When You Are the Writer

1. Prepare your draft in readable form. Double-space your work and print it on standard 8.5" × 11" paper. Use only one side of the paper.
2. When you receive your peers' comments, weigh them carefully. Keep an open mind, but do not feel that you must accept every suggestion that is made.

3. If you have questions or are uncertain about your peers' advice, talk with your instructor.

When You Are the Reviewer

1. Read the draft through at least once before making any suggestions.

2. As you read, keep the writer's intended audience in mind (see Chapter 11). The draft should be appropriate for that audience.

3. Offer positive comments first. Say what the writer did well.

4. Use the Revision Checklists in Chapters 12–17 to guide your reading and comments. Be specific in your review and offer suggestions for improvement.

SELF-TEST SUMMARY

To test yourself, cover the Answer column with a sheet of paper and answer each question in the left column. Evaluate each of your answers as you work by sliding the paper down and comparing your answer with what is printed in the Answer column.

	QUESTION	ANSWER
Goal 1 Use the writing process	What are the steps in the writing process?	The five steps in the writing process are • generating ideas • organizing ideas • writing a first draft • revising • proofreading
Goal 2 Generate ideas	What techniques can help you generate ideas?	Three techniques that can help you generate ideas are freewriting, brainstorming, and branching.
Goal 3 Organize ideas	What are two methods of organizing ideas?	Two common methods of organizing ideas are outlining and idea mapping.
Goal 4 Write a paragraph	What is a paragraph?	A paragraph is a group of sentences that expresses one main idea.
Goal 5 Write an essay	What is an essay and how is an essay organized?	An essay is a group of paragraphs about one subject. An essay usually has an introductory paragraph, a body, and a concluding paragraph.
Goal 6 Prepare to write	How can you improve your writing?	Improve your writing by attending and participating in your writing class, taking a positive approach to writing, keeping a writing journal, and using peer review.

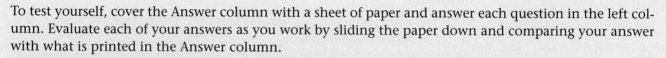 **MyWritingLab** *Visit Ch. 1 An Introduction to Writing in MyWritingLab to test your understanding of the chapter objectives.*

2

The Reading-Writing Connection

WRITE ABOUT IT!

Although the people in the two photos seemingly have nothing to do with one another, they are connected. Write a sentence stating how they are connected.

The journalist in the first photo is writing a news article; the person in the second photo is reading the article he wrote. Readers and writers are always connected in this way. In this chapter you will learn about the reading-writing connection. You will learn reading and critical-thinking skills that will make an immediate, noticeable change in how well you understand and remember what you read. As you work through this chapter, you will see that there is a strong connection between reading and writing. Improving one skill often improves the other.

EXPLORING THE READING-WRITING-CRITICAL THINKING CONNECTION

At first, reading and writing may seem like very different, even opposite, processes. A writer starts with a blank page or computer screen and creates and develops ideas, while a reader starts with a full page and reads someone else's ideas. Although reading and writing may seem very different, they are actually parts of the same communication process.

Writers begin with a message they want to communicate; readers attempt to understand that message through their own experiences. Because reading and writing work together, improving one often improves the other. By learning to read more effectively, you'll become a better writer as well as a better reader. For example, as you learn more about writing paragraphs, you will be able to read them more easily. Similarly, as you learn more about how an essay is organized, you will find it easier to read essays and to organize your own ideas into essay form. Finally, by becoming a more critical thinker and reader, you improve your ability to communicate and persuade when you write.

NEED TO KNOW

The Relationship Between Reading, Writing, and Critical Thinking

- Reading and writing are parts of the same communication process.

- Writers begin with a message they want to communicate.

- Readers try to understand the message by connecting it to their own experiences.

- Critical thinking makes you a better reader and a more persuasive writer.

PREVIEWING BEFORE READING

GOAL 1 Preview before reading

Do you wish you could remember more of what you read? **Previewing** is a way of becoming familiar with what a reading is about and how it is organized *before* you read it. Previewing will make an assignment easier to read and remember, as well as make it more interesting. It will also help you discover what you already know about the topic before you begin reading.

Previewing is like looking at a map before you begin to drive in an unfamiliar city. It familiarizes you with the organization and content of a reading. Then, when you read the selection, you are able to understand it more easily. Previewing is not time-consuming. You can preview a brief selection in several minutes by following these basic steps:

1. **Read and think about the title of the selection.** What does it tell you about the subject? Does it offer any clues as to how the author feels about the subject or how the author will approach it? What do you already know about the subject?

2. **Check the author's name.** If it is familiar, what do you know about the author?

3. **Read the first paragraph.** Here the author often introduces the subject. Look for a statement of the main point of the entire reading. If the first paragraph is lengthy, read only the first few sentences.

4. **Read all boldfaced headings.** Headings divide the reading into sections and announce the topic of each section.

5. **Read the first sentence under each heading.** This sentence often states the main point of the section.

6. **If the reading lacks headings, read the first sentence of each of a few paragraphs on each page.** You will discover many of the main ideas of the article.

7. **Read the last paragraph.** Often this paragraph summarizes or concludes the reading. If the last paragraph is lengthy, read only the last few sentences.

The more you practice previewing and get in the habit of previewing, the more effectively it will work. Use the preview strategy for all your college textbooks, as well as for assigned chapters and readings in this book. Before each professional reading in this book, you will be reminded to preview it.

Demonstration of Previewing

Now, preview the following reading, "Studying for Exams." The portions you should preview have been highlighted. Preview this reading now, reading only the shaded portions.

READING

STUDYING FOR EXAMS: CRAMMING IS NOT AN OPTION

Saundra K. Ciccarelli and J. Noland White

How should you approach studying for exams, and why do different kinds of test questions require different study approaches?

1   There is a right way to study for a test, believe it or not. Here are some good things to remember when preparing for an exam, whether it's a quiz, a unit test, a midterm, or a final:

2   **Timing is everything.** One of the worst things that students can do is to wait until the last minute to study for an exam. Remember the analogy about "chewing" the steak? (Just as a steak has to be chewed to be enjoyed and to be useful to the body, textbook material has to be "chewed" with the mind.) The same concept applies to preparing for an exam: You have to give yourself enough time. If you've read your text material and taken good notes as discussed in the previous sections, you'll be able to save a lot of time in studying for the exam, but you still need to give yourself ample time to go over all of those notes. The time management tips given earlier in this chapter will help you prioritize your studying.

Could this be you? The scattered materials, the frantic phone call to a friend or professor, and the tense and worried expression are all hallmarks of that hallowed yet useless student tradition, cramming. Don't let this happen to you.

3   **Find out as much as you can about the type of test and the material it will cover.** The type of test can affect the way in which you want to study the material. An objective test, for example, such as multiple-choice or true/false, is usually fairly close to the text material, so you'll want to be very familiar with the wording of concepts and definitions in the text, although this is not a suggestion to memorize a lot of material.

4   **These kinds of tests can include one of three types of questions:**

- **Factual:** Questions that ask you to remember a specific fact from the text material. For example, "Who built the first psychological laboratory?" requires that you recognize a person's name. (The answer is Wilhelm Wundt.)

- **Applied:** Questions that ask you to use, or apply, information presented in the text. For example, consider the following question:

  Ever since she was scared by a dog as a young child, Angelica has been afraid of all dogs. The fact that she is not only afraid of the original dog but all types of dogs is an example of

  a. stimulus generalization.
  b. stimulus discrimination.
  c. spontaneous recovery.
  d. shaping.

  This question requires you to take a concept (in this case, generalization) and apply it to a real-world example.

- **Conceptual**: Questions that demand that you think about the ideas or concepts presented in the text and demonstrate that you understand them by answering questions like the following:

  "Freud is to _____ as Watson is to _____." (The answers could vary, but a good set would be "the unconscious" and "observable behavior.")

5   **Memorization is not enough.** Notice that although memorizing facts might help on the first type of question, it isn't going to help at all on the last two. Memorization doesn't always help on factual questions either, because

the questions are sometimes worded quite differently from the text. It is far better to understand the information rather than be able to "spit it back" without understanding it. "Spitting it back" is memorization; understanding it is true learning. There are different levels of analysis for information you are trying to learn, and the higher the level of analysis, the more likely you are to remember. *Factual questions* are the lowest level of analysis: knowledge. *Applied questions* are a higher level and are often preferred by instructors for that reason—it's hard to successfully apply information if you don't really understand it. *Conceptual questions* are a kind of analysis, a level higher than either of the other two. Not only do you have to understand the concept, you have to understand it well enough to compare and contrast it with other concepts. They might be harder questions to answer, but in the long run, you will get more "bang for your buck" in terms of true learning.

6   **Prepare for subjective tests.** Subjective tests, such as essay tests and short-answer exams, require that you not only are able to recall and understand the information from the course but also that you are able to organize it in your own words. To study for a subjective test means that you need to be familiar with the material *and* that you need to be able to write it down. Make outlines of your notes. Rewrite both reading and lecture notes and make flash cards, charts, and drawings. Practice putting the flash cards in order. Talk out loud or study with someone else and discuss the possible questions that could be on an essay test.

7   You may find that only a few of these methods work best for you, but the more ways in which you try to study, the better you will be able to retrieve the information when you need it. It may sound like a big investment of your time, but most students vastly underestimate how long it takes to study—and fail to recognize that many of these techniques are doable when first reading the textbook assignment and preparing for the classroom lecture.

DON'T CRAM!

■ ■ ■ ■

Although you may not realize it, you learned a great deal about how to study for exams in the minute or two you spent previewing.

EXERCISE 2-1   Testing Your Recall

Directions: Without referring to the above reading, "Studying for Exams," make a list of ideas or suggestions you recall. ■

Connecting the Reading to Your Own Experience

Once you have previewed a reading, try to connect the topic to your own experience. Take a moment to recall what you already know or have read about the topic. This activity will make the reading more interesting and easier to write about. Here are a few suggestions to help you make connections:

1. **Ask questions and answer them.** Suppose you have just previewed a reading titled "Advertising: Institutionalized Lying." Ask questions such as: Do

ads always lie? If not, why not? What do I already know about deceptive advertising?

2. **Brainstorm.** Jot down everything that comes to mind about the topic on a sheet of paper or a computer file. For example, if the topic of a reading is "The Generation Gap," write down ideas as they occur to you. You might list reasons for such a gap, try to define it, or mention names of families in which you have observed it. For more about brainstorming, see Chapter 11, page 273.

3. **Think of examples.** Try to think of situations, people, or events that relate to the topic. For instance, suppose you have previewed a reading titled "Fashions, Fads, and Crazes." You might think of recent examples of each: pajamas as casual attire, iPods, or tattoos.

Each of these techniques will help you identify ideas or experiences that you may share with the writer and that will help you focus your attention on the reading. In this book, the section titled "Interactive Reading: Thinking Before and Responding During Reading," which comes before each reading, lists several questions that will help you make connections to your own experiences.

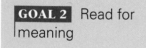

EXERCISE 2-2   **Connecting the Reading to Your Own Experience**

Writing in Progress

Directions: Based on your preview of "Studying for Exams," use one or more of the above techniques to connect the reading to your own experience. You might think of study approaches you already use or types of exam questions you find difficult (or easy). ■

READING FOR MEANING

GOAL 2 Read for meaning

Reading is much more than moving your eyes across a line of print. To get the most out of a reading, you should search for, grasp, and react to the author's ideas. To do so, you'll need to know how essays and paragraphs are organized, how to develop strategies for dealing with difficult or confusing sentences or passages, and how to handle unfamiliar vocabulary.

What to Look for in Paragraphs

Paragraphs will be easier to understand and remember if you look for their three essential parts:

- **The topic** A paragraph is about one topic. This topic is discussed throughout the paragraph.

- **The main idea** A paragraph expresses one idea about its topic. Often this idea is expressed in a sentence called the topic sentence.

- **The supporting details** All the other sentences in the paragraph explain its main idea. Supporting details are facts that explain more about the main idea.

You can visualize a paragraph as follows:

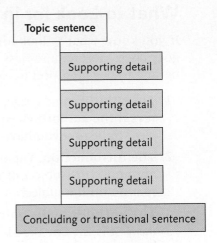

In the diagram above, the topic sentence appears first. The topic sentence is usually placed first in a paragraph, but it can appear anywhere in the paragraph. (You will learn much more about topic sentences and supporting details in Chapters 12 and 13.)

As you read, search for the topic sentence of each paragraph and notice how the other sentences in the paragraph explain it. This process will help you keep your mind on the reading and will direct your attention to the reading's key points. Try underlining or highlighting each topic sentence as you find it.

Directions: Complete the idea map for the paragraph below. Notice how the writer states and then explains ideas.

Verbal Mnemonics

Sometimes the easiest way to remember a list of items is to use verbal mnemonics, or "memory tricks." Chances are, you have already used popular methods such as *rhymes* ("*i* before *e*, except after *c*" is my favorite; "thirty days hath September, April, June, and November" is another) and *acronyms* that reduce the amount of information to be stored (for example, *ROY G BIV* can be used to recall the colors of the light spectrum: *r*ed, *o*range, *y*ellow, *g*reen, *b*lue, *i*ndigo, and *v*iolet). Relying on verbal mnemonics, advertisers create slogans to make their products memorable.
—Kassin, *Psychology*, pp. 244–245.

Topic sentence: _____
_____

Major detail: _____

Minor detail: *i* before *e*, except after *c*

Minor detail: thirty days hath September, April, June, and November

Major detail: _____

Minor detail: *ROY G BIV*

Conclusion: _____
_____
_____

What to Look for in Essays

If you know what to look for as you read, you'll find reading an essay is easier, goes faster, and requires less rereading. When you read the essays in this book, be sure to pay attention to each of the following parts:

1. **The title** In some essays, the title announces the topic of the essay and may reveal the author's viewpoint. In others, the meaning of the title becomes clear only after you have read the essay.

2. **The introduction** The opening paragraph of an essay should interest you, announce the subject of the essay, and provide necessary background information on the subject.

3. **The author's main point** The main point is often called the *thesis statement*. It is the one big idea that the entire essay explains. Often it appears in the first paragraph, but it can be placed anywhere in the essay. Don't confuse the phrase *thesis statement* with *topic sentence*. The sentence that states the main idea of a paragraph is a topic sentence. (For more on thesis statements, see pages 441–445.)

4. **Support and explanation** The body of the essay should explain, give reasons for, or offer support for the author's thesis. Each supporting paragraph should have a topic sentence that identifies the paragraph's main idea.

5. **The conclusion** The last paragraph brings the essay to a close. Often, it will restate the author's main point. It may also suggest directions for further thought.

Now, reread "Studying for Exams," which has been marked here to identify each of the parts described above.

READING

STUDYING FOR EXAMS: CRAMMING IS NOT AN OPTION

Saundra K. Ciccarelli and J. Noland White

How should you approach studying for exams, and why do different kinds of test questions require different study approaches?

Title and subtitle: identify the topic and focus of the reading

Thesis statement

Introduction: Explains that the reading will offer tips.

Topic sentence: First point to remember when preparing for an exam

1   There is a right way to study for a test, believe it or not. Here are some good things to remember when preparing for an exam, whether it's a quiz, a unit test, a midterm, or a final:

2   **Timing is everything.** One of the worst things that students can do is to wait until the last minute to study for an exam. Remember the analogy about "chewing" the steak? (Just as a steak has to be chewed to be enjoyed and to be useful to the body, textbook material has to be "chewed" with the mind.) The same concept applies to preparing for an exam: You have to give yourself enough time. If you've read your text material and taken good notes as discussed in the previous sections, you'll be able to save a lot of time in studying for the exam, but you still need to give yourself ample time to go over all of

Could this be you? The scattered materials, the frantic phone call to a friend or professor, and the tense and worried expression are all hallmarks of that hallowed yet useless student tradition, cramming. Don't let this happen to you.

those notes. The time management tips given earlier in this chapter will help you prioritize your studying.

Topic sentence: Second point to remember

3   **Find out as much as you can about the type of test and the material it will cover.** The type of test can affect the way in which you want to study the material. An objective test, for example, such as multiple-choice or true/false, is usually fairly close to the text material, so you'll want to be very familiar with the wording of concepts and definitions in the text, although this is not a suggestion to memorize a lot of material.

Support in the form of examples of types of exam questions

4   **These kinds of tests can include one of three types of questions:**

- **Factual:** Questions that ask you to remember a specific fact from the text material. For example, "Who built the first psychological laboratory?" requires that you recognize a person's name. (The answer is Wilhelm Wundt.)

- **Applied:** Questions that ask you to use, or apply, information presented in the text. For example, consider the following question:

    Ever since she was scared by a dog as a young child, Angelica has been afraid of all dogs. The fact that she is not only afraid of the original dog but all types of dogs is an example of

    e. stimulus generalization.
    f. stimulus discrimination.
    g. spontaneous recovery.
    h. shaping.

    This question requires you to take a concept (in this case, generalization) and apply it to a real-world example.

- **Conceptual:** Questions that demand that you think about the ideas or concepts presented in the text and demonstrate that you understand them by answering questions like the following:

    "Freud is to _____ as Watson is to _____." (The answers could vary, but a good set would be "the unconscious" and "observable behavior.")

Topic sentence: Third point to remember and further explanation/support

5   **Memorization is not enough**. Notice that although memorizing facts might help on the first type of question, it isn't going to help at all on the last two. Memorization doesn't always help on factual questions either, because the questions are sometimes worded quite differently from the text. It is far better to understand the information rather than be able to "spit it back" without understanding it. "Spitting it back" is memorization; understanding it is true learning. There are different levels of analysis for information you are trying to learn, and the higher the level of analysis, the more likely you are to remember. *Factual questions* are the lowest level of analysis: knowledge. *Applied questions* are a higher level and are often preferred by instructors for that reason—it's hard to successfully apply information if you don't really understand it. *Conceptual questions* are a kind of analysis, a level higher than either of the other two. Not only do you have to understand the concept, you have to understand it well enough to compare and contrast it with other concepts. They might be harder questions to answer, but in the long run, you will get more "bang for your buck" in terms of true learning.

Topic sentence: Fourth point to remember

6   **Prepare for subjective tests.** Subjective tests, such as essay tests and short-answer exams, require that you not only are able to recall and understand the information from the course but also that you are able to organize it in your own words. To study for a subjective test means that you need to be familiar with the material *and* that you need to be able to write it down. Make outlines of your notes. Rewrite both reading and lecture notes and make flash cards, charts, and drawings. Practice putting the flash cards in order. Talk out loud or study with someone else and discuss the possible questions that could be on an essay test.

Conclusion: draws reading to a close

7   You may find that only a few of these methods work best for you, but the more ways in which you try to study, the better you will be able to retrieve the information when you need it. It may sound like a big investment of your time, but most students vastly underestimate how long it takes to study—and fail to recognize that many of these techniques are doable when first reading the textbook assignment and preparing for the classroom lecture.

DON'T CRAM!

■ ■ ■ ■

HOW TO HANDLE DIFFICULT READINGS

GOAL 3 Read more effectively

All of us, at one time or another, come across a piece of material that is difficult or confusing. An entire reading may be difficult, or just a paragraph or two within an otherwise comfortable reading may be troublesome. Don't give in to the temptation to skip over difficult parts or just give up. Instead, try to approach challenging readings using the methods in the box on the next page.

Tips for Reading Difficult Material

1. **Analyze the time and place in which you are reading.** If you have been reading or studying for several hours, mental fatigue may be the source of the problem. If you are reading in a place with numerous distractions, lack of concentration may contribute to poor comprehension.

2. **Look up unfamiliar words.** Often, a few unfamiliar words can block understanding. Keep a dictionary handy and refer to it as needed.

3. **Do not hesitate to reread difficult or complicated sections.** In fact, sometimes several rereadings are appropriate and necessary.

4. **Rephrase each paragraph in your own words.** You might approach extremely complicated material sentence by sentence, expressing each idea in your own words.

5. **Read aloud sentences or sections that are particularly difficult.** Hearing ideas aloud often aids comprehension.

6. **Make a brief outline of the major points of the reading.** An outline will help you see the overall organization and progression of ideas.

7. **Slow down your reading rate if you feel you are beginning to lose comprehension.** On occasion, simply reading more slowly will boost your comprehension.

8. **Summarize.** Test your recall by summarizing each section after you read it.

9. **Work with a classmate.** Working through and discussing a reading with a classmate often will increase your understanding of it.

HOW TO RECORD YOUR THINKING: MARKING AND ANNOTATION

GOAL 4 Mark and annotate text

Annotation is a way of jotting down your ideas, reactions, and opinions as you read. Think of annotation as recording your ideas while you read. It is a way to "talk back" to the author—to question, agree, disagree, or comment. Annotations are particularly useful when you will be writing about what you have read.

Three different types of annotations are useful: *symbols and abbreviations, highlights,* and *statements and questions.* Depending on your preferences, you may choose to use one, two, or all three of these methods.

Symbols and Abbreviations

Marking key parts of an essay with symbols or abbreviations can help you clarify meaning and remember key information. Table 2-1 below provides a list of useful symbols and abbreviations. You should feel free to add to this list in any way that suits your reading and learning styles.

Here is an example of an annotated reading:

Sitting on the top rung of the class ladder is a powerful elite that consists of just 1 percent of the U.S. population. This capitalist class is so wealthy that it owns one-third of all the nation's assets. This tiny 1 percent is worth more than the entire bottom 90 percent of the country. Power and influence cling to this small elite. They have direct access to politicians, own major media and entertainment outlets (newspapers, magazines, TV stations, sports franchises), and control the boards of directors of our most influential colleges and universities.

TABLE 2-1   ANNOTATION SYMBOLS AND ABBREVIATIONS

Type of Annotation	Symbol and Example
1. **Underlining key ideas**	The <u>most prominent unions in the United States are among public-sector employees</u> such as teachers and police.
2. **Circling unknown words**	One goal of labor unions is to address the apparent (asymmetry) of power in the employer-worker relationship.
3. **Marking definitions** *def.*	To say that the balance of power favors one party over another is to introduce a disequilibrium.
4. **Marking examples** *ex.*	Concessions may include additional benefits, increased vacation time, or higher wages.
5. **Numbering lists of ideas, causes, reasons, or events**	The components of power include self-①range, ②population, ③natural resources, and ④geography.
6. **Placing asterisks (stars) next to important passages**	* Once a dominant force in the United States economy, labor unions have been shrinking over the last few decades.
7. **Putting question marks next to confusing passages** ?	Strikes can be averted through the institutionalization of mediated bargaining.
8. **Marking possible test items** ⊤	A *closed shop* is a form of union agreement in which the employer agrees to hire only union workers.
9. **Drawing arrows to show relationships**	Standing between managers and employees is the (shop steward), who is both a union employee and a rank-and-file worker within the company that employs union members.
10. **Marking summary statements** *sum.*	The greater the degree of conflict between labor and management, the more sensitive the negotiations need to be.
11. **Marking essential information that you must remember**	The largest and most important trade union in the United States, and the one that has had the most influence on labor-union relations, is the AFL-CIO. ⏋!
12. **Noting author's opinion of or attitude toward the topic** *opinion*	In a world where the gap between rich and poor is increasing, labor unions are essential to ensuring that workers are paid and treated fairly.
13. **Indicating material to reread later** *RR*	At the apex of union density in the 1940s, only about 9.8 percent of public employees were represented by unions, while 33.9 percent of private, nonagricultural workers had such representation. In this decade, those proportions have essentially reversed, with 36 percent of public workers being represented by unions while private sector union density had plummeted to around 7 percent.

The capitalist class can be divided into "old money" and "new money." <u>The longer that wealth has been in a family, the more it adds to the family's prestige.</u> The *def.* <u>children of old money</u> (sometimes called (blue-bloods)) seldom mingle with "common" folk. Instead, they attend exclusive <u>private</u> schools where they learn ways of life that support their <u>privileged positions</u>. They don't work for wages; instead, many study business or become lawyers so that they can manage the family fortune. The people *def.* with "new money" are also known as the (nouveau riche). Although they have made fortunes in business, entertainment, or sports, they are <u>outsiders to the upper class</u>.

They have not attended the "right" schools, and they don't share the social networks that come with old money. Children of the new-moneyed can ascend into the top part of the capitalist class—if they go to the right schools *and* marry old money.

—Henslin, *Sociology*, p. 272.

Highlights

In some cases, the easiest and fastest way to mark important facts and ideas is to highlight them with a pen or highlighter. (Many students prefer highlighters because they come in different colors, such as bright yellow or pink, which draw the eye to important material.) When highlighting, you mark the portions of a reading that you need to study, remember, or locate quickly.

Here are a few suggestions for highlighting effectively.

1. **Read a paragraph or section first**, then go back and highlight what is important.

2. **Highlight the topic sentence and any important details you want to remember.**

3. **Be accurate.** Make sure your highlighting reflects the content of the reading. Incomplete highlighting may cause you to miss the main point.

4. **Use a system for highlighting.** For instance, use two different highlighter colors to distinguish between topic sentences and supporting details.

5. **Highlight the right amount.** By highlighting too little, you miss valuable information. By highlighting too much, you are not identifying the most important ideas. As a general rule, the only complete sentences that should be highlighted are topic sentences. In all other sentences, highlight only key phrases or words.

Here is an example of effective highlighting:

> Money (or actually the lack of it) is a major source of stress for many people. In a sense, this is one of the most "valid" stressors because so many of our basic survival needs require money. Anyone struggling to survive on a small income is likely to feel plenty of stress. But money has significance beyond its obvious value as a medium of exchange. Even some of the wealthiest people become stressed over money-related issues. To some people, wealth is a measurement of human value, and their self-esteem is based on their material assets. Stress management for such people requires taking an objective look at the role money plays for them.

—Byer and Shainberg, *Living Well*, pp. 78–79.

Statements and Questions

In many of your writing assignments, you'll be asked to respond to an author's presentation, opinion, or suggestions. By recording your responses in the margin as you read, you take the first step toward writing about your own ideas.

Table 2-2 (p. 30) lists some types of statements and questions you might write in the margins of a reading. Note that it is perfectly acceptable to use abbreviations in your statements and questions! You should feel free to expand this list in any way that helps you "talk" with the reading.

TABLE 2-2. RESPONDING TO A READING IN THE MARGIN

Based on "Studying for Exams," pages 19–21

Ways of Responding	Example of Marginal Annotation
1. **Ask questions.**	What is the best way to prioritize studying?
2. **Challenge the author's ideas.**	Memorization and cramming are better than nothing if I run out of time!
3. **Look for inconsistencies.**	Reading refers to time management tips—where are they in the chapter?
4. **Add examples.**	Matching and true/false questions would also fall under the *Factual* category.
5. **Note exceptions.**	The problem is, my teachers don't always reveal how the test will be set up so I can't find out about the type of test.
6. **Disagree with the author.**	Rewrite reading and lecture notes? It took enough of my time to write them the first time!
7. **Make associations with other sources.**	We talked about different levels of learning and analysis in Psychology last semester. Same ideas about knowledge, application, analysis.
8. **Make judgments.**	This reading has some good ideas, but not all of them will work for my life and schedule.
9. **Make notes to yourself.**	Talk to Gus and Mbulungi about studying together this week. What are they thinking will be on the essay part of our next test?
10. **Ask instructor to clarify.**	Ask Prof: Where can I get a copy of the graph she showed in class?

EXERCISE 2-3   Using Marking and Annotating

Directions: Annotate or mark the following readings using any of the techniques described above. Use whichever techniques work best for you.

1. Amusement Parks

The first amusement parks, which were called pleasure gardens, were built in England and France. Some of the largest and most popular amusement parks such as Gardaland on Italy's Lake Garda and Tivoli in Denmark attract millions of visitors each year. As the name *pleasure garden* implies, these attractions began as manicured gardens designed to provide a temporary escape for city dwellers from the everyday drudgeries of life. Rides such as carousels, games, and food and drink stands were added to these pleasure gardens to meet visitors' needs.

The idea of parks with rides and other entertainment activities soon found its way to the United States. Interest in amusements in the United States heightened when the Ferris wheel was introduced at the 1893 Chicago World's Fair. The name for this new amusement, which became the centerpiece of most modern amusement parks, was taken from its inventor, George Washington Gales Ferris.

—adapted from Cook, Yale, and Marqua, *Tourism*, p. 214.

2. Dieting

Millions of people in the United States want to lose weight without sacrificing their favorite foods, without pain, and without great effort. If only we could be thin and firm by waving a magic wand! It is very popular to resort to well-publicized weight-loss programs that involve special food requirements such as high-fat, low-protein, low-carbohydrate, or liquid protein. There are hundreds of such programs that continue to come and go. Many of them are reported as "breakthroughs," but if this were the case, even newer breakthroughs would not be needed.

There is usually at least one fad diet book on the best-seller list in any given week. Some fad diets are simple variations of a basic 1000–1100-calorie balanced diet. Others may be dangerous because they emphasize one food or food group and the elimination of others, and advise people to follow diets low in energy and nutrients. Some fad diets are more hazardous to a person's health than the obesity they propose to cure, creating adverse reactions ranging from headaches to death. Of 29,000 claims, treatments, and therapies for losing weight, fewer than 6 percent are effective, and 13 percent are downright dangerous. Ultimately, the problem is that most diet plans focus on short-term (and often futile) weight loss, which results in weight cycling, or "yo-yo" dieting, and psychological problems that result from repeated failures to keep weight off. Only 5 percent of people who try are able to maintain their weight losses. Much better is a program of lifetime weight management, which involves learning new eating and exercise habits.

—adapted from Byer and Shainberg, *Living Well*, p. 311. ∎

USING IDEA MAPS

GOAL 5 Create idea maps

Many students have difficulty remembering what they have read and find they have to reread frequently in order to write about a reading. One solution to this problem is to draw an idea map: a diagram that helps you both understand and remember how the writer's ideas relate to one another and how the essay is organized. Idea maps work because they force you to think about and analyze the relationships between ideas. They also are effective because they require you to express ideas from the reading in your own words; this activity increases your recall of those ideas.

Here is a sample idea map for the reading "Studying for Exams." Notice that it includes all of the key ideas.

 Visualize It!

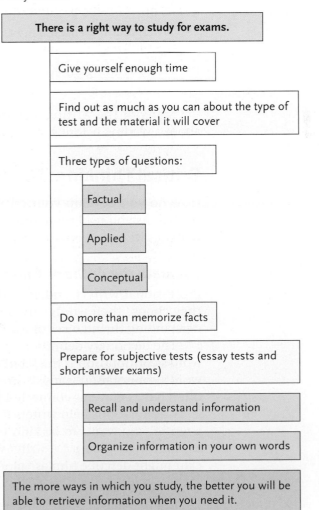

There is a right way to study for exams.

Give yourself enough time

Find out as much as you can about the type of test and the material it will cover

Three types of questions:

Factual

Applied

Conceptual

Do more than memorize facts

Prepare for subjective tests (essay tests and short-answer exams)

Recall and understand information

Organize information in your own words

The more ways in which you study, the better you will be able to retrieve information when you need it.

PREPARING TO WRITE: THINKING CRITICALLY

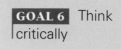

GOAL 6 Think critically

College writing assignments are not just about reading and memorization. They are also about *thinking*. You may have noticed that annotation skills require you not only to identify key material, but also to *analyze* what you are reading. **Critical thinking** is another term for analytical thinking.

In this context, *critical* does not mean "negative." Critical thinking requires you to evaluate what you read, rather than to accept everything as *the truth*. Thinking critically sometimes requires you to disagree with the author or express a different opinion.

The Benefits of Critical Thinking

The ability to think and read critically offers many benefits to writers. Specifically, critical thinking allows you to:

- Distinguish good information from incomplete, inaccurate, or misleading information.
- Write paragraphs, essays, term papers, and essay exams that exhibit a strong understanding of what you've read.

Critical reading should take place at all times, no matter what you read. For example:

- When reading a college textbook, you might ask yourself if the author is trying to influence your opinions.
- When reading a newspaper, you might ask yourself if the journalist is telling the full story or if she is leaving something out.
- When reading an advertisement, you might ask yourself what techniques the ad is using to get you to buy the product.

Many of the writing assignments in this book ask you to think critically about a reading before you begin writing.

Critical Thinking: The Basics

How do you develop your critical-thinking abilities? Here are six tips to get started. As you read these tips, remember that they will help make you a better writer as well as a better reader.

Evaluate the Author's Choice of Words

Professional writers understand that words influence the reader greatly, and they choose their words carefully. For this reason, reading critically means understanding the nuances of words and how they affect the reader.

The dictionary definition of a word, its literal meaning, is its **denotation**. A word's **connotation** is the set of additional associations that it takes on. Often, a word's connotation is much stronger than its denotation because connotations often have emotions connected to them.

Connotations help writers influence the reader's opinion on the topic. Thus a writer who wants to be kind to an overweight politician might describe him as "pleasingly plump." A writer who wants to be negative about the same politician might describe him as "morbidly obese" or "grossly fat."

As you evaluate the writer's choice of words, ask yourself:

- What adjectives (descriptive words) does the writer use, and how do they affect me?
- Do any of the words have a strong emotional component to them? What is the writer's purpose in using these words?

For more on choosing the best words in your own writing, see Writers' Workshops: Using Words Effectively, pp. 76–81.

Distinguish Between Facts and Opinions

Facts are statements that can be verified—that is, proven to be true. Opinions are statements that express feelings, attitudes, or beliefs and are neither true nor false.

Facts

Martin Luther King, Jr., was assassinated in 1968.
The main source of food for Native Americans was the buffalo.

Opinions

Americans should give up their cars and take public transportation instead.
By the year 2025, food shortages will be a major problem in most Asian countries.

Opinions are sometimes signaled by the use of such key words or phrases as *apparently, this suggests, some believe, it is likely that, seemingly, in my view,* and *one explanation is.*

Opinions can be divided into two categories. Informed opinions are made by people whose learning and experience qualify them to offer expert opinions. Uninformed opinions are made by those who have few qualifications. To determine whether an opinion is informed or not, ask these questions:

- What experience does this person have regarding the subject matter?
- What do other respected authorities think of this person?
- Is the opinion expressed in a respectful way? Or is it expressed in a manner that is disrespectful or intolerant?
- Does the opinion appear in a respected publication, or is it found on a Web site where people can say whatever they want?

Be sure to read the directions for your writing assignments carefully. If the assignment calls for strictly factual reporting, do not offer your opinion.

Recognize and Evaluate Generalizations

A **generalization** is a statement made about a large group based on observation or experience with a portion of that group. For example, "College freshmen are disoriented during their first week on campus" is a generalization. By visiting colleges and observing freshman, you could make the generalization that freshmen are disoriented. However, unless you observe every student on every campus in the world, you could not be certain your generalization applies to all students.

Much of what you read will contain generalizations, and you will sometimes be asked to write generalizations yourself. Because writers usually do not have the space to describe all available evidence, they often make a general statement of what the evidence shows. To evaluate a generalization, ask yourself:

- **Does the author provide evidence to support the generalization?** Generalizations without any supporting evidence are often untrustworthy.
- **What is the basis of the author's generalization?** Is it based on many years of observation or reading (reliable) or on just one observation or source (unreliable)?

Your own writing will be the most persuasive when you give evidence to support any generalizations you make.

Look for Bias

Read the following statements and determine what they have in common:

- Laboratory experiments using live animals are forms of mutilation and torture.
- The current vitamin fad is a distortion of sound medical advice.

Each statement reflects a **bias**—a preference for or prejudice against a person, object, or idea. Biased material is one-sided. Other facts, such as the advantages of using animals for laboratory research, or research that has confirmed the value of taking vitamins, are not mentioned. (Notice, too, the use of emotional words such as *mutilation, torture,* and *distortion.*)

Much of what you read and hear expresses a bias. In many newspapers and magazine articles, nonfiction books, and essays you will find the opinions and beliefs of the author revealed. Some writers reveal their attitudes directly by stating how they feel. Others do so less directly, expressing their attitudes through the manner in which they write. As you read, ask yourself the following questions:

- What facts were omitted? What additional facts are needed?
- What impression would I have if different words had been used?

Evaluate Different Viewpoints and Develop Your Own Opinion

College reading and writing assignments provide you with opportunities to encounter new ideas and viewpoints. Some of these ideas may force you to reexamine how you think about a particular issue. An instructor may raise a controversial or current topic or issue by asking you to read different articles with different viewpoints, and then ask you to write about them.

When reading materials that challenge your beliefs:

- Put aside or suspend temporarily what you already think about the issue.
- Look for and evaluate evidence that suggests the viewpoint is well thought out.
- To overcome the natural tendency to pay more attention to points of view you agree with, deliberately spend more time reading, thinking about, and examining ideas that differ from your own.

To fully grasp varying viewpoints, try writing a summary of each in your own words.

Understand the Power of Images

A writer can choose visual aids that reflect his or her opinions. Consider the following excerpt and the photo that accompanies it.

> Is alcohol bad for health? This beverage cuts both ways. One to two drinks a day for men and one drink for women reduces the risk of heart attacks, strokes, gallstones, and diabetes. Beyond these amounts, however, alcohol scars the liver, damages the heart, and increases the risk of breast cancer. It also increases the likelihood of birth defects. One-third of the 43,000 Americans who die each year in vehicle accidents are drunk. Each year, 700,000 Americans seek treatment for alcohol problems.

—adapted from Henslin, *Sociology*, pp. 580–581.

A Vermont state trooper in Newport, VT, checks the wrecked car that four teens died in while returning from a night drinking in Quebec.

The passage is very matter-of-fact. It summarizes the benefits and drawbacks of drinking alcohol. But also note how intense the photo is. Just looking it at, you know that a horrible accident has occurred and someone has probably died. Thus the photo makes the author's message about the drawbacks of alcohol much stronger than his message about its benefits.

When viewing a photo or other visual aid, ask yourself:

- What is the author's reason for including this photo? Is it meant to appeal to my emotions?

- Does the photo reinforce the author's opinions or biases?

EXERCISE 2-4   Reading Critically

Directions: Read the following paragraph, and think analytically and critically when you answer the questions that follow.

> In survey after survey, 60 to 80 percent of food shoppers say they read food labels before selecting products; they consume more vegetables, fruits, and lower-fat foods; and they are cutting down on portion sizes and total calories. Diet-book sales are at an all-time high as millions of people make the leap toward what they think is healthy eating. But we still have a long way to go. In fact, although reports indicate that increasing numbers of us read labels and are trying to eat more healthfully, nearly 78% of all adults indicate that they are not eating the recommended servings of fruits and vegetables and that they are still eating too many refined carbohydrates and high-fat foods.

—Donatelle, *Health*, p. 255.

1. The passage talks about "surveys," which is another word for "question-naires." Why might the survey results not truly reflect reality?

   _____

   _____

2. Does the fact that diet-book sales are at an all-time high mean that more people are going on diets and/or eating more healthfully? In a sentence or two, explain why or why not.

   _____

   _____

3. Write a sentence or two summarizing the author's opinion regarding a good way to eat more healthfully. Do you agree or disagree with this opinion?

   _____

   _____

4. Have you ever watched a friend, co-worker, or family member start a diet? On a separate sheet of paper, write a paragraph describing that person's approach to dieting. For example, did he or she decide to start exercising every morning? Did his or her approach work? ■

EXERCISE 2-5   Taking Notes

Directions: If your instructor conducts a class discussion of the reading "Studying for Exams," take brief notes during the discussion and fill them in when the class is over. Possible discussion questions are:

1. How do you approach studying for exams?
2. What are the three types of questions? Give an example of each type.
3. Why is cramming a bad idea? ■

EXERCISE 2-6   Applying Your Skills
Working Together

Directions: Select two or more techniques suggested in "Studying for Exams." Write a journal entry in response to the following question: How can you apply these techniques to your studies? Compare your entry with that of a classmate, and create a Tip Sheet that would be useful to other students not in your writing class. ■

HOW TO WRITE ABOUT A READING

GOAL 7 Write about a reading

Once you've read, annotated, and thought critically about a reading, you are ready to write. Each reading in this book is followed by a series of exercises to help you develop your skills.

1. **"Examining the Reading Using an Idea Map"** asks you to map the reading visually.

2. **"Strengthening Your Vocabulary"** helps you expand your vocabulary.

3. **"Reacting to Ideas: Discussion and Journal Writing"** offers questions that can stimulate discussion with your peers, as well as ideas for writing in your journal. As you prepare to discuss or write, ask yourself the following questions to direct your thinking:

   - Why did the author write this? What was his or her purpose?

   - For what audience was the essay written?

   - What issue, problem, concern, or question does the essay address?

   - What is the author's main point or position on the issue?

   - What types of words and visuals did the author use? Why?

4. **"Writing About the Reading"** offers both paragraph and essay assignments on topics related to the reading. When your instructor gives you an assignment, use the following suggestions to help you produce a solid, well-written paper:

   - **Read the assignment several times before you begin.** Express in your own words what the assignment requires. If you have a choice of assignments, take a fair amount of time to choose. It is worthwhile to spend a few minutes thinking about and weighing possible topics. You don't want to work your way through a first draft and then realize that you don't have enough to say or you cannot work well with the topic.

   - **Try discussing the assignment with a classmate.** By talking about it, you can make sure you are on the right track, and you may discover new or additional ideas to write about. Also consider asking the classmate to react to your paper once you have a draft.

   - **Review your journal entries and notes of class discussions for possible topics or approaches to the assignment.** (Chapter 11, "Planning and Organizing," offers several strategies for discovering and selecting ideas to write about.)

   - **Don't be satisfied with the first draft that you write.** As you will discover in Chapter 12, "Drafting and Revising," you need to rethink and revise both what you have said and how you said it.

THINK AS YOU READ: A USER'S GUIDE

Throughout this chapter you have seen that reading is an active process of thinking and responding to what you read. Before you read, you preview and connect the reading to your own experience. While reading you are searching for meaning, noticing the author's flow and organization of ideas, and paying attention to paragraph and essay structure. After reading, you respond to the text by marking, annotating, and drawing ideas maps. Thinking critically and responding to the reading occurs both while and after reading. As you read you may have initial thoughts and reactions. They may be better formed and more complete when you reflect after reading.

To guide you through the process of thinking before, during, and after reading, each of the professional readings at the end of the chapters of this book is structured as a guide to demonstrate how an active reader thinks and questions before, during, and after reading. Here is a sample of the guide, excerpted from the professional reading for this chapter, starting on page 39. Arrows and annotations explain to you the parts of this guide. Questions and activities appear before you read that help you get ready to read. Marginal bubbles appear in the blue margin titled, "Think As You Read" along the side of the reading to guide your thinking as you read. Questions and writing assignments appear after the reading to guide your response to the reading.

To get the most benefit from this guide, read the essay, answering the questions asked in the bubbles as they appear in the blue margin. It is fine to move back and forth between the paragraph or sentence in the reading and the bubble. As you get in the habit of thinking as you read, you will find that you understand more, can recall more of what you read, and are better prepared to write about what you have read. Be sure to follow the model of this guide as you read essays in Part VI: A Thematic Reader, starting on page 483, and in everything you read for all of your other courses. Expect results! You will experience a big difference.

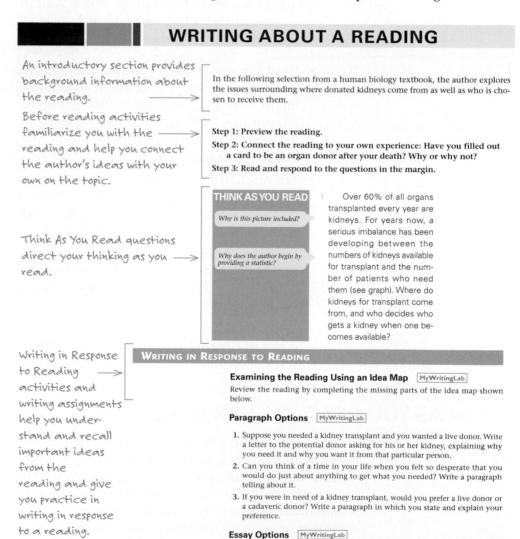

WRITING ABOUT A READING

An introductory section provides background information about the reading.

In the following selection from a human biology textbook, the author explores the issues surrounding where donated kidneys come from as well as who is chosen to receive them.

Before reading activities familiarize you with the reading and help you connect the author's ideas with your own on the topic.

Step 1: Preview the reading.

Step 2: Connect the reading to your own experience: Have you filled out a card to be an organ donor after your death? Why or why not?

Step 3: Read and respond to the questions in the margin.

Think As You Read questions direct your thinking as you read.

THINK AS YOU READ

Why is this picture included?

Why does the author begin by providing a statistic?

Over 60% of all organs transplanted every year are kidneys. For years now, a serious imbalance has been developing between the numbers of kidneys available for transplant and the number of patients who need them (see graph). Where do kidneys for transplant come from, and who decides who gets a kidney when one becomes available?

Writing in Response to Reading activities and writing assignments help you understand and recall important ideas from the reading and give you practice in writing in response to a reading.

WRITING IN RESPONSE TO READING

Examining the Reading Using an Idea Map [MyWritingLab]

Review the reading by completing the missing parts of the idea map shown below.

Paragraph Options [MyWritingLab]

1. Suppose you needed a kidney transplant and you wanted a live donor. Write a letter to the potential donor asking for his or her kidney, explaining why you need it and why you want it from that particular person.

2. Can you think of a time in your life when you felt so desperate that you would do just about anything to get what you needed? Write a paragraph telling about it.

3. If you were in need of a kidney transplant, would you prefer a live donor or a cadaveric donor? Write a paragraph in which you state and explain your preference.

Essay Options [MyWritingLab]

4. Write an essay in which you discuss your reasons, as a live donor, for donating/not donating a kidney to a total stranger.

5. Critics charge that the current system of kidney allocation is discriminatory. Write an essay in which you discuss the reasons for these charges and improvements that could be made to the system to render it fairer.

6. Should donors or families of donors be paid for their donation? Write an essay in which you take and defend a stand on this issue.

WRITING ABOUT A READING

In the following selection from a human biology textbook, the author explores the issues surrounding where donated kidneys come from as well as who is chosen to receive them.

Step 1: Preview the reading.

Step 2: Connect the reading to your own experience: Have you filled out a card to be an organ donor after your death? Why or why not?

Step 3: Read and respond to the questions in the margin.

THINK AS YOU READ

Why is this picture included?

Why does the author begin by providing a statistic?

Why is this sentence italicized?

What is the main point of the graph?

HOW SHOULD WE ALLOCATE SCARCE KIDNEYS?

Michael D. Johnson

1   Over 60% of all organs transplanted every year are kidneys. For years now, a serious imbalance has been developing between the numbers of kidneys available for transplant and the number of patients who need them (see graph). Where do kidneys for transplant come from, and who decides who gets a kidney when one becomes available?

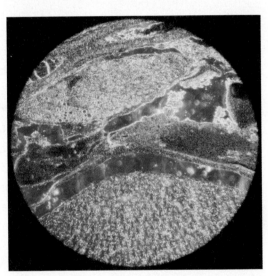

SEM of kidney glomeruli (red) and the blood vessels that supply them. The glomerular capsule and the nephron tubules have been removed.

2   About 40% of all donated kidneys come from living donors; the rest come from cadavers. Patient and donor must have the same blood type and be tested for six key tissue antigens that determine the closeness of the immunological match. Living donors are usually close relatives, but even among close relatives the chances of a perfect match are not all that good. Matches between unrelated donors are rare. *The responsibility for finding a living donor rests with the patient.* There is no national registry of living unrelated potential donors.

3   If a patient cannot find his/her own living donor, the only source is a deceased person (a cadaver). Organs may be harvested from a cadaver only when permission has been granted by the deceased or by the deceased's relatives. Persons who wish to donate their organs after death can make their wishes known by signing and carrying a uniform donor card available through most state motor vehicle departments or on the web. To make it easy for you, some states will indicate "organ donor" on your driver's license, with your permission.

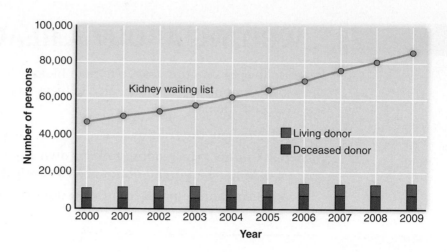

How are Cadaver Kidneys Currently Allocated?

4   Cadaver kidneys are allocated to patients according to federal rules established by the Department of Health and Human Services (DHHS). Patients who need a kidney place themselves on the transplant list of 1 of 11 regional Organ Procurement Organizations (OPO), linked together by the United Network for Organ Sharing (UNOS), a national private nonprofit corporation. UNOS maintains the national waiting lists of potential transplant recipients. When a kidney becomes available in a particular region it is tested for blood type and the six antigens. Perfect matches—the same blood type and the same six antigens—are so rare that a patient anywhere in the country has first priority for a perfectly matched kidney.

5   For all partial matches, the kidney is first made available to all patients in the region of the OPO that procured the kidney. If none of the patients in that region is considered suitable, the kidney is made available (by UNOS) to patients in all other OPOs. A patient's income is not supposed to be a consideration, but people who are willing to pay for the transplant themselves can put themselves on the transplant lists of several OPOs simultaneously. (Insurance generally pays for a transplant only in the patient's primary OPO.)

6   Critics charge that the current system is unfair because organs do not always go to the sickest patients, who need them the most. The current system may also discriminate against minorities and the poor because they live in regions that have lower rates of organ donation.

Developments to Watch

7   Currently it is against the law to sell a kidney—they can only be donated. Studies show that only about 50% of families of a deceased potential donor give their consent, even when asked. To increase this number, the American Medical Association suggests that families who donate cadaveric kidneys from a loved one should be "compensated" in some way, but so far it isn't allowed.

8   At least 24 countries have adopted "presumed consent" laws. Under presumed consent, organs are presumed to be available for donation unless the donor (or family) explicitly states otherwise. Presumed consent laws have dramatically increased donations in countries that have adopted them. In the

Why are prefect matches rare?

How can a patient's income become a factor?

Why is the current system unfair?

What are "presumed consent" laws?

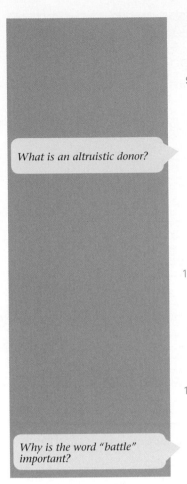

What is an altruistic donor?

Why is the word "battle" important?

United States, however, presumed consent laws have not gained widespread acceptance, because they can be viewed as a subtle form of government coercion or religious discrimination.

9   In desperation, some patients are finding their own unrelated living donors on the Internet. The first commercial Web site to match living "altruistic donors" with patients was MatchingDonors.com. Patients who need an organ make an appeal on the site, and potential donors read through them and choose a patient to help, provided the immunological match is good. They also have a "paired exchange program," in which the patient finds a donor (perhaps a relative) who is willing to donate a kidney on the patient's behalf but is not a good match. Then they search the site for another patient/donor pair with exactly the opposite incompatibility, and an exchange is made. That way, two transplants are possible even though neither patient initially had a compatible donor.

10   There are also Web sites that can increase your chances of finding a cadaveric kidney privately, outside the government-sanctioned UNOS system. LifeSharers (www.lifeshares.org) is a non-profit national network of people who are willing to donate their organs to the network after death, in exchange for the chance of receiving an organ from the network should they need one during their lifetimes.

11   At least five states (Kentucky, Louisiana, Oklahoma, South Carolina, and Wisconsin) have passed laws mandating that organs donated in their states must be offered first to in-state patients. Whether these laws will stand up under challenge is an open question. The battle for scarce organs continues.

Questions to Consider

1. How do you think we should allocate cadaveric kidneys and other organs? What improvements, if any, would you suggest to the present system?

2. Would you be willing to donate your kidneys or other organs after death? Have you completed a donor card?

3. Should the government set up a national registry to match living donors with unrelated patients? Why or why not?

The Facts...

- There are not enough donated cadaveric kidneys to meet the growing need for kidney transplants.

- The responsibility for finding a living donor rests with the patient.

- Under current federal allocation rules, where you live may affect your chances of receiving a cadaveric kidney.

- Some patients are using Web sites to find unrelated living or cadaveric donors.

WRITING IN RESPONSE TO READING

Examining the Reading Using an Idea Map   MyWritingLab

Review the reading by completing the missing parts of the idea map shown below.

Visualize It!

Title   **How Should We Allocate Scarce Kidneys?**

Thesis   Both the source of donated kidneys and who is chosen to receive them are issues.

How are cadaver kidneys _____?

UNOS _____ _____.

Patients anywhere in the country have priority if they are _____

For a partial match, _____ have priority.

_____ is not supposed to be a factor, but in some cases, it is.

Developments to watch

Compensation _____ _____.

Presumed Consent laws presume that the organs of a deceased person are available unless _____ _____.

Some patients are using the _____ to find altruistic donors.

LifeSharers.com is a website that helps patients find _____.

Some states have also passed _____ _____.

Conclusion   The scarcity of available kidneys is a continuing problem.

Strengthening Your Vocabulary   `MyWritingLab`

Using the word's context, word parts, or a dictionary, write a brief definition of each of the following words as it is used in the reading.

1. cadavers (paragraph 2) _____

2. procured (paragraph 5) _____

3. altruistic (paragraph 9) _____

4. compatible (paragraph 9) _____

5. mandating (paragraph 11) _____

Reacting to Ideas: Discussion and Journal Writing   `MyWritingLab`

Get ready to write about the reading by discussing the following:

1. What was the author's purpose in writing this article?

2. What do you think of the presumed consent law described in this reading?

3. In one word, how would you describe the current system of allocating kidneys?

4. Why do some people argue that the current system of allocating kidneys is unfair?

5. What message does the graph accompanying this reading communicate?

Paragraph Options   `MyWritingLab`

1. Suppose you needed a kidney transplant and you wanted a live donor. Write a letter to the potential donor asking for his or her kidney, explaining why you need it and why you want it from that particular person.

2. Can you think of a time in your life when you felt so desperate that you would do just about anything to get what you needed? Write a paragraph telling about it.

3. If you were in need of a kidney transplant, would you prefer a live donor or a cadaveric donor? Write a paragraph in which you state and explain your preference.

Essay Options   `MyWritingLab`

4. Write an essay in which you discuss your reasons, as a live donor, for donating/not donating a kidney to a total stranger.

5. Critics charge that the current system of kidney allocation is discriminatory. Write an essay in which you discuss the reasons for these charges and improvements that could be made to the system to render it fairer.

6. Should donors or families of donors be paid for their donation? Write an essay in which you take and defend a stand on this issue.

■ ■ ■ ■

SELF-TEST SUMMARY

To test yourself, cover the Answer column with a sheet of paper and answer each question in the left column. Evaluate each of your answers as you work by sliding the paper down and comparing your answer with what is printed in the Answer column.

	QUESTION	ANSWER
GOAL 1 Preview before reading	What is previewing?	Previewing is a way of becoming familiar with what a reading is about and how it is organized *before* you read it.
GOAL 2 Read for meaning	What should you look for in paragraphs and essays?	In paragraphs, look for the three main parts: the topic, the main idea, and the supporting details. In essays, pay attention to the title, the introduction, the author's main point, support and explanation, and the conclusion.
GOAL 3 Read more effectively	What are some methods for handling difficult readings?	To approach difficult material, begin by analyzing where and when you are reading. Look up unfamiliar words and try to rephrase material in your own words. Reread or read aloud difficult sections, outline major points, and slow down your reading rate. (See the complete list of "Tips for Reading Difficult Material" on page 27.)
GOAL 4 Mark and annotate text	What is annotation? What are different types of annotation?	Annotation is a way of jotting down your ideas, reactions, and opinions as you read. Different types of annotation include symbols and abbreviations, highlights, and statements and questions.
GOAL 5 Create idea maps	What are idea maps and how do they work?	Idea maps are diagrams that help you understand and remember how the writer's ideas relate to one another and how the essay is organized. They work because they force you to think about the relationships between ideas.
GOAL 6 Think critically	How do you develop your critical-thinking abilities?	Develop your critical thinking abilities by evaluating the author's choice of words, distinguishing between facts and opinions, recognizing and evaluating generalizations, looking for bias, evaluating different viewpoints, and understanding the power of images.
GOAL 7 Write about a reading	How should you approach writing about a reading?	Read the assignment several times before you begin, discuss the assignment with a classmate, look for topic ideas or approaches in your journal entries and notes, and don't be satisfied with your first draft.

MyWritingLab *Visit Ch. 2 The Reading-Writing Connection in MyWritingLab to test your understanding of the chapter objectives.*

3 Expanding Your Vocabulary

Learning Goals

In this chapter, you will learn how to

GOAL 1 Use dictionaries and thesauruses effectively

GOAL 2 Use context clues to figure out unfamiliar words

GOAL 3 Use word parts to figure out the meanings of words

GOAL 4 Understand idioms

GOAL 5 Develop a system for learning new words

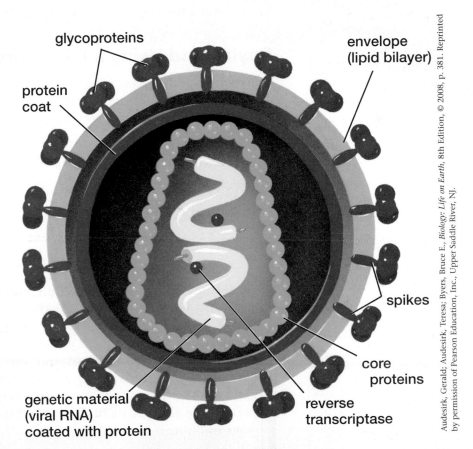

glycoproteins

protein coat

envelope (lipid bilayer)

spikes

core proteins

genetic material (viral RNA) coated with protein

reverse transcriptase

Audesirk, Gerald; Audesirk, Teresa; Byers, Bruce E., *Biology: Life on Earth*, 8th Edition, © 2008, p. 381. Reprinted by permission of Pearson Education, Inc., Upper Saddle River, NJ.

WRITE ABOUT IT!

The labels that accompany the diagram above contain several unfamiliar words. Write a list of ways you can figure out their meanings. In this chapter you will learn numerous strategies for figuring out and learning unfamiliar words.

VOCABULARY

Your vocabulary is one of your most valuable assets. Because words are the basic building blocks of language, you need a strong vocabulary to express yourself clearly in both speech and writing. A strong vocabulary identifies you as an effective communicator—an important skill both in college and in the workplace. Further, a solid vocabulary is the mark of an educated person—someone who is able to think, write, read critically, and speak effectively. Vocabulary building is well worth your while, and will pay off hundreds of times both in college and on the job. Let's get started!

GET THE RIGHT TOOLS

GOAL 1 Use dictionaries and thesauruses effectively

Building your vocabulary is much easier if you have the right tools to help you. Be sure you have a dictionary, and consider purchasing a thesaurus.

Buying and Using a Dictionary

Every writer needs access to a dictionary, not only to check spellings, but also to check meanings and the appropriate usages of words. You may use a desk or collegiate dictionary, or a pocket dictionary or an online dictionary. Widely used print dictionaries include:

The American Heritage Dictionary of the English Language

Webster's New Collegiate Dictionary

Webster's New World Dictionary of the American Language

> **Tip for Writers**
>
> ESL students will find an ESL dictionary extremely helpful for speaking and writing. Written for the nonnative speaker of English, it gives definitions in the simplest language possible, contains sample sentences to show how words are used, explains the differences between easily confused words, contains lots of labeled pictures, and offers many additional features. For students ready to write paragraphs and essays, the *Longman Advanced American Dictionary* is a good choice. (There are also ESL dictionaries for British English and for both American and British English.)

Several dictionaries are available online. One of the most widely used is Merriam-Webster's (http://www.m-w.com). This site features an audio component that allows you to hear how a word is pronounced. You might also refer to http://www.dictonary.com. This site allows you to view and compare entries from several different dictionaries for a given word.

Here is a brief review of the information a dictionary entry contains. As you read, refer to the sample dictionary entry shown below.

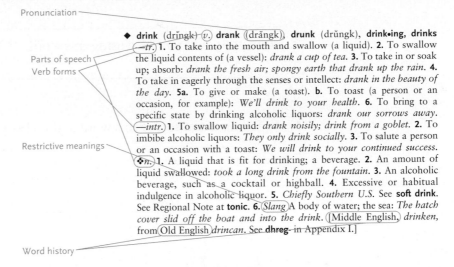

American Heritage Dictionary of the English Language

1. **Pronunciation** The pronunciation of the word is given in parentheses. Symbols are used to indicate the sounds letters make within specific words. Refer to the pronunciation key printed on each page or on alternate pages of your dictionary.

2. **Grammatical information** The part of speech is indicated, as well as information about different forms the word may take. Most dictionaries include

   - principal forms of verbs (both regular and irregular).
   - plural forms of irregular nouns.
   - comparative and superlative forms of adjectives and adverbs.

3. **Meanings** Meanings are numbered and are usually grouped by the part of speech they represent.

4. **Restrictive meanings** Meanings that are limited to special situations are labeled. Some examples are

   - *Slang*—casual language used only in conversation.
   - *Biol.*—words used in specialized fields, in this case biology.
   - *Regional*—words used only in certain parts of the United States.

5. **Synonyms** Words with similar meanings may be listed.

6. **Word history** The origin of the word (its etymology) is described. (Not all dictionaries include this feature.)

EXERCISE 3-1   Using a Dictionary 1

Directions: Use a dictionary to complete each of the following items.

word: *reconstitute*

1. Write one definition of this word and identify its part of speech.

   _____

2. Write your own sentence using this word.

   _____

word: *launch*

1. Write one definition of this word and identify its part of speech.

_____

2. Write your own sentence using this word.

_____

word: *console*

1. Write one definition of this word and identify its part of speech.

_____

2. Write your own sentence using this word.

_____

■

EXERCISE 3-2   Using a Dictionary 2

Directions: Use a dictionary to answer the following questions.

1. What does the abbreviation *obs.* mean?

_____

2. What does the symbol *c.* stand for?

_____

3. How many meanings are listed for the word *fall*?

_____

4. How is the word *phylloxera* pronounced? (Record its phonetic spelling.)

_____

5. What is the plural spelling of *addendum*?

_____

6. Can the word *protest* be used other than as a verb? If so, how?

_____

7. The word *prime* can mean first or original. List some of its other meanings.

_____

8. What does the French expression *savoir faire* mean?

_____

9. List three synonyms for the word *fault*.

_____

10. List several words that are formed using the word *dream*.

_____

■

Finding the Right Meaning in a Dictionary Entry

Most words have more than one meaning. When you look up the meaning of a new word, you must choose the meaning that best fits the way the word is used in the context of the sentence. The following sample entry for the word *green* contains many meanings for the word.

Meanings grouped by parts of speech

7 Nouns

12 Adjectives

1 Verb

Many different meanings

Type of vegetable

Part of golf course

Unripe fruit

Inexperienced person

green (grēn) *n.* **1.** The hue of that portion of the visible spectrum lying between yellow and blue, evoked in the human observer by radiant energy with wavelengths of approximately 490 to 570 nanometers; any of a group of colors that may vary in lightness and saturation and whose hue is that of the emerald or somewhat less yellow that that of growing grass; one of the additive or light primaries; one of the psychological primary hues. **2.** Something green in color. **3. greens** Green growth or foliage, especially: **a.** The branches and leaves of plants used for decoration. **b.** Leafy plants or plant parts eaten as vegetables. **4.** A grassy lawn or plot, especially: **a.** A grassy area located usually at the center of a city or town and set aside for common use; a common. **b.** *Sports* A putting green. **5. greens** A green uniform: "A young...sergeant in dress greens" (Nelson DeMille). **6.** *Slang* Money. **7. Green** A supporter of a social and political movement that espouses global environmental protection, bioregionalism, social responsibility, and nonviolence. ❖*adj.* **green•er, green•est 1.** Of the color green. **2.** Abounding in or covered with green growth or foliage: *the green woods.* **3.** Made with green or leafy vegetables: *a green salad.* **4.** Characterized by mild or temperate weather: *a green climate.* **5.** Youthful; vigorous: *at the green age of 18.* **6.** Not mature or ripe; young: *green tomatoes.* **7.** Brand-new; fresh. **8.** Not yet fully processed, especially: **a.** Not aged: *green wood.* **b.** Not cured or tanned: *green pelts.* **9.** Lacking training or experience. See synonyms at **young. 10a.** Lacking sophistication or worldly experience; naive. **b.** Easily duped or deceived; gullible. **11.** Having a sickly or unhealthy pallor indicative of nausea or jealousy, for example. **12a.** Beneficial to the environment: *green recycling policies.* **b.** Favoring or supporting environmentalism: *green legislators who strengthened pollution controls.* ❖*tr. & intr. v.* greened, green•ing, greens To make or become green.
—*idiom:* **green around** (or **about) the gills** Pale or sickly in appearance. [Middle English *grene,* from Old English *grēne,* see **ghrē-** in Appendix I. N., sense 7, translation of German *(die) Grünen,* (the) Greens, from *grün,* green.] —**green'ly** *adv.* —**green'ness** *n.*

American Heritage Dictionary of the English Language

Tip for Writers

A bilingual dictionary translates from your native language to English and vice versa. However, these dictionaries may not give all the different meanings that a word has in English. This type of dictionary is useful but not sufficient for academic writing. ESL students should have an ESL dictionary with a vocabulary of at least 80,000 words and also use a standard desk-size college dictionary.

The meanings are grouped by part of speech and are numbered consecutively in each group. Generally, the most common meanings of the word are listed first, with more specialized, less common meanings appearing toward the end of the entry. Now find the meaning that fits the use of the word *green* in the following sentence:

The local veterans' organization held its annual fund-raising picnic on the village **green**.

In this sentence, *green* refers to "a common or park in the center of a town or village." Since this is a specialized meaning of the word, it appears toward the end of the entry.

Here are a few suggestions for choosing the correct meaning from among those listed in an entry:

1. **If you are familiar with the parts of speech, try to use these to locate the correct meaning.** For instance, if you are looking up the meaning of a word that names a person, place, or thing, you can save time by reading only those entries given after *n.* (noun).

2. **For most types of college reading, you can skip definitions that give slang and colloquial (abbreviated as *colloq.*) meanings.** Colloquial meanings refer to informal or conversational language.

3. **If you are not sure of the part of speech, read each meaning until you find a definition that seems correct.** Skip over restrictive meanings that are inappropriate.

4. **Test your choice by substituting the meaning in the sentence with which you are working.** Substitute the definition for the word and see whether it makes sense in the context of the sentence.

EXERCISE 3-3   Writing Different Meanings

Directions: The following words have two or more meanings. Look them up in your dictionary and write two sentences with different meanings for each word.

1. culture

_____

_____

2. perch

_____

_____

3. surge

_____

_____

4. extend

_____

_____

5. irregular

_____

_____

EXERCISE 3-4   Finding Appropriate Meanings

Directions: Use the dictionary to help you find an appropriate meaning for the boldfaced word in each of the following sentences.

1. The last contestant did not have a **ghost** of a chance.

   _____

2. The race-car driver won the first **heat**.

   _____

3. The police took all possible **measures** to protect the witness.

   _____

4. The orchestra played the first **movement** of the symphony.

   _____

5. The plane stalled on the **apron**.

   _____

   ■

Using a Thesaurus

A **thesaurus** is a dictionary of synonyms. It groups together words with similar meanings. A thesaurus is particularly useful when you want to do the following:

- Locate the precise or exact word to fit a particular situation. (Example: Replace "a _boring_ movie" with "an _uneventful_ movie.")
- Find an appropriate descriptive word. (Example: Choose from among the following words to describe _happiness_: _delight, pleasure, joy, glee_.)
- Replace an overused or unclear word. (Example: Replace "a _good_ television program" with "a _thrilling_ or _refreshing_ television program.")
- Convey a more specific shade of meaning. (Example: Use one of the following words to describe _walking_: _swagger, strut, stroll_.)

Suppose you are looking for a more precise word for the phrase _will tell us about_ in the following sentence:

In class today, our chemistry instructor **will tell us about** our next assignment.

The thesaurus lists the following synonyms for "tell" or "explain":

10 **explain, explicate, expound,** exposit; **give the meaning,** tell the meaning of; **spell out,** unfold; **account for,** give reason for; **clarify, elucidate,** clear up; **make clear,** make plain; **simplify,** popularize; **illuminate,** enlighten, **shed** _or_ **throw light upon**; rationalize, euhemerize, demythologize, allegorize; tell _or_ show how, show the way; **demonstrate, show, illustrate,** exemplify; decipher, crack, unlock, find the key to, unravel, **solve;** explain oneself; explain away.

11 **comment upon,** commentate, remark upon; **annotate,** gloss; **edit,** make an edition.

12 **translate, render,** transcribe, transliterate, put _or_ turn into, transfuse the sense of; construe; English.

13 paraphrase, **rephrase, reword, restate,** rehash; give a free _or_ loose translation.

The American Heritage College Thesaurus

Read the previous entry and underline words or phrases that you think would be more descriptive than *tell about*. You might underline words and phrases such as *comment upon, illustrate, demonstrate,* and *spell out.*

The most widely used thesaurus is *Roget's Thesaurus.* Inexpensive paperback editions are available in most bookstores; online thesauruses are also available.

When you first consult a thesaurus, you will need to familiarize yourself with its format and learn how to use it. The following is a step-by-step approach:

1. **Locate the word you are trying to replace in the index.** Following the word, you will find the number(s) of the section(s) in the main part of the thesaurus that list(s) the synonyms of that word.

2. **Turn to those sections, scanning each list and jotting down all the words you think might work as synonyms.**

3. **Test each of the words you selected in the sentence in which you will use it.** The word should fit the context of the sentence.

4. **Select the word that best expresses what you are trying to say.**

5. **Choose only words whose shades of meaning you know.** Check unfamiliar words in a dictionary before using them. Remember, misusing a word is often a more serious error than choosing an overused or general word.

 **Analyze It!**

Directions: Read the paragraph on the left, taken from a college textbook. Use context, word parts, and a dictionary, if necessary, to figure out the meanings of the words listed on the right. Write the meanings in the space provided.

Human communication, in one way or another, inevitably involves the body in sending and receiving messages. Beyond the mechanics of speaking, hearing, gesturing, and seeing, the body itself can function as a "text" that conveys messages. The full range of body language includes eye movements, posture, walking style, the way of standing and sitting, cultural inscriptions on the body such as tattoos and hairstyles, and accessories such as dress, shoes, and jewelry. Body language follows patterns and rules just as verbal language does. Like verbal language, the rules and meanings are learned, often unconsciously. Without learning the rules and meanings, one will commit communication errors, which are sometimes funny and sometimes serious.

—Miller, *Anthropology,* p. 284.

inevitably _____

_____

mechanics _____

_____

body language _____

_____

accessories _____

_____

unconsciously _____

_____

▌EXERCISE 3-5   Using a Thesaurus

Directions: Using a thesaurus, replace the boldfaced word or phrase in each of the following sentences with a more precise or descriptive word. Write the word in the space provided. Rephrase the sentence, if necessary.

1. Although the movie was **good**, it lasted only an hour and 20 minutes.

   _____

2. The judge **looked at** the criminal as she pronounced the sentence.

   _____

3. The accident victim was awarded a **big** cash settlement.

   _____

4. The lottery winner was **happy** to win the $100,000 prize, but he was surprised to learn that a sizable portion had already been deducted for taxes.

   _____

5. On the first day of class, the instructor **talked to** the class about course requirements.

   _____

                                                                    ▪

USE CONTEXT CLUES TO FIGURE OUT UNFAMILIAR WORDS

GOAL 2 Use context clues to figure out unfamiliar words

Context refers to the words around a given word. Often you can use context to figure out a word you do not know. Try it in the following sentence:

> **Phobias,** such as a fear of heights, water, or confined spaces, are difficult to overcome.

From the clues in the rest of the sentence, you can figure out that *phobias* are fears of specific objects or situations. Such clues are called **context clues**. There are five types of context clues that can help you figure out a word you do not know: *definition, synonym, example, contrast,* and *inference.* These are summarized in the "Need to Know" box shown on the following page.

Context clues do not always appear in the same sentence as the unknown word. They may appear anywhere in the passage, or in an earlier or later sentence. So if you cannot find a clue immediately, look before and after the word. Here is an example:

> Betsy took a *break* from teaching in order to serve in the Peace Corps. Despite the **hiatus**, Betsy's school was delighted to rehire her when she returned.

Notice that the clue for the word *hiatus, break,* appears in the sentence before the one containing the word you want to define.

NEED TO KNOW

Five Useful Types of Context Clues

Type of Context Clue	How It Works	Examples
Definition	Writers often define a word after using it. Words such as *means*, *refers to*, and *can be defined as* provide an obvious clue that the word's meaning is to follow. Sometimes writers use dashes, parentheses, or commas to separate a definition from the rest of the sentence.	**Corona** refers to the outermost part of the sun's atmosphere. Broad flat noodles that are served covered with sauce or butter are called **fettuccine**. The judge's **candor**—his sharp, open frankness—shocked the jury. **Audition**, the process of hearing, begins when a sound wave reaches the outer ear.
Synonym	Rather than formally define a word, some writers include a word or brief phrase that is close in meaning to a word you may not know.	The main character in the movie was an **amalgam**, or combination, of several real people the author met during the war.
Example	Writers often include examples to help explain a word. From the examples, you can often figure out what the unknown word means.	**Toxic** materials, such as arsenic, asbestos, pesticides, and lead, can cause bodily damage. (You can figure out that *toxic* means "poisonous.") Many **pharmaceuticals**, including morphine and penicillin, are not readily available in some countries. (You can figure out that *pharmaceuticals* are drugs.)
Contrast	Sometimes a writer gives a word that is opposite in meaning to a word you don't know. From the opposite meaning, you can figure out the unknown word's meaning. (Hint: watch for words such as *but, however, though, whereas*.)	Uncle Sal was quite **portly**, but his wife was very thin. (The opposite of *thin* is *fat*, so you know that *portly* means "fat.") The professor **advocates** the testing of cosmetics on animals, but many of her students oppose it. (The opposite of *oppose* is *favor*, so you know that *advocates* means "favors.")
Inference	Often your own logic or reasoning skills can lead you to the meaning of an unknown word.	Bob is quite **versatile**: he is a good student, a top athlete, an excellent auto mechanic, and a gourmet cook. (Because Bob excels at many activities, you can reason that *versatile* means "capable of doing many things.") On hot, humid afternoons, I often feel **languid**. (From your experience you may know that you feel drowsy or sluggish on hot afternoons, so you can figure out that *languid* means "lacking energy.")

EXERCISE 3-6   Using Context Clues 1

Directions: Using the definition or synonym clues in each sentence, write a brief definition of each boldfaced word in the following sentences.

1. After taking a course in **genealogy**, Diego was able to create a record of his family's history dating back to the eighteenth century.

   _____

2. Louie's **dossier** is a record of his credentials, including college transcripts and letters of recommendation.

   _____

3. There was a **consensus**—or unified opinion—among the students that the exam was difficult.

   _____

4. After each course heading there was a **synopsis**, or summary, of the content and requirements for the course.

   _____

5. When preparing job application letters, Serena develops one standard letter or **prototype**. Then she changes that letter to fit the specific jobs for which she is applying.

   _____

EXERCISE 3-7   Using Context Clues 2

Directions: Using the example clues in each sentence, write a brief definition of each boldfaced word in the following sentences.

1. **Histrionics**, such as wild laughter or excessive body movements, are usually inappropriate in business settings.

   _____

2. Jerry's child was **reticent** in every respect; she would not speak, refused to answer questions, and avoided looking at anyone.

   _____

3. Most **condiments**, such as pepper, mustard, and catsup, are used to improve the flavor of foods.

   _____

4. Dogs, cats, parakeets, and other **sociable** pets can provide senior citizens with companionship.

   _____

5. Paul's grandmother is a **sagacious** businesswoman; once she turned a small ice cream shop into a popular restaurant and sold it for a huge profit.

   _____

EXERCISE 3-8   Using Context Clues 3

Directions: Using the contrast clues in each sentence, write a brief definition of each boldfaced word in the following sentences.

1. Freshmen are often **naive** about college at first, but by their second semester they are usually quite sophisticated in the ways of their new school.

   _____

2. Although most members of the class agreed with the instructor's evaluation of the film, several strongly **objected**.

   _____

3. Little Jill hid shyly behind her mother when she met new people, yet her brother Matthew was very **gregarious**.

   _____

4. The child remained **demure** while the teacher scolded, but became violently angry afterward.

   _____

5. Some city dwellers are **affluent**; others live in poverty.

   _____

EXERCISE 3-9   Using Context Clues 4

Directions: Using logic and your own reasoning skills, choose the correct definition of each boldfaced word in the following sentences.

_____ 1. To **compel** Clare to hand over her wallet, the mugger said he had a gun.
   a. discourage   c. force
   b. entice   d. imagine

_____ 2. Student journalists are taught how to be **concise** when writing in a limited space.
   a. peaceful   c. proper
   b. clear and brief   d. wordy

_____ 3. There should be more **drastic** penalties to stop people from littering.
   a. extreme   c. dirty
   b. suitable   d. dangerous

_____ 4. To **fortify** his diet while weightlifting, Monty took 12 vitamins a day.
   a. suggest   c. avoid
   b. strengthen   d. approve of

_____ 5. On our wedding anniversary, my husband and I **reminisced** about how we first met.
   a. sang   c. argued
   b. remembered   d. forgot

| **EXERCISE 3-10** | **Using Context Clues in a Passage** |

Directions: Read the following passage and then choose the answer that best defines each boldfaced word appearing in the text.

Worms and *viruses* are rather unpleasant terms that have entered the **jargon** of the computer industry to describe some of the ways that computer systems can be invaded.

A worm can be defined as a program that transfers itself from computer to computer over a network and plants itself as a separate file on the target computer's disks. One worm was **injected** into an electronic mail network where it multiplied uncontrollably and clogged the memories of thousands of computers until they could no longer function.

A virus is a set of illicit instructions that passes itself on to other programs or documents with which it comes in contact. It can change or delete files, display words or obscene messages, or produce bizarre screen effects. In its most **vindictive** form, a virus can slowly **sabotage** a computer system and remain undetected for months, contaminating data or wiping out an entire hard drive. A virus can be dealt with using a vaccine, or antivirus, which is a computer program that stops the virus from spreading and often **eradicates** it.

—adapted from Capron, *Computers.*

_____ 1. jargon
    a. language   **c.** confusion
    b. system   **d.** security

_____ 2. injected
    a. avoided   **c.** removed
    b. introduced   **d.** discussed

_____ 3. vindictive
    a. creative   **c.** spiteful
    b. simple   **d.** typical

_____ 4. sabotage
    a. prevent   **c.** transfer
    b. disable   **d.** produce

_____ 5. eradicates
    a. produces   **c.** repeats
    b. allows   **d.** eliminates ■

PAY ATTENTION TO WORD PARTS

GOAL 3 Use word parts to figure out the meanings of words

Suppose that you came across the following sentence in a human anatomy textbook:

Trichromatic plates are used frequently in the text to illustrate the position of body organs.

If you did not know the meaning of *trichromatic*, how could you determine it? There are no clues in the sentence context. One solution is to look up the word in a dictionary. An easier and faster way is to break the word into parts and analyze the meaning of each part. Many words in the English language are made up of word parts called **prefixes**, **roots**, and **suffixes**. These word parts have specific meanings that, when added together, can help you determine the meaning of the word as a whole.

The word *trichromatic* can be divided into three parts: its prefix, root, and suffix.

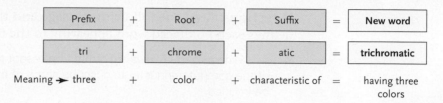

You can see from this analysis that *trichromatic* means "having three colors." Here are a few other examples of words that you can figure out by using prefixes, roots, and suffixes:

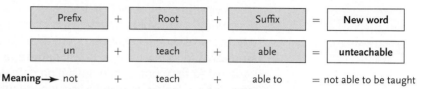

The parents thought their child was unteachable.

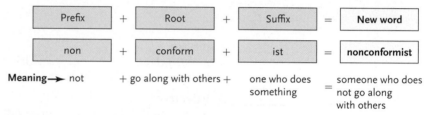

The student was a nonconformist.

The first step in using the prefix-root-suffix method is to become familiar with the most commonly used word parts. The prefixes and roots listed in Table 3-1 and Table 3-2 (see p. 59 and p. 60) will give you a good start in determining the meanings of thousands of words without looking them up in the dictionary. For instance, more than 10,000 words can begin with the prefix *non-*. Not all these words are listed in a collegiate dictionary, but they would appear in an unabridged dictionary. Another common prefix, *pseudo-*, is used in more than 400 words. A small amount of time spent learning word parts can yield a large payoff in new words learned.

Before you begin to use word parts to figure out new words, here are a few things you need to know:

1. **In most cases, a word is built upon at least one root.**

2. **Words can have more than one prefix, root, or suffix.**

   a. Words can be made up of two or more roots (geo/logy).

   b. Some words have two prefixes (in/sub/ordination).

   c. Some words have two suffixes (beauti/ful/ly).

3. **Words do not always have a prefix and a suffix.**

   a. Some words have neither a prefix nor a suffix (read).

   b. Others have a suffix but no prefix (read/ing).

   c. Others have a prefix but no suffix (pre/read).

4. **The spelling of roots may change as they are combined with suffixes.** Some common variations are included in Table 3-2.

TABLE 3-1 COMMON PREFIXES

Prefix	Meaning	Sample Word
Prefixes referring to amount or number		
mono/uni	One	monocle/unicycle
bi/di/du	Two	bimonthly/divorce/duet
tri	Three	Triangle
quad	Four	Quadrant
quint/pent	Five	quintet/pentagon
deci	Ten	decimal
centi	hundred	centigrade
milli	thousand	milligram
micro	small	microscope
multi/poly	many	multipurpose/polygon
semi	half	semicircle
equi	equal	equidistant
Prefixes meaning "not" (negative)		
a	not	asymmetrical
anti	against	antiwar
contra	against, opposite	contradict
dis	apart, away, not	disagree
in/il/ir/im	not	incorrect/illogical/irreversible/impossible
mis	wrongly	misunderstand
non	not	nonfiction
pseudo	false	pseudoscientific
un	not	unpopular
Prefixes giving direction, location, or placement		
ab	away	absent
ad	toward	adhesive
ante/pre	before	antecedent/premarital
circum/peri	around	circumference/perimeter
com/col/con	with, together	compile/collide/convene
de	away, from	depart
dia	through	diameter
ex/extra	from, out of, former	ex-wife/extramarital
hyper	over, excessive	hyperactive
inter	between	interpersonal
intro/intra	within, into, in	introduction
post	after	posttest
re	back, again	review
retro	backward	retrospect
sub	under, below	submarine
super	above, extra	supercharge
tele	far	telescope
trans	across, over	transcontinental

TABLE 3-2 TWENTY COMMON ROOTS

Common Root	Meaning	Sample Word
aud/audit	hear	audible
bio	life	biology
cap	take, seize	captive
cede	go	precede
chron(o)	time	chronology
cred	believe	incredible
dict/dic	tell, say	predict
duc/duct	lead	introduce
graph	write	autograph
mit/mis(s)	send	permit/dismiss
path	feeling	sympathy
photo	light	photosensitive
port	carry	transport
scrib/script	write	inscription
sen/sent	feel	insensitive
spec/spic/spect	look, see	retrospect
sym/syn	same, together	synonym
ven/vent	come	convention
vert/vers	turn	invert
voc	call	vocation

5. **Different prefixes, roots, or suffixes may have the same meaning.** For example, the prefixes *bi-, di-,* and *duo-* all mean "two."

6. **Word parts may have more than one meaning.** A dictionary listing that begins or ends with a hyphen is a word part, not a complete word. The hyphen is usually not used in the spelling of the word. Be careful when interpreting the meaning of these word parts. Many have more than one meaning. For example, *ex-* means "former" (as in *ex-president*), but it can also mean "out" or "outside" (as in *exit* or *exterior*).

7. **Use a dictionary to find out which prefix to use.** Several word parts mean "not" and make the word they precede mean the opposite of its original meaning. For example, the following are some common negative prefixes: *in-* (*incomplete*), *im-* (*impossible*), *un-* (*unbearable*), *non-* (*nonsense*), *il-* (*illegal*), *ir-* (*irregular*), and *dis-* (*disobey*). Which one should you use? In many cases, the correct prefix is determined by the word's part of speech (such as *dis-* before a verb) and the first letter of the base word. Base words beginning with *m* or *p* usually use *im-*, words beginning with *l* usually use *il-*, and most words beginning with *r-* use *ir-* as their negative prefixes. If you're not sure which prefix to use, consult a dictionary.

8. **Sometimes you may identify a group of letters as a prefix or root but find that it does not carry the meaning of that prefix or root.** For example, the letters *mis* in the word *missile* are part of the root and are not the prefix *mis-*, which means "wrong or bad."

Prefixes

Prefixes appear at the beginnings of many English words. They alter the meaning of the root to which they are connected. For example, if you add the prefix *re-* to the word *test*, the word *retest* is formed, meaning to test again. If *pre-* is added to the word *test*, the word *pretest* is formed, meaning a test given before something else. If the prefix *post-* is added, the word *posttest* is formed, meaning a test given after something else. Table 3-1 groups common prefixes according to meaning.

EXERCISE 3-11   Using Prefixes 1

Directions: Use the list of common prefixes in Table 3-1 (p. 59) to determine the meaning of each of the following words. Write a brief definition or synonym for each. If you are unfamiliar with the root, you may need to check a dictionary.

1. interoffice _____
2. supernatural _____
3. nonsense _____
4. introspection _____
5. prearrange _____
6. reset _____
7. subtopic _____
8. transmit _____
9. multidimensional _____
10. imperfect _____

EXERCISE 3-12   Using Prefixes 2

Directions: Read each of the following sentences. Use your knowledge of prefixes to fill in the blanks and complete the words.

1. A person who speaks two languages is _____ **lingual**.
2. A letter or number written beneath a line of print is called a _____ **script**.
3. The new sweater had a snag, and I returned it to the store because it was _____ **perfect**.
4. The flood damage was permanent and _____ **reversible**.
5. People who speak several different languages are _____ **lingual**.
6. A musical _____ **lude** was played between the events in the ceremony.
7. I decided the magazine was uninteresting, so I _____ **continued** my subscription.
8. Merchandise that does not pass factory inspection is considered _____ **standard** and is sold at a discount.
9. The tuition refund policy approved this week will apply to last year's tuition as well; the policy will be _____ **active** to January 1 of last year.
10. The elements were _____ **acting** with each other when they began to bubble and their temperature rose.

EXERCISE 3-13   Using Prefixes 3
Working Together

Directions: Working with a classmate, list as many words as you can think of for two of the following prefixes: *multi-, mis-, trans-, com-, inter-*. Then share your lists with the class. ■

Roots

Roots carry the basic or core meaning of a word. Hundreds of root words are used to build other words in the English language. Twenty of the most common and most useful are listed in Table 3-2 on page 60. Knowledge of the meanings of these roots will enable you to unlock the meanings of many words. For example, if you knew that the root *dic/dict* means "tell or say," then you would have a clue to the meanings of such words as *dictate* (to speak while someone writes down your words), *diction* (wording or manner of speaking), or *dictionary* (a book that "tells" what words mean).

EXERCISE 3-14   Using Roots 1

Directions: Complete each of the following sentences using one of the words listed below. Not all of the words will be used.

Apathetic	dictated	graphic	scriptures	tendon
captivated	extensive	phonics	spectators	verdict
deduce	extraterrestrial	prescribed	synchronized	visualize

1. The jury brought in its _____ after one hour of deliberation.
2. Religious or holy writings are called _____.
3. The _____ watching the football game were tense.
4. The doctor _____ two types of medication.
5. The criminal appeared _____ when the judge pronounced his sentence.
6. The runners _____ their watches before beginning the race.
7. The textbook contained numerous _____ aids, including maps, charts, and diagrams.
8. The district manager _____ a new policy on business expenses.
9. Through his attention-grabbing performance, he _____ the audience.
10. By putting together the clues, the detective was finally able to _____ who committed the crime. ■

EXERCISE 3-15   Using Roots 2

Directions: List two words for each of the following roots: *dict/dic; spec/spic/spect; cred; photo; scrib/script*.

_____

_____

■

Suffixes

Suffixes are word endings that often change the part of speech of a word.

For example, adding the suffix -*y* to the noun *cloud* forms the adjective *cloudy*. Accompanying the change in part of speech is a shift in meaning (*cloudy* means "resembling clouds; overcast with clouds; dimmed or dulled as if by clouds").

Often, several different words can be formed from a single root word by adding different suffixes.

EXAMPLES

Root: class
root + suffix = class/ify, class/ification, class/ic
Root: right
root + suffix = right/ly, right/ful, right/ist, right/eous

If you know the meaning of the root word and the ways in which different suffixes affect the meaning of the root word, you will be able to figure out a word's meaning when a suffix is added. A list of common suffixes and their meanings appears in Table 3-3 below.

TABLE 3-3   COMMON SUFFIXES

Suffix	Sample Word
Suffixes that refer to a state, condition, or quality	
able	touchable
ance	assistance
ation	confrontation
ence	reference
ible	tangible
ion	discussion
ity	superiority
ive	permissive
ment	amazement
ness	kindness
ous	jealous
ty	loyalty
y	creamy
Suffixes that mean "one who"	
an	Italian
ant	participant
ee	referee
eer	engineer
ent	resident
er	teacher
ist	activist
or	advisor
Suffixes that mean "pertaining to or referring to"	
al	autumnal
hood	brotherhood
ship	friendship
ward	homeward

You can expand your vocabulary by learning the variations in meaning that occur when suffixes are added to words you already know. When you find a word that you do not know, look for the root. Then, using the sentence in which the word appears, figure out what the word means with the suffix added. Occasionally you may find that the spelling of the root word has been changed. For instance, a final *e* may be dropped, a final consonant may be doubled, or a final *y* may be changed to *i*. Consider the possibility of such changes when trying to identify the root word.

EXAMPLES

The article was a **compilation** of facts.
root + suffix

compil(e) + -ation = compilation (something that has been compiled, or put together into an orderly form)

We were concerned with the **legality** of our decision to change addresses.
root + suffix
legal + -ity = legality (pertaining to legal matters)

The couple **happily** announced their engagement.
root + suffix
happ(y) + -(i)ly = happily (in a pleased or contented way)
Note: The letter *y* is changed to *i* when the suffix is added.

EXERCISE 3-16   Using Suffixes 1

Directions: On a sheet of paper, for each suffix shown in Table 3-3, write another example of a word you know that contains that suffix. ■

EXERCISE 3-17   Using Suffixes 2

Directions: For each of the words listed below, add a suffix so that the word will complete the sentence. Write the new word in the space provided. Check a dictionary if you are unsure of the spelling.

1. **converse**
   Our phone _____ lasted ten minutes.

2. **assist**
   The medical _____ labeled the patient's blood samples.

3. **qualify**
   The job applicant outlined his _____ to the interviewer.

4. **intern**
   The doctor completed her _____ at Memorial Medical Center.

5. **audio**
   She spoke so softly that her voice was not _____ .

6. **permit**
   The professor granted her _____ to miss class.

7. **instruct**
   The lecture on Freud was very _____ .

8. **mortal**
   The _____ rate in Ethiopia is very high.

9. **feminine**

She called herself a _____, although she never actively supported the movement for equal rights for women.

10. **hazard**

The presence of toxic waste in the lake is _____ to health. ∎

EXERCISE 3-18   Using Suffixes 3

Directions: For each word listed below, write as many new words as you can create by adding suffixes.

1. compare _____

2. adapt _____

3. right _____

4. identify _____

5. will _____

6. prefer _____

7. notice _____

8. like _____

9. pay _____

10. promote _____

∎

How to Use Word Parts

Think of roots as being at the root or core of a word's meaning. There are many more roots than are listed in Table 3-2. You already know many of these because they are used in everyday speech. Think of prefixes as word parts that are added before the root to qualify or change its meaning. Think of suffixes as add-ons that make the word fit grammatically into the sentence in which it is used.

When you come upon a word you do not know, keep the following pointers in mind:

1. **First, look for the root.** Think of this as looking for a word inside a larger word. Often a letter or two will be missing.

    EXAMPLES

un/<u>utter</u>/able	<u>defens</u>/ible
inter/<u>colleg</u>/iate	re/<u>popular</u>/ize
post/<u>operat</u>/ive	non/<u>adapt</u>/able
im/<u>measur</u>/ability	non/<u>commit</u>/tal

2. **If you do not recognize the root, then you will probably not be able to figure out the word.** The next step is to check its meaning in a dictionary.

3. **If you did recognize the root word, look for a prefix.** If there is one, determine how it changes the meaning of the word.

    EXAMPLES

un/utterable	un- = not
post/operative	post- = after

4. **Locate the suffix.** Determine how it further adds to or changes the meaning of the root word.

EXAMPLES

| unutter/able | -able = able to |
| postoperat/ive | -ive = state or condition |

5. **Next, try out the meaning in the sentence in which the word was used.** Substitute your meaning for the word and see whether the sentence makes sense.

EXAMPLES

Some of the victim's thoughts were unutterable at the time of the crime.

unutterable = not able to be spoken

My sister was worried about the cost of postoperative care.

postoperative = state or condition after an operation

EXERCISE 3-19   Using Word Parts 1

Directions: Use the steps listed previously to determine the meaning of each boldfaced word. Underline the root in each word, and then write a brief definition of the word that fits its use in the sentence.

1. The doctor felt the results of the X-rays were **indisputable**.

   _____

2. The **dissimilarity** among the three brothers was surprising.

   _____

3. The **extortionist** demanded two payments of $10,000 each.

   _____

4. It is **permissible** to camp in most state parks.

   _____

5. The student had **retentive** abilities.

   _____

6. The **traumatic** event changed the child's attitude toward animals.

   _____

7. We were surprised by her **insincerity**.

   _____

8. The child's **hypersensitivity** worried his parents.

   _____

9. The English instructor told Peter that he had written a **creditable** paper.

   _____

10. The rock group's agent hoped to **repopularize** their first hit song.

   _____

EXERCISE 3-20   Using Word Parts 2

Directions: Read each of the following paragraphs and determine the meaning of each boldfaced word. Write a brief definition for each in the space provided.

A. Exercising in hot weather can create stress on the circulatory system due to the high **production** of body heat. In hot weather the **distention** of blood vessels in the skin **diverts** increased quantities of blood to the body surfaces, where heat is released. As the body heats, skin heat evaporates the sweat, cooling the skin and the blood **circulating** near the skin.

—Byer and Shainberg, *Living Well*, p. 360.

1. production _____
2. distention _____
3. diverts _____
4. circulating _____

B. In addition to being **irreversible**, interpersonal communication is also **unrepeatable**. The reason is simple: Everyone and everything are constantly changing. As a result, you can never **recapture** the exact same situation, frame of mind, or relationship that defined a previous interpersonal act. For example, you can never repeat meeting someone for the first time, comforting a grieving friend, or resolving a specific conflict.

—DeVito, *Building Interpersonal Communication Skills*, p. 22–23.

1. irreversible _____
2. unrepeatable _____
3. recapture _____

C. People with positive emotional **wellness** can function **independently**. They can think for themselves, make decisions, plan their lives, and follow through with their plans. **Conversely**, people who have difficulty making decisions are often immature and **insecure**. They are afraid to face the consequences of the decisions they make, so they make as few decisions as possible. Growth involves making **mistakes** as well as achieving success. Our mistakes are best viewed as learning experiences. We must take some risks in order to live our lives most fully.

—Byer and Shainberg, *Living Well*, p. 67.

1. wellness _____
2. independently _____
3. conversely _____
4. insecure _____
5. mistakes _____

D. We could probably greatly reduce the risks associated with nuclear power by simply exercising more care and common sense. There are a **multitude** of published accounts that attest to our carelessness, however. For example, it has been revealed that the Diablo Canyon nuclear power plant in California was built on an earthquake fault line. Of course it was girded for that risk. **Incredibly**, however, the blueprints were somehow **reversed** and the earthquake supports were put in backwards. Furthermore, the mistake was not noticed for four years. At the

Comanche Peak Plant in Texas, supports were **constructed** 45 degrees out of line. At the Marble Hill in Indiana, the concrete surrounding the core was found to be full of air bubbles. At the WNP-2 plant in Washington state, the concrete contained air bubbles and pockets of water as well as shields that had been **incorrectly** welded. At the San Onofre plant in California, a 420-ton reactor vessel was installed backwards and the error was not detected for months.

—Wallace, *Biology*, p. 834.

1. multitude _____

2. incredibly _____

3. reversed _____

4. constructed _____

5. incorrectly _____

■

LEARN IDIOMS

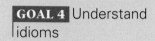

GOAL 4 Understand idioms

An **idiom** is a phrase that has a meaning other than the common meaning of the words in the phrase. For example, the phrase *turn over a new leaf* is not about the leaves on a tree. It means to "start fresh" or "begin over again in a new way." You can locate idioms in a dictionary by looking up the key words in the phrase. To find the meaning of the idiom *as the crow flies*, look up the entry for *crow*. Idioms are usually identified by the label "—idiom," followed by the complete phrase and its meaning.

If you need more help figuring out idioms, consult a handbook or dictionary of American idioms, such as *Webster's New World American Idioms Handbook*. It is usually best not to use idioms in your own writing. Many are overused and will not express your ideas in a clear or concise way.

▌EXERCISE 3-21   Understanding Idioms

Directions: Explain the meaning of each of the following idioms.

1. to keep tabs on _____

2. to steal someone's thunder _____

_____

_____

3. in the dark _____

4. to bite the bullet _____

5. to make no bones about _____

_____

■

DEVELOP A SYSTEM FOR LEARNING NEW WORDS

GOAL 5 Develop a system for learning new words

Here are two effective ways to organize and learn specialized or technical vocabulary for each of your courses.

The Vocabulary Card System

One of the most efficient and practical ways to organize words for study and review is the vocabulary card system. Use a 3-by-5-inch index card for each new term. Record the word on the front and its meaning on the back. If the word is particularly difficult, you might also include a guide to its pronunciation. Underneath the correct spelling of the word, indicate in syllables how the word sounds. For the word *eutrophication* (a term used in chemistry to mean "over-nourishment"), you could indicate its pronunciation as "you-tro-fi-kay'-shun." On the back of the card, along with the meaning, you might want to include an example to help you remember the term more easily. A sample vocabulary card, front and back, is shown below.

Sample Vocabulary Card

ostracize (ŏs´ trə sīz)	*to banish from social or political favor* *Ex.: A street gang will ostracize a member who refuses to wear the gang emblem.*
Front	**Back**

Use these cards for study, for review, and for testing yourself. Go through your pack of cards once, looking at the front and trying to recall the meaning on the back. Then reverse the procedure; look at the meanings and see whether you can recall the terms. As you go through the pack in this way, sort the cards into two piles: words you know and words you don't know. The next time you review the cards, use only cards in the "don't know" pile for review. This sorting procedure will help you avoid wasting time reviewing words you have already learned. Continue to review the cards until you are satisfied that you have learned each new term. To avoid forgetting a word, review the entire pack of cards periodically.

The Computerized Vocabulary File

Using a word processing program, create a computer file for each of your courses. Daily or weekly, review both textbook chapters and lecture notes and enter specialized and technical terms that you need to learn. Use a two-column or table format, entering the word in one column and its meaning in the other. You might subdivide or code your file by textbook chapter so that you can review easily when exams or quizzes on particular chapters are announced.

Your files can be used in several different ways. If you alphabetize the words, you will have created a glossary that will serve as a handy reference. Keep a print copy handy as you read new chapters and review lecture notes. When studying the words in your file, try scrambling the words to avoid learning them in a fixed order.

WRITING ABOUT A READING

In the following article from *The Washington Post*, the author describes the consequences of one woman's efforts to escape an arranged marriage in Afghanistan.

Step 1: Preview the reading.

Step 2: Connect the reading to your own experience: Does the government have the right to refuse to let a woman cancel her engagement?

Step 3: Read and respond to the questions in the margin.

THINK AS YOU READ

Predict the conflict that will arise in this reading.

What does this subtitle tell you about the content of the reading? Does it suggest the thesis?

This a shocking opening; What questions does it raise?

What does this paragraph suggest about how the author will approach the subject?

How does this photograph support the author's message?

AFGHANISTAN: WHERE WOMEN HAVE NO CHOICE

For an Afghan girl dreading marriage to a man she hates, death is often the only escape.

Kevin Sieff

1   Just before she leapt from her roof into the streets of Kabul, Farima thought of the wedding that would never happen and the man she would never marry. Her fiancé would be pleased to see her die, she later recalled thinking. It would offer relief to them both.

2   Farima, 17, had resisted her engagement to Zabiullah since it was ordained by her grandfather when she was 9. In post-Taliban Kabul, where she walked to school and dreamed of becoming a doctor, she still clawed against a fate dictated by ritual. After 11 years of Western intervention in Afghanistan, a woman's right to study and work had long since been codified by the government. Modernity had crept into Afghanistan's capital, Farima thought, but not far enough to save her from a forced marriage to a man she despised.

3   Farima's father, Mohammed, was eating breakfast when he heard her body hit the dirt like a tiny explosion. He ran outside. His daughter's torso was contorted. Her back was broken, but she was still alive. In a quick burst of consciousness, Farima recognized that she had survived. It was God's providence, she thought. It was

Why was living not a miracle that Farima had prayed for?

Predict the answer to this question.

What does liberal *mean as used here?*

Based on the information revealed thus far, answer Farima's question.

What does the family's shame suggest about the culture?

Predict the author's answer to this question.

How do you think Mohammed feels about Farima's behavior at the party?

Why does the author include this information at this point in the essay?

a miracle she hadn't prayed for. But it left her without an escape. Suddenly, she was a mangled version of herself, still desperate to avoid the marriage her family had ordered.

4   She didn't know it yet, but her survival meant that she would become a test case in one of her country's newest and most troubled experiments in modernity: a divorce court guided by Afghanistan's version of Islamic **sharia**[1] law. Could a disabled teenager navigate a legal system still stacked against women?

5   "We still must get married," Zabiullah told his brother when he heard about Farima's suicide attempt. "The engagement must remain." Her father agreed that Farima's pursuit of a separation was unwise. "We are not a liberal family," Mohammed said. "This is not how we handle our problems."

6   When her marriage was fixed, a 9-year-old Farima crawled into her mother's lap, confused about what it meant to be engaged. Even as Kabul grew more modern, that traditional engagement was unbreakable, her parents told her. The man she was destined to spend her life with was a distant cousin. If the marriage didn't happen, the family could splinter. But when Farima got to know Zabiullah, she couldn't stand him. They talked on the phone, and he chastised her for venturing outside her home. He demanded that she stop speaking even with members of her family. "She was too close with her relatives, getting ice cream and going to the market with her father's cousin," he said.

7   "If he was like that when we were engaged, what would marriage have been like?" Farima said. "I couldn't bear it."

8   Less than a minute after Farima hit the ground, Mohammed scooped up his daughter. He hailed a taxi, and they sped to Ali Ahmed Hospital, where Taher Jan Khalili performed surgery for three hours. The family was ashamed to tell Khalili the truth. Her father said Farima had fallen by accident.

9   "I wasn't sure if she would survive. Her back was badly broken," Khalili said. In the past year, he has handled nearly a dozen attempted female suicides. Farima spent nine days in the hospital, flickering in and out of consciousness. When she re-entered the world in late September, bandaged and carried on a stretcher, her relatives cried and thanked God that she had survived. "But if not death, then what?" Farima thought.

10   Zabiullah, a plumber, was insistent that the wedding date remain unchanged. He had spent $30,000 on gifts for his fiancée, he said. He had paid for a big engagement party, during which Farima had sat sullen for hours, while relatives sang and danced and ate kebab. "Everyone was having a great night, but she did not," Mohammed said.

11   Dozens of women in Afghanistan kill themselves each year to escape failed, and often violent, marriages. Those tragedies are widely mourned, but they nonetheless offer a resolution recognized by Islamic law: A woman's death, even by her own hand, marks the end of a marriage or engagement. Women who run away face prison sentences of several years.

[1]**sharia** religious law based on the Quran and the example set by the prophet Muhammad

12   A failed suicide is more complicated to untangle. When Farima awoke in the hospital bruised and broken, her wedding had not yet been canceled. Nearly all of her relatives expected her to follow through with the marriage. She gave up on the prospect of another suicide attempt; she could not walk without assistance and was too weak to inflict much damage on herself. The girl accused of being "too modern" would make another modern decision: She opted to resolve her failing engagement in Kabul's nascent family court. She would have to plead her case in front of a room full of judges and lawyers, who would decide whether she was entitled to a separation. In traditional Afghan culture, men can divorce their wives without the approval of any justice system.

How does this system compare to the legal system in the United States?

13   Two months after she left the hospital, her mother and father helped carry her to the third floor of the family court—a faded yellow guesthouse, where a line of **burqa**[2]-clad women are nearly always waiting outside. Farima wore a black headscarf. Her skin was pallid. She hadn't been outside in weeks, spending most of her time reading novels in her room. The chief judge, Rahima Rasai, looked across the room at Farima while she adjusted her back brace. "You have ruined your life," Rasai said.

14   The court is a place where a woman is entitled to plead for divorce or custody of her children, but only if she has five male "witnesses," or defenders, and often only if her husband or fiancé condones the separation. The court is funded by Western organizations but adheres strictly to sharia law. Farima sat on the opposite side of the room from her fiancé. She looked at the judge and tried hard not to cry.

Do you think that Farima stands to receive a fair trial?

15   Every year, Kabul's family court handles about 300 cases, mostly women seeking to divorce their negligent or abusive husbands. Established in 2003, it was seen widely as a leap of progress after the Taliban's stoning of adulterers and dismantling of women's rights. Women whose fiancés emigrated from Afghanistan line up to seek separation from absent partners. Girls whose husbands sold them as prostitutes sink into the court's cushioned chairs, begging for divorce certificates stamped with a government insignia.

16   Last month was a typical one at the court: Some women screamed at their husbands. Some brought their small children to testify. Some beat themselves with their fists to demonstrate the abuse they had endured. Some watched as their husbands were dragged out in handcuffs. Some arrived in burqas, and some in blue jeans. Many were crying as they left the courtroom.

What is Mohammed's primary concern about the court proceedings?

17   On Farima's day in court, her father sat in the corner of the room. For years, he had been trying to avoid this moment. "I told my daughter not to do this. We don't want a bad name. We don't want our family to fall apart," Mohammed said. Farima had told him many times that she was thinking about killing herself, he said. When he looked at her, crumpled and frail, he knew what he could have prevented. "I just never thought she would really do it," he said.

18   "What is wrong with this man?" Rasai asked Farima, pointing to Zabiullah. "He treats me terribly," Farima said. "Our marriage would be hell."

[2]**burqa** a loose outer garment covering the entire body and veiling the face, with an opening for the eyes

19   Then the judge looked to Zabiullah. He wanted badly not to be there, objecting to the whole idea of a family court. "She is confused," he said. "She has become so liberal," he said.

20   There was a hush in the courtroom. Rasai sipped her tea. She was tired. It was the last case of the morning. Already, the court had heard four women pleading for divorce and protracted arguments over dowry compensation and physical abuse. None of those cases had been resolved. There weren't enough male witnesses, or Rasai wasn't convinced that a separation was warranted; she is reluctant to grant too many. "It haunts me. Even when I'm praying, I think about the sadness of my job," Rasai said later.

What does Rasai mean when she speaks of the "sadness" of her job?

21   Although she is one of Afghanistan's few female judges, Rasai is hardly a Western-style advocate of women's rights. She sometimes recommends that men "subdue their wives." Even in seemingly clear-cut cases of domestic abuse, she often resists defendants' initial pleas for separation.

22   When Rasai finally spoke again, she asked Farima what gifts Zabiullah had given her for their engagement. Farima's mother left the courtroom and returned dragging a metal trunk, full of clothes, jewelry and cosmetics. Her mother pulled out one item at a time and held it above her head for the court to see. "Where are the other rings?" Zabiullah burst out. "That's all that you gave me," Farima replied, exasperated.

23   "Even if **Karzai**[3] demands it, I will not allow my daughter to marry this man!" Farima's mother suddenly exclaimed. It was the kind of support Farima had never received from her parents.

Is this the verdict that you expected?

24   Rasai started scribbling. "Your engagement is scrapped," she said. "You no longer have any relation to each other."

25   Farima looked defiant, but she did not smile. She and Zabiullah dipped their thumbs in ink and touched them to certificates pronouncing their separation. "Keep this with you forever," Rasai said, giving each a copy.

26   Farima's parents helped carry her down the stairs. She had lived to get what her family had denied her. Her Afghanistan again showed a flash of modern promise.

Why was her mother crying?

27   "I have defended my rights," Farima said in the lobby. Her mother was crying.

28   Two weeks later, Farima was back to spending her days at home. She was reading a book called *The Gift of the Bride*. "It's about relationships between wives and husbands and children," she said. She was no longer attending school. Her father and brothers had asked her to stop during her engagement, and they would not allow her to return.

29   Farima was still basking in the court's judgment. But it left her feeling unmoored. Even in the country's most developed city, opportunities are limited for a single woman unable to walk on her own. "I'm worried that no one will marry my daughter now," her mother said. Zabiullah is sure that he will marry another woman. He has a trunk full of gifts ready for her. Farima has started considering the prospect of a life alone, in her childhood bedroom. "I'm not sure what I will do," she said. "I'm not sure what I can do."

Compare the futures of Farima and Zabiullah.

30   In the Afghanistan of her novels, the girls grow up to be happy and marriages are full of love. Husbands are patient and accepting. "For me, it is not always like that," Farima said. "Life is complicated."

How does Zabiullah feel about the divorce?

[3]**Karzai** Hamid Karzai, the former president of Afghanistan

WRITING IN RESPONSE TO READING

Examining the Reading Using an Idea Map

Review the reading by completing the missing parts of the idea map shown below.

Visualize It!

Title | **Afghanistan: Where Women Have No Choice**

Thesis |
The ritual of arranged marriages is next to impossible to escape. _____ . Farima _____ from her roof onto the _____ . Her _____ finds her broken but _____ . Mohammed, Farima's father, says her fall was an _____ . Farima decides to fight her engagement in court. Her fiancé says that the wedding date should _____ . Farima plans to fight her _____ in _____ court. She will have to present her case to _____ and _____ . Farima has her day in court. Farima's parents carry her into court. Farima's _____ comes to her defense. The judge proclaims, _____ Farima faces life as a single woman. After her court victory, Farima's father and brothers _____ . Her parents are worried that she will never _____ . Farima feels that her life has become very complicated.

Conclusion | Life is difficult and does not always produce happy endings.

Strengthening Your Vocabulary   MyWritingLab

Using the word's context, word parts, or a dictionary, write a brief definition of each of the following words as it is used in the reading.

1. contorted (paragraph 3) _____

2. chastised (paragraph 6) _____

3. sullen (paragraph 10) _____

4. nascent (paragraph 12) _____

5. pallid (paragraph 13) _____

6. condones (paragraph 14) _____

7. protracted (paragraph 20) _____

8. unmoored (paragraph 29) _____

Reacting to Ideas: Discussion and Journal Writing   MyWritingLab

Get ready to write about the reading by discussing the following:

1. What was the author's purpose in writing this article?

2. What do you think of the method of matchmaking described in this reading?

3. How would you describe Farima's relationship with her father?

4. What does Farima's father mean when he says, "We are not a liberal family?"

5. What details do you notice about the photograph that corresponds to the reading?

Paragraph Options   MyWritingLab

1. Suppose you lived in a culture in which arranged marriages were the norm. What type of mate would your parents select for you? Write a paragraph describing that mate.

2. Can you think of a time in your life when you felt so strongly about something that you took a risk and went against the popular opinion? Write a paragraph telling about it.

3. Choose a friend, a boyfriend/girlfriend, or your mate and write a paragraph about how you met.

Essay Options   MyWritingLab

4. What can you tell from this reading about the author's attitude toward arranged marriages? Write an essay examining the ways the author reveals his attitude. Include in your essay specific examples from the reading.

5. Write an essay in which you compare and contrast the status of women in Afghanistan and women in the United States.

6. In the novels that Farima reads, "the girls grow up to be happy and marriages are full of love. Husbands are patient and accepting." In an essay, describe your concept of the ideal marriage.

SELF-TEST SUMMARY

To test yourself, cover the Answer column with a sheet of paper and answer each question in the left column. Evaluate each of your answers as you work by sliding the paper down and comparing your answer with what is printed in the Answer column.

	QUESTION	ANSWER
GOAL 1 Use dictionaries and thesauruses effectively	How do you use a dictionary effectively? What is a thesaurus?	Using a dictionary effectively involves understanding the information provided and choosing the correct meaning of a word. A thesaurus is a dictionary of synonyms; it groups together words with similar meanings.
GOAL 2 Use context clues to figure out unfamiliar words	What is context? What are the five types of context clues?	Context refers to the words around a given word. Types of context clues include definition, synonym, example, contrast, and inference.
GOAL 3 Use word parts to figure out the meaning of words	What are word parts?	Many words are made up of word parts called prefixes, roots, and suffixes. Prefixes appear at the beginning of words and alter the word's core meaning, roots carry the basic meaning of a word, and suffixes are endings that often change the word's part of speech.
GOAL 4 Understand idioms	What are idioms?	An idiom is a phrase that has a meaning other than the common meaning of the words in the phrase.
GOAL 5 Develop a system for learning new words	What are two systems for organizing and learning new vocabulary?	The vocabulary card system and a computerized vocabulary file will help you organize and learn new words.

MyWritingLab *Visit Ch. 3 Expanding Your Vocabulary in MyWritingLab to test your understanding of the chapter objectives.*

WRITERS' WORKSHOPS: Using Words Effectively

The goal of *Pathways* is to help you become a better writer. Learning how to write is an ongoing process. But everyone needs a place to start, and everyone likes to see improvement quickly. The purpose of these Writers' Workshops is to give you some simple, easy-to-remember guidelines that will improve your writing skills immediately.

WRITERS' WORKSHOP

1

YOU'RE A GREAT WRITER? YOUR A GREAT WRITER?

Don't Make These Common Mistakes

The English language can be tricky. Words that sound exactly alike are often spelled different ways and have completely different meanings.

Everyone—including your instructor and potential employers—will be impressed if you avoid the mistakes they see every day. Familiarize yourself with these commonly confused words and phrases, and commit the correct spellings and usage to memory.

affect: A verb meaning "to influence."

The rain *affected* everyone's mood negatively. When will the sun come out and make life worth living again?

effect: A noun meaning "the result."

The medication had many negative *effects* on me. I could live with the sleepiness, but I didn't appreciate all my hair falling out.

a lot: *A lot* is the correct spelling. *Alot* is incorrect.

English teachers correct *a lot* of errors when they grade papers. What a hassle!

all right: *All right* is the correct spelling. *Alright* is incorrect.

As the rock group *The Who* once sang, "The kids are *all right.*"

fewer: Refers to items that can be counted.

The express checkout line is for people buying eight items or *fewer*. Then why do so many people try to get away with nine items or more?

less: Refers to a general amount that cannot be counted.

I consume *less* caffeine now than I used to when I was working full-time.

good: Should be used as an adjective only.

I enjoy a *good* horror movie, but not when I'm alone.

well: Should be used as an adverb. Tip: Many times, *well* is the correct word to use when it appears after the verb.

Thanks to her new hearing aid, she hears *well*. Now I wish she'd get glasses, too.

its: Means "belonging to it."

He absentmindedly scratched the dog behind *its* ears.

it's: A contraction meaning "it is."

It's not unusual for dogs to have fleas in the summer. Confusing *its* and *it's* is probably the most common mistake in English!
It's great that you stopped the cat from using *its* claws to teach the neighbor's dog a lesson.

loose: An adjective meaning "not tight" or "not securely attached."

In hot weather, *loose* clothing is the way to go.

lose: A verb meaning "misplace" or "not win."

Did you really *lose* your keys again?

their: A possessive form meaning "belonging to them."

The harried store employees kept looking at *their* watches.

there: An adverb indicating place.

She put her computer over *there*, next to the lamp.

they're: Means "they are."

They're here—your Aunt Maud and that awful man she met in Aruba.

to: A preposition indicating direction, or part of an infinitive.

I'm going *to* the mall with Marcie *to* see if I can find something to wear for the office party.

too: Means "also."

Can I come *too*?

Paragraph Options   MyWritingLab

1. Suppose you lived in a culture in which arranged marriages were the norm. What type of mate would your parents select for you? Write a paragraph describing that mate.
2. Can you think of a time in your life when you felt so strongly about something that you took a risk and went against the popular opinion? Write a paragraph telling about it.
3. Choose a friend, a boyfriend/girlfriend, or your mate and write a paragraph about how you met.

Essay Options   MyWritingLab

4. What can you tell from this reading about the author's attitude toward arranged marriages? Write an essay examining the ways the author reveals his attitude. Include in your essay specific examples from the reading.
5. Write an essay in which you compare and contrast the status of women in Afghanistan and women in the United States.
6. In the novels that Farima reads, "the girls grow up to be happy and marriages are full of love. Husbands are patient and accepting." In an essay, describe your concept of the ideal marriage.

SELF-TEST SUMMARY

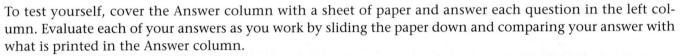

To test yourself, cover the Answer column with a sheet of paper and answer each question in the left column. Evaluate each of your answers as you work by sliding the paper down and comparing your answer with what is printed in the Answer column.

	QUESTION	ANSWER
GOAL 1 Use dictionaries and thesauruses effectively	How do you use a dictionary effectively? What is a thesaurus?	Using a dictionary effectively involves understanding the information provided and choosing the correct meaning of a word. A thesaurus is a dictionary of synonyms; it groups together words with similar meanings.
GOAL 2 Use context clues to figure out unfamiliar words	What is context? What are the five types of context clues?	Context refers to the words around a given word. Types of context clues include definition, synonym, example, contrast, and inference.
GOAL 3 Use word parts to figure out the meaning of words	What are word parts?	Many words are made up of word parts called prefixes, roots, and suffixes. Prefixes appear at the beginning of words and alter the word's core meaning, roots carry the basic meaning of a word, and suffixes are endings that often change the word's part of speech.
GOAL 4 Understand idioms	What are idioms?	An idiom is a phrase that has a meaning other than the common meaning of the words in the phrase.
GOAL 5 Develop a system for learning new words	What are two systems for organizing and learning new vocabulary?	The vocabulary card system and a computerized vocabulary file will help you organize and learn new words.

MyWritingLab *Visit Ch. 3 Expanding Your Vocabulary in MyWritingLab to test your understanding of the chapter objectives.*

WRITERS' WORKSHOPS: Using Words Effectively

The goal of *Pathways* is to help you become a better writer. Learning how to write is an ongoing process. But everyone needs a place to start, and everyone likes to see improvement quickly. The purpose of these Writers' Workshops is to give you some simple, easy-to-remember guidelines that will improve your writing skills immediately.

WRITERS' WORKSHOP

1

YOU'RE A GREAT WRITER? YOUR A GREAT WRITER?

Don't Make These Common Mistakes

The English language can be tricky. Words that sound exactly alike are often spelled different ways and have completely different meanings.

Everyone—including your instructor and potential employers—will be impressed if you avoid the mistakes they see every day. Familiarize yourself with these commonly confused words and phrases, and commit the correct spellings and usage to memory.

affect: A verb meaning "to influence."

The rain *affected* everyone's mood negatively. When will the sun come out and make life worth living again?

effect: A noun meaning "the result."

The medication had many negative *effects* on me. I could live with the sleepiness, but I didn't appreciate all my hair falling out.

a lot: *A lot* is the correct spelling. *Alot* is incorrect.

English teachers correct *a lot* of errors when they grade papers. What a hassle!

all right: *All right* is the correct spelling. *Alright* is incorrect.

As the rock group *The Who* once sang, "The kids are *all right.*"

fewer: Refers to items that can be counted.

The express checkout line is for people buying eight items or *fewer*. Then why do so many people try to get away with nine items or more?

less: Refers to a general amount that cannot be counted.

I consume *less* caffeine now than I used to when I was working full-time.

good: Should be used as an adjective only.

I enjoy a *good* horror movie, but not when I'm alone.

well: Should be used as an adverb. Tip: Many times, *well* is the correct word to use when it appears after the verb.

Thanks to her new hearing aid, she hears *well*. Now I wish she'd get glasses, too.

its: Means "belonging to it."

He absentmindedly scratched the dog behind *its* ears.

it's: A contraction meaning "it is."

It's not unusual for dogs to have fleas in the summer. Confusing *its* and *it's* is probably the most common mistake in English!
It's great that you stopped the cat from using *its* claws to teach the neighbor's dog a lesson.

loose: An adjective meaning "not tight" or "not securely attached."

In hot weather, *loose* clothing is the way to go.

lose: A verb meaning "misplace" or "not win."

Did you really *lose* your keys again?

their: A possessive form meaning "belonging to them."

The harried store employees kept looking at *their* watches.

there: An adverb indicating place.

She put her computer over *there*, next to the lamp.

they're: Means "they are."

They're here—your Aunt Maud and that awful man she met in Aruba.

to: A preposition indicating direction, or part of an infinitive.

I'm going *to* the mall with Marcie *to* see if I can find something to wear for the office party.

too: Means "also."

Can I come *too*?

two: The number 2.

I'm afraid there's only room for *two* in her car.

whose: The possessive form of *who*.

Whose iPhone is this? I found it in the ladies' room.

who's: Means "who is."

Who's ringing my doorbell?

your: The possessive form of *you*. Used for something belonging to *you*.

I really like *your* shades, but *your* shoes are seriously out of style.

you're: Means "you are."

But *you're* still the best looking guy I know.

An extended list of commonly confused, misunderstood, and misspelled words appears in Part VII E, pages 573–581.

➡ TRY IT OUT!

Directions: Underline the word that completes each sentence correctly.

1. (Its / It's) really frustrating when you screen my calls!

2. I would ask you out on a date, but (your / you're) a very boring person.

3. My boss wants me to be more polite. When someone calls, I should ask, "(Whose / Who's) calling, please?" instead of saying, "Who is this and what do you want?"

4. I suspected that the knot in the rope attaching the boat to my car was (loose / lose). That fear was confirmed when my boat went flying into a ditch alongside the highway.

5. Would it be (all right / alright) with you if I bought (a lot / alot) of lottery tickets instead of paying the rent?

WRITERS' WORKSHOP

2

THERE ARE SOME THINGS NOT TO DO . . .

Such as Overusing *There Is* and *There Are*

Sentences beginning with *There is*, *There are*, or *There were* make use of **expletive construction**. These sentences can be effective when you want to emphasize the subject:

There is a particularly ugly spider spinning an amazingly beautiful web on my window.

There are many good reasons not to eat a carton of ice cream in one sitting.

Often, however, sentences that begin with *There is* or *There are* can be wordy and dull.

Wordy: *There were* errors and unexpected costs that delayed construction of the new football stadium.

Better: Errors and unexpected costs delayed the construction of the new football stadium.

Note: If you must use *There is* or *There are*, be sure to use the correct verb. Use *is* if a singular noun follows. Use *are* if a plural noun follows.

There *is* a woman on the show who lost 150 pounds!

There *are* three benefits of a healthy diet: you live longer, you feel better, and you look great.

→ **TRY IT OUT!**

Directions: Rewrite each sentence, making it more direct and concise.

1. There were all sorts of delays that caused the airplane to be late, including a rainstorm, thunder, and an antiquated air-traffic control system.

2. There's a great deal of debate over whether or not the average person should take multivitamins.

3. There is a tendency for teenagers to think that everyone is looking at them all the time, something that psychologists call the *spotlight effect*.

4. There are ghosts, poltergeists, wraiths, and phantasms in the dusty old house, but no people.

5. There is no one thing that everyone believes about Twitter accounts: some believe they are fun, while others think they are a waste of time.

WRITERS' WORKSHOP

3

GOOD WRITING IS WHEN . . .

You Don't Use *Is When*

Speech patterns don't always translate well into college writing. Common phrases or sayings that work well in conversation are not necessarily appropriate in essays. Consider the phrases *is when* and *is where*. In a conversation you might hear:

An exam *is when* you are tested on what you know.

A marathon *is where* you run a long distance, ruin your feet, and wonder why you ever thought it was a good idea.

Each sentence provides a definition (which is the function of the verb *is*). In college writing, definitions require nouns on both sides of the verb, which means you must eliminate *is when* and *is where*. Consider the following rewrites.

An examination is a test of what you know. So you'd better read the textbook and attend lectures.

A marathon is a long-distance run that ruins your feet and tests both your endurance and sanity.

Another construction to avoid is *reason is because*. By definition, *reason* equals *because*, so using both together is redundant.

Redundant: *The reason the Yankees lost the game is because* the pitcher doesn't know what he's doing.

Revised: The Yankees lost the game because their pitcher doesn't know how to throw a strike.

→ **TRY IT OUT!**

Directions: Revise the following sentences, eliminating awkward or redundant phrases.

1. A dream that always bothers me is when I dream I am a waiter and everyone in the restaurant is making demands on me at the same time.

2. A "talkback" after a play is where the audience gets to talk to the actors and ask them questions.

3. The reason that I am so irritable is because the baby has kept me awake all night for the last two weeks.

4. A dropped call is when you go into an area with bad cell service, and the phone just loses service.

5. You wonder why I am going to college? The reason is because I want to get a good job, earn a good living, and provide for my family.

WRITERS' WORKSHOP

4

WHAT MAKES A GOOD SENTENCE?

One Possible Answer: Not Using the Verb *Make*

Every sentence has two essential parts—the *subject* and the *verb*. Your sentences will be most effective if they emphasize these two parts. Think of the subject and verb as the key actors in a film. Do you want your actors to be weak and fade into the background, or do you want them to dominate the screen and grab your attention? Do not hide them among phrases that have no significant meaning.

Empty phrases that can almost always be eliminated from your sentences include:

As far as I'm concerned	For all intents and purposes
In my opinion	And stuff
In a manner of speaking	Last but not least

Some particularly weak verbs are *is*, *has*, and *makes*.

Weak: Greenpeace *is* a world leader in environmental awareness.

Revised: Greenpeace leads other environmental groups in making the public aware of ecological issues.

Weak: *Grand Theft Auto has* several different difficulty settings, from easy to impossible.

Revised: *Grand Theft Auto* allows players to choose their level of difficulty, from beginner through expert.

Weak: The climbers *make* slow progress up the steep rock face.

Revised: The climbers progress slowly up the steep rock face.

 **TRY IT OUT!**

Directions: Rewrite the following sentences, eliminating empty phrases and weak verbs.

1. I was amazed by all the types of food available at the carnival: fried dough, pizza, corn on the cob, Chinese noodles, and stuff.

2. In my opinion, the use of surveillance cameras in public spaces is a threat to the right to privacy.

3. *American Idol* is a trendsetter in terms of the music that young people buy and listen to.

4. All things considered, I'd rather live in the city than in the country.

5. As far as I'm concerned, the chef at Dino's makes the best tacos I've ever eaten.

WRITERS' WORKSHOP

5

AN ESSAY IS NOT A TEXT MESSAGE

Formal Versus Informal Writing

It has been said that the single biggest challenge facing today's college writers is the text message. Text messages have nothing in common with college and professional writing. Why?

1. Text messages are short. College writing requires thought and space to develop your ideas.

2. Text messages are based on abbreviations and shorthand. Serious writing requires you to spell out your words and explain your ideas.

3. Text messages are a form of entertainment. College and professional writing is intended to convey important information and ideas.

4. In a text message, spelling and punctuation don't matter. In college and professional writing, spelling and punctuation matter a great deal.

The way you write a text message should have nothing in common with the way you write a college paper. Text messages are a type of **informal** writing, in which the rules don't matter. In college and the workplace, you are expected to write formally. In **formal** English, the rules do matter. And the better you understand the rules, the better your chances of good grades and a good job offer.

Table 1 outlines some common abbreviations used in text messages. *Never* use these abbreviations in any type of formal writing. Spell out the entire word, and don't forget the capitals and punctuation.

TABLE 1 COMMON TEXT ABBREVIATIONS

Word or Phrase	Abbreviation(s)
as soon as possible	asap
because	cuz
before	b4
by the way	btw
face to face	f2f
great	gr8
I don't know	idk
in my humble/honest opinion	imho
just kidding	jk
laughing out loud	lol
later	l8r
rolling on the floor laughing	rofl
talk to you later	ttyl8r, ttyl, t2yl
tomorrow	2mro
why?	y
you are	u r
your	ur

→ TRY IT OUT!

Directions: Convert the following text messages into formal English sentences.

1. i wuz w1dering how u r doin 2day

   _____

2. can i talk 2 u b4 u leave 4 the day

   _____

3. my sister cant make it until l8r, what time r u free?

   _____

4. the kidz did gr8 on the test

   _____

5. prof wants 2 know y u wuz late 4 class

   _____

4

Complete Sentences
Versus Fragments

Learning Goals

*In this chapter, you will
learn how to*

GOAL 1 Identify
sentence fragments

GOAL 2 Recognize
and correct fragments
caused by missing
subjects

GOAL 3 Recognize
and correct fragments
caused by missing verbs

GOAL 4 Recognize
and correct fragments
caused by dependent
clauses

2008 World Wildlife Fund Public Service Announcement.

Protecting the Future of Nature
WWF works around the world developing responsible fishing practices to
protect marine populations from overfishing and ensure a catch that will feed
fishermen, their families and you.
Be Part of Our Work   **worldwildlife.org**

WRITE ABOUT IT!

When you read the caption under the picture in the advertisement—"Protecting the Future of Nature"—does it make sense? No doubt your answer is yes.
Write a sentence stating the message it communicates about the World Wildlife Federation (WWF). From the caption, the photo, and the accompanying
text, you know that the WWF is working toward the development of responsible fishing practices.

Now suppose you saw the caption alone, without the accompanying photograph and text. Would it make sense? Would you understand the message of the advertisement? Probably not. You do not know who is protecting the future of nature. The caption is a sentence fragment. A fragment is an incomplete sentence. It lacks a subject. It does have a verb—*protecting*. How can you make the caption into a complete sentence? You must add a subject.

Here are a few ways to make the caption a complete sentence:

FRAGMENT   Protecting the future of nature.

                                 subject   verb

COMPLETE SENTENCE   The World Wildlife Federation is protecting the future of nature.

The new version now makes sense even without the photograph. This version has a subject and a verb and expresses a complete thought. In this chapter you will learn to identify fragments and correct them.

NEED TO KNOW

Complete Sentences

Remember that every sentence must have a subject and a verb. The usual word order in **statements** is to put the subject before the verb:

          subject   verb

The clowns are coming!

However, occasionally, the verb is put first:

       verb   subject   verb   subject

Here come the clowns! There are ten clowns!

The usual **question pattern** has the helping verb before the subject and the main verb after.

  helping verb   subject main verb

Why are ten clowns getting into that little tiny car?

WRITING

WHAT IS A FRAGMENT?

GOAL 1 Identify sentence fragments

A **fragment** is an incomplete sentence that lacks either a subject, a verb, or both. Following are a few more statements taken from magazine ads. Each one is a sentence fragment because each one lacks a subject and a verb and does not express a complete thought. As you read the fragments that follow, notice how difficult they are to understand. Try to guess what product each sentence fragment describes. Correct answers appear at the bottom of page 85.

FRAGMENT	PRODUCT
1. "Got milk"?	1. _____
2. "Eat Fresh"	2. _____
3. "Mmm mmm Good"	3. _____
4. "Healthy Beautiful Smile for Life"	4. _____

Because advertisers use pictures to complete their messages, they do not have to worry about the confusing nature of sentence fragments. Also, no one requires writers of ads to use complete sentences. Your instructors, however, expect you to write sentences that are complete and correct. You will, therefore, need to know how to spot and correct sentence fragments. To do so, you need to understand three sentence elements:

1. subjects
2. verbs
3. dependent clauses (also called subordinate clauses)

SUBJECTS AND FRAGMENTS

> **GOAL 2** Recognize and correct fragments caused by missing subjects

The **subject** of a sentence is usually a **noun**. (For a review of nouns, see Part VII, "Reviewing the Basics," p. 517.)

The <u>Babylonians</u> wrote the first advertisements.

The <u>advertisements</u> were inscribed on bricks.

The <u>kings</u> conducted advertising campaigns for themselves.

NEED TO KNOW

Subjects, Verbs, and Sentence Fragments

- The **subject** of a sentence tells you who or what the sentence is about—who or what does or receives the action of the verb.

- A **verb** expresses action or state of being. Sometimes a verb consists of only one word. (The doorbell *rang*.) Often, however, the main verb has a helping verb. (The guest *had arrived*.)

SUBJECT	VERB
Heat	rises.
Joyce	laughed.
Weeds	grow.
Opportunities	exist.

- A **sentence fragment** is not a complete idea because it lacks either a subject or a verb, or both. It needs to be connected to a nearby sentence, or to be expanded into a new sentence.

The subject of a sentence can also be a **pronoun**, a word that refers to, or substitutes for, a noun. For example, *I, you, he, she, it, they,* and *we* are all familiar pronouns. (For a review of pronouns, see Part VII, p. 519.)

Early <u>advertisements</u> were straightforward. <u>They</u> carried the names of temples.

The <u>wall</u> was built. <u>It</u> was seen by thousands of people.

The subject of a sentence can also be a group of words:

<u>Inscribing the bricks</u> was a difficult task.

<u>Uncovering the bricks</u> was a surprise.

<u>To build the brick wall</u> was a time-consuming task.

Compound Subjects

Some sentences contain two or more subjects joined together with a coordinating conjunction (*and, but, or, nor, for, so,* or *yet*). The subjects that are linked together form a **compound subject**.

compound subject

<u>Carter's Little Liver Pills</u> and <u>Ivory Soap</u> are examples of early brand-name advertising.

Note that when there are two subjects, there is no comma before the *and*. When there is a series of subjects, however, commas appear after each subject except the last.

compound subject

<u>Calendars</u>, <u>toys</u>, <u>posters</u>, and <u>clocks</u> carried advertisements for early brand-name products.

Distinguishing Subjects from Prepositional Phrases

Do not mistake a noun in a prepositional phrase for the subject of a sentence. The subject of a sentence is *never* in a prepositional phrase. A **prepositional phrase** is a group of words that begins with a preposition (such as *after, in, of*). A prepositional phrase usually ends with a noun or pronoun that tells what or whom is the object of the preposition.

preposition   noun that is object of preposition

<u>on</u> the house

preposition   noun that is object of preposition

<u>from</u> my instructor

Here are a few more prepositional phrases using common prepositions. (For a review of prepositions and more examples, see Part VII, p. 5.)

> **Tip for Writers**
>
> Be sure to use a plural verb with a compound subject even if each of the two nouns or pronouns is singular.
>
> The <u>library</u> and the <u>gym</u> <u>are</u> at the northern end of campus.

Answers to sentence fragments on page 000: 1. Milk; 2. Subway; 3. Campbell's soup. 4. Crest toothpaste.

across the lawn	until last night
throughout history	to Maria
before the judge	between friends

Remember, the noun within a prepositional phrase is *never* the subject of a sentence.

PREPOSITIONAL PHRASE   subject

Beneath the chair, the cat dozed.

subject   PREPOSITIONAL PHRASE

The students in the art class painted a mural.

PREPOSITIONAL PHRASE   subject

Inside the house, the temperature was 75 degrees.

It is especially easy to mistake the noun in the prepositional phrase for the subject of the sentence when the prepositional phrase comes between the subject and verb.

subject   PREPOSITIONAL PHRASE

The idea of killing animals disturbs Brian.

EXERCISE 4-1   Identifying Subjects and Prepositional Phrases

Directions: Circle each prepositional phrase. Then underline the subject in each of the following sentences.

EXAMPLE   The superintendent of our school was quoted in the newspaper.

1. A crowd of teenagers had purchased tickets for the concert.

2. Rows of birds perched on the telephone wires in the cornfields.

3. The strap on my backpack was tattered.

4. Trash from the festival covered the grounds inside the park.

5. Patches of blue sky are visible above the horizon. ■

EXERCISE 4-2   Writing Sentences

Directions: Write a sentence using each of the following words as a subject. Then circle any prepositional phrases in your sentence.

EXAMPLE   sister   My sister has the best sense of humor.

1. history _____

2. movie actresses _____

3. dancing _____

4. telephone calls _____

5. studying _____

■

Fragments Without a Subject

A common sentence-writing error is to write a sentence without a subject. The result is a sentence fragment. Writers often make this mistake when they think the subject of a previous sentence or a noun in a previous sentence applies to the next sentence as well.

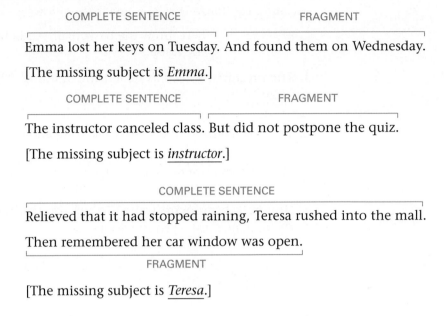

COMPLETE SENTENCE   FRAGMENT

Emma lost her keys on Tuesday. And found them on Wednesday.

[The missing subject is *Emma*.]

COMPLETE SENTENCE   FRAGMENT

The instructor canceled class. But did not postpone the quiz.

[The missing subject is *instructor*.]

COMPLETE SENTENCE

Relieved that it had stopped raining, Teresa rushed into the mall.

Then remembered her car window was open.

FRAGMENT

[The missing subject is *Teresa*.]

You can revise a fragment that lacks a subject in two ways:

1. **Add a subject, often a pronoun referring to the subject of the preceding sentence.**

   FRAGMENT   And found them on Wednesday.

                    subject

   REVISED   She found them on Wednesday.

   FRAGMENT   Then remembered her car window was open.

                        subject

   REVISED   Then she remembered her car window was open.

2. **Connect the fragment to the preceding sentence.**

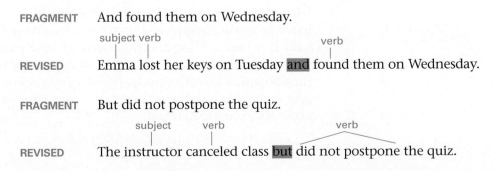

   FRAGMENT   And found them on Wednesday.

                    subject verb   verb

   REVISED   Emma lost her keys on Tuesday and found them on Wednesday.

   FRAGMENT   But did not postpone the quiz.

                        subject   verb   verb

   REVISED   The instructor canceled class but did not postpone the quiz.

Each of these sentences now has a subject and a compound verb (see Part VII, p. 559).

EXERCISE 4-3   Revising Fragments by Adding Subjects

Directions: Each of the following items consists of a complete sentence followed by a sentence fragment that lacks a subject. Make each fragment into a complete sentence by adding a subject. You may need to take out words, add new ones, capitalize words, or make them lowercase as you revise.

EXAMPLE   Bert threw the basketball. ⌃He cheered when it went in the hoop.

1. The president waved as he left the building. Then got in the car and drove away.

2. The novel was complex. Was also long and drawn out.

3. The scissors were not very sharp. Were old and rusty, you see.

4. Hundreds of students waited to get into the bookstore. Milled around until the manager unlocked the door.

5. My roommate, whose name is Speed, is an excellent skater. Gets teased sometimes about her name.

6. The computer printed out the list of names. Then beeped loudly.

7. Fans crowded the stadium. And cheered after each touchdown.

8. Many guests arrived early for the wedding. Unfortunately, were not seated until ten o'clock.

9. The delivery man put the large package down. Then rang the doorbell.

10. The big black dog sat obediently. But growled nonetheless. ■

EXERCISE 4-4   Writing About an Advertisement

Writing in Progress

Directions: Write a paragraph describing an advertisement you have seen or heard recently. Explain to whom the advertisement appeals and why. After you have finished revising and proofreading your paragraph, underline the subject of each sentence. Exchange papers with a peer reviewer and see if you agree on the identification of subjects. Discuss any differences of opinion with another peer reviewer or with your instructor. Save your paper. You will need it for other exercises in this chapter. ■

VERBS AND FRAGMENTS

GOAL 3 Recognize and correct fragments caused by missing verbs

A **verb** is a word or word group that indicates what the subject does or what happens to the subject. Most verbs express action or a state of being, for example, *run, invent, build, know, be*. (For a review of verbs, see Part VII, p. 522.)

Advertising <u>is</u> bland without a slogan.

Slogans <u>promote</u> a specific product.

Sometimes a verb consists of only one word.

The announcer <u>speaks</u>.

Often, however, the main verb is accompanied by one or more **helping (auxiliary) verbs** such as *will, can*, and forms of *be, have*, or *do*. (For a review of helping verbs, see Part VII, p. 522.)

helping verb   main verb

The announcer <u>will</u> <u>speak</u>.

helping verb   main verb

The announcer <u>will be</u> <u>speaking</u>.

helping verb   main verb

The first trademark <u>was</u> <u>registered</u> in 1870.

helping verb   main verb

<u>Do</u> any companies <u>use</u> animals as trademarks?

helping verb   main verb

The lion <u>has been</u> MGM's trademark for a long time.

Compound Verbs

Some sentences have two or more verbs joined together with a coordinating conjunction (such as *and, or*, or *but*).

subject   compound verb

The "Uncle Sam Wants You" poster <u>stirred</u> patriotism and <u>increased</u> enlistments.

coordinating conjunction

subject   compound verb

The posters <u>appeared</u> on billboards and <u>hung</u> on buildings.

coordinating conjunction

EXERCISE 4-5   Identifying Verbs

Directions: Underline the verb(s), including any helping verb(s), in each of the following sentences.

> EXAMPLE   The lectures in psychology <u>have been focusing</u> on instinctive behavior lately.

1. Preschools teach children social and academic skills.

2. Exercise clubs offer instruction and provide companionship.

3. Millions of people have watched soap operas.

4. Essay exams are given in many college classes.

5. The audience will be surprised by the play's ending. ■

Fragments Without Complete Verbs

Fragments often occur when word groups begin with words ending in *-ing* or with phrases beginning with the word *to*. These words and phrases are verb forms and may look like verbs, but they cannot function as verbs in sentences.

-ing *Fragments*

Note the *-ing* word in the fragment below:

> FRAGMENT   <u>Walking</u> across campus after lunch.

In this word group, *walking* has no subject. Who is walking? Now let's add a subject and see what happens:

> *Allison* <u>walking</u> across campus after lunch.

The word group still is not a complete sentence; the verb form *walking* cannot be used alone as a sentence verb. You can make the word group a complete sentence by adding a helping verb (for example, *is, was, has been*) or by using a different verb form (*walked* or *walks*).

> helping verb added
> |
> REVISED   Allison <u>was</u> <u>walking</u> across campus after lunch.

> form changed to present tense
> |
> REVISED   Allison <u>walks</u> across campus after lunch.

Now the word group is a complete sentence.

Tip for Writers

The simple present tense is used for repeated action. "Allison <u>walks</u> across campus after lunch" means she does this regularly. On the other hand, "Allison is walking" (present continuous tense) means right now or at some stated future time (perhaps tomorrow) she is or will be walking.

You can correct fragments beginning with *-ing* words in four ways:

1. **Add a subject and change the verb form to a sentence verb.**

   FRAGMENT

   FRAGMENT   Morris was patient. Waiting in line at the bank.

   subject   verb changed to past tense

   REVISED   Morris was patient. He waited in line at the bank.

2. **Add a subject and a form of *be* (such as *am, are, will be, has been, is, was, were*) as a helping verb.**

   FRAGMENT

   FRAGMENT   Juan was bored. Listening to his sister complain about her boyfriend.

   subject   form of be   main verb

   REVISED   Juan was bored. He was listening to his sister complain about her boyfriend.

3. **Connect the fragment to the sentence that comes before or after it.**

   FRAGMENT

   FRAGMENT   Mark finished lunch. Picking up his tray. Then he left the cafeteria.

   modifies he

   REVISED   Mark finished lunch. Picking up his tray, he left the cafeteria.

4. **If the *-ing* word is *being*, change its form to another form of *be* (*am, are, is, was, were*).**

   FRAGMENT

   FRAGMENT   Jayla failed the math quiz. Her mistakes being careless errors.

   verb from changed

   REVISED   Jayla failed the math quiz. Her mistakes were careless errors.

Fragments with To Phrases

A phrase beginning with *to* cannot be the verb of the sentence. When it stands alone, it is a sentence fragment.

   FRAGMENT   To review for the psychology test.

This word group lacks a subject and a sentence verb. To make a complete sentence, you need to add a subject and a sentence verb.

   subject   verb

   REVISED   Deon plans to review for the psychology test.

You can revise fragments that begin with *to* in two ways:

1. **Add a subject and a sentence verb.**

   FRAGMENT   To reach my goal.

   subject   verb

   REVISED   I hope to reach my goal.

2. **Connect the *to* phrase to a nearby sentence.**

   FRAGMENT   To earn the highest grade. Antonio studied eight hours.

   REVISEDS   To earn the highest grade, Antonio studied eight hours.

EXERCISE 4-6
Working Together

Correcting Fragments by Adding Verbs

Directions: Each of the following word groups is a fragment. Revise each one to form a complete sentence, and then compare your revisions with those of a classmate.

EXAMPLE

FRAGMENT   Walking along the waterfront.

COMPLETE SENTENCE   Andrea was walking along the waterfront.

1. Photographing the wedding.

   _____

2. To have a family.

   _____

3. Hanging up the suit in the closet.

   _____

4. Deciding what to have for dinner.

   _____

5. To attend the awards ceremony.

   _____

6. Writing the speech.

   _____

7. To sketch a diagram.

   _____

8. To quit her job.

_____

9. Making the paper less repetitious.

_____

10. Being old and in disrepair.

_____

■

EXERCISE 4-7 *Writing in Progress*	**Revising Your Paragraph**

Directions: Go back to the paragraph you wrote in Exercise 4-4 and circle the verb or verbs in each sentence. Exchange papers with a peer reviewer and check each other's work. ■

CLAUSES AND FRAGMENTS

GOAL 4 Recognize and correct fragments caused by dependent clauses

A sentence must not only contain a subject and a verb; *it must also express a complete thought.* That is, a sentence should not leave a question in your mind as to its meaning or leave an idea unfinished. To spot and avoid sentence fragments in your writing, you must be able to recognize the difference between independent and dependent (or subordinate) clauses. A **clause** is a group of related words that contains a subject and its verb. There are two types of clauses, independent and dependent. An **independent clause** expresses a complete thought and can stand alone as a complete sentence. A **dependent (or subordinate) clause** does not express a complete thought. When a dependent clause stands alone, it is a fragment.

Independent Clauses

An **independent clause** has a subject and a verb and can stand alone as a complete and correct sentence. It expresses a complete thought.

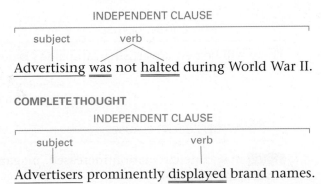

COMPLETE THOUGHT

INDEPENDENT CLAUSE

subject   verb

Advertising was not halted during World War II.

COMPLETE THOUGHT

INDEPENDENT CLAUSE

subject   verb

Advertisers prominently displayed brand names.

Dependent (or Subordinate) Clauses

A **dependent clause** has a subject and a verb but cannot stand alone as a complete and correct sentence. It does not express a complete thought. A dependent clause makes sense only when it is joined to an independent clause. When a dependent clause stands alone, it is a **dependent clause fragment**. A dependent clause fragment leaves an unanswered question in your mind.

INCOMPLETE THOUGHT
DEPENDENT CLAUSE FRAGMENT

subject   verb

After World War II ended. [What happened after World War II ended?]

INCOMPLETE THOUGHT
DEPENDENT CLAUSE FRAGMENT

subject   verb

If new products are developed. [What happens if new products are developed?]

INCOMPLETE THOUGHT
DEPENDENT CLAUSE FRAGMENT

subject   verb

When magazine circulation increased. [What happened when circulation increased?]

How can you spot dependent clauses? A dependent clause often begins with a word or group of words called a **subordinating conjunction**.

Subordinating conjunctions signal dependent clauses. When you see a clause beginning with one of these words, as shown in the "Need to Know" box on page 95, make sure the clause is attached to an independent clause. A subordinating conjunction explains the relationship between the dependent clause and the independent clause to which it is joined.

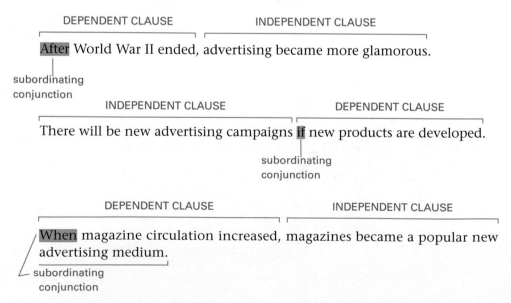

DEPENDENT CLAUSE   INDEPENDENT CLAUSE

After World War II ended, advertising became more glamorous.

subordinating
conjunction

INDEPENDENT CLAUSE   DEPENDENT CLAUSE

There will be new advertising campaigns if new products are developed.

subordinating
conjunction

DEPENDENT CLAUSE   INDEPENDENT CLAUSE

When magazine circulation increased, magazines became a popular new advertising medium.

subordinating
conjunction

EXERCISE 4-8   Identifying Clauses

Directions: Decide whether the following clauses are independent or dependent. Write "I" for independent or "D" for dependent before each clause.

_____ 1. While Arturo was driving to school.

_____ 2. *Sesame Street* is a children's educational television program.

_____ 3. Samantha keeps a diary of her family's holiday celebrations.

_____ 4. Because Aretha had a craving for chocolate.

_____ 5. Exercise can help to relieve stress.

_____ 6. When Peter realized he would be able to meet the deadline.

_____ 7. A snowstorm crippled the eastern seaboard states on New Year's Eve.

_____ 8. Unless my uncle decides to visit us during spring break.

_____ 9. Long-distance telephone rates are less expensive during the evening than during the day.

_____ 10. As long as Jacqueline is living at home. ■

NEED TO KNOW

Subordinating Conjunctions

A clause beginning with a subordinate conjunction is a dependent clause. It cannot stand alone. It must be connected to an independent clause. Here is a list of common subordinating conjunctions:

after	If	though
although	inasmuch as	unless
as	in case	until
as far as	in order that	when
as if	in order to	whenever
as long as	now that	where
as soon as	once	whereas
as though	provided that	wherever
because	rather than	whether
before	since	while
during	so that	
even if	than	
even though	that	

Correcting Dependent Clause Fragments

You can correct a dependent clause fragment in two ways:

1. **Join the dependent clause to an independent clause to make the dependent clause fragment part of a complete sentence.**

FRAGMENT	Although competition increased.
COMPLETE SENTENCE	Although competition increased, the sales staff was still getting new customers.
FRAGMENT	Because market research expanded.
COMPLETE SENTENCE	The company added new accounts because market research expanded.
FRAGMENT	Although statistics and market research have become part of advertising.
COMPLETE SENTENCE	Although statistics and market research have become part of advertising, consumers' tastes remain somewhat unpredictable.

2. **Take away the subordinating conjunction, and the dependent clause fragment becomes an independent clause that can stand alone as a complete sentence.**

FRAGMENT	Although competition increased.
COMPLETE SENTENCE	Competition increased.
FRAGMENT	Because market research expanded.
COMPLETE SENTENCE	Market research expanded.
FRAGMENT	Although statistics and market research have become part of advertising.
COMPLETE SENTENCE	Statistics and market research have become part of advertising.

Note: When you join a dependent clause to an independent clause, you need to think about punctuation:

1. **If the *dependent* clause comes first, follow it with a comma.** The comma separates the dependent clause from the independent clause and helps you know where the independent clause begins.

DEPENDENT CLAUSE   INDEPENDENT CLAUSE

COMMA NEEDED   After World War II ended, humor and sex were used in commercials.

2. **If the *independent* clause comes first, do *not* use a comma between the two clauses.**

INDEPENDENT CLAUSE

NO COMMA NEEDED   Humor and sex were used in commercials after World War II ended.

DEPENDENT CLAUSE

EXERCISE 4-9   **Revising Fragments by Adding Independent Clauses**

Directions: Make each of these dependent clause fragments into a sentence by adding an independent clause before or after the fragment. Add or remove punctuation if necessary.

EXAMPLE   After we got to the beach,/ we put on sunscreen.

1. Since the surgery was expensive.

   _____

2. As long as my boss allows me.

   _____

3. Because I want to be a journalist.

   _____

4. Until the roof is repaired.

   _____

5. Once I returned the library books.

   _____

6. So that I do not miss class.

   _____

7. Provided that Marietta gets the loan.

   _____

8. Unless you would rather go to the movies.

   _____

9. If the thunderstorm comes during the barbecue.

   _____

10. Although we visited Pittsburgh last summer.

   _____

Dependent Clauses Beginning with Relative Pronouns

Dependent clauses also may begin with **relative pronouns**. (For more information on relative pronouns, see Part VII, p. 551.)

RELATIVE PRONOUNS			
RELATIVE PRONOUNS THAT REFER TO PEOPLE		**RELATIVE PRONOUNS THAT REFER TO THINGS**	
who	whom	that	whichever
whoever	whomever	which	whatever
whose			

The relative pronoun that begins a dependent clause connects the dependent clause to a noun or pronoun in the independent clause. However, the verb in the dependent clause is *never* the main verb of the sentence. The independent clause has its own verb, the main verb of the sentence, and expresses a complete thought.

The following sentence fragments each consist of a noun followed by a dependent clause beginning with a relative pronoun. They are not complete sentences because the noun does not have a verb and the fragment does not express a complete thought.

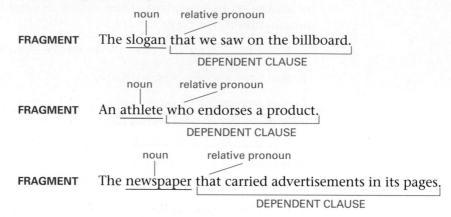

You can correct this type of fragment by adding a verb to make the noun the subject of an independent clause. Often the independent clause will be split, and the dependent clause will appear between its parts.

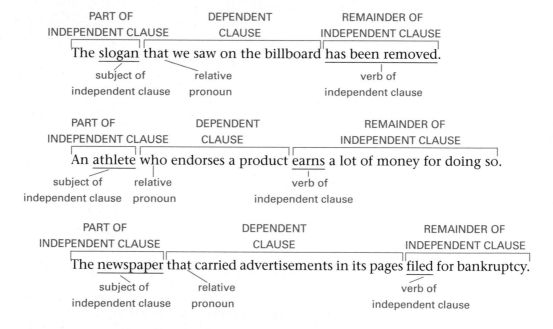

EXERCISE 4-10   Revising Fragments

Directions: Make each of these fragments into a complete sentence. Add words, phrases or clauses, and punctuation as needed.

EXAMPLE   The usher who was available, led us to our seats.

1. The radio that Trevor had purchased last night.

2. The official who had signed the peace treaty.

3. The athlete who won the tennis tournament.

4. Mark, whose nose had been broken in a fight.

_____

5. The advice that his lawyer gave him.

_____

6. The student who needed the scholarship the most.

_____

7. The answering machine that is in the kitchen.

_____

8. Sarah, whom I knew in high school.

_____

9. The problems that the professor assigned.

_____

10. The men who signed the Declaration of Independence.

_____

HOW TO SPOT AND REVISE FRAGMENTS: A BRIEF REVIEW

Now that you have learned to identify subjects, verbs, and dependent clauses, you will be able to spot and correct fragments. The "Need to Know" boxes provide a brief review.

NEED TO KNOW

How to Spot Fragments

Use the following questions to check for fragments:

1. **Does the word group have a subject?** The subject is a noun or pronoun that performs or receives the action of the sentence. To find the subject, ask *who* or *what* performs or receives the action of the verb.

2. **Does the word group have a verb?** Be sure that the verb is a complete and correct sentence verb. Watch out for sentences that begin with an -ing word or a *to* phrase.

3. **Does the word group begin with a subordinating conjunction (*since, after, because, as, while, although, and so forth*) introducing a dependent clause?** Unless the dependent clause is attached to an independent clause, it is a fragment.

4. **Does the word group begin with a relative pronoun (*who, whom, whose, whoever, whomever, that, which, whatever*) introducing a dependent clause?** Unless the dependent clause forms a question, is part of an independent clause, or is attached to an independent clause, it is a fragment.

NEED TO KNOW

How to Revise Fragments

Once you spot a fragment in your writing, correct it in one of the following ways:

1. **Add a subject if one is missing.**

   FRAGMENT   Appeared on television ten times during the game.

   REVISED   The advertisement for Pepsi appeared on television ten times during the game.

2. **Add a verb if one is missing. Add a helping verb if one is needed, or change the verb form.**

   FRAGMENT   An action-packed commercial with rap music.

   REVISED   An action-packed commercial with rap music advertised a new soft drink.

3. **Combine the fragment with an independent clause to make a complete sentence.**

   FRAGMENT   Because advertising is expensive.

   REVISED   Because advertising is expensive, companies are making shorter commercials.

4. **Remove the subordinating conjunction or relative pronoun so the group of words can stand alone as a sentence.**

   FRAGMENT   Since viewers can "zap" out commercials on video-recorders.

   REVISED   Viewers can "zap" out commercials on video-recorders.

EXERCISE 4-11   Revising Fragments

Directions: Make each of the following sentence fragments a complete sentence by combining it with an independent clause, removing the subordinating conjunction or relative pronoun, or adding the missing subject or verb.

EXAMPLE

FRAGMENT   Many environmentalists are concerned about the spotted owl. Which is almost extinct.

COMPLETE SENTENCE   Many environmentalists are concerned about the spotted owl, which is almost extinct.

1. Renting a DVD of the movie *The King's Speech.*

   _____

   _____

2. Spices that had been imported from India.

   _____

   _____

3. The police officer walked to Jerome's van. To give him a ticket.

_____

_____

4. My English professor, with the cup of tea he brought to each class.

_____

_____

5. After the table was refinished.

_____

_____

6. Roberto memorized his lines. For the performance tomorrow night.

_____

_____

7. A tricycle with big wheels, painted red.

_____

_____

8. On the shelf an antique crock used for storing lard.

_____

_____

9. Because I always wanted to learn to speak Spanish.

_____

_____

10. Looking for the lost keys. I was late for class.

_____

_____

■

 Analyze It!

Directions: The following paragraph is correct except that it contains sentence fragments. Underline each fragment. Then revise the paragraph in the space provided by rewriting or combining sentences to eliminate fragments.

Social networks such as Facebook and Twitter appeal to college students for a variety of reasons. Social networks are a way of having conversations. Staying in touch with friends without the inconvenience of getting dressed and meeting them somewhere. Friends can join or drop out of a conversation whenever they want. Social networks also allow college students to meet new people and make new friends. Members can track who is friends with whom. Students may choose to share only portions of their profiles. To protect their privacy. Some students use social networks to form groups. Such as clubs, study groups, or special interest groups. Other students use networks to screen dates. And discover who is interested in dating or who is already taken.

EXERCISE 4-12   Revising Sentence Fragments

Writing in Progress

Directions: Review the paragraph you wrote for Exercise 4-4, checking for sentence fragments. If you find a fragment, revise it. ■

Paragraph Writing Scenarios

Friends and Family

1. Choose a close friend and write a paragraph that explains the characteristics that make him or her a good friend.

2. Write a paragraph that begins with the topic sentence, "There are three main ways to ruin a friendship."

Classes and Campus Life

1. Choose one of your courses and a particular class session for that course. Explain what you learned from that class session. Discuss how you can use what you learned.

2. Which of your classes do you expect to be the most difficult or challenging? Write a paragraph explaining your reasons.

Working Students

1. Write a paragraph on the value of work. Other than a paycheck, what are its benefits?

2. Write a paragraph describing the perfect or ideal job. If you could choose any job you wanted, what would you pick?

Communities and Cultures

1. Everyone belongs to various communities. A community is a group of people who share a common goal or purpose. Clubs, colleges, ethnic groups, and religious groups are all communities. Employees working in the same business form a community, as do members of a sports team or diners in a restaurant. Choose one of your classes and write a paragraph describing why it is a community. That is, explain what you share or have in common with other students.

2. Choose a community (see #1 for a definition of community), other than your classes, that you belong to. Write a paragraph explaining your common goals or purposes.

WRITING ABOUT A READING

In the following reading, the author provides a behind-the-scenes look at prison dog programs.

Step 1: Preview the reading.

Step 2: Connect the reading to your own experience: What do you know about training dogs?

Step 3: Read and respond to the questions in the margin.

THINK AS YOU READ

What do the title and subtitle suggest about the content of the reading?

How can a prisoner be an "emblem?

What are the benefits of prison-dog programs?

TAILS IN JAIL

A BEHIND-THE-SCENES LOOK AT PRISON DOG PROGRAMS

Denise Flaim

1   They are the oddest of couples.

2   One is an emblem of violence and lawlessness, of everything that is awry in American society.

3   The other is a greeting-card image of furry innocence, radiating promise and optimism and unsullied loyalty.

4   But together they have forged a bond that has been in the human-canine DNA for millennia, one that transcends steel bars and barbed wire and guard towers, and returns some of society's most isolated and ostracized members to a long-ago place of pride within themselves.

5   Today, there are about a hundred programs around the country that use prisoners to raise and train puppies and dogs for service organizations and rescue groups. Some of the dogs go on to serious jobs, from bomb detection to guiding the blind. Others simply become beloved house pets. But the premise behind using the incarcerated for their caretakers is universal, and starkly simple: Dog training takes time, which is many of these men and women have in abundance.

6   Prison-dog programs are a winning proposition on all sides: For service-dog and adoption groups, they provide full-time foster homes and trainers. Prison officials say the programs increase empathy, lower stress and tension, teach new skills that might one day lead to employment outside the concrete walls, and serve as a powerful motivation to keep a clean disciplinary record. And for the prisoners themselves, the dogs represent something that they had long ago given up any hope of experiencing again: trust.

7   "Dogs show an unconditional love," says Brian Harkness, 41, of Sacramento, Calif., who socialized dogs for Pen Pals of San Quentin during his almost 4-year sentence, which ended only a few months ago. "If you treat them right, they love you, no matter who you are, what you look like," he says. "I can honestly say I never had that before."

8   Sister Pauline Quinn knows firsthand how a bundle of fur can change not only how a person feels inside, but how society values them. Institutionalized 36 times as a youngster, she experienced abuse on the street and at the hands of authority figures that was literally unspeakable—at one point in her life, Quinn, who later became a nun, was so shattered she found herself unable to talk.

9   "I was able to pull myself up after I received a German shepherd named Joni," says Quinn, who had a movie about her life made for cable television, starring Laura Dern in her role. "Through Joni, my self-esteem started to be rebuilt."

Why does Quinn call Joni an "image dog?"

10   Quinn calls Joni an "image dog": A big, beautiful, serious shepherd, she commanded respect—something Quinn had had little of in her life–and that transferred to the other end of the leash. "People didn't treat me the same way as they did before. It was interesting how a dog can bring back your self-esteem, or empower you if you don't have it within yourself."

11   Recognizing how Joni had transformed her, Quinn decided to do the same for others in the nation's institutions. So in 1981, with the help of a vet-school dean, she started what is believed to be the first prison-dog program in the country, which continues to this day at Washington State Corrections Center for Women in Gig Harbor.

What does "other-centered" mean?

12   "Our own dogs were trained, and we brought them in there so the inmates could have that feeling of success right away," Quinn explains. "The dogs helped the prisoners to become 'other centered'—even if we have pain in our lives, helping others helps our pain."

13   More than a quarter-century after Quinn started her program, today prison-dog programs are flourishing. Here are three, each in a different part of the country, and each training dogs from different backgrounds, for different purposes. But all are rooted in the same belief: That dogs, magical creatures that they are, have the power to bring out the best in us, no matter how far we have strayed.

Pen Pals of San Quentin

What is the meaning of "no cakewalk"?

14   San Quentin is no cakewalk: California's only death-row prison was home to the likes of Robert Kennedy's assassin Sirhan Sirhan and mass murderer Charles Manson. But well-behaved inmates in the minimum-security firehouse on the 440-acre island also share their 8-foot-square sleeping quarters with strays from The Marin Humane Society.

What is the message of the photograph to the right?

Inmates at Blackburn Correctional Complex in Lexington, Kentucky, walk the dogs they have trained (so they will be more adoptable) to the Lexington Humane Society truck after their graduation ceremony on Thursday, March 19, 2009. The inmates are assigned in teams, two per each animal, and are responsible for their dogs 24 hours a day, seven days a week.

15   Larry Carson of the humane society, who coordinates the prison's Pen Pals program, says about 10 to 12 of the firehouse prisoners work with a total of three to four dogs at a time.

16   More than half the dogs are medical fosters, recuperating from everything from heartworm to starvation. Another 20 percent are shy, "shut down" dogs that need more socialization to come out of their shells and be good adoption prospects. And an equivalent amount are adolescent dogs who have never had training or structure.

17   "They really do relate to the dogs," Carson says of the prisoners. "These are homeless dogs, and in some cases dogs that people don't want, and they can relate to that in their own lives."

18   To date, 135 dogs have gone through the San Quentin program. Harkness, the recently released convict, remembers his first dog, Arthur, a Shar-Pei rescued from a Chinese food market where he was likely on the menu.

19   Arthur had a skin condition so severe he had lost all his hair, and he was so gaunt he had lost the breed's characteristic wrinkles. "He was a poor old beat-up dog," Harkness remembers proudly. "But I totally nursed him back to health."

Second Chance Greyhounds

How are second chance Greyhounds similar to prisoners?

20   Greyhounds who are bred and raised on race tracks have a few things in common with prisoners: Deprived of socialization and life "on the outside," these delicate-looking sighthounds are unfamiliar with everyday objects and occurrences that other dogs simply take for granted.

21   Second Chance Greyhounds is a fledgling rescue group that has partnered with correctional facilities in Georgia and Florida to train former racing greyhounds to transition to life on the couch.

22   Greyhounds from Birmingham Race Course in Alabama spend two months at the minimum-security Gaston Correctional Facility in Florida, whose dormitory set-up is as conducive to a home environment as any prison gets. The prisoners teach basic things that most other dogs know from puppyhood: No, you cannot walk through a sliding glass door. Yes, it's OK to walk across that slippery tile floor. Look, here are steps . . . this is how you climb them. "Sit" means recline back on your haunches; "hurry" means go outside and do your business.

23   Caring for the greyhounds affords the prisoners special privileges, such as taking them outdoors to an enclosed football field to let them exercise. "Watching these greyhounds run is a thrill in itself," says Patti Peterson, who chairs the greyhound group. "They're beautiful runners."

24   The prisoners, many of whom have been incarcerated for fraud or identity theft, write weekly reports on how their dogs have progressed. When dogs finish their stay, they write letters to the new families, who are adopting them sight unseen. And their emotions are displayed in every penstroke.

Why do you think the author described the stationery in such vivid detail?

25   "Please give him lots of love—he needs it. Upon his arrival he had no idea what affection was," reads one neatly scripted letter, written by an inmate named Jenifer on tasteful flower-print stationery. "I hope you have lots of fun, as I have. I will miss him dearly."

Puppies Behind Bars

26   When Gloria Gilbert Stoga founded Puppies Behind Bars 13 years ago, there were all of three prison-dog programs in the country. Today, the program is in place at six correctional facilities in New York, New Jersey and Connecticut, and has graduated almost 600 dogs, many of which have gone on to be service dogs for the disabled, as well as explosives-detection dogs.

27   One concern about any prison-dog program is for the dogs themselves: Are these innocent animals targets for violence and mishandling in a population convicted of serious crimes like murder and rape?

What is the author suggesting here?

28   Stoga says any potential for abuse is forestalled by a vigorous screening process. "We take into consideration the nature of the crime, length of sentence, disciplinary record and mental health," she says. "And anyone who has directly hurt a child or been convicted of a sex crime is not accepted into the program."

29   Applicants for the program are interviewed using psychologist-written questions, and "puppy raisers," as they are called, are required to sign a contract with Puppies Behind Bars that outlines all of their responsibilities in the program, which include mandatory attendance at weekly puppy class, reading assignments, homework and exams.

Why are psychologist-written questions a part of the application process?

30   "This dog is gonna be useful and this dog is gonna love somebody and this dog is just gonna be somebody's everything," says Jasmine, a prisoner at the women's maximum-security Bedford Hills Correctional Facility in Bedford Hills, NY, adding that she thinks her success in training a dog for service or bomb-detection work will translate to employment outside the prison walls. And Stoga confirms that a number of former inmates are working in animal-related fields after their release.

31   In the meantime, the dewy-eyed Golden and Labrador Retriever puppies remind their handlers that that even within their world of lock downs and cinderblock cells, there are ample opportunities for trust, redemption . . . and second chances.

What is the purpose of this paragraph?

WRITING IN RESPONSE TO READING

Examining the Reading Using an Idea Map MyWritingLab

Review the reading by completing the missing parts of the idea map shown below.

Visualize It!

Title — **Tails in Jail**

Thesis — Dogs and prisoners both benefit from prison dog training programs.

Prison dog programs are beneficial in several ways.

_____

_____

Prisoners also experience trust and unconditional love from the dogs.

Sister Pauline Quinn experienced how a dog could help transform a life.

Her dog helped her recover from a traumatic early life.

_____

Three different prison programs are described.

Pen Pals of San Quentin:
1. _____
2. _____

Second Chance Greyhounds:
1. _____
2. _____

Puppies Behind Bars:
Almost 600 dogs have graduated from six prisons in the program.

_____

Conclusion — Prison dog programs improve the lives of dogs and prisoners.

Strengthening Your Vocabulary   MyWritingLab

Using the word's context, word parts, or a dictionary, write a brief definition of each of the following words as it is used in the reading

1. transcends (paragraph 4) _____
2. ostracized (paragraph 4) _____
3. incarcerated (paragraph 5) _____
4. flourishing (paragraph 13) _____
5. recuperating (paragraph 16) _____
6. fledgling (paragraph 21) _____
7. forestalled (paragraph 28) _____
8. redemption (paragraph 31) _____

Reacting to Ideas: Discussion and Journal Writing   MyWritingLab

Get ready to write about the reading by discussing the following:

1. How did the author capture your attention in the opening paragraph?
2. The author quotes prison inmates, program coordinators, and a nun in this article. Which of these were most effective in convincing you of the value of prison dog programs?
3. How would you feel about adopting a dog that had been trained by a prisoner?
4. What details do you notice about the photograph of the inmates walking with dogs at the Blackburn Correctional Complex? How does this photograph reinforce the author's message?

Paragraph Options   MyWritingLab

1. What questions do you have about the dog training programs that were not answered in this article? Write a paragraph about what else you would like to know about these programs.
2. Write a paragraph discussing pet ownership, including the pros and cons.
3. Do you agree that "dogs . . . have the power to bring out the best in us, no matter how far we have strayed"? Write a paragraph explaining your answer, or substitute a different word for *dogs* and write a paragraph based on that statement.

Essay Options   MyWritingLab

4. If you support the idea of a prison dog program, compose a letter to the editor of your newspaper, arguing in favor of creating such a program. If you do not see the benefit of a prison dog program, write a letter arguing against it. Be sure to give reasons to support your case.
5. When have you been given a second chance in your life? Write an essay describing your experience.

6. What can you tell about the author's attitude toward dogs and the prison dog programs she describes in the article? Write an essay examining the ways the author reveals her feelings toward the subject, including specific examples from the article. Consider her tone, choice of words, and what she has included as well as what she may have omitted.

■ ■ ■ ■

SELF-TEST SUMMARY

To test yourself, cover the Answer column with a sheet of paper and answer each question in the left column. Evaluate each of your answers as you work by sliding the paper down and comparing your answer with what is printed in the Answer column.

	QUESTION	ANSWER
Goal 1 Identify sentence fragments	What is a sentence fragment?	A fragment is an incomplete sentence that lacks either a subject, a verb, or both.
Goal 2 Recognize and correct fragments caused by missing subjects	What are two ways to correct fragments caused by missing subjects?	Revise a fragment that lacks a subject by adding a subject or by connecting the fragment to the preceding sentence.
Goal 3 Recognize and correct fragments caused by missing verbs	How do fragments without verbs occur? How can you correct fragments caused by missing verbs?	Fragments without verbs often occur when word groups begin with *-ing* words or with *to* phrases. Correct *to* fragments by adding a subject and a sentence verb or by connecting the *to* phrase to a nearby sentence. Ways to correct *-ing* fragments include • adding a subject and changing the verb form to a sentence form; • adding a subject and a form of *be* as a helping verb; • connecting the fragment to the sentence before or after it; • if the *-ing* word is *being*, change it to another form of *be*.
Goal 4 Recognize and correct fragments caused by dependent clauses	What is a dependent clause? What are two ways to correct dependent clause fragments?	A dependent clause has a subject and a verb but does not express a complete thought; a dependent clause often begins with a subordinating conjunction. Correct dependent clause fragments by joining the dependent clause to an independent clause or by taking away the subordinating conjunction.

MyWritingLab *Visit Chapter 4: Complete Sentences Versus Fragments in MyWritingLab to test your understanding of the chapter objectives.*

Run-On Sentences and Comma Splices

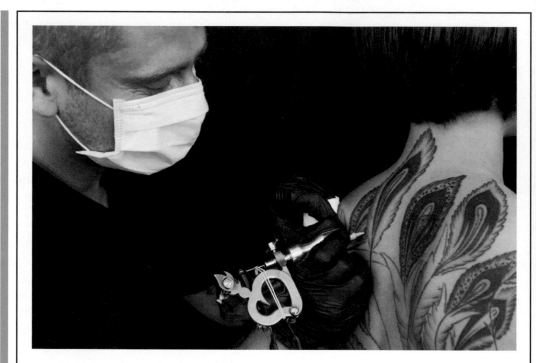

WRITE ABOUT IT!

Study the paragraph below. Why is it difficult to read?

Tattoos are a popular but permanent form of body decoration tattoos similar to body painting used by primitive societies in fact the word *tattoo* comes from the Tahitian word *ta-tu* they are used to communicate things about the wearer to those who view them a tattoo may be used to identify the person wearing the tattoo as part of a group they have recently become popular within a wide range of age groups people getting tattoos are cautioned to be sure to choose a safe clean tattoo parlor and be sure that sterile procedures are used.

Did you have trouble reading this paragraph? Why? Write a sentence explaining your difficulty.

Most likely you said that the paragraph lacked punctuation. You could not see where one idea ended and another began. It is important to remember this confusion when you are writing. If you run sentences together, you run the risk of confusing your readers. In this chapter you will learn how to avoid this problem. Specifically, you will learn to use punctuation to connect or distinguish separate ideas within a sentence.

WRITING

THE FUNCTION OF PUNCTUATION: HOW TO USE IT CORRECTLY

GOAL 1 Use punctuation correctly within and between sentences

All punctuation serves one primary purpose—to separate. Periods, question marks, and exclamation points separate complete sentences from one another. Think of these punctuation marks as *between*-sentence separators. All other punctuation marks—commas, colons, semicolons, hyphens, dashes, quotation marks, and parentheses—separate parts *within* a sentence. To correct and avoid run-on sentences and comma splices, you need a good grasp of both between-sentence and within-sentence punctuation.

Between-Sentence Punctuation

The period, question mark, and exclamation point all mark the end of a sentence. Each has a different function.

BETWEEN-SENTENCE PUNCTUATION

Punctuation	Function	Example
Period (.)	Marks the end of a statement or command	The lecture is about to begin. Please be seated.
Question mark (?)	Marks the end of a direct question	Are you ready?
Exclamation point (!)	Marks the end of statements of excitement or strong emotion	We are late! I won an award!

Within-Sentence Punctuation

Commas, colons, semicolons, hyphens, dashes, quotation marks, and parentheses all separate parts of a sentence from one another. For a complete review of how and when to use each, refer to Part VII, "Reviewing the Basics," pages **555–564**.

The **comma** is the most commonly used within-sentence punctuation mark and also the most commonly misused. The comma separates parts of a sentence from one another. In this chapter, we'll be concerned with just one type of separation: the separation of two complete thoughts. *Note:* Some instructors refer to a complete thought as an independent clause. An independent clause has a subject and a verb and can stand alone as a sentence. (For a review of independent clauses, see Chapter 4, p. **93**.)

The comma can be used to separate two complete thoughts within a sentence *if and only if* it is used along with one of the coordinating conjunctions (*and, but, for, nor, or, so, yet*). Coordinating conjunctions are words that link and relate equally important parts of a sentence. The comma is not a strong enough separator to be used between complete thoughts without one of the coordinating conjunctions.

complete thought   coordinating conjunction   complete thought

I work now for a big company, but I am hoping someday to take over my father's business.

complete thought   coordinating conjunction   complete thought

I am undecided about a career, so I am majoring in liberal arts.

When you do not insert punctuation and a coordinating conjunction between two complete thoughts, you create an error called a **run-on sentence.** (This is sometimes called a **fused sentence** because two sentences are incorrectly fused, or joined together.) When you use *only* a comma to separate two complete thoughts, you make an error called a **comma splice.**

RUN-ON SENTENCES

GOAL 2 Recognize and correct run-on sentences

When you do not separate two complete thoughts (two independent clauses) with the necessary punctuation, the two clauses run together and form a run-on sentence.

How to Recognize Run-On Sentences

1. **Read each sentence aloud.** Listen for a break or change in your voice midway through the sentence. Your voice automatically pauses or slows down at the end of a complete thought. If you hear a break but have no punctuation at that break, you may have a run-on sentence. Try reading the following run-on sentences aloud. Place a slash mark (/) where you hear a pause.

   RUN-ON   The library has a copy machine it is very conveniently located.

   RUN-ON   The Career Planning Center on campus is helpful one of the counselors suggested I take a career-planning course.

   RUN-ON   My major is nursing I do enjoy working with people.

Did you mark the sentences as follows?

> The library has a copy machine / it is very conveniently located.
>
> The Career Planning Center on campus is helpful / one of the counselors suggested I take a career-planning course.
>
> My major is nursing / I do enjoy working with people.

The pause in each indicates the need for punctuation.

Tip for Writers

Then cannot be used to connect two independent clauses even if it is preceded by a comma. When using *then* as a connector, write the sentence one of these ways:

- We adopted a dog, **and then** we adopted four cats.
- We adopted a dog; **then** we adopted four cats.
- We adopted a dog **and then** four cats.

2. Look for sentences that contain two complete thoughts (independent clauses) without punctuation to separate them.

complete thought (independent clause)

RUN-ON   Houseplants are pleasant additions to a home or office they add color and variety.

complete thought (independent clause)

complete thought (independent clause)   complete thought (independent clause)

RUN-ON   My sister decided to wear black I chose red.

complete thought (independent clause)

RUN-ON   Having a garage sale is a good way to make money it unclutters the house, too.

complete thought (independent clause)

complete thought (independent clause)   complete thought (independent clause)

RUN-ON   We bought a portable phone then we had to connect the base unit into our phone line.

3. Look for long sentences. Not every long sentence is a run-on, but run-ons do tend to occur more frequently in longer sentences than in shorter ones.

RUN-ON   Choosing a mate is one of the most important decisions you will ever make unless you make the right choice, you may be unhappy.

RUN-ON   I plan to work in a day-care center some days taking care of my own kids is enough to make me question my career choice.

EXERCISE 5-1   Identifying Run-On Sentences

Directions: Read each sentence aloud. Place a check mark in the blank before each sentence that is a run-on. Use a slash mark to show where punctuation is needed. Not all of these sentences are run-ons.

_____ 1. Parking spaces on campus are limited often I must park far away and walk.

_____ 2. Before exercising, you should always stretch and warm up to prevent injury.

_____ 3. Theodore's car wouldn't start fortunately Phil was able to use jumper cables to help him get it started.

_____ 4. The skydiver jumped from the plane when she had fallen far enough she released her parachute.

_____ 5. Radio stations usually have a morning disc jockey whose job is to wake people and cheer them up on their way to work.

_____ 6. It continued to rain until the river overflowed many people had to be evacuated from their homes.

_____ 7. Calla bought a bathrobe for her brother as a birthday gift it was gray with burgundy stripes.

_____ 8. The rooms in the maternity section of the hospital have colorful flowered wallpaper they are cheerful and pleasant.

_____ 9. Because my cousin went to nursing school and then to law school, she is going to practice medical malpractice law.

_____ 10. We rented *The Fighter* to watch on the DVD player later we practiced boxing moves. ■

How to Correct Run-On Sentences

1. **Create two separate sentences.** Split the two complete thoughts into two separate sentences. End the first thought with a *period* (or a *question mark* or an *exclamation point* if one is needed). Begin the second thought with a capital letter.

Complete thought.   Complete thought.

RUN-ON   Many students do not have a specific career goal they do have some general career directions in mind.

CORRECT   Many students do not have a specific career goal. They do have some general career directions in mind.

RUN-ON   Some students choose courses without studying degree requirements these students may make unwise choices.

CORRECT   Some students choose courses without studying degree requirements. These students may make unwise choices.

RUN-ON   Some people love their jobs they are delighted that someone is willing to pay them to do what they enjoy.

CORRECT   Some people love their jobs. They are delighted that someone is willing to pay them to do what they enjoy.

RUN-ON   Some people hate their jobs going back to school may be a good idea in these cases.

CORRECT   Some people hate their jobs. Going back to school may be a good idea in these cases.

The separation method is a good choice if the two thoughts are not closely related or if joining the two thoughts correctly (by one of the methods described next) creates an extremely long sentence.

2. Use a semicolon. Use a **semicolon** (;) to connect two complete thoughts that will remain parts of the same sentence.

Complete thought   ;   complete thought.

RUN-ON   Our psychology instructor is demanding he expects the best from all his students.

CORRECT   Our psychology instructor is demanding; he expects the best from all his students.

RUN-ON   Sunshine is enjoyable it puts people in a good mood.

CORRECT   Sunshine is enjoyable; it puts people in a good mood.

RUN-ON   A course in nutrition may be useful it may help you make wise food choices.

CORRECT   A course in nutrition may be useful; it may help you make wise food choices.

Use this method when your two complete thoughts are closely related and the relationship between them is clear and obvious.

EXERCISE 5-2
Writing in Progress
Correcting Run-On Sentences by Making Separate Sentences

Directions: Revise the run-on sentences you identified in Exercise 5-1 by creating two separate sentences in each case. ■

EXERCISE 5-3   Correcting Run-On Sentences Using Semicolons

Directions: Place a check mark in the blank before each sentence that is a run-on. Correct each run-on by using a semicolon. Not all of these sentences are run-ons.

_____ 1. The economic summit meeting was held in Britain many diplomats attended.

_____ 2. I especially enjoy poetry by Emily Dickinson her poems are intense, concise, and revealing.

_____ 3. The Use and Abuse of Drugs is a popular course because the material is geared for nonscience majors.

_____ 4. The food festival offered a wide selection of food everything from hot dogs to elegant desserts was available.

_____ 5. Since the flight was turbulent, the flight attendant suggested that we remain in our seats.

_____ 6. The bowling alley was not crowded most of the lanes were open.

_____ 7. Swimming is an excellent form of exercise it gives you a good aerobic workout.

_____ 8. When the disabled aircraft landed safely, the onlookers cheered.

_____ 9. The two-lane highway is being expanded to four lanes even that improvement is not expected to solve the traffic congestion problems.

_____ 10. Before visiting Israel, Carolyn read several guidebooks they helped her plan her trip. ■

NEED TO KNOW

How to Use Coordinating Conjunctions

There are seven coordinating conjunctions. An easy way to remember them is the acronym FANBOYS (for, and, nor, but, or, yet, and so). Choose the one that shows the right relationship between the two complete thoughts in a sentence.

COORDINATING CONJUNCTION	MEANING	EXAMPLE
for	since, because	Sarah is taking math, *for* she is a chemistry major.
and	added to, in addition, along with	Budgeting is important, *and* it is time well spent.
nor	and not, or not, not either	Sam cannot choose a career, *nor* can he decide upon a major.
but	just the opposite, on the other hand	I had planned to visit Chicago, *but* I changed my mind.
or	either	I will major in liberal arts, *or* I will declare myself "undecided."
yet	but, despite, nevertheless	I plan to become a computer programmer, *yet* a change is still possible.
so	as a result, consequently	Yolanda enjoys mathematics, *so* she is considering it as a career.

3. **Use a comma and a coordinating conjunction.** Use a **comma** and a **co-ordinating conjunction** to separate two complete thoughts placed within one sentence.

   Note: When you separate two complete thoughts by using a coordinating conjunction, you must also use a comma.

   The seven coordinating conjunctions are listed below:

Complete thought	, for	complete thought.
Complete thought	, and	complete thought.
Complete thought	, nor	complete thought.
Complete thought	, but	complete thought.
Complete thought	, or	complete thought.
Complete thought	, yet	complete thought.
Complete thought	, so	complete thought.

When you use a coordinating conjunction to separate two complete thoughts, be sure to use the right one. Since each coordinating conjunction has a particular meaning, you should choose the one that shows the right relationship between the two thoughts. For example, the conjunction *and* indicates the ideas are equally important and similar. The words *but* and *yet* indicate that one idea is contrary to or in opposition to the other. *For* and *so* emphasize cause-and-effect connections. *Or* and *nor* indicate choice.

The following examples show how to use a comma and a coordinating conjunction to correct a run-on sentence:

RUN-ON   Interests change and develop throughout life you may have a different set of interests 20 years from now.

comma and conjunction *so* used to show cause-and-effect relationship

CORRECT   Interests change and develop throughout life, so you may have a different set of interests 20 years from now.

RUN-ON   Take courses in a variety of disciplines you may discover new interests.

comma and conjunction *for* used to show cause-and-effect relationship

CORRECT   Take courses in a variety of disciplines, for you may discover new interests.

RUN-ON   Alexis thought she was not interested in biology by taking a biology course, she discovered it was her favorite subject.

comma and conjunction *but* used to show contrast

CORRECT   Alexis thought she was not interested in biology, but, by taking a biology course, she discovered it was her favorite subject.

RUN-ON   The weather forecast threatened severe thunderstorms just as the day ended, the sky began to cloud over.

comma and conjunction *and* used to show addition

CORRECT   The weather forecast threatened severe thunderstorms, and just as the day ended, the sky began to cloud over.

This method of correcting run-ons allows you to indicate to your reader how your two ideas are connected. Use this method for correcting run-on sentences when you want to explain the relationship between the two thoughts.

EXERCISE 5-4
Working Together

Correcting Run-On Sentences Using Commas and Conjunctions

Directions: Working with a classmate, correct each of the following run-on sentences by using a comma and a coordinating conjunction. Think about the relationship between the two thoughts, and then choose the best coordinating conjunction. (These are the coordinating conjunctions you should use: *for, and, nor, but, or, yet, so.*)

EXAMPLE   I thought I had left for class in plenty of time ,but I was two minutes late.

1. Jameel got up half an hour late he missed the bus.

2. My creative-writing teacher wrote a book our library did not have a copy.

3. *Ford* is an interesting first name we did not choose it for our son.

4. Smoking cigarettes is not healthy it can cause lung cancer.

5. My paycheck was ready to be picked up I forgot to get it.

6. The window faces north the room gets little sun.

7. I may order Chinese food for dinner I may bake a chicken.

8. Miranda had planned to write her term paper about World War I she switched her topic to the Roaring Twenties.

9. The journalist arrived at the fire she began to take notes.

10. The table is wobbly we keep a matchbook under one leg to stabilize it. ■

4. **Make one thought dependent.** Make one thought dependent by making it a dependent clause. A **dependent clause** depends on an independent clause for its meaning. It cannot stand alone because it does not express a complete thought. In a sentence, a dependent clause must always be linked to an independent clause, which expresses a complete thought. By itself, a dependent clause always leaves a question in your mind; the question is answered by the independent clause to which it is joined.

dependent clause raises a question

Because I missed the bus   [What happened?]

                     independent clause answers the question

Because I missed the bus, I was late for class.

dependent clause raises a question

When I got my exam back   [What did you do?]

                     independent clause answers the question

When I got my exam back, I celebrated.

Did you notice that each dependent clause began with a word that made it dependent? In the above sentences, the words that make the clauses dependent are *Because* and *When*. These words are called **subordinating conjunctions.** Subordinating conjunctions let you know that the sense of the clause that follows them depends on another idea, an idea you will find in the independent clause of the sentence. Some common subordinating conjunctions are *after, although, before, if, since,* and *unless.* (For a more complete list of subordinating conjunctions, see p. 95.)

You can correct a run-on sentence by changing one of the complete thoughts into a dependent clause and joining the ideas in the two clauses with a subordinating conjunction. This method places more emphasis on the idea expressed in the complete thought (independent clause) and less emphasis on the idea in the dependent clause.

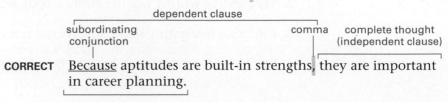

RUN-ON   Aptitudes are built-in strengths they are important in career planning.

                          dependent clause

         subordinating   comma   complete thought
         conjunction   (independent clause)

CORRECT   <u>Because</u> aptitudes are built-in strengths, they are important in career planning.

RUN-ON   Emotional involvement can interfere with job performance
be sure to keep work and friends and family separate.

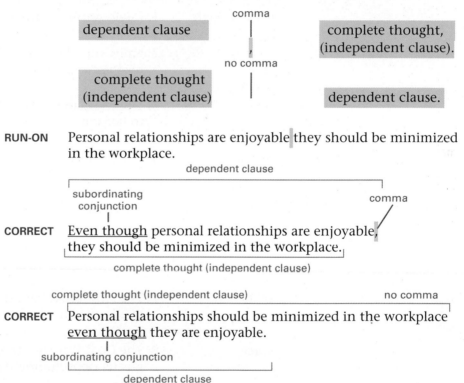

dependent clause

subordinating
conjunction

CORRECT   <u>Since</u> emotional involvement can interfere with job
performance, be sure to keep work and family and friends separate.

comma   complete thought (independent clause)

Note: A dependent clause can appear before or after an independent clause. If
the dependent clause appears first, it must be followed by a comma, as in the
examples above. No comma is needed when the complete thought comes first.

comma

| dependent clause | | complete thought, (independent clause). |

no comma

| complete thought (independent clause) | | dependent clause. |

RUN-ON   Personal relationships are enjoyable they should be minimized
in the workplace.

dependent clause

subordinating
conjunction

comma

CORRECT   <u>Even though</u> personal relationships are enjoyable,
they should be minimized in the workplace.

complete thought (independent clause)

complete thought (independent clause)   no comma

CORRECT   Personal relationships should be minimized in the workplace
<u>even though</u> they are enjoyable.

subordinating conjunction

dependent clause

NEED TO KNOW

How to Correct Run-On Sentences

You can correct run-on sentences in four ways:

Method 1   Separate the two complete thoughts into two sentences.

Method 2   Separate the two complete thoughts with a semicolon.

Method 3   Join the two complete thoughts with a comma and a
coordinating conjunction (*and, but, for, nor, or, so, yet*).

Method 4   Make one thought dependent upon the other by
using a subordinating conjunction (see the list on p. 95).

EXERCISE 5-5

EXERCISE 5-5	# Revising Run-On Sentences Using Subordinating Conjunctions

Directions: In each of the following run-on sentences, make one thought dependent on the other by using the subordinating conjunction in boldface. Don't forget to use a comma if the dependent clause comes first.

EXAMPLE

until   _Until w_
              ∧ We called the plumber , we were without water.
                                                    ∧

SUBORDINATING CONJUNCTION

even though   1. David wants a leather jacket it is very expensive.

so that   2. Emily runs ten miles every day she can try out for the cross-country squad in the spring.

when   3. The television program ended Estefania read a book to her son.

because   4. The pool was crowded it was 95 degrees that day.

although   5. Industry is curbing pollution our water supply still is not safe.

because   6. I always obey the speed limit speeding carries a severe penalty in my state.

while   7. The crowd fell silent the trapeze artist attempted a quadruple flip.

since   8. The Cold War with the USSR is over, there are greater opportunities for cultural exchange.

as   9. The storm approached I stocked up on batteries.

whenever   10. The moon is full our dog is restless.   ■

EXERCISE 5-6	## Revising Sentences

Directions: Write five sentences, each of which has two complete thoughts. Then revise each sentence so that it has one dependent clause and one complete thought (independent clause). Use a comma, if needed, to separate the two clauses. You may want to refer to the list of subordinating conjunctions on page 95. ■

COMMA SPLICES

GOAL 3 Recognize and correct comma splices

Like run-ons, comma splices are serious sentence errors that can confuse and annoy your readers. Also, like run-ons, they are easy to correct once you know what to look for. In fact, they are corrected in the same way that run-ons are. A comma splice occurs when you use *only* a comma to separate two complete thoughts. A comma alone is not sufficient to divide the two thoughts. A stronger, clearer separation is necessary. You can visualize a comma splice this way:

COMMA SPLICE	Complete thought , complete thought.

COMMA SPLICE   Spatial aptitude is the ability to understand and visualize objects in physical space, it is an important skill for engineers and designers.

COMMA SPLICE   Some people have strong mechanical ability, they often prefer hands-on tasks.

COMMA SPLICE   Verbal reasoning is important to many careers, it is the ability to think through problems.

How to Recognize Comma Splices

To avoid comma splices, you have to make sure that you do not place *only a comma* between two complete thoughts. To test a sentence to see if you have written a comma splice, take the sentence apart at the comma. If the part before the comma is a complete thought and the part after the comma is a complete thought, then you need to check whether the second clause starts with a coordinating conjunction (*for, and, nor, but, or, yet, so*). If you do not have a coordinating conjunction to separate the two complete thoughts, then you have a comma splice.

How to Correct Comma Splices

To correct comma splices, use any one of the four methods you used to correct run-ons:

1. **Separate the thoughts into two complete sentences, deleting the comma.**

   Complete thought.   Complete thought.

2. **Separate the two thoughts with a semicolon, deleting the comma.**

   Complete thought ; complete thought.

3. **Separate the two thoughts by adding a coordinating conjunction after the comma.**

Complete thought	, for	complete thought.
Complete thought	, and	complete thought.
Complete thought	, nor	complete thought.
Complete thought	, but	complete thought.
Complete thought	, or	complete thought.
Complete thought	, yet	complete thought.
Complete thought	, so	complete thought.

4. **Make one thought dependent on the other by using a subordinating conjunction to separate the two thoughts.** (For a complete list of subordinating conjunctions, see p. 95.)

   Subordinating conjunction dependent clause , independent clause.

   Independent clause subordinating conjunction dependent clause.

NEED TO KNOW

How to Correct Comma Splices

Correct comma splices the same way you correct run-on sentences:

Method 1	Separate the two complete thoughts into two sentences.
Method 2	Separate the two complete thoughts with a semicolon.
Method 3	Join the two complete thoughts with a comma and a coordinating conjunction (*for, and, nor, but, or, yet, so*).
Method 4	Make one thought dependent upon the other by using a subordinating conjunction. (See the list on p. **95**.)

EXERCISE 5-7   Correcting Comma Splices

Directions: Some of the following sentences have comma splices. Correct each comma splice by using one of the four methods described in this chapter. Write "OK" in the blank before each sentence that is correct.

_____ 1. The stained glass window is beautiful, it has been in the church since 1880.

_____ 2. Replacing the spark plugs was simple, replacing the radiator was not.

_____ 3. School buses lined up in front of the school, three o'clock was dismissal time.

_____ 4. The gymnast practiced her balance-beam routine, she did not make a single mistake.

_____ 5. A huge branch fell on the driveway, it just missed my car.

_____ 6. The receptionist answered the phone, she put the caller on hold.

_____ 7. The couple dressed up as Raggedy Ann and Andy for Halloween, but their red-yarn wigs kept falling off.

_____ 8. Bill left his notebook in the cafeteria, he was confused later when he was unable to find the notebook.

_____ 9. The strawberries are red and sweet, the blueberries are not ripe yet.

_____ 10. There had been a severe drought, so the waterfall dried up.

EXERCISE 5-8   Identifying and Correcting Run-On Sentences and Comma Splices

Directions: In the blanks, identify each sentence as a run-on sentence (RO), a comma splice (CS), or a correct sentence (C). Then correct the faulty sentences using one of the four methods discussed.

EXAMPLE   _CS_   *When t*/The children chased the ball into the street, cars screeched to a halt.

_____ 1. Inez packed for the camping trip she remembered everything except insect repellant.

_____ 2. A limousine drove through our neighborhood, everybody wondered who was in it.

_____ 3. The defendant pleaded not guilty the judge ordered him to pay the parking fine.

_____ 4. Before a big game, Louis, who is a quarterback, eats a lot of pasta and bread he says it gives him energy.

_____ 5. Four of my best friends from high school have decided to go to law school, I have decided to become a legal secretary.

_____ 6. Felicia did not know what to buy her parents for their anniversary, so she went to a lot of stores she finally decided to buy them a camera.

_____ 7. After living in a dorm room for three years, Jason found an apartment the rent was very high, so he had to get a job to pay for it.

_____ 8. The cherry tree had to be cut down it stood right where the new addition was going to be built.

_____ 9. Amanda worked every night for a month on the needlepoint pillow that she was making for her grandmother.

_____ 10. Driving around in the dark, we finally realized we were lost, Dwight went into a convenience store to ask for directions. ■

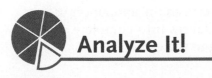

Analyze It!

Directions: Find and correct the run-on sentences and comma splices in the following paragraph. You should find one run-on and three comma splices.

If you work in an office with cubicles—small partitioned workspaces—make sure to observe cubicle etiquette. Most cubicles are composed of three chest-high partitions, the fourth side is an open entryway. Cubicle etiquette is designed to minimize invasions of personal space for example as you walk past a cubicle, resist the temptation to peer down at the person. If you need to talk to a cubicle occupant, do not startle the person by entering abruptly or speaking loudly. Similarly, do not silently lurk in the entryway if the person's back is turned, speak quietly to announce your presence. Try to keep cubicle conversations or phone calls brief, in deference to your co-workers in adjacent cubicles. Finally, remember that odors as well as noise can "pollute" the cubicle environment, don't even think about eating leftover garlic pasta at your desk!

Paragraph Writing Scenarios

Friends and Family

1. Choose someone close to you. Make a list of how that person looks: his or her eyes, skin, hair, clothing, etc. Now write a paragraph describing that person in detail, using the items from your list. Make sure you write complete sentences and avoid run-on sentences.

2. Write a paragraph that begins with the topic sentence: "If I could change one thing about . . ." Describe what you might change about one of your relatives.

Classes and Campus Life

1. Choose an assignment from one of your courses. Explain what you have been asked to do for that assignment. Discuss three steps you will take in order to complete the assignment.

2. Write a paragraph that explains why you chose to apply to your college. Describe any other colleges that you considered as well.

Working Students

1. Write a paragraph on the kind of work you do. Is it boring or fun; easy or hard? How did you find this job?

2. Write a paragraph describing someone else's job at the same place. Would you rather have that job than the one you currently have? Why or why not?

Communities and Cultures

1. Think about American culture. Write a paragraph describing one thing from another culture that has become part of everyday life in America. It could be a food Americans like, a popular style of dress or music, or words from a language other than English that most Americans would know.

2. Listen to the broadcast of a game, tournament, or other athletic competition. Make a list of dependent clauses the announcer uses in calling the play. Now turn these clauses into complete sentences that describe what is happening in the game.

WRITING ABOUT A READING

Marine Capt. Timothy Kudo, a graduate student at New York University, deployed to Iraq in 2009 and to Afghanistan from 2010 to 2011. This essay first appeared in *The Washington Post*.

Step 1: Preview the reading.

Step 2: Connect the reading to your own experience: Do you know any veterans of war? What do you think are the consequences of war?

Step 3: Read and respond to the questions in the margin.

THINK AS YOU READ

Based on your preview, predict the author's answer to this question.

Why is this background information included?

Highlight the two contradictory beliefs.

I KILLED PEOPLE IN AFGHANISTAN. WAS I RIGHT OR WRONG?

Timothy Kudo

1   When I joined the Marine Corps, I knew I would kill people. I was trained to do it in a number of ways, from pulling a trigger to ordering a bomb strike to beating someone to death with a rock. As I got closer to deploying to war in 2009, my lethal abilities were refined, but my ethical understanding of killing was not.

2   I held two seemingly contradictory beliefs: Killing is always wrong, but in war, it is necessary. How could something be both immoral and necessary? I didn't have time to resolve this question before deploying. And in the first few months, I fell right into killing without thinking twice. We were simply too busy to worry about the morality of what we were doing.

3   But one day in Afghanistan in 2010, my patrol got into a firefight and ended up killing two people on a motorcycle who we thought were about to attack us. They ignored or didn't understand our warnings to stop, and according to the military's "escalation of force" guidelines, we were authorized to shoot them in self-defense. Although we thought they were armed, they turned out to be civilians. One looked no older than 16.

4   It's been more than two years since we killed those people on the motorcycle, and I think about them every day. Sometimes it's when I'm reading the news or watching a movie, but most often it's when I'm taking a shower or walking down my street in Brooklyn.

5   They are not the only deaths I carry with me. I also remember the first time a Marine several miles away asked me over the radio whether his unit could kill someone burying a bomb. The decision fell on me alone. I said yes. Those decisions became commonplace over my deployment. Even more frightening than the idea of what we were doing was how easy it became for me. I never shot someone, but I ordered bomb strikes and directed other people to shoot.

6   Many veterans are unable to reconcile such actions in war with the biblical commandment "Thou shalt not kill." When they come home from an environment where killing is not only accepted but is a metric of success, the transition to one where killing is wrong can be incomprehensible.

7   This incongruity can have devastating effects. After more than 10 years of war, the military lost more active-duty members last year to suicide than to enemy fire. More worrisome, the Department of Veterans Affairs [VA] estimates that one in five Americans who commit suicide is a veteran, despite the fact that veterans make up just 13 percent of the population.

8   While I don't know why individual veterans resort to suicide, I can say that the ethical damage of war may be worse than the physical injuries we sustain. To properly wage war, you have to recalibrate your moral compass. Once you return from the battlefield, it is difficult or impossible to repair it.

9   VA has started calling this problem "moral injury," but that's as deceptive a **euphemism**[1] as "collateral damage." This isn't the kind of injury you recover from with rest, physical therapy and pain medication. War makes us killers. We must confront this horror directly if we're to be honest about the true costs of war.

10   I didn't return from Afghanistan as the same person. My personality is the same, or at least close enough, but I'm no longer the "good" person I once thought I was. There's nothing that can change that; it's impossible to forget what happened, and the only people who can forgive me are dead.

Sidebar questions:
Why would Kudo think of these people while showering or walking?
Did Kudo "kill" the person burying the bomb?
How are attitudes about killing different at home and at war?
What do these statistics seem to indicate about veterans?
How does the author's reference to the "ethical damage of war" suggest his thesis? What is a moral compass?
What do these euphemisms mean?
What does "good" mean?

[1] **euphemism** an inoffensive expression used to replace one thought to be offensive or grim

What does the author want civilians to understand?

Why does this question make veterans angry? What does it mean to the author?

What does the author hope for by answering the question?

11   I will never know whether my actions in Afghanistan were right or wrong. On good days, I believe they were necessary. But instead, I want to believe that killing, even in war, is wrong.

12   America will participate in other wars in my lifetime. But if the decision to do so is a collective responsibility, then civilians need to have a better understanding of the consequences. The immorality of war is not a wound we can ignore—as is painfully obvious with so many veterans committing suicide.

13   Civilians can comprehend the casualties of war because most people know someone who has died. But few know someone who has killed. When I tell people I'm a Marine, the next question many ask is: "Did you kill anyone?" To my ears, this sounds like: "What's the worst thing you've ever done?" They don't realize they're asking about an intensely private matter.

14   Many veterans I know are incensed by this question. It reinforces the isolation they feel in a society that doesn't seem to care about Iraq or Afghanistan. But to me, it speaks to the fact that civilians' curiosity about war overwhelms their understanding of it. Most Americans have little idea what war means. Our battles are fought with volunteers, making an intimate knowledge of war voluntary as well—and therefore avoidable.

15   Veterans are the only ones who can explain the ethical impact of war. For me, this means being open and honest about the deaths I caused and how they have changed me.

16   The question "Did you kill anyone?" isn't easy to answer—and it's certainly not one every veteran wants to. But when civilians ask, I think I have a duty to respond. And if explaining what I did 6,000 miles away in a conflict far from the public's consciousness makes the next war less likely, then maybe my actions weren't in vain.

WRITING IN RESPONSE TO READING

Examining the Reading Using an Idea Map   MyWritingLab

Review the reading by completing the missing parts of the idea map shown below.

 Visualize It! →

Title   **I killed people in Afghanistan. Was I right or wrong?**

Thesis   Soldiers who kill people in war sustain moral and ethical damage.

The author was trained to kill but had no _____ _____ .

He believed killing was wrong but _____ in war.

He frequently thinks of _____ _____ .

Many veterans experience conflict between actions in war and at home.

More active-duty military died last year from suicide than from enemy fire.

One in five Americans who commit suicide is ____ _____ .

The _____ of war may be worse than the physical injuries.

VA calls the problem _____ .

The author was changed by his war experience.

He is no longer the "good" person he once thought he was.

He wants to believe that _____ .

Civilians need to have a better understanding of the _____ .

Asking soldiers if they killed someone is intensely private.

This question reinforces many veterans' sense of _____ .

_____ are the only ones who can explain the ethical impact of war.

Conclusion   By explaining his actions during war, Kudo hopes _____ .

Strengthening Your Vocabulary   MyWritingLab

Using the word's context, word parts, or a dictionary, write a brief definition of each of the following words as it is used in the reading.

1. lethal (paragraph 1) _____

2. ethical (paragraph 1) _____

3. escalation (paragraph 3) _____

4. incongruity (paragraph 7) _____

5. recalibrate (paragraph 8) _____

6. collective (paragraph 12) _____

Reacting to Ideas: Discussion and Journal Writing   MyWritingLab

Get ready to write about the reading by discussing the following:

1. Discuss the title. Would another title have been as effective or appropriate? Why or why not?

2. Evaluate the kinds of supporting details the author uses in this article. Which details were most compelling? How important was the author's personal experience as support for his thesis?

3. Why did the author find it frightening that killing (or making decisions that caused death) became easy for him?

4. Why do you think the author wrote this essay and for what audience? Do you think he accomplished what he hoped to? Why or why not? ■

Paragraph Options   MyWritingLab

1. What other euphemisms can you think of, either war-related or otherwise? Write a paragraph explaining the meaning of at least two euphemisms.

2. Did this article change your understanding of the costs of war? In what ways? Write a paragraph explaining your answer.

3. Have you ever held two contradictory beliefs? Write a paragraph describing the experience and whether you were able to reconcile the conflicting beliefs. ■

Essay Options   MyWritingLab

4. Write an essay in the form of a letter to the author. Explain what you learned or gained by reading about his experience, and describe your response to the last paragraph of the article.

5. Write an essay about your own moral compass. Have you ever had to "recalibrate" it for any reason? How did you determine the right settings for your compass?

6. If civilians had a better understanding of the consequences of war, do you think war would be less likely? Why or why not? Write an essay explaining your answer. ■

■ ■ ■ ■

SELF-TEST SUMMARY

To test yourself, cover the Answer column with a sheet of paper and answer each question in the left column. Evaluate each of your answers as you work by sliding the paper down and comparing your answer with what is printed in the Answer column.

	QUESTION	ANSWER
Goal 1 Use punctuation correctly within and between sentences	What is the primary purpose of punctuation? What are examples of between-sentence punctuation and within-sentence punctuation?	The primary purpose of punctuation is to separate. Periods, question marks, and exclamation points are used *between* sentences to separate sentences from one another. Commas, colons, semicolons, hyphens, dashes, quotation marks, and parentheses are used to separate parts *within* a sentence.
Goal 2 Recognize and correct run-on sentences	What is a run-on sentence? What are four ways to correct a run-on sentence?	A run-on sentence occurs when two complete thoughts are not separated with the necessary punctuation. Correct run-on sentences by • creating two separate sentences; • using a semicolon; • using a comma and a coordinating conjunction; • making one thought dependent.
Goal 3 Recognize and correct comma splices	What is a comma splice and how can it be corrected?	A comma splice occurs when only a comma separates two complete thoughts. Correct comma splices by using any of the four methods for correcting run-on sentences.

MyWritingLab *Visit Ch. 5: Run-On Sentences and Comma Splices in MyWritingLab to test your understanding of the chapter objectives.*

6

Combining and Expanding Your Ideas

WRITE ABOUT IT!

Study the six photographs shown above one at a time (cover the others with your hand as you look at them). What is happening in each one? It is probably difficult to tell because there is so little information in each one. Then look at the six photographs all together. Now it is clear what is happening. Write a sentence that states the main point of the combined photograph.

The six photographs seen separately are difficult to understand because each one contains so little information, and it is unclear if and how each is related to the others. A similar uncertainty can occur in writing when a writer uses too many very short sentences in a paragraph in which the relationship between them is unclear.

In this chapter, you will learn to combine your ideas to make your sentences more effective as well as more interesting. You will also learn how to use sentence arrangement to show the relationships and the logical connections between and among ideas.

WRITING

UNDERSTANDING INDEPENDENT AND DEPENDENT CLAUSES

GOAL 1 Recognize independent and dependent clauses

If you are financially independent, you alone accept full responsibility for your finances. If you are financially dependent, you depend on someone else to pay your living expenses. Clauses, too, are either independent or dependent. (A clause is a group of words that contains a subject and a verb.) Clauses either stand alone and accept responsibility for their own meaning, or they depend on another clause to complete their meaning. Independent clauses can stand alone as sentences. Dependent clauses can never stand alone because they are not complete sentences. The key to combining and expanding your ideas is to recognize this difference between independent and dependent clauses.

The various combinations of independent and dependent clauses shown in the "Need to Know" box on the next page allow you to link your ideas to one another.

COMBINING IDEAS OF EQUAL IMPORTANCE

GOAL 2 Combine ideas of equal importance

Many times, ideas are of equal importance. For example, in the following sentence, it is just as important to know that the writer never has enough time as it is to know that she always rushes.

I never have enough time, so I always rush from task to task.

Complete thoughts (independent clauses) of equal importance are combined by using a technique called **coordination**. *Co-* means "together." *Coordinate* means "to work together." When you want two complete thoughts to work together equally, you can combine them into a single sentence by using coordination.

Method 1: Use a Comma and a Coordinating Conjunction

The most common way to join ideas is by using a comma and a coordinating conjunction. Use a semicolon only when the two ideas are *very* closely related and the connection between the ideas is clear and obvious. In this section, we will concentrate on using a comma and a coordinating conjunction.

The following two sentences contain equally important ideas:

Samantha works 20 hours per week.

Samantha manages to find time to study.

NEED TO KNOW
Independent and Dependent Clauses

Sentences are made up of various combinations of independent and dependent clauses. Here are the possible combinations:

1. **Simple sentence**   A simple sentence has one independent clause and no dependent clauses.

   independent clause

   Richard hurried to his car.

2. **Compound sentence**   A compound sentence has two or more independent clauses and no dependent clauses.

   independent clause   independent clause

   Richard hurried to his car, but he was already late for work.

3. **Complex sentence**   A complex sentence has one independent clause and one or more dependent clauses.

   independent clause   dependent clause

   Richard hurried to his car because he was late for work.

4. **Compound-complex sentence**   A compound-complex sentence has two or more independent clauses and one or more dependent clauses.

   dependent clause   independent clause

   As Richard hurried to his car, he knew he would be late for work,
   but he hoped that he would not be docked an hour's pay.

   independent clause   dependent clause

You can combine these ideas into one sentence by using a comma and a coordinating conjunction.

idea 1   comma   conjunction   idea 2

Samantha works 20 hours per week, but she manages to find time to study.

As we saw in the section on correcting run-ons (see Chapter 5, p. 114), a **coordinating conjunction** joins clauses and adds meaning to a sentence. A coordinating conjunction indicates how the ideas are related. Here is a brief review of the meaning of each coordinating conjunction and the relationship it expresses:

COORDINATING CONJUNCTION	MEANING	RELATIONSHIP
and	in addition	The two ideas are added together.
but	in contrast	The two ideas are opposite.
for	because	The idea that follows *for* is the cause of the idea in the other clause.
nor, or	not either, either	The ideas are choices or alternatives.
so	as a result	The second idea is the result of the first.
yet	in contrast	The two ideas are opposite.

Note: Do *not* use the words *also, plus*, and *then* to join complete thoughts. They are *not* coordinating conjunctions.

NEED TO KNOW

How to Join Independent Clauses

There are two basic ways to join two ideas that are equally important:

Method 1.   Join them by using a **comma** and a **coordinating conjunction** (*and, but, for, nor, or, so, yet*).

Complete thought , coordinating conjunction complete thought.

Method 2.   Join them by using a **semicolon**.

Complete thought ; complete thought.

Here are a few more examples:

SIMPLE SENTENCES	Time is valuable. I try to use it wisely.
COMBINED SENTENCE	Time is valuable, so I try to use it wisely.
SIMPLE SENTENCES	Many students try to set priorities for work and study. Many students see immediate results.
COMBINED SENTENCE	Many students try to set priorities for work and study, and they see immediate results.
SIMPLE SENTENCES	I tried keeping lists of things to do. My friend showed me a better system.
COMBINED SENTENCE	I tried keeping lists of things to do, but my friend showed me a better system.

Tip for Writers

Sample Sentences Using Coordinating Conjunctions

COORDINATING CONJUNCTION	SAMPLE SENTENCE
and	The sky darkened, <u>and</u> it began to rain.
but	I thought it would rain, <u>but</u> the sun shone instead.
for	Be sure to study both the textbook chapter and your lecture notes, <u>for</u> the instructor may test on both.
nor	You cannot smoke in the lecture hall, <u>nor</u> are you allowed to consume food.
or	In sociology, you can take the written final exam, <u>or</u> you can make an oral presentation instead.
so	I was early for class, <u>so</u> I reread my notes from the previous class.
yet	My brother promised to call, <u>yet</u> I have not heard from him.

EXERCISE 6-1 Using Coordinating Conjunctions

Directions: For each of the following sentences, add the coordinating conjunction that best expresses the relationship between the two complete thoughts.

EXAMPLE   I never learned to manage my time, __so__ I am planning to attend a time-management workshop.

1. I might study math, _____ I might review for my history exam.
2. The average person spends 56 hours a week sleeping, _____ the average person spends seven hours a week eating dinner.
3. Watching television is tempting, _____ I usually shut the set off before I start studying.
4. I do not feel like typing, _____ do I feel like reviewing math.
5. I am never sure of what to work on first, _____ I waste a lot of time deciding.
6. A schedule for studying is easy to follow, _____ it eliminates the need to decide what to study.
7. My cousin has a study routine, _____ she never breaks it.
8. Frank studies his hardest subject first, _____ then he takes a break.
9. I know I should not procrastinate, _____ I sometimes postpone an unpleasant task until the next day.
10. I had planned to study after work, _____ my exam was postponed.

EXERCISE 6-2 Completing Sentences

Directions: Complete each of the following sentences by adding a second complete thought. Use the coordinating conjunction shown in bold.

EXAMPLE   I feel torn between studying and spending time with friends, **but** _I usually choose to study._

1. My psychology class was canceled, **so** _____
2. I waste time doing unimportant tasks, **and** _____
3. My cell phone used to be a constant source of interruption, **but** _____
   _____
4. I had extra time to study this weekend, **for** _____
   _____
5. I had hoped to finish reading my biology chapter, **but** _____
   _____
6. Every Saturday I study psychology, **or** _____
7. I had planned to finish work early, **yet** _____
8. I can choose a topic to write about, **or** _____
9. I had hoped to do many errands this weekend, **but** _____
   _____
10. I tried to study and watch television at the same time, **but** _____
    _____

EXERCISE 6-3   Combining Sentences Using Coordinating Conjunctions

Directions: Combine each of the following pairs of sentences by using a comma and a coordinating conjunction (*and, but, for, nor, or, so, yet*). Change punctuation, capitalization, and words as necessary. Be sure to insert a comma before the coordinating conjunction.

EXAMPLE
a. I have a free hour between my first and second classes.
b. I use that free hour to review my biology notes.

I have a free hour between my first and second classes, so I use that hour to review my biology notes.

1. a. Some tasks are more enjoyable than others.
   b. We tend to put off unpleasant tasks.

2. a. Many people think it is impossible to do two things at once.
   b. Busy students soon learn to combine routine activities.

3. a. Marita prioritizes her courses.
   b. Marita allots specific blocks of study time for each.

4. a. Marcus may try to schedule his study sessions so they are several hours apart.
   b. Marcus may adjust the length of his study sessions.

5. a. Sherry studies late at night.
   b. Sherry does not accomplish as much as she expects to.

6. a. Marguerite studies without breaks.
   b. Marguerite admits she frequently loses her concentration.

7. **a.** Alfonso studies two hours for every hour he spends in class.
   b. Alfonso earns high grades.

   _____

   _____

8. **a.** Deadlines are frustrating.
   b. Deadlines force you to make hasty decisions.

   _____

   _____

9. **a.** Juan thought he was organized.
   b. Juan discovered he was not.

   _____

   _____

10. **a.** Monica sets goals for each course.
    b. Monica usually attains her goals.

    _____

    _____

■

Method 2: Use a Semicolon

A semicolon can be used alone or with a transitional word or phrase to join independent clauses. These transitional words and phrases are called **conjunctive adverbs**. Conjunctive adverbs are adverbs that *join*.

Independent clause   ; therefore,   independent clause.
                      ; however,
                      ; consequently,

independent clause   independent clause

semicolon   conjunctive adverb

I had hoped to earn a good grade; however, I never expected an A.

independent clause   independent clause

semicolon   conjunctive adverb

I lost my wallet; consequently, I had to cancel two credit cards.

As you can see in these examples, a comma follows the conjunctive adverb.

Use this method when the relationship between the two ideas is clear and requires no explanation. Be careful to choose the correct conjunctive adverb. A list of conjunctive adverbs and their meanings follows on the next page.

CONJUNCTIVE ADVERB	MEANING	EXAMPLE
therefore, consequently, thus, hence	cause and effect	I am planning to become a nurse; *consequently*, I'm taking a lot of science courses.
however, nevertheless, nonetheless, conversely	differences or contrast	We had planned to go bowling; *however*, we went to hear music instead.
furthermore, moreover, also	addition; a continuation of the same idea	To save money I am packing my lunch; *also*, I am walking to school instead of taking the bus.
similarly, likewise	similarity	I left class as soon as I finished the exam; *likewise*, other students left.
then, subsequently, next	sequence in time	I walked home; *then* I massaged my aching feet.

Note: If you join two independent clauses with only a comma and fail to use a coordinating conjunction or semicolon, you will produce a comma splice. If you join two independent clauses without using a punctuation mark and a co-ordinating conjunction, you will produce a run-on sentence.

Tip for Writers

These words mean the same as *and: also, besides, furthermore,* and *in addition.* These mean the same as *but: however, nevertheless, on the other hand,* and *still.* These mean the same as *so* when it is used to introduce a result: *therefore, consequently,* and *as a result. Otherwise* and *unless* usually mean *if not.*

NEED TO KNOW

How to Use Conjunctive Adverbs

Use a conjunctive adverb to join two equal ideas. Remember to put a semi-colon before the conjunctive adverb and a comma after it. Here is a list of common conjunctive adverbs:

also	in addition	otherwise
as a result	instead	similarly
besides	likewise	still
consequently	meanwhile	then
finally	nevertheless	therefore
further	next	thus
furthermore	now	undoubtedly
however	on the other hand	

EXERCISE 6-4   Completing Sentences

Directions: Complete each of the following sentences by adding a coordinating conjunction or a conjunctive adverb and the appropriate punctuation.

EXAMPLE   Teresa vacationed in Denver last year ____; similarly,____ Jan will go to Denver this year.

1. Our professor did not complete the lecture _____ did he give an assignment for the next class.

2. A first-aid kit was in her backpack _____ the hiker was able to treat her cut knee.

3. The opening act performed at the concert _____ the headline band took the stage.

4. I always put a light on when I leave the house _____ I often turn on a radio to deter burglars.

5. Sue politely asked to borrow my car _____ she thanked me when she returned it.

6. My roommate went to the library _____ I had the apartment to myself.

7. Steve and Todd will go to a baseball game _____ they will go to a movie.

8. Cheryl looks like her father _____ her hair is darker and curlier than his.

9. Maureen took a job at a bookstore _____ she was offered a job at a museum.

10. Our neighbors bought a barbecue grill _____ we decided to buy one. ■

EXERCISE 6-5   **Writing Compound Sentences**

Directions: Write five compound sentences about how you study for tests or how you spend your weekends. Each sentence should contain two complete thoughts. Join the thoughts by using a comma and a coordinating conjunction. Use a different coordinating conjunction in each sentence. ■

EXERCISE 6-6   **Writing Using Compound Sentences**

Directions: Write a paragraph evaluating how well you manage your time. Use at least two compound sentences. ■

COMBINING IDEAS OF UNEQUAL IMPORTANCE

GOAL 3 Combine ideas of unequal importance

Consider the following two simple sentences:

Pete studies during peak periods of attention.
Pete accomplishes a great deal.

Reading these sentences, you may suspect that Pete accomplishes a great deal *because* he studies during peak periods of attention. With the sentences separated, however, that cause-and-effect relationship is only a guess. Combining the two sentences makes the relationship between the ideas clear.

Because Pete studies during peak periods of attention, he accomplishes a great deal.

The combined sentence makes it clear that one event is the cause of another. Let's look at another pair of sentences:

Yolanda analyzed her time commitments for the week.
Yolanda developed a study plan for the week.

You may suspect that Yolanda developed the study plan *after* analyzing her time commitments. Combining the sentences makes the connection in time clear.

> After Yolanda analyzed her time commitments for the week, she developed a study plan.

In each of these examples, the two complete thoughts were combined so that one idea depended on the other. This process of combining ideas so that one idea is dependent on another is called **subordination**. *Sub-* means "below." Think of subordination as a way of combining an idea of lesser or lower importance with an idea of greater importance.

Ideas of unequal importance can be combined by making the less important idea depend on the more important one. Notice how, in the following sentence, the part before the comma doesn't make sense without the part after the comma.

> While Malcolm was waiting for the bus, he studied psychology.

If you read only the first half of the sentence, you'll find yourself waiting for the idea to be completed, wondering what happened while Malcolm was waiting. The word *while* (a subordinating conjunction) makes the meaning of the first half of the sentence incomplete by itself. Thus, the first half of the sentence is a **dependent clause**. It depends on the rest of the sentence to complete its thought. A dependent clause can never be a complete sentence. It must always be joined to an *independent* clause to make a complete thought. The dependent clause can go at the beginning, in the middle, or at the end of a sentence.

Review the following list for other words that are commonly used to begin dependent clauses. Such words are called **subordinating conjunctions**. Use these words to indicate how a less important idea (a dependent clause) relates to another, more important idea (an independent clause).

SUBORDINATING CONJUNCTION	MEANING	EXAMPLE
before, after, while, during, until, when, once	time	*When* you set time limits, you are working toward a goal.
because, since, so that	cause or effect	*Because* I felt rushed, I made careless errors.
whether, if, unless, even if	condition	*If* I finish studying before nine o'clock, I will read more of my mystery novel.
as, as far as, as soon as, as long as, as if, as though, although, even though, even if, in order to	circumstance	*Even if* I try to concentrate, I still am easily distracted.

Note: Relative pronouns (*who, whom, whose, that, which, whoever, whomever, whichever*) can also be used to show relationships and to join a dependent clause with an independent clause. The topic of relative pronouns is covered in detail in Chapter 8, page 186.

When you combine a dependent clause with an independent clause, use a comma to separate the clauses if the dependent clause comes *first* in the sentence.

Dependent clause , independent clause.

dependent clause   comma independent clause

When I follow a study schedule, I accomplish more.

When the dependent clause comes in the *middle* of the sentence, set it off with a *pair* of commas.

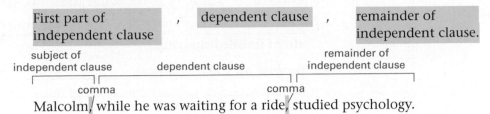

First part of independent clause   ,   dependent clause   ,   remainder of independent clause.

subject of independent clause   dependent clause   remainder of independent clause

comma   comma

Malcolm, while he was waiting for a ride, studied psychology.

If the dependent clause comes at the end of the sentence, do not use a comma to separate it from the rest of the sentence.

Independent clause   dependent clause.

independent clause   no comma   dependent clause

I accomplish more when I follow a study schedule.

EXERCISE 6-7   Adding Subordinating Conjunctions

Directions: For each of the following sentences, add a subordinating conjunction that makes the relationship between the two ideas clear. Try to use as many different subordinating conjunctions as possible.

EXAMPLE   <u>When</u>   I finish studying, I am mentally exhausted.

1. _____ math requires peak concentration, I always study it first.

2. _____ Andres starts to lose concentration, he takes a short break.

3. Julia never stops in the middle of an assignment _____ she is too tired to finish.

4. _____ she likes to wake up slowly, Shannon sets her alarm for ten minutes before she needs to get up.

5. _____ Maria took a five-minute study break, she felt more energetic.

6. Alan worked on his math homework _____ he did the laundry.

7. _____ Jamille increases his study time, he may not earn the grades he hopes to receive.

8. _____ Marsha completes an assignment, she crosses it off her "To do" list.

9. _____Robert did not know when he wasted time, he kept a log of his activities for three days.

10. _____ noises and conversation do not interfere with my concentration, I wear a headset with soft music playing. ■

EXERCISE 6-8   Completing Sentences

Directions: Make each of the following sentences complete by adding a complete thought. Be sure the meaning fits the subordinating conjunction used in the sentence.

EXAMPLE   <u>I edited my essay</u>   while the ideas were fresh in my mind.

1. _____
   after I finished studying.

2. Because my job is part-time, _____
   _____

3. Once I finish college, _____
   _____

4. _____
   while I was studying.

5. If you schedule blocks of study time, _____
   _____

6. _____
   unless I carry a pocket calendar.

7. Although English is my favorite subject, _____
   _____

8. _____
   as far as I can tell.

9. Even if I finish by eight o'clock, _____
   _____

10. As soon as I decide what to do, _____
    _____

EXERCISE 6-9   Combining Sentences

Directions: Combine each of the following pairs of sentences by using a subordinating conjunction and a comma. Change punctuation, capitalization, and words as necessary. You may wish to refer to the list of subordinating conjunctions on page 95.

EXAMPLE   a. Yi-Min is taking voice lessons.
           b. Yi-Min always sings scales in the shower.

           <u>Because Yi-Min is taking voice lessons, she always sings scales</u>
           <u>in the shower.</u>

1. a. Christine has a six-month-old child.
   b. She must study while the baby sleeps.

   _____

   _____

2. **a.** Taj jots stray thoughts on a notepad to clear them from his mind.
   b. Taj can concentrate for long periods of time.

   _____

   _____

3. **a.** Gary finished a difficult biology assignment.
   b. He rewarded himself by ordering a pizza.

   _____

   _____

4. **a.** It takes Anthony 45 minutes to drive to school.
   b. Anthony records lectures and listens while he drives.

   _____

   _____

5. **a.** Ada felt disorganized.
   b. Ada made a priority list of assignments and due dates.

   _____

   _____

6. **a.** Juanita walked from her history class to her math class.
   b. She observed the brilliant fall foliage.

   _____

   _____

7. **a.** Kevin skipped meals and ate junk food.
   b. Kevin signed up for a cooking class.

   _____

   _____

8. **a.** Lian joined the soccer team.
   b. Lian became the first woman to do so.

   _____

   _____

9. **a.** John ate dinner on Saturday night.
   b. John reviewed his plans for the week with his less-than-fascinated date.

   _____

   _____

10. **a.** Frank waited for his history class to begin.
    b. He wondered if he was in the right room.

    _____

    _____

| | |

EXERCISE 6-10 **Writing Complex Sentences**
Working Together

Directions: Working with a classmate, write ten complex sentences on a subject that interests both of you. Each must contain one dependent clause and one independent clause. Use a comma to separate the clauses when the dependent clause comes first. Use two commas to set off a dependent clause in the middle of the sentence. You do not need a comma when the dependent clause comes last. ■

EXERCISE 6-11 **Writing Complex Sentences**

Directions: Write a paragraph on one of the following topics. Include at least two complex sentences.

1. Renting videos
2. Online shopping
3. Visiting the dentist or doctor
4. Advantages or disadvantages of credit cards
5. A favorite possession or a favorite piece of clothing ■

WRITING COMPOUND-COMPLEX SENTENCES

GOAL 4 Write compound-complex sentences

A compound-complex sentence is made up of two or more independent clauses and one or more dependent clauses. This type of sentence is often used to express complicated relationships. Look at the following examples of compound-complex sentences. Here, a dependent clause is followed by two independent clauses:

dependent clause / independent clause

Even though Mara needed to be better organized, she avoided weekly study plans, and she ended up wasting valuable time.

independent clause

Here, an independent clause containing a dependent clause is followed by a second independent clause with a dependent clause:

first part of independent clause | dependent clause | remainder of independent clause

The new students who had just arrived wanted a tour of the town; Lamar told them that he had no time.

independent clause | dependent clause

Here, the sentence is made up of a dependent clause, an independent clause containing a dependent clause, and another independent clause:

independent clause
dependent clause | dependent clause

Although Amanda changed her work schedule, she found that she still needed more time to study, and she ended up quitting her job.

independent clause

The key to writing effective and correct compound-complex sentences is to link each clause to the one that follows it in the correct way. The rules you have already learned in this chapter apply. For example, if you have two independent clauses followed by a dependent clause, link the two independent clauses as you would in a compound sentence by using a comma and a coordinating conjunction. Then link the second independent clause to the dependent clause by using a subordinating conjunction.

independent clause   independent clause   dependent clause

I got up early, and I left the house before rush hour because I wanted to be on time for my interview.

EXERCISE 6-12   Adding Conjunctions

Directions: Each of the following sentences is made up of at least three clauses. Read each sentence, and then make it correct by adding the necessary subordinating and/or coordinating conjunctions in the blanks.

EXAMPLES   _Because_ they both got home from work late, Ted grilled hamburgers_while_ Alexa made a salad.

1. _____ Sarah's sociology class required class discussion of the readings, she scheduled time to review sociology before each class meeting _____ she would have the material fresh in her mind.

2. _____ making a "To do" list takes time, Deka found that the list actually saved her time, _____ she accomplished more when she sat down to study.

3. _____ Terry's history lecture was over, he reviewed his notes, _____ when he discovered any gaps, he was usually able to recall the information.

4. Many students have discovered that distributing their studying over several evenings is more effective than studying in one large block of time _____ it gives them several exposures to the material, _____ they feel less pressured.

5. We have tickets for the concert, _____ we may not go _____ Jeff has a bad cold. ■

EXERCISE 6-13   Writing a Compound-Complex Sentence

Directions: Write a compound-complex sentence. Then label its dependent and independent clauses. ■

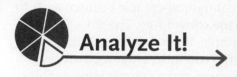 **Analyze It!**

Directions: The following paragraph consists of simple sentences and lacks details. Revise the paragraph by expanding or combining sentences. Write your revised paragraph on a separate sheet of paper.

Texting causes many problems. Texts are a nuisance. They come in all the time. They often come in when I am busy doing something important. They are a distraction. They interrupt me when I am studying. They interrupt me at work. Texting is sometimes a safety hazard. I see people texting while doing other things. They are not paying attention. And then there is the social aspect. Cell phones disrupt conversations with friends. My cell phone rings when I am out with friends. I have to ignore them to answer the phone. I try to enjoy dinner in a restaurant. People around me are talking on their cell phones.

Paragraph Writing Scenarios

Friends and Family

1. Choose a casual acquaintance and write a paragraph about what makes you want to know him or her better.
2. Write a paragraph that begins with the topic sentence: "I really hated the way . . ."

Classes and Campus Life

1. Describe the way you feel before an exam. Explain the difference in how you feel when you are prepared and when you're not.
2. Write a paragraph describing the things you have to carry with you throughout a day on campus.

Working Students

1. Write a paragraph on one thing a working student could do to manage his or her time better. Is there something that you do to stay organized that might work for others?
2. Write a paragraph describing the shoes (or other apparel) you wear to work. Do you choose them for looks or comfort?

Communities and Cultures

1. Choose a culture or country whose people you find particularly interesting or one that you would like to learn more about. Describe what makes this culture or country interesting to you.
2. Describe a family ritual that you know—or guess—came from another country. Who in your family is the one who keeps the ritual going?

WRITING ABOUT A READING

This article first appeared in *Contexts*, a quarterly magazine published by the American Sociological Association.

Step 1: Preview the reading.

Step 2: Connect the reading to your own experience: Do you believe that becoming a parent is essential to your happiness? What has your experience with children taught you up to this point in your life?

Step 3: Read and respond to the questions in the margin.

BUNDLE OF TROUBLE

KIDS ARE SUPPOSED TO BRING JOY. SO WHY ARE PARENTS SO UNHAPPY?

Robin W. Simon

1   Americans harbor a widespread, deeply held belief that no adult can be happy without becoming a parent. Parenthood, we think, is pivotal for developing and maintaining emotional well-being, and children are an essential ingredient for a life filled with happiness, joy, excitement, satisfaction, and pride.

Do these facts surprise you?

Predict the author's answer to this question.

Summarize the positive effects provided by children.

What social conditions would be ideal for parenting?

What factors contribute to stress from the "second shift," according to Hochschild?

2   That's not exactly the case. Although studies indicate parents derive more purpose and meaning from life than nonparents, as a group, moms and dads in the United States also experience depression, emotional distress, and negative emotions (such as fear, anxiety, worry, and anger) far more than their child-free peers. What's more, parents of grown children report no greater well-being than adults who never had children.

3   Such facts fly in the face of cultural dogma that proclaims it impossible for people to have an emotionally fulfilling life unless they become parents. And yet: Why doesn't parenthood have the positive emotional effects on adults that our cultural beliefs suggest?

4   Children provide parents with an important social identity. They help them forge emotional connections to extended family members and their communities. Children fulfill basic human desires, including having someone to love and nurture, carrying on family traditions, and allowing us to become grandparents. Watching children grow is enjoyable, and parents often feel comforted by the perception that they won't be alone in old age.

5   The disconnect lies in the social conditions in which Americans now parent; they're far from ideal for allowing parents to reap the emotional benefits of having children. Parents cope with stressors that cancel out and often exceed the emotional rewards of having children. Making matters worse, parents and others perceive the strain as a private matter and a reflection of their inability to cope with the "normal" demands of parenthood.

6   A significant source of parental stress simply comes from the high financial cost of raising a child to adulthood. Even the basics such as food, clothing, and (for those who have it) health care are expensive, not to mention extracurricular activities and the astronomical cost of college education. Demographers estimate that 70 percent of children in the United States are raised in households in which all adults work outside the home—and there's a fundamental incompatibility between employment as we know it and raising children.

7   Sociologist Arlie Hochschild was the first to document how the lack of flexible work schedules, high-quality and affordable child care for preschool-age children, and after-school care for elementary-age children all contribute to stress from what's now commonly referred to as the "second shift" for employed parents, who leave their jobs at five o'clock only to start another job caring for children at home. There are few policies or programs to alleviate this stress. In the end, the collective response to stressed out employed parents is that they need to become better organized.

8   Although financial stress and the strain of the "second shift" subside as children become more independent, the majority of parents continue to be involved in the lives of their adult offspring. Among other things, parents worry about their grown children's financial well-being, social relationships, happiness, and mental and physical health. Our culture also places

high expectations on parents for the way children "turn out." Irrespective of their children's age, we question parents' child-rearing skills when kids have problems. In fact, the way children turn out seems to be the only measure our culture offers for assessing whether men and women are good parents.

Is it the parents' fault when children have problems?

9   Yet unlike other societies, ours offers comparatively little preparation for parenthood, and most parents raise their children in relative social isolation with little assistance from extended family members, friends, neighbors, and the larger community. We lack institutional supports that would help ease the social and economic burdens—and subsequent stress and social disadvantages—associated with parenthood. Instituting better tax credits, developing more and better day care and after-school options, as well as offering flexible work schedules for employed mothers and fathers would go far toward alleviating some of the difficulty of raising children.

Highlight three institutional changes that would help alleviate the difficulty of raising children.

10   Of equal importance is the need to take stock of and reevaluate existing cultural beliefs that children improve the emotional health and well-being of adults. These cultural beliefs—and our expectation that children guarantee a life filled with happiness, joy, excitement, contentment, satisfaction, and pride—are an additional, though hidden, source of stress for all parents. The feelings of depression and emotional distress that parents experience can cause them to question what they're doing wrong. These negative emotions can also lead parents to perceive themselves as inadequate, since their feelings clearly aren't consistent with the cultural ideal.

Express the author's conclusion in your own words.

11   Reducing the enormous and unrealistic cultural expectations we have for parenthood is as important as greater cultural recognition of the unrelenting challenges and difficulties associated with having children. Hallmark stores stock baby cards filled with happy wishes for new parents, celebrating their precious bundles of joy. Perhaps the selection should also include cards to acknowledge the difficult emotions that often accompany parenthood.

WRITING IN RESPONSE TO READING

Examining the Reading Using an Idea Map   MyWritingLab
Review the reading by completing the missing parts of the idea map shown below.

Visualize It! →

Title   **Bundle of Trouble**

Thesis   Our culture promotes unrealistic expectations and ideals about _____.

The facts about parenthood being essential to happiness are mixed.

> Parents get more purpose and meaning from life than _____ .

> Parents experience more_____ _____ than nonparents.

> Parents of adult children report _____ than nonparents.

Parenthood has positive emotional effects because children:

> Provide parents with an important _____ .

> Help parents forge _____ .

> Fulfill basic _____ .

> Provide enjoyment and potential comfort in old age.

Social conditions lead to parental stress that cancels the benefits of parenthood. Parental stress comes from:

> The high cost of raising a child.

> Lack of_____ .

> Lack of high-quality, affordable _____ .

> The "second shift" for employed parents.

> Continued involvement and worry about _____ .

> High cultural expectations for _____ .

> Lack of_____ to ease social and economic burdens.

> Cultural beliefs that children improve adults' lives.

Conclusion   _____
_____

Strengthening Your Vocabulary   MyWritingLab

Using the word's context, word parts, or a dictionary, write a brief definition of each of the following words as it is used in the reading.

1. harbor (paragraph 1) _____
2. pivotal (paragraph 1) _____
3. dogma (paragraph 3) _____
4. reap (paragraph 5) _____
5. incompatibility (paragraph 6) _____
6. alleviate (paragraph 7) _____
7. irrespective (paragraph 8) _____
8. unrelenting (paragraph 11) _____ ■

Reacting to Ideas: Discussion and Journal Writing   MyWritingLab

Get ready to write about the reading by discussing the following:

1. Evaluate the effectiveness of the title, "Bundle of Trouble." How does it reveal the author's approach to her subject? What other titles might be appropriate?
2. Evaluate the kinds of supporting evidence the author uses in this article. What other evidence might be used to support or refute her thesis?
3. How would you describe the tone of this article? Identify examples of language that reveal the author's attitude toward her subject.
4. Discuss the statistic that 70 percent of American children are raised in households in which all adults work outside the home. Do you agree that raising children is fundamentally incompatible with employment?
5. What is the purpose of the photo that accompanies the reading? What details illustrate the author's message? ■

Paragraph Options   MyWritingLab

1. Consider the author's suggestion that there should be baby cards that acknowledge the difficult emotions accompanying parenthood. What would such a card say? Write a paragraph suggesting ideas for supportive parenting cards.
2. In your opinion, do the positive effects of parenthood outweigh the negatives? Why or why not? Write a paragraph explaining your answer.
3. Is it fair that our culture holds parents responsible when their children have problems? Why or why not? What other measures could our culture use for assessing whether someone is a good parent? Write a paragraph exploring these questions. ■

Essay Options MyWritingLab

4. What do you believe are the essential ingredients for a life filled with happiness, joy, excitement, satisfaction, and pride? Are children one of the ingredients? Why or why not? Write an essay exploring the answers to these questions.

5. What cultural expectations are placed upon you? What expectations have you set for yourself? Consider the various aspects of your identity (e.g., student), and write an essay about the different expectations and the support—or lack of support—that you receive from individuals and from society.

6. Consider the author's claim that, in our society, most parents raise children without assistance from extended family, friends, neighbors, and the larger community. Was this your experience growing up? Write an essay describing your own experience and explaining whether your parents benefited from the kinds of social and institutional supports described in the article. ■

■ ■ ■ ■

SELF-TEST SUMMARY

To test yourself, cover the Answer column with a sheet of paper and answer each question in the left column. Evaluate each of your answers as you work by sliding the paper down and comparing your answer with what is printed in the Answer column.

	QUESTION	ANSWER
Goal 1 Recognize independent and dependent clauses	What are independent and dependent clauses?	Independent clauses can stand alone as sentences. Dependent clauses can never stand alone because they are not complete sentences.
Goal 2 Combine ideas of equal importance	What are two ways to combine ideas of equal importance (independent clauses)?	Join independent clauses by using a comma and a coordinating conjunction or by using a semicolon.
Goal 3 Combine ideas of unequal importance	What is subordination?	Subordination is the process of combining ideas so that one idea is dependent on another.
Goal 4 Write compound–complex sentences	What is a compound-complex sentence?	A compound-complex sentence is made up of two or more independent clauses and one or more dependent clauses.

MyWritingLab *Visit Ch. 6 Combining and Expanding Your Ideas in MyWritingLab to test your understanding of the chapter objectives.*

7

Using Adjectives and Adverbs to Describe

WRITE ABOUT IT!

Study the photo above, and then write a few sentences that describe it in detail.

Some of the words you wrote are probably adjectives—words that describe a noun or pronoun. In this chapter you will learn to use adjectives and adverbs. Adverbs are words that describe verbs or other adverbs. You will see how they are essential to effective communication and how to use them to make your sentences lively and interesting.

WRITING

USING ADJECTIVES TO DESCRIBE

GOAL 1 Use adjectives to add descriptive details

Adjectives describe nouns and pronouns. Notice that the following sample student paragraph uses very few adjectives.

Sample Paragraph

The congregation had just finished singing a hymn as the minister stepped up to the pulpit. Just as the man asked the congregation to pray, a boy screamed. The grandmother tried to calm the child as she placed a hand over the lips of the child. The child obviously didn't enjoy this because he bit her hand. The minister continued with the prayer and tried to ignore the cries of the boy. Somehow the boy slipped away from the grip of the grandmother and ran down the aisle to the front of the church. The minister walked down from the pulpit and picked up the child. "Lord," he said as he continued the prayer, "help all the children of this world and bless all of the grandmothers, ministers, and members of the congregation who have to put up with them! Amen." With that he ended the service.

This paragraph, which contains no adjectives, gives the bare bones of an interesting story, but how well does it enable you to visualize the people involved? Adjectives give you details about the nouns and pronouns they modify. They can add four kinds of information to your writing:

WHICH?	the <u>young</u> man, the <u>largest</u> stove
WHOSE?	<u>Sam's</u> application, <u>my</u> mug
WHAT KIND?	the <u>job</u> interviewer, the <u>traffic</u> helicopter
HOW MANY?	<u>thirty</u> résumés, <u>no</u> cookies

Thus, we say that adjectives *describe* and *identify* (which? whose?), *qualify* (what kind?), or *limit* (how many?) nouns and pronouns. (For more on adjectives, see Part VII, "Reviewing the Basics," p. 527.) The following revised version of the above paragraph uses adjectives (underlined) to add interesting and important information.

Revised Paragraph

The congregation had just finished singing a <u>sacred</u> hymn as the <u>tall</u>, <u>young</u> minister stepped up to the <u>well-lit</u> pulpit. Just as the man asked the <u>reverent</u> congregation to pray, a <u>red-headed, four-year-old</u> boy screamed. His <u>embarrassed</u> grandmother tried to calm the <u>angry</u> child as she placed a <u>firm</u> hand over his <u>quivering</u> lips. The <u>squirming</u> child obviously didn't enjoy this because he bit his <u>grandmother's</u> hand. The <u>calm</u> minister continued with the prayer and tried to ignore the <u>little</u> boy's <u>loud, shrill</u> cries. Somehow, the <u>determined, tearful</u> boy slipped away from his grandmother's <u>firm</u> grip and ran down the <u>long center</u> aisle to the front of the church. The <u>patient</u> minister walked down from the pulpit and picked up the <u>screaming</u> child. "Lord," he said as he continued the prayer, "help all the children of this world and bless all of the <u>loving</u> grandmothers, <u>patient</u> ministers, and <u>long-suffering</u> members of the congregation who have to put up with them! Amen." With that he ended the service.

EXERCISE 7-1
Working Together

Writing Adjectives

Directions: *The Adjective Contest:* The time limit for this exercise is three minutes. List as many positive adjectives as you can that describe one of your instructors. This is your chance to flatter an instructor! Exchange lists with a partner, verify that each word listed is an adjective, and count the words on the list. The winner is the student who has listed the most positive adjectives.

"The face of the pear-shaped man reminded me of the mashed turnips that Aunt Mildred used to serve alongside the Thanksgiving turkey. As he got out of the strawberry-hued car, his immense fists looked like two slabs of slightly gnawed ham. He waddled over to the counter and snarled at me under his lasagna-laden breath, 'Something, my little bonbon, is fishy in Denmark.' Slowly, I lowered my grilled cheese sandwich . . ."

Using Adjectives Correctly

To use adjectives effectively, you must also use them correctly. Keep the following points in mind:

1. **Adjectives are usually placed in front of the word they describe.**
   the <u>wet</u> raincoat
   the <u>purple</u> dragon

2. **An adjective can follow a <u>linking verb</u>, such as** *be*, *seem*, **or** *feel*. A linking verb expresses a state of being.
   Serafina seems <u>sleepy</u>. [*Sleepy* describes Serafina.]
   The room was <u>warm</u>. [*Warm* describes the room.]

3. **Several adjectives can describe the same noun or pronoun.**
   <u>George's</u> <u>three</u> <u>biology</u> assignments
   the <u>worn</u>, <u>ragged</u> <u>denim</u> jacket

Tip for Writers

A verb is called a *linking verb* when its subject and the information following the verb both refer to the same person, place, or thing. The word(s) after the linking verb describe or rename the subject.

Joe <u>seems nice</u>. (linking verb + adjective)

Joe <u>is an accountant</u>. (linking verb + noun)

Verbs of sensory perception (taste, smell, etc.) often (but not always) function as linking verbs.

This cake <u>tastes delicious</u>. (linking verb + adjective)

<u>Sam tasted the cake</u>. (In this sentence, <u>tasted</u> is not a linking verb. Sam isn't the cake.)

4. **When two or more adjectives describe the same noun or pronoun, there are specific rules concerning when to use a comma between the adjectives.**

- First, *never* place a comma between an adjective and the noun or pronoun it describes.

  no comma

  a soft-spoken, understanding|counselor

  no comma

  an interesting, appealing|job

- *Do* place a comma between two adjectives when each describes the same noun (or pronoun) separately.

  comma

  a soft-spoken,|understanding counselor

- *Do not* place a comma between two adjectives when the adjective closest to the noun (or pronoun) describes the noun and the other adjective describes the combination of those two words.

  no comma

  a worn|English dictionary

  no comma

  a broken|glass bottle

  no comma

  an accurate|job description

Use the following test to decide whether you need to place a comma between two adjectives: if the word *and* makes sense when placed between the two adjectives, a comma is needed.

MAKES SENSE	a soft-spoken <u>and</u> understanding counselor
USE A COMMA	a soft-spoken, understanding counselor
DOES NOT MAKE SENSE	a new <u>and</u> Mexican restaurant
DO NOT USE A COMMA	a new Mexican restaurant

EXERCISE 7-2   Adding Commas

Directions: If needed, add commas to each of the following phrases.

EXAMPLE   the lazy, sleepy pot-bellied pig

1. an elderly California senator
2. the gentle quiet waves
3. a folded used newspaper
4. the dedicated cancer specialist
5. the sharp cat's claw
6. valuable family photographs
7. a weathered twisted pine tree
8. excited happy children
9. brown leather wallet
10. worthless costume jewelry ■

NEED TO KNOW

Adjectives

- **Adjectives** describe nouns and pronouns.

- An **adjective** is usually placed before the word it describes.

- An **adjective** can follow a linking verb.

- Use **adjectives** to add interest and detail to your sentences.

Using Adjectives to Expand Sentences

Adjectives are powerful words. They can create vivid pictures and impressions in the mind of your reader. Consider the following sentence:

EXAMPLE   The applicant greeted the interviewer.

This sentence has two nouns: *applicant* and *interviewer*. Without adjectives, however, what do we know about them or the situation? With adjectives, the same sentence becomes more informative.

REVISED   The <u>eager</u>, <u>excited</u> applicant greeted the <u>friendly</u>, <u>welcoming job</u> interviewer.

REVISED   The <u>nervous</u>, <u>insecure</u> applicant greeted the <u>cool</u>, <u>polished job</u> interviewer.

Now can you imagine the people and the situation each sentence describes? Let's take another sentence and expand it several ways by using adjectives.

EXAMPLE   The building houses the lab.

REVISED   The <u>ivy-covered brick</u> building houses the <u>well-equipped</u>, <u>up-to-date</u> biology lab.

REVISED   The <u>dilapidated</u>, <u>unpainted</u> building houses the <u>time-worn</u>, <u>outdated biology</u> lab.

As you can see from the examples above, you can drastically alter and expand your meaning by using adjectives. Think of adjectives as words that allow you to choose details that create the impression you want to convey.

EXERCISE 7-3   Expanding and Revising Sentences Using Adjectives

Directions: Expand and revise each of the following sentences in two different ways by adding adjectives. Each of your two revisions should create a different impression. Underline your adjectives.

EXAMPLE   The interviewer asked Julie a question.

REVISED   The <u>skillful</u> interviewer asked Julie an <u>indirect</u> question.

REVISED   The <u>young</u>, <u>inexperienced</u> interviewer asked Julie a <u>personal</u> question.

1. Mr. Lindgren's parrot was able to speak several words.

   a. _____

   b. _____

2. The department store made sales.

   a. _____

   b. _____

3. The Wildlife Rehabilitation Center sponsored an exhibit.

   a. _____

   b. _____

4. A professor published an article on campus reform.

   a. _____

   b. _____

5. The chef prepared a dish.

   a. _____

   b. _____

6. The diner serves food throughout the night.

   a. _____

   b. _____

7. The disc jockey plays music.

   a. _____

   b. _____

8. The book was read by each member of the club.

   a. _____

   b. _____

9. The newspaper lay on the table.

   a. _____

   b. _____

10. The teacher calmed the child by showing her books.

    a. _____

    b. _____

EXERCISE 7-4   Revising by Adding Adjectives

Directions: Rewrite the following paragraph by adding adjectives. You can also add new phrases and sentences anywhere in the paragraph—beginning, middle, or end—as long as they have adjectives in them. Underline the adjectives.

I had been looking forward to my vacation for months. I was going to lie on the beach all day and dance all night. I didn't get off to a good start. On the flight to Miami, I had the middle seat between a big man and a mother with a baby. Then we sat on the ground for two hours because of fog. It was hot and noisy. When we did get off the ground, the flight was very bumpy. Finally we got to Miami. I waited and waited for my suitcase. Needless to say, it didn't arrive. I could just picture all my new clothes sitting in some other city. Actually, though, all I needed for my week in Miami was a raincoat, because it rained every day. I didn't need my party clothes either because the first morning, I slipped getting out of the shower and sprained my ankle. I need a vacation from my vacation. ■

EXERCISE 7-5   Writing Using Adjectives

Directions: Write a paragraph on one of the following topics. After you have written your first draft, revise your paragraph by adding adjectives. Underline your adjectives.

1. A full- or part-time job you held
2. A trip you took
3. A valued possession
4. Searching for _____
5. Interviewing for _____ ■

USING ADVERBS TO DESCRIBE

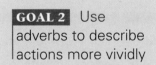
GOAL 2 Use adverbs to describe actions more vividly

Adverbs describe, qualify, or limit verbs, adjectives, or other adverbs. The following paragraph uses no adverbs:

Sample Paragraph

The old door opened on its rusty hinges. A young woman entered the attic. She searched for the box of costumes. She saw a carton on the shelf across the room. She lifted the box and undid its dusty strings. She opened it. She began laughing. A huge chicken costume was in the box!

Did this paragraph give you enough details to visualize the scene? Imagine you are directing this scene in a movie: How would the rusty door hinges sound? How would the young woman walk when she entered the attic? Where would she look for the costumes? Adverbs give you details about the verbs, adjectives, and other adverbs they modify.

Adverbs can add five kinds of information to your writing:

HOW?	He announced his intentions <u>cautiously</u>.
WHEN?	We will leave <u>tomorrow</u>.
WHERE?	We searched <u>everywhere</u>.
HOW OFTEN?	I exercise <u>daily</u>.
TO WHAT EXTENT?	The caller was <u>very</u> polite.

The following revised version of the above paragraph uses adverbs to add details that let you visualize the scene more fully:

Revised Paragraph

The old door opened <u>creakily</u> on its rusty hinges. A young woman <u>quickly</u> entered the attic. She searched <u>everywhere</u> for the box of costumes. <u>Finally</u>, she saw a carton on the shelf across the room. <u>Gingerly</u>, she lifted the box down and undid its dusty strings. <u>Very carefully</u>, she opened it. She began laughing <u>gleefully</u>. A huge chicken costume was in the box!

From this revision, you can see that adverbs help bring actions alive.

EXERCISE 7-6
Working Together

Writing Adverbs

Directions: *The Adverb Contest*: The time limit for this exercise is ten minutes. Expand the "attic" paragraph above and see how many more adverbs you can add. You can add new phrases and sentences anywhere in the present paragraph—beginning, middle, or end—as long as they have adverbs in them. Underline your adverbs and exchange your expanded story with a partner to verify how many adverbs you have added. The winner is the student who has added the most adverbs. ■

Using Adverbs Correctly

To use adverbs effectively, you must also use them correctly. Keep the following points in mind:

1. **Many adverbs end in** *-ly.* Some do not, however, such as *often, now, always,* and *not.* To determine whether a word is an adverb, look at how it functions in your sentence.

2. **Adverbs can modify verbs, adjectives, or other adverbs.**

   • Here are adverbs describing verbs (a verb expresses action or state of being):

                  verb
   Clara <u>patiently</u> waited for the appointment.

                  verb
   The building crumbled <u>quickly</u>.

                  verb
   The winning team <u>proudly</u> watched the DVD of the playoff game.

- Here are adverbs describing adjectives (an adjective modifies a noun or pronoun):

adjective

An <u>extremely</u> long interview is tiring.

adjective

The reporters asked <u>briskly</u> efficient questions.

adjective

<u>Microscopically</u> small plankton live in the ocean.

- Here are adverbs describing other adverbs:

adverb

Read a want ad <u>very</u> carefully.

adverb

Microscopes allow one to view an object <u>more</u> closely.

adverb

The automated door opened <u>quite</u> easily.

3. **Adverbs <u>can be placed</u> almost anywhere in a sentence.** Three common placements are:

AT THE BEGINNING OF THE SENTENCE	<u>Briefly</u>, Mark explained.
IN FRONT OF THE VERB	Mark <u>briefly</u> explained.
AFTER THE VERB	Mark explained <u>briefly</u>.

4. **Adverbs should be followed by a comma only when they begin a sentence.**

comma

Slowly, Jim walked into the reception area.

comma

Cautiously, he asked to see Mr. Stoneface.

When adverbs are used elsewhere in a sentence, they are *not* set off by commas.

no comma   no comma

Jim walked slowly into the reception area.

no comma   no comma

He cautiously asked to see Mr. Stoneface.

Using Adverbs to Expand Sentences

Like adjectives, adverbs are powerful words. Adverbs can create a more complete impression of the action within a sentence. Consider the following sentence and its two revisions:

EXAMPLE	The car runs.
REVISED	The car runs <u>smoothly</u>.
REVISED	The car runs <u>haltingly</u>.

Tip for Writers

When using a two-word verb, you *can* place the adverb between the two words:

He <u>has often driven</u> to New York.

I <u>will carefully finish</u> this work.

In one revised sentence, the car runs well; in the other revision, the car barely runs at all. Notice how adverbs, like adjectives, let you change the meaning of a sentence.

In the following examples, adverbs provide extra details about the action:

EXAMPLE   The president prepared his State of the Union address.

adverb adverb   adverb

REVISED   The president <u>very</u> <u>carefully</u> and <u>thoroughly</u> prepared his State of the Union address.

EXAMPLE   The swim team accepted the gold medal.

adverb   adverb

REVISED   <u>Proudly</u> and <u>excitedly</u>, the swim team accepted the gold medal.

Like adjectives, adverbs allow you to choose details that expand your sentences and refine your meaning.

NEED TO KNOW
Adverbs

- **Adverbs** qualify or limit verbs, adjectives, or other adverbs.
- Many adverbs end in *-ly,* but some do not.
- Use a comma after an adverb only when the adverb begins the sentence.
- Use adverbs to qualify and expand your ideas.

EXERCISE 7-7   Expanding and Revising Sentences Using Adverbs

Directions: Expand and revise each of the following sentences in two different ways by adding adverbs. Each revision should create a different impression. Underline your adverbs.

EXAMPLE   The employment agency lists hundreds of management positions.

REVISED   The employment agency <u>usually</u> lists hundreds of management positions.

REVISED   The employment agency <u>seldom</u> lists hundreds of management positions.

1. The gymnast performed his routine.

    a. _____

    b. _____

2. The chemistry experiment was completed.

    a. _____

    b. _____

3. Botanists study newly discovered plant life.

   a. _____

   b. _____

4. The furniture in our office breaks.

   a. _____

   b. _____

5. The businesspeople in my office use cell phones.

   a. _____

   b. _____

6. The professor will post the exam grades.

   a. _____

   b. _____

7. Mirrors should be handled carefully.

   a. _____

   b. _____

8. Many people lived through the Depression.

   a. _____

   b. _____

9. Seat belts have saved thousands of lives.

   a. _____

   b. _____

10. The boat left the dock.

   a. _____

   b. _____

EXERCISE 7-8   Writing and Revising Using Adverbs

Directions: Write a paragraph on one of the following topics. After you have written your first draft, revise your paragraph by adding adverbs. Underline your adverbs.

1. A long-lasting or vivid memory
2. The lack of privacy in apartments
3. How to make a(n) _____
4. Learning to _____
5. How to avoid _____

Directions: Rewrite the following paragraph by adding adjectives and adverbs. You can also add phrases and sentences anywhere in the beginning, middle, or end of the paragraph, as long as they have adjectives and adverbs in them. Underline the adjectives and circle the adverbs.

> Every family has someone who's eccentric—someone who's lovable but strange. In my family, that's Aunt Irma. Aunt Irma lives in an apartment filled with souvenirs from her many trips. She has souvenirs of all kinds—big and small—from everywhere in the world. If you want to sit down at Aunt Irma's, you have to move a souvenir, and probably what you're sitting on is a souvenir, too. Aunt Irma also has unusual eating habits. She eats only soup and sandwiches. She always makes her own soups, and they are unusual. The sandwiches are strange, too. You'll never see one on a menu. Aunt Irma is also an exercise nut. She has several sets of weights in different rooms. She runs in place whenever she watches TV. Finally, Aunt Irma has a distinctive way of dressing. I have seen her wear some really strange outfits. But she is lovable and, when all's said and done, what would we do without Aunt Irma stories? ■

USING ADJECTIVES AND ADVERBS TO COMPARE

> **GOAL 3** Use adjectives and adverbs to make comparisons

Adjectives and adverbs modify, describe, explain, qualify, or restrict the words they modify. **Adjectives** modify nouns and pronouns. **Adverbs** modify verbs, adjectives, and other adverbs; adverbs can also modify phrases, clauses, or whole sentences.

ADJECTIVES	the red car; the quiet one
ADVERBS	quickly finish; only four reasons; very angrily

Comparison Using Adjectives and Adverbs

1. **Positive** adjectives and adverbs modify but do not involve any comparison: *green, bright, lively*.

2. **Comparative** adjectives and adverbs compare two persons, things, actions, or ideas.

COMPARATIVE ADJECTIVE	Michael is taller than Phoebe.
COMPARATIVE ADVERB	Antonio reacted more calmly than Robert.

Here is how to form comparative adjectives and adverbs. (Consult your dictionary if you are unsure of the form of a particular word.)

- **If the adjective or adverb has one syllable, add -er. For some two-syllable words, also add -er.**

  cold → colder   slow → slower   narrow → narrower

- **For most words of two or more syllables, place the word *more* in front of the word.**

  reasonable → more reasonable   interestingly → more interestingly

- **For two-syllable adjectives ending in -y, change the -y to -i and add -er.**

  drowsy → drowsier   lazy → lazier

3. **Superlative** adjectives and adverbs compare more than two persons, things, actions, or ideas.

SUPERLATIVE ADJECTIVE   Michael is the <u>tallest</u> member of the team.

SUPERLATIVE ADVERB   Of everyone in the class, she studied the <u>most diligently</u> for the test.

Here is how to form superlative adjectives and adverbs:

- **Add** *-est* **to one-syllable adjectives and adverbs and to some two-syllable words.**

  cold → coldest   slow → slowest   narrow → narrowest

- **For most words of two or more syllables, place the word *most* in front of the word.**

  reasonable → most reasonable   interestingly → most interestingly

- **For two-syllable adjectives ending in *-y*, change the *-y* to *-i* and add *-est*.**

  drowsy → drowsiest   lazy → laziest

EXERCISE 7-10   Using Adjectives and Adverbs

Directions: Fill in the blank with the comparative form of the adjective or adverb given.

1. seriously   Mary was injured _____ than Tom.

2. lively   I feel a lot _____ than I did yesterday.

3. pretty   This bouquet of flowers is _____ than that one.

4. interesting   My biology teacher is _____ than my history teacher.

5. softly   Speak _____, or you'll wake the baby. ■

EXERCISE 7-11   Using Adjectives and Adverbs

Directions: Fill in the blank with the superlative form of the adjective or adverb given.

1. beautiful   It was the _____ wedding I'd ever seen.

2. slow   I always get in the _____ checkout line at the grocery store.

3. early   This is the _____ Jana has ever arrived.

4. difficult   That is the _____ trick the magician performs.

5. loud   It was by far the _____ band that played last Saturday. ■

Irregular Adjectives and Adverbs

Some adjectives and adverbs form their comparative and superlative forms in irregular ways.

<table>
<tr><td>Tip for Writers</td><td colspan="3"></td></tr>
</table>

> **Tip for Writers**
>
> *Littler* and *littlest* are used to describe size. *Less* and *least* describe amounts.
>
> Joe is the <u>littlest boy</u> in his class.
>
> I have <u>less money</u> than I had last week.

Positive	Comparative	Superlative
Adjectives		
good	better	best
bad	worse	worst
little	<u>littler, less</u>	<u>littlest, least</u>
Adverbs		
well	better	best
badly	worse	worst
Adjectives and Adverbs		many
many	more	most
some	more	most
much	more	most

EXERCISE 7-12   Using Adjectives and Adverbs

Directions: Fill in the blanks with the correct positive, comparative, or superlative form of the adjective or adverb given.

1. good   Bob's barbecue sauce is _____ than Shawna's, but I think Leo's recipe is the _____ of all.

2. little   Please give me just a _____ piece of pie. You can give me even _____ ice cream.

3. well   I don't feel _____ today, but I'm still _____ than I was yesterday.

4. much   I have _____ homework this semester than last semester. Of all my classes, I get the _____ homework in math.

5. bad   It rained _____ on Thursday than on Friday, but it rained the _____ on Saturday. ■

Common Mistakes to Avoid

1. **Do not use adjectives to modify verbs, other adjectives, or adverbs.**

   INCORRECT   Peter and Mary take each other <u>serious</u>.

   CORRECT   Peter and Mary take each other <u>seriously</u>. [Modifies the verb *take*.]

2. **Do not use the adjectives *good* and *bad* when you should use the adverbs *well* and *badly*.**

   INCORRECT   Juan did <u>good</u> on the exam.

   CORRECT   Juan did <u>well</u> on the exam. [Modifies the verb *did*.]

3. **Do not use the adjectives *real* and *sure* when you should use the adverbs *really* and *surely*.**

   INCORRECT   Jan scored <u>real</u> well on the exam.

   CORRECT   Jan scored <u>really</u> well on the exam. [Modifies the verb *well*.]

   INCORRECT   I <u>sure</u> was surprised to win the lottery.

   CORRECT   I <u>surely</u> was surprised to win the lottery. [Modifies the verb *was surprised*.]

4. **Do not use *more* or *most* with the *-er* or *-est* form of an adjective or adverb.** Use one form or the other, according to the rules above.

   INCORRECT   That was the <u>most</u> <u>tastiest</u> dinner I've ever eaten.

   CORRECT   That was the <u>tastiest</u> dinner I've ever eaten.

5. **Avoid double negatives—that is, two negatives in the same clause.**

   INCORRECT   He did <u>not</u> want <u>nothing</u> in the refrigerator.

   CORRECT   He did <u>not</u> want <u>anything</u> in the refrigerator.

6. **When using the comparative and superlative forms of adverbs, do not create an incomplete comparison.**

   INCORRECT   The heater works more <u>efficiently</u>. [More efficiently than what?]

   CORRECT   The heater works <u>more efficiently than it did before we had it repaired</u>.

7. **Do not use the comparative or superlative form for adjectives and adverbs that have no degree.** It is incorrect to write, for example, *more square*, *most perfect*, *more equally*, or *most unique*. Do not use a comparative or superlative form for any of the following adjectives and adverbs:

Adjectives				
complete	equal	infinite	pregnant	unique
dead	eternal	invisible	square	universal
empty	favorite	matchless	supreme	vertical
endless	impossible	parallel	unanimous	whole
Adverbs				
endlessly	infinitely	uniquely		
equally	invisibly	universally		
eternally	perpendicularly			
impossibly	straight			

EXERCISE 7-13   Revising Adjective and Adverb Use

Directions: Revise each of the following sentences so that all adjectives and adverbs are used correctly.

EXAMPLE   I answered the question polite*ly*.

1. Matteo's apartment was more expensive.

2. When I heard the man and woman sing the duet, I decided that the woman sang best.

3. Our local movie reviewer said that the film's theme song sounded badly.

4. The roller coaster was excitinger than the merry-go-round.

5. *The Scarlet Letter* is more good than *War and Peace*.

6. Lia sure gave a rousing speech.

7. Last week's storm seemed badder than a tornado.

8. Some women thought that the Equal Rights Amendment would guarantee that women would be treated more equally.

9. Taking the interstate is the more fast route to the outlet mall.

10. Professor Reed had the better lecture style of all my instructors. ■

 Analyze It!

Directions: Revise the following paragraph by adding adjectives and adverbs. You can also add phrases and sentences anywhere in the beginning, middle, or end of the paragraph, as long as they have adjectives or adverbs in them. Underline the adjectives and circle the adverbs.

When I think back on all my college professors, one stands out as the best. His name was Thomas P. Meyerson, but he was known as Professor M. His lectures were legendary; every student seemed to have at least one story about Professor M's teaching style. I was fortunate to take the last American history class he taught before retiring. At that time, he still had a full head of hair and a moustache with waxed tips. He always wore a suit and tie, with a handkerchief spilling from his pocket. For a lecture on the Revolution, he donned the type of hat worn during that period. For a lecture on Abraham Lincoln, he showed up wearing a stovepipe hat. During a presentation about Civil War battles, he flourished a sword. His lectures were not only entertaining but also educational, as his voice and teaching style brought the past to life, leaving me with images as well as knowledge.

Paragraph Writing Scenarios

Friends and Family

1. Every family has its own rituals, things they do together over and over again. Write a paragraph on one ritual your family has. It can be the way you practice your religion, share a weekly meal, or celebrate a particular holiday.

2. Write a paragraph that begins with the topic sentence "My ideal day with my family would be. . . ."

Classes and Campus Life

1. Think of one task you have trouble with in school. Write a paragraph about what makes it difficult.

2. Do you procrastinate or get right to work on your assignments? Write a paragraph that describes the way you approach homework.

Working Students

1. Write a paragraph on what makes good customer service. What personality traits do you have that would make you a good or a poor customer service representative?

2. Write a paragraph describing what you wear to work. Even if it's as simple as a T-shirt and jeans, use plenty of details.

Communities and Cultures

1. Choose a hobby, activity, or interest that introduced you into a new community. What else, if anything, did you have in common with the members of this group?

2. Describe an article of clothing or a fashion trend that came out of a particular culture and is now worn by people of all different cultures.

WRITING ABOUT A READING

In the following reading from a sociology textbook, the author discusses the functions of sports as well as the conflicts created by sports within society.

Step 1: Preview the reading.

Step 2: Connect the reading to your own experience: Why do you play and/or watch sports?

Step 3: Read and respond to the questions in the margin.

THINK AND RESPOND

What is the meaning of the title?

What is the function of the question in the introductory paragraph? To what audience is the author appealing?

Summarize the functions of sports.

Explain the meaning of "dysfunctional consequences."

THE GAMES PEOPLE PLAY

John J. Macionis

1   Who doesn't enjoy sports? Children as young as six or seven take part in organized sports, and many teens become skilled at three or more. Weekend television is filled with sporting events for viewers of all ages, and whole sections of our newspapers are devoted to teams, players, and scores. In the United States, top players such as Joe Flacco (football), Michael Phelps (swimming), LeBron James (basketball), and Serena Williams (tennis) are among our most famous celebrities. Sports in the United States are also a multibillion-dollar industry. What can we learn by applying sociology's major theoretical approaches to this familiar part of everyday life?

The Functions of Sports

2   The functions of sports include providing recreation as well as offering a means of getting in physical shape and a relatively harmless way to let off steam. Sports have important latent functions as well, which include building social relationships and also creating tens of thousands of jobs across the country. Participating in sports encourages competition and the pursuit of success, both of which are values that are central to our society's way of life.

3   Sports also have dysfunctional consequences. For example, colleges and universities try to field winning teams to build a school's reputation and also to raise money from alumni and corporate sponsors. In the process, however, these schools sometimes recruit students for their athletic skill rather than their academic ability. This practice not only lowers the academic standards of the college or university but also shortchanges athletes, who spend little time doing the academic work that will prepare them for later careers.

Sports and Conflict

What is the author suggesting here?

4   The games that people play reflect their social standing. Some sports—including tennis, swimming, golf, sailing, and skiing—are expensive, so taking part is largely limited to the well-to-do. Football, baseball, and basketball, however, are accessible to people at almost all income levels. Thus the games people play are not simply a matter of individual choice but also a reflection of their social standing.

5   Throughout history, men have dominated the world of sports. In the nineteenth century, women had little opportunity to engage in athletic competition, and those that did received little attention. For example, the first modern Olympic Games, held in 1896, barred women from competition. The 2012 Olympics, by contrast, included women competing in twenty-six sports, including boxing. Throughout most of the twentieth century, Little League teams barred

What does this imply about female athletes?

girls based on the traditional ideas that girls and women lack the strength to play sports and risk losing their femininity if they do. Like the Olympics, Little League is now open to females as well as males. But even today, our society still encourages men to become athletes while expecting women to be attentive observers and cheerleaders. At the college level, men's athletics attracts a greater amount of attention and resources compared to women's athletics, and men greatly outnumber women as coaches, even in women's sports. At the professional level, women also take a back seat to men, particularly in the sports with the most earning power and social prestige.

6   For decades, big league sports excluded people of color, who were forced to form leagues of their own. Only in 1947 did Major League Baseball admit the first African American player when Jackie Robinson joined the Brooklyn Dodgers. More than fifty years later, professional baseball honored Robinson's amazing career by retiring his number 42 on *all* of the teams in the league. In 2011, African Americans (13 percent of the U.S. population) accounted for 9 percent of Major League Baseball players, 67 percent of National Football League (NFL) players, and 78 percent of National Basketball Association (NBA) players.

Explain the significance of the picture.

What type of support does the author use in this paragraph?

Legendary baseball player Jackie Robinson was the first African American to play in Major League Baseball. Sports remain an important element of social life in countless communities across the United States, a evidenced by Robinson's appearance on a U.S. postage stamp.

7   One reason for the high number of African Americans in some professional sports is that athletic performance—in terms of batting average or number of points scored per game—can be precisely measured and is not influenced by racial prejudice. It is also true that some people of color make a particular effort to excel in athletics, where they see greater opportunity than in other careers. In recent years, in fact, African American athletes have earned higher salaries, on average, than white players. *Forbes* (2012) reports that four of the five highest-earning athletes are people who are racial or ethnic minorities.

8   But racial discrimination still exists in professional sports. For one thing, race is linked to the *positions* athletes play on the field, in a pattern called "stacking." Figure A shows the results of a study of race in professional baseball. Notice that white athletes are more concentrated in the central "thinking" positions of pitcher (66 percent) and catcher (58 percent). By contrast, African Americans represent only 3 percent of pitchers and there are no black catchers at all. At the same time, 8 percent of infielders are African Americans, as are 27 percent of outfielders, positions characterized as requiring "speed and reactive ability".

> *What is "stacking"?*

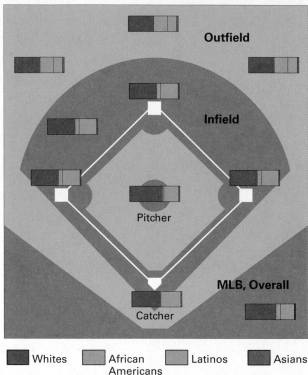

Whites   African Americans   Latinos   Asians

Figure A "Stacking" in Professional Baseball *Does race play a part in professional sports? Looking at the various positions in professional baseball, we see that white players are more likely to play the central positions in the infield, while people of color are more likely to play in the outfield. What do you make of this pattern?*
Source: Lapchick (2012).

> *Does this information surprise you?*

9   More broadly, African Americans have a large share of players in only five sports: baseball, basketball, football, boxing, and track. In baseball, this share has been declining, from 19 percent in 1995 to 9 percent in 2012. And across all professional sports, the vast majority of managers, head coaches, and team owners are white.

> *Does the concluding paragraph create a positive or negative feeling about the effect of sports on society?*

10   Who benefits most from professional sports? Although many individual players get sky-high salaries and millions of fans enjoy following their teams, the vast profits sports generate are controlled by a small number of people—predominantly white men. In sum, sports in the United States are bound up with inequalities based on gender, race, and wealth.

WRITING IN RESPONSE TO READING

Examining the Reading Using an Idea Map   MyWritingLab

Review the reading by completing the missing parts of the idea map shown below.

 Visualize It!

Title	**The Games People Play**
Thesis	Sports serves many functions and also creates conflicts within society.

Sports have numerous functions and effects.

Recreation.

_____.

_____.

_____.

_____.

_____.

Lowering _____ and shortchanging _____.

Sports are a reflection of social standing.

_____ have dominated sports.

Discriminatory toward_____ and _____.

Conclusion	Although sports contributes positively to society, it also can have dysfunctional consequences and create gender, race, and economic inequalities.

Strengthening Your Vocabulary MyWritingLab

Using the word's context, word parts, or a dictionary, write a brief definition of each of the following words as it is used in the reading.

1. sociology (paragraph 1) _____

2. latent (paragraph 2) _____

3. prestige (paragraph 5) _____ ■

Reacting to Ideas: Discussion and Journal Writing MyWritingLab

Get ready to write about the reading by discussing the following:

1. What was the author's purpose in writing this article?

2. How do sports help to build social relationships?

3. According to the article, what do Little League and the Olympics have in common?

4. How do sports contribute to racial inequality?

5. Explain the significance of the number 42. ■

Paragraph Options MyWritingLab

1. What do you think is the most positive contribution of sports to society? Write a paragraph in which you describe the contribution and explain your reasons for choosing it.

2. Write a paragraph telling about the impact—positive or negative—that sports have had on your life.

3. Do you have a favorite college or professional athlete? Write a paragraph in which you describe this athlete fully and tell why he or she is your favorite.

Essay Options MyWritingLab

4. Write an essay in which you discuss the functional and dysfunctional ways that sports function in society. Be sure to use examples to support your major points.

5. Critics charge that sports contribute to race, gender, and economic inequality in society. Write an essay in which you agree or disagree with this charge. Be sure to use examples to support your major points.

6. Write an essay in which you contrast men and women's athletics at the college and/or professional level. ■

■ ■ ■ ■

SELF-TEST SUMMARY

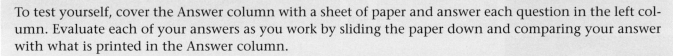

To test yourself, cover the Answer column with a sheet of paper and answer each question in the left column. Evaluate each of your answers as you work by sliding the paper down and comparing your answer with what is printed in the Answer column.

	QUESTION	ANSWER
Goal 1 Use adjectives to add descriptive details	What are adjectives? How are adjectives used correctly?	Adjectives describe nouns and pronouns. An adjective is usually placed before the word it describes, or it can follow a linking verb. Several adjectives can describe the same noun or pronoun.
Goal 2 Use adverbs to describe actions more vividly	What are adverbs? How are adverbs used correctly?	Adverbs describe, qualify, or limit verbs, adjectives, or other adverbs. Many adverbs end in -*ly*. Adverbs can be placed almost anywhere in a sentence, but they should be followed by a comma only when they begin a sentence.
Goal 3 Use adjectives and adverbs to make comparisons	What are comparative and superlative adjectives and adverbs?	Comparative adjectives and adverbs compare two persons, things, actions, or ideas; you can form comparative adjectives and adverbs by adding -*er* or the word *more*. Superlative adjectives and adverbs compare more than two persons, things, actions, or ideas; you can form superlative adjectives and adverbs by adding -*est* or the word *most*.

MyWritingLab *Visit Ch. 7 Using Adjectives and Adverbs to Describe in MyWritingLab to test your understanding of the chapter objectives.*

8

Using Modifiers to Add Detail

Learning Goals

In this chapter, you will learn how to

GOAL 1 Use prepositional phrases to add detail

GOAL 2 Use *-ing* phrases to add detail

GOAL 3 Use relative (*who, which, that*) clauses to add detail

WRITE ABOUT IT!

Compare the two images above. Write a sentence explaining how they differ.

    These two images demonstrate what a paragraph looks like without words and phrases that add detail. A paragraph is just a skeleton, as is the first image, without words and phrases that explain or change the meaning. In this chapter you will learn to use **modifiers**—words that change or limit the meaning of another word or word group.

WRITING

To further understand the value of modifiers, read this sample paragraph and the revised paragraph that follows it:

Sample Paragraph

Eyes produce tears. Tears wash the eye. Tears clean away dust and germs. People cry sometimes when happy, sad, or in pain. No one knows why. The eye also waters if something touches it or if the person has a cold or other infection. Used tear fluid drains away. It goes to a chamber in the nose. Crying produces a runny nose.

Did this paragraph seem choppy and underdeveloped to you? Now read the revised paragraph below. To add information and improve flow, the writer has used modifiers, such as prepositional phrases, -*ing* phrases, and relative clauses, which are underlined.

Revised Paragraph

Eyes produce tears <u>in the lachrymal glands behind the upper eyelids.</u> <u>Cleaning away dust and germs with every blink</u>, tears wash the eye. <u>For reasons not well understood</u>, people who are happy, sad, or in pain sometimes produce extra tears, <u>which flood down their cheeks.</u> The eye also waters if something touches it or if the person has a cold or other infection. Used tear fluid drains away <u>through two tiny holes in the eyelids near the nose, entering small tubes that are called the tear ducts.</u> These ducts empty into a chamber in the nose. This fact explains why someone <u>who is having a good cry</u> will often get a runny nose as well.

This chapter will help you learn to write more interesting, effective sentences by using three types of modifiers: prepositional phrases, -*ing* phrases, and *who*, *which*, and *that* relative clauses.

USING PREPOSITIONAL PHRASES TO ADD DETAIL

GOAL 1 Use prepositional phrases to add detail

A **preposition** links its object (a noun or pronoun) to the rest of the sentence. Prepositions often show relationships of *time*, *place*, *direction*, or *manner*.

TIME	Let's study after class.
PLACE	Meet me behind Hayes Hall.
DIRECTION	Who's that coming toward us?
MANNER	I acted according to my principles.

Prepositions show other relationships as well, usually variations on *time*, *place*, *direction*, or *manner*.

DURATION	We walked until dark.
REASON	They were late because of the snow.
RELATION	She looks like her sister.
QUALIFICATION	Everyone attended except Suzanna.
ORIGIN	In the beginning, I thought I couldn't write.
DESTINATION	We're going to the Grand Canyon in May.
LOCATION	The book is in my car.

Become familiar with the following common prepositions. They will help you link your ideas and make your sentences more varied and interesting.

COMMON PREPOSITIONS			
about	beneath	in spite of	round
above	beside	instead of	since
according to	between	into	through
across	beyond	like	throughout
after	by	near	till
against	concerning	next to	to
along	despite	of	toward
along with	down	off	under
among	during	on	underneath
around	except	onto	unlike
as	except for	out	until
aside from	excepting	out of	up
at	for	outside	upon
because of	from	over	with
before	in	past	within
behind	in addition to	regarding	without
below	inside		

A **prepositional phrase** consists of a preposition and the object of the preposition (a noun or pronoun). It may also include words that modify the object.

preposition   object of preposition   preposition   modifier   object of preposition
Sam sat beside me.   Turn left at the red barn.

You can add a prepositional phrase to a sentence to describe a noun, pronoun, verb, or adjective.

Prepositional Phrase Describing a . . .

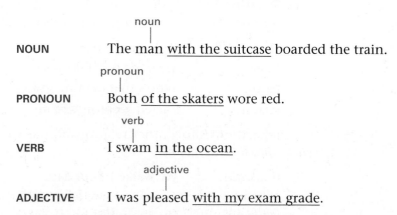

noun
NOUN   The man with the suitcase boarded the train.

pronoun
PRONOUN   Both of the skaters wore red.

verb
VERB   I swam in the ocean.

adjective
ADJECTIVE   I was pleased with my exam grade.

Using Prepositional Phrases to Expand Sentences

Now let's look at how you can use prepositional phrases to add detail to your sentences and expand them:

BASIC SENTENCE	I met an old friend.
ADDITIONAL DETAIL	My old friend was <u>from California</u>. [location] We met <u>at a quiet restaurant</u>. [place] We met <u>on Saturday night</u>. [time]
EXPANDED SENTENCE	On Saturday night, I met an old friend from California at a quiet restaurant.
BASIC SENTENCE	Molly got a job.
ADDITIONAL DETAIL	Her job is <u>at the bakery</u>. [place] The bakery is <u>on Seventh Street</u>. [place] She got the job <u>on Monday</u>. [time]
EXPANDED SENTENCE	On Monday, Molly got a job at the bakery on Seventh Street.

Punctuating Prepositional Phrases

To use prepositional phrases effectively, you must also punctuate them correctly. Keep the following points in mind:

1. **A preposition is never separated from its object by a comma.**

   comma
   |
   INCORRECT   <u>According to</u>, the newspaper

   no comma
   |
   CORRECT   According to the newspaper

2. **A prepositional phrase is never a complete sentence.** It lacks both a subject and a verb. Be sure you do not punctuate a prepositional phrase as a sentence. Doing so creates a fragment.

   INCORRECT   We went for a walk. <u>Along the road</u>.

   CORRECT   We went for a walk <u>along the road</u>.

3. **A prepositional phrase that introduces a sentence is set apart from the rest of the sentence by a comma, unless the prepositional phrase is very short (two or three words).**

   comma
   |
   <u>According to my sister and my cousin</u>, the party lasted until midnight.

   no comma
   |
   <u>On Tuesday</u> I missed class.

4. **When a prepositional phrase interrupts a sentence and is not essential to the meaning of the sentence, it is set apart from the sentence with commas.**

   comma   comma
   | |
   The president, <u>unlike those before him</u>, intends to establish new policies.

EXERCISE 8-1　Identifying Prepositional Phrases

Directions: Underline each prepositional phrase. Add punctuation if it is needed.

EXAMPLE　The mayor according to the television news report has approved the proposed school budget.

The mayor, <u>according to the television news report</u>, has approved the proposed school budget.

1. The family walked toward the museum.
2. Throughout the film, the man next to me kept sneezing.
3. A tree branch crashed to the ground and slid down the hill.
4. Over the past few years, the sculptor has created many works.
5. Barbara bought an iPod instead of a CD player with her bonus check.
6. After dinner Dominic gave me a gift.
7. Over the phone, the salesman tried to convince me to buy his product.
8. The dog and the squirrel ran around the tree.
9. We were busy talking and drove past the restaurant.
10. Firemen broke into the building and rescued seven people. ■

EXERCISE 8-2　Expanding Sentences Using Prepositional Phrases

Directions: Expand each of the following basic sentences by using prepositional phrases to add additional detail. Your new sentence should have only one subject and one verb. Add punctuation if it is needed. Underline the prepositional phrases.

EXAMPLE

BASIC SENTENCE	I ordered a pizza.
ADDITIONAL DETAIL	I ordered it from Mazia's.
	I ordered it with mushrooms and anchovies.
	I ordered it before noon.
EXPANDED SENTENCE	<u>Before noon</u> I ordered a pizza <u>with mushrooms and anchovies from Mazia's.</u>

1. BASIC SENTENCE	Maria plays the drums.
ADDITIONAL DETAIL	She plays in a band.
	The band plays at the Rathskeller.
	She plays on weekends.
EXPANDED SENTENCE	_____
	_____
	_____

2. **BASIC SENTENCE** The construction crew is building a skyscraper.

  ADDITIONAL DETAIL They are building it next to a church.

  They are building it on Ivy Street.

  EXPANDED SENTENCE _____

  _____

  _____

3. **BASIC SENTENCE** The folders should be organized and filed.

  ADDITIONAL DETAIL They should be organized by subject.

  The folders are beside the phone.

  They should be filed under "Marketing Ideas."

  EXPANDED SENTENCE _____

  _____

  _____

4. **BASIC SENTENCE** Jason will buy a house.

  ADDITIONAL DETAIL The house is in Williamsville.

  He will buy it as an investment.

  The house has a two-car garage.

  EXPANDED SENTENCE _____

  _____

  _____

5. **BASIC SENTENCE** The library is a popular place.

  ADDITIONAL DETAIL It is popular for socializing.

  The library is in the Humanities Building.

  Many students study there during the exam period.

  EXPANDED SENTENCE _____

  _____

  _____

6. **BASIC SENTENCE** The vice president was honored.

  ADDITIONAL DETAIL He was honored for his volunteer work.

  He was honored after the staff meeting.

  He volunteered throughout his career.

  EXPANDED SENTENCE _____

  _____

  _____

7. BASIC SENTENCE   Tamara joined a sorority.

ADDITIONAL DETAIL   She joined along with her friend Marion.

This was unlike her sister Shara.

She joined despite her busy schedule.

EXPANDED SENTENCE   _____

_____

_____

8. BASIC SENTENCE   The movie is playing at the theater.

ADDITIONAL DETAIL   The theater is behind the mall.

The movie is about dinosaurs.

It is playing during the afternoon only.

EXPANDED SENTENCE   _____

_____

_____

9. BASIC SENTENCE   Women are waiting to get married.

ADDITIONAL DETAIL   They are waiting until they are older and have careers.

This is happening throughout the country.

This is true according to a recent survey.

EXPANDED SENTENCE   _____

_____

_____

10. BASIC SENTENCE   The museum is famous.

ADDITIONAL DETAIL   The museum is outside the city.

It is famous for its Monet paintings.

It is famous despite its out-of-the-way location.

EXPANDED SENTENCE   _____

_____

_____

■

EXERCISE 8-3   Expanding Sentences Using Prepositional Phrases

Directions: Expand each of the following sentences by adding at least two prepositional phrases anywhere in the sentence. Underline your prepositional phrases.

EXAMPLE

BASIC SENTENCE   Jack rented an apartment.

EXPANDED SENTENCE   Jack rented an apartment <u>with a beautiful view</u> <u>of the</u> <u>waterfront</u>.

1. The bank was recently taken over.

_____

_____

2. The grocery store closed permanently.

_____

_____

3. The publisher uses only recycled paper.

_____

_____

4. The children heard a story.

_____

_____

5. Lightning struck the old oak tree.

_____

_____

6. The tanker spilled oil.

_____

_____

7. Alaskan brown bears catch salmon.

_____

_____

8. The road was being paved.

_____

_____

9. The Bach sonata was played.

_____

_____

10. The show dog won a ribbon.

_____

_____

EXERCISE 8-4
Working Together

Writing a Paragraph Using Prepositional Phrases

Directions: Write a paragraph on one of the following topics. After you have written your first draft, make sure your paragraph includes at least five prepositional phrases. Underline these phrases. Exchange paragraphs with a classmate and evaluate each other's paragraphs. Add additional prepositional phases, if needed.

1. When the unexpected happened
2. Something simple that became difficult
3. A lost and never-found item
4. Signs of laziness
5. A phobia (fear) of _____ ■

USING -*ING* PHRASES TO ADD DETAIL

GOAL 2 Use -*ing* phrases to add detail

Another way to add detail to your writing is to use -*ing* phrases to expand your sentences. An -*ing* phrase begins with the -*ing* verb form (*running, calling*) and functions as an adjective—that is, it modifies a noun or pronoun.

Walking slowly, the couple held hands.

Sitting on the sofa, Sally watched a video.

The phrase *walking slowly* describes the couple. The phrase *sitting on the sofa* describes Sally.

You can also use -*ing* phrases to combine ideas from two sentences into a single sentence.

TWO SENTENCES	Matt grilled a steak.
	He was standing on the patio.
COMBINED	Standing on the patio, Matt grilled a steak.
TWO SENTENCES	The couple discovered an injured pelican.
	The couple searched for sea shells.
COMBINED	Searching for sea shells, the couple discovered an injured pelican.
TWO SENTENCES	The photographer slipped off his step stool.
	He fell two feet.
COMBINED	The photographer slipped off his step stool, falling two feet.

Punctuating -*ing* Phrases

Remember the following rules for punctuating -*ing* phrases:

1. **A comma must follow an -*ing* phrase that appears at the beginning of the sentence.** Its purpose is to separate the -*ing* phrase from the independent thought that follows.

comma

Driving home, I saw a shooting star.

2. **If the *-ing* phrase appears at the end of the sentence, a comma separates the *-ing* phrase from the independent thought that comes before the phrase.**

comma
|

I explored the flooded basement, wishing I had worn my boots.

3. **When the *-ing* phrase interrupts a sentence and is not essential to the meaning of the sentence, it is set apart from the sentence with commas.**

ESSENTIAL   The cows munching grass were facing us; the other cows were facing the other way.

comma   comma
| |

NOT ESSENTIAL   The cows, munching grass, all stood with their backs to the wind.

EXERCISE 8-5   Combining Sentences

Directions: Combine each pair of sentences into a single sentence that begins with an *-ing* phrase. Underline each *-ing* phrase.

EXAMPLE

TWO SENTENCES   Art wished it would stop raining.
                       Art was walking home without a raincoat.

COMBINED   <u>Walking home without a raincoat</u>, Art wished it would stop raining.

1. a. Kedra did not listen to the lecture.
   b. Kedra was thinking about her essay.
   COMBINED _____
   _____

2. a. Kenyon was driving to the bookstore.
   b. Kenyon was singing to himself.
   COMBINED _____
   _____

3. a. The plumber entered the house.
   b. The plumber carried a toolbox.
   COMBINED _____
   _____

4. a. The baby was crying for her mother.
   b. The baby was standing in her crib.
   COMBINED _____
   _____

5. a. The press secretary held a press conference.
   b. The press secretary was wearing a navy pin-striped suit.
   COMBINED _____
   _____

■ **EXERCISE 8-6**   **Expanding Sentences Using *-ing* Phrases**

Directions: Expand each of the following sentences by adding an *-ing* phrase. You may add your *-ing* phrase at the beginning, in the middle, or at the end of the sentence. Underline each *-ing* phrase.

EXAMPLE   The man stood on a ladder.

EXPANDED SENTENCE   <u>Painting his garage</u>, the man stood on a ladder.

1. The programmer sat at her desk.

   _____

2. The doctor walked through the hospital.

   _____

3. Rafael climbed the tree.

   _____

4. The teenagers walked through the mall.

   _____

5. The instructor returned the exams.

   _____

6. Ellen waited for a bus.

   _____

7. The clerk bagged the groceries.

   _____

8. The movie star accepted the award.

   _____

9. They spent a quiet evening.

   _____

10. The kitten was curled up on the sofa.

   _____

                                                                    ■

■ **EXERCISE 8-7**   **Writing a Paragraph Using *-ing* Phrases**

Writing in Progress

Directions: Review the paragraph you wrote for Exercise 8-4. Double-underline any *-ing* phrases. If you have not used any *-ing* phrases, revise your paragraph to include at least one. ■

USING *WHO, WHICH,* AND *THAT* RELATIVE CLAUSES TO ADD DETAIL

GOAL 3 Use relative (*who, which, that*) clauses to add detail

A **clause** is a group of words that has a subject and a verb. Clauses that begin with the pronoun *who, which,* or *that* are called **relative** (or **adjective**) **clauses** because they relate one idea to another. The pronoun

   who refers to people.

   which refers to things.

   that refers to people or things.

Relative clauses add variety to your writing, as well as interesting detail. Here are a few examples of relative clauses used to expand sentences by adding detail:

BASIC SENTENCE	My sister is a football fan.
ADDITIONAL DETAIL	She is ten years old.
EXPANDED SENTENCE	My sister, <u>who is ten years old</u>, is a football fan.
BASIC SENTENCE	My favorite movie is *The Fighter*.
ADDITIONAL DETAIL	I saw *The Fighter* ten times.
EXPANDED SENTENCE	My favorite movie is *The Fighter*, <u>which I've seen ten times</u>.
BASIC SENTENCE	I own a large van.
ADDITIONAL DETAIL	The van can haul camping equipment.
EXPANDED SENTENCE	I own a large van <u>that can haul camping equipment</u>.

> **Tip for Writers**
>
> **Using Relative Pronouns**
>
> Be sure to use relative pronouns, not personal pronouns, to introduce a clause that explains a noun.
>
> **INCORRECT** Laptop computers, <u>they</u> are convenient to use and easy to carry, are costly.
>
> **CORRECT** Laptop computers, <u>which</u> are convenient to use and easy to carry, are costly.

Placement of Relative Clauses

Who, *which*, and *that* clauses usually come directly after the words they relate to or modify.

My math instructor, <u>who lives in Baltimore</u>, has a British accent.

Mickey's, <u>which serves 32 varieties of coffee</u>, is part of a national chain.

Punctuating Relative Clauses

Note the following guidelines for punctuating relative clauses:

1. **A relative clause is never a sentence by itself.** Alone, a relative clause is a fragment. It must be combined with a complete sentence.

FRAGMENT	That has two fireplaces.
REVISED	The house <u>that has two fireplaces</u> is for sale.
FRAGMENT	Who lives next door.
REVISED	The woman <u>who lives next door</u> is a plumber.
SENTENCE + FRAGMENT	I needed my notebook. Which I left at home.
REVISED	I needed my notebook, <u>which I left at home</u>.

2. **If the relative clause is essential to the meaning of the sentence, no punctuation is needed.**

   Pens <u>that have refillable cartridges</u> are expensive.

The sentence above states that not all pens are expensive. Only those pens that have refillable cartridges are expensive. Here the relative clause is essential to the meaning of the sentence, so no commas are needed. Essential relative clauses always use the word *that*.

3. **If the relative clause is *not* essential to the meaning of the sentence, then it should be separated from the remainder of the sentence by commas.** To discover whether the clause is essential, try reading the sentence without the clause. If the basic meaning does not change, the clause is not essential. Nonessential clauses use the word *which* for things and *who* for a person or people.

My car, <u>which is a Nissan</u>, has over 100,000 miles on it.

In this sentence, the additional information that the car is a Nissan does not change the basic meaning of the sentence.

People <u>who talk constantly</u> are annoying.

In this sentence, the clause is essential: only people who talk constantly are annoying.

NEED TO KNOW

Modifiers

- Use *prepositional phrases* to show relationships of time, place, direction, or manner.

- Use *-ing phrases* to describe or modify a noun or pronoun.

- Use *relative clauses* (*who*, *which*, and *that*) to add detail by showing relationships.

- Be sure to check the punctuation of each of these phrases and clauses.

EXERCISE 8-8   Identifying Relative Clauses

Directions: Underline each relative clause. Add punctuation if it is needed. Circle the word to which each clause relates.

EXAMPLE   My bicycle which I rode all summer needs repair.

REVISED   My (bicycle), <u>which I rode all summer</u>, needs repair.

1. An apartment that has three bedrooms is expensive.

2. The flash drive that I handed you has the graduation pictures saved on it.

3. Becky, who has been there before, said the food is terrific.

4. Trees that lose their leaves are called deciduous.

5. Animals that live both on land and in water are called amphibians.

6. The fence, which was put up to keep rabbits out of the garden, is becoming rusted.

7. My car, which I bought at an auction, is seven years old.

8. The professor asked a question of Michael, who had not done the reading.

9. Bettina reconditions outboard motors, which she buys at marinas.

10. Brady, who visited France last year, speaks six languages fluently. ■

EXERCISE 8-9   Combining Sentences

Directions: Combine each pair of sentences into a single sentence that has a relative clause. Underline the relative clause, and circle the word to which each clause relates.

EXAMPLE

TWO SENTENCES   a. Sam lives in New Orleans.
b. Sam travels around the country demonstrating computer software.

COMBINED   (Sam) who lives in New Orleans, travels around the country demonstrating computer software.

1. a. The trunk was old.
   b. The trunk contained antique clothing.
   COMBINED   _____
   _____

2. a. The coins were valuable.
   b. The coins had sunk on a boat hundreds of years ago.
   COMBINED   _____
   _____

3. a. The students attended the Garth Brooks concert.
   b. The students enjoy country music.
   COMBINED   _____
   _____

4. a. Einstein stated the theory of relativity.
   b. Einstein was a very humorous man.
   COMBINED   _____
   _____

5. a. The truck had a flat tire.
   b. The truck was going to the repair shop.
   COMBINED   _____
   _____

6. **a.** The wreath was hung on the door.
   b. The wreath was made of dried flowers and leaves.
   COMBINED _____

   _____

7. **a.** An appointment book was found on the desk.
   b. The appointment book was filled with writing.
   COMBINED _____

   _____

8. **a.** Roberto was hired as an accountant.
   b. Roberto has a degree from this college.
   COMBINED _____

9. **a.** The pool sold for 300 dollars.
   b. The pool had a tear in its lining.
   COMBINED _____

   _____

10. **a.** Test questions should be approached systematically.
    b. Some test questions are multiple choice.
    COMBINED _____

    _____

EXERCISE 8-10   Evaluating and Revising Your Writing
Writing in Progress

Directions: Review the paragraph you wrote for Exercise 8-4. Bracket any relative clauses. If you have not included any relative clauses, revise your paragraph to include at least one. ■

EXERCISE 8-11   Expanding Sentences Using Relative Clauses

Directions: Expand each of the following sentences by adding a relative clause. Underline all relative clauses and set off unessential ones with commas.

EXAMPLE   Mr. Schmidt had a heart attack.

EXPANDED SENTENCE   Mr. Schmidt, who had always been healthy, had a heart attack.

1. "The Three Little Pigs" is a popular children's story.

   _____

2. Our dog is afraid to climb the spiral staircase.

   _____

3. A paper plate lay in the garbage.

_____

_____

4. The stereo was too loud.

_____

_____

5. I picked up my screwdriver and tightened the screw.

_____

_____

6. The student called the Records Office.

_____

_____

7. The wineglass shattered.

_____

_____

8. The lottery jackpot is one million dollars.

_____

_____

9. Jackie stepped on the thistle.

_____

_____

10. The train crossed the bridge.

_____

_____

■

EXERCISE 8-12   Expanding Sentences

Directions: Expand the following sentences by adding prepositional phrases, _-ing_ phrases, and relative clauses. Underline the phrases and clauses that you add.

EXAMPLE	The sportscaster reported the game.
EXPANDED	The sportscaster, who was wearing a really wild tie, reported the game with great enthusiasm.

1. Randall will graduate.

_____

2. The race began.

_____

3. The Smiths are remodeling.

_____

4. Hillary walked alone.

_____

5. Manuel repairs appliances.

_____

6. The motorcycle was loud.

_____

7. My term paper is due on Tuesday.

_____

8. I opened my umbrella.

_____

9. Austin built a garage.

_____

10. Lucas climbs mountains.

_____

■

EXERCISE 8-13   Writing a Paragraph

Directions: Write a paragraph describing what you think is happening in the photograph below. To make your writing vivid, use adjectives and adverbs, prepositional phrases, *-ing* phrases, and relative clauses.

■

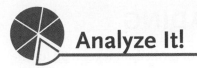 **Analyze It!**

Directions: Revise the following paragraph by adding modifiers for each blank line.

Going to the dentist terrified me until I discovered an effective strategy for _____. I dreaded dental work so much that I would put off making an appointment _____. At the dentist's office, I would sit nervously in the waiting room, _____. Minutes seemed like hours as I flipped through old magazines, trying to distract myself _____. _____, I would smile weakly at the reception-ist, _____. When I finally sat in the dentist's chair, I would literally tremble with fear _____. Recently, a friend suggested that music might calm my fear of the dentist, so I took my MP3 player and headphones _____. In the waiting room, I put on my headphones, _____. Right away I could feel some of the tension leaving my body. In the dentist's chair, I switched to mellow jazz and was amazed that my anxiety remained _____. _____, the dentist even commented on how relaxed I was. When the drilling started, I flinched but soon discovered that the drill was no match for the music _____.

Paragraph Writing Scenarios

Friends and Family

1. Think of something you recently discussed with a friend about which you had very different opinions. Write a paragraph explaining how your viewpoints differed.

2. Write a paragraph about a movie you have seen. Begin with the topic sentence: "My friend (name of friend) has to see (include name of movie)." Describe what you think your friend would like about this film.

Classes and Campus Life

1. Different awards and scholarships are given to students for excellence in various fields of study and activities. Describe something you do very well and what an award for that specialty might be called.

2. Write a paragraph about what you do—or wish you did—to stay in shape. If your campus has a gym, explain what you use it for.

Working Students

1. Write a paragraph on one authority figure at school or work whom you admire. What are the qualities that person has that make him or her a good leader?

2. Make a list of chores you don't ever seem to have the time to do. Which one would you like to get done the most? Why?

Communities and Cultures

1. Describe your family's attitude toward education. How is your own attitude different? How is it the same?

2. Write a paragraph that begins with the phrase "I have always wanted to visit . . . ." Pick a country you've never been to, and explain why you'd like to go there.

WRITING ABOUT A READING

The author of the following reading is the mother of basketball legend Shaquille O'Neal. In this excerpt from her autobiography *Walk Like You Have Somewhere to Go*, Lucille O'Neal describes some of the experiences that have shaped her relationship with her famous son.

Step 1: Preview the reading.

Step 2: Connect the reading to your own experience: Why did your parents choose to name you as they did? Does your name have any special meaning?

Step 3: Read and respond to the questions in the margin.

THINK AS YOU READ

Based on the title, what do you expect the reading to be about?

What information is incomplete or not fully explained in this paragraph?

What tough circumstance does this paragraph reveal?

THE LITTLE WARRIOR

Lucille O'Neal

1   I will always believe that the tough circumstances surrounding his birth are just one of the many reasons Shaquille and I have always had a special bond. Now, that's not to say that I don't share a special bond with all four of my children, because I most certainly do. But as mothers, we often interact differently with each child depending on their needs, personalities, and circumstances. My relationship with my oldest son remains strong to this day, and I know I'm truly blessed to have it.

2   I named him Shaquille, and that's what I call him every time I see him. I've never called him Shaq, and I never will. I don't mind others calling him that, but I named him Shaquille for a reason. More than a few people in my family and a few more outside of it were baffled as to why I decided to give all four of my children Muslim names. I'd grown up in such a strict Christian household that I suppose, in some ways, that was how I chose to rebel against my grandparents' suffocating rules that had irked me all my life—as if being pregnant without the benefit of marriage wasn't enough.

Here, Shaq plays for the Celtics in 2010: his mother's "Little Warrior" has become a basketball superstar.

What other tough circumstances does this paragraph discuss?

What does Lucille reveal about her own life as she was growing up?

What statement did her choice of names make?

Why did Shaquille and his mother have to be warriors?

3   Shaquille was born in 1972, an all-at-once thrilling and uncertain time for African Americans everywhere. Black power, black pride, African garb, and Afros were all the rage, and I was fascinated by the unity and optimism of the moment. I'd already witnessed the 1967 Newark riots, and along with the rest of the country, I felt deeply the pain of Martin Luther King Jr.'s death in 1968. The world was changing rapidly, and I wanted to be a part of it in any way I could. But what could I do? My family wasn't exactly the activist type, and any civil unrest that led to jail (right or wrong) would result in me staying there. All I knew was that I had to make my mark somehow.

4   Divine intervention sometimes comes in the most unexpected ways. A few years before I became pregnant with Shaquille, an Islamic mosque was built in our neighborhood, no doubt a result of the popularity of the Nation of Islam and Malcolm X. I caught headlines here and there about the Muslim movement, but for the most part, I never fully appreciated what they were doing or what they stood for. In our house, politics were rarely discussed, and when they were, we as children were not included in the conversation. The old adage that children were to be seen and not heard was in full effect in my house, which made the Black Muslim platform seem eons way from my little block in New Jersey.

5   Maybe it was that lack of knowledge that had me so fascinated with the mosque and what it represented in our neighborhood. Its teachings were the polar opposite of all I'd learned as a child, and that was right up my alley. Some days I'd go into the mosque's gift store in the mornings and wander the book aisles for hours, looking for anything that caught my eye. One book that did catch my eye was a collection of Islamic names and their meanings. This was the period when blacks were actually giving their children names that stood for something, and I decided this could be my way of making a statement—giving my firstborn child a name that spoke to the times in which we were living.

6   The name Shaquille stuck in my mind immediately because it meant "little one," and the middle name I gave him, Rashaun, meant "warrior." I liked the idea of my son being a warrior in a world that could be pretty harsh, particularly toward African Americans. Since his father had abandoned his parental responsibilities, my firstborn and I were both going to have to be true warriors together in order to survive.

WRITING IN RESPONSE TO READING

Examining the Reading Using an Idea Map   MyWritingLab

Review the reading by completing the missing parts of the idea map shown below.

 Visualize It! →

Title   **The Little Warrior**

Thesis   Lucille O'Neal has a special bond with her oldest son, Shaquille.

The circumstances surrounding his birth were tough.

She named him Shaquille and always calls him that.

She gave all her children Muslim names to _____

_____

When her son was born in 1972, it was an exciting time for African Americans.

_____
_____

_____
_____

She wanted to make her mark on the world _____
_____

Divine intervention came unexpectedly.

She was attracted to the neighborhood mosque and its teachings.

_____
_____

She decided to give her firstborn a name that _____
_____

She chose the name Shaquille Rashaun.

Shaquille meant _____
_____

She liked the idea that her son was a warrior in a harsh world.

She and her son would be _____

Conclusion   Lucille O'Neal made a statement by giving her son a meaningful name.

Strengthening Your Vocabulary   MyWritingLab

Using the word's context, word parts, or a dictionary, write a brief definition of each of the following words as it is used in the reading.

1. interact (paragraph 1) _____

2. baffled (paragraph 2) _____

3. irked (paragraph 2) _____

4. garb (paragraph 3) _____

5. adage (paragraph 4) _____

Reacting to Ideas: Discussion and Journal Writing   MyWritingLab

Get ready to write about the reading by discussing the following:

1. How would you describe Lucille's relationship with her son?

2. How did Lucille respond to the strictness of her upbringing?

3. Why did Lucille consider it "divine intervention" when a mosque was built in her neighborhood?

4. Identify some of the descriptive words that were used in this reading. Which words have a strong emotional component or connotative meaning?

5. How does the photo of Shaquille playing basketball add to the story?

Paragraph Options   MyWritingLab

1. Have you ever experienced something like divine intervention? Write a paragraph describing what happened.

2. Write a paragraph describing a time when you felt like you had to become a warrior to survive.

Essay Options   MyWritingLab

3. Write an essay describing the household in which you grew up. How do you think your choices today are influenced by your upbringing?

4. To illustrate her point in paragraph. 3, the author mentions people and events that defined the times and signified a changing world. Write an essay describing some of the people and events that define the times you live in today.

■ ■ ■ ■

SELF-TEST SUMMARY

To test yourself, cover the Answer column with a sheet of paper and answer each question in the left column. Evaluate each of your answers as you work by sliding the paper down and comparing your answer with what is printed in the Answer column.

	QUESTION	ANSWER
Goal 1 Use prepositional phrases to add detail	What is a preposition?	A preposition links its object (a noun or pronoun) to the rest of the sentence. Prepositions often show time, place, direction, or manner.
Goal 2 Use *-ing* phrases to add detail	How do *-ing* phrases add detail to sentences?	An *-ing* phrase begins with the *-ing* verb form and acts as an adjective to modify a noun or pronoun. You can also use *-ing* phrases to combine ideas from two sentences into one.
Goal 3 Use relative (*who, which, that*) clauses to add detail	What are relative clauses?	Clauses that begin with *who, which,* or *that* are called relative clauses because they relate one idea to another. The pronoun *who* refers to people, *which* refers to things, and *that* refers to people or things. *Who, which,* and *that* clauses usually come directly after the words they relate to.

MyWritingLab   *Visit Ch. 8 Using Modifiers to Add Detail in MyWritingLab to test your understanding of the chapter objectives.*

WRITERS' WORKSHOPS: Using Language Effectively

WRITERS' WORKSHOP

6

DON'T (-_-) BE (^_^) (TRANSLATION: DON'T WORRY, BE HAPPY)

Convey Your Feelings with Words, Not Emoticons

The smiley ☺ and sad ☹ faces you see all over e-mail and text messages are called **emoticons**, and they play an important role in electronic communication. In face-to-face conversations, you can watch people's faces, and listen to their tone of voice, to understand if they are joking. Without these visual and verbal cues, a joke may be misunderstood. Emoticons developed as a way of indicating tone through images on the computer screen.

Emoticons are never appropriate in college or business writing. Their use implies that the writer is unable to convey his or her feelings through words. Think of it this way: if you need to use an emoticon, you have not expressed your thoughts effectively.

Inappropriate/Ineffective: I'm not feeling so great after flunking that test. ☹

Appropriate/Effective: I am feeling depressed after failing that test.

Inappropriate/Ineffective: The Cowboys won the Super Bowl!!!!!☺☺☺☺☺

Appropriate/Effective: I am overjoyed. The Cowboys won the Super Bowl!

Note also that one piece of punctuation is enough; never use multiple exclamation points or question marks in formal writing.

➡ TRY IT OUT!

Directions: Rewrite each sentence in formal English.

1. The Democrats were bummed that they lost control of the Senate. ☹

   _____

2. Madame Curie must have wondered why she was feeling so sick after she discovered uranium ????

   _____

   _____

3. I am totally looking forward to my vacation!!!!!

   _____

   _____

4. My sister is my favorite sibling, but my brother gives me money when I need it. ☺

_____

_____

5. Howard Stern's autobiography is hilarious. ROFL ☺

_____

_____

■

WRITERS' WORKSHOP

7

86 THE SLANG, OK?

Write in Standard English

Slang is a set of informal, casual expressions used by a group of people. Many groups have their own slang. Hip-hop artists and their fans sometimes use the term _benjamins_ to refer to $100 bills (because Benjamin Franklin's portrait appears on the bill). Skateboarders will say something is _sick_ when they think it's cool.

Slang is colorful, expressive, fun, and funny. It shows the living and evolving nature of language, and it often creates feelings of friendship and camaraderie. It is not, however, appropriate for use in any formal writing in college or the workplace, which requires the use of **Standard English**.

Why? Because slang words are not understood by large portions of the population. Consider the title of this workshop. Did you know that "86" means "to get rid of"? Most likely you did not, because the slang term "86" was used by an older generation and is no longer used much. When you write, your goal is to communicate effectively with your readers regardless of their age, gender, or any other category. That's why you need to use Standard English, which everyone understands.

Slang: Jay has a sketchy board, but he can do some sick tricks.

Standard: My friend Jay has a beat-up skateboard, but he can do really impressive tricks with it.

Slang: My bro is always _buggin'_. I wish he'd just _marinate_.

Standard: My brother is always nervous about something. I wish he'd just relax.

You know what is slang and what isn't. If you're not sure, you can decide by asking yourself: Would my parents know what this means? Would my teacher? Would I use this word in a job interview?

➡ TRY IT OUT!

Directions: Rewrite each sentence, converting the slang into Standard English. If you don't understand the slang, check its meaning at http://www.urbandictionary.com.

1. I need to get the 411 on that car before I decide to buy it.

_____

_____

2. In Jane Austen's novel *Emma*, Mr. Knightley does a major smackdown on Emma Woodhouse.

    _____

    _____

3. Of all the people in America with the most dough, Bill Gates is #1.

    _____

    _____

4. The nutritionist told me to chill on the french fries and eat rabbit food instead.

    _____

    _____

5. Bud had so much to drink at the party he was yacking all night.

    _____

    _____

WRITERS' WORKSHOP

8

STOP BEATING A DEAD HORSE

Avoid Trite Expressions and Clichés

Have you ever had a friend who says the same thing over and over again? In writing, a cliché is the equivalent of hearing the same boring words so often that you tune out.

Clichés, sometimes known as *trite expressions*, are words, phrases, and sayings that are used so often that they've become stale. They hurt your writing by making it seem lazy and bland. The following are some clichés you probably have heard or used:

add insult to injury	hit the nail on the head
all work and no play	raining cats and dogs
better late than never	singing the blues
easier said than done	strong as an ox
face the music	work like a dog

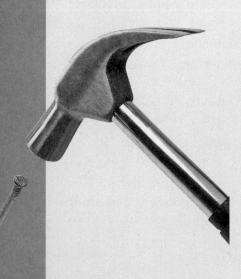

Trite expressions like these take the place of original, specific, meaningful descriptions in your writing. When you use a cliché, you have lost a chance to convey a fresh, precise impression. In the following examples, note that the revised version gives much more complete information.

Trite: I worked like a dog to finish my writing assignment.

Revised: I worked until midnight every night last week to finish my writing assignment.

Trite: He smokes like a chimney.

Revised: He smokes two packs of Marlboro Lights a day.

Rewriting clichés is fun. Rethinking them makes you re-visualize them and use words that convey a better mental picture.

→ **TRY IT OUT!**

Directions: Rewrite the following cliché-ridden sentences to give them fresh meaning. Feel free to add descriptions and further details!

1. The trainer at my gym is fit as a fiddle.

   _____

   _____

2. If there's one thing I've learned about clichés, it's that you should avoid them like the plague.

   _____

   _____

3. When push comes to shove, Mr. Pearson always has your back.

   _____

   _____

4. You need an umbrella; it's raining cats and dogs out there!

   _____

   _____

5. Have you ever noticed that people who gossip want you to keep their secrets, but they're always the first to let the cat out of the bag?

   _____

   _____

WRITERS' WORKSHOP

9

STOP REPEATING YOURSELF AND ELIMINATE REDUNDANCY

Say It Once, Effectively

Have you ever known someone who takes way too long to tell a story? The person suffering from **wordiness** uses more words than necessary to get to the point.

Wordiness can be a problem in writing, too. Wordy writers mistakenly believe that more words are better. But the opposite is often true: the clearest writing is short, concise, and sharp.

> **Wordy:** The *rushed and pressured nature of nursing is due to the fact* that hospitals lack adequate staff.

> **Concise:** Nurses are rushed and pressured because hospitals lack adequate staff.

To eliminate wordiness:

1. Look for words that do not add meaning, and eliminate them. You may need to rearrange the words in your sentence, as in the above example.

2. Eliminate empty words and phrases.

Do you need all these words . . .	When you can instead say . . .
spell out in detail	explain
the only difference being that	except
it is clear that	clearly
in the vicinity of	near
on the grounds that	because
for the reason that	because
at this point in time	now

3. Avoid saying the same thing twice in two different ways (redundancy).

square in shape	square [square is a shape]
mental attitude	attitude [the only type of attitude is a mental one]
the year 2009	2009 [2009 is a year]

→ TRY IT OUT!

Directions: Rewrite each sentence, eliminating redundancy and unnecessary words.

1. The "Corn Cob Towers" in Chicago are apartment buildings that are round in shape.

   _____

   _____

2. At this stage of the game, Lady Gaga is one of the most popular singers in the United States.

   _____

   _____

3. Stop walking immediately and instantaneously.

   _____

   _____

4. I decided to take the introductory psychology course in my first semester of college for the reason that I am giving thought to majoring in the discipline of psychology.

   _____

   _____

5. I am sorry to report that my daughter is sick and is not feeling well.

   _____

   _____

WRITERS' WORKSHOP

10

LET EVERYONE INTO YOUR WRITING

Avoiding Sexist Language

The goal of writing is to communicate with as many people as possible: therefore, it is important to use language that includes both women and men. Using gender-specific, or sexist, language can prevent some people from feeling that they are part of the intended audience, or even make them feel excluded. (For more on audience, review Chapter 11, pp.271–272.) Also, by using certain expressions and pronouns, you may unintentionally make unfair statements or offend your readers.

Sexist: A student will get good grades if *he* knows how to take good lecture notes. (This statement fails to recognize that many students are women.)

Nonsexist: A student will get good grades if *he or she* knows how to take good lecture notes. OR *Students* will get good grades if *they* know how to take good lecture notes.

Sexist: The *girl* at the customer service desk was helpful and efficient. (The term *girl* implies childishness, immaturity, and perhaps condescension.)

Nonsexist: The *customer service rep* was helpful and efficient. OR The *woman* at the customer service desk was helpful and efficient.

Sexist: The *male nurse* gave my grandmother the prescribed medications. (This statement makes an unnecessary distinction between male and female nurses. The nurse's sex doesn't matter.)

Nonsexist: The *nurse* gave my grandmother the prescribed medications.

Here are a few guidelines to help you to avoid sexist language:

1. When referring to people in general, rewrite your sentence using the phrase *he or she*, *she or he*, or plural nouns.

   Sexist: A writer should proofread *his* paper.

   Nonsexist: A writer should proofread *her or his* paper.
   Writers should proofread *their* papers.

2. Avoid using the words *man* or *mankind* to refer to people in general. Also avoid occupational terms ending in *-man*.

Sexist	**Nonsexist**
any man who gives . . .	anyone who gives . . .
policeman	police officer
salesman	salesperson

3. Avoid expressions that make negative or unfair references to men or women.

Sexist	**Nonsexist**
my old man	my husband
career gal	career-oriented woman

4. Refer to a woman by her own name, not by her husband's name.

   Sexist: Mrs. Samuel Goldstein was named Educator of the Year.

   Nonsexist: Rita Goldstein was named Educator of the Year.

5. When possible, use a term that includes both men and women.

Rather than using . . .	Use . . .
actress	actor
stewardess	flight attendant
waitress	server

The key to wring in an inclusive, nonsexist way is to remain focused on your audience. By not excluding people from your writing, you are inviting them into it.

→ TRY IT OUT!

Directions: Rewrite each sentence to eliminate sexism or phrases that might exclude certain readers. Convert any slang into Standard English.

1. As your candidate for governor, my goal is to represent the interests of all men in the state.

_____

_____

2. The chick at the DMV was way rude.

_____

_____

3. A doctor should always turn off his cell phone before he sees a patient.

_____

_____

4. Mrs. Bill Clinton, sometimes known as Hillary, was highly regarded in her role as secretary of state.

_____

_____

5. The stewardess poured the coffee into my lap before going ballistic and jumping out of the airplane.

_____

_____

Part III
COMMON
SENTENCE
PROBLEMS
AND HOW TO
AVOID THEM

9

Revising Confusing and Inconsistent Sentences

Learning Goals

In this chapter, you will learn how to

GOAL 1 Use pronouns clearly and correctly

GOAL 2 Avoid shifts in person, number, and verb tense

GOAL 3 Avoid misplaced and dangling modifiers

GOAL 4 Use parallelism

WRITE ABOUT IT!

The situation shown in the photo does not "seem right." Inconsistencies in your writing can also make it seem "not right" or confusing. Here are a few examples from a book titled *Anguished English* by Richard Lederer that show how errors create confusion and sometimes unintentional humor.

1. We do not tear your clothing with machinery. We do it carefully by hand.

2. Have several very old dresses from grandmother in beautiful condition.

3. Tired of cleaning yourself? Let me do it.

Sometimes sentence errors create unintentional humor, as in Lederer's examples. Most often, though, they distract or confuse your reader. They may also convey the impression that you have not taken time to check and polish your work. In this chapter you will learn to avoid several common types of sentence errors.

WRITING

USING PRONOUNS CLEARLY AND CORRECTLY

GOAL 1 Use pronouns clearly and correctly

A **pronoun** is a word that substitutes for, or refers to, a noun or another pronoun. *I, you, he, she, it, we, they, his, mine, yours, who,* and *whom* are all examples of pronouns. The noun or pronoun to which a pronoun refers is called the pronoun's **antecedent.** To use pronouns correctly, you need to make sure that the antecedent of the pronoun (your pronoun reference) is clear to your reader and that the pronoun and antecedent agree in number (singular or plural) and in gender.

Pronoun Reference

If your pronoun reference is unclear, your sentence may be confusing and difficult to follow. Note the confusing nature of the following sentences:

> The aerobics instructor told the student that *she* made a mistake. [Who made the mistake?]

> *They* told Kevin that he was eligible for a Visa card. [Who told Kevin?]

> Aaron bought a bowling ball at the garage sale *that* he enjoyed. [Did Aaron enjoy the garage sale or the bowling ball?]

The following suggestions will help you make sure that all your pronoun references are clear:

1. **Make sure there is only one possible antecedent for each pronoun.** The antecedent (the word to which the pronoun refers) comes before the pronoun (*ante-* means "before") in the sentence. The reader should not be left wondering what the antecedent of any given pronoun is.

UNCLEAR	The father told the child that *he* was sunburned.
REVISED	The father told the child, "I am sunburned."

2. **Avoid using vague pronouns that lack an antecedent.** *They* and *it* are often mistakenly used this way.

UNCLEAR	*They* told me my loan application needs a cosigner.
REVISED	The loan officer told me my loan application needs a cosigner.

3. **Eliminate unnecessary pronouns.** If a sentence is clear without a pronoun, delete the pronoun.

UNCLEAR	The manager, *he* says that the store will close at midnight.
REVISED	The manager says that the store will close at midnight.

4. **Always place the pronoun as close as possible to its antecedent.**

UNCLEAR	Lucia saw a dress at the mall *that* she wanted.
REVISED	At the mall, Lucia saw a dress that she wanted.

5. **Use the pronoun *you* only if you are directly addressing the reader.**

UNCLEAR	*You* need daily exercise to keep physically fit.
REVISED	Everyone needs daily exercise to keep physically fit.

Tip for Writers

Don't write both a noun and a pronoun for the same subject.

INCORRECT My teacher she is very tall.

CORRECT My teacher is very tall. (or) She is very tall.

EXERCISE 9-1   Correcting Pronoun Reference Errors

Directions: Revise each of the following sentences to correct problems in pronoun reference.

EXAMPLE   The glass, ~~it~~ ^was^ filled to the rim.

1. You should try to be honest at all times.

2. When I bought the shirt, I told him that I would pay with my credit card.

3. Jamal told Rob he had received an A in the course.

4. James talked with Bill because he did not know anyone else at the party.

5. The teachers told the school board members, that they needed more preparation time.

6. The board of directors, they decided that the company would have to declare bankruptcy.

7. The gallery owner hung a painting on the wall that was blue.

8. They sent our grades at the end of the semester.

9. The Constitution says you have the right to bear arms.

10. They filled the parking lot on Sunday. ■

EXERCISE 9-2   Revising Sentences

Directions: Revise each of the following sentences to correct problems in pronoun reference. If a sentence contains no errors, write *Correct* beside it.

EXAMPLE   ~~It~~ ^The professor's note^ said that the grades would be posted on Tuesday.

_____ 1. On the bulletin board it says there will be a fire drill today.

_____ 2. Laverne and Louise they pooled their money to buy a new CD player.

_____ 3. They said on the news that the naval base will be shut down.

_____ 4. The street that was recently widened is where I used to live.

_____ 5. Ivan sat on the couch in the living room that he bought yesterday.

_____ 6. "Sarah," the tutor advised, "you should underline in your textbooks for better comprehension."

_____ 7. Christina handed Maggie the plate she had bought at the flea market.

_____ 8. Bridget found the cake mix in the aisle with the baking supplies that she needed for tonight's dessert.

_____ 9. Rick told Larry, he was right.

_____ 10. It said in the letter that my payment was late. ■

EXERCISE 9-3
Writing in Progress

Writing a Paragraph

Directions: Write a paragraph on one of the following topics. After you have written your first draft, reread it to be certain your pronoun references are clear. Make corrections if needed.

1. A recent clothing fad
2. Advice columns
3. Horoscopes
4. Remembering names
5. An extreme weather condition (heat wave, storm, blizzard, flood) that you lived through ■

Pronoun-Antecedent Agreement

A pronoun must "agree" with its antecedent—that is, a pronoun must have the same number (singular or plural) as the noun or pronoun it refers to or replaces. Singular nouns and pronouns refer to one person, place, or thing; plural nouns and pronouns refer to more than one.

Always check your sentences for pronoun-antecedent agreement.

	plural singular
INCORRECT	The dogs are in its kennels.
REVISED	The dogs are in their kennels.

	plural singular
INCORRECT	Marcia and Megan called all her friends about the party.
REVISED	Marcia and Megan called all their friends about the party.

Use the following guidelines to make sure the pronouns you use agree with their antecedents:

1. **Use singular pronouns with singular nouns.**

   singular noun   singular pronoun

   Teresa sold her bicycle.

2. **Use plural pronouns with plural nouns.**

   plural noun   plural pronoun

   The neighbors always shovel their walks when it snows.

3. **Use a plural pronoun to refer to a compound antecedent joined by *and* unless both parts of the compound refer to the same person, place, or thing.**

plural antecedent   plural pronoun

Mark and Keith bought their concert tickets.

singular antecedent   singular pronoun

The pitcher and team captain broke her ankle.

4. **When antecedents are joined by *or, nor, either . . . or, neither . . . nor, not . . . but,* or *not only . . . but also,* the pronoun agrees in number with the nearer antecedent.**

plural noun   plural pronoun

Either the professor or the students will present their views.

Note: When one antecedent is singular and the other is plural, avoid awkwardness by placing the plural antecedent second in the sentence.

AWKWARD   Neither the salespersons nor the manager has received his check.

REVISED   Neither the manager nor the salespersons have received their checks.

5. **Avoid using *he, him,* or *his* to refer to general, singular words such as *child, person, everyone.* These words exclude females. Use *he or she, him or her,* or *his or hers,* or rewrite your sentence to use a plural antecedent and a plural pronoun that do not indicate gender.**

INCORRECT   A person should not deceive his friends.

REVISED   A person should not deceive his or her friends.

BETTER   People should not deceive their friends.

6. **With collective nouns (words that refer to a group of people, such as *army, class, congregation, audience*), use a singular pronoun to refer to the noun when the group acts as a unit.**

The audience showed its approval by applauding.

The team chose its captain.

Use a plural pronoun to refer to the noun when each member of the group acts individually.

The family exchanged their gifts.

The team changed their uniforms.

To avoid using a plural verb or pronoun after a collective noun, write "the members of the team," which gives you a plural subject (members).

▮ EXERCISE 9-4   Correcting Agreement Errors

Directions: Revise each of the following sentences to correct errors in pronoun-antecedent agreement.

> *he or she*
> EXAMPLE   Usually when a driver has been caught speeding, ~~they~~ readily
> admit the mistake.

1. Each gas station in town raised their prices in the past week.

2. Neither the waitress nor the hostess received their paycheck from the restaurant.

3. The committee put his or her signatures on the document.

4. An infant recognizes their parents within the first few weeks of life.

5. The Harris family lives by his or her own rules.

6. Lonnie and Jack should put his ideas together and come up with a plan of action.

7. An employee taking an unpaid leave of absence may choose to make their own health-insurance payments.

8. The amount of time a student spends researching a topic depends, in part, on their familiarity with the topic.

9. Alex and Susana lost her way while driving through the suburbs of Philadelphia.

10. Neither the attorney nor the protesters were willing to expose himself to public criticism. ■

Agreement with Indefinite Pronouns

Indefinite pronouns (such as *some, everyone, any, each*) are pronouns without specific antecedents. They refer to people, places, or things in general. When an indefinite pronoun is an antecedent for another pronoun, mistakes in pronoun agreement often result. Use the following guidelines to make your pronouns agree with indefinite pronoun antecedents:

1. **Use singular pronouns to refer to indefinite pronouns that are singular in meaning.**

another	either	nobody	other
anybody	everybody	no one	somebody
anyone	everyone	nothing	someone
anything	everything	one	something
each	neither		

singular antecedent   singular pronoun

Someone left his dress shirt in the locker room.

singular antecedent   singular compound pronoun

Everyone in the office must pick up his or her paycheck.

Note: To avoid the awkwardness of *his or her*, use plural antecedents and pronouns.

plural antecedent   plural pronoun

Office workers must pick up their paychecks.

2. **Use a plural pronoun to refer to indefinite pronouns that are plural in meaning.**

both   few   many   More   several

plural antecedent   plural pronoun

Both of the police officers said that as far as they could tell, no traffic violations had occurred.

3. **The indefinite pronouns *all*, *any*, *more*, *most*, and *some* can be singular or plural, depending on how they are used.** If the indefinite pronoun refers to something that cannot be counted, use a singular pronoun to refer to it. If the indefinite pronoun refers to two or more of something that can be counted, use a plural pronoun to refer to it.

Most of the students feel they can succeed.

Most of the air on airplanes is recycled repeatedly, so it becomes stale.

NEED TO KNOW

Pronouns

- **Pronouns** substitute for, or refer to, nouns or other pronouns.

- The noun or pronoun to which a pronoun refers is called its **antecedent**.

- Make sure that it is always clear to which noun or pronoun a pronoun refers.

- A pronoun must agree with its antecedent in number (singular or plural) and gender. Singular nouns and pronouns refer to one thing; plural nouns and pronouns refer to more than one.

- **Indefinite pronouns** are pronouns without specific antecedents. Follow the rules given in this chapter to make indefinite pronouns agree with their antecedents.

EXERCISE 9-5   Correcting Pronoun-Antecedent Errors

Directions: Revise each of the following sentences to correct errors in pronoun-antecedent agreement.

EXAMPLE	No one could remember their student number.
REVISED	No one could remember his or her student number.
BETTER	The students could not remember their student numbers.

1. Someone left their jacket in the car.

2. Everything Todd said was true, but I did not like the way he said them.

3. In my math class, everyone works at their own pace.

4. When someone exercises, they should drink plenty of liquids.

5. No one should be forced into a curriculum that they do not want.

6. No one will receive their exam grades before Friday.

7. Many of the club members do not pay his or her dues on time.

8. Both of the cooks used her own secret recipes.

9. No one was successful on their first attempt to run the race in less than two hours.

10. Each of the workers brought their own tools. ■

EXERCISE 9-6   Correcting Agreement Errors

Directions: Revise the sentences below that contain agreement errors. If a sentence contains no errors, write *Correct* beside it.

EXAMPLE   Somebody dropped their ring down the drain. *(his or her)*

_____ 1. Many of the residents of the neighborhood have had their homes tested for radon.

_____ 2. Each college instructor established their own grading policies.

_____ 3. The apples fell from its tree.

_____ 4. Anyone may enter their painting in the contest.

_____ 5. All the engines manufactured at the plant have their vehicle identification numbers stamped on them.

_____ 6. No one requested that the clerk gift wrap their package.

_____ 7. Either Professor Judith Marcos or her assistant, Maria, graded the exams, writing their comments in the margins.

_____ 8. James or his parents sails the boat every weekend.

_____ 9. Most classes were not canceled because of the snowstorm; it met as regularly scheduled.

_____ 10. Not only Ricky but also the Carters will take his children to Disneyland this summer. ■

EXERCISE 9-7   Revising a Paragraph
Writing in Progress

Directions: Reread the paragraph you wrote for Exercise 9-3 to be certain that there are no errors in pronoun-antecedent agreement. Revise as needed. ■

AVOIDING SHIFTS IN PERSON, NUMBER, AND VERB TENSE

GOAL 2 Avoid shifts in person, number, and verb tense

The parts of a sentence should be consistent. Shifts in person, number, or verb tense within a sentence make it confusing and difficult to read.

Shifts in Person

Person is the grammatical term used to identify the speaker or writer (**first person:** *I, we*), the person spoken to (**second person:** *you*), and the person or thing spoken about (**third person:** *he, she, it, they,* or any noun, such as *Joan, children*). Be sure to refer to yourself, your audience (or readers), and people you are writing about in a consistent way throughout your sentence or paragraph.

In the following paragraph, note how the writer shifts back and forth when addressing her audience:

> A <u>person</u> should know how to cook. <u>You</u> can save a lot of money if <u>you</u> make your own meals instead of eating out. <u>One</u> can also eat more healthily at home if <u>one</u> cooks according to principles of good nutrition.

Here the writer shifts from sentence to sentence, first using the indefinite phrase *a person,* then the more personal *you,* then the more formal *one.*

In the next paragraph, the writer shifts when referring to himself.

> Arizona has many advantages for year-round living, so <u>I</u> am hoping to move there when <u>I</u> graduate. One reason <u>I</u> want to live in Arizona is that <u>you</u> never need to shovel snow.

In this paragraph, the writer shifts from the direct and personal *I* to the indirect and more general *you.*

To avoid making shifts in references to yourself and others, decide before you begin to write how you will refer to yourself, to your audience, and to those about whom you are writing. Base your decision on whether you want your paragraph to be direct and personal or more formal. In academic writing, most instructors prefer that you avoid using the personal pronoun *I* and try to write in a more formal style.

PERSONAL	I want to live in Florida for a number of reasons.
MORE FORMAL	Living in Florida is attractive for a number of reasons.
PERSONAL	I have difficulty balancing school and a part-time job.
MORE FORMAL	Balancing school and a part-time job is difficult.

Shifts in Number

Number distinguishes between singular and plural. A pronoun must agree in number with its antecedent. Related nouns within a sentence must also agree in number.

SHIFT	All the <u>women</u> wore a <u>dress</u>.
CONSISTENT	All the <u>women</u> wore <u>dresses</u>.

EXERCISE 9-8   Correcting Shift in Person Errors

Directions: Revise each of the following sentences to correct shifts in person or number.

> **EXAMPLE**   I perform better on exams if the professor doesn't hover over ~~you~~ *me*.

1. Each student has to plan their schedules for the semester.

2. Eva said she doesn't want to go to the wedding because you would have to bring a gift.

3. In some states, continuing education is required for doctors or lawyers; after you pass the board or bar exam, you are required to take a specified number of credits per year in brush-up courses.

4. Construction workers must wear a hard hats.

5. I swim with a life vest on because you could drown without it.

6. A good friend is always there when you need them most.

7. The first and second relay racers discussed his strategies.

8. I always tell yourself to think before acting.

9. Patients often expect their doctors to have all the answers, but you should realize doctors are not miracle workers.

10. Each giraffe stretched their neck to reach the leaves in the trees. ■

Shifts in Verb Tense

Tip for Writers

When the main clause is in a future tense, the verb in the dependent time clause is put in the present tense even though the entire sentence is about the future.

Use the same verb tense (past, present, future, etc.) throughout a sentence and paragraph unless meaning requires you to make a shift.

                             present   future

REQUIRED SHIFT   After the moon <u>rises</u>, we <u>will go</u> for a moonlight swim.

Incorrect shifts in verb tense can make a sentence confusing. One of the most common incorrect shifts is between present and past tenses.

                                   past   present

INCORRECT   After Marguerite <u>joined</u> the food co-op, she <u>seems</u> healthier.

                                   past   past

CORRECT   After Marguerite <u>joined</u> the food co-op, she <u>seemed</u> healthier.

NEED TO KNOW

Shifts in Person, Number, and Verb Tense

- *Person* is a term used to identify the speaker or writer (**first person**: *I*, *we*), the person spoken to (**second person**: *you*), and the person or thing spoken about (**third person**: *he, she, it, they*, or any noun, such as *desk* or *Robert*).

- Be sure to use a consistent person throughout a piece of writing.

- **Number** distinguishes between singular and plural. A pronoun must agree in number with its antecedent.

- **Verb tense** is the form of a verb that indicates whether the action or state of being that the verb tells about occurs in the past, present, or future. Unless there is a specific reason to switch tenses, be sure to use a consistent tense throughout a piece of writing.

EXERCISE 9-9   **Correcting Shift in Verb Tense Errors**

Directions: Revise each of the following sentences to correct shifts in verb tense.

                                    waited

    EXAMPLE   I ~~was waiting~~ for the hailstorm to end, and then I dashed into the restaurant.

1. In the morning, the factory workers punch in, but have not punched out at night.

2. José looked muscular; then he joined a gym and looks even more so.

3. I run two miles, and then I rested.

4. Quinne called me but hangs up on my answering machine.

5. Until I took physics, I will not understand the laws of aerodynamics.

6. While the rain fell, the campers take shelter in their tent.

7. Because the moon will be full, the tide was high.

8. Katie drives me to work, and I worked until 9:30 p.m.

9. Richard went to the mall because he need to buy a suit for his job interview.

10. The speaker stands at the podium and cleared his throat. ■

EXERCISE 9-10   Revising Sentences

Directions: Revise each of the following sentences to correct errors in shift of person, number, or verb tense. If a sentence contains no errors, write *Correct* beside it.

EXAMPLE   Boats along the river were tied to their ~~dock~~. *docks*

_____   1. When people receive a gift, you should be gracious and polite.

_____   2. When we arrived at the inn, the lights are on and a fire is burning in the fireplace.

_____   3. Before Trey drove to the cabin, he packs a picnic lunch.

_____   4. The artist paints portraits and weaves baskets.

_____   5. The lobsterman goes out on his boat each day and will check his lobster traps.

_____   6. All the cars Honest Bob sells have a new transmissions.

_____   7. Rosa ran the 100-meter race and throws the discus at the track meet.

_____   8. Public schools in Florida an have air-conditioning system.

_____   9. Office workers sat on the benches downtown and are eating their lunches outside.

_____   10. Before a scuba diver goes underwater, you must check and recheck your breathing equipment. ■

EXERCISE 9-11   Revising a Paragraph
Writing in Progress

Directions: Reread the paragraph you wrote for Exercise 9-3. Check for shifts in person, number, and verb tense. Revise as needed. ■

AVOIDING MISPLACED AND DANGLING MODIFIERS

GOAL 3 Avoid misplaced and dangling modifiers

A **modifier** is a word, phrase, or clause that describes, qualifies, or limits the meaning of another word. Modifiers that are not correctly placed can confuse your reader.

Types of Modifiers

The following list will help you review the main types of modifiers:

1. **Adjectives modify nouns and pronouns.**

   It is an interesting photograph.

   She is very kind.

2. **Adverbs modify verbs, adjectives, or other adverbs.**

   I walked quickly.

   The cake tasted very good.

   The flowers are very beautifully arranged.

3. **Prepositional phrases modify nouns, adjectives, verbs, or adverbs.**

   The woman in the green dress is stunning.

   They walked into the store to buy milk.

4. ***-ing* phrases modify nouns or pronouns.**

   Waiting for the bus, Joe studied his history notes.

5. **Dependent clauses modify nouns, adjectives, verbs, or adverbs.** (A dependent clause has a subject and verb but is incomplete in meaning.)

   After I left campus, I went shopping.

   I left because classes were canceled.

   The kitten that I found in the bushes was frightened.

Misplaced Modifiers

Placement of a modifier in a sentence affects meaning:

   I need only to buy Marcos a gift.

   Only I need to buy Marcos a gift.

   I need to buy only Marcos a gift.

If a modifier is placed so that it does not convey the meaning you intend, it is called a **misplaced modifier**. Misplaced modifiers can make a sentence confusing.

MISPLACED	Anthony found a necklace at the mall <u>that sparkled and glittered</u>. [Which sparkled and glittered—the mall or the necklace?]
MISPLACED	The president announced that the club picnic would be held on August 2 <u>at the beginning of the meeting</u>. [Is the picnic being held at the beginning of the meeting on August 2, or did the president make the announcement at the beginning of the meeting?]

You can avoid a misplaced modifier if you make sure that the modifier immediately precedes or follows the word it modifies.

CORRECT	Anthony found a necklace <u>that sparkled and glittered</u> at the mall.
CORRECT	The club president announced <u>at the beginning of the meeting</u> that the picnic would be held on August 2.

Dangling Modifiers

Dangling modifiers are words or phrases that do not clearly describe or explain any part of the sentence. Dangling modifiers create confusion and sometimes unintentional humor. To avoid dangling modifiers, make sure that each modifying phrase or clause has a clear antecedent.

DANGLING	<u>Uncertain of which street to follow</u>, the <u>map</u> indicated we should turn left. [The opening modifier suggests that the map was uncertain of which street to follow.]
CORRECT	<u>Uncertain of which street to follow</u>, <u>we</u> checked a map, which indicated we should turn left.
DANGLING	My <u>shoes</u> got wet <u>walking across the street</u>. [The modifier suggests that the shoes were walking across the street by themselves.]
CORRECT	My shoes got wet <u>as I crossed the street</u>.
DANGLING	<u>To pass the test</u>, careful review is essential. [Who will pass the test?]
CORRECT	<u>To pass the test</u>, I must review carefully.

There are two common ways to revise dangling modifiers.

1. **Add a word or words that the modifier clearly describes.** Place the new material immediately after the modifier, and rearrange other parts of the sentence as necessary.

DANGLING	<u>While walking in the garden</u>, <u>gunfire</u> sounded. [The opening modifier implies that the gunfire was walking in the garden.]
CORRECT	<u>While walking in the garden</u>, <u>Carol</u> heard gunfire.

2. **Change the dangling modifier to a dependent clause.** You may need to change the verb form in the modifier.

DANGLING	<u>While watching television</u>, the cake burned.
CORRECT	<u>While Pat was watching television</u>, the cake burned.

NEED TO KNOW

Misplaced and Dangling Modifiers

- A **modifier** is a word, phrase, or clause that describes, qualifies, or limits the meaning of another word.

- A **misplaced modifier** is placed so that it does not convey the intended meaning.

- To avoid misplaced modifiers, be sure that you place the modifier immediately before or after the word it modifies.

- A **dangling modifier** is a word or phrase that does not clearly describe or explain any part of the sentence.

- To revise a dangling modifier you can add a word or words that the modifier clearly describes, or change the dangling modifier to a dependent clause.

EXERCISE 9-12   Correcting Misplaced or Dangling Modifiers

Directions: Revise each of the following sentences to correct misplaced or dangling modifiers.

EXAMPLE   Jerome mailed a bill at the post office that was long overdue.

REVISED   At the post office, Jerome mailed a bill that was long overdue.

1. Running at top speed, dirt was kicked up by the horse.

   _____

   _____

2. Swimming to shore, my arms got tired.

   _____

   _____

3. The helmet on the soldier's head with a red circle represented his nationality.

   _____

   _____

4. In order to answer your phone, the receiver must be lifted.

   _____

   _____

5. Walking up the stairs, the book dropped and tumbled down.

   _____

   _____

6. Twenty-five band members picked their instruments up from chairs that were gleaming and began to play.

_____

7. Laughing, the cat chased the girl.

_____

_____

8. When skating, skate blades must be kept sharp.

_____

_____

9. The ball bounced off the roof that was round and red.

_____

_____

10. Ducking, the snowball hit Andy on the head.

_____

_____

EXERCISE 9-13   Correcting Misplaced or Dangling Modifiers

Directions: Revise each of the following sentences to correct misplaced or dangling modifiers.

EXAMPLE   Deciding which flavor of ice cream to order, another customer cut in front of Roger.

REVISED   While Roger was deciding which flavor of ice cream to order, another customer cut in front of him.

1. Tricia saw an animal at the zoo that had black fur and long claws.

_____

_____

2. Before answering the door, the phone rang.

_____

_____

3. I could see large snowflakes falling from the bedroom window.

_____

_____

4. Honking, Felicia walked in front of the car.

_____

_____

5. After leaving the classroom, the door automatically locked.

_____

_____

6. Applauding and cheering, the band returned for an encore.

_____

_____

7. The waiter brought a birthday cake to our table that had 24 candles.

_____

_____

8. Books lined the library shelves about every imaginable subject.

_____

_____

9. While sobbing, the sad movie ended and the lights came on.

_____

_____

10. Turning the page, the book's binding cracked.

_____

_____

EXERCISE 9-14   Revising a Paragraph

Writing in Progress

Directions: Reread the paragraph you wrote for Exercise 9-3. Check for dangling or misplaced modifiers. Revise as needed. ■

USING PARALLELISM

GOAL 4 Use parallelism

Study the following pairs of sentences. Which sentence in each pair reads more smoothly?

Pair 1
1. Seth, a long-distance biker, enjoys swimming and drag races cars.
2. Seth enjoys long-distance biking, swimming, and drag racing.

Pair 2
3. The dog was large, had a beautiful coat, and it was friendly.
4. The dog was large, beautiful, and friendly.

Do sentences 2 and 4 sound better than 1 and 3? Sentences 2 and 4 have balance. Similar words have similar grammatical form. In sentence 2, *biking*, *swimming*, and *drag racing* are all nouns ending in -*ing*. In sentence 4, *large*, *beautiful*, and *friendly* are all adjectives. The method of balancing similar elements within a sentence is called **parallelism**. Parallelism makes your writing smooth and makes your ideas easier to follow.

EXERCISE 9-15   Examining Parallelism

Directions: In each group of words, circle the element that is not parallel.

EXAMPLE   walking, running, (to jog,) dancing

1. intelligent, successful, responsibly, mature

2. happily, quickly, hurriedly, hungry

3. wrote, answering, worked, typed

4. to fly, parachutes, to skydive, to drive

5. were painting, drew, were carving, were coloring

6. sat in the sun, played cards, scuba diving, ate lobster

7. thoughtful, honestly, humorous, quick-tempered

8. rewrote my résumé, arranging interviews, buying a new suit, getting a haircut

9. buy stamps, cash check, dry cleaning, return library books

10. eating sensibly, eight hours of sleep, exercising, drinking a lot of water ■

What Should Be Parallel?

When you write, be sure to keep each of the following elements parallel:

1. **Nouns in a series**

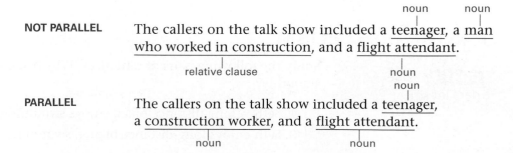

NOT PARALLEL   The callers on the talk show included a teenager, a man who worked in construction, and a flight attendant.

PARALLEL   The callers on the talk show included a teenager, a construction worker, and a flight attendant.

2. **Adjectives in a series**

		adjective	"-ing" phrase

NOT PARALLEL   The students in the class seemed <u>tired</u> and <u>not paying attention</u>.

		adjective	adjective

PARALLEL   The students in the class seemed <u>tired</u> and <u>inattentive</u>.

3. **Verbs in a series** (They should have the same tense.)

		simple past	past progressive

NOT PARALLEL   The couple <u>danced</u> and <u>were joking</u>.

		simple past	simple past

PARALLEL   The couple <u>danced</u> and <u>joked</u>.

4. **Clauses within sentences**

prepositional phrase

NOT PARALLEL   The students were angry <u>about the parking difficulties</u> and <u>that no one was concerned</u>.

dependent clause

dependent clause

PARALLEL   The students were angry <u>that it was difficult to park</u> and <u>that no one was concerned</u>.

dependent clause

5. **Items being compared or contrasted**

noun   infinitive phrase

NOT PARALLEL   <u>Honesty</u> is better than <u>to be dishonest</u>.

infinitive phrase   infinitive phrase

PARALLEL   It is better <u>to be honest</u> than <u>to be dishonest</u>.

noun   pronoun

NOT PARALLEL   The students wanted <u>parking spaces</u>, not <u>someone to feel sorry for them</u>.

infinitive phrase

noun   noun

PARALLEL   The students wanted <u>parking spaces</u>, not <u>sympathy</u>.

NEED TO KNOW

Parallelism

- **Parallelism** is a method of balancing similar elements within a sentence.

- The following elements of a sentence should be parallel: nouns in a series, adjectives in a series, verbs in a series, clauses within a sentence, and items being compared or contrasted.

EXERCISE 9-16   Correcting Parallelism Errors

Directions: Revise each of the following sentences to correct errors in parallel structure.

EXAMPLE   The instructor ~~was demanding~~ *demanded hard work* and insisted on high standards.

1. Accuracy is more important than being speedy.

2. The teller counted and recounts the money.

3. Newspapers are blowing away and scattered on the sidewalk.

4. Judith was pleased when she graduated and that she received an honors diploma.

5. Thrilled and exhausting, the runners crossed the finish line.

6. Our guest speakers for the semester are a radiologist, a student in medicine, and a hospital administrator.

7. Students shouted and were hollering at the basketball game.

8. We enjoyed seeing the Grand Canyon, riding a mule, and photography.

9. Laughing and relaxed, the co-workers enjoyed lunch at the Mexican restaurant.

10. Professor Higuera is well known for his humor, clear lecturing, and scholarship. ■

EXERCISE 9-17   Correcting Parallelism Errors

Directions: Revise each of the following sentences to achieve parallelism.

EXAMPLE   Rosa has decided to study nursing instead of ~~going into~~ accounting.

1. The priest baptized the baby and congratulates the new parents.

2. We ordered a platter of fried clams, a platter of corn on the cob, and fried shrimp.

3. Lucy entered the dance contest, but the dance was watched by June from the side.

4. Léon purchased the ratchet set at the garage sale and buying the drill bits there, too.

5. The exterminator told Brandon the house needed to be fumigated and spraying to eliminate the termites.

6. The bus swerved and hit the dump truck, which swerves and hit the station wagon, which swerved and hit the bicycle.

7. Channel 2 covered the bank robbery, but a python that had escaped from the zoo was reported by Channel 7.

8. Sal was born when Nixon was president, and Johnson was president when Rob was born.

9. The pediatrician spent the morning with sore throats, answering questions about immunizations, and treating bumps and bruises.

10. Belinda prefers to study in the library, but her brother Marcus studies at home. ■

EXERCISE 9-18   Revising a Paragraph
Writing in Progress

Directions: Reread the paragraph you wrote for Exercise 9-3. Correct any sentences that lack parallelism. ■

EXERCISE 9-19   Revising Sentences

Directions: Now that you have learned about common errors that produce confusing or inconsistent sentences, turn back to the confusing sentences used to introduce the chapter on page 207. Identify each error, and revise the sentences so they convey the intended meaning. ■

EXERCISE 9-20   Revising a Paragraph
Working Together

Directions: Working with a classmate, revise this student paragraph by correcting all instances of misplaced or dangling modifiers, shifts in verb tense, and faulty parallelism.

Robert Burns said that the dog is "man's best friend." To a large extent, this statement may be more true than you think. What makes dogs so special to humans is their unending loyalty and that they love unconditionally. Dogs have been known to cross the entire United States to return home. Unlike people, dogs never made fun of you or criticize you. They never throw fits, and they seem happy always to see you. This may not necessarily be true of your family, friends, and those who live near you. A dog never lies to you, never betrays your confidences, and never stayed angry with you for more than five minutes. Best of all, he or she never expects more than the basics from you of food and shelter and a simple pat on the head in return for his or her devotion. The world would be a better place if people could only be more like their dogs. ■

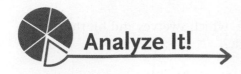 **Analyze It!** **Directions:** Revise any sentences in the paragraphs that contain errors in pronoun reference, shifts in person, number, or verb tense, or dangling or misplaced modifiers.

As a child growing up in Hawaii, and even as an adult, I would sit on the beach anywhere from Waiamea to Makupa or from Kaneohe to Waikiki and look out onto the horizon thinking that one day I would go beyond that horizon to see what was really out there. There were things happening in my life at that time that you would not believe. It was spinning out of control. I need to get away from it all and start over. I knew that I was the only one who would have the final say in the decision to sail beyond the horizon, to experience the thrill, test my endurance, and to turn it in a new direction. This would be my turning point; I would follow my heart and begin my journey at sea. My dream seemed unreachable. What are the chances that I would be given the opportunity to sail beyond the horizon? I had friends—both male and female—who had followed his or her dreams, but they all had people to help them. I had no one. As a student attending a community college, some information proved to be very valuable later on. While glancing through the college catalog, I found a course named Marine Technology. I was intrigued by the title of the class. Perhaps this might be the chance I was waiting for. Excitedly, I signed up for the class in hopes that it would help me to better my life and fulfill my lifelong dream.

Paragraph Writing Scenarios

Friends and Family

1. Think of a relative you were close to as a child. Write a paragraph about a time you did something together that made you laugh.

2. Write a paragraph that begins "I thought (choose a person) was my friend, but . . . ."

Classes and Campus Life

1. Think of a place on campus where you usually have to wait in line. Write a paragraph about that place, what you are waiting for, and how you feel about lines.

2. Some instructors allow food and drinks in class; others don't. Write a paragraph expressing your opinion on whether or not you should be allowed to eat in class.

Working Students

1. Write a paragraph about the worst day in your week. What makes this day more difficult than the others?

2. Write a paragraph describing the perfect day off.

Communities and Cultures

1. Think of a country you've never seen but would like to visit. Write a paragraph explaining why you would like to go there. Use your imagination and plenty of details to describe what appeals to you about this country.

2. Transportation varies from place to place. Bus or plane passengers, for example, form a community. Write a paragraph about a kind of transportation you use on a regular basis. What behaviors do you share with other passengers or drivers?

WRITING ABOUT A READING

In the following reading, the author discusses what happens to our discarded electronics.

Step 1: Preview the reading.

Step 2: Connect the reading to your own experience: What happens to your old cell phones and other electronic devices when you have finished using them?

Step 3: Read and respond to the questions in the margin.

THINK AS YOU READ

What does the title indicate about the author's attitude toward waste?

How effective in capturing the reader's attention is the first sentence?

Give an example of e-waste.

Does this information surprise you?

What type of support does the author use in this paragraph, and how effective is it?

WASTE WOES

Chris Jozefowicz

1   Matthew Gallagher has skeletons in his attic—and stuffed into a drawer. The 19-year-old from Louisville, Ky., is holding on to the skeletons of electronics past. His family has an old TV and a computer in the attic. Gallagher keeps an obsolete MP3 player and a collection of abandoned handheld games in a drawer. While the old electronics languish, Gallagher is dreaming of new gadgets. "Oh, I definitely want to upgrade," he says. He hopes to get a new smart phone and a laptop computer during his first year of college. So why keep the old stuff? "Subconsciously, I guess I think I'll use them again," admits Gallagher. But he rarely does. Instead, they pile up as electronic waste, or e-waste, inside the Gallagher house.

2   E-waste is junk with significant electronic components. "Basically, it is anything with a circuit board," says Barbara Kyle, the national coordinator for the Electronics TakeBack Coalition, an organization that fights e-waste. Electronic equipment contains chemicals that can be dangerous if people come in contact with them. Yet tons of electronics are thrown away each day. Some companies even ship e-waste to other countries, where it may be taken apart by people for little money and with a big risk of damage to their health. "The problem is growing exponentially," says Kyle. "Think about all the stuff we have that wasn't even around five years ago."

21st-Century Trash

3   Some consumers, such as the Gallagher family, hoard old equipment, but most electronics end up as part of the waste stream. In 2007, Americans discarded 2.5 million tons of TVs, cell phones, computers, and printers, according to the Environmental Protection Agency (EPA). Worldwide, people throw away 10 to 20 times as much each year. That's enough e-waste to fill a train that stretches around the globe.

4   A fraction of those electronics gets recycled. Greg Spears is vice president of American Industrial Services, an Indiana company involved in recycling e-waste. "We're seeing a lot of TVs because of the switch over to digital

TV last year," he says. Recyclers break down electronics and separate the plastic, metal, glass, and other parts to reuse. Spears estimates that 90 percent of appliances, such as TVs or computer monitors, can be recycled, but EPA figures suggest that more than 80 percent of electronics in the United States are not recycled. Some of those electronics end up in landfills close to home. Many more are shipped overseas—sometimes illegally—and left in huge e-waste dumps in Asia, Africa, and Latin America.

Passing the Problem

What do you expect the section titled "Passing the Problem" to be about?

5   Chemicals can leach into the ground, water, or air if e-waste is not disposed of properly. Professor Valerie Thomas studies recycling at the Georgia Institute of Technology in Atlanta. She says dangerous chemicals are the biggest problem related to e-waste. "E-waste contains chemicals that are toxic," Thomas says. "It can pollute if it goes into a landfill or **incinerator**,[1] and it can pollute if it is recycled because it has to be opened up."

Does the author approve of this means of disposal?

6   So why would other countries take dangerous waste? For money, of course. Spears says junk can often be shipped overseas for less money than it takes to dismantle and sell the parts in the United States. Poor people living in countries such as China or Ghana will then break apart the old electronics and sell the parts for a few dollars a day. Often, children work beside adults in the e-waste scrap yards. In most cases, laws to protect those workers are weak or nonexistent. "The electronics land in places where people earn next to nothing," Kyle says. "The system relies on low-wage workers to basically bash open electronics. People remove the metals and junk the rest. They burn the plastics. It's literally poisoning people."

What does the photograph below add to the reading?

7   Those old, thick TVs that are being replaced by flat-screen models can contain more than 5 pounds of lead in each screen. The lead may poison workers who break apart the TVs, and it often pollutes the environment around e-waste dumps. More than 80 percent of kids living in one e-waste recycling town in China had high levels of lead in their blood, according to a recent study. That's a huge health problem because elevated lead levels can damage nerves and kidneys, and slow bone and muscle growth. Lead is particularly dangerous for kids'

Will your discarded TV end up in a ditch in Ghana?   [1]**incinerator** a furnace for burning trash

brains, which are still developing. Additional studies have shown that people who live and work near e-waste dumps have high levels of other dangerous chemicals in their bodies, raising the risk for cancer and a range of other diseases.

Buyers Beware

8   To prevent e-waste pollution from spreading, people in countries that generate millions of tons of waste—such as the United States—must work to recycle responsibly. Many communities have e-waste recycling collections, but people still need to call the recycler to make sure their e-waste is not shipped overseas. Some large store chains offer free recycling for old electronics and batteries. Even the U.S. Postal Service runs a program that allows people to mail small electronics to a recycler free of charge.

9   Kyle and the Electronics TakeBack Coalition want the federal government to pass laws forbidding the export of e-waste to other nations. "We think manufacturers should take back and recycle our old products when we are done with them, and that the price of the products should include the cost of recycling," Kyle says. "Otherwise, people pay for it [with their health] in China." Consumers can also help solve e-waste problems by buying electronics made with fewer toxic chemicals. Everyone should keep some simple goals in mind to help reduce waste in their electronics, Thomas says. "People should ask themselves, 'Can I upgrade my old one instead of getting a new one? How long will this product last?'"

10   Young people buy and use so many electronic gadgets that they have the power to influence better e-waste practices. One such activist is Jennifer Roberts, who helped fight e-waste at the University of California (UC) in Santa Cruz, where she was recently a student. She helped create Toxic Free UC, a group that succeeded in inspiring the university to commit to buying electronics that are low in toxins and easy to recycle. "Students can make their own campaigns," Roberts says. "There has to be a grassroots campaign of consumers. People have to say, 'I'm not going to support your company if you are putting all these horrible chemicals in your computers and cell phones and not taking care of them at the end of their lives.'"

Are these solutions realistic and practical?

What is a grassroots campaign?

State the conclusion of the reading in one sentence.

WRITING IN RESPONSE TO READING

Examining the Reading Using an Idea Map   MyWritingLab

Review the reading by completing the missing parts of the idea map shown below.

Visualize It!

Title   **Waste Woes**

Thesis   Discarded electronics often become toxic waste at home and around the world.

E-waste is trash with electronic components.

_____

Americans discarded 2.5 million tons of electronics in 2007.

_____
_____

A fraction of electronics gets recycled.

Most appliances, including TVs and computers, can be recycled.

_____
_____

E-waste can release toxic chemicals into the ground, water, or air.

Other countries accept electronic waste for money.

_____
_____

_____
_____

_____
_____

Consumers can stop e-waste from spreading in several ways.

Work to recycle responsibly.

_____
_____

_____
_____

_____
_____

Conclusion   The author concludes with a call to action for consumers.

Strengthening Your Vocabulary   MyWritingLab

Using the word's context, word parts, or a dictionary, write a brief definition of each of the following words as it is used in the reading.

1. obsolete (paragraph 1) _____
2. languish (paragraph 1) _____
3. exponentially (paragraph 2) _____
4. hoard (paragraph 3) _____
5. leach (paragraph 5) _____
6. toxic (paragraph 5) _____
7. dismantle (paragraph 6) _____

Reacting to Ideas: Discussion and Journal Writing   MyWritingLab

Get ready to write about the reading by discussing the following:

1. What was the author's purpose in writing this article?
2. Why do you think some people hoard their old electronics? Why don't more people recycle their old electronics instead of just throwing them away?
3. Analyze the kinds of supporting evidence the author uses in this article. In your opinion, which types of evidence—opinions, facts, statistics, examples—were most persuasive?
4. What other photographs would be useful to add to the reading?

Paragraph Options   MyWritingLab

1. Did this article change your opinion about recycling your old electronics? Write a paragraph explaining why or why not.
2. Do you think the federal government should make it illegal to export e-waste to other countries? Write a paragraph explaining your answer.
3. Would you be willing to pay more for an electronic product if the price included the cost of recycling? Write a paragraph explaining why you think this is or is not a good idea.

Essay Options   MyWritingLab

4. The article describes the power of young people to create campaigns that influence e-waste policies. For what purpose or cause would you be willing to create a grassroots campaign? Write an essay explaining your answer.
5. Write an essay in the form of a letter to the editor of your newspaper, explaining the problem of e-waste and calling for specific actions on the part of consumers.
6. Write an essay examining the ways that you could reduce the amount of e-waste that you generate in your own life.

SELF-TEST SUMMARY

To test yourself, cover the Answer column with a sheet of paper and answer each question in the left column. Evaluate each of your answers as you work by sliding the paper down and comparing your answer with what is printed in the Answer column.

	QUESTION	ANSWER
Goal 1 Use pronouns clearly and correctly	What is a pronoun? How do you use pronouns correctly?	A pronoun is a word that substitutes for a noun or another pronoun, called the antecedent. Use pronouns correctly by making sure that your pronoun reference (the antecedent) is clear and that the pronoun and antecedent agree in number and gender.
Goal 2 Avoid shifts in person, number, and verb tense	What is meant by person, number, and verb tense?	Person identifies: • the speaker or writer (first person: *I, we*), • the person spoken to (second person: *you*), • the person or thing spoken about (third person: *he, she, they,* etc.). Number distinguishes between singular and plural. Verb tense is the form of the verb that indicates whether the action occurs in the past, present, or future.
Goal 3 Avoid misplaced and dangling modifiers	What is a modifier? How do you avoid misplaced and dangling modifiers?	A modifier is a word, phrase, or clause that describes, qualifies, or limits the meaning of another word. Avoid misplaced modifiers by making sure the modifier immediately precedes or follows the word it modifies. Avoid dangling modifiers by making sure each modifying phrase or clause has a clear antecedent.
Goal 4 Use parallelism	What is parallelism? What elements of a sentence should be parallel?	Parallelism is a method of balancing similar elements within a sentence. The elements of a sentence that should be parallel are: • nouns in a series, • adjectives in a series, • verbs in a series, • clauses within sentences, • items being compared or contrasted.

MyWritingLab *Visit Ch. 9 Revising Confusing and Inconsistent Sentences in MyWritingLab to test your understanding of the chapter objectives.*

10 Using Verbs Correctly

Learning Goals

In this chapter, you will learn how to

GOAL 1 Use verb tenses correctly

GOAL 2 Use irregular verbs correctly

GOAL 3 Avoid subject-verb agreement errors

GOAL 4 Use active instead of passive voice in most situations

"Then she's like, 'I gotta go,' and I'm like, 'Okay,' and she's like, 'Later,' and I'm like, 'Go already!'"

WRITE ABOUT IT!

Have you ever stopped to listen to the way people misuse verbs? Write a sentence evaluating this teenager's use of language.

Did you notice that, in this sentence, the speaker has used *like* instead of more interesting and descriptive verbs like *yelled, retorted, said, replied, snorted,* or *exclaimed*? Verbs are words that express action. Using them correctly is essential to good writing and can make the difference between something that is dull or difficult to read and something that is interesting or fun to read. In this chapter you will focus on forming verb tenses with regular and irregular verbs.

WRITING

USING VERB TENSES CORRECTLY

GOAL 1 Use verb tenses correctly

The primary function of verbs is to express action or a condition. However, verbs also indicate time. **Verb tenses** tell us whether an action takes place in the present, past, or future.

The three basic verb tenses are the **simple present**, **simple past**, and **simple future**. There are also nine other verb tenses in English. To review these tenses, see Part VII, "Reviewing the Basics," page **525**. Using verb tenses consistently (avoiding shifts in tense) is discussed in Chapter 9, on page 217.

There are two types of verbs: *regular* and *irregular*. The forms of **regular verbs** follow a standard pattern of endings; the forms of **irregular verbs** do not. The English language contains many more regular verbs than irregular verbs.

The Simple Present Tense

The **present tense** indicates action that is occurring at the time of speaking or describes regular, habitual action.

HABITUAL ACTION	Maria works hard.
ACTION AT TIME OF SPEAKING	I see a rabbit on the lawn.

In the **simple present tense**, the verb for first person (*I* or *we*), second person (*you*), or third-person plural (*they*) is the same as the infinitive; no ending is added. The verb for third-person singular subjects (noun or pronoun) must end in -*s*.

To most third-person singular infinitive verbs, just add -*s*. If the verb ends in -*s*, -*sh*, -*ch*, -*x*, or -*z*, add -*es* to make the third-person singular form. If the verb ends in a consonant plus -*y*, change the *y* to *i*, and then add -*es* (*I hurry, he hurries*). If the verb ends in a vowel plus -*y*, just add -*s*. (*I stay, he stays*).

Third-person singular subjects include the pronouns *he, she,* and *it* and all singular nouns (*a desk, the tall man*). In addition, uncountable nouns (*money, music, homework*, abstractions such as *beauty* and *happiness*, liquids, and so on) are followed by third-person singular verbs. (*Water is essential for life.*) Singular collective nouns, such as *family, orchestra, team,* and *class*, also usually take a third-person singular verb since they refer to one group.

SIMPLE PRESENT TENSE

Singular		Plural	
Subject	*Verb*	*Subject*	*Verb*
I	like	we	like
you	like	you	like
he, she, it	likes	they	like
Sam	likes	Sam and Brenda	like

In speech we often use nonstandard verb forms, and these are perfectly acceptable in informal conversation. However, these nonstandard forms are *not* used in college writing or in career writing.

In the examples on the next page, note the nonstandard forms of the verb *lift* and the way these forms differ from the correct, standard forms that you should use in your writing.

NONSTANDARD PRESENT	STANDARD PRESENT
Singular	*Singular*
I lifts	I lift
you lifts	you lift
she (he) lift	she (he) lifts
Plural	*Plural*
we lifts	we lift
you lifts	you lift
they lifts	they lift

EXERCISE 10-1   Identifying Verb Forms

Directions: The sentences below are in the simple present tense. First, underline the subject or subjects in each sentence. Then circle the correct verb form.

    EXAMPLE   <u>Sal</u> (pick, (picks)) apples.

1. Planes (take, takes) off from the runway every five minutes.

2. I (enjoy, enjoys) sailing.

3. She (own, owns) a pet bird.

4. We (climb, climbs) the ladder to paint the house.

5. Engines (roar, roars) as the race begins.

6. They always (answer, answers) the phone on the first ring.

7. That elephant (walk, walks) very slowly.

8. You (speak, speaks) Spanish fluently.

9. He (say, says) his name is Luis.

10. Dinosaur movies (scare, scares) me. ■

EXERCISE 10-2   Using the Present Tense

Directions: For each of the following verbs, write a sentence using the simple present tense. Use a noun or *he, she, it,* or *they* as the subject of the sentence.

    EXAMPLE   prefer   *Art prefers to sit in the front of the bus.*

1. call _____

2. request _____

3. laugh _____

4. grow _____

5. hide _____

    ■

The Simple Past Tense

The **past tense** refers to action that was completed in the past. To form the **simple past tense** of regular verbs, add -*d* or -*ed* to the verb. Note that with the simple past tense, the verb form does not change with person or number.

SIMPLE PAST TENSE

Singular		Plural	
Subject	*Verb*	*Subject*	*Verb*
I	worked	we	worked
you	worked	you	worked
he, she, it	worked	they	worked
Sam	worked	Sam and Brenda	worked

In nonstandard English, the -*d* or -*ed* is often dropped. You may hear "Last night I work all night" instead of "Last night I work*ed* all night." In written English, be sure to include the -*d* or -*ed* ending.

The Simple Future Tense

The **future tense** refers to action that *will* happen in the future. Form the **simple future tense** by adding the helping verb *will* before the verb. Note that the verb form does not change with person or number.

SIMPLE FUTURE TENSE

Singular		Plural	
Subject	*Verb*	*Subject*	*Verb*
I	will work	we	will work
you	will work	you	will work
he, she, it	will work	they	will work
Sam	will work	Sam and Brenda	will work

NEED TO KNOW
Verb Tense

- **Verb tense** indicates whether an action takes place in the present, past, or future.

- There are three basic verb tenses: **simple present**, **simple past**, and **simple future**.

- The **simple present tense** is used to describe regular, habitual action or can be used for nonaction verbs. It can also indicate action that is occurring at the time of speaking. The ending of a simple present tense verb must agree with the subject of the verb.

- The **simple past tense** refers to action that was completed in the past. For regular verbs, the simple past tense is formed by adding *-d* or *-ed*.

- The **simple future tense** refers to action that will happen in the future. The simple future tense is formed by adding the helping verb *will* before the verb.

EXERCISE 10-3 Using the Simple Past and Simple Future Tenses

Directions: For each of the following verbs, write a sentence using the simple past tense and one using the simple future tense.

EXAMPLE   overcook   *The chef overcooked my steak.*
I know he will overcook my steak.

1. dance _____

_____

2. hunt _____

_____

3. joke _____

_____

4. watch _____

_____

5. photograph _____

_____

EXERCISE 10-4   Writing a Paragraph
Writing in Progress

Directions: Write a paragraph on one of the following topics, using either the simple past tense or the simple future tense.

1. Selecting a movie to rent
2. Cleaning the attic or garage
3. Selecting courses for next semester
4. Buying groceries
5. Caring for a three-year-old child ■

USING IRREGULAR VERBS CORRECTLY

GOAL 2 Use irregular verbs correctly

Errors in verb tense can occur easily with irregular verbs. Irregular verbs do not form the simple past tense according to the pattern we have studied. A regular verb forms the simple past tense by adding *-d* or *-ed*. An irregular verb forms the simple past tense by changing its spelling internally (for example, "I feed" becomes "I fed") or by not changing at all (for example, "I cut" remains "I cut").

Tip for Writers

Helping Verbs

A helping verb is used before the main verb to form certain tenses.

helping verb main verb

Ericka <u>will</u> <u>sit</u> in front of the television for hours.

Common helping verbs include:

have	has	had
be	am	is
do	does	did
are	was	were
being	been	

The following verbs can only be used as helping verbs:

can	could
will	would
shall	should
may	might
must	ought to

EXAMPLE   I <u>can</u> leave tomorrow.
I <u>may</u> cancel my insurance.

Three Troublesome Irregular Verbs

The verbs *be, do,* and *have* can be especially troublesome. You should master the correct forms of these verbs in both the present tenses and the past tenses since they are used so often.

1. **Irregular Verb:** *Be*

	PRESENT	PAST
Singular	I am	I was
	you are	you were
	he, she, it is	he, she, it was
Plural	we are	we were
	you are	you were
	they are	they were

- It is nonstandard to use *be* for all present tense forms.

  INCORRECT   I <u>be</u> finished.

  CORRECT   I <u>am</u> finished.

  INCORRECT   They <u>be</u> surprised.

  CORRECT   They <u>are</u> surprised.

- Another error is to use *was* instead of *were* for plural past tenses or with *you.*

  INCORRECT   We <u>was</u> late.

  CORRECT   We <u>were</u> late.

  INCORRECT   You <u>was</u> wrong.

  CORRECT   You <u>were</u> wrong.

- Note that the verb *to be* never takes an object.

Tip for Writers

The pronoun *you* is always grammatically plural in English. Use plural verbs (*are, have,* or *were*) with *you,* not singular forms such as *is, has,* or *was.* Use a plural verb with *you* even when you are speaking or writing to one person.

Tip for Writers

Does, as a main verb or a helping verb, is used only with third-person singular or uncountable subjects, such as *he, Maria, the book, homework, music,* or *an idea.* Use *do,* not *does,* after *I, you,* or *they.*

2. Irregular Verb: *Do*

	PRESENT	PAST
Singular	I do	I did
	you do	you did
	he, she, it does	he, she, it did
Plural	we do	we did
	you do	you did
	they do	they did

- A common error is to use *does* instead of *do* for present plural forms.

INCORRECT   We <u>does</u> our best.

CORRECT   We <u>do</u> our best.

INCORRECT   They <u>doesn't</u> know the answer.

CORRECT   They <u>don't</u> know the answer.

- Another error is to use *done* instead of *did* for past plural forms.

INCORRECT   We <u>done</u> everything. You <u>done</u> finish.

CORRECT   We <u>did</u> everything. You <u>did</u> finish.

3. Irregular Verb: *Have*

	PRESENT	PAST
Singular	I have	I had
	you have	you had
	he, she, it has	he, she, it had
Plural	we have	we had
	you have	you had
	they have	they had

- A common, nonstandard form uses *has* instead of *have* for the present plural.

INCORRECT   We <u>has</u> enough. They <u>has</u> a good reason.

CORRECT   We <u>have</u> enough. They <u>have</u> a good reason.

- Another error occurs in the past singular.

INCORRECT   I <u>has</u> nothing to give you. You <u>has</u> a bad day.

CORRECT   I <u>had</u> nothing to give you. You <u>had</u> a bad day.

EXERCISE 10-5   Using Standard Verb Forms

Directions: Circle the correct, standard form of the verb in each of the following sentences.

> EXAMPLE   Last April Anne (was, were) in Nevada.

1. After I watched the news, I (does, did) my homework.
2. You (be, were) lucky to win the raffle.
3. The electrician (have, has) enough time to complete the job.
4. When I am reading about the Civil War, I (am, be) captivated.
5. All the waitresses I know (have, has) sore feet.
6. We (was, were) at the grocery store yesterday.
7. He (do, does) his studying at the library.
8. We (did, done) the jigsaw puzzle while it rained.
9. Alice Walker (be, is) a favorite author of mine.
10. You (was, were) in the audience when the trophy was awarded. ■

EXERCISE 10-6   Using Irregular Verbs

Directions: Write sentences for each pair of irregular verbs shown below. Try to write several sentences that ask questions.

> EXAMPLE   am   *I am going to the Bulls game tonight.*
>
>   be   *Will you be at home tonight?*

1. do   _____

   does   _____

2. was   _____

   were   _____

3. is   _____

   be   _____

4. do   _____

   did   _____

5. am   _____

   was   _____ ■

EXERCISE 10-7   Using Irregular Verbs

Directions: Write sentences for each pair of irregular verbs shown below. Use a plural pronoun (*we, you, they*) or a plural noun.

EXAMPLE   be   _We will be at my dad's house._

were   _They were happy to see us._

1. do   _____

did   _____

2. are   _____

be   _____

3. have   _____

had   _____

4. are   _____

were   _____

5. be   _____

were   _____

EXERCISE 10-8   Correcting Verb Errors

Working Together

Directions: Working with a classmate, read the following student paragraph and correct all verb errors.

Sometimes first impressions of people is very inaccurate and can lead to problems. My brother, Larry, learn this the hard way. When he was 17, Larry and I was driving to the mall. Larry decided to pick up a hitchhiker because he looks safe and trustworthy. After the man got in the car, we notice that he was wearing a knife. A few miles later, the man suddenly tell us to take him to Canada. So my brother said we'd have to stop for gas and explained that he did not have any money. The man get out of the car to pump the gas. When he goes up to the attendant to pay for the gas, we took off. We do not stop until we reach the police station, where we tell the officer in charge what happens. The police caught the man several miles from the gas station. He be serving time in prison for burglary and had escaped over the weekend. Later, Larry said, "I was lucky that my first impression were not my last!" ■

Other Irregular Verbs

Among the other verbs that form the past tense in irregular ways are *become (became)*, *drive (drove)*, *hide (hid)*, *stand (stood)*, and *wear (wore)*. For a list of the past-tense forms of other common irregular verbs, see Part VII, page 524. If you have a question about the form of a verb, consult this list or your dictionary.

Confusing Pairs of Irregular Verbs

Two particularly confusing pairs of irregular verbs are *lie/lay* and *sit/set*.

Lie/Lay

Lie means to recline. *Lay* means to put something down. The past tense of *lie* is *lay*. The past tense of *lay* is *laid*.

SIMPLE PRESENT	SIMPLE PAST
Command the dog to <u>lie</u> down.	The dog <u>lay</u> down.
<u>Lay</u> the boards over here.	The carpenter <u>laid</u> the boards over there.

Sit/Set

Sit means to be seated. *Set* means to put something down. The past tense of *sit* is *sat*. The past tense of *set* is *set*.

SIMPLE PRESENT	SIMPLE PAST
Please <u>sit</u> over here.	We <u>sat</u> over here.
<u>Set</u> the books on the table.	He <u>set</u> the books on the table.

NEED TO KNOW
Irregular Verbs

- An **irregular verb** does not form the simple past tense with *-d* or *-ed*.

- Three particularly troublesome irregular verbs are *be*, *do*, and *have*.

- Two confusing pairs of verbs are *lie/lay* and *sit/set*. Each has a distinct meaning.

EXERCISE 10-9 Using Correct Verbs

Directions: Circle the correct verb in each of the following sentences.

EXAMPLE   Eric plans to (lay, (lie)) in bed all day.

1. The chef (sat, set) the mixer on "high" to beat the eggs.

2. I prefer to (lie, lay) on the hammock rather than on a chaise.

3. The students (sit, set) in rows to take the exam.

4. After putting up the wallboard, James (lay, laid) the hammer on the floor.

5. Bags of grain (set, sat) on the truck.

6. I'm going to (lie, lay) down and take a short nap.

7. Because we came late, we (sat, set) in the last row.

8. The kitten (lay, laid) asleep in the laundry basket.

9. Bob (sat, set) the groceries on the counter.

10. Completely exhausted, Shawna (lay, laid) on the sofa. ■

AVOIDING SUBJECT-VERB AGREEMENT ERRORS

GOAL 3 Avoid subject-verb agreement errors

A subject and its verb must agree (be consistent) in person (first, second, third) and in number (singular, plural). (For more on pronoun forms, see p. 519; for more on verb forms in all persons and number, see p. 523.)

The most common problems with subject-verb agreement occur with third-person present-tense verbs, which are formed for most verbs by adding *-s* or *-es*. (For the present-tense and past-tense forms of certain irregular verbs, see p. 524.)

Agreement Rules

1. **Use the present-tense ending *-s* or *-es* if a verb's subject is third-person singular.** For first and second person, no ending is added.

Singular Subject	Verb	Singular Subject	Verb
I	talk	it	talks
you	talk	Sally	talks
he	talks	a boy	talks
she	talks		

2. **For a plural subject (more than one person, place, thing, or idea), use a plural form of the verb.**

Plural Subject	Verb	Plural Subject	Verb
we	talk	Sally and James	talk
you	talk	boys	talk
they	talk		

Common Errors

The following circumstances often lead to errors in subject-verb agreement:

1. **Third-person singular** A common error is to omit the *-s* or *-es* in a third-person singular verb in the present tense. The subjects *he, she,* and *it,* or a noun that could be replaced with *he, she,* or *it,* all take a third-person singular verb.

   INCORRECT   She act like a professional.

   CORRECT   She acts like a professional.

   INCORRECT   Professor Simmons pace while he lectures.

   CORRECT   Professor Simmons paces while he lectures.

2. **Verbs before their subjects** When a verb comes before its subject, as in sentences beginning with *Here* or *There*, it is easy to make an agreement error. *Here* and *there* are never subjects of a sentence and do not determine the correct form of the verb. Look for the subject *after* the verb and, depending on its number, choose a singular or plural verb.

   singular verb   singular subject

   There is a pebble in my shoe.

   plural verb   plural subject

   There are two pebbles in my shoe.

3. **Words between the subject and its verb** Words, phrases, and clauses coming between the subject and its verb do not change the fact that the verb must agree with the subject. To check that the verb is correct, mentally remove everything between the subject and its verb, and make sure that the verb agrees in number with its subject.

   singular subject   singular verb

   A list of course offerings is posted on the bulletin board.

   plural subject   plural verb

   Details of the accident were not released.

   Note: Phrases beginning with prepositions such as *along with, together with, as well as,* and *in addition to* are not part of the subject and should not be considered in determining the number of the verb.

   singular subject   singular verb

   The stereo, together with the radios, televisions, and lights, goes dead during electrical storms.

   Note: Using contractions such as *here's* and *there's* leads to mistakes because you cannot "hear" the mistake. "Here's two pens" may not sound incorrect, but "Here is two pens" does.

4. **Compound subjects** Two or more subjects joined by the coordinating conjunction *and* require a plural verb, even if one or both of the subjects are singular.

   INCORRECT   Anita and Mark plays cards.

   CORRECT   Anita and Mark play cards.

When a compound subject is joined by the conjunctions *or, nor, either . . . or, neither . . . nor, not . . . but,* or *not only . . . but also,* the verb should agree with the subject nearer to it.

<u>Neither</u> the <u>book</u> nor the <u>article</u> <u>was</u> helpful to my research.

<u>Sarah</u> <u>or</u> the <u>boys</u> <u>are</u> coming tomorrow.

NEED TO KNOW
Subject-Verb Agreement

- A **subject** of a sentence must agree (be consistent) with the **verb** in person (first, second, or third) and in number (singular or plural).

- Watch for errors when using the third-person singular, placing verbs before their subjects, using compound subjects, and adding words, phrases, or clauses between the subject and the verb.

EXERCISE 10-10 Choosing Correct Verbs

Directions: Circle the verb that correctly completes each sentence.

EXAMPLE   The newspapers (is, (are)) on the desk.

1. The hubcaps that fell off the car (was, were) expensive to replace.
2. The conductor and orchestra members (ride, rides) a bus to their concerts.
3. A Little League team (practice, practices) across the street each Tuesday.
4. Here (is, are) the book I borrowed.
5. Not only the news reporters but also the weather forecaster (are broadcasting, is broadcasting) live from the circus tonight.
6. Nobody older than 12 (ride, rides) the merry-go-round.
7. The discussion panel (offer, offers) its separate opinions after the debate.
8. Terry's green shorts (hang, hangs) in his gym locker.
9. Several of the cookies (taste, tastes) stale.
10. A mime usually (wear, wears) all-black or all-white clothing. ■

EXERCISE 10-11 Choosing Correct Verbs

Directions: Circle the verb that correctly completes each sentence.

EXAMPLE   Everybody (like, (likes)) doughnuts for breakfast.

1. Physics (is, are) a required course for an engineering degree.
2. Most of my courses last semester (was, were) in the morning.
3. The orchestra members who (is, are) carrying their instruments will be able to board the plane first.

4. Suzanne (sing, sings) a touching version of "America the Beautiful."
5. Here (is, are) the performers who juggle plates.
6. Kin Lee and his parents (travel, travels) to Ohio tomorrow.
7. A box of old and valuable stamps (is, are) in the safe-deposit box at the bank.
8. The family (sit, sits) together in church each week.
9. Judith and Erin (arrive, arrives) at the train station at eleven o'clock.
10. Directions for the recipe (is, are) on the box. ■

EXERCISE 10-12 Correcting Subject-Verb Agreement Errors

Directions: Revise any sentences that contain errors in subject-verb agreement.

Los Angeles have some very interesting and unusual buildings. There is the Victorian houses on Carroll Avenue, for example. The gingerbread-style trim and other ornate architectural features makes those houses attractive to tourists and photographers. The Bradbury Building and the Oviatt Building was both part of the nineteenth-century skyline. They was restored as office buildings that now houses twentieth-century businesses. Some of the architecture in Los Angeles seem to disguise a building's function. One of the most startling sights are a building that look like a huge ship. ■

USING ACTIVE INSTEAD OF PASSIVE VOICE

GOAL 4 Use active instead of passive voice in most situations

When a verb is in the active voice, the subject performs the action of the verb.

subject   active-voice verb

ACTIVE VOICE   Mr. Holt opened his briefcase.

When a verb is in the **passive voice**, the subject is the receiver of the action of the verb.

subject   passive-voice verb

PASSIVE VOICE   The briefcase was opened.

This passive-voice sentence does not name the person who opened the brief-case. Passive-voice sentences seem indirect, as if the writer were purposefully avoiding giving information the reader might need or want.

PASSIVE VOICE   The fingerprints had been carefully wiped away.
PASSIVE VOICE   The vase had been broken.

Both active and passive voices are grammatically correct. However, the active voice is usually more effective because it is simpler, more informative, and more direct. Use the active rather than the passive voice unless

1. **you do not know who or what performs the action of the verb.**

   PASSIVE   The broken window <u>had been wiped</u> clean of fingerprints.

2. **you want to emphasize the object of the action rather than who or what performs the action.**

   PASSIVE   The poem "The Chicago Defender Sends a Man to Little Rock" by Gwendolyn Brooks <u>was discussed</u> in class. [Here, exactly who discussed the poem is less important than what poem was discussed.]

As a general rule, try to avoid writing passive-voice sentences. Get in the habit of putting the subject—the person or thing performing the action—at the beginning of each sentence. If you do this, you will usually avoid the passive voice.

NEED TO KNOW

Active and Passive Voices

- When a verb is in the **active voice**, the subject performs the action.

- When a verb is in the **passive voice**, the subject receives the action.

- Because the active voice is straightforward and direct, use it unless you do not know who or what performed the action or want to emphasize the object of the action rather than who or what performed it.

EXERCISE 10-13 Using Active Voice

Directions: Revise each of the following sentences by changing the verb from passive to active voice.

EXAMPLE   The china cups and saucers were painted carefully by Lois and her friends.

REVISED   *Lois and her friends carefully painted the china cups*

and saucers.

1. *Goodnight Moon* was read by the mother to her daughter.

   _____

2. The maple tree was trimmed by the telephone company.

   _____

3. The vacuum cleaner was repaired by Mr. Fernandez.

   _____

4. Many bags of flour were donated by the fraternity.

_____

5. Six quarts of strawberries were made into jam by Alice.

_____

6. Cornrows were braided into Pam's hair by Felicia.

_____

7. Tanya was driven to Weston City by Janice.

_____

8. The transmission was repaired by Mike.

_____

9. Potholes were filled by the city employees.

_____

10. Grapes were pressed into juice by the winemaker.

_____

EXERCISE 10-14 Using Active Voice

Directions: Revise each of the following sentences by changing the verb from passive to active voice.

EXAMPLE   The patient was operated on by an experienced surgeon.

REVISED   *An experienced surgeon operated on the patient.*

1. The coin collection was inherited by Roderick from his grandfather.

_____

2. A large bunch of roses was cut by my sister.

_____

3. The president's advisers were relied on by the president.

_____

4. Ice cream was served to the children at the birthday party by one of the adults.

_____

5. Tools were packed in a box by Terry.

_____

6. Scuba-diving equipment was handed to the students by the licensed instructor.

_____

7. Alaska was visited by my parents last fall.

_____

8. A large rock bass was caught by James.

_____

9. The newspaper was delivered by a 12-year-old girl on her bike.

_____

10. Trash was collected and disposed of by the picnickers before they left for home.

_____

■

EXERCISE 10-15 **Revising a Paragraph**
Writing in Progress

Directions: Reread the paragraph you wrote in Exercise 10-4. Check for subject-verb agreement errors and for sentences you wrote in the passive voice. Revise as necessary. ■

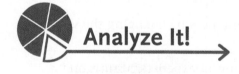 Analyze It!

Directions: Revise the following paragraph by correcting all verb usage errors.

The summer I turned ten, I learned the difference between being alone and being lonely. Growing up in a large family, I never had much time to myself, but that summer I visit my aunt for three weeks. She lived in the country, and I was the only kid for miles around. At first, I had felt lonely without my brothers and sisters, but then I discover the boulders in the woods. The jumble of huge rocks was endlessly fascinating. Some days I was an explorer, moving from one rock to another, surveying the countryside from the tallest boulder. Some days, I retired to my secret fort, tucked in a shadowy crevice. I furnished my rocky fort with an old cushion to set on and a cigar box for collecting treasures. On sunny mornings, before the air has lost its early chill, I laid on the flattest boulder, its smooth surface warming my skinny arms and legs. The boulders were my audience when I read aloud the stories I had wrote. I remember many things about my time alone in the woods that summer, but I don't recall ever feeling lonely.

Paragraph Writing Scenarios

Friends and Family

1. Think of a family member who works very hard. Write a paragraph about the kind of dream vacation you would treat this person to if you could.

2. Write a paragraph about a pet owned by someone you know. Use details to describe what makes this animal special, cute, annoying, sweet, or unusual.

Classes and Campus Life

1. Some people are "morning people." Others would describe themselves as "night people." Write a paragraph about your own daily energy levels—when you're the most awake and ready to go and when you're the most sluggish. Include information about what are your ideal times for going to sleep and waking up. Explain how this fits with your college class schedule.

2. Some campuses are sprawling, stately, or spacious places. Others are crammed into cement corners of urban neighborhoods. Write a paragraph that describes the physical place and atmosphere of your school's campus. Use details and plenty of descriptive words to "paint a picture" for your reader.

Working Students

1. Some employers are hesitant about hiring students, while others particularly like having students work for them. Write a paragraph about what you think might make an employer nervous about hiring a student. What would you say about yourself to overcome that employer's fears?

2. A job application asks for references. Choose someone you would use as a reference, and write a paragraph describing what you think they would say about you.

Communities and Cultures

1. When we say "culture" we are usually talking about a way of life. Some people identify more closely with the traditional culture of their ancestors, while others follow the trends and fashions of popular culture. Write a paragraph describing which influences you more, the customs, religion, dress, foods, arts, or language of your traditional culture, or the fashions, music, trends, and news from the TV, movies, magazines, or newspapers of popular culture.

2. People migrate from all over the world to the United States in search of "the American dream." To some, this means religious freedom. To others, it means fame and fortune. Write a paragraph describing your idea of "the American dream."

WRITING ABOUT A READING

In the following reading, the author discusses the difficult working conditions faced by workers in the seafood industry in Santa Rosalia, Mexico.

Step 1: Preview the reading.

Step 2: Connect the reading to your own experience: What are the working conditions like at your current job?

Step 3: Read and respond to the questions in the margin.

THINK AS YOU READ

What is a sweatshop?

What feelings does the author create in the first paragraph?

How does this feeling change in paragraph 2?

SWEATSHOPS AT SEA

Virginia Sole-Smith

1   It was a little after eight in the evening, and the sun was just beginning to set over the Gulf of California. Our small motorboat, known here in Santa Rosalia, Mexico, as a *panga*, sped out over the shimmering water. The breezy sea air felt good and clean after the heat of the day, and soon Delmar, the 26-year-old squid fisherman who had agreed to take us out for his night's work, was cracking open cans of **Tecate**.[1] When we reached Delmar's fishing spot, he cut the engine and flipped on a tiny lightbulb duct-taped to a pole on the middle bench of the *panga*. Floating all around us were dozens of other *pangas*, and as night fell, the dots of light twinkled like a hundred fallen stars. It was beautiful and peaceful. Then we began to fish.

2   Delmar unraveled a glow-in-the-dark plastic tube fitted with sharp metal hooks that was attached to a thousand feet of clear fishing line. He tossed it overboard, wrapping the other end around a piece of scrap wood. When

Tightening U.S. seafood regulations could improve human rights in Mexico.

[1] **Tecate** a brand of Mexican beer

the line went tight after a few minutes, he began to pull, bare hand over bare hand, hauling the line back up through hundreds of feet of water. Seconds later, a 40-pound Humboldt squid splashed up from the depths with an enormous spray of salt water and sticky black ink. From tentacles to tail, it was almost as long as the *panga* was wide.

3   In one fluid movement, Delmar yanked the squid out of the water, slapped it down, grabbed a rusty *machete*, and chopped off its head. Four hours later, the piles of red squid bodies and heads had grown so large that we had to balance with our feet braced awkwardly against the slick benches. When we had to move around the boat, we'd slip on spare eyeballs and black slime, and occasionally a spastic tentacle would wrap itself around the odd ankle. To make matters even worse, there were no life vests, radios, or emergency lights on board Delmar's *panga*.

4   It's no wonder that, every season, at least two or three fishermen like Delmar die at sea. The unsafe, grotesque working conditions on the water are just one of the many problems facing the working people of Santa Rosalia, a town of around 10,000 that is located in Baja California Sur. There are no spring break parties here. The dirty waterfront is devoted to three squid factories and the *panga* docks, because fishing the millions of Humboldt squid swimming in 25 square miles of Santa Rosalia's waters is the only game in town.

5   The squid processing plants—Korean-owned Brumar de San Bruno, Korean-owned Hanjin Mexico, and Chinese-owned Pesquera de Longing, SA—buy each day's catch from middlemen who have frozen the price the fishermen receive for their squid at just two pesos per kilo. That means most consider a $50 paycheck for a 10-hour fishing trip to be a good night. And it is, at least when you compare those wages to what the fishermen's wives, mothers, and daughters make working in the plants themselves, which—far from the federal labor offices in Mexico City—operate Wild West style.

6   Rosa Ceseña Ramirez began working in the Hanjin Mexico factory in 1994. She never knew when a shift was going to start or how long it would last. "You can either drink coffee for hours to stay awake, or sleep on the factory floor like an animal," Rosa explains. "Once the squid arrives, we have to work until it's all processed, even if it takes until the next afternoon. Then we go home for a few hours to sleep and see our kids, and have to come right back that evening."

7   The breaking point for Rosa came in November 2002, when Hanjin Mexico allegedly failed to pay its workers a federally mandated annual bonus and shortchanged their weekly paychecks. Rosa gathered signatures and filed a complaint with the Santa Rosalia labor office. Rosa says Hanjin Mexico responded by firing her and more than 90 workers. Eight years later, the former Hanjin Mexico workers are still waiting for the labor office to resolve their dispute, and conditions at all three Santa Rosalia factories have worsened.

8   At the neighboring Pesquera de Longing, workers report that only two toilets are available for more than 80 workers. Conditions at Brumar de San Bruno are no better. Most of the workers are migrant laborers who come from other Mexican states and live at the plant in a long, barracks-style dorm. "There are six of us sleeping in one room and whenever it's time to go back

---

Why is the work on the panga dangerous?

What makes the working conditions grotesque?

Why do you think the author reveals the nationalities of the owners of the squid processing plants?

What caused Rosa to reach her breaking point, and how did the employer respond?

Is comparing the workers to slaves a fair comparison?

to work, the Koreans just open the door and yell, 'Let's go,'" worker Sonia Sanchez says. "They don't care if you're undressed or sleeping. We're treated like slaves."

What is the goal of Enlace International?

9   The owners of the Santa Rosalia factories vehemently deny all of their workers' complaints, which is why Enlace International, a coalition of unions and worker centers in Mexico and the United States, is now approaching year eight of a campaign to create better working conditions for Santa Rosalia's labor force. "There will never be any enforcement of the labor laws in Mexico because this is a country with $212 billion in foreign debts," says Garrett Brown, coordinator of the Maquiladora Health and Safety Support Network. "If Americans want to help these workers, getting our government and banks to forgive Mexico's debt would be a big first step."

10   Another big step would be to tighten U.S. regulation of imported seafood. According to U.S. Department of Agriculture data, imports of processed squid from China totaled more than 1.1 million pounds in 2009 (along with 120 million pounds of unprocessed squid). But figuring out which U.S. retailers to hold accountable for the dire conditions in Santa Rosalia is all but impossible. "Seafood is often shipped from port to port before it reaches the United States, and it can be relabeled upon entry and exit, so we have no way of telling where it originally came from," explains Patrick Woodall of Food and Water Watch, a nonprofit consumer advocacy organization in Washington, D.C. "Companies can catch squid in Mexico, then ship it back to China for processing so they can take advantage of even cheaper labor markets and lower food safety regulations, then send it back to the United States. . . . There's just no way to trace it all."

What emotion/feeling does Rosa share in the final paragraph?

11   Meanwhile Rosa balances her day job at a local supermarket with raising funds for the local union. She holds meetings for interested workers in the playground of the local school and writes letters to government officials. The process is slow, and more workers suffer every day. But Rosa is not deterred. "We know that one day it will be our daughters working in those factories," she says. "One part of my heart is sad for all the bad things that have happened. But the other part of my heart is happy because I know we are supporting one another."

WRITING IN RESPONSE TO READING

Examining the Reading Using an Idea Map   MyWritingLab

Review the reading by completing the missing parts of the idea map shown below.

 Visualize It!

Title	**Sweatshops at Sea**

Thesis	Working conditions for a Mexican town's labor force are dangerous and inhumane.

The only industry in Santa Rosalia is based on fishing and processing squid.

Local fishermen work in unsafe conditions for low wages.

_____

The town has three foreign-owned squid processing plants.

Rosa Ceseña Ramirez worked at one of the plants.

_____

Working conditions in the factory were difficult.

In 2002 a factory allegedly failed to pay bonuses and shortchanged paychecks.

Rosa filed a complaint with the town's labor office.

_____

_____

Two steps might improve working conditions.

_____

_____

Conclusion	The author ends with a description of Rosa's continuing efforts to improve conditions.

Strengthening Your Vocabulary MyWritingLab

Using the word's context, word parts, or a dictionary, write a brief definition of each of the following words as it is used in the reading.

1. grotesque (paragraph 4) _____

2. allegedly (paragraph 7) _____

3. mandated (paragraph 7) _____

4. vehemently (paragraph 9) _____

5. coalition (paragraph 9) _____

6. dire (paragraph 10) _____

7. deterred (paragraph 11) _____

Reacting to Ideas: Discussion and Journal Writing MyWritingLab

Get ready to write about the reading by discussing the following:

1. Evaluate the introductory paragraphs of the essay. How does the initial description of the fishing trip contrast with the work that takes place on the boat and in the factories?

2. Discuss why this essay is called "Sweatshops at Sea."

3. Explain what the author means when she says that the seafood processing plants operate "Wild West style."

4. Identify descriptive words in the essay and indicate which words have positive or negative connotations. What is the author's purpose in using these words?

5. Can you identify any bias in this piece? Consider whether facts or opposing viewpoints were omitted.

6. What aspects of the essay are illustrated by the photograph? Discuss details in the photograph that correspond to descriptions in the essay.

Paragraph Options MyWritingLab

1. What is the most difficult work you have ever done? Write a paragraph describing your experience and what made it difficult.

2. Did this essay make you sympathetic to the plight of these workers? Write a paragraph explaining your answer.

3. Were you surprised to learn about the business practices surrounding imported seafood? Write a paragraph explaining your answer and whether this information will affect your consumption of seafood or other imported foods.

WRITING IN RESPONSE TO READING

Examining the Reading Using an Idea Map   MyWritingLab

Review the reading by completing the missing parts of the idea map shown below.

 Visualize It! →

Title   **Sweatshops at Sea**

Thesis   Working conditions for a Mexican town's labor force are dangerous and inhumane.

The only industry in Santa Rosalia is based on fishing and processing squid.

Local fishermen work in unsafe conditions for low wages.

_____

The town has three foreign-owned squid processing plants.

Rosa Ceseña Ramirez worked at one of the plants.

_____

Working conditions in the factory were difficult.

In 2002 a factory allegedly failed to pay bonuses and shortchanged paychecks.

Rosa filed a complaint with the town's labor office.

_____

_____

Two steps might improve working conditions.

_____

_____

Conclusion   The author ends with a description of Rosa's continuing efforts to improve conditions.

Strengthening Your Vocabulary   MyWritingLab

Using the word's context, word parts, or a dictionary, write a brief definition of each of the following words as it is used in the reading.

1. grotesque (paragraph 4) _____
2. allegedly (paragraph 7) _____
3. mandated (paragraph 7) _____
4. vehemently (paragraph 9) _____
5. coalition (paragraph 9) _____
6. dire (paragraph 10) _____
7. deterred (paragraph 11) _____

Reacting to Ideas: Discussion and Journal Writing   MyWritingLab

Get ready to write about the reading by discussing the following:

1. Evaluate the introductory paragraphs of the essay. How does the initial description of the fishing trip contrast with the work that takes place on the boat and in the factories?
2. Discuss why this essay is called "Sweatshops at Sea."
3. Explain what the author means when she says that the seafood processing plants operate "Wild West style."
4. Identify descriptive words in the essay and indicate which words have positive or negative connotations. What is the author's purpose in using these words?
5. Can you identify any bias in this piece? Consider whether facts or opposing viewpoints were omitted.
6. What aspects of the essay are illustrated by the photograph? Discuss details in the photograph that correspond to descriptions in the essay.

Paragraph Options   MyWritingLab

1. What is the most difficult work you have ever done? Write a paragraph describing your experience and what made it difficult.
2. Did this essay make you sympathetic to the plight of these workers? Write a paragraph explaining your answer.
3. Were you surprised to learn about the business practices surrounding imported seafood? Write a paragraph explaining your answer and whether this information will affect your consumption of seafood or other imported foods.

Essay Options   MyWritingLab

4. What can you tell from this reading about the author's attitude toward the workers and the owners of the factories? Write an essay examining the ways in which the author reveals her feelings toward each.

5. Why do you think Rosa Ceseña Ramirez is undeterred after eight years? Write an essay from her point of view explaining her motivations and her commitment to this cause.

6. Consider the two steps that are suggested as ways to improve conditions for the labor force. Do you agree or disagree that these actions should be taken? Can you think of other steps that might be effective? Write an essay explaining your answers.

■ ■ ■ ■

SELF-TEST SUMMARY

To test yourself, cover the Answer column with a sheet of paper and answer each question in the left column. Evaluate each of your answers as you work by sliding the paper down and comparing your answer with what is printed in the Answer column.

	QUESTION	ANSWER
Goal 1 Use verb tenses correctly	What are the three basic verb tenses, and what type of action is shown by each tense?	The three basic verb tenses are simple present, simple past, and simple future. The present tense indicates action that is occurring at the time of speaking or describes regular, habitual action. The past tense refers to action that was completed in the past. The future tense refers to action that will happen in the future.
Goal 2 Use irregular verbs correctly	How does an irregular verb form the past tense? What are examples of irregular verbs?	An irregular verb does not form the past tense with -d or -ed; it does so by changing its spelling internally or by not changing at all. Irregular verbs include *be*, *do*, and *have*.
Goal 3 Avoid subject-verb agreement errors	How do you avoid subject-verb agreement errors?	Avoid errors by making sure the subject of a sentence agrees with the verb in person (first, second, or third) and in number (singular or plural).
Goal 4 Use active instead of passive voice in most situations	What is the difference between active and passive voice? When should you use passive voice?	When a verb is in the active voice, the subject performs the action. When a verb is in the passive voice, the subject receives the action. Use passive voice when you do not know who performed the action or when you want to emphasize the object of the action rather than who performed the action.

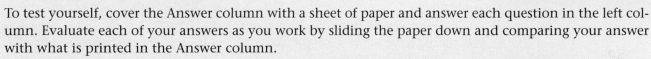

MyWritingLab *Visit Ch. 10 Using Verbs Correctly in MyWritingLab to test your understanding of the chapter objectives.*

WRITERS' WORKSHOPS: Digital Literacy in the Wired Classroom

WRITERS' WORKSHOP

11

A COMPUTER ON EVERY DESK

Digital Literacy in Today's Classroom

Recent studies suggest that more than 75 percent of U.S. households have at least one computer.[2] That number will likely continue to grow as the classroom and the workplace become even more dependent on computers and applications.

To be successful in today's classroom, you should have a core set of digital skills.

Essential Digital Literacy Skills

You need to know how to . . .

- **Be comfortable with computers, keyboards, and peripherals** like a wireless or built-in mouse. (This includes knowing how to type.)

- **Access the Internet via a browser** such as Google Chrome, Firefox, Internet Explorer, or Safari.

- **Set your computer up so that it can access wireless networks**, not only on campus but also anywhere else you may work or study.

- **Search for information using an Internet search engine.**

- **Use the key software applications in the Microsoft Office suite:** Word (for word processing), Excel (for spreadsheets), and PowerPoint (for presentations).

- **Use your school's electronic course management system**, which will be the online portal for many of your courses. Some common course management systems are BlackBoard, Moodle, Desire2Learn, and Canvas.

- **Take graded quizzes and exams online.** Find out how the online quizzing system works. For example, once you click your answer, will you be able to change it, or will the answer be submitted immediately? Does the system allow you to go back and review your work if you have extra time at the end of the exam?

Where to Get Help

Take a moment to assess your skills in these areas. If you are weak in any of them, seek assistance in developing them. Visit your campus computer lab, take a basic course in computer usage, or sign up for courses (or buy books) that help you learn the Microsoft Office programs step-by-step.

[2]https://www.census.gov/hhes/computer/files/2012/Computer_Use_Infographic_FINAL.pdf

WRITERS' WORKSHOP

12

IT ISN'T TRUE JUST BECAUSE IT'S ON THE INTERNET

Evaluating Online Source Materials

Many people mistakenly believe that the first page of hits on a Google search contains the "best" links. However, the best, most valuable information may be found on (for example) the fourth page of the search results. Google allows advertisers to buy placement for their links on the first page of results, and various companies offer a service called "search engine optimization" to make a business's Web site one of the first to appear on the Google results page.

What does this mean? It means you must think critically about the sources of any material you find online. Who wrote the material, and why? Is it trustworthy? To evaluate Web-based materials, consider their content, accuracy, reliability, authorship/authority, timeliness, and objectivity.

Content

- **To be worthwhile, the source should contain the information you need.** If the source does not answer your question, check other sources for more information. Some Web sites provide additional links to more detailed sites with more complete information.

- **A good source should contain the level of technical detail that suits your purpose.** Some sources may provide information that is too sketchy or incomplete; others assume a level of background knowledge or technical sophistication that you may lack. Closely examine the source to determine whether it matches your needs and background knowledge.

- **Good sources try to provide complete information on the topic.** For example, if a Web site about important English poets does not mention William Shakespeare, then it is incomplete. If you discover a source that is incomplete (and many are), search for other sources that provide a more thorough treatment of the topic.

Accuracy and Reliability

- **Accurate, reliable Web sites are usually professionally edited and presented.** Check to see whether the Web site has been published by a professional organization or reputable publisher. Look for information about the site's sponsor and authors. Misspellings, grammatical mistakes, messy or cluttered layouts, or unclear graphics often signal an unreliable source.

- **Reliable Web sites contain information that can be verified elsewhere.** Compare the information you find on the site with the information in other sources (periodicals, books, reference works) on the same topic. If you find a discrepancy, conduct further research to determine which sources are trustworthy and which are not.

- **In all serious research, the sources of information and the techniques used to collect and analyze data are fully documented.** If the Web site does not contain a References or Works Cited section, you should question its accuracy and reliability.

Authorship and Authority

- **Identifying the publisher or sponsor is often the key to evaluating the Web site's credibility.** Material published by the U.S. government either in print form or on the Web (any URL ending in .gov) is highly authoritative and reliable. In general, if the author, business, publisher, or sponsoring agency is not identified, the source lacks authority and reliability.

- **If the author's name is not given anywhere, the Web site lacks credibility.** If the author's name is given, ask yourself whether the author is an expert in his or her field. (Check the site for an author biography.)

- **Credible Web sites often provide an e-mail address or other address at which the writers or editors can be reached.** If no contact information is provided, the source may not be reliable.

Timeliness

Although the Web often provides up-to-the-minute information, not all Web sites are current. Evaluate a Web site's timeliness by checking the following:

- the date on which the materials were posted to the Web site.
- the date when the site was last revised or updated.
- the date when the links were last checked.

Objectivity

Much of what you read and hear expresses a **bias**—a partiality, preference, or prejudice for or against a person, object, or idea. Reliable, credible Web sites fall into two categories:

- sources that treat the subject in a fair, unbiased manner, or
- sources that exhibit bias by supporting a particular viewpoint and acknowledging their bias.

A Web site with a specific viewpoint is not necessarily unreliable. In fact, many people who write blogs strongly argue in favor of or against a particular policy, practice, or government action. You can use these blogs to inform your thinking and open your mind to alternative viewpoints, but in the end you must evaluate the competing viewpoints and decide your own opinions.

To assess a source's **objectivity**—that is, the extent to which it is free of bias—ask yourself the following questions:

- **What is the author's goal?** Is it to present information objectively, to persuade you to accept a particular viewpoint, to take a specific action? If it is not to present balanced information, you can justifiably question the author's objectivity.

- **Are opinions clearly identified?** An author is free to express opinions, but these should be clearly identified as such. Look for words and phrases that identify ideas as opinions (such as *in my opinion*, *I would argue that*, *many people believe*). If a Web site presents opinions as facts or does not distinguish between facts and opinions, the site is most likely unreliable.

- **Is the site a mask for advertising?** Be cautious of Web sites that present information to persuade you to purchase a product or service. If a Web site resembles an infomercial you might see on television, be just as suspicious of it as you would be of the infomercial.

→ TRY IT OUT!

Directions: Conduct a Google search on an academic topic of your choice. Some examples might be "how does photosynthesis work?" or *"Grapes of Wrath* criticism." Visit five of the sites that appear on the first page of the Google results, and evaluate each of them on the criteria above. Which of them seems the most reliable? Which seems the least reliable? ■

WRITERS' WORKSHOP

13

IF IT'S ONLINE, IT'S ALWAYS THERE

Communication and Self-Presentation in a Digital Age

Remember those photos from your younger years that you would never want your friends to see? You used to be able to rip up those photos, toss them in the trash bin, and never worry that they'd come back to embarrass you. But once those photos are put into digital form and uploaded to the Web, they'll be there forever. Even files that you think you've deleted can live on someone else's hard drive for a very long time.

More and more employers are searching the Web for information about job candidates. If they find unflattering or unpleasant things you've written, or photos that you wouldn't want an employer to see, you likely won't get the job.

How do you use the Web to communicate effectively while maintaining a positive image in the digital world? Here are a few suggestions.

- **Whenever you are posting on the Web under your own name, be sure to use proper spelling, grammar, and punctuation.** If you post strong opinions on any topic, remember that those opinions will always be there for others to read.

- **If you play online games or have an online avatar, use a name that can never be traced to your real identity.** It's one thing to have fun online; but you may not want potential employers to see the sexy avatar you've created for yourself on Second Life.

- **Express yourself clearly and intelligently.** Those who express profanity-laden ideas or opinions are generally not taken seriously.

- **Use emoticons (☺, ☹, and so on) only in personal communications to friends.** Never use them in writing that will be read by a wide audience.

- **Don't post images of yourself drunk or stoned.**

- **Don't post matter that can be construed as immature, prejudiced, or closed-minded.**

→ **TRY IT OUT!**

Directions: If you have a Facebook account or blog, examine your postings over the past month or so. How many of these would you be comfortable with a potential employer seeing? If you don't have a Facebook account or blog, examine somebody else's postings as if you were an employer trying to decide whether to hire the person. Based on the person's online activity, would you hire him or her? Why or why not? ■

WRITERS' WORKSHOP

14

FINDING THE HELP YOU NEED

Useful Online Resources

A Google search will turn up hundreds of Web sites that are useful for college writers. Here are some particularly useful sites.

Simmons 3

Works Cited

Neuharth, Al. "Google Is Gutsy to Spit in China's Eye." *USA Today* 26 Mar. 2010:

15a. Print.

Pember, Don R., and Clay Calvert. *Mass Media Law.* Boston: MCGraw-Hill, 2009.

Print.

Pillai, Prabhakar. "Pros and Cons of Censorship." *Buzzle Web Protal: Intelligent Life*

on the Web. Buzzle.com, n.d. Web.8 Apr. 2012.

"Pros of Censorship." *Laws.com.* n.d. Web. 8 Apr. 2012.

"What Is Censorship?" American Civil Liberties Union. 30 Aug. 2006. Web. 08 Apr.

2012.

THE WRITING PROCESS

1. **OWL (Online Writing Lab) at Purdue University**
   https://owl.english.purdue.edu/owl/
   This site offers many resources regarding all the elements of the writing process, from paragraph and essay writing through grammar and punctuation.

2. **The Writing Center at the University of North Carolina (UNC)**
   https://writingcenter.unc.edu/
   This site includes a section for students whose second language is English, as well as links and handouts on a wide variety of writing topics (many of which are accompanied by a video).

3. **The Fun Side of Grammar**

   Grammar Girl's Quick and Dirty Tips

   http://www.quickanddirtytips.com/grammar-girl

   This site, written by best-selling author Mignon Fogarty, describes itself as "your friendly guide to the world of grammar, punctuation, usage, and fun developments in the English language."

4. **Citing Your Sources**

   Giving proper credit to your sources is essential in academic writing. Your instructor will likely ask you to use either MLA (Modern Language Association) style or APA (American Psychological Association) style.

   - **MLA Style** *www.mla.org/style*
   - **APA** *Style www.apastyle.org*

   You can also find information about the specifics of MLA and APA style on the OWL and UNC Web sites listed above.

BIBLIOGRAPHY GENERATOR

www.easybib.com
This site helps you create a correctly formatted bibliography, provided that you input all the needed information.

ONLINE REFERENCE SOURCES

1. **The Internet Public Library**

   http://www.ipl.org/

   This site offers free access to online encyclopedias, dictionaries, and more.

2. **Ref Desk**

   http://www.refdesk.com/

   This site is an enormous collection of reference works that quickly allow you to check facts and find critical pieces of information.

3. **American Fact Finder**

   http://factfinder2.census.gov/faces/nav/jsf/pages/index.xhtml

   Published by the U.S. Census Bureau, the American Fact Finder contains a wealth of information about U.S. housing, geographic, and economic data.

4. **Online Thesaurus**

   www.thesaurus.com

   This site helps you quickly identify synonyms and antonyms for any given word.

→ TRY IT OUT!

Directions: Choose three of the Web sites listed above and spend about ten minutes exploring each. Which resources do you find most useful? Which are you likely to use frequently in your college writing assignments, and why? ■

11 Planning and Organizing

Learning Goals

In this chapter, you will learn how to

GOAL 1
Choose a topic

GOAL 2 Keep your reader in mind as you write

GOAL 3
Generate ideas

GOAL 4
Organize your ideas

WRITE ABOUT IT!

Imagine for a moment that this is your kitchen, and you have only one hour to prepare a meal for someone important. It could be your grandmother, your future in-laws, or someone else you want to impress. Write a sentence describing how you would feel about this task, explaining whether you could pull it together in time and whether it would be as good as you'd like it to be.

You would probably have trouble preparing a meal in an hour because the kitchen is disorganized. Planning and organization are important in writing as well as in meal preparation. First, you have to choose a topic, just as you have to choose a main dish. Next, you have to plan and organize the details you'll write about, just as you have to plan a menu and organize the order in which you prepare each item. Plan properly, and you'll have a delicious meal. Organize well, and you won't be looking for the onions while the garlic burns.

Finally, planning and organizing your paragraph or paper will help to ensure its success, just as planning and organizing the details of your dinner will help to impress your guests. In this chapter you will learn to choose a topic, consider your audience, and generate and organize ideas.

WRITING

CHOOSING A TOPIC

GOAL 1
Choose a topic

Many times, your instructor will assign a topic to write about. Other times, however, instructors will ask you to write a paragraph or essay on a topic of your own choice. The topic you choose often determines how successful your writing will be. The following tips will help you choose a workable topic:

1. **Look for an idea, not just for a topic.** An idea makes a point or states an opinion about a topic. For example, instead of deciding to write about children, start with an idea: "Children often reflect their parents' attitudes." Or, "Children need their own personal space." Or, instead of trying to write about computers, start with the idea that computers are becoming more and more important in everyone's life. Start with an idea!

2. **Look for familiar topics and ideas.** It is easier to think of ideas about topics that you know a lot about. Therefore, examine your own experiences and areas of knowledge.

3. **Look for topics and ideas that interest you.** What subjects or problems grab your attention? What current events or issues spark your interest? You will feel more like writing and will write more successfully if you focus on something interesting and important to you.

4. **Keep an ongoing list of topics.** If a topic doesn't work for one assignment, it may be right for another.

Sources of Ideas

As long as you are aware of, and interacting with, the world around you, you will have ideas to write about. Never think that your ideas are unimportant or worthless. You can develop very simple, ordinary ideas into interesting, effective paragraphs and essays. Here is a list of some good sources of ideas:

SOURCES OF IDEAS	WHAT TO LOOK FOR
daily or weekly activities	likes, dislikes, problems; best, worst, unexpected, exciting events
your physical surroundings	surprising, beautiful, ugly, unusual objects or places
local, national, or world events	memorable, shocking, surprising, interesting, tragic, happy, or amusing occurrences
people (family, friends)	predictable or unpredictable behavior, personalities, actions, histories, insights gained from acquaintances
television or other media	news events, documentaries, trends in programming or advertising, likes, dislikes

"Write about dogs!"

EXERCISE 11-1   Choosing a Topic
Writing in Progress

Directions: Make a list of five to ten topics or ideas that you know about and are interested in.

_____

_____

_____

_____

_____

_____

_____

_____

_____

Choosing a Manageable Topic

If your topic is either too broad or too narrow, you will have difficulty writing an effective paragraph or essay about it. If it is too broad, you will have too much to say. If your topic is too narrow, you won't have enough to say. Some warning signals for each situation are as follows:

A TOPIC MAY BE TOO BROAD IF

- you don't know where to start writing.
- you don't know where to stop.

- you feel as if you are going in circles.
- the topic seems overwhelming.

A TOPIC MAY BE TOO NARROW IF

- you end up repeating ideas.

- your paragraph is too short and you have nothing to add.
- you find yourself focusing again and again on small details.
- the topic seems unimportant.

Narrowing a Topic

If your topic is too broad, try to divide it into smaller topics. Just as a large house can be divided into apartments, a large topic can be divided into smaller, more manageable topics.

Suppose you were asked to write a paragraph about a perfect vacation. Let's say you chose New York City as your destination and decided to write a paragraph about your choice. Most likely you would not be able to cover the reasons for your choice in a single paragraph. Because the topic is too broad, you need to divide it into smaller parts. Try to think in terms of ideas, not topics, as shown in the diagram below:

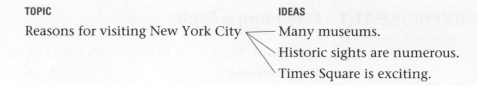

TOPIC   **IDEAS**

Reasons for visiting New York City ⟨— Many museums.

Historic sights are numerous.

Times Square is exciting.

Instead of writing about all of your reasons, you could limit your paragraph to any one of the above reasons.

The diagram below gives you a few other examples of ways to divide large topics into smaller, more manageable ones. Remember to think in terms of *ideas*.

TOPIC   **IDEAS**

1. parades   Parades are festive, happy occasions.

Parades are often patriotic.

Parades attract crowds.

2. campus newspaper   There are many types of articles.

Advertisements fill the paper.

Announcements are usually important.

3. compliments   There are many types of compliments.

Giving compliments is an art.

Accepting compliments is often awkward.

A **topic** is a thing, a person, or an object. Parades, newspapers, and compliments are things. An **idea** makes a statement about a topic. The statement "Parades are festive, happy occasions" makes a point about parades.

For each topic you consider, think to yourself, "What are the various angles on this subject?" This will help you find *ideas* about the topic. Sometimes more than one narrowing is necessary. Note that the divisions for topics 2 and 3 above can still be considered *topics*, not *ideas*, and that some of them are still too broad to be covered in a single paragraph. For example, in topic 2, "advertisements" (one division of "campus newspaper") is still a topic, not an idea, and is still very broad. The diagram below shows how you can narrow this topic down still further using ideas.

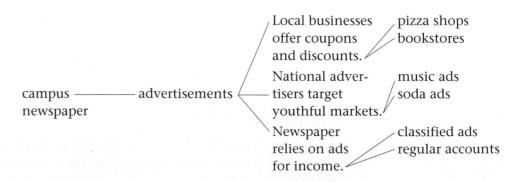

In the diagram above, the first narrowing of the topic "advertisements" yields ideas about the topic (for example, "National advertisers target youthful markets"). Note that each idea is further broken down into examples that support the idea (for instance, "soda ads" and "music ads" are examples of ads that target youthful markets). You'll be working more with supporting your ideas in Chapter 13.

EXERCISE 11-2
Working Together

Narrowing a Topic

Directions: Working with a classmate, divide each of the following topics into at least three smaller topics or ideas. Then, choose one division and narrow it further until you've produced an idea that seems manageable to cover in one paragraph.

1. Child-care problems
2. The importance of holidays
3. The value of friends ■

KEEPING YOUR READER IN MIND

GOAL 2 Keep your reader in mind as you write

Whenever you speak, you are addressing a specific person or group of people. You usually have some knowledge about whom you are addressing. You may know your listeners personally—for example, friends or family. At other times, you may know your listeners in a more distant way. According to your level of familiarity with your listeners and your knowledge about them, you automatically adjust both what you say and how you say it. You speak differently with friends than with your instructors, for example. Suppose the following people made the following comments to you. What would you say to each person? Write your response in the space provided.

PERSON	COMMENT	YOUR RESPONSE
Parent or guardian	"Don't you think you should take a course in psychology?"	_____
Employer	"Have you taken a psychology course yet? If not, you should."	_____
College instructor	"I advise you to register for a psychology course."	_____
Close friend	"Why don't you take a psych class?"	_____

Now analyze your responses. Did you choose different words? Did you express and arrange your ideas differently? Did your tone change? Were some responses casual and others more formal?

Your reaction to each person was different because you took into account who the speaker was as well as what each one said. In writing, your readers are your listeners. They are called your **audience**. As you write, keep your audience in mind. What you write about and how you explain your ideas must match the needs of your audience. Through your language and word choice, as well as through the details you include in your paragraphs, you can communicate effectively with your audience.

Remember, your audience cannot see you when you write. Listeners can understand what you say by seeing your gestures, posture, and facial expressions and hearing your tone of voice and emphasis. When you write, all these non-verbal clues are missing, so you must make up for them. You need to be clear, direct, and specific to be sure you communicate your intended meaning.

EXERCISE 11-3 Considering Your Audience

Directions: Select two people from the list below. For each one, write an explanation of why you decided to attend college.

1. Your best friend
2. Your English instructor
3. Your employer

Do not label which explanation is for which person. In class, exchange papers with a classmate. Ask your classmate to identify the intended audience of each explanation. When you've finished, discuss how the two pieces of writing differ. Then decide whether each piece of writing is appropriate for its intended audience. ■

GENERATING IDEAS

GOAL 3
Generate ideas

Once you have a topic and an audience in mind, the next step is to generate ideas that you can use to write about that topic. This section describes three techniques for generating ideas.

1. Brainstorming
2. Freewriting
3. Branching

You can use these techniques for both essay and paragraph writing, and they can help you narrow your topic if it is too broad or expand it if it is too narrow. If you are writing an essay, these techniques will help you break your general topic down into paragraphs. In paragraph writing, you can use these techniques for generating details that will fill out your paragraphs and support your main ideas.

Brainstorming

For **brainstorming**, make a list of everything you know about your topic. Include facts, ideas, examples, questions, or feelings. Do not stop to decide whether your ideas are good or bad; write down *all* of them. Concentrate on generating *ideas*, not topics. Don't worry about grammar or correctness. Give yourself a time limit. You can brainstorm alone or with another person. After you finish brainstorming, read through your list and mark usable ideas. If you have trouble putting ideas down on paper, consider recording your ideas or discussing ideas with a friend or classmate. The following is a list of ideas a student came up with while brainstorming on the topic of radio talk shows.

Sample Brainstorming

Radio Talk Shows

lots of them

some focus on sports

some deal with issues of the day

some hosts are rude

don't let callers finish talking

some crazy callers, though!

some lack knowledge

some get angry

can learn a lot

get other viewpoints

sometimes hosts get too opinionated

fun to listen to

some topics too controversial

overkill on some issues

The topic of radio talk shows is too broad for a single paragraph. This student's brainstorming produced several paragraph-sized ideas:

characteristics of callers

characteristics of hosts

characteristics of topics covered on radio talk shows

EXERCISE 11-4
Writing in Progress

Brainstorming About a Topic

Directions: Select a topic you listed in Exercise 11-1, or choose one of the following topics. Brainstorm for about five minutes. When you finish, review your work and mark ideas you could use in writing a paragraph.

1. Your dream vacation
2. Physical-education courses
3. Street gangs
4. Photographs
5. Magazines ■

Freewriting

Freewriting is a way to generate ideas on a topic by writing nonstop for a specified period. Here's how it works:

1. **Write whatever comes to your mind, regardless of whether it is about the topic.** If you cannot think of anything to write, rewrite your last interesting phrase or idea until a new idea comes to mind.

2. **Don't worry about complete sentences, grammar, punctuation, or spelling.** Just record ideas as they come to mind. Don't even worry about whether they make sense. If you are writing on a computer, it may be helpful to darken the screen so you aren't distracted by errors and typos.

3. **The most important things are to keep writing and to write fast.**

4. **Give yourself a time limit: three to five minutes is reasonable.**

5. **After you have finished, underline or highlight ideas that might be usable in your paragraph.**

A sample of student freewriting on the topic of visiting the zoo is shown below.

Sample Freewriting

Pat and I went to the zoo Sunday. Great weather. Sunny. Warm. Warm . . . warm . . . warm . . . Oh! I know what I want to say. I didn't have as much fun as I thought I would. I used to love to go to the zoo as a kid. My parents would take us and we'd have a picnic. But I still could get cotton candy at the refreshment stand. It was a really big treat. My dad would carry me on his shoulders and my mother would be pushing my baby brother in the stroller. I loved the giraffes with their long necks and spots. And the tigers. But this time the animals looked so sad. The tiger was in an enclosed area, and he'd worn a path around the edges. He paces constantly. It was awful.

Notice that this sample contains numerous errors, including sentence fragments; this student was focusing on ideas, not correctness. Notice, too, that the student repeats the word *warm*, probably because she was stuck and needed to get her ideas flowing.

This freewriting contains two possible topics:

a childhood memory of the zoo
the quality of life for animals in a zoo

Once you have selected a topic, it may be helpful to freewrite again to generate more ideas.

EXERCISE 11-5   Using Freewriting

Directions: Freewrite for five minutes each on two of the following topics. Be sure to write without stopping. When you finish, underline or highlight any ideas that might be usable in writing a paragraph on that topic.

1. Movies
2. Cigarette smoke
3. Common sense
4. Bad motorists
5. Hitchhikers ■

Branching

Branching uses freestyle diagrams to generate ideas. Branching begins with a trunk—that is, with a general topic. Related ideas branch out from the trunk like limbs on a tree. As on a tree, branches also can originate from other branches. To do branching, just follow these simple steps:

1. **Write your general topic in the center of a full sheet of 8.5-by-11-inch paper.** Draw a circle around the topic.
2. **As you think of ideas related to the topic, write them down around the central circle.** Draw a line connecting each idea to the central circle. In the following diagram, a student has used branching to generate ideas on the topic of homeless people.

First Branching Diagram

3. **Now begin to think of ideas that relate to the branches.** Write them down near the appropriate branch. You don't need to work with each branch. Choose only one or two to develop further. You may need to use separate sheets of paper to give yourself room to develop each branch, as in the second branching diagram shown on the next page. Here the student chose to develop further the idea of shelters for the homeless.

4. **Continue to draw branches until you are satisfied you have enough for the assignment at hand.** The student who made the second branching diagram decided to write about one of the experiences she had when she volunteered to serve food in a shelter for the homeless.

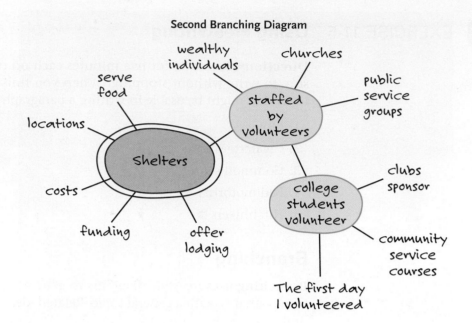

Second Branching Diagram

EXERCISE 11-6   Using Branching

Directions: Use branching to develop two of the following topics:

1. Car-safety devices
2. Noise
3. Borrowing money
4. Sales tax
5. Convenience food stores ■

Choosing a Technique That Works

Now that you have tried these techniques, you may have a sense that one of them works best for you.

However, don't judge the techniques too quickly. Try each of them three or four times. As you continue working with them, another preference may develop. You will also find that for certain topics, one technique may work better than another. For example, suppose you are writing a paragraph about snowmobiling. You may find that freewriting about it does not yield as many fresh ideas as branching. If you're describing a close friend, you may find that branching doesn't work as well as brainstorming or freewriting.

Identifying Usable Ideas

Brainstorming, freewriting, and branching each produce a large assortment of ideas. Your job is to decide which ideas are useful for the writing assignment at hand. Don't feel as if you have to use them all. Sometimes you might select just one idea and develop it further by doing a second freewriting, branching, or brainstorming. For example, suppose you brainstormed on the topic of radio talk shows and selected from your brainstorming list the subtopic of sports talk shows; then you might generate more ideas about sports talk shows by further brainstorming. Your goal is to produce ideas that you can use to develop a paragraph on your selected topic.

NEED TO KNOW
Techniques for Generating Ideas

TECHNIQUE	DESCRIPTION
Brainstorming	1. List all ideas about your topic.
	2. Use words and phrases.
	3. Give yourself a time limit.
Freewriting	1. Write nonstop about your topic.
	2. Write whatever comes to mind.
	3. Give yourself a time limit.
Branching	1. Write your topic in the middle of your page and circle it.
	2. As you think of related ideas, write them down around the center circle. Connect the ideas with lines.
	3. Draw additional branches as needed.

EXERCISE 11-7   Comparing Methods of Generating Ideas

Directions: Select one of the topics listed below. Try brainstorming, freewriting, and branching to generate ideas about it. When you have finished, mark the usable ideas in each method and compare your results. Then answer the questions below.

1. The value of exercise
2. Dressing stylishly
3. Choosing an apartment
4. Managing money
5. Amusement parks

1. Which technique worked best this time? Why?

_____

_____

2. Which technique was least successful this time? Why?

_____

_____

ORGANIZING YOUR IDEAS

GOAL 4
Organize your ideas

After you have developed usable ideas to include in your paragraph or essay, the next step is to decide how to organize them. Ideas should flow logically from one to another. There are many ways to group or arrange ideas in both paragraphs and essays so that they are clear and easy to follow. The list below describes three of the most common types of organization:

1. **Least/most arrangement** Arrange your ideas from most to least or least to most, according to some standard. For example, you might arrange ideas from most to least important, likeable, interesting, controversial, serious, or familiar.

2. **Time sequence** Arrange events in the order in which they happened. Whatever happened first is placed first in the paragraph. Whatever occurred last is placed last. A time-sequence organization would be good to use if, for example, you wanted to describe events at a surprise party. This type of organization is also what you would use to describe a process, such as how to change a flat tire.

3. **Spatial arrangement** Arrange descriptions of persons, places, or things according to their positions in space. You could describe your topic from outside to inside, right to left, or top to bottom. For example, you might use a left-to-right organization to describe your psychology classroom, or you might use a front-to-back organization to describe your friend's pickup truck.

These methods of organization are discussed in more detail in Chapter 14.

NEED TO KNOW
Planning and Organizing

Planning and organizing contribute to successful writing. Be sure to

- focus on ideas, not general topics.

- use events, activities, physical surroundings, media, and people around you as sources of ideas.

- make sure your topic is manageable—neither too broad nor too narrow.

- choose a topic that is well suited to your audience.

- use brainstorming, freewriting, and branching to generate ideas.

- organize your ideas using a logical method. Three common methods are least/most arrangement, time sequence, and spatial arrangement.

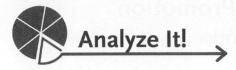

Analyze It!

Directions: The following is one student's freewriting on the topic of summer camps. Study the freewriting and in the space provided, list possible topics that could be used for a short essay.

The other day my son asked if he could go to summer camp. His friend is going to the YMCA sleep-away camp for two weeks next summer. I didn't know what to say. He's only 8, for crying out loud! I didn't go to camp until I was 10, and man, was I homesick. I cried myself to sleep every night the first week. I guess I'm glad he's curious about it. Adventurous spirit. Unlike me as a kid. Although, come to think of it, camp did build my confidence. And maybe improved my social skills. I loved canoeing and roasting marshmallows around the campfire. Oh, and we played some great pranks! But I got a wicked case of swimmer's ear. I'd be a wreck worrying that my kid might get hurt. He may be ready for sleep-away camp, but I'm not sure I'm ready to let him go. He likes sleeping over at friend's houses. How much does the Y camp cost anyway? I've heard good things about the staff. How DO you decide if your kid's ready? Wonder if there's financial aid available . . .

A STUDENT ESSAY

The Writing Task

For her writing class, Jessica Nantka was asked to write an essay explaining what she learned from a work experience. As you read, notice that she uses correct and consistent verbs throughout.

I Don't Want a Promotion

Jessica Nantka

1   At every job, there are different levels of seniority. You might think that getting promoted to the highest position is always better. I work at Picasso's Pizzeria and I've been there for almost two years now. I believe a promotion is not always better, and after experiencing and observing different positions at the pizza shop, a promotion doesn't sound good to me.

2   When I first started, I was promoted quickly. I worked making wings. Within a month I moved up to making subs, and then to being the weekend sub and wing opener. Three months after I started, I became a sub and wing closer and fourteen months into my job, I became a store opener. Now there is talk that I might become the next manager. I have moved from the bottom of the roster to almost the top in a matter of fifteen months. Although it's flattering to be considered for a manager position, I don't think that I want the job.

3   The positions I've held have shown me that with each promotion comes more responsibility. All new employees start out making wings, and that's all they have to do. Once you're promoted to subs, you not only have to make subs, but you have to be ready to help the wing makers if they need help. The manager will blame you if things go wrong with the wings, so you have to keep an eye on them all the time. There is a lot more to remember on the sub side of the shop and it's a busier job. Promotion to subs comes with a small raise, but a lot more responsibility.

4   The manager's job is diverse and has its benefits. It includes cashiering, waiting tables, answering phones, lots and lots of paperwork, and watching over the other employees. Managers get tips for waiting tables, do not have to wear hats, or do any of the dirty jobs. The manager is the one in charge if the owner or general manager is gone, so there is a lot of authority to the job. There's also a nice raise.

5   Being manager really is a lot of work, though. The current managers complain about their jobs a lot. Managers are the first to get yelled at if something goes wrong. They even get in trouble if the other workers do something wrong, like making a pizza wrong. Furthermore, if someone forgets to do part of their closing or cleaning list, the managers get in trouble because they are responsible for checking everyone's work. Managers have to put up with rude people on the phone and in the dining room. Managing is really a hard job with a lot of work, especially since managers have to do not only their own work, but have to watch over the work all the other employees do in the entire shop all the time. Sometimes managers even have to step in and do the general manager's work too.

6   You can get many raises without getting to the top and that's what I have done. Being in the middle can be a good thing. I like it just where I am. Becoming a manager would mean a lot more responsibility and headaches. I'm glad to have gotten the promotions I've had, but I'm happiest not having all the responsibility in the shop. Some people may think I am not ambitious. That's not true—I am smart, smart enough to spend my time and energy on college where the payoff will be bigger and longer lasting.

EXAMINING STUDENT WRITING

1. Reread Nantka's introduction. Does it draw you into the essay?

2. Reread Nantka's thesis statement. Is it adequately explained and supported throughout the essay?

3. Are Nantka's topic sentences clear? Is each one supported and explained in the remainder of the paragraph?

4. Is more detail or explanation needed? If so, where?

Paragraph Writing Scenarios

Friends and Family

1. Choose a friend and write a paragraph about how you met.

2. Think of someone you consider old-fashioned. Write a paragraph about the things this person does or says that are not contemporary or up-to-date.

Classes and Campus Life

1. Imagine that you are filling out a financial aid application. Write a paragraph explaining why you need an extra $1,000 this semester.

2. Write a paragraph about whether you would prefer to live at home with your family, on your own in an apartment or house, or in a dorm.

Working Students

1. You need a day off to prepare for an exam. Write a letter to your boss explaining why this test is so important. Include a suggestion for how you might make up the missed hours.

2. Write a paragraph describing the perfect job.

Communities and Cultures

1. Think of a place you like to go—other than school, work, or home—where you feel like you belong. Write a paragraph about what it is about this place that makes you comfortable.

2. Many Americans originally came from all over the world. Choose a friend or relative, living or deceased, and write a paragraph about where they came from and why they emigrated to this country.

WRITING ABOUT A READING

In this article from *Business Week* magazine, the author discusses the wasteful habits of American households as well as efforts to reduce food waste in the United States.

Step 1: Preview the reading.

Step 2: Connect the reading to your own experience: Which types of food do you typically spend the most money on? Which types of food represent the most waste in your own household?

Step 3: Read and respond to the questions in the margin.

LIVING IN THE UNITED STATES OF FOOD WASTE

Ira Sager

1   It's Sunday morning and I'm rummaging through our refrigerator for items we haven't finished, tossing everything—cold cuts, cheese, vegetables, fruit, bread, tomato sauce, yogurt, and various unidentifiable leftovers. This is my weekly routine before heading to the supermarket. The stuffed shells prepared a few days earlier—mostly uneaten: out, too.

Why is this background information included?

2   It's usually at this time I hear my father's voice, chiding his kids for being picky eaters. "You're lucky," he'd say, "you don't know what it's like to go hungry." Hunger was a constant childhood companion, following him and his brothers and sisters from Europe to America.

What are these details intended to show?

3   So I tuck away a few items to eat later or for lunch tomorrow. Roughly, I calculate $12 worth of food is in the garbage, about 8 percent of our weekly grocery bill. That figure varies every week, of course. What doesn't is the garbage pail I fill.

Do these statistics surprise you or make you feel guilty?

4   I am not alone in my wasteful habits. I live in the United States of Food Waste. On average, my fellow citizens throw away 20 pounds of food each month, which amounts to $2,275 a year for a family of four, according to the U.S. Department of Agriculture.

What trend is described here?

5   As a nation, we waste 40 percent of the food we produce, according to estimates from the National Institute of Health. Last year, Americans threw out the equivalent of about $180 billion[1] worth of food—an 8 percent increase from 2008, the last time the USDA calculated the total value of food loss from households, supermarkets, restaurants, and other food-service providers.

Highlight each source of waste.

6   That's only the last links in the food chain—albeit the largest source of waste in this country. (The USDA doesn't factor in what farmers leave in the field.) Waste happens at every step further up the supply chain—at the farm, getting crops to market, during processing, and transportation to distribution centers. Jonathan Bloom, author of *American Wasteland*, a chronicle of waste throughout the food system, estimates that in the U.S. $250 billion worth of food is lost throughout the entire supply chain.

7   All that uneaten food ends up in our landfills—where else? Food scraps are the No. 1 material sent to landfills in the U.S.—more than paper or plastic, according to the Environmental Protection Agency. Our uneaten refuse accounts for about 14 percent of all municipal solid waste, contributing almost 25 percent of methane emissions and costing roughly $1.3 billion to transport and dump in landfills.

What is the common theme of the statistics in this reading? How do the statistics support the thesis? Highlight the thesis when you encounter it.

What is a cultural habit?

8   Wasting food is a cultural habit. When I shop, I expect my grocer to have only the freshest, unblemished vegetables and fruits. Supermarket managers do a daily version of my refrigerator-cleansing routine. If you're in the food-service industry, waste is simply the cost of doing business. The USDA estimates that supermarkets lose $15 billion annually in unsold fruits and vegetables alone. ("Freegan" movement aside, a growing number of people are living off what supermarkets toss.)

What is the "freegan" movement?

Why do you think weighing the food makes a difference in cutting waste?

9   Breaking our wasteful habit requires a cultural adjustment. Food-service giant Sodexo gets workers to help cut waste using a scale connected to a touchscreen terminal developed by LeanPath. Before the food is discarded, a worker places it on the scale and enters the type of food and why it's being tossed. The terminal then records the date, time, and weight, and sets

[1]Bloomberg BusinessWeek updated the USDA food waste numbers using inflation rates for each food category.

What does grassroots mean?

What solution to food waste is suggested here?

What does the expression "on our radar" mean?

What does the Serrano ham example reveal about the author's own attempt to reduce food waste?

a value for the item. The data are used to adjust ordering. In tests on seven college campuses, the company cut food waste nearly 50 percent, by dollar and weight, says Christy Cook, senior manager of sustainability. "It creates **waste** experts [in every kitchen]. It's a grassroots program." So far, Sodexo uses the system in 50 college cafeterias with plans to add more.

10   Some food advocates believe the government should have a more direct role in cutting waste. "We are just now recognizing that we squander a good amount of our food," says Bloom. "The next step is getting people to see it as a problem and act." In a recent report for the Natural Resources Defense Council, Dana Gunders calls for the U.S. to conduct a comprehensive study and set national goals for waste reduction, among other efforts.

11   It's doubtful the government will go so far as to set national goals, as some countries like Britain have. Elise Golan, director for sustainable development, says there is a "brainstorming" effort under way at the USDA to identify programs it can tweak or start new efforts to address the problem. "It's on our radar," she says.

12   I have to admit it's on my radar, too. I'm more aware of the apples we haven't eaten, so I'll buy fewer or none at all. Have my buying habits radically changed? Not really. I'm still a sucker for the impulse buy. I know it's pure manipulation, but that sale on Serrano ham (OK, so they post the price by the quarter pound to make it look less expensive), why not get half a pound—even though I've already stocked up on other cold cuts. Maybe I won't throw it out next week.

WRITING IN RESPONSE TO READING

Examining the Reading Using an Idea Map   MyWritingLab

Review the reading by completing the missing parts of the idea map shown below.

 Visualize It!

Title   **Living in the United States of Food Waste**

Thesis   Americans waste incredible amounts of food.

Waste happens throughout the food chain.

The author wasted _____

We waste _____ of food monthly, or _____ annually.

As a nation _____

We wasted _____ worth of food last year, _____ from 2008.

_____ worth of food is lost through the entire supply chain.

Wasted food ends up in _____.

_____ are the number one material sent to landfills:

Accounting for 14% of _____

_____

_____

Wasting food is a cultural habit.

We expect fresh produce from grocers.

Markets lose $15 billion in _____ _____ annually.

Breaking wasteful habits requires cultural adjustments.

_____ is cutting waste at colleges.

_____ wants direct government role.

USDA is trying to identify programs to _____ .

Conclusion   The author is aware of the problem and is making small changes.

Strengthening Your Vocabulary `MyWritingLab`

Using the word's context, word parts, or a dictionary, write a brief definition of each of the following words as it is used in the reading.

1. rummaging (paragraph 1) _____
2. refuse (paragraph 7) _____
3. unblemished (paragraph 8) _____
4. advocates (paragraph 10) _____
5. squander (paragraph 10) _____
6. tweak (paragraph 11) _____

Reacting to Ideas: Discussion and Journal Writing `MyWritingLab`

Get ready to write about the reading by discussing the following:

1. What was the author's purpose in writing this article?
2. Evaluate the kinds of supporting evidence the author uses in this article. How accurate and reliable do you think his sources are?
3. Why does the author mention his father in paragraph 2? How does his father's "voice" change his own behavior?
4. Based on the last paragraph, how likely do you think the author is to make significant changes to address food waste in his own household?
5. What is the purpose of the photograph that accompanies the reading? How effectively does it illustrate the author's message?

Paragraph Options `MyWritingLab`

1. Write a paragraph evaluating the effectiveness of the title and exploring the meaning of "the United States of Food Waste."
2. How well does the author's personal tone suit the material? What phrases or word choices does the author use to establish a relationship with the reader? Write a paragraph evaluating his style in approaching the material.
3. Which facts or statistics about food waste were most shocking or compelling to you? Choose three facts or statistics in the reading, and write a paragraph explaining why they are shocking or compelling.

Essay Options `MyWritingLab`

4. Do you agree that it is important to change our cultural habit of wasting food? Why or why not? In what other ways are we wasteful in our culture? Write an essay exploring the answers to these questions.
5. Think about your food consumption over the past week or weekend. Write a short essay analyzing approximately how much money you spent on food, what percentage of the food you actually consumed, and what percentage was wasted. Does your own experience confirm or differ from what is described in the reading?
6. What should be the government's role in cutting waste? Should there be national goals for waste reduction? Why or why not? Write an essay addressing these questions.

■ ■ ■ ■

SELF-TEST SUMMARY

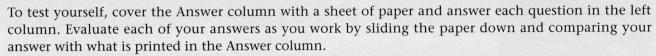

To test yourself, cover the Answer column with a sheet of paper and answer each question in the left column. Evaluate each of your answers as you work by sliding the paper down and comparing your answer with what is printed in the Answer column.

	QUESTION	ANSWER
Goal 1 Choose a topic	What are tips for choosing a workable topic?	In order to choose a workable topic, look for an idea that makes a point, consider topics and ideas that you know a lot about and that interest you, and keep an ongoing list of topics for other assignments.
Goal 2 Keep your reader in mind as you write	How do you communicate effectively with your audience?	Communicate effectively with your audience through your language and word choice as well as through the details you include in your paragraphs.
Goal 3 Generate ideas	What are three techniques for generating ideas, and how does each technique work?	Three techniques for generating ideas are brainstorming, freewriting, and branching. Brainstorming involves making a list of everything you know about your topic. Freewriting involves writing nonstop about your topic for a specified period. Branching involves creating freestyle diagrams to generate ideas.
Goal 4 Organize your ideas	What are three common methods of organizing ideas?	Three common ways to organize ideas are least/most arrangement, time sequence, and spatial arrangement.

MyWritingLab *Visit Ch. 11 Planning and Organizing in MyWritingLab to test your understanding of the chapter objectives.*

12

Drafting and Revising

To grow up big and strong like his Dad he should eat Mini Bonio too.

Like Father, like Son, like Mini Bonio a lot. That's because it's been specially made for smaller dogs and puppies. It's also enriched with calcium and minerals for healthy teeth and bones.

And if that's not enough there are four

SPILLERS MINI BONIO

Spillers takes the biscuit.

other nutritious biscuits in the Spillers range – Mini Chops, Cheese Crunches, Bonio and Shapes.

But even with Mini Bonio he may never grow up to be a Great Dane but he will grow up to be a great Sausage Dog.

WRITE ABOUT IT!

Study the advertisement above. Write a sentence that states what message the advertisement conveys.

Advertisements often begin with a general announcement that catches your interest and suggests what the ad is about. This is called a *headline statement*.

In the ad shown on the preceding page, the headline, "To grow up big and strong like his Dad he should eat Mini Bonio too" catches your attention and suggests the message the ad is trying to convey. The remainder of the ad, called the *body copy,* offers more information about the headline. Ads often end with either a *close* or a *tagline* intended to create a final, lasting impression or to urge action.

Paragraphs follow a similar structure. First, a paragraph must have a sentence that is similar to a headline statement. This sentence identifies the topic of the paragraph, indicates a main point (idea) about the topic, and catches the reader's interest. This sentence is called a **topic sentence**. Writers often place the topic sentence at the beginning of the paragraph. Paragraphs must also have details that support and explain the topic sentence. Finally, like ads, paragraphs need to draw to a close. Usually one or more sentences serve this function. The conclusion of a paragraph makes a strong statement. It leaves the reader with a summary of the paragraph's main point or a point related to what has come before.

In this chapter you will learn how to write topic sentences and develop details to support them. You will also learn how to revise paragraphs to make them more effective.

WRITING

CHOOSING A MANAGEABLE TOPIC

GOAL 1 Choose a manageable topic

The topic you choose for a paragraph must not be too broad or too narrow. It must be the right size to cover in a single paragraph. If you choose a topic that is too broad, you will have too much to say. Your paragraph will wander and seem unfocused. If you choose a topic that is too narrow (too small), you will not have enough to say. Your paragraph will seem skimpy.

Suppose you want to write a paragraph about pollution. You write the following topic sentence:

Pollution is everywhere.

Clearly, the topic of global pollution is too broad to cover in a single paragraph. Pollution has numerous types, causes, effects, and potential solutions. Would you write about causes? If so, could you write about all possible causes in one paragraph? What about effects? Are you concerned with immediate effects? Long-term effects? You can see that the topic of widespread global pollution is not a manageable one for a single paragraph. You could make this topic more manageable by limiting it to a specific pollutant, an immediate source or effect, and a particular place. Your revised topic sentence might read:

Fuel emissions from poorly maintained cars greatly increase air pollution in the United States.

This topic may still prove too broad to cover in a single paragraph. You could narrow it further by limiting the topic to a particular city in the United States, or even a particular type of fuel emission.

Shown below are a few more examples of topics that are too broad. Each one has been revised to be more specific.

TOO BROAD	Water conservation
REVISED	Lawn-watering restrictions
TOO BROAD	Effects of water shortages
REVISED	Sinkholes caused by water shortages
TOO BROAD	Crop irrigation
REVISED	A system for allocating water for crop irrigation in the San Joaquin Valley

If your topic is too narrow, you will run out of things to say in your paragraph. You also run the risk of straying from your topic as you search for ideas to include. Suppose you want to write a paragraph about environmental waste. You write the following topic sentence:

Each year Americans discard 2 billion disposable razors.

This sentence is too specific. It could work as a detail, but it is too narrow to be a topic sentence. To turn this statement into a good topic sentence, try to make your topic more general. Your revised topic sentence could be

Each year Americans strain their landfills with convenient but environmentally damaging products.

You then could develop a paragraph such as the following:

Sample Paragraph

Each year Americans strain their landfills with convenient but environmentally damaging products. For example, Americans discard billions of disposable razors. Disposable diapers are another popular product. Parents use mountains of them on their children instead of washable cloth diapers. Milk, which used to come in reusable glass bottles, is now sold mainly in plastic or cardboard cartons that can only be used once. Other items, such as Styrofoam cups, aluminum cans, disposable cameras, and ballpoint pens, add to the solid-waste problem in this country. Eventually people will need to realize it's not OK to "use it once, then throw it away."

Here are a few other examples of topic sentences that are too narrow. Each one has been revised to be less specific.

TOO NARROW	Americans discard 250 million used tires per year.
REVISED	Several companies are tackling the problem of what to do with used tires.
TOO NARROW	Less than 4 percent of plastics are recycled.
REVISED	Consumers need to take recycling more seriously.
TOO NARROW	Americans in some states are paid five cents per can to recycle aluminum cans.
REVISED	Money motivates many consumers to recycle.

EXERCISE 12-1 **Evaluating Sentences**

Directions: For each of the following pairs of topic sentences, place a check mark on the line before the sentence that is more effective (neither too broad nor too narrow).

1. _____ a. Power tools can be dangerous.

   _____ b. To avoid injury, users of power saws should follow several safety precautions.

2. _____ a. A Barbie doll from the 1950s recently sold for $3,000.

   _____ b. Barbie dolls from the 1950s are valued by collectors.

3. _____ a. Parachuting is a sport.

   _____ b. Parachuting is a sport that requires skill and self-confidence.

4. _____ a. Learning keyboarding skills requires regular practice.

   _____ b. Learning a new skill is difficult.

5. _____ a. Children's toys should be fun.

   _____ b. A toy should stimulate a child's imagination. ■

EXERCISE 12-2 **Narrowing a Topic**
Writing in Progress

Directions: Choose three of the following topics and narrow each one to a topic manageable in a single paragraph. Use branching (p. 275) to help you.

1. Packaging of products
2. The value of parks and "green spaces"
3. Garbage
4. Water pollution or conservation
5. Building environmental awareness
6. Recycling ■

WRITING TOPIC SENTENCES

GOAL 2 Write an effective topic sentence

An effective **topic sentence** must

1. identify what the paragraph is about (the topic).
2. make a point (an idea) about that topic.

Suppose your topic is acid rain. You could make a number of different points about acid rain. Each of the following is a possible topic sentence:

1. Acid rain has caused conflict between the United States and Canada.
2. Acid rain could be reduced by controlling factory emissions.
3. Acid rain has adversely affected the populations of fish in our lakes.

Each of the sentences identifies acid rain as the topic, but each expresses a different point about acid rain. Each would lead to a different paragraph and be supported by different details.

Think of your topic sentence as a headline; it states what your paragraph will contain. You can also think of a topic sentence as a promise. Your topic sentence promises your reader what you will deliver in the paragraph.

What does each of the following topic sentences promise the reader?

1. There are three basic ways to dispose of sewage sludge.
2. Each year we discard valuable raw materials into landfills.
3. Many people do not understand how easy composting is.

Sentence 1 promises to explain three ways to dispose of sewage sludge. Sentence 2 promises to tell what valuable resources we discard. Sentence 3 promises to explain how easy composting is.

Your topic sentence must be a clear and direct statement of what the paragraph will be about. Use the following suggestions to write effective topic sentences:

1. **Be sure your topic sentence is a complete thought.** If your sentence is a fragment, run-on sentence, or comma splice, your meaning will be unclear or incomplete.

FRAGMENT	People who don't throw their litter in the bin.
RUN-ON SENTENCE	The audience was captivated by the speaker no one spoke or moved.
COMMA SPLICE	Many children's games copy adult behavior, playing nurse or doctor is an example.

   Chapter 4 and Chapter 5 discuss how to spot and correct these errors.

2. **Place your topic sentence first in the paragraph.** You *may* place your topic sentence anywhere in the paragraph, but you will find it easier to develop your paragraph around the topic sentence if you put it first.

3. **Avoid direct announcements or statements of intent.** Avoid sentences that sound like formal announcements, such as the following examples:

ANNOUNCEMENT	In this paragraph, I will show that the average American is unaware of the dangers of smog.
REVISED	The average American is unaware of the dangers of smog.
ANNOUNCEMENT	This paragraph will explain why carbon monoxide is a dangerous air pollutant.
REVISED	There are three primary reasons why carbon monoxide is a dangerous air pollutant.

EXERCISE 12-3   Writing a Topic Sentence

Writing in Progress

Directions: Write a topic sentence for each of the three topics that you selected in Exercise 12-2. ■

DEVELOPING THE PARAGRAPH

GOAL 3 Develop a paragraph using supporting details

Once you've written a preliminary topic sentence, your next step is to include the details that support your sentence. Just as an advertiser provides facts and information that support the headline, so must you provide details that support your topic sentence. Let's look at advertising copy on a milk carton.

In the ad copy shown below, the subject is organic chocolate milk. Now study the body copy. What kinds of information are provided? Notice that only information that supports the subject is included: all the details describe organic milk and convince readers that it is a source of plant-based DHA, calcium and vitamin D, 8 essential nutrients, and does not contain added hormones, antibiotics, pesticides, or cloning. These are called **relevant details**. *Relevant* means that the details directly relate to or explain the headline. Notice, too, that a reasonable number of facts are included—enough to make the headline believable and convincing. In other words, a **sufficient** number of **details** are provided to make the headline effective. When you select details to support a topic sentence, they must also be *relevant* and *sufficient*. You must provide a sufficient number of details to make your topic sentence understandable and convincing. However, a detail that is interesting and true must be left out if it does not support the topic sentence.

Tip for Writers

Relevant information is about the topic being discussed. The opposite is *irrelevant.* If your teacher marks a sentence *irrelevant,* that means it doesn't belong where you've placed it, so it should be deleted or moved to another paragraph.

Choosing Relevant Details

Relevant details directly support the topic sentence. The following paragraph contains two details that do not support the topic sentence, which is shaded. Can you spot them?

Sample Paragraph

(1) Corporations are beginning to recognize the importance of recycling. (2) Our landfills are getting too full, and we are running out of room for our garbage. (3) Many companies are selling products with reusable containers. (4) Tide laundry soap and Jergens hand cream, for example, sell refills. (5) It bothers me that some manufacturers charge the same or even more, for refills as for the original containers. (6) I believe all cities and towns should have recycling bins to make it easy for individuals to recycle. (7) By recycling tin, glass, plastic, and paper, companies can save valuable natural resources. (8) Some corporations recycle plastic and paper bags to conserve energy and natural resources. (9) Through these methods, corporations are helping to save our environment.

Sentence 5 is not relevant because what companies charge for reusable containers does not relate to the importance of recycling. Sentence 6 is not relevant because it is about towns and individuals, not corporations.

EXERCISE 12-4   Selecting Relevant Details
Working Together

Directions: Each of the topic sentences listed below is followed by a set of details. Working with a classmate, place check marks on the lines before those statements that are relevant supporting details.

1. **TOPIC SENTENCE** People should take safety precautions when outside temperatures reach 95 degrees or above.

   DETAILS
   _____ a. It is important to drink plenty of fluids.
   _____ b. If you are exposed to extreme cold or dampness, you should take precautions.
   _____ c. To prevent heat exhaustion, reduce physical activity.
   _____ d. Infants and elderly people are particularly at risk for heat exhaustion.

2. **TOPIC SENTENCE** Cuba is one of the last nations with a communist government.

   DETAILS
   _____ a. Cuba is an island nation and thus is able to keep out other political philosophies and opponents of communism.
   _____ b. Cuba earns high revenues from cigar sales despite the U.S. boycott against Cuba.

_____ c. Fidel Castro was not chosen by the Cuban people.

_____ d. The movement to overthrow communism in Cuba is centered in Miami and thus is not very effective within Cuba itself.

3. TOPIC SENTENCE   Freedom of speech, the first amendment to the United States Constitution, does not give everyone the right to say anything at any time.

DETAILS   _____ a. The Constitution also protects freedom of religion.

_____ b. Freedom of speech is a right that citizens of most Western countries take for granted.

_____ c. Freedom of speech is restricted by slander and libel laws, which prohibit speaking or publishing harmful, deliberate lies about people.

_____ d. Citizens may sue if they feel their freedom of speech has been unfairly restricted.

4. TOPIC SENTENCE   Family violence against women is a growing problem that is difficult to control or prevent.

DETAILS   _____ a. Abusive partners will often ignore restraining orders.

_____ b. Violence shown on television may encourage violence at home.

_____ c. New laws make it easier for observers of child abuse to report the violence.

_____ d. Battered women frequently do not tell anyone that they have been battered because they are ashamed.

_____ e. Violence against the elderly is increasing at a dramatic rate. ■

Including Sufficient Details

Including **sufficient details** means including _enough_ details to make your topic sentence believable and convincing. Your details should be as exact and specific as possible. The following paragraph lacks sufficient detail:

Sample Paragraph

Recycling has a lot of positive sides. When you recycle, you receive money if you return used containers. When you recycle, you clean up the earth, and you also save the environment. Less waste and more space are our goals.

Notice that the paragraph is very general. It does not describe any specific benefits of recycling, nor does it explain how recycling saves the environment or creates more space.

A revised version is shown below. Notice the addition of numerous details and the more focused topic sentence.

Revised Paragraph

Recycling offers benefits for consumers and manufacturers, as well as for the environment. Consumers benefit from recycling in several ways. Recycling generates revenue, which should, in the long run, reduce costs of products. Soda bottles and cans returned to the store produce immediate return for cash. Manufacturers benefit, too, since their costs are reduced. Most important, however, are benefits to the environment. Recycling reduces landfills. It also produces cleaner air by reducing manufacturing. Finally, recycling paper saves trees.

If you have difficulty thinking of enough details to include in a paragraph, try brainstorming, freewriting, or branching. Also, try to draft a more focused topic sentence, as the writer did in the paragraph above. You may then find it easier to develop supporting details. If you are still unable to generate additional details, your topic may be too narrow or you may need to do some additional reading or research on your topic. If you use information from printed sources, be sure to give the author credit by using a citation. Indicate the author, title, place of publication, publisher, and year.

NEED TO KNOW

Drafting Paragraphs

To draft effective paragraphs, be sure to
- choose a manageable **topic**. Your topic should be neither too broad nor too narrow.
- write a clear **topic sentence**. Your topic sentence should identify the topic and make a point about that topic.
- develop your paragraph by providing **relevant** and **sufficient details**. Relevant details are those that directly support the topic. Including sufficient details means providing enough details to make your topic sentence believable and convincing.

EXERCISE 12-5   Writing a Paragraph
Writing in Progress

Directions: Write a paragraph developing one of the topic sentences you wrote in Exercise 12-3. Then, check to see if you can improve your topic sentence by making it more focused. Make the necessary changes. Finally, be sure you have included relevant and sufficient details in the rest of your paragraph. ■

Avoiding Plagiarism and Citing Sources

Plagiarism is using another person's words or ideas without giving that person credit. (*Plagiarism* comes from a Latin word meaning "to kidnap.") An author's writing is considered legal property. To take an author's words or ideas and use them as your own is dishonest.

How to Avoid Plagiarism

To avoid plagiarism, keep in mind the following points:

1. **It is not necessary to credit information that is common knowledge—the major facts of history, for example—or information that is available in many reference books.**

2. **You should credit unique ideas, little-known facts, interpretations of facts, and unique wording.**

3. **If you copy in your notes a phrase, sentence, or paragraph from a source, always put quotation marks around it.** Then you'll never make the mistake of presenting it as your own. Following the quotation, indicate the title of the source and the author's name.

4. **When taking notes on someone else's unique ideas, place brackets around your notes to indicate that the information was taken from a source.** In your notes, include information on the source.

How to Credit Sources

When you do use someone else's words or ideas, you must indicate from where and whom you took the information. To credit sources accurately, use the following suggestions.

1. **Be sure to record complete information on each source you use.** On a 3-by-5-inch index card, in a computer file, or on a photocopy of the source materials you have found, write the source's title and author and the page number of the quotation or other information you want to use. If the source is a book, include the publisher and the year and place of publication. If the source is a magazine article, include the volume and issue numbers and the beginning and ending page numbers of the article. For Internet sources, include the author's name, the title, the date of publication, the site's URL, and the date you accessed the site.

2. **In your paper, use the documentation style that your instructor specifies.** Two common documentation methods are the MLA (Modern Language Association) style and the APA (American Psychological Association) style. With both styles, you place a brief reference to the source within your paper, giving the author, the title, and the page number for the material you used. You then give complete information on your sources in a list of references at the end of your paper.

3. **To obtain further information about MLA and APA styles, consult the most recent edition of the *MLA Handbook for Writers of Research Papers* or the *Publication Manual of the American Psychological Association.*** Your library or bookstore will have copies. You can also find summaries of these styles in some writing handbooks or online.

REVISING PARAGRAPHS

> **GOAL 4** Revise a paragraph by adding, deleting, and changing text

Did you know that it takes an advertising agency months to develop and write a successful ad? Copy writers and editors work through many drafts until they decide on a final version of the ad. Often, too, an agency may test an ad on a sample group of consumers. Then, working from consumer responses, the agency makes further changes in the ad.

To produce an effective paragraph, you will need to revise and test your work. Revision is a process of examining and rethinking your ideas. It involves adding text, deleting text, and changing both *what* you have said and *how* you have said it.

When to Revise

It is usually best, after writing a draft of a paragraph, to wait a day before beginning to revise it. You will have a fresh outlook on your topic and will find that it is easier to see what you need to change.

How to Revise

Sometimes it is difficult to know how to improve your own writing. Simply rereading your own work may not help you discover flaws, weaknesses, or needed changes. This section presents two aids to revision that will help you identify what and how to revise: (1) a **revision map** and (2) a **revision checklist**.

Using Revision Maps

A **revision map**, as shown on **the next page**, is a visual display of the ideas in your paragraph or essay. It is similar to an idea map. While an idea map shows how ideas in someone else's writing are related, a revision map will show you how ideas in your writing fit together. A revision map will also help you identify ideas that do not fit and those that need further explanation.

To draw a revision map of a paragraph, follow these steps:

1. **Write a shortened topic sentence at the top of your paper, as in the sample revision map on the next page.** Be sure your topic sentence has both a subject and a verb and expresses an *idea*. Do *not* simply write the topic of your paragraph.

2. **Work through your paragraph sentence by sentence.** On your revision map, underneath the topic sentence, list each detail that directly supports the topic sentence.

3. **If you spot a detail that is an example or a further explanation of a detail already listed, write it underneath the first detail and indent it.**

4. **If you spot a detail that does not seem to support anything you've written, write it to the right of your list, as in the sample revision map.**

The diagram on the next page is a sample revision map.

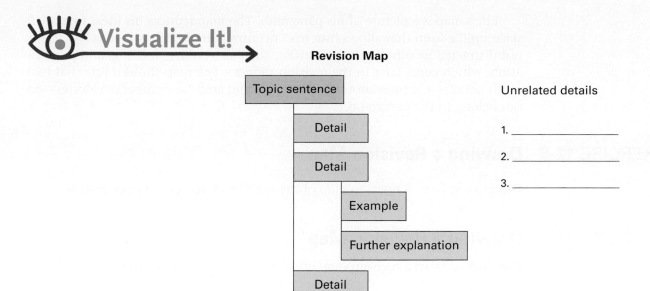

Visualize It!

Revision Map

| Topic sentence |
| Detail |
| Detail |
| Example |
| Further explanation |
| Detail |

Unrelated details

1. _____
2. _____
3. _____

The following paragraph is a first draft written by a student named Eric. His revision map follows the paragraph.

Sample First Draft

Pizza is a surprisingly nutritious food. It has cheese, tomato sauce, and crust. Each of these is part of a basic food group. However, nutritionists now talk about the food pyramid instead of food groups. Toppings such as mushrooms and peppers also add to its nutritional value. Pepperoni, sausage, and anchovies provide protein. Pizza is high in calories, though, and everyone is counting calories. But pizza does provide a wide variety of nutrients from vegetables, dairy products, meats, and carbohydrates. And the best part is that it is tasty, as well as nutritious.

Visualize It!

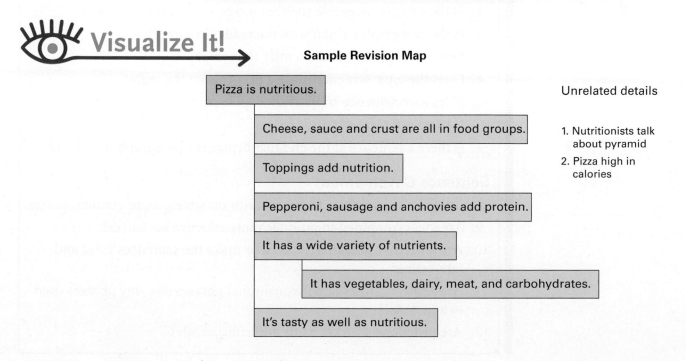

Sample Revision Map

| Pizza is nutritious. |
| Cheese, sauce and crust are all in food groups. |
| Toppings add nutrition. |
| Pepperoni, sausage and anchovies add protein. |
| It has a wide variety of nutrients. |
| It has vegetables, dairy, meat, and carbohydrates. |
| It's tasty as well as nutritious. |

Unrelated details

1. Nutritionists talk about pyramid
2. Pizza high in calories

Eric's map is a picture of his paragraph. The map reduces his ideas to a brief, skeletonlike form that allows him to concentrate on the ideas themselves. He is not distracted by other revision matters, such as wording, spelling, and punctuation, which come later in the revision process. The map showed Eric that two of his details—the ones about the food pyramid and the number of calories—do not belong in the paragraph.

EXERCISE 12-6   Drawing a Revision Map

Directions: Draw a revision map of the sample paragraph on page 294. ■

EXERCISE 12-7   Drawing a Revision Map

Writing in Progress

Directions: Draw a revision map of the paragraph you wrote in Exercise 12-5. ■

Using the Revision Checklist

Focused questions can help you evaluate a piece of writing. The revision checklist is a list of questions in checklist form to help you look closely and critically at your writing and to identify parts that need improvement. It will also help you confirm that you have mastered certain skills. The revision checklist is divided into two parts: paragraph development and sentence development. The sentence development section covers what you learned in Chapter 4 through Chapter 10. As you learn more about writing paragraphs in later chapters, we will add items to the paragraph development section.

Revision Checklist

Paragraph Development

1. Is the topic manageable (neither too broad nor too narrow)?
2. Is the paragraph written with the reader in mind?
3. Does the topic sentence identify the topic?
4. Does the topic sentence make a point about the topic?
5. Does each sentence support the topic sentence?
6. Is there sufficient detail?
7. Is there a sentence at the end that brings the paragraph to a close?

Sentence Development

8. Are there any sentence fragments, run-on sentences, or comma splices?
9. Are ideas combined to produce more effective sentences?
10. Are adjectives and adverbs used to make the sentences vivid and interesting?
11. Are relative clauses and prepositional phrases like *-ing* phrases used to add detail?
12. Are pronouns used correctly and consistently?

Now let's apply the questions from the paragraph development section of the checklist to a sample student paragraph. Read the paragraph and then answer the questions in the revision checklist that follows.

Sample Paragraph

The world is experiencing a steady decline in water quality and availability. About 75 percent of the world's rural population and 20 percent of its urban population have no ready access to uncontaminated water. Many states have a limited water supply, and others waste water. Bans on lawn sprinkling and laws restricting water use would help solve the problem. Building more reservoirs would also help.

Revision Checklist

Paragraph Development

1. Is the topic manageable (neither too broad nor too narrow)?

   _____

2. Is the paragraph written with the reader in mind?

   _____

3. Does the topic sentence identify the topic? (What is the topic?)

   _____

4. Does the topic sentence make a point about the topic? (What is the point?)

   _____

5. Does each sentence support the topic sentence? (List any that do not.)

   _____

6. Is there sufficient detail?

   _____

7. Is there a sentence at the end that brings the paragraph to a close? (What is it?)

   _____

The topic of the paragraph above—water quality and availability throughout the world—is too broad. Water quality and water availability are two separate topics, and both vary greatly throughout the world. To revise this paragraph, the writer first narrowed the topic to one idea. Choosing the topic of increasing water availability in the United States, he wrote the revised paragraph on the following page.

Revised Paragraph

There are several easy-to-take actions that could increase water availability in the United States. First, lawn-sprinkling bans would reduce nonessential use of water in areas in which water is in short supply. Second, laws limiting the total amount of water a household could use would require people to cut down on their water use at home. Increasing the cost of water to households is a third way to restrict its use. Each of these actions could produce an immediate increase in water availability.

NEED TO KNOW
Revising Paragraphs

Revision is a process of examining and rethinking your ideas. It involves adding text, deleting text, and changing both what you say and how you say it. To know what to revise, do the following:

1. Draw a **revision map**. A revision map is similar to an idea map. It shows how your ideas relate to one another.
2. Use a **revision checklist**. The revision checklist offers focused questions that will help you evaluate your writing.

EXERCISE 12-8   Using a Revision Checklist
Writing in Progress

Directions: Apply all the questions in the revision checklist—about both sentences and paragraphs—to the paragraph you wrote in Exercise 12-5. ■

 Analyze It!

Directions: In the following paragraph, underline the topic sentence. Then cross out sentences that contain unrelated details that do not support the topic sentence.

If you are a diner who loves to eat a little bit of everything, you should definitely sample the Spanish-based cuisine known as tapas. Tapas originated in Spain as small snacks—olives, almonds, cubes of cheese, slices of ham—eaten while drinking beer or wine in a neighborhood bar during the early evening. According to one legend. Alfonso, the king of Castile, acquired the habit of eating small snacks with wine when he was recovering from an illness, and he later advocated the practice for his subjects. Alfonso was a tyrant and not well-liked. Today, many diners order a selection of tapas for lunch or dinner rather than eating them only as cocktail appetizers. These diners are obviously not concerned with costs or calories Some tapas consist of toasted bread with toppings such as grilled anchovies, smoked ham, or marinated tomatoes. Other tapas are fried and served with sauces: for example, Patatas Bravas consists of fried potatoes in a spicy sauce, and Albondigas are meatballs in garlic-tomato sauce. Spanish cuisine is known for delicious stews and soups as well as tapes If your taste buds are bored, and you want more variety, try some tapas!

WRITING IN PROGRESS: THREE VERSIONS OF "PROFESSIONAL ATHLETES AS ROLE MODELS"

This essay by Jacob Frey illustrates the process of discovering and narrowing a topic, writing a first draft, and revising. As you read through Frey's drafts, pay particular attention to the changes he makes.

Topic Selection

Celebrities

(Sports)

Defining Success in Life

Adjusting to College

New Year's Resolutions

Social Media

Cyberbullying

College Student Finances

Narrowing a Topic

Playing sports in school

(Athletes as role models)

Benefits of sports in society

Hardcore sports fans

(Professional athletes as good role models)

Professional athletes as poor role models

Lessons learned from professional athletes

Female role models vs. male role models

Stress young children feel when playing sports

College athletics vs. Professional athletics

Paying college athletes

Managing school and sports

Steroids and sports

FIRST DRAFT SHOWING REVISIONS
PROFESSIONAL ATHLETES AS GOOD ROLE MODELS

Jacob Frey

LeBron, Kobe, Jordan, Shaq, Rice just the start of a list of names that have their names in lights and that have fans googley eying their every move. Every move they do is watched and every word coming out of their mouth is recorded and dispersed to the world through the media. Professional athletes have basically no privacy and how they act and what they do inspire people of all ages. Some people base their entire lives off of what professional athletes are saying and how they are acting and they try and copy their style and show themselves off like a pro athlete. Pro athletes are good role because they inspire people to have a strong work ethic and to go out and try and achieve their dream.

Athletes can inspire people with anything they do, especially in the words that they speak. Post-game press conferences give athletes an opportunity to talk about how they gave their full effort and put all their work they have done into the game they just played. If they loose and they are being interviewed they can show how to be a gracious loser and congratulate the other team for playing hard and give their word that they will be in the gym working harder to win next time. When people here these words they can take them and apply them to their own lives and personal battles. If they have a victory they can give credit to their hard work, and if they have a loss they can dedicate themselves to working harder.

It's not just in interviews that athletes have the ability to be positive role models but also in their game attitude. Some athletes just flat out quit when there team gets behind by a lot they stop caring they give up and throw in the towel. There are other athletes though that go harder and try to motivate their teammates to do the same to work harder to show that even though they may be down they are not yet out. It is not always possible for them to win the game though and it is more as a symbol that they are willing to play to the last minute of the game by showing their toughness. People can take this practice into their lives and apply it to every day and not quitting even if they are behind. If someone is failing a class midyear, they can push through and give it their all and make a passing grade.

Most professional athletes play on a team and weather they are playing a game or just in practice they have to make sure that they are getting along with their teammates and functioning all together. Athletes have to create relationships with their teammates, and even if they do not like their teammates all that much, they still have to be able to play with them night after night. This is good for people to see because not everyone likes everyone else but they may have to work with some people they do not like and so they can do like the athletes and form relationships and work with the people they may not like.

Athletes are where they are because of the hard work they put in when they were younger and not just because they are able to play on a team. Athletes put in hours and hours of hard work and kept dreaming about one day making it pro and they worked to achieve that goal. People should dream big like athletes and then take what they are dreaming and make it reality. They should work their hardest every day in order to capture and make their dream come true. The hard work they put in can pay off and put them at the top of whatever they are striving for.

Athletes teach people to go and capture their dreams and be humble in a win or a loss and that sometimes teammates aren't necessarily people that are liked, but they have to work with them anyways. Athletes are very positive role models and live everyday showing that hard work can pay off and many athletes try to model their lives in positive ways to make sure that people see them as role models. While not all athletes are perfect and good role models, many are and can help people work their hardest and achieve their goals.

SECOND DRAFT SHOWING REVISIONS
PROFESSIONAL ATHLETES AS ROLE MODELS
Jacob Frey

LeBron, Kobe, Jordan, Shaq, Rice. This is just the start of a list of people who have their names in lights and that have fans googley eying their every move. Every move they make is watched and every word coming out of their mouth is recorded and dispersed to the world through the media. Professional athletes have basically no privacy, and how they act and what they do inspire people of all ages. Some people base their entire lives off of what professional athletes are saying and how they are acting and they try and copy their style and show themselves off like a pro athlete. Pro athletes are good role models because they inspire people to have a strong work ethic and to go out and try and achieve their dream.

Athletes can inspire people with anything they do, especially in the words that they speak. Post-game press conferences give athletes an opportunity to talk about how they gave their full effort to the game they just played. If they loose and they are being interviewed, they can model how to be a gracious loser by congratulating the other team for playing hard and giving their word that they will be in the gym working harder to win next time. When fans here these words, they can take them and apply them to their own lives and personal battles. If they have a victory, they can give credit to their hard work, and if they have a loss they can dedicate themselves to working harder.

Not only do athletes serve as positive role models in interviews, but they also have the ability to be good role models in their game attitude. Some athletes just flat out quit when there team gets behind by a lot. They stop caring, they give up, and throw in the towel. There are other athletes, though, that work harder and try to motivate their teammates to do the same - to work harder to show that even though they may be down, they are not yet out. It is not always possible for them to win the game though and it is more as a symbol that they are willing to play to the last minute of the game by showing their toughness. People can take this practice into their lives and apply it to every day and not quitting even if they are behind. If someone is failing a class midyear, he can push through and give it his all and make a passing grade.

Most professional athletes play on a team and weather they are playing a game or just in practice they have to make sure that they are getting along with their teammates and functioning all together. Athletes have to create relationships with their teammates, and even if they do not like their teammates all that much, they still have to be able to play with them night after night. This is good for people to see because not everyone likes everyone else but they may have to work with some people they do not like. In school and work, collaboration is required, and sometimes, a grade or an evaluation is based on how well one works' with others. Athletes model this behavior well on their playing field. They function as a team, not as individuals.

Another positive trait that athletes model is their commitment to training. Athletes are where they are because of the hard work they put in when they were younger and not just because they are able to play on a team. Athletes put in hours and hours of hard work and kept dreaming about one day making it to the professional level and they worked to achieve that goal. People should dream big like athletes and then take what they are dreaming and make it reality. They should work their hardest every day in order to capture and make their dream come true. The hard work they put in can pay off and put them at the top of whatever they are striving for.

Athletes are very positive role models and live everyday showing that hard work can pay off and many athletes try to model their lives in positive ways to make sure that people see them as role models. They teach people to go and capture their dreams and be humble in a win or a loss and that sometimes teammates aren't necessarily people that are liked, but they have to work with them anyways. While not all athletes are good role models, many are and can encourage people to work their hardest and achieve their goals.

FINAL DRAFT THE WRITING TASK
PROFESSIONAL ATHLETES AS ROLE MODELS

Jacob Frey

LeBron, Kobe, Jordan, Shaq, Rice. This is just the start of a list of people who have their names in lights and fans eying their every move. Every move they make is watched, and every word coming out of their mouth is recorded and dispersed to the world through the media. Professional athletes have no privacy, and how they act and what they do inspire people of all ages. Some people base their entire lives off of what professional athletes are saying and how they are acting, and they try to copy their style and show themselves off like a professional athlete. Pro athletes are good role models because they inspire people to have a strong work ethic and to go out and try to achieve their dream.

Athletes can inspire people with anything they do, especially in the words that they speak. Post-game press conferences give athletes an opportunity to talk about how they gave their full effort to the game they just played. If they lose and they are being interviewed, they can model how to be a gracious loser by congratulating the other team for playing hard and giving their word that they will be in the gym working harder to win next time. When fans hear these words, they can take them and apply them to their own lives and personal battles. For example, if they have a victory, they can give credit to their hard work, and if they have a loss, they can dedicate themselves to working harder.

Not only do athletes serve as positive role models in interviews, but they also have the ability to be good role models in their game attitude. Some athletes just flat out quit when their team gets behind by a lot. They stop caring, they give up, and they throw in the towel. There are other athletes, though, that work harder and try to motivate their teammates to do the same—to work harder to show that even though they may be down, they are not yet out. Though it is not always possible for them to win the game, their attitude serves more as a symbol that they are willing to play to the last minute of the game by showing their toughness. People can take this practice into their lives and persevere even if they are behind. If someone is failing a class midyear, he can push through and give it his all and make a passing grade.

Most professional athletes play on a team, and whether they are playing a game or just in practice, they have to make sure that they are getting along with their teammates and functioning as a team. Athletes have to create relationships with their teammates, and even if they do not like their teammates all that much, they still have to be able to play with them night after night. This is good for people to see because not everyone likes everyone else, but they may have to work with some people they do not like. In school and work, collaboration is required, and sometimes, a grade or an evaluation is based on how well one works with others. Athletes model this behavior well on their playing field. They function as a team, not as individuals.

Another positive trait that athletes model is their commitment to training. Athletes are where they are because of the hard work they put in when they were younger and not just because they are able to play on a team. As they were developing their skill, athletes put in hours and hours of hard work and kept dreaming about one day making it to the professional level, and they worked hard to achieve that goal. People should dream big like athletes and then take what they are dreaming and make it a reality. They should work their hardest every day in order to capture and make their dream come true. The hard work they put in can pay off and put them at the top of whatever they are striving for.

Athletes are positive role models, and they live everyday showing that hard work can pay off. They teach people to pursue their dreams and be humble in a win or a loss. They also model teamwork and acceptance of others. Sometimes teammates aren't necessarily best friends, but they have to work together to achieve a goal. While not all athletes are good role models, many are, and they encourage people to work their hardest and achieve their goals.

EXAMINING STUDENT WRITING

1. Evaluate the structure and content of the essay.
    a. Does the essay follow a logical plan? Describe its organization.
    b. What is Frey's thesis?
    c. In what ways does he support his thesis?
    d. Evaluate the effectiveness of the title, introduction, and conclusion.
2. Study the changes Frey made in his revisions. What kinds of changes did he make?
3. What further revisions would you suggest?

The Writing Task

Jessica Beebe submitted this essay for a psychology class. Her assignment was to examine a current social media outlet and explain what makes it attractive to Internet users.

Title: identifies the subject of the essay

Pinterest: Social Media with a Twist

Jessica Beebe

Introduction: Beebe engages the reader by describing Pinterest

Pinterest, the visual social media site with a scrapbook or "pin board" interface, is sometimes called the site where women go to plan imaginary weddings, dress children that don't exist, and decorate homes they can't afford. Any person with a familiarity with Pinterest will likely smile at the humorous, vastly oversimplified criticism. Indeed, the vast majority of Pinterest users are women and a quick perusal of the most popular "pins" on the site will show that wedding planning, children's clothing, and home decorating are prevalent on the site.

Thesis statement

However, closer inspection reveals that Pinterest is not merely a deluge of pictures, but a tool for organization on a wide variety of topics, a useful way to share visual plans and ideas, and a unique social media site amongst other social media sites like Facebook, LinkedIn, and Twitter.

Topic sentence

Pinterest is not only a place for women to plan imaginary weddings or dress imaginary children. Pinterest is a social media site designed to serve as a visual scrapbook and discovery tool, helping users to find images and articles and "pin" them to user-created boards centered on any number of topics and interests. Though it is true that the vast majority of pins tend to center on domestic concerns like home decorating, craft ideas, and recipes, pins can be anything from a beautiful piece of artwork to a diagram of the latest gadget. From cars to cartoons, users can arrange pins onto themed boards for organization, and sort these boards into categories. Users can also find others who share their tastes and "follow" boards to generate a feed of images on a user's home Pinterest page.

Topic sentence

Some users merely take pleasure in looking at the myriad of images tailored to their interests, but Pinterest often serves a more utilitarian purpose. Users will often use Pinterest for planning events or keeping lists. Instead of creating a bulky binder to keep track of details for a large birthday party, users can simply pin party ideas onto a board. Designers, artists, stylists, bloggers, and other creative professionals use Pinterest as a way to generate inspiration and to find and audience for their work. Travellers can pin ideas for a vacation and create maps based on their pinned points of interest. Pinterest users can even search for gift ideas and share boards with others to collaborate on projects.

Topic sentence

Though Pinterest is often considered alongside other major social media websites like Facebook, LinkedIn, and Twitter, it is important to differentiate between them. Facebook and LinkedIn are social media sites built around personal profiles. Individuals are encouraged to represent themselves on a profile page and to share information about themselves. On Facebook, this information is meant to be personal and on LinkedIn, professional. Twitter strips down much of the extraneous content on these other social media sites by focusing not on a profile, but almost entirely on user "tweets" or short, 140-character status updates. Contrastingly, Pinterest users are given no platform to provide personal or professional status updates. Instead, the site is entirely designed around discovering, organizing, and sharing images.

Because Pinterest is so unique among social media sites for sharing and organizing images, it is easy to see why the site has been able to grow so greatly in popularity since it launched in 2010. Not only is the site a unique social media outlet, but it offers utility, making it easier to visualize plans and to share these visions with others. Pinterest also offers great flexibility by not limiting the content on its site to only a few topics. Users are free to make pin boards about dogs, hats, or even dogs wearing hats. The possibilities are almost limitless. Pinterest's distinctiveness, utility, and flexibility make it an attractive site for Internet users around the globe.

> **Conclusion: a summary of the main points and a restatement of the thesis bring the essay to a close.**

EXAMINING STUDENT WRITING

1. Does Beebe follow a logical plan of organization? Suggest how the organization could be improved.

2. Do you think further details are needed? If so, suggest which paragraphs need more detail. What types of detail would improve the essay?

3. Do you think the major aspects of Pinterest are adequately explained?

4. What details could Beebe have included that might make Pinterest more appealing to men?

Paragraph Writing Scenarios

Friends and Family

1. Write a paragraph describing an ancestor or relative you've never met, but about whom you've heard a lot. Include things others have said about this person that make him or her sound interesting.

2. Every family has its own idea of success. Write a paragraph about something you've done or could do to make your family proud of you.

Classes and Campus Life

1. You have an important assignment due tomorrow, but classes may be canceled because of the weather. Write a paragraph about how you will spend the evening, preparing for classes or hoping for a storm.

2. A book you need from the library has been out for weeks. Write a paragraph explaining how you will solve the problem.

Working Students

1. Imagine you are going to a job interview. Write a paragraph describing specific strengths you have that will enable you to handle both school and work.

2. Describe in a paragraph something you do to pass the time when work is slow.

Communities and Cultures

1. Some people do best as part of a team, and others prefer to do things alone. Write a paragraph describing one thing you'd rather do on your own and another in which you'd rather be part of a group or team.

2. Society has become very casual, with people wearing jeans in most places. Write a paragraph describing one place where you think jeans or other casual clothes are inappropriate.

WRITING ABOUT A READING

The following reading, "Finding a Mate: Not the Same as It Used to Be," is taken from a textbook by James M. Henslin titled *Sociology: A Down-to-Earth Approach to Core Concepts*.

Step 1: Preview the reading.

Step 2: Connect the reading to your own experience: How did your parents meet? What is the best way to find a mate?

Step 3: Read and respond to the questions in the margin.

THINK AS YOU READ

Based on your preview, what aspect of finding a mate does the author focus on?

What is the purpose of this paragraph?

Do you expect this statement to be the thesis? Why or why not?

What criteria do Chinese matchmakers use to identify compatability?

How do Chinese parents retain input?

What do these descriptions reveal about the author's attitude?

FINDING A MATE: NOT THE SAME AS IT USED TO BE

James M. Henslin

1   THINGS HAVEN'T CHANGED ENTIRELY. Boys and girls still get interested in each other at their neighborhood schools, and men and women still meet at college. Friends still serve as matchmakers and introduce friends, hoping they might click. People still meet at churches and bars, at the mall and at work.

2   But technology is bringing about some fundamental changes.

3   Among traditional people—Jews, Arabs, and in the villages of China and India—for centuries matchmakers have brought couples together. They carefully match a prospective couple by background—or by the position of the stars, whatever their tradition dictates—arranging marriages to please the families of the bride and groom, and, hopefully, the couple, too.

4   In China, this process is being changed by technology. Matchmakers use computerized records—age, sex, personal interests, and, increasingly significant, education and earnings—to identify compatibility and predict lifelong happiness.

5   But parents aren't leaving the process up to technology. They want their input, too. In one park in Beijing, hundreds of mothers and fathers gather twice a week to try to find spouses for their adult children. They bring photos of their children and share them with one another, talking up their kid's virtues while evaluating the sales pitch they get from the other parents. Some of the parents even sit on the grass, next to handwritten ads they've written about their children.

6   Closer to home, Americans are turning more and more to the Internet. Dating sites advertise that they offer thousands of potential companions, lovers, or spouses. For a low monthly fee, you, too, can meet the person of your dreams.

7   The photos are fascinating in their variety. Some seem to be lovely people, attractive and vivacious, and one wonders why they are posting their photos and personal information online. Do they have some secret flaw that they need to do this? Others seem okay, although perhaps, a bit needy. Then there are the pitiful, and one wonders if they will ever find a mate, or even a hookup, for that matter. Some are desperate, begging for someone—

anyone—to make contact with them: women who try for sexy poses, exposing too much flesh, suggesting the promise of at least a good time; and men who try their best to look like hulks, their muscular presence promising the same.

8   Many regular, ordinary people post their profiles. And some do find the person of their dreams—or at least adequate matches. With Internet postings losing their stigma, electronic matchmaking is becoming an acceptable way to find a mate.

What is the purpose of the cartoon?

Tall, Dark, and Handsome chats with Buxom Blonde.

9   Matchmaking sites tout "thousands of eligible prospects." Unfortunately, the prospects are spread over the nation, and few people want to invest in a plane ticket only to find that the "prospect" doesn't even resemble the posted photo. You can do a search for your area, but there are likely to be few candidates from it.

What does "not to worry" really mean?

10   Not to worry. More technology to the rescue.

How does "dating on demand" work?

11   The ease and comfort of "dating on demand." You sit at home, turn on your TV, and use your remote to search for your partner. Your local cable company has done all the hard work—hosting singles events at bars and malls, where they tape singles talking about themselves and what they are looking for in a mate.

12   You can view the videos free. And if you get interested in someone, for just a small fee you can contact the individual.

Does the author seem enthusiastic or skeptical about how the process of finding a mate has changed?

13   Now all you need to do is to hire a private detective—also available online for another fee—to see if this engaging person is already married, has a dozen kids, has been sued for paternity or child support, or is a child molester or a rapist.

WRITING IN RESPONSE TO READING

Examining the Reading Using an Idea Map   MyWritingLab

Review the reading by completing the missing parts of the idea map shown below.

Visualize It!

Title	**Finding a Mate: Not the Same as It Used to Be**
Thesis	Technology is changing how people go about _____

Traditional people—Jews, Arabs, those in villages of China and India—have relied for centuries on _____

In China, technology is changing the matchmaking process.

Computerized records base compatibility on:
- _____
- _____
- _____
- _____
- _____

In America, people are also turning to technology to find a mate.

Internet dating sites offer:
- Wide variety of people
- _____
- _____

Dating on demand:
- Cable TV company helps singles make tapes of themselves
- _____
- _____
- _____
- _____

Conclusion	Author concludes with comment about the uncertainty of modern electronic dating.

Strengthening Your Vocabulary   `MyWritingLab`

Using the word's context, word parts, or a dictionary, write a brief definition of each of the following words as it is used in the reading.

1. prospective (paragraph 3) _____
2. compatibility (paragraph 4) _____
3. virtues (paragraph 5) _____
4. vivacious (paragraph 7) _____
5. pitiful (paragraph 7) _____
6. stigma (paragraph 8) _____

Reacting to Ideas: Discussion and Journal Writing   `MyWritingLab`

Get ready to write about the reading by discussing the following:

1. What do you think of the traditional methods of matchmaking described in this selection? How might technology improve upon these methods?
2. Evaluate the criteria that matchmakers use in China to identify compatibility and predict happiness. What traits would you add to the list? Which ones would you remove?
3. Would you trust the description of a person you met online? Why or why not? If you became interested in a person you met online, would you use a detective service to look into his or her background?
4. Why was the cartoon included in the reading? What key point does it emphasize? ■

Paragraph Options   `MyWritingLab`

1. Write a paragraph describing how you first met a person who is important in your life.
2. If you are single, have you considered using an electronic dating site? Write a paragraph explaining why or why not.
3. Do you agree that Internet dating sites are losing their stigma? Write a paragraph explaining your answer.

Essay Options   `MyWritingLab`

4. Imagine the scene described in paragraph 5, with hundreds of parents trying to make matches for their children in a park in Beijing. If your parents were there, what would they say about you in their "sales pitch" to other parents? Write an essay explaining how you think your parents would describe you. In addition, try writing an ad that your parents might write about you.
5. What can you tell from the reading about the author's attitude toward Internet dating? Write an essay examining the ways the author reveals his feelings toward the subject. Include in your essay specific examples from the selection that show he is sympathetic, suspicious, disapproving, etc. Also, explain how the selection would be different if it were entirely objective. How does the author's tone add to or detract from the reading?

6. What if you were to make a recording for a dating-on-demand video? Write an essay describing what you would want to include about yourself and the person you are hoping to meet. ■

Revision Checklist

Paragraph Development

1. Is the topic manageable (neither too broad nor too narrow)?
2. Is the paragraph written with the reader in mind?
3. Does the topic sentence identify the topic?
4. Does the topic sentence make a point about the topic?
5. Does each sentence support the topic sentence?
6. Is there sufficient detail?
7. Is there a sentence at the end that brings the paragraph to a close?

Sentence Development

8. Are there any sentence fragments, run-on sentences, or comma splices?
9. Are ideas combined to produce more effective sentences?
10. Are adjectives and adverbs used to make the sentences vivid and interesting?
11. Are relative clauses and prepositional phrases like *-ing* phrases used to add detail?
12. Are pronouns used correctly and consistently?

■ ■ ■ ■

SELF-TEST SUMMARY

To test yourself, cover the Answer column with a sheet of paper and answer each question in the left column. Evaluate each of your answers as you work by sliding the paper down and comparing your answer with what is printed in the Answer column.

	QUESTION	ANSWER
GOAL 1 Choose a manageable topic	Why is it important to choose a manageable topic?	The topic you choose for a paragraph must not be too broad or too narrow. If you choose a topic that is too broad, you will have too much to say; if you choose a topic that is too narrow, you will not have enough to say.
GOAL 2 Write an effective topic sentence	What must an effective topic sentence do? How do you write effective topic sentences?	An effective topic sentence must identify what the paragraph is about and make a point about that topic. Write effective topic sentences by • making sure your topic sentence is a complete thought • placing your topic sentence first in the paragraph • avoiding direct announcements or statements of intent
GOAL 3 Develop a paragraph using supporting details	What does it mean to provide relevant and sufficient details? What is plagiarism?	Relevant details are those that directly support the topic. Including sufficient details means providing enough details to make your topic sentence understandable and convincing. Plagiarism is using another person's words or ideas without giving that person credit.
GOAL 4 Revise a paragraph by adding, deleting, and changing text	How can a revision map and a revision checklist help you identify what and how to revise?	A revision map is a visual display of the ideas in your paragraph or essay; it will show you how your ideas fit together and help you identify ideas that do not fit or need further explanation. The revision checklist offers focused questions that will help you evaluate your writing. (See the Revision Checklist on page 315.)

MyWritingLab *Visit Ch. 12 Drafting and Revising in MyWritingLab to test your understanding of the chapter objectives.*

13

Developing, Arranging, and Connecting Details

Learning Goals

In this chapter, you will learn how to

GOAL 1 Develop paragraphs using specific, vivid details

GOAL 2 Arrange details in a logical fashion and use transitions effectively

"It was a dark and stormy night. Rain fell in torrents, soaking through the thin cardboard that passed for a roof in the old mansion. Alone in the attic, Sarah sobbed, imagining her mother dancing while she shivered in the cold."

WRITE ABOUT IT!

The caption below the photograph presents one possible description of what is happening in the house. Write an alternative scenario for what could be happening in the photo. Be as detailed as possible.

What would horror stories or mysteries be without carefully arranged details like those in the caption above and the one you wrote? They would be boring, for one thing. Imagine how quickly you'd lose interest if this story began, "Sarah's mother went out and left her home with a babysitter. But then the babysitter's boyfriend called, so she left, and it was raining and Sarah got scared." Maybe Sarah *was* scared, but it's doubtful that you, the reader, feel any tension.

Details—how things happen and when they happen—are what drive a story. The way you arrange details is called **time sequence**. Words and phrases that lead readers from one step in a story to the next are called **transitions**. Your writing will improve as you learn to use details and arrange them well. In this chapter you will learn how to develop details and arrange them using time-sequence, spatial, and least/most arrangements to make your paragraphs clear, lively, and interesting. You will also learn how to use transitions to connect your details.

WRITING

DEVELOPING A PARAGRAPH USING SPECIFIC DETAILS

GOAL 1 Develop paragraphs using specific, vivid details

Read the following pairs of statements. For each pair, place a check mark on the line before the statement that is more vivid and that contains more information.

1. _____ a. Professor Valquez gives a lot of homework.

   _____ b. Professor Valquez assigns 20 problems during each class and requires us to read two chapters per week.

2. _____ a. In Korea, people calculate age differently.

   _____ b. In Korea, people are considered to be one year old at birth.

3. _____ a. It was really hot Tuesday.

   _____ b. On Tuesday the temperature in New Haven reached 97 degrees.

These pairs of sentences illustrate the difference between vague statements and specific statements. Statement a in each pair conveys little information and also lacks interest and appeal. Statement b offers specific, detailed information and, as a result, is more interesting.

As you generate ideas and draft paragraphs, try to include as many specific details as possible. These details (called **supporting details** because they support your topic sentence) make your writing more interesting and your ideas more convincing.

The sample paragraph below lacks detail. Compare it with the revised paragraph that follows it. Notice how the revision has produced a much more lively, informative, and convincing paragraph.

Sample Paragraph

Being a waiter or waitress is a more complicated job than most people think. First of all, you must have a friendly personality. You must be able to maintain a smile no matter what your inner feelings may be. Proper attire and good hygiene are also essential. You have to be good at memorizing what your customers want and make sure each order is made to their specifications. If you are friendly, neat, and attentive to your customers, you will be successful.

Revised Paragraph

Being a waitress is a more complicated job than the average customer thinks. First of all, a friendly, outgoing personality is important. No one wants to be greeted by a waitress who has an angry, indifferent, or "I'm bored with this job" expression on her face. A waitress should try to smile, regardless of the circumstances. When a screaming child hurls a plate of french fries across the table, smile and wipe up the ketchup. Proper attire and good hygiene are important, too. A waitress in a dirty dress and with hair hanging down into the food does not please customers. Finally, attentiveness to customers' orders is important. Be certain that each person gets the correct order and that the food is prepared according to his or her specifications. Pay particular attention when serving salads and steaks, since different dressings and degrees of rareness are easily confused. Following these suggestions will lead to happy customers as well as larger tips.

In this revision, the writer added examples, included more descriptive words, and made all details more concrete and specific.

Here are a few suggestions for how to include more specific details:

1. **Add names, numbers, times, and places.**

VAGUE	My uncle bought a used car.
MORE SPECIFIC	Yesterday afternoon my uncle bought a vintage red, two-door 1996 Toyota Tercel at the new "Toy-a-Rama" dealership.

2. **Add more facts and explanation.**

VAGUE	My fax machine works well.
MORE SPECIFIC	My fax machine allows me to send letters and documents through a phone line in seconds and at minimal cost.

3. **Use examples.**

VAGUE	Dogs learn their owners' habits.
MORE SPECIFIC	As soon as I reach for my wire garden basket, my golden retriever knows this means I'm going outside, and he rushes to the back door.

4. **Draw from your personal experience.**

VAGUE	People sometimes eat to calm down.
MORE SPECIFIC	My sister relaxes every evening with a bowl of popcorn.

Tip for Writers

Concrete is the opposite of *abstract*. Something concrete can be experienced through the senses (by seeing, hearing, tasting, etc.). In contrast, abstractions are ideas, not physical things.

Specific is the opposite of *general*. There are many levels of specificity. For example, *beverage* is more specific than *liquid; coffee* is more specific than *beverage; Joe's black coffee* is even more specific.

Depending on your topic, you may need to do research to get more specific details. Dictionaries, encyclopedias, and magazine articles are often good sources. Think of research as interesting detective work and a chance to learn. For example, if you are writing a paragraph about the safety of air bags in cars, you may need to locate some current facts and statistics. Your college library and the Internet will be two good sources; a car dealership and a mechanic may be two others.

EXERCISE 13-1   Revising Sentences

Directions: Revise each of the following statements to make it more specific.

EXAMPLE   Biology is a difficult course.

Biology involves memorizing scientific terms and learning

some of life's complex processes.

1. I rode the train.

   _____

   _____

2. Pizza is easy to prepare.

   _____

   _____

3. The Fourth of July is a holiday.

   _____

   _____

4. I bought a lawnmower.

   _____

   _____

5. The van broke down.

   _____

   _____

▌ EXERCISE 13-2   **Writing a Paragraph Using Specific Details**

Directions: Write a paragraph on one of the following topics. Develop a topic sentence that expresses one main point about the topic. Then develop your paragraph using specific details.

1. Your favorite food (or junk food)
2. How pets help people
3. Why shopping is (or is not) fun
4. A sport (or hobby) you would like to take up
5. An annoying habit ▉

METHODS OF ARRANGING DETAILS

GOAL 2 Arrange details in a logical fashion and use transitions effectively

Your paragraph can have many good details in it, but if they are arranged in a jumbled fashion, your writing will lack impact. You must arrange your details logically within each paragraph. Let us look at three common ways of arranging details:

1. Time-sequence arrangement
2. Spatial arrangement
3. Least/most arrangement

Time-Sequence Arrangement

When you are describing an event or series of events, it is often easiest to arrange them in the order in which they happened. This arrangement is called **time sequence**. The following time-sequence map will help you visualize this arrangement of details.

 Visualize It! ➜

Time-Sequence Map

Here is how to build a low-fat deli select sandwich.

Start with two slices of whole-grain bread.

Add fat-free smoked chicken breast.

Add low-fat pastrami.

Add one slice of fat-free cheese.

Slather with fat-free mayo.

You can also use time sequence to explain how events happened or to tell a story. For example, you can explain how you ended up living in Cleveland or tell a story about a haunted house. This is called a narrative and is discussed in more detail in Chapter 14, page 337. In the following sample paragraph, the student has arranged details in time sequence. Read the paragraph and then fill in the blanks in the time-sequence map that follows it.

Sample Time-Sequence Paragraph

Driving a standard-shift vehicle is easy if you follow these steps. First, push the clutch pedal down. The clutch is the pedal on the left. Then start the car. Next, move the gearshift into first gear. On most cars this is the straight-up position. Next, give the car some gas, and slowly release the clutch pedal until you start moving. Finally, be ready to shift into higher gears—second, third, and so on. A diagram of where to find each gear usually appears on the gearshift knob. With practice, you will learn to start up smoothly and shift without the car making grinding noises or lurching.

Time-Sequence Map

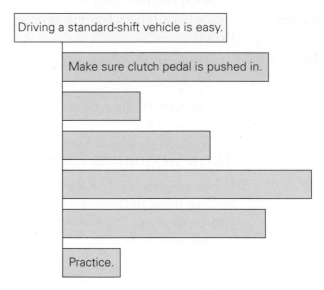

Driving a standard-shift vehicle is easy.

Make sure clutch pedal is pushed in.

Practice.

Time-Sequence Transitions

Look again at the sample paragraph. Notice that transitions are used to lead you from one step to another. Try to pick them out; underline those that you find. Did you underline *first, then, next,* and *finally*? Using transitions like those listed below will help you to link details in a time-sequence paragraph.

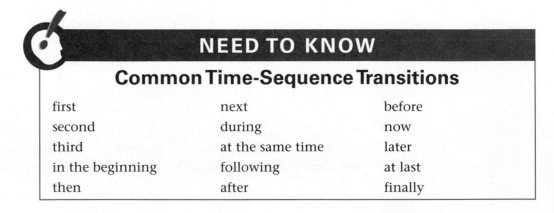

NEED TO KNOW

Common Time-Sequence Transitions

first	next	before
second	during	now
third	at the same time	later
in the beginning	following	at last
then	after	finally

EXERCISE 13-3 Arranging Details

Directions: Arrange in time sequence the supporting-detail sentences that follow the topic sentence below. Place a "1" on the line before the detail that should appear first in the paragraph, a "2" before the detail that should appear second, and so on.

TOPIC SENTENCE   Registration for college classes requires planning and patience.

SUPPORTING-DETAIL SENTENCES

_____ a. Find out which of the courses that you need are being offered that particular semester.

_____ b. Study your degree requirements and figure out which courses you need to take before you can take others.

_____ c. Then start working out a schedule.

_____ d. For example, a math course may have to be taken before an accounting or a science course.

_____ e. Then, when you register, if one course or section is closed, you will have others in mind that will work with your schedule.

_____ f. Select alternative courses that you can take if all sections of one of your first-choice courses are closed. ■

EXERCISE 13-4 Writing a Paragraph

Directions: Write a paragraph on one of the following topics. First, write a topic sentence that identifies your topic and expresses your main point about it. Then arrange your supporting-detail sentences in order. Be sure to use transitions to connect your ideas. When you have finished, draw a time-sequence map of your paragraph (see p. 321 for a model). Use your map to check that you have included sufficient details and that you have presented your details in the correct sequence.

1. Making up for lost time

2. Closing (or beginning) a chapter of your life

3. Getting more (or less) out of an experience than you expected

4. Having an adventure

5. Having an experience that made you feel like saying, "Look who's talking!" ■

Spatial Arrangement

Suppose you are asked to describe a car you have just purchased. You want your reader, who has never seen the car, to visualize it. How would you organize your description? You could describe the car from bottom to top or from top to bottom, or from front to back. This method of presentation is called **spatial arrangement**. For other objects, you might arrange your details from inside to outside, from near to far, or from east to west. Notice how, in the following paragraph, the details are arranged from top to bottom.

Sample Spatial–Arrangement Paragraph

My dream house will have a three-level outdoor deck that will be ideal for relaxing on after a hard day's work. The top level of the deck will be connected by sliding glass doors to the family room. On this level there will be a hot tub, a large picnic table with benches, and a comfortable padded chaise. On the middle level there will be a sun-tanning area, a hammock, and two built-in planters for a mini-herb garden. The lowest level, which will meet the lawn, will have a built-in stone barbeque pit for big cookouts and a gas grill for everyday use.

Can you visualize the deck?

Spatial-Arrangement Transitions

In spatial-arrangement paragraphs, transitions are particularly important since they often reveal placement or position of objects or parts. Using transitions like those listed in the "Need to Know" box below will help you to link details in a spatial-arrangement paragraph.

NEED TO KNOW
Common Spatial-Arrangement Transitions

above	next to	nearby
below	inside	on the other side
beside	outside	beneath
in front of	behind	the west (or other direction)

EXERCISE 13-5   Using Spatial Arrangement

Directions: Use spatial arrangement to order the supporting-detail sentences that follow the topic sentence below. Write a "1" in the blank before the detail that should appear first in the paragraph, a "2" before the detail that should appear second, and so on.

TOPIC SENTENCE   My beautiful cousin Audry always looks as if she has dressed quickly and given her appearance little thought.

SUPPORTING-DETAIL SENTENCES

_____ a. She usually wears an oversized, baggy sweater, either black or blue-black, with the sleeves pushed up.

_____ b. Black slip-on sandals complete the look; she wears them in every season.

_____ c. On her feet she wears mismatched socks.

_____ d. Her short, reddish hair is usually wind-blown, hanging every which way from her face.

_____ e. She puts her makeup on unevenly, if at all.

_____ f. The sweater covers most of her casual, rumpled skirt. ■

EXERCISE 13-6   Writing a Paragraph Using Spatial Arrangement

Directions: Write a paragraph on one of the following topics. First, write a topic sentence that identifies your topic and expresses your main point about it. Then use spatial arrangement to develop your supporting details.

1. The room you are in now
2. The building where you live
3. A photograph or painting that you like
4. Your dream car
5. Your favorite chair or place ■

Least/Most Arrangement

Another method of arranging details is to present them in order from least to most or most to least, according to some quality or characteristic. For example, you might choose least to most important, serious, frightening, or humorous. In writing a paragraph explaining your reasons for attending college, you might arrange details from most to least important. In writing about an exciting evening, you might arrange your details from most to least exciting.

As you read the following paragraph, note how the writer has arranged details in a logical way.

Sample Least/Most Paragraph

This week has been filled with good news. One night when balancing my checkbook, I discovered a $155 error in my checking account—in my favor, for once! I was even happier when I finally found a buyer for my Chevy Blazer that I had been trying to sell all winter. Then my boss told me he was submitting my name for a 50-cent hourly raise; I certainly didn't expect that. Best of all, I learned that I'd been accepted into the Radiology curriculum for next fall.

In this paragraph, the details are arranged from least to most important.

Least/Most Transitions

In least/most paragraphs, transitions help your reader to follow your train of thought. Using transitions like those listed in the "Need to Know" box below will help you link details in a least/most paragraph.

NEED TO KNOW

Common Least/Most Transitions

most important	particularly important	moreover
above all	even more	in addition
especially	best of all	not only . . . but also

EXERCISE 13-7   Writing a Paragraph Using Least/Most Arrangement

Directions: Write a paragraph on one of the following topics. First, write a topic sentence that identifies your topic and expresses your main point about it. Then use a least/most arrangement to order your details. When you have finished, draw a map of your paragraph. Use your map to check that you have included sufficient details and that you have arranged your details in least/most order.

1. Your reasons for choosing the college you are attending
2. Changes in your life since you began college
3. Three commercials you saw on television recently
4. Why you like a certain book or movie
5. Good (or bad) things that have happened to you recently ■

EXERCISE 13-8   Writing Topic Sentences
Working Together

Directions: Working with a classmate, write a topic sentence for each of the following topics. Then indicate what method (time sequence, spatial, or least/most) you would use to arrange supporting details.

TOPIC	relationship with a friend
TOPIC SENTENCE	Whenever George and I get together, he always takes over the conversation.
METHOD OF ARRANGEMENT	time sequence

1. **TOPIC** — animals that have humanlike behaviors
   TOPIC SENTENCE _____
   METHOD OF ARRANGEMENT _____

2. **TOPIC** — a difficulty that I faced
   TOPIC SENTENCE _____
   METHOD OF ARRANGEMENT _____

3. **TOPIC** — feeling under pressure
   TOPIC SENTENCE _____
   METHOD OF ARRANGEMENT _____

4. **TOPIC** — a favorite dinner menu
   TOPIC SENTENCE _____
   METHOD OF ARRANGEMENT _____

5. TOPIC   an exciting sporting event

    TOPIC SENTENCE   _____
                            _____

    METHOD OF   _____
    ARRANGEMENT   ■

EXERCISE 13-9   Identifying Methods of Arrangement

Working Together

Directions: Find several magazine or newspaper ads. Working in a group, identify the method of arrangement of the advertising copy. ■

NEED TO KNOW

Developing, Arranging, and Connecting Details

Be sure to use interesting and lively **details** to support your topic sentence.

- Choose details that are specific and concrete.

- Within your paragraphs, arrange details in a **logical order**. Three techniques for arranging details are

  - **time-sequence arrangement**; information is presented in the order in which it happened.

  - **spatial arrangement**; descriptive details are arranged according to their position in space.

  - **least/most arrangement**; ideas are arranged from least to most or most to least according to some quality or characteristic.

- Use **transitions** to help your reader move easily from one key detail to the next.

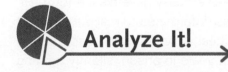 Analyze It!

Directions: The following paragraph lacks concrete details to make it interesting and informative. Revise the paragraph by adding details to help readers visualize the writer's shopping experience.

If I go grocery shopping before supper, without taking a list of items that I really need, the results can be disastrous. Because I'm hungry, everything looks good, and I tend to overload my cart. The problem starts in the produce department. Perhaps I need bananas and broccoli. After placing these items in my cart, I find myself adding a lot of other fruits and vegetables. Then I go to the fish department, where I get two kinds of fish instead of one. I proceed to the cereal aisle and put three boxes in my cart. On the way to get yogurt, I end up buying ice cream. "This has got to stop!" I say to myself, but myself does not listen.

A Student Essay

The Writing Task

Sarah Frey wrote this essay for her sociology class. In the assignment, she was asked to define an abstract concept using concrete examples. As you read, pay particular attention to the technique that the writer has used to organize the major details in the essay.

Title: suggests main point of the essay

Leadership: Moving Others Forward
Sarah Frey

Introduction: Frey engages the reader by including the names of well-known leaders.

1   Martin Luther King, Jr. Hillary Clinton. Nelson Mandela. Oprah Winfrey. These incredible people have many individual traits and characteristics, but the reason they are grouped together, more often than not, is because of the incredible leadership they have provided to the world. Leaders compel their followers to be moving forward constantly, but how they achieve this phenomenon is specific to the person. There is no one way to lead. In fact, there are so many ways to lead that one could say that there are as many ways to lead as there are people in the world. Everyone does it just a little dif-

Thesis Statement

ferently. However different the individual styles and characteristics might be, leadership is about compelling people to reach places where they would not normally go alone.

Topic Sentence

2   There is no cookie cutter pattern for what leaders should look like; the important thing is that they are willing to be determined, passionate, and responsible for what they believe. Leaders can be quiet and unassuming, like Mother Teresa, or leaders can be bold and boisterous, like Barack Obama. Leaders

Interesting Details

can be organized, such as Eleanor Roosevelt, or leaders can be spontaneous, like Rosa Parks. Leaders come in all shapes and sizes; they come from all walks of life. More specifically, leadership is about passion. It is about having the drive and the willingness to pursue the beliefs that the leader holds dear. Martin Luther King, Jr. believed in a better life for his children and his people, and his passion for his cause is evident. He eventually gave his life for it. He made a statement about his passion and was determined to make the rest of the country and even the rest of the world hear it. Additionally, leadership is about determination. Nelson Mandela spent years in prison, silently fighting for the ending of Apartheid in South Africa. Never once did the world hear him complain, for he was determined to make the world see the injustice that was occurring in the country he held dear. Leadership is also about responsibility, a responsibility to speak up for those who cannot speak. Michelle Obama is taking responsibility for the well-being and education of America's children. She is passionate about a social issue that is near to her heart and taking it into her own hands. She is compelling the nation to understand that childhood obesity is a problem and that the needs must be addressed.

Topic Sentence 3   Although leadership entails the above mentioned character traits, it is also an abstract concept. Leadership is the line between going too far and not far enough. It means possessing enough passion and determination and knowledge to break the boundaries that society has arbitrarily set. Leaders are challengers of the norms; they are brave enough to push through the ridicule and the persecution because they believe in the cause for which they are fighting. They fight for their beliefs and their values, even if it means that they are by themselves. Leaders are not always the center of attention; in fact, many times they are not even recognized as leaders until months or even years have passed. They fight for their values with the constant possibility of failure. Leadership is about not knowing what comes next but venturing into the unknown anyway.

Topic Sentence 4   Perhaps the most important characteristic of leadership is simply respect for all people. Being a leader means that there is an innate obligation to respect everyone. A leader does not attract followers just because he declares **Good use of concrete detail** himself a leader; followers fall into line because a leader earns their respect and respects each of them. Time and time again, history paints the picture of the leader sitting back while his troops are in battle, when in all reality, a leader is at the forefront of the battle lines, right along with his troops encouraging and compelling them to move forward. Leadership is about earning the right to lead the people who believe in the same values. It is about knowing that nothing is set in stone, that nothing is for sure, and yet still caring enough to being in the trenches. Leadership is about respect.

5   In his play *Twelfth Night*, William Shakespeare wrote, "some are born great, some achieve greatness, and some have greatness thrust upon them." This **Conclusion: refers back to the title** same phrase can be applied to leaders. Some people are born leaders, with leadership running through their veins, waiting for the right moment to break through. Some achieve the title of being a leader. They work hard and push through adversity to earn the ability to lead. And there are some who have leadership thrust upon them. These people are asked by situations and society to step into the limelight to give the public someone to look to in hard and trying times. Leaders come into this world in a multitude of ways. They come from broken homes and happy families. They are bright and shining, and they are shy and reserved. But the aspect that each of them has in common is that they encourage those around them to go to places that they never would have dreamed. They push the world to the limits and ask it to step up and join them.

EXAMINING STUDENT WRITING

1. Does Frey follow a logical plan of organization? Suggest how the organization could be improved.

2. Do you think further details are needed? If so, suggest which paragraphs need more detail.

3. Examine Frey's thesis statement. How accurately does it suggest the topics Frey covers in her essay?

4. Do you think that the concept of leadership is adequately explained? Cite examples from the essay to support your answer.

Paragraph Writing Scenarios

Friends and Family

1. Think of a good friend with whom you once had a major argument. Write a paragraph explaining what that argument was about and how you got over it.

2. Write a paragraph describing a relative other than your parents who you were close to as a child.

Classes and Campus Life

1. Think about the teachers you have this year. Write a paragraph comparing two of them. What are the main differences in their styles of teaching?

2. If there is a campus store, write a paragraph about the things you regularly would buy there or would not buy there. If there is not a store on your campus, write a paragraph explaining why you think your school should add one.

Working Students

1. Write an imaginary letter to your boss explaining what you would do to improve your workplace.

2. Write a paragraph explaining why you deserve a raise.

Communities and Cultures

1. People often form ideas about a culture without knowing anyone from that culture. Describe one incorrect idea, misconception, or stereotype that people have about a culture.

2. People live in a variety of communities. Choosing from urban, suburban, rural, or small-town neighborhoods, write a paragraph describing the one you'd most like to live in and why.

WRITING ABOUT A READING

The following reading, "A Brother's Murder," explains how a man feels about the circumstances surrounding the death of his street-smart younger brother.

Step 1: Preview the reading.

Step 2: Connect the reading to your own experience: What would you say or do to help a relative or friend headed for trouble?

Step 3: Read and respond to the questions in the margin.

THINK AS YOU READ

Based on your preview, what happens in this essay?

Do you sense the author's disapproval of Blake's lifestyle?

Why does the author describe his life after leaving his hometown? What does the phrase "upwardly mobile" mean?

How does the author use details to make the essay interesting and real? Highlight details that are concrete, vivid, and specific.

What negative words and phrases does the author use to describe Blake and his street life?

A BROTHER'S MURDER

Brent Staples

1   It has been more than two years since my telephone rang with the news that my younger brother Blake—just 22 years old—had been murdered. The young man who killed him was only 24. Wearing a ski mask, he emerged from a car, fired six times at close range with a massive .44 Magnum, then fled. The two had once been inseparable friends. A senseless rivalry—beginning, I think, with an argument over a girlfriend—escalated from posturing, to threats, to violence, to murder. The way the two were living, death could have come to either of them from anywhere. In fact, the assailant had already survived multiple gunshot wounds from an incident much like the one in which my brother lost his life.

2   I left the East Coast after college, spent the mid- and late-1970s in Chicago as a graduate student, taught for a time, then became a journalist. Within 10 years of leaving my hometown, I was overeducated and "upwardly mobile," ensconced on a quiet, tree-lined street where voices raised in anger were scarcely ever heard. The telephone, like some grim **umbilical**,[1] kept me connected to the old world with news of deaths, imprisonings, and misfortune. I felt emotionally beaten up. Perhaps to protect myself, I added a psychological dimension to the physical distance I had already achieved. I rarely visited my hometown. I shut it out.

3   As I fled the past, so Blake embraced it. On Christmas of 1983, I traveled from Chicago to a black section of Roanoke, Virginia, where he then lived. The desolate public housing projects, the hopeless, idle young men crashing against one another—these reminded me of the embittered town we'd grown up in. It was a place where once I would have been comfortable, or at least sure of myself. Now, hearing of my brother's forays into crime, his scrapes with police and street thugs, I was scared, unsteady on foreign terrain.

4   I saw that Blake's romance with the street life and the hustler image had flowered dangerously. One evening that late December, standing in some Roanoke dive among drug dealers and grim, hair-trigger losers, I told him I feared for his life. He had affected the image of the tough he wanted to be.

---

[1] **umbilical** connecting cord, similar to the cord that joins a baby to the placenta in the womb

What does the author mean when he says "We embraced as though through glass"?

What effects did Blake's death have on the author?

But behind the dark glasses and the swagger, I glimpsed the baby-faced toddler I'd once watched over. I nearly wept. I wanted desperately for him to live. The young think themselves immortal, and a dangerous light shone in his eyes as he spoke laughingly, of making fools of the policemen who had raided his apartment looking for drugs. He cried out as I took his right hand. A line of stitches lay between the thumb and index finger. Kickback from a shotgun, he explained, nothing serious. Gunplay had become part of his life.

5   I lacked the language simply to say: Thousands have lived this for you and died. I fought the urge to lift him bodily and shake him. This place and the way you are living smells of death to me, I said. Take some time away, I said. Let's go downtown tomorrow and buy a plane ticket anywhere, take a bus trip, anything to get away and cool things off. He took my alarm casually. We arranged to meet the following night—an appointment he would not keep. We embraced as though through glass. I drove away.

6   As I stood in my apartment in Chicago holding the receiver that evening in February 1984, I felt as though part of my soul had been cut away. I questioned myself then, and I still do. Did I not reach back soon or earnestly enough for him? For weeks I awoke crying from a recurrent dream in which I chased him, urgently trying to get him to read a document I had, as though reading it would protect him from what had happened in waking life. His eyes shining like black diamonds, he smiled and danced just beyond my grasp. When I reached for him, I caught only the space where he had been.

—from *Bearing Witness*

WRITING IN RESPONSE TO READING

Examining the Reading Using an Idea Map   MyWritingLab

Review the reading by completing the missing parts of the idea map shown below.

 Visualize It! ➔

Title | **A Brother's Murder**

Thesis | As a result of becoming involved with street life, guns, and drug dealers, Blake Staples was murdered at the age of 22.

Staples left hometown after college.

_____

Ten years after leaving, he lived different lifestyle.

_____

_____

_____

He was not comfortable in that environment anymore.

_____

He told Blake he feared for Blake's life.

He tried to get him to leave town.

_____

_____

Conclusion | _____

Strengthening Your Vocabulary   `MyWritingLab`

Using the word's context, word parts, or a dictionary, write a brief definition of each of the following words as it is used in the reading.

1. rivalry (paragraph 1)_____
2. escalated (paragraph 1) _____
3. ensconced (paragraph 2) _____
4. desolate (paragraph 3) _____
5. forays (paragraph 3) _____
6. terrain (paragraph 3) _____

Reacting to Ideas: Discussion and Journal Writing   `MyWritingLab`

Get ready to write about the reading by discussing the following:

1. Why did Brent Staples rarely visit his hometown?
2. Staples wonders whether he could have done more to protect and rescue his brother. Do you think there was more he could or should have done? Explain.
3. Why do you think Staples keeps dreaming about his brother? What does his dream mean?
4. The author chose not to include a visual with this reading. What type of visual might have been meaningful and helpful?

Paragraph Options   `MyWritingLab`

1. Staples describes embracing his brother as if through glass. This description and others throughout the reading suggest that Staples and his brother could not communicate well, although they seemed to care about one another. Write a paragraph describing your relationship with someone you had difficulty communicating with or your relationship with someone you could communicate with easily.

2. Members of the same family often are very different, and sometimes the opposite of each other. Write a paragraph explaining how you are either very similar to or very different from a member of your family.

Essay Option   `MyWritingLab`

3. Staples's brother lost his life to the violence of street crime. Write an essay describing what you feel can or should be done to avoid such a tragic waste of life.

■ ■ ■ ■

> ## Revision Checklist
>
> **Paragraph Development**
>
> 1. Is the topic manageable (neither too broad nor too narrow)?
> 2. Is the paragraph written with the reader in mind?
> 3. Does the topic sentence identify the topic?
> 4. Does the topic sentence make a point about the topic?
> 5. Does each sentence support the topic sentence?
> 6. Is there sufficient detail?
> 7. Is there a sentence at the end that brings the paragraph to a close?
>
> **Sentence Development**
>
> 8. Are there any sentence fragments, run-on sentences, or comma splices?
> 9. Are ideas combined to produce more effective sentences?
> 10. Are adjectives and adverbs used to make the sentences vivid and interesting?
> 11. Are relative clauses and prepositional phrases like -ing phrases used to add detail?
> 12. Are pronouns used correctly and consistently?

■ ■ ■ ■

SELF-TEST SUMMARY

To test yourself, cover the Answer column with a sheet of paper and answer each question in the left column. Evaluate each of your answers as you work by sliding the paper down and comparing your answer with what is printed in the Answer column.

	QUESTION	ANSWER
Goal 1 Develop paragraphs using specific, vivid details	What are four ways to include more specific details?	Include more specific details by • adding names, numbers, times, and places • adding more facts and explanation • using examples • drawing from your personal experience
Goal 2 Arrange details in a logical fashion and use transitions effectively	What are three techniques for arranging details in a logical order?	Three techniques for arranging details are • *time sequence*: information is presented in the order in which it happened • *spatial*: details are arranged according to their position in space • *least/most*: ideas are arranged from least to most or most to least according to some quality or characteristic

MyWritingLab *Visit Ch. 13 DEVELOPING, ARRANGING, AND CONNECTING DETAILS in MyWritingLab to test your understanding of the chapter objectives.*

14 Using Methods of Organization

WRITE ABOUT IT!

Study the photograph above and then write a paragraph about it.

You could have developed your paragraph in a number of ways. For example, perhaps you told a story about the special occasion for which the cake was served. If so, you used a method of development called **narration** (discussed in Section A of this chapter). If your paragraph described the delicious taste, texture, or flavors of the cake, you used a method of development called **description** (Section B of this chapter). There are other possible ways to write a paragraph about the cake, using different methods of development. In this chapter you will learn the different methods for developing and organizing a paragraph.

WRITING

METHODS OF ORGANIZATION

Separate sections of this chapter are devoted to each of the following methods of development:

Section A: Narration	Tells a story that involves cake
Section B: Description	Describes the taste, texture, or flavor of cake
Section C: Example	Gives examples of celebrations in which cake is often served.
Section D: Definition	Defines what cake is to someone unfamiliar with it
Section E: Comparison and Contrast	Compares different flavors of cake
Section F: Classification	Explains the different types of cake (chocolate, layer, pound cakes, etc.)
Section G: Process	Explains how cake is made or explains how to make a cake
Section H: Cause and Effect	Explains why people enjoy cake
Section I: Argument	Makes the case that cake should be on every restaurant menu
Section J: Multiple Methods of Organization	Compares the ingredients in the traditional holiday cakes made in different countries while providing specific examples from countries around the world

Each of these methods of development produces an entirely different paragraph. The method you use depends on what you want to say and how you want to say it. For example, if you wanted your readers to visualize or imagine something, you might use description. If you wanted your readers to understand how something works, you would use process. If you wanted to convince your readers of something, you would use argument. The method you choose, then, should suit your purpose for writing. The nine methods of development described in this chapter offer you a wide range of choices for developing and organizing your writing. By learning to use each of them, you will develop a variety of new approaches to paragraph writing. Once you understand each method, you will be able to combine multiple methods of development into a single paragraph or multi-paragraph essay.

A: NARRATION

GOAL 1 Write using narration

What Is Narration?

The technique of making a point by telling a story is called **narration**. Narration is *not* simply listing a series of events—"this happened, then that happened." Narration shapes and interprets events to make a point. Notice the difference between the two paragraphs below.

Paragraph 1: Series of Events

Last Sunday we visited the National Zoo in Washington, D.C. As we entered, we decided to see the panda bear, the elephants, and the giraffes. All were outside enjoying the springlike weather. Then we visited the bat cave. I was amazed at how closely bats pack together in a small space. Finally, we went into the monkey house. There we spent time watching the giant apes watch us.

Paragraph 2: Narrative

Last Sunday's visit to the National Zoo in Washington, D.C., was a lesson to me about animals in captivity. First, we visited the panda, the elephants, and the giraffes. All seemed slow moving and locked into a dull routine—pacing around their yards. Then we watched the seals. Their trainer had them perform stunts for their food; they would never do these stunts in the wild. Finally, we stopped at the monkey house, where sad, old apes stared at us and watched kids point at them. The animals did not seem happy or content with their lives.

The first paragraph retells events in the order in which they happened, but with no shaping of the story. The second paragraph, a narrative, also presents events in the order in which they happened, but uses these events to make a point: animals kept in captivity are unhappy. Thus, all details and events work together to support that point. You can visualize a narrative paragraph as follows. Study the model and the map for paragraph 2.

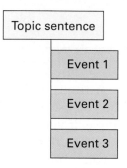 **Visualize It!** →

Model Idea Map for Narration

Topic sentence

> Event 1

> Event 2

> Event 3

Note: The number of events will vary.

Idea Map of Paragraph 2

The visit to the zoo was a lesson to me.

> Pandas, elephants, and giraffes followed a dull routine.

> Seals performed stunts.

> Kids pointed at sad, old apes.

How to Develop a Narrative Paragraph

Developing a narrative paragraph involves writing a topic sentence and presenting sufficient details to support it.

Write a Clear Topic Sentence

Your topic sentence should accomplish two things:

1. **It should identify your topic.**
2. **It should reveal your attitude toward your topic.**

For example, suppose you are writing about visiting a zoo. Your topic sentence could take your narrative in a variety of directions, each of which would reveal a very different attitude toward the experience.

- During my recent visit to the zoo, I was saddened by the animals' behavior in captivity.

- A recent visit to the zoo gave my children a lesson in geography.

- My recent visit to the zoo taught me more about human nature than about animals.

 **Examine It!**

Directions: The following paragraph uses the narrative method of development. Study its annotations to discover how the writer supports the topic sentence and organizes her ideas.

Author establishes the importance of the narrative

Topic sentence

Description of events

Final comment reveals McPherson's mental state

    I can't eat. I can't sleep. And I certainly can't study. I stare at a single paragraph for a quarter of an hour but can't absorb it. How can I, when behind the words, on the white background of the paper, I'm watching an endless loop of my parents' deaths? Watching as their cream-colored Buick flies through the guardrail and over the side of the bridge to avoid old Mr. McPherson's red truck? Old Mr. McPherson, who confessed as he was led from the scene that he wasn't entirely sure what side of the road he should have been on and thinks that maybe he hit the gas instead of the brake? Old Mr. McPherson, who showed up at church one legendary Easter without trousers?

—Gruen, *Water for Elephants*, p. 21.

EXERCISE A-1   Writing Topic Sentences

Writing in Progress

Directions: Complete three of the following topic sentences by adding information that describes an experience you have had related to the topic.

    EXAMPLE   My first job *was an experience I would rather forget.*

1. Holidays _____

2. A frightening event _____

3. My first day on campus _____

4. Cell phones _____

5. My advisor/instructor _____

Include Sufficient Details

A narrative paragraph should include enough detail to support your topic sentence and allow your reader to fully understand the experience you are writing about. Be sure you have answered most of the following questions:

- *What* events occurred?
- *Where* did they happen?
- *When* did they happen?
- *Who* was involved?
- *Why* did they happen?
- *How* did they happen?

EXERCISE A-2

Writing in Progress

Brainstorming Details

Directions: Using one of the topic sentences you wrote in Exercise A-1, brainstorm a list of relevant and sufficient details to support it. ■

How to Organize a Narrative Paragraph

The events in a narrative are usually arranged in the order in which they happened. This method of organization is called **time-sequence arrangement** (see Chapter 13, p. 321, for a discussion of this method). Transitions are especially important in narrative paragraphs because they identify and separate events from one another. Useful transitions are shown below.

NARRATION: USEFUL TRANSITIONS			
first	then	in the beginning	next
second	later	after	during
third	at last	following	after that
finally			while

EXERCISE A-3

Writing in Progress

Using Time-Sequence Order

Directions: Using the topic sentence you wrote in Exercise A-1, and the relevant and sufficient details you generated in Exercise A-2, present your details in time-sequence order, using transitions as needed. ■

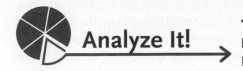

Analyze It!

Directions: The paragraph on the left is a professional example of a narrative paragraph. Read the paragraph and then complete the idea map below.

Foxy came over early in the evening of July 3 to help Dayton load Babe into the back of the pickup for her ride to the rodeo. Fencing had been fixed to the sides of the bed, which was pulled against the open gate of the corral. A runway made of thick boards covered with a piece of shag carpet was rigged to the tailgate. I watched from the open window while Dayton spread the flat bottom of the truck with fresh hay, then waited while Foxy rustled and spooked Babe. It took awhile. She raced by the ramp, flicking her tail and shaking her head, kicking dust into Foxy's new rodeo clothes. Her hooves struck the ground hard as hammers, and she shook the bit, flapping the rope out of Foxy's reach. Finally, as if she knew what she was doing, she charged into the truck so fast that Dayton backed against the cab and waved his arms to ward her off, but the next minute, she had lowered her head to chew some hay, her heaving sides the only sign she was excited.

—Dorris, *A Yellow Raft in Blue Water,*
pp. 276–277.

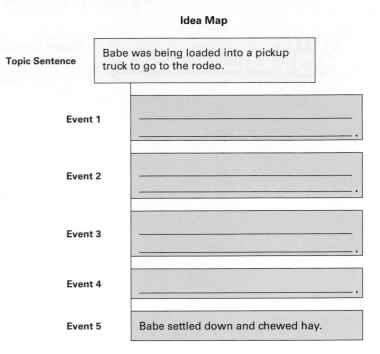

Idea Map

Topic Sentence — Babe was being loaded into a pickup truck to go to the rodeo.

Event 1 — _____

Event 2 — _____

Event 3 — _____

Event 4 — _____

Event 5 — Babe settled down and chewed hay.

B: DESCRIPTION

GOAL 2 Write using description

What Is Description?

Descriptive writing uses words and phrases that appeal to the senses—taste, touch, smell, sight, hearing. Descriptive writing helps your reader imagine an object, person, place, or experience. The details you use should also leave your reader with an overall impression of what you are describing. Here is a sample descriptive paragraph written by a student, Ted Sawchuck. Notice how he makes you feel as if you are in the kitchen with him as he prepares chili.

My favorite chili recipe requires a trip to the grocery store and a day to hang around the kitchen stirring, but it is well worth the expense and time. Canned, shiny red kidney beans and fat, great white northern beans simmer in the big pot, while ground beef and kielbasa sizzle and spit in a cast-iron skillet. Raw white onions bring tears to one's eyes, and they are quickly chopped. Plump yellow and orange peppers are chopped to add fiber and flavor, while six cloves of garlic, smashed, make simmering all day a necessity. When it cooks, this chili makes the whole house smell mouthwateringly good. When eaten, chunks of kielbasa stand out in a spicy, garlicky sauce with small nuggets of ground beef.

Notice that this paragraph describes tastes, smells, sounds, and colors. You even learn how it feels to chop an onion. Notice, too, that all of the details directly support an overall impression that is expressed in the first sentence. You can visualize a descriptive paragraph as follows. Study the model and the map for Sawchuck's paragraph.

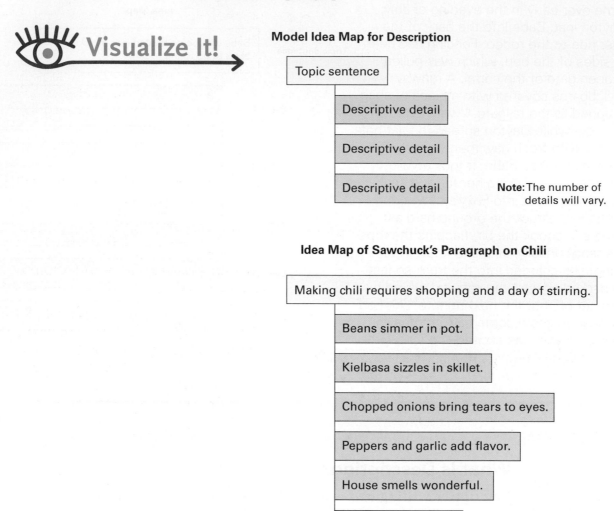

Visualize It!

Model Idea Map for Description

Topic sentence

Descriptive detail

Descriptive detail

Descriptive detail

Note: The number of details will vary.

Idea Map of Sawchuck's Paragraph on Chili

Making chili requires shopping and a day of stirring.

Beans simmer in pot.

Kielbasa sizzles in skillet.

Chopped onions bring tears to eyes.

Peppers and garlic add flavor.

House smells wonderful.

Chili tastes garlicky.

How to Develop a Descriptive Paragraph

A descriptive paragraph has three key features, an overall impression, sensory details, and descriptive language.

1. **Create an overall impression.** The **overall impression** is the *one* central idea you want to present to your reader. It is the single, main point that all of your details prove or support. For example, if you are writing a paragraph about your math instructor's sense of humor, then all of your details should be about amusing things he or she has said or done. Your overall impression should be expressed in your topic sentence, usually at the beginning of the

paragraph. Notice that each of the following topic sentences expresses a different overall impression of Niagara Falls:

a. Niagara Falls is stunningly beautiful and majestic.
b. The beauty of Niagara Falls is hidden by its tourist-oriented, commercial surroundings.
c. Niagara Falls would be beautiful to visit if I could be there alone, without the crowds of tourists.

Your overall impression is often your first reaction to a topic. Suppose you are writing about your college snack bar. Think of a word or two that sums up how you feel about it. Is it noisy? Smelly? Relaxing? Messy? You could develop any one of these descriptive words into a paragraph. For example, your topic sentence might be:

The snack bar is a noisy place that I try to avoid.

The details that follow would then describe the noise—the clatter of plates, loud conversations, chairs scraping the floor, and music blaring.

Examine It!

Directions: The following paragraph, about the eruption of Mount St. Helens, a volcano in Washington state, uses the descriptive method of development. Notice how each of the highlighted words and phrases helps you visualize the eruption.

The slumping north face of the mountain produced the greatest landslide witnessed in recorded history; about 2.75 km³ (0.67 mi³) of rock, ice, and trapped air, all fluidized with steam, surged at speeds approaching 250 kmph (155 mph). Landslide materials traveled for 21 km (13 mi) into the valley, blanketing the forest, covering a lake, filling the rivers below. The eruption continued with intensity for 9 hours, first clearing out old rock from the throat of the volcano and then blasting new material.

—Christopherson, *Geosystems*, p. 368.

EXERCISE B-1
Writing in Progress

Brainstorming, Reacting, and Writing Topic Sentences

Directions: Brainstorm a list of words that sum up your reaction to each of the following topics. Then develop each list of words into a topic sentence that expresses an overall impression and could lead to a descriptive paragraph.

TOPIC	A parent or guardian
REACTION	Dad: loving, accepting, smart, helpful, calm, generous
TOPIC SENTENCE	My whole life, my father has been generous and helpful in the way he let me be myself.

1. TOPIC   A library, gym, or other public place that you have used

   REACTION _____

   TOPIC SENTENCE _____

_____

_____

2. **TOPIC**   A part-time job, past or present

   REACTION   _____

   TOPIC SENTENCE _____
                      _____
                      _____

3. **TOPIC**   A small shop or a shopkeeper familiar to you

   REACTION   _____

   TOPIC SENTENCE _____
                      _____
                      _____

4. **TOPIC**   A music video, movie, or song

   REACTION   _____

   TOPIC SENTENCE _____
                      _____
                      _____

5. **TOPIC**   A person in the news

   REACTION   _____

   TOPIC SENTENCE _____
                      _____
                      _____

   ■

2. **Include sensory details. Sensory details** appeal to your senses—your sense of touch, taste, sight, sound, and smell. Try to imagine your topic—the person, place, thing, or experience. Depending on what your topic is, write down what it makes you see, hear, smell, taste, or feel.

EXERCISE B-2   Brainstorming Details
Writing in Progress

Directions: Using one of the topic sentences you wrote in Exercise B-1, brainstorm details that support the overall impression it conveys.

3. **Use descriptive language. Descriptive language** uses words that help your readers imagine your topic and make it exciting and vivid to them. Consider the following sentences. The first is dull and lifeless; the second describes what the writer sees and feels.

   NONDESCRIPTIVE   The beach was crowded with people.

   DESCRIPTIVE   The beach was overrun with teenagers wearing neon Lycra suits and slicked with sweet-smelling oil.

   ■

Making your details more descriptive is not difficult. Use the guidelines below.

NEED TO KNOW

Using Descriptive Details

1. **Use verbs that help your reader picture the action.**

   NONDESCRIPTIVE   The boy walked down the beach.

   DESCRIPTIVE   The boy ambled down the beach.

2. **Use exact names.** Include the names of people, places, brands, animals, flowers, stores, streets, products—whatever will make your description more precise.

   NONDESCRIPTIVE   Kevin parked his car near the deserted beach.

   DESCRIPTIVE   Kevin parked his maroon Saturn convertible at Burke's Garage next to the deserted beach.

3. **Use adjectives to describe.** Adjectives are words that describe nouns. Place them before or after nouns to add detail.

   NONDESCRIPTIVE   The beach was deserted.

   DESCRIPTIVE   The remote, rocky, windswept beach was deserted.

4. **Use words that appeal to the senses.** Use words that convey touch, taste, smell, sound, and sight.

   NONDESCRIPTIVE   I saw big waves roll on the beach.

   DESCRIPTIVE   Immense black waves rammed the shore, releasing with each crash the salty, fishy smell of the deep ocean.

How to Organize a Descriptive Paragraph

Among the common methods of ordering details in descriptive writing are

- **Spatial arrangement.** You organize details according to their physical location. (See Chapter 13, p. 323, for a discussion of this method.) For example, you could describe a favorite newsstand by arranging your details from right to left or from front to back.

- **Least/most arrangement.** You organize details in increasing or decreasing order, according to some quality or characteristic, such as importance. (See Chapter 13, p. 325, for a discussion of this method.) Suppose your overall impression of a person is that she is disorganized. You might start with some minor traits (she can never find a pen) and move to more serious and important characteristics of disorganization (she misses classes and forgets appointments).

Whatever method you choose to arrange your details, you will want to use good transitional words and phrases between details.

DESCRIPTION: USEFUL TRANSITIONS	
SPATIAL	**LEAST/MOST**
above, below, inside, outside, beside	first, second, primarily, secondarily
next to, facing, nearby, to the right, to the left, in front of, across	most important, also important

 **Analyze It!**

Directions: The paragraph on the left is a professional example of a descriptive paragraph. For each part of the house listed below, list several descriptive words that help you visualize its appearance.

The earth by the front door was worn flat, smoothed by the dumping and drying of dishwater. Shingles were blown off the roof in an irregular pattern that reminded me of notes on a music sheet, and tan cardboard replaced glass in a pane of the attic window. The house and the land had been through so many seasons, shared so much rain and sun, so much expanding and shrinking with heat and cold, that the seams between them were all but gone. Now the walls rose from the ground like the sides of a short, square hill, dug out by the wind and exposed.

—Dorris, *A Yellow Raft in Blue Water*, p. 251.

Roof: _____

_____

Attic window: _____

_____

Walls: _____

_____

_____

EXERCISE B-3
Writing in Progress

Writing a Descriptive Paragraph

Directions: Using the details you developed in Exercise B-2, write a paragraph. Assume that your reader is unfamiliar with what you are describing. Use descriptive language and organize your paragraph using a spatial or least/most arrangement, and use transitions as needed. ■

C: EXAMPLE

What Is an Example?

 **GOAL 3** Write using example

An **example** is a specific instance or situation that explains a general idea or statement. Apples and grapes are examples of fruit. Martin Luther King Day and Thanksgiving Day are examples of national holidays. Here are a few sample general statements along with specific examples that illustrate them:

GENERAL STATEMENT	EXAMPLES
1. I had an exciting day.	a. My sister had her first baby.
	b. I got a bonus check at work.
	c. I reached my goal of 20 laps in the pool.
2. Joe has annoying habits.	a. He interrupts me when I am talking.
	b. He is often late and makes no apologies.
	c. He talks with his mouth full.

Here is a sample paragraph written by Annie Lockhart that uses examples to explain the general idea of superstitious beliefs:

> Superstition affects many people on a daily basis. For example, some people think it is very unlucky if a black cat crosses their path, so they go to great lengths to avoid one. Also, according to another superstitious belief, walking under a ladder brings bad luck. Putting shoes on a bed is thought to be a sign that a death will occur in the family. People tend either to take superstitions very seriously or to reject them out of hand as fanciful imagination; regardless, they play an important part in our culture.

Notice that the paragraph gives three examples of superstitions. You can visualize an example paragraph as follows. Study the model and the map for the paragraph on superstitions.

Model Idea Map for Example

Topic sentence

Example

Example

Example

Note: The number of examples will vary.

Idea Map for Lockhart's Paragraph on Superstition

Superstition affects many people on a daily basis.

Black cats are unlucky.

Walking under ladders brings bad luck.

Shoes on a bed mean death.

How to Develop an Example Paragraph

Developing an example paragraph involves writing a topic sentence and selecting appropriate examples to support it.

Write a Topic Sentence

Your topic sentence should accomplish two things:

1. **It should identify your topic.**
2. **It should make a general statement that the examples support.**

Here are a few examples of topic sentences. Can you predict the types of examples each paragraph would contain?

- Consumers often purchase brand names they have seen advertised in the media.
- Advertisers use attention-getting devices to make a lasting impression in the minds of their consumers.
- Some teenagers are obsessed with instant messaging, using it to the extreme and forsaking other forms of communication.

Choose Appropriate Examples

Make sure the examples you choose directly support your topic sentence. Use the following guidelines in choosing examples:

1. **Choose clear examples.** Do not choose an example that is complicated or has too many parts; your readers may not be able to see the connection to your topic sentence clearly.

2. **Use a sufficient number of examples to make your point understandable.** The number you need depends on the complexity of the topic and your readers' familiarity with it. One example is sufficient only if it is well developed. The more difficult and unfamiliar the topic, the more examples you will need. For instance, if you are writing about how purchasing books at the college bookstore can be viewed as an exercise in patience, two examples may be sufficient. However, if you are writing about religious intolerance, you probably will need more than two examples.

3. **Include examples that your readers are familiar with and understand.** If you choose an example that is out of the realm of your readers' experience, the example will not help them understand your main point.

4. **Vary your examples.** If you are giving several examples, choose a wide range from different times, places, people, etc.

5. **Choose typical examples.** Avoid outrageous or exaggerated examples that do not accurately represent the situation you are discussing.

6. **Each example should be as specific and vivid as possible, accurately describing an incident or situation.** Include as much detail as is necessary for your readers to understand how the situation illustrates your topic sentence.

7. **Make sure the connection between your example and your main point is clear to your readers.** If the connection is not obvious, include an explanation. For instance, if it is not clear that poor time management is an example of poor study habits, explain how the two relate.

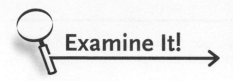

Examine It!

Directions: The following paragraph is a good model of an example paragraph. Study its annotations to discover how the writers use examples to develop their paragraph.

Alternative Energy Sources

Topic sentence

Example 1 (new technology)

Example 2 (wind power)

Example 3 (applications)

New technologies are helping to make alternative sources of energy cost effective. In Pennsylvania and Connecticut, *for example,* the waste from landfills is loaded into furnaces and burned to generate electricity for thousands of homes. Natural sources of energy, *such as* the sun and the wind, are also becoming more attractive. The electricity produced by 300 wind turbines in northern California, *for instance,* has resulted in a savings of approximately 60,000 barrels of oil per year. Solar energy also has many applications, from pocket calculators to public telephones to entire homes, and is even used in spacecraft, where conventional power is unavailable.

—adapted from Bergman and Renwick, *Introduction to Geography,* p. 343, and Carnes and Garraty, *The American Nation,* p. 916.

EXERCISE C-1
Writing in Progress

Brainstorming Examples

Directions: Select one of the topics listed below, narrow it, and write a topic sentence for it. Then brainstorm a list of examples that support it.

1. The behavior of professional athletes
2. The value of travel or a vacation
3. People's eating habits
4. Television commercials
5. Restaurant dining ■

How to Organize an Example Paragraph

Be sure to arrange your examples logically. You might arrange them from most to least important or least to most important. (See Chapter 13, p. 325 and Section B of this chapter, p. 345.) You might also arrange them chronologically, in order of time, if the examples are events in the past. For example, if you are reporting on how early educational experiences influenced you, you might begin with the earliest situation and progress to the most recent.

Regardless of the order you use, be sure to connect your examples with transitional words and phrases like those shown below.

EXAMPLE: USEFUL TRANSITIONS		
for example	for instance	to illustrate
one example	another example	such as
also		

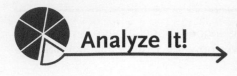

Analyze It!

Directions: The following paragraph is a good model of an example paragraph. Read the paragraph and highlight each example. Then underline the sentences that the examples support.

Controlling Information and Using Technology

To maintain their positions of power, elites try to control information. Fear is a favorite tactic of dictators. To muffle criticism, they imprison, torture, and kill reporters who dare to criticize their regime. Under Saddam Hussein, the penalty for telling a joke about Hussein was having your tongue cut out. Lacking such power, the ruling elites of democracies rely on more covert means. The new technology is another tool for the elite. Telephones can be turned into microphones even when they are off the hook. Machines can read the entire contents of a computer in a second, without leaving evidence that they have done so. Security cameras—"Tiny Brothers"—have sprouted almost everywhere. Face-recognition systems can scan a crowd of thousands, instantly matching the scans with digitized files of individuals. With these devices, the elite can monitor citizens' activities without anyone knowing that they are being observed. Dictatorships have few checks on how they employ such technology, but in democracies, checks and balances, such as requiring court orders for search and seizure, at least partially curb their abuse. The threat of bypassing such restraints on power are always present, as with the Homeland Security laws.

—Henslin, *Sociology*, p. 249.

EXERCISE C-2

Writing in Progress

Writing an Example Paragraph

Directions: Using the topic sentence and examples you generated in Exercise C-1, write an example paragraph. Present your details in a logical order, using transitions as needed. ■

D: DEFINITION

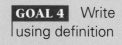
GOAL 4 Write using definition

What Is Definition?

A **definition** is an explanation of what something is. It has three essential parts:

1. The term being defined
2. The group, or category, to which the term belongs
3. Its distinguishing characteristics

Suppose you had to define the term *cheetah*. If you said it was a cat, then you would be stating the group to which it belongs. **Group** means the general category of which something is a part. If you said a cheetah lives in Africa and southwest Asia, has black-spotted fur, is long-legged, and is the fastest animal on land, you would be giving some of its distinguishing characteristics. **Distinguishing characteristics** are those details that allow you to tell an item apart from others in its same group. The details about the cheetah's fur, long legs, and speed enable a reader to distinguish it from other large cats in Africa and southwest Asia. Here are a few more examples:

TERM	GROUP	DISTINGUISHING CHARACTERISTICS
opal	gemstone	greenish blue colors
comedian	entertainer	makes people laugh
fear	emotion	occurs when a person feels threatened or in danger

Here is a sample definition paragraph written by a student, Ted Sawchuck.

Sushi is a Japanese food consisting of small cakes of cooked rice wrapped in seaweed. While it is commonly thought of as raw fish on rice, it is actually any preparation of vinegared rice. Sushi can also take the form of conical hand rolls and the more popular sushi roll. The roll is topped or stuffed with slices of raw or cooked fish, egg, or vegetables. Slices of raw fish served by themselves are commonly mistaken for sushi but are properly referred to as *sashimi*.

In the paragraph above, the term being defined is *sushi*. Its group is Japanese food, and its distinguishing characteristics are detailed. You can visualize a definition paragraph as follows. Study the model and the map for the paragraph on sushi shown below.

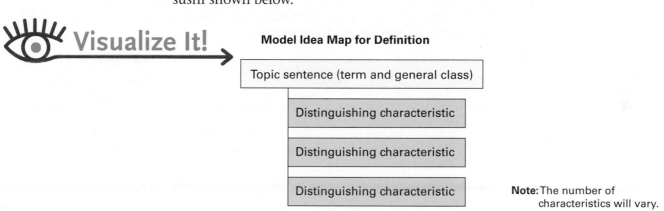

Model Idea Map for Definition

Topic sentence (term and general class)

Distinguishing characteristic

Distinguishing characteristic

Distinguishing characteristic

Note: The number of characteristics will vary.

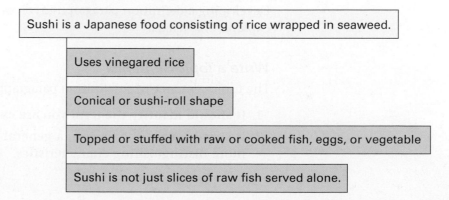

Idea Map of Sawchuck's Paragraph on Sushi

Sushi is a Japanese food consisting of rice wrapped in seaweed.

Uses vinegared rice

Conical or sushi-roll shape

Topped or stuffed with raw or cooked fish, eggs, or vegetable

Sushi is not just slices of raw fish served alone.

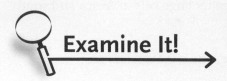
Examine It!

Directions: The following paragraph is a good model of a definition paragraph. Study the annotations to discover how the writer defines the term *nervous system*.

The Nervous System

Topic sentence

First distinguishing feature

Second distinguishing feature

Third distinguishing feature

Example

The nervous system, the master controlling and communicating system of the body, has three overlapping functions. (1) It uses millions of sensory receptors to monitor changes occurring both inside and outside the body. These changes are called stimuli and the gathered information is called *sensory input.* (2) It processes and interprets the sensory input and decides what should be done at each moment—a process called *integration.* (3) It causes a response by activating our muscles or glands; the response is called *motor output.* An example will illustrate how these functions work together. When you are driving and see a red light ahead (sensory input), your nervous system integrates this information (red light means "stop"), and your foot goes for the brake (motor output).

—Marieb, *Anatomy and Physiology*, p. 387.

EXERCISE D-1   Classifying Terms

Directions: For each term listed below, give the group it belongs to and at least two of its distinguishing characteristics.

TERM	GROUP	DISTINGUISHING CHARACTERSTICS
1. baseball	_____	_____
2. a role model	_____	_____
3. blogging	_____	_____
4. terrorism	_____	_____
5. facial expressions	_____	_____

How to Develop a Definition Paragraph

Developing a definition paragraph involves writing a topic sentence and adding explanatory details.

Write a Topic Sentence

The topic sentence of a definition paragraph should accomplish two things:

1. **It should identify the term you are explaining.**

2. **It should place the term in a general group. It may also provide one or more distinguishing characteristics.**

In the topic sentence below, the term being defined is *psychiatry*, the general group is "a branch of medicine," and its distinguishing feature is that it "deals with mental and emotional disorders."

Psychiatry is a branch of medicine that deals with mental and emotional disorders.

EXERCISE D-2	**Writing a Topic Sentence**
Writing in Progress	

Directions: Write a topic sentence that includes a group and a distinguishing characteristic for each of the following items.

1. shirt _____
2. horror _____
3. hip-hop _____
4. age discrimination _____
5. ballroom dancing _____

Add Explanatory Details

Your topic sentence will usually *not* be sufficient to give your reader a complete understanding of the term you are defining. You will need to explain it further in one or more of the following ways:

1. **Give examples.** Examples can make a definition more vivid and interesting to your reader. (To learn more about using examples, see Section C of this chapter, p. 346.)

2. **Break the term into subcategories.** Breaking your subject down into subcategories helps to organize your definition. For example, you might explain the term *discrimination* by listing some of its types: racial, gender, and age.

3. **Explain what the term is not.** To bring the meaning of a term into focus for your reader, it is sometimes helpful to give counterexamples, or to discuss in what ways the term means something different from what one might expect. Notice that Sawchuck does this in the paragraph on sushi.

4. **Trace the term's meaning over time.** If the term has changed or expanded in meaning over time, it may be useful to trace this development as a way of explaining the term's current meaning.

5. **Compare an unfamiliar term to one that is familiar to your readers.** If you are writing about rugby, you might compare it to football, a more familiar sport. Be sure to make the connection clear to your readers by pointing out characteristics that the two sports share.

How to Organize a Definition Paragraph

You should logically arrange the distinguishing characteristics of a term. You might arrange them from most to least familiar or from more to less obvious, for example. Be sure to use strong transitional words and phrases to help your readers follow your presentation of ideas, guiding them from one distinguishing characteristic to another. Useful transitional words and phrases are shown below.

DEFINITION: USEFUL TRANSITIONS			
can be defined as	means	is	
one	a second	another	also

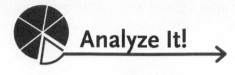 **Analyze It!**

Directions: The paragraph on the left is a good model of a paragraph that uses definition as a method of development. Complete the outline below using information given in the paragraph.

What Is a Tale?

The name *tale* is sometimes applied to any story, whether short or long, true or fictitious. But defined in a more limited sense, a **tale** is a story, usually short, that sets forth strange and wonderful events in more or less bare summary, without detailed character-drawing. *Tale* implies a story in which the goal is to reveal something marvelous rather than to reveal the character of someone. In the English folk tale "Jack and the Beanstalk," for instance, we take away a more vivid impression of the miraculous beanstalk and the giant who dwells at its top than of Jack's mind or personality.

—adapted from Kennedy and Gioia, *Literature*, p. 7.

I.   Tale

A.   Often defined as _____ .

    _____

B.   In a more limited sense, it has specific characteristics.

   1.   It is usually _____ .

   2.   It describes events _____ form.

   3.   Its goal is to _____, rather than to reveal someone's character.

     a.   Example: _____ : the _____ is memorable, but Jack's personality is not.

EXERCISE D-3

Writing in Progress

Writing a Definition Paragraph

Directions: Select one of the topic sentences you wrote for Exercise D-2. Write a paragraph defining that topic, using transitions as needed. ■

E: COMPARISON AND CONTRAST

GOAL 5 Write using comparison and contrast

What Are Comparison and Contrast?

Comparison and contrast are two ways of organizing information about two or more subjects. **Comparison** focuses on similarities; **contrast** focuses on differences. When writing paragraphs, it is often best to focus either on similarities or on differences, instead of trying to cover both in a short piece of writing. Essay-length pieces can focus on both similarities and differences, but it is often easier to concentrate on one or the other. Here is a sample contrast paragraph written by Ted Sawchuck:

> Every time I go out for Mexican food, I have to choose between tacos de carne asada and tacos al pastor—they are tasty, but different. The tacos de carne asada are three small tortillas stuffed with chopped steak, served with a dish each of cilantro, onion, tomato, and fiery salsa. The tacos al pastor are similar, but chorizo is added to the chopped steak. While the tacos al pastor are a little greasier, they also have more spice and heat. Tacos de carne asada are drier with less flavor, but there's more room to add the vegetables, and that often makes for more dynamic flavor possibilities.

In this paragraph, Sawchuck discusses the differences between two types of tacos. He examines their ingredients, their spiciness, and their overall flavor. You can visualize a comparison or contrast paragraph as follows. Study the models and the map for Sawchuck's paragraph.

Model Idea Map for Comparison

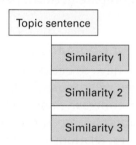

Topic sentence

Similarity 1

Similarity 2

Similarity 3

Note: The number of similarities will vary.

Model Idea Map for Contrast

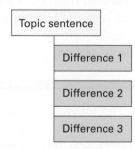

Topic sentence

Difference 1

Difference 2

Difference 3

Note: The number of differences will vary.

Idea Map for Sawchuck's Paragraph on Tacos

Tacos de carne asada and tacos al pastor taste different.

Contents: de carne asada have steak; al pastor have steak and chorizo

Texture: al pastor are greasier

Heat: al pastor have more heat

Vegetables: de carne asada have more room for vegetables

How to Develop a Comparison or Contrast Paragraph

Developing a comparison or contrast paragraph involves writing a topic sentence and developing points of comparison or contrast.

Write a Topic Sentence

Your topic sentence should do two things:

1. **It should identify the two subjects that you will compare or contrast.**
2. **It should state whether you will focus on similarities, differences, or both.**

Here are a few sample topic sentences that meet the requirements above:

- Judaism is one of the smallest of the world's religions; Hinduism is one of the largest.
- Neither Judaism nor Hinduism limits worship to a single location, although both hold services in temples.
- Unlike Hinduism, Judaism teaches belief in only one God.

Be sure to avoid topic sentences that announce what you plan to do. Here's an example: "I'll compare network news and local news and show why I prefer local news."

Develop Points of Comparison or Contrast

The first thing you have to decide in writing a comparison or contrast paragraph is on what bases you will compare your two subjects. These bases are called **points of comparison** or **contrast**. Suppose you are comparing two different jobs that you have held. Points of comparison could be your salary, work schedule, required tasks, responsibilities, relationships with other employees, relationship with your boss, and so forth. The points of comparison you choose should depend on what you want your paragraph to show—your purpose for writing. If your purpose is to show what you learned from the jobs, then you might compare the tasks you completed and your responsibilities. If you want to make a case that working conditions in entry level jobs are poor, then you might use responsibilities, work schedule, and relationship with your boss as points of comparison.

Examine It!

Directions: The following paragraph is a good model of a comparison and contrast paragraph. Study the annotations to discover how the writer explains the differences between two types of tumors.

Malignant and Benign Tumors

Topic Sentence

Difference #1

Difference #2

Not all tumors are **malignant** (cancerous); in fact, more are **benign** (noncancerous). Benign and malignant tumors differ in several key ways. Benign tumors are generally composed of ordinary-looking cells enclosed in a fibrous shell or capsule that prevents their spreading to other body areas. Malignant tumors, in contrast, are usually not enclosed in a protective capsule and can therefore spread to other organs. Unlike benign tumors, which merely expand to take over a given space, malignant cells invade surrounding tissue, emitting clawlike protrusions that disrupt chemical processes within healthy cells.

—adapted from Donatelle, *Health*, p. 324.

EXERCISE E-1
Writing in Progress

Brainstorming and Writing Topic Sentences

Directions: For two of the topics below, brainstorm lists of similarities or differences. Review your lists and choose points of comparison. Then write topic sentences for them.

1. Two special places
2. Two favorite pastimes
3. Two styles of dress
4. Two cars
5. Two public figures
6. Two sports
7. Two college classes
8. Two relatives ■

How to Organize a Comparison or Contrast Paragraph

Once you have identified similarities or differences and drafted a topic sentence, you are ready to organize your paragraph. There are two ways you can organize a comparison or contrast paragraph:

* subject by subject
* point by point

Subject-by-Subject Organization

In the **subject-by-subject method**, you write first about one of your subjects, covering it completely, and then about the other, covering it completely. Ideally, you cover the same points of comparison or contrast for both and in the same order. With subject-by-subject organization, you begin by discussing your first job—its salary, working conditions, and responsibilities. Then you discuss your second job—its salary, working conditions, and responsibilities. You can visualize the arrangement with the idea map shown below.

 **Visualize It!**

Model Idea Map for Subject-by-Subject Organization

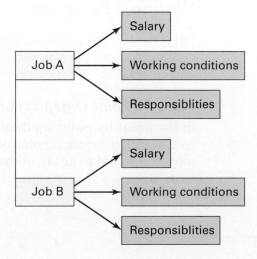

To develop each subject, focus on the same kinds of details and discuss the same points of comparison in the same order. Organize your points within each topic, using a most-to-least or least-to-most arrangement.

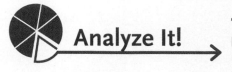 **Analyze It!**

Directions: The paragraph on the left is a good model of a paragraph that uses comparison and contrast as a method of development. Complete the map below using information given in the paragraph.

Types of Leaders

Groups have two types of leaders. The first is easy to recognize. This person, called an **instrumental leader** (or *task-oriented leader*), tries to keep the group moving toward its goals. These leaders try to keep group members from getting sidetracked, reminding them of what they are trying to accomplish. The **expressive leader** (or *socioemotional leader*), in contrast, usually is not recognized as a leader, but he or she certainly is one. This person is likely to crack jokes, to offer sympathy, or to do other things that help to lift the group's morale. Both type of leadership are essential: the one to keep the group on track, the other to increase harmony and minimize conflicts.

—*Henslin, Sociology,* p. 169.

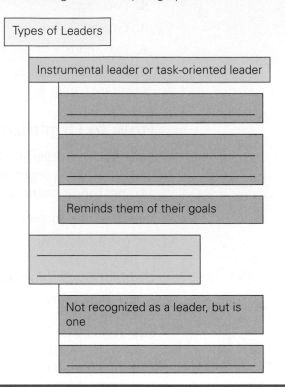

EXERCISE E-2
Writing in Progress

Writing a Paragraph

Directions: Using the subject-by-subject method of organization, write a comparison or contrast paragraph on one of the topics you worked with in Exercise E-1. ■

Point-by-Point Organization

In the **point-by-point method of organization,** you discuss both of your subjects together for each point of comparison or contrast. For the paragraph on jobs, you would write about the salary for Job A and Job B, and then you would write about working conditions for Job A and Job B, and so on.

You can visualize the organization this way:

Model Idea Map for Point-by-Point Organization

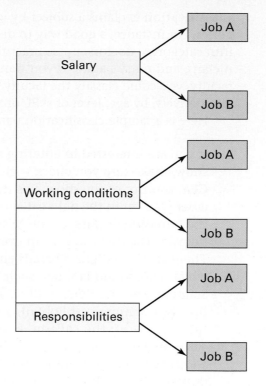

When using this organization, maintain consistency by discussing the same subject first for each point. (For example, always discuss Job A first and Job B second.)

If your paragraph focuses only on similarities or only on differences, arrange your points in a least-to-most or most-to-least pattern.

Transitions are particularly important in comparison and contrast writing. Because you are discussing two subjects and covering similar points for each, your readers can easily become confused. Useful transitions are shown below.

COMPARISON AND CONTRAST USEFUL TRANSITIONS	
To show similarities	likewise, similarly, in the same way, too, also
To show differences	however, on the contrary, unlike, on the other hand, but, although

EXERCISE E-3   Using Transitions
Writing in Progress

Directions: Review the paragraph you wrote for Exercise E-2. Add transitions as needed. ▪

F: CLASSIFICATION

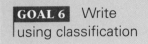

GOAL 6 Write using classification

What Is Classification?

Classification explains a subject by identifying and describing its types or categories. For instance, a good way to discuss medical personnel is to arrange them into categories: doctors, nurse practitioners, physician's assistants, nurses, technicians, and nurse's aides. If you wanted to explain who makes up your college faculty, you could classify the faculty members by the disciplines they teach (or, alternatively, by age, level of skill, or some other factor).

Here is a sample classification paragraph written by Elsie Hunter:

> If you are interested in entering your pedigreed pet in the upcoming cat show, make sure you check with the Cat Fanciers' Association first. The CFA, sponsor of the show, has strict rules regarding eligibility. You must enter your cat in the right category. Only cats in the Championship Class, the Provisional Class, or the Miscellaneous Class will be allowed to participate. The first category in every cat show is the Championship Class. There are 37 pedigreed breeds eligible for showing in this class, some of which may sound familiar, such as the Abyssinian, the Maine Coon, the Siamese, and the Russian Blue. The Provisional Class allows only three breeds: the American Bobtail, a breed that looks like a wildcat but acts like a pussycat; the LaPerm, a curly-haired cutie that's descended from early American barn cats; and the semi-longhaired Siberian, a breed that was first imported from Russia in 1990. The Miscellaneous Class allows only one breed—the big Ragamuffin with its silky, rabbitlike coat. So, before you rush out and pay the entry fee, make sure you have something fancy enough for the Cat Fanciers' Association.

This paragraph explains the eligibility for a cat show by describing the three categories of cats allowed to enter the show.

You can visualize the process of classification as follows. Study the model and the map for Hunter's paragraph below.

Model Idea Map for Classification

Topic sentence

Category 1

Category 2

Category 3

Note: The number of categories will vary.

Idea Map for Hunter's Paragraph on Cats

Cats eligible for the show must fit into one of three categories.

Championship class

Provisional class

Miscellaneous class

How to Develop a Classification Paragraph

Developing a classification paragraph involves deciding on a basis of classification for the subject you are discussing, writing a topic sentence, and explaining each subgroup.

Decide on What Basis to Classify Information

To write a paper using classification, you must first decide on a basis for breaking your subject into subgroups. Suppose you are given an assignment to write about some aspect of campus life. You decide to classify the campus services into groups. You could classify them by benefit, location, or type of facility, depending on what you wanted the focus of your writing to be.

The best way to plan your classification paragraph is to find a good general topic and then brainstorm different ways to break it into subgroups or categories.

Directions: The following paragraph is a good model of a classification paragraph. Study the annotations to discover how the writers classify strategies used by companies.

Company Strategies

Topic sentence

Category 1

     Three types of strategy are usually considered by a company. The purpose of **corporate strategy** is to determine the firm's overall attitude toward growth and the way it will manage its businesses or product lines. A company may decide to *grow* by increasing its activities or investment or to *retrench* by reducing them. **Business** (or **competitive**)

Category 2

strategy, which takes place at the level of the business unit or product line, focuses on improving the company's competitive position. At the

Category 3

level of **functional strategy**, managers in specific areas decide how best to achieve corporate goals by being as productive as possible.

—adapted from Ebert and Griffin, *Business Essentials*, p. 117.

EXERCISE F-1   Using Brainstorming

Working Together

Directions: For each of the following topics, brainstorm to discover different ways you might classify them. Compare your work with that of a classmate and select the two or three most effective classifications.

   1. **TOPIC** Crimes
      WAYS TO CLASSIFY _____

      _____

      _____

   2. **TOPIC** Movies
      WAYS TO CLASSIFY _____

      _____

      _____

   3. **TOPIC** Web sites
      WAYS TO CLASSIFY _____

      _____

      _____

Most topics can be classified in a number of different ways. Stores can be classified by types of merchandise, prices, size, or customer service provided, for example. Use the following tips for choosing an appropriate basis of classification:

- **Consider your audience.** Choose a basis of classification that will interest them. Classifying stores by size may not be as interesting as classifying them by merchandise, for example.

- **Choose a basis that is uncomplicated.** If you choose a basis that is complicated or lengthy, your topic may be difficult to write about. Categorizing stores by prices may be unwieldy, since there are thousands of products sold at various prices.

- **Choose a basis with which you are familiar.** While it is possible to classify stores by the types of customer service they provide, you may have to do some research or learn more about available services in order to write about them.

EXERCISE F-2   Using Brainstorming

Writing in Progress

Directions: Choose one of the following topics. Brainstorm a list of possible ways to classify the topic.

1. Professional athletes or their fans
2. Bad drivers
3. Diets
4. Cell phone users
5. Friends ■

Write a Topic Sentence

Once you have chosen a way to classify a topic and have identified the subgroups you will use, you are ready to write a topic sentence. Your topic sentence should accomplish two things:

1. **It should identify your topic.**
2. **It should indicate how you will classify items within your topic.**

The topic sentence may also mention the number of subgroups you will use. Here are a few examples:

- Three relatively new types of family structures are single-parent families, blended families, and families without children.

- Since working as a waiter, I've discovered that there are three main types of customer complaints.

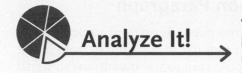

Analyze It!

Types of Burns

Burns are classified according to their severity (depth) as first-, second-, or third-degree burns. In **first-degree burns,** only the epidermis is damaged. The area becomes red and swollen. Except for temporary discomfort, first-degree burns are not usually serious and generally heal in two to three days without any special attention. **Second-degree burns** involve injury to the epidermis and the upper region of the dermis. The skin is red and painful, and *blisters* appear. Because sufficient numbers of epithelial cells are still present, regrowth (regeneration) of the epithelium can occur. Ordinarily, no permanent scars result if care is taken to prevent infection. **Third-degree burns** destroy the entire thickness of the skin. The burned area appears blanched (gray-white) or blackened, and because the nerve endings in the area are destroyed, the burned area is not painful. In third-degree burns, regeneration is not possible, and skin grafting must be done to cover the underlying exposed tissues.

—Marieb, *Essentials of Human Anatomy and Physiology,* p.124.

Directions: The paragraph on the left is a good model of a paragraph that uses classification as a method of development. Complete the chart on the right using information given in the paragraph.

Characteristic	First-Degree Burns	Second-Degree Burns	Third-Degree Burns
Appearance	_____ _____	_____ _____	_____ _____
Degree of Skin Damage	_____ _____ _____	_____ _____ _____	_____ _____ _____
Healing Properties	_____ _____	_____ _____	_____ _____ _____

EXERCISE F-3   Writing a Topic Sentence

Writing in Progress

Directions: For one of the topics in Exercise F-2, write a topic sentence that identifies the topic and explains your method of classification. ■

Explain Each Subgroup

The details in your paragraph should explain and provide further information about each subgroup. Depending on your topic and/or your audience, it may be necessary to define each subgroup. If possible, provide an equal amount of detail for each subgroup. If you define or offer an example for one subgroup, you should do the same for each of the others.

How to Organize a Classification Paragraph

The order in which you present your categories depends on your topic. Possible ways to organize the categories include from familiar to unfamiliar, from oldest to newest, or from simpler to more complex. Be sure to use transitions to signal your readers that you are moving from one category to another. Useful transitions are shown below.

CLASSIFICATION: USEFUL TRANSITIONS		
first	second	third
one	another	also
in addition	then	last

EXERCISE F-4

Writing in Progress

Writing a Classification Paragraph

Directions: For the topic sentence you wrote in Exercise F-3, write a classification paragraph. Be sure to identify and explain each group. Use transitions as needed. ■

G: PROCESS

GOAL 7 Write using process

What Is Process?

A process is a series of steps or actions that one follows in a particular order to accomplish something. When you assemble a toy, bake a cake, rebuild an engine, or put up a tent, you do things in a specific order. A **process paragraph** explains the steps to follow in completing a process. The steps are given in the order in which they are done. Here is a sample process paragraph. In it, the student writer, Ted Sawchuck, explains how copyediting is done at his college's student newspaper.

> The Fourth Estate's copyediting process is not very complicated. First, articles are submitted in electronic format and are read by Merren, the copy editor. Next, she makes changes and ensures all the articles are in their proper place. Then, section editors have a day to read the stories for their sections and make changes. Finally, all articles, photographs, cartoons, and anything else to be included in the upcoming issue is read and fact-checked by the editor-in-chief.

In this paragraph the writer identifies four steps. Notice that they are presented in the order in which they happen. You can visualize a process paragraph as follows. Study the model and the map on the following page for the paragraph above.

There are two types of process paragraphs—a "how-to" paragraph and a "how-it-works" paragraph:

- **A "how-to" paragraph explains how something is done.** For example, it may explain how to change a flat tire, aid a choking victim, or locate a reference source in the library.

- **A "how-it-works" paragraph explains how something operates or happens.** For example, it may explain the operation of a pump, how the human body regulates temperature, or how children acquire speech.

Model Idea Map for Process

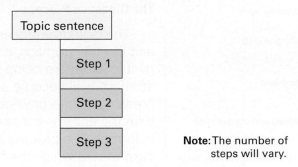

Note: The number of steps will vary.

Idea Map of Sawchuck's Essay on Copyediting

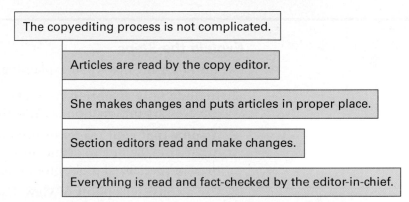

How to Develop a Process Paragraph

Developing a process paragraph involves writing a topic sentence and explaining each step clearly and thoroughly.

Write a Topic Sentence

For a process paragraph, your topic sentence should accomplish two things:

1. **It should identify the process or procedure.**
2. **It should explain to your reader why familiarity with it is useful, interesting, or important (*why* he or she should learn about the process).** Your topic sentence should state a goal, offer a reason, or indicate what can be accomplished by using the process.

Here are a few examples of topic sentences that contain both of these important elements:

- Reading maps, a vital skill if you are taking vacations by car, is a simple process, except for the final refolding.
- Because reading is an essential skill, all parents should know how to interest their children in recreational reading.
- To locate information on the Internet, you must know how to use a search engine.

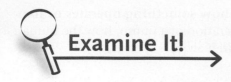

Examine It!

Directions: The following paragraph is a good model of a process paragraph. Study the annotations to discover how the writer describes the process of digestion.

Heading announces topic	**The Digestive Process**
Step 1: stretching of wall	The digestive process involves three basic steps. As food enters and fills the stomach, its wall begins to stretch. At the same time the
Step 2: gastric juices	gastric juices are being secreted. Then the three muscle layers of the stomach wall become active. They compress and pummel the food,
Step 3: pummeling and compression	breaking it apart physically, all the while continuously mixing the food with the enzyme-containing gastric juice so that the semifluid chyme is formed. The process looks something like the preparation of a
Comparison to something familiar helps reader understand three steps	cake mix, in which the floury mixture is repeatedly folded on itself and mixed with the liquid until it reaches uniform texture.

—Marieb, *Essentials of Human Anatomy and Physiology*, p. 487.

Explain the Steps

Use the following tips when explaining each step in a process:

1. **Include only essential, necessary steps.** Avoid comments, opinions, and unnecessary information because they may confuse your reader.

2. **Assume that your reader is unfamiliar with your topic (unless you know otherwise).** Be sure to define unfamiliar terms and describe clearly any technical or specialized tools, procedures, or objects.

3. **Use a consistent point of view.** Use either the first person (*I*) or the second person (*you*) throughout. Don't switch between them.

4. **List needed equipment.** For how-to paragraphs, tell your readers what they will need to complete the process. For a how-to paragraph on making chili, list the ingredients, for example.

5. **Identify pitfalls and problems.** Alert your readers about potential problems and places where confusion or error may occur. For instance, warn your chili-making readers to add chili peppers gradually and to taste the chili frequently along the way.

EXERCISE G-1   Writing a Topic Sentence

Writing in Progress

Directions: Write a topic sentence for one of the topics listed below. Then write a paragraph using the techniques listed above.

1. How to have an exciting vacation

2. How to cure an illness

3. How to shop on the Internet

4. How to build or repair _____

5. How _____ works ■

How to Organize a Process Paragraph

Process paragraphs should be organized sequentially according to the order in which the steps are done or occur. It is usually a good idea to place your topic sentence first. Placing it in this position provides your reader with a purpose for reading. Be sure to use transitional words and phrases to signal your readers that you are moving from one step to another. Useful transitions are listed below.

PROCESS: USEFUL TRANSITIONS		
first	then	next
second	later	after
third	while	following
after	finally	afterward
before		

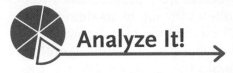 **Analyze It!**

Directions: The paragraph on the left is a good model of a paragraph that uses process as a method of development. On the right, list the steps in the method of loci process using information given in the paragraph.

The Method of Loci

The *method of loci* is a memory device that can be used when you want to remember a list of items such as a grocery list or when you give a speech or a class report and need to make your points in order without using notes. The word *loci* (pronounced "LOH-sye") is the plural form of *locus,* which means "location" or "place." Here's how to use the method of loci. Select any familiar place—your home, for example—and simply associate the items to be remembered with locations there. Progress in an orderly fashion. For example, visualize the first item or idea you want to remember in its place on the driveway, the second in the garage, the third at the front door, and so on, until you have associated each item you want to remember with a specific location. You may find it helpful to conjure up oversized images of the items that you place at each location. When you want to recall the items, take an imaginary walk starting at the first place—the first item will pop into your mind. When you think of the second place, the second item will come to mind, and so on.

—Wood et al., *Mastering the World of Psychology,* p. 181.

List the steps involved in the method of loci memory device.

Step 1: _____

_____

Step 2: _____

Step 3: _____

_____

Step 4: _____

_____

EXERCISE G-2   Adding Transitions
Writing in Progress

Directions: Revise the draft you wrote for Exercise G-1. Check transitional words and phrases and add more, if necessary, to make your ideas clearer. ■

H: CAUSE AND EFFECT

GOAL 8 Write using cause and effect

What Are Cause and Effect?

Causes are explanations of why things happen. **Effects** are explanations of what happens as a result of an action or event. Each day we face situations that require cause-and-effect analysis. Some are daily events; others mark important life decisions. Why won't my car start? Why didn't I get my student loan check? What will happen if I skip class today? How will my family react if I decide to get married? Here is a sample cause-and-effect paragraph. The student writer, Ted Sawchuck, discusses what can go wrong when preparing guacamole.

> Adding too many ingredients to guacamole will ruin the delicate flavor created by the interplay between fatty avocado, spicy peppers, and sweet tomatoes. Adding yogurt, for example, dilutes the dip to an almost souplike consistency and ruins the flavor. Dumping in salsa overpowers the delicate avocado so that you don't know what you are eating. Another common error, adding too much salt, masks the luxurious flavor of the avocado found in the best guacamole.

In this paragraph the student writer identifies three causes and three effects. You can visualize a cause-and-effect paragraph as follows. Study the model and the map for Sawchuck's paragraph.

Model Idea Map for Cause and Effect

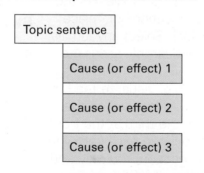

Topic sentence

Cause (or effect) 1

Cause (or effect) 2

Cause (or effect) 3

Note: The number of causes or effects will vary.

Idea Map of Sawchuck's Paragraph on Guacamole

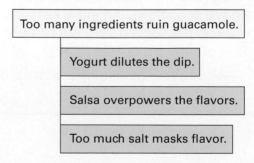

Too many ingredients ruin guacamole.

Yogurt dilutes the dip.

Salsa overpowers the flavors.

Too much salt masks flavor.

How to Develop a Cause-and-Effect Paragraph

Developing a cause-and-effect paragraph involves distinguishing between causes and effects, writing a topic sentence, and providing relevant and sufficient details.

Distinguish Between Cause and Effect

How can you distinguish between causes and effects? To determine causes, ask:

"Why did this happen?"

To identify effects, ask:

"What happened because of this?"

Let's consider an everyday situation: you lost your set of keys, so you are locked out of your apartment. This is a simple case in which one cause produces one effect. You can diagram this situation as follows:

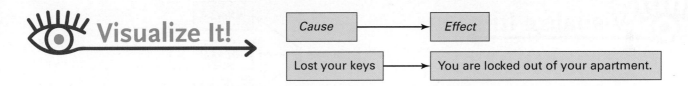

Most situations, however, are much more complicated than the one shown above. Sometimes cause and effect work like a chain reaction: one cause triggers an effect, which in turn becomes the cause of another effect. In a chain reaction, each event in a series influences the next, as shown in the following example:

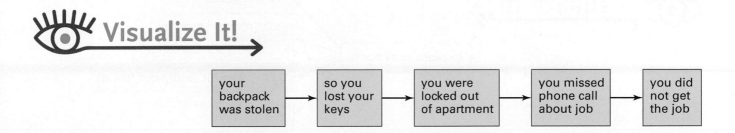

At other times, many causes may contribute to a single effect, as shown in the following diagram.

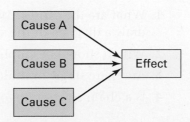

For example, there may be several reasons why you decided to become a veterinarian:

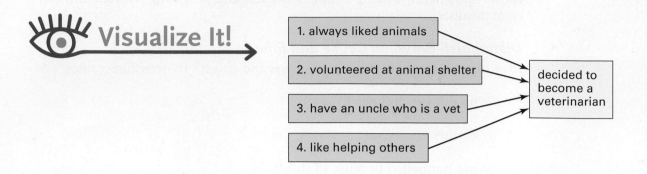

At other times, a single cause can have multiple effects, as shown below:

Suppose, for example, you decide to take a second part-time job:

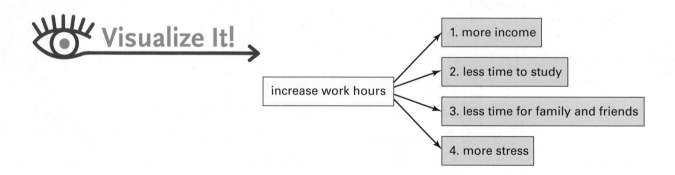

When analyzing a cause-and-effect situation that you plan to write about, ask yourself the following questions:

1. What are the causes? What are the effects? (To help answer these questions, draw a diagram of the situation.)
2. Which should be emphasized—cause or effect?
3. Are there single or multiple causes? Single or multiple effects?
4. Is a chain reaction involved?

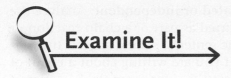

Examine It!

Directions: The following paragraph is a good model of a cause-and-effect paragraph. Study the annotations to discover how the writer explains the effects of marijuana.

Chronic Use of Marijuana

Most current information about chronic marijuana use comes from countries such as Jamaica and Costa Rica, where the drug is not illegal. These studies of long-term users (for 10 or more years) **[Effect #1]** indicate that marijuana causes lung damage comparable to that caused by tobacco smoking. Indeed, smoking a single joint may **[Effect #2]** be as bad for the lungs as smoking three tobacco cigarettes. Other risks associated with marijuana include suppression of the immune system, blood pressure changes, and impaired memory function. Recent studies suggest that pregnant women who smoke marijuana are at a higher risk for stillbirth or miscarriage and for delivering low– **[Effect #3]** birth weight babies and babies with abnormalities of the nervous system. Babies born to marijuana smokers are five times more likely to have features similar to those exhibited by children with fetal alcohol syndrome.

—Donatelle, *Access to Health*, p. 436.

EXERCISE H-1   Identifying Causes and Effects

Writing in Progress

Directions: Identify possible causes and effects for three of the following situations:

1. Spending too much time surfing the Internet
2. Academic cheating or dishonesty
3. An important decision you made
4. The popularity of cell phones
5. Earning good grades ■

Write a Topic Sentence

To write effective topic sentences for cause-and-effect paragraphs, do the following:

1. **Clarify the cause-and-effect relationship.** Before you write, carefully identify the causes and the effects. If you are uncertain, divide a sheet of paper into two columns. Label one column "Causes" and the other "Effects." Brainstorm about your topic, placing your ideas in the appropriate column.

2. **Decide whether to emphasize causes or effects.** In a single paragraph, it is best to focus on either causes or effects—not both. For example, suppose you are writing about students who work two part-time jobs. You need to decide whether to discuss why they work two jobs (causes) or what happens to students who work two jobs (effects). Your topic sentence should indicate whether you are going to emphasize causes or effects. (In essays, you may consider both causes and effects.)

3. Determine whether the events are related or independent. Analyze the causes or effects to discover if they occurred as part of a chain reaction or are not related to one another. Your topic sentence should suggest the type of relationship you are writing about. If you are writing about a chain of events, your topic sentence should reflect this—for example, "A series of events led up to my brother's decision to join the military." If the causes or effects are independent, then your sentence should indicate that—for example, "Young men and women join the military for a number of different reasons."

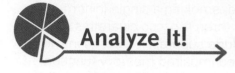

Analyze It!

Directions: The paragraph on the left is a good model of a paragraph that uses cause and effect as a method of development. Read it and then complete the outline on the right using information given in the paragraph.

Risk Factors for Ulcers

Although ulcers are commonly associated with stress, they can be brought on by other risk factors. Chronic use of aspirin and other non-steroidal anti-inflammatory drugs increases the risk of ulcer because these agents suppress the secretion of both mucus and bicarbonate, which normally protect the lining of the GI tract from the effects of acid and pepsin. The risk of ulcer is also increased by chronic alcohol use or the leakage of bile from the duodenum into the stomach, both of which can disrupt the mucus barrier. Surprisingly, ulcers are usually not associated with abnormally high rates of stomach-acid secretion; more often than not, acid secretion is normal or even below normal in most people with ulcers.

—adapted from Germann and Stanfield,
Principles of Human Physiology, p. 622.

A. List four causes of ulcers.

1. _____

   _____

2. _____

   _____

3. _____

   _____

4. _____

   _____

EXERCISE H-2   Writing a Topic Sentence
Writing in Progress

Directions: For one of the topics you chose in Exercise H-1, decide whether you will focus on causes or effects. Then write a topic sentence for a paragraph that will explain either causes *or* effects. ■

Provide Relevant and Sufficient Details

Each cause or effect you describe must be relevant to the situation introduced in your topic sentence. Each cause or reason requires explanation, particularly if it is *not* obvious. Jot down a list of the causes or reasons you plan to include.

This process may help you think of additional ones and will give you a chance to consider how to explain or support each cause or reason. You might decide to eliminate one or to combine several.

How to Organize a Cause-and-Effect Paragraph

There are several ways to arrange the details in a cause-and-effect paragraph. The method you choose depends on your purpose in writing, as well as on your topic. Suppose you are writing a paragraph about the effects of a hurricane on a coastal town. Several different arrangements of details are possible:

1. **Chronological** A chronological organization arranges your details in the order in which situations or events happened. For example, the order in which damage occurs during the course of a hurricane would become the order in which you present your details about the event. This arrangement is similar to the arrangement you learned in Section A of this chapter, "Narration," page 000. A chronological arrangement works for situations and events that occurred in a specific order.

2. **Order of importance** In an order-of-importance organization, the details are arranged from least to most important or from most to least important. In describing the effects of a hurricane, you could discuss the most severe damage first and then describe lesser damage. Alternatively, you could build up to the most important damage for dramatic effect.

3. **Spatial** Spatial arrangement of details uses physical or geographical position as a means of organization. In recounting the hurricane damage, you could start by describing damage to the beach and then work toward the center of town.

4. **Categorical** This method of arrangement divides the topic into parts or categories. Using this arrangement to describe hurricane damage, you could recount what the storm did to businesses, roads, city services, and homes.

Because cause-and-effect relationships can be complicated, be sure to use transitional words and phrases to signal your reader which are causes and which are effects. Useful transitions are shown below.

CAUSE AND EFFECT: USEFUL TRANSITIONS	
FOR CAUSES	**FOR EFFECTS**
because, due to, one cause is . . . , another is . . . , since, for, first, second	consequently, as a result, thus, resulted in, one result is . . . , another is . . . , therefore

EXERCISE H-3
Writing in Progress

Writing a Cause-and-Effect Paragraph

Directions: Write a paragraph developing the topic sentence you wrote for Exercise H-2. Be sure to include relevant and sufficient details. Organize your paragraph according to one of the methods described on page 373. ■

I: ARGUMENT

GOAL 9 Write using argument

What Is Argument?

An **argument** is a line of reasoning intended to persuade the reader or listener to agree with a particular viewpoint or to take a particular action. An argument presents reasons and evidence for accepting a belief or position or for taking a specific action. For example, you might argue that testing cosmetic products on animals is wrong, or that a traffic signal should be installed at the end of your street. An argument has three essential parts:

- **An issue** This is the problem or controversy that the argument addresses. It is also the topic of an argument paragraph. Gun control legislation is an example of an issue.

- **A position** A position is the particular point of view a writer has on an issue. There are always at least two points of view on an issue—pro and con. For example, you may be for or against gun control. You may favor or oppose lowering the legal drinking age.

- **Support** Support consists of the details that demonstrate your position is correct and should be accepted. There are three types of support: reasons, evidence, and emotional appeals.

Here is a sample argument paragraph:

> I strongly urge residents to vote "NO" on a referendum to withdraw funding for the proposed renovation of the Potwine town soccer fields. The town's other available fields are at capacity, and the number of children trying out for soccer is still growing. There are now more than 2,000 children between the ages of 6 and 13 playing on recreational and travel soccer teams. Meanwhile, the number of fields the college is willing to let us use has been reduced from 19 to 2. We are now having to rent fields in neighboring towns to accommodate all of the teams playing on Saturday afternoons! Opponents of the renovation always cite money as an obstacle. In fact, the money to fix the fields has been sitting in a Community Preservation Act fund for more than 15 years. Let the upcoming election be the final one, and make it one for the children—our own and the generations to come. Vote NO.

In this paragraph, the issue is the renovation of soccer fields. The writer's claim is that the renovation is necessary. The paragraph then offers reasons for the renovation.

Study the model and the map for this paragraph on the following page.

Model Idea Map for Argument

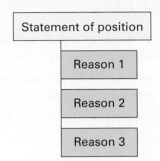

Statement of position

Reason 1

Reason 2

Reason 3

Note: The number of reasons will vary.

Idea Map of Paragraph on Soccer Fields

Residents should oppose withdrawal of funding for renovation of soccer fields.

Town's other fields are filled to capacity.

Number of children trying out is increasing.

Number of available college fields is decreasing.

Town must rent space from neighboring towns.

The money is available.

How to Develop an Argument Paragraph

Developing an argument paragraph involves writing a topic sentence, supporting your position with reasons and evidence, and addressing opposing viewpoints.

Write a Topic Sentence

Your topic sentence should do the following:

1. **Identify the issue.**
2. **State your position on the issue.**

The following topic sentence makes it clear that the writer will argue against the use of animals for medical research:

> The testing of cosmetics on animals should be outlawed because it is cruel, unnecessary, and disrespectful of animals' place in the chain of life.

Notice that this thesis identifies the issue and makes it clear that the writer opposes animal testing. It also suggests the three major reasons she will present: (1) it is cruel, (2) it is unnecessary, and (3) it is disrespectful. You do not always have to include the major points of your argument in your topic sentence statement, but including them does help the reader know what to expect. This topic sentence also makes clear what action the author thinks is appropriate: using animals in medical research should be outlawed.

Here are a few more topic sentences. Notice that they use the verbs *should, would,* and *must.*

- If we expect industries to be environmentally responsible, then we should provide tax breaks to help cover their costs.
- It would be a mistake to assume sexual discrimination has been eliminated or even reduced significantly over the decade.
- The number of women on our college's Board of Trustees must be increased.

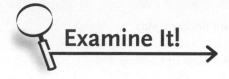 **Examine It!**

Directions: The following paragraph is a good model of an argument paragraph. Study the annotations to discover how the writer argues that animals should be used in medical research.

Heading announces the issue

Animals Should Be Used in Medical Research

Topic sentence:
States a position

Reason 1

Reason 2

Reason 3

Laboratory animal research is fundamental to medical progress. Vaccines for devastating human diseases like polio and smallpox and equally serious animal diseases like rabies, feline leukemia, and distemper were all developed through the use of research animals. The discovery, development, and refinement of drugs that could arrest, control, or eliminate such human diseases as AIDS, cancer, and heart disease all require the use of laboratory animals whose physiological mechanisms are similar to humans. I have only noted above a few of the many examples where animals have been used in human and veterinary medical research. It's also important to note that studies in behavior, ecology, physiology, and genetics all require the use of animals, in some capacity, to produce valid and meaningful knowledge about life on this planet.

—Tuff, "Animals and Research" from *NEA Higher Education Advocate.*

EXERCISE I-1
Writing in Progress

Writing a Topic Sentence

Directions: For three of the following issues, take a position and write a topic sentence.

1. Professional athletes' salaries
2. Drug testing in the workplace
3. Using cell phones while driving
4. Mandatory counseling for drug addicts
5. Buying American-made products
6. Adopting shelter animals
7. A topic of your choice ■

Support Your Position

There are two primary types of support that you can use to explain why your position should be accepted:

- **Reasons** Reasons are general statements that back up a position. Here are a few reasons to support an argument in favor of parental Internet controls:

  The Internet contains sites that are not appropriate for children.

  The Internet is a place where sexual predators can find victims.

  No one else polices the Internet, so parents must do so.

- **Evidence** The most common types of evidence are facts and statistics, quotations from authorities, examples, and personal experience.

- **Emotional Appeals** Emotional appeals are ideas that are targeted toward needs and values that the reader is likely to care about. Needs include physiological needs (food, drink, shelter) and psychological needs (sense of belonging, sense of accomplishment). An argument on gun control, for example, may appeal to a reader's need for safety. An argument against banks sharing clients' personal or financial information may appeal to a reader's need for privacy.

Use a Variety of Evidence

Facts and Statistics

When including facts and statistics, be sure to do the following:

1. **Obtain statistics from reliable online or print sources.** These include databases, almanacs, encyclopedias, articles in reputable journals and magazines, or other trustworthy reference materials from your library.

2. **Use up-to-date information, preferably from the past year or two.** Outdated statistics may be incorrect or misleading.

3. **Make sure you define terms and units of measurement.** For example, if you say that 60 percent of adults regularly play the lottery, you should define what *regularly* means.

Quotations from Authorities

You can also support your position by using expert or authoritative statements of opinion or conclusions. Experts or authorities are those who have studied a subject extensively, conducted research on it, or written widely about it. For example, if you are writing an essay calling for stricter preschool-monitoring requirements to prevent child abuse, the opinion of a psychiatrist who works extensively with abused children would provide convincing support.

Examples

Examples are specific situations that illustrate a point. Refer to Section C of this chapter for a review of how to use them as supporting details. In a persuasive essay, your examples must represent your position and should illustrate as many aspects of your position as possible. Suppose your position is that a particular television show should be cancelled because it contains excessive use of inappropriate language. The evidence you choose to support this position should be specific examples of the language used.

Personal Experience

If you are knowledgeable about a subject, your personal experiences can be convincing evidence. For example, if you were writing an essay supporting the position that being a child in a single-parent household encourages a teenager or young adult to mature earlier, you could discuss your own experiences with assuming new responsibilities.

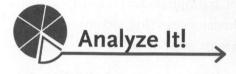

Analyze It!

Directions: The paragraph on the left is a good model of a paragraph that uses argument as a method of development. Complete the map on the right using information given in the paragraph.

Animals Should Not Be Used in Medical Research

I cannot accept the argument that research on animals is necessary to discover "cures" for humans. Many diseases and medications react very differently in animals than they do in humans. Aspirin, for example, is toxic to cats, and there are few diseases directly transmittable from cats to humans. I particularly abhor the "research" conducted for cosmetic purposes. The Draise test—where substances are introduced into the eyes of rabbits and then examined to see if ulcers, lesions or other observable reactions take place—is archaic and inefficient. Other alternatives exist that are more accurate and do not cause unnecessary suffering to our fellow creatures. Household products are also tested needlessly on animals using the LD-50 test. Animals, in many cases puppies, are force-fed these toxic chemicals to determine the dosage at which exactly 50 percent of them die. These tests are not necessary and do not give very useful information.

—adapted from Molina, "Animals and Research" from *NEA Higher Education Advocate*.

Statement of position: _____

_____

Reason 1: _____

_____

Reason 2: _____

_____

Reason 3: _____

_____

EXERCISE I-2

Writing in Progress

Generating Reasons and Evidence

Directions: Generate reasons and evidence to support one of the topic sentences you wrote for Exercise I-1. ■

Address Opposing Viewpoints

An opposing viewpoint is the position that is the opposite of the one you take. It is effective to recognize opposing viewpoints because it builds your credibility and shows that you are open-minded. For example, suppose you are arguing that children should wear uniforms to school. You could also recognize or acknowledge that opponents believe uniforms stifle creativity and individuality. You may also decide to refute, or argue against, opposing viewpoints. *Refute* means "to present evidence that a statement is wrong." You could refute the notion that uniforms stifle individuality by stating that children will find more useful and important ways of expressing their individuality if uniforms are required. Think of refutation as a process of finding weaknesses in your opponent's argument.

How to Organize an Argument Paragraph

There are two common ways to organize an argument paragraph.

1. **Place the topic sentence first and then give the supporting evidence and reasons.**
2. **Give your evidence and reasons first and conclude with the topic sentence.**

Because argumentation is complex, be sure to use transitional words and phrases to guide your reader from one reason or piece of evidence to another. Useful transitions are shown below.

ARGUMENT: USEFUL TRANSITIONS		
one reason	furthermore	therefore
a second reason	another reason	because

EXERCISE I-3   Writing an Argument Paragraph

Directions: Using the reasons and evidence you generated in Exercise I-2, write an argument paragraph. Be sure to recognize and/or refute opposing viewpoints. ■

J: USING MULTIPLE METHODS OF ORGANIZATION

GOAL 10 Write using multiple methods of organization

How Can a Paragraph Use Multiple Methods of Organization?

A paragraph that uses multiple methods of organization generally relies on a *primary method* and a *secondary method*. For example, a narrative paragraph about your first day on the job may include examples of the tasks you performed. In this case, narration is your primary method and example is your secondary method. A paragraph that defines love may do so by dividing it into categories, such as the love between parents and their children and the love between two spouses. In this paragraph, definition is the primary pattern and classification is the secondary pattern.

Below is a classification paragraph about the biological concept of asexual reproduction. The inclusion of three categories helps the reader better visualize and understand the concept. Note that the paragraph also includes *definition* (in the first sentence), *process* (because it explains how each category of asexual reproduction occurs), and *example* (because it provides examples of three organisms: amoebas, yeast, and starfish).

	Asexual reproduction occurs when offspring arise from a single parent rather than from two parents. Three common forms of asexual reproduction are fission, budding, and fragmentation. In fission, the parent literally splits into two separate organisms of approximately the same size. The single-celled blobs called amoebas that we learned about in our early science classes reproduce by fission. In budding, the parent splits into one larger organism and one smaller organism (called the bud). The yeast used to make bread reproduces through budding. In fragmentation, a new organism grows from a fragment of the parent. Starfish reproduce this way. The arm of a starfish can split off from the parent and then grow into its own organism.
Definition →	
Classification (primary pattern) →	
Category #1 →	
Category #2 →	
Category #3→	

Because the methods of organization can be combined in an infinite number of ways, there is no single visual map that can be used for all multi-method paragraphs. However, here is an idea map of the paragraph above.

 Visualize It!

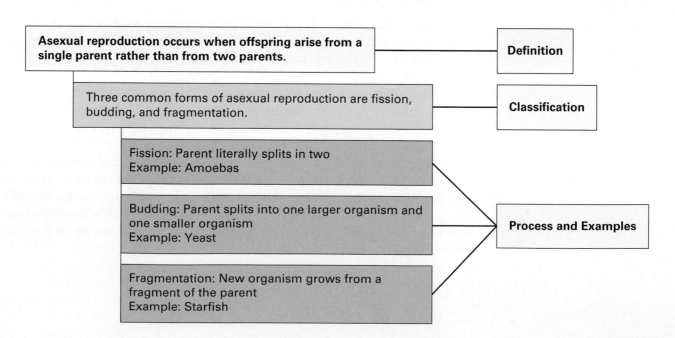

How to Develop a Multi-Method Paragraph

Developing a multi-method paragraph involves choosing a primary method of development, writing a topic sentence and selecting secondary methods of development, revising the topic sentence to reveal secondary patterns, providing support for your topic sentence, and using effective transitions.

 **Visualize It!** →

Writing a Multi-Method Paragraph
Select a primary method.
Write a preliminary topic sentence and choose secondary methods of development.
Revise your topic sentence to reveal seconday methods of development.
Provide support for your topic sentence.
Use transitions to help your reader.

Select a Primary Method

Suppose you are given the following assignment:

> Write a paragraph about gardening.

The topic "gardening" is quite broad, so think about how you can use different methods of development to focus the topic. Using *narration*, you could tell the story of a family member who is an avid gardener. Using *process*, you could explain how to prepare soil for planting or the best techniques for caring for seedlings. Using *argument*, you could argue that home gardening is both organic and healthy, and urge your readers to grow more of the foods they eat. Your key goal is to narrow the topic and select a primary pattern of organization for your paragraph.

EXERCISE J-1

Writing in Progress

Selecting a Primary Method of Organization for a Multi-Method Paragraph

Directions: You have received an assignment to write a paragraph on the topic of music. Narrow your topic and select a primary method of organization. ■

Write a Preliminary Topic Sentence and Choose Secondary Methods

Because paragraphs must be focused and tight, you will not want to use all the methods of development in a single paragraph. However, you can write a preliminary topic sentence and then choose secondary patterns to help support it. For instance, you might begin with the following topic sentence:

> Different types of tomatoes are used for different purposes in cooking.

Based on this topic sentence, you signal that you will use *classification* as your primary pattern: You will be listing the different types of tomatoes and how they are used in cooking. You can then incorporate definition, description, and cause and effect to write an effective, interesting paragraph. For example, you might provide the *definition* of a tomato (many people are surprised to learn that tomatoes are fruits, not vegetables); briefly *describe* each type of tomato; and list the *effects* of eating organically grown tomatoes (tomatoes contain high levels of lycopene, which are powerful natural antioxidants with positive health effects).

EXERCISE J-2

Writing in Progress

Selecting Secondary Methods of Organization and Writing a Topic Sentence for a Multi-Method Paragraph

Directions: Write a preliminary topic sentence for your paragraph on music and select the secondary patterns your paragraph will use. ■

Revise Your Topic Sentence to Reveal Secondary Methods

Your preliminary topic sentence should reveal your primary method of development. But you can revise it to suggest other patterns your paragraph will use. Remember to select and use only those secondary patterns that support the topic sentence. Using too many patterns can make the paragraph long, unfocused, and difficult to follow.

Here is an example of a good topic sentence that combines patterns:

Tomatoes, which are pulpy fruits native to South America and a source of many important nutrients, have become a favorite ingredient of chefs around the world because their many varieties offer varying tastes and textures in sauces, salads, and garnishes.

This topic sentence makes it clear that classification is the predominant pattern. It also suggests that the paragraph will use definition and cause and effect.

EXERCISE J-3

Writing in Progress

Revising a Topic Sentence for a Multi-Method Paragraph

Directions: Revise the topic sentence for your paragraph on music so that it reflects your primary and secondary methods of organization. ■

Provide Support for Your Topic Sentence

Providing support for your topic sentence is essential to writing a good paragraph. To support the topic sentence above, you will want to list and describe some of the common tomato varieties and their uses. For example, beefsteak tomatoes are large and juicy, and they are often used in sandwiches. Plum tomatoes are more solid and less juicy, and they are therefore used to make tomato sauce and paste. Cherry tomatoes are small and round, and they are often used in salads.

Use Transitions to Help Your Reader

Use the transitional words and phrases you learned in this chapter to help readers follow your train of thought.

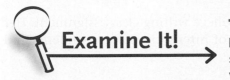

Examine It!

Directions: The following multi-method paragraph provides an effective topic sentence, support, and transitions. Study its annotations to discover how writers compose an effective multi-method paragraph.

Topic sentence includes definition →	Tomatoes, which are pulpy fruits native to South America and a source of many important nutrients, have become a favorite ingredient of chefs around the world because their many varieties offer
Category #1 with description →	varying tastes and textures in sauces, salads, and garnishes. Beefsteak tomatoes are large, juicy tomatoes with a thin skin and a short shelf life. Their juiciness
Category #2 with description →	makes them popular in sandwiches. Plum tomatoes (which are shaped like small plums or pears) are more solid and less juicy, which makes them perfect for creating tomato sauces and pastes. Cherry
Category #3 with description →	tomatoes and grape tomatoes, named for the fruits they resemble, are small, bite-sized tomatoes that are often used in salads or as garnishes. Regardless of their
Transitional phrase leading to effect →	size or type, tomatoes are high in lycopene, a natural antioxidant, which makes tomatoes a healthy, low-calorie choice for any diet.

EXERCISE J-4   Writing a Multi-Method Paragraph

Directions: Using your work in Exercises J-1 through J-3, write a multi-method paragraph, being sure to provide support for your topic sentence and use transitions to help guide your reader. ■

A STUDENT ESSAY

The Writing Task

Aurora Gilbert wrote this essay for a college writing class assignment. Her assignment was to identify a subject of interest to college students and explain the importance or benefit of it.

Title: identifies the subject of the essay

Employment: Not Just a Post-Graduation Agenda

The perks of having a job as a student

Aurora Gilbert

Introduction: Gilbert engages the reader by describing college life

1   A light course load with minimal study obligations, an on-campus commitment such as the school newspaper or recreational soccer team, and ample time for social activities; this is the luxurious life that television and films have portrayed as typical of a college student. However, many college students can testify that life on campus is not quite that luxurious. Courses may be tougher than expected, study requirements may necessitate more than a few late nights in the library, on-campus activities may be demanding, and these commitments may cut into that much-idolized collegiate social calendar as well as put a significant dent in the typical college student's budget. Time spent in college can be a tough reminder that success requires hard work and, furthermore, that most things in life are not free. To cover the basic living expenses as well as the costs of any fee-based campus activities or social and personal indulgences, many college students take up part-time jobs. Despite the initial concern that a job might add stress to the demands of schoolwork and on-campus obligations, there are several benefits to having a part-time position, such as developing financial independence, learning useful skills that will prepare the student for the full-time workplace, building a strong professional network, and taking a break from schoolwork and campus life.

Thesis statement

Topic sentence

2   Clearly, having a part time job allows a student to make money to support herself. Unless she has worked extensively on breaks from school and saved up money for the school year, it is almost inevitable that a student without a job will end up asking her parents or guardians for money to aid in living expenses and additional "luxury" costs. Regardless of the school, all students will most likely have to pay for textbooks, food, transportation, toiletries, and any fun activities outside of school such as movies, concerts, or dinner with friends. Making money will take the burden off parents and guardians, and it is also a great way to prepare for making a living in the real world. Having a part-time job and depending on a regular paycheck makes a student more aware of her spending and savings, and more able to make well planned purchases.

Details explain benefit #1 – extra money

Topic sentence

Details explain benefit #2 – building
technical and social skills

3   Along with building financial independence, a student with a part-time job will build skills, both technical and social, that she will need in the workplace after graduation. Though every position will have different requirements, it is guaranteed that the daily responsibilities will be useful tasks that will prepare a student for success in any workplace. These tasks may include providing administrative support, preparing presentations in PowerPoint, communicating with coworkers through Outlook, or working on spreadsheets in Excel. It is also important to learn how to behave properly in an office environment, how to dress appropriately, and how to work with different kinds of people. Developing these skills will help the student learn more about what she wants to do after graduation, what type of a job she wants, and what type of office environment she prefers.

Topic sentence

Details explain benefit #3 – building
a strong professional network

4   Working alongside professionals will also allow the student to build a strong professional network of individuals who will give advice, serve as role models, and serve as references for future applications. Chances are that all of these individuals have been through the same process of college and career-preparation and are excited to share their experiences and suggestions. This is also a great way to begin to develop one's professional network; one can never have too many connections (both in real life and on LinkedIn!). Future jobs will ask for references from previous employers, so holding a part-time job or two in college is a great way to collect some of these potential references. The student's employer may also consider hiring the student for a full-time position following graduation or even later on in the graduate's career.

Topic sentence

Details explain benefit #4 – providing
a break from campus

5   Despite these perks, some students worry that a job may distract from schoolwork, but a part-time position actually awards a much-needed, enjoyable break from campus. It is important to take a step back and realize that the campus is not all there is to the real world. Even if the job is on campus, it is helpful to take this respite from schoolwork and academic stress. At a part-time job, a student can briefly devote her entire brain activity to non-school-related tasks. Some students may be intimidated by the extra responsibility, but it is important to remember that the job is only a part-time commitment and that an employer will not ask the student to devote outside time to the job; most companies understand that students with jobs are juggling multiple commitments and will even ask the student to stay focused on schoolwork.

Conclusion: reemphasis of the thesis
statement and closure

6   Every student will find that being in college is not a walk in the park. Taking up a part-time job while in school may seem daunting, but it is actually a great way to alleviate the stress of school while building useful skills and a great professional network to prepare for life after graduation and earning a small income that will cover expenses. College is designed to prepare students for the real world, providing them with the skills they need in order to pursue their interests in a certain career field after they graduate. In this time of preparation, taking a part-time job is a great way to supplement this education and learn skills that can only be taught in the workplace itself. Though it may consume some time and add one more task to that weekly to-do list, a part-time job will be exponentially beneficial as the years go on, as the student finds herself able to live comfortably throughout college, well-equipped with skills and etiquette when she enters the workplace, and backed up by a strong network of professionals as she navigates her career path.

Examining Student Writing

1. Does Gilbert provide an adequate number of relevant details? What types of details could be added?

2. Evaluate Gilbert's introduction. What other ways could she have introduced her topic while building interest?

3. Examine Gilbert's thesis statement. How accurately does it suggest the topics Gilbert covers?

4. Choose a paragraph from the essay and evaluate it with the paragraph development questions on page 392.

Paragraph Writing Scenarios

Friends and Family

1. Write a paragraph defining friendship.

2. Choose a parent or close family member whom you admire. Write a paragraph giving examples that demonstrate this person's admirable characteristics.

Classes and Campus Life

1. Write a paragraph classifying the types of problems that may lead to dropping out of college.

2. Write a paragraph explaining how you studied for a particular exam.

Working Students

1. Write a paragraph describing an employer or supervisor for whom you have worked. Be sure to create an overall impression about this person.

2. Write a paragraph comparing or contrasting two co-workers.

Communities and Cultures

1. Write a paragraph about a tradition that you value. Write a narrative paragraph that details the events related to the tradition.

2. Choose a community to which you belong. Write a paragraph about an activity that you share with other members. Be sure to explain why you chose to participate.

WRITING ABOUT A READING

This selection originally appeared in NYU Local, a student-run blog for New York University. The author is a senior staff writer and a member of the technologically connected population he writes about in this article.

Step 1: Preview the reading.

Step 2: Connect the reading to your own experience: How dependent are you on technology? What aspects of technology and social media are most important in your life?

Step 3: Read and respond to the questions in the margin.

THINK AS YOU READ

Based on your preview, predict the author's attitude toward smartphones. What does it mean to "go off the grid"?

Which of these activities are familiar or typical in your own life?

Does it seem that the author suggests that only students depend on technology?

Predict how the author will answer the questions he is asking here.

Why did the author begin the essay with a photo? What effect does this have?

IN A SEA OF SMARTPHONES, GOING OFF THE GRID

Aaron Marks

1   When Brittany Siler wants to figure out her Friday plans, she doesn't log onto Facebook to check which events she signed up for that week. She doesn't look at her Twitter stream to see what events are trending. She doesn't pull up Foursquare to learn about the hottest restaurants her friends have been checking into.

2   Brittany does not, *cannot,* do any of these, because she does not have accounts on those sites. She doesn't have an account on *any* website, in fact, besides Gmail and a Google Plus account—where her only friend is her sister, who posts pictures of her children. Nor does she have a smartphone, opting instead to carry "a little Nokia that was made before common cellphones could access the internet."

3   That Siler lives without these "always-on" technologies wouldn't be particularly strange—millions of Americans live without smartphones, Facebook, or even (*gasp*) high-speed Internet—were she not a student at NYU, where it seems that every elevator is packed with students on their smartphones, the last time anyone got invited to a party over anything but Facebook was back in high school, and through its various digital initiatives, the university embraces technology with open arms.

4   Among a student population which thrives at the forefront of the latest tech, why would someone like Siler forego these tools? Does living off the grid make her happier, more focused, or just out of touch? As it turns out, it's a bit of everything for this digital exile. And she's not the only one.

Highlight each advantage of being "off the grid" as you read the remaining paragraphs.

5   "I had Facebook for 3 years," Siler, a Gallatin sophomore studying Psychology and Creative Writing told us, "and I used it as regularly as anyone." But after a few months at NYU, "I deleted the account because it made the world seem too big." Getting off of social media gave Siler a feeling of control over her social life. "Facebook streamed a lot of excess information into my awareness," she said, adding that "I just like having the option of seeking out [what I'm interested in] myself instead of having it presented to me."

6   Siler acknowledges that people might consider a digital-free social life strange (or altogether impossible,) but thinks that's not true. "Relative to my peers, you might say I'm a hermit. I don't think that's really true, though. I have a few close friends (my roommates being three of them) that I don't need Facebook to communicate with." Her biggest complaint? "The only thing is I'm out of the loop on memes."

What are memes?

How are the examples of students similar? How are they different?

7   Other students have indulged the desire to go off the grid, if not so completely. Kristina Jaku, a Steinhardt senior, decided to delete her Facebook account for her semester abroad, wanting to enjoy the time without the distress brought on by the site. "10 seconds into logging on Facebook," Jaku said, "I would silently hate myself and think 'I don't even care about all of this!'" Dan Zavaro, another senior, also felt wary of social media's sway on his life. "I felt like I was living my life thinking, 'How would this translate into a Facebook status?'" Zavaro said. "And that's not good."

8   After deleting her account, Jaku "felt very much at ease without it and felt more able to concentrate on important things more." She noted that "It did lead me to finding other websites to procrastinate on," but "nothing as soul sucking as Facebook." Zavaro said he felt that after going off the proverbial grid, he could "focus more on my life and growing and not catering to my Facebook identity."

Explain what Jaku means by "soul sucking."

9   Going off the "always-on" grid seems to make a larger statement than riding a bike instead of taking the train, going vegetarian or not buying Nike sneakers. Smartphones and the social networks they support permeate society. Sitting in Think Coffee now writing this, I can glance outside and see more than half the passersby strolling, jogging or cavorting with smartphone in hand, scrolling idly, listening to music or, as you sometimes see, holding the thing in a limp wrist anticipating the next buzz.

Why does the author mention that he is writing in a café? Has he gone off the grid?

Does this paragraph suggest the author's thesis? Express his thesis in your own words.

10   To extricate oneself from the digital web reflects concerns not only of one's own life, but about how society functions (which is, on the web). "Our brains are very plastic," Silar said, "and if we don't know how to practice self control when it comes to tools like GPS and Google, I think we run the frightening risk of losing self-sufficiency."

11   Plenty a think piece has been written bemoaning our relationship to technology, the zenith of which trend was probably Nicholas Carr's "Is Google Making Us Stupid?" Carr ended up with a book deal. But that was two years ago. The techno-phobic star may be fading, and even some former holdouts are no longer buying the argument:

Do you agree with Smith's statements here and in the next paragraph?

12   "I can see how it limits real-world social interaction just like your great-aunt in Ithaca says it does," Sydney Smith, a junior who until recently used an old phone without a camera or data plan, told us. "On trains, at restaurants,

at parties, and in class, the ubiquity of the iPhone makes it impossible to talk to people when they have a spare moment. So that sucks. But while people aren't talking during those moments, they are accomplishing a lot of other useful stuff, including social bonding."

13   Before getting an iPhone, Smith said "I had romanticized the notion of going off the grid, phoneless in a world gone mad—as we all have I think." But she is no longer convinced that such a thing exists. "There is no off-grid world in the spheres we occupy (western youth culture) that you can find through externally distancing yourself from technology. You have to deal with the impulse to want or use technology in the first place. I've deleted my Facebook in the past, and I got back on because it turns out I was still implicated in the Facebook-tainted world and not having one proved to be a nuisance."

Why does the author ask these questions here?

14   Is that really the best reason to ignore the little voice in your head that says take your iPhone and throw it into the East River? That everyone else is doing it and it's too difficult to get by in a society where everyone else is doing it? Maybe so. Jaku returned to Facebook after her semester abroad not for the deeply personal reasons she left it, but for reasons more practical: "My friends kept bothering me about wanting to see my photos from abroad, and Facebook seemed to be the easiest way to do that . . . I also wanted to be in the loop with the NYU Sydney group on Facebook, haha. Nothing more than that, really."

15   My own experience confirms this tendency to hop back on the wagon for a relatively trivial reason; after six months off of Facebook, a new friend said they would invite me to a party and to "just friend me on Facebook." Not wanting to be a stick in the mud, I reactivated my account and, a year later, am back to checking it five times a day like the rest of us.

What does it mean to be "a stick in the mud"?

16   Despite the abstainers, the relentless march of new technologies into our lives carries on. Even the strictest Luddites don't always advocate for abstention. "I wouldn't recommend my technological lifestyle to other people," Siler said. "Being on Facebook just doesn't work for me personally." And with mommy and daddy not there to remind you of "Just because Sally is doing it . . ." logic, "always-on" smartphone usage is spreading like wildfire: According to a new study, you are twice as likely to pretend to look busy on your smartphone if companions are doing the same.

Explain what "Just because Sally is doing it" logic means.

17   "Ultimately [an iPhone] is just a tool like a bottle opener or a pen, and can't shape your personality or your disposition to make friends or be an observant person," Smith, the pragmatist, said. "The idea that it's somehow morally "better" to have no phone or to distance ourselves from technology proves to be a false dialectic, because it only deals with censuring the tools which allow us to behave the ways we've chosen. Maybe that's valid, in the way that gun control would certainly cause fewer murders, but in both cases the underlying problem would not be addressed by our collective disarmament. We wouldn't do this because although we might feel the pull towards a distance from iPhon-ery, it's a pull which is clearly outweighed by something else."

What does it mean to be a pragmatist?

Express Smith's analogy about gun control in your own words.

18   Perhaps in the end, our underlying concern is not with the technology but with the people using it, with ourselves.

Is the author's conclusion what you expected?

WRITING IN RESPONSE TO READING

Examining the Reading Using an Idea Map [MyWritingLab]

Review the reading by completing the missing parts of the idea map shown below.

Visualize It! →

Title   **In a Sea of Smartphones, Going Off the Grid**

Thesis   Removing oneself from technology reflects concerns about one's own life and about how society uses technology.

College populations generally thrive on using technology.

Students choose to forego technology for different reasons.

Gain control over _____ .

_____
_____

_____ makes a major statement.

Smartphones and social networks permeate society.

Much has been written about our relationship to technology.

Smith claims it is not possible to _____
_____ .

Deal with the impulse to _____
_____ .

Smartphones limit_____ but accomplish_____ .

Most people in our society use technology so functioning without it is difficult.

Even those who limit use do not _____
_____ .

Study shows we may_____
_____ if companions are doing the same.

Technology is a tool.

Conclusion   _____
_____

Strengthening Your Vocabulary   MyWritingLab

Using the word's context, word parts, or a dictionary, write a brief definition of each of the following words as it is used in the reading.

1. initiatives (paragraph 3) _____

2. exile (paragraph 4) _____

3. permeate (paragraph 9) _____

4. extricate (paragraph 10) _____

5. zenith (paragraph 11) _____

6. ubiquity (paragraph 12) _____

7. abstention (paragraph 16) _____

Reacting to Ideas: Discussion and Journal Writing   MyWritingLab

Get ready to write about the reading by discussing the following:

1. How effective is the title "In a Sea of Smartphones, Going Off the Grid"? Can you think of other titles that would be appropriate?

2. Who are the primary sources the author uses in this article? How accurate and reliable do you think his sources are? What other types of evidence could he have used to support his thesis?

3. Discuss what it means to go off the grid. Do you know anyone who has decided to limit or remove technology from his or her life?

4. Do you ever feel that social media makes the world seem too big? Would deleting your social media account(s) make you feel more or less control over your social life?

5. What is the purpose of the photograph that accompanies the reading? What details in the photograph reflect the author's message?

Paragraph Options   MyWritingLab

1. Are there any aspects of your life in which you could be described as a Luddite, or one who is opposed to change or prefers the "old ways" of doing things? Write a paragraph explaining your answer.

2. What are the "always-on" technologies in your life? Which of these technologies could you do without and which would you miss most? Write a paragraph listing each one and describing its importance to you.

3. Do you agree that a smartphone is "just a tool like a bottle opener or a pen"? Write a paragraph explaining why or why not.

Essay Options   MyWritingLab

4. What aspects of this essay are reflected in your own routine? Are there aspects of your digital life that you would like to change? Why or why not? Write an essay exploring your own relationship to technology.

5. Consider your use of technology and social media over the past month. Did any of your online experiences create distress or concern about social media's influence on your life? Write an essay analyzing approximately how much time you spent on social media or other forms of technology in the past month and your feelings about this time spent. In what ways, if any, does your experience reflect the reading?

6. Do you agree that going off the grid makes a larger statement than riding a bike, going vegetarian, or not buying Nike sneakers? Why or why not? If you wanted to "make a statement" about smartphones and social media, what would it be? Write an essay explaining your answers.

■ ■ ■ ■

Revision Checklist

Paragraph Development

1. Is the topic manageable (neither too broad nor too narrow)?
2. Is the paragraph written with the reader in mind?
3. Does the topic sentence identify the topic?
4. Does the topic sentence make a point about the topic?
5. Does each sentence support the topic sentence?
6. Is there sufficient detail?
7. Is there a sentence at the end that brings the paragraph to a close?

Sentence Development

8. Are there any sentence fragments, run-on sentences, or comma splices?
9. Are ideas combined to produce more effective sentences?
10. Are adjectives and adverbs used to make the sentences vivid and interesting?
11. Are relative clauses and prepositional phrases like *-ing* phrases used to add detail?
12. Are pronouns used correctly and consistently?

SELF-TEST SUMMARY

To test yourself, cover the Answer column with a sheet of paper and answer each question in the left column. Evaluate each of your answers as you work by sliding the paper down and comparing your answer with what is printed in the Answer column.

	QUESTION	ANSWER
Goal 1 Write using narration	What is narration? How are the events in a narrative usually organized?	Narration is the technique of making a point by telling a story. The events in a narrative are usually arranged in the order in which they happened (time-sequence arrangement).
Goal 2 Write using description	What is descriptive writing? What are three key aspects of writing a descriptive paragraph?	Descriptive writing uses words and phrases that appeal to the senses and help the reader imagine an object, person, place, or experience. Writing a descriptive paragraph involves creating an overall impression, including sensory details, and using descriptive language.
Goal 3 Write using example	What is an example? What are some guidelines for choosing examples?	An example is a specific instance or situation that explains a general idea or statement. Choose examples that are clear, sufficient in number, familiar and understandable to readers, varied, typical, specific, and vivid.
Goal 4 Write using definition	What is a definition? What are the three essential parts of a definition?	A definition is an explanation of what something is. The three essential parts of a definition are • the term being defined • the group or category to which the term belongs • its distinguishing characteristics
Goal 5 Write using comparison and contrast	What are comparison and contrast? What are two ways to organize a comparison or contrast paragraph?	Comparison and contrast are two ways of organizing information about two or more subjects. Comparison focuses on similarities; contrast focuses on differences. Two ways to organize a comparison or contrast paragraph are • subject by subject • point by point

SELF-TEST SUMMARY *(CONTINUED)*

	QUESTION	ANSWER
Goal 6 Write using classification	What is classification? What is involved in writing a classification paragraph?	Classification explains a subject by identifying and describing its types or categories. Writing a classification paragraph involves deciding on a basis of classification for the subject, writing a topic sentence, and explaining each subgroup.
Goal 7 Write using process	What does a process paragraph do? What are the two types of process paragraphs?	A process paragraph explains the steps to follow in completing a process. The two types of process paragraphs are • how-to paragraphs, which explain how something is done • how-it-works paragraphs, which explain how something operates or happens
Goal 8 Write using cause and effect	What are cause and effect? How do you distinguish between causes and effects?	Causes are explanations of why things happen; effects are explanations of what happens as a result of an action or event. To determine causes, ask "Why did this happen?" To identify effects, ask "What happened because of this?"
Goal 9 Write using argument	What is argument? What are the three essential parts of an argument?	An argument is a line of reasoning intended to persuade the reader or listener to agree with a particular viewpoint or to take a particular action. An argument consists of an issue (the problem that the argument addresses), a position (the writer's point of view), and support (the details that show the writer's position is correct).
Goal 10 Writing using multiple methods of organization	What is involved in developing a multi-method paragraph?	Developing a multi-method paragraph involves choosing a primary method of development, writing a topic sentence and selecting secondary methods of development, revising the topic sentence to reveal secondary patterns, providing support for your topic sentence, and using effective transitions.

MyWritingLab *Visit Chapter 14: Using Methods of Organization in MyWritingLab to test your understanding of the chapter objectives.*

WRITERS' WORKSHOPS:
Using Visuals in Your Writing

WRITERS' WORKSHOP

15

A PICTURE'S WORTH A THOUSAND WORDS

Using Visual Aids to Help Your Readers

Photographs, images, and graphics are visual ways of summarizing and communicating information. Writers often choose to include these with their writing to clarify or emphasize important concepts. The following table summarizes the different types of visual aids and how writers use them.

Type of Graphic	Writers Use These To . . .	Example
Bar graphs	Compare quantities or amounts using bars of different lengths.	
Cartoons	Make a point quickly or simply; lighten the text by adding a touch of humor; often help to make abstract concepts more concrete or real.	"I'm sending you to a job hunting seminar. Trust me when I say you're going to need it."
Charts	Display quantitative (numbers-based) or cause-and-effect relationships.	ORGANIZATIONAL CHART

Type of Graphic	Writers Use These To . . .	Example
Circle graphs (Pie charts)	Show whole/part relationships or how parts of a unit have been divided or classified.	
Diagrams	Explain an object, idea, or process by outlining parts or steps or by showing the object's organization.	
Infographics	Combine several types of visual aids into one, often merging photos with text, diagrams, or tables.	
Line graphs	Plot information along a horizontal axis (line) and a vertical axis, with one or more variables plotted between the two axes. The line graph connects all these points, thus showing a progression.	

Type of Graphic	Writers Use These To . . .	Example
Maps	Show the exact positions of physical objects such as cities, states, or countries; provide statistical or factual information about a particular area or region.	
Photographs	Introduce new ideas; provide examples; create emotional responses; provide perspective; help readers visualize an event, concept or feeling.	
Tables	Display facts, figures, statistics and other data in a condensed orderly sequence for clarity and convenient reference.	

→ **TRY IT OUT!**

Directions: Identify at least one type of visual aid that would be appropriate for each writing assignment below. Explain your choices. (Each assignment may lend itself to more than one type of visual aid.)

1. A term paper for your history class that discusses the Partition of India into two separate countries: India and Pakistan (and, later, Bangladesh). _____

   _____

   _____

1. An article you are writing for a parents' magazine about how to interpret the facial expressions of toddlers. _____

   _____

   _____

1. A senior thesis you are writing for your economics class comparing the growth rates of the United States and China over the period 2000–2010. _

   _____

   _____

   _____

WRITERS' WORKSHOP

16

THINKING LIKE AN ARTIST

Using Visual Aids to Support Your Ideas: Be Creative

Visual aids should not be just window dressing. They should support, enhance, or explain your ideas. Keep in mind that visual aids can support various aspects of your writing:

- your thesis
- your main points
- major details

As you examine the following paragraph, make notes about possible effective visual aids that would help your reader understand your main point.

The Social Components of Hunger

People often eat when they are not really hungry. There are all sorts of social cues that tell people to eat, such as the convention of eating breakfast, lunch, and dinner at certain times. A large part of that "convention" is actually the result of what psychologists call "classical conditioning." The body becomes conditioned to respond with the hunger reflex at certain times of day; through association with the act of eating, those times of the day have become conditioned stimuli for hunger. Sometimes a person who has eaten a late breakfast will still "feel" hungry at noon, simply because the clock say it's time to eat. People also respond to the appeal of food. How many times has someone finished a huge meal only to be tempted by that luscious-looking cheesecake on the dessert cart?

—Ciccarelli and White, *Psychology*, p. 357.

What ideas did you come up with? For example, you might have chosen to provide an illustration of three clocks indicating the times that most people eat breakfast, lunch, and dinner. But how interesting would that visual be for your readers? Most people already know the typical meal times. It might be more interesting to show two sets of clocks: one set that shows meal times in the United States and another set that shows meal times in another country, such as Spain or Italy. These images would reinforce the message that people are socially conditioned to eat at certain times.

Now look at the last sentence of the paragraph. You might be tempted to include a photo of a delicious-looking cheesecake. But your readers understand more if you provided two photos—one of cheesecake and one of something very unappealing, such as a wilted salad—and wrote a caption that simply states, "Not all foods are equally appealing."

→ TRY IT OUT!

Directions: Come up with at least three ideas for creative visual aids to accompany the following paragraph. What would you say in the caption that accompanies each visual aid?

Insomnia

Insomnia—a term that literally means "no sleep"—is a condition characterized by difficulty falling or staying asleep, a pattern of waking too early, or poor-quality sleep. Although 30% of Americans occasionally suffer from insomnia, about 10% experience chronic insomnia; that is, insomnia that lasts for more than a month.

There are two types of insomnia. Secondary insomnia is by far the most common, and is due to behavior such as substance abuse or another medical disorder such as heart disease. Primary insomnia occurs in only about 20% of people with insomnia, and almost always develops as a result of stress. Before diagnosing primary insomnia, a physician will conduct an interview and a series of tests to rule out behaviors (such as alcohol or caffeine intake) and medical disorders that could be causing secondary insomnia.

—Lynch et al., *Health: Making Choices for Life*, p. 93. ∎

WRITERS' WORKSHOP

17

SO MANY IMAGES, SO LITTLE SPACE

Finding Visuals to Accompany Your Writing

How do you go about finding images to accompany your writing? Most writers start with the Internet, which is home to millions of diagrams, photos, and other visual aids. Some places to begin your search are:

- **Google Images:** On the Google home page, click on "Images," then type your query in the search bar.
- **Creative Commons:** This Web site gathers millions of images from a variety of sources, such as Fotopedia, Google Images, and Open Clip Art Library.
- **Flickr:** This is a popular Web site that allows users to upload and share photos and other images.
- **Social Media:** Some social media platforms, such as Pinterest, Instagram, and Tumblr, are heavily image based.

An important note: Whenever you use an image created by someone else, you must give credit to the source. Check your writer's handbook for specific details on how to cite the sources of your visual aids. Do not publish any of your writing (whether on the Internet or anywhere else) without first getting permission from the original image source.

You might also consult non-Internet sources of visual aids, including the following:

- photographs you have taken (or family photographs taken by earlier generations)
- images you have sketched, either by hand or on computer
- clip art files that accompany the word processing program you use (such as Microsoft Word)
- tabular data you have found in printed sources, such as government publications

→ TRY IT OUT!

Directions: Using the sources listed above, find and print out visual aids that effectively illustrate each of the following. If you have artistic talent, you might try drawing visual aids based on the results of your image research.

1. the process of photosynthesis
2. the difference between dragonflies and damselflies
3. Albert Einstein as a boy, young man, and older man
4. four actors who have played Sherlock Holmes
5. fjords in Scandinavia

WRITERS' WORKSHOP

18

WATCH OUT FOR PHOTOSHOP . . .

Using Visual Aids Ethically

Just as writers can use words with strong connotations to persuade and influence their readers, they can use powerful images to strengthen their message. When using images, you must consider whether you are using them ethically. In general, the images you use should

- fairly represent the situation.
- not be manipulated through computer programs (such as Photoshop) or other means.
- be faithful to the original source's intention.

Suppose you are fund-raising for an environmental organization that seeks to protect baby seals. It is well known that hunters club baby seals to death for their skins. You are writing about this practice in your newsletter. Is it ethical for you to include a photo of a hunter clubbing a baby seal to death? This image is likely to be graphic and shocking—and effective in terms of getting people to donate to your cause. Use of the image would likely be considered ethical in these circumstances, because the image (while illustrating a horrible practice) presents a hard truth that you want people to know about.

Now consider the following image, which was mailed to all the houses in a particular school district by the local board of education. This graphic was part of a flyer intended to convince people that the school budget must be increased (that is, people must pay higher property taxes to finance the school budget). Is this image reflective of reality, or is it deceptive?

If you look closely at the image, you can see that it is deceptive. Between 2000 and 2010, the number of children in the school district increased by 2,350 (8,600 − 6,250 = 2,350). That is a 37 percent increase. But the size of the image on the right is nearly four times the size of the image on the left—which implies an increase in the student body of 400 percent, not 37 percent.

→ **TRY IT OUT!**

Directions: Examine the following visual aid and answer the question that follows.

Marital Satisfaction Over the Life Span

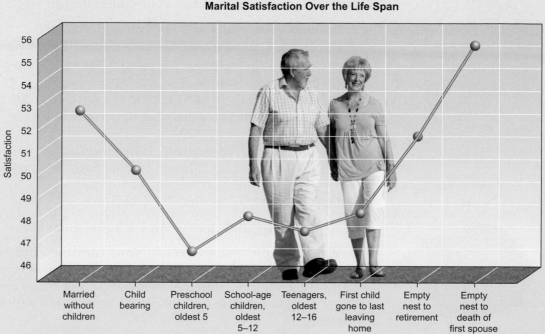

Source: Rollins & Feldman, 1970.

Which of the following are ethical uses of the visual aid? Which are unethical uses?

_____ 1. Using the graph in a textbook that describes the general progression of happiness over the course of a long-term marriage.

_____ 2. Using the graph in an essay that argues in favor of euthanasia (that is, mercy killings). The author's thesis is that spouses should be comfortable euthanizing their partners because their own happiness is likely to increase after their spouse is dead.

_____ 3. Using the graph in a parenting magazine that provides tips on how to keep a marriage healthy and strong when there are young children in the home.

_____ 4. Using the graph in an advertisement for an expensive boarding school. The advertisement states that research has shown that parents' happiness drops when there are children in the home, and adults can increase their happiness by sending their children away to school.

WRITERS' WORKSHOP

19

CONTEXT + CAPTIONS = GOOD COMMUNICATION

Providing Context for and Writing Captions to Accompany Visual Aids

To achieve maximum effectiveness, your visual aids should be solidly anchored to your writing. That is, you should provide direction for your readers, telling them when to examine the visual aids that accompany your writing. You should also provide a brief write-up, or caption, that ties each visual aid back to your writing.

Context

There are several ways to direct your readers to your visual aids.

- **Number each visual aid.** For example, you might have Figure 1, Figure 2, and Figure 3. In your writing, steer readers toward your visuals with in-text references. You might say, "As Figure 1 shows," "Figure 2 illustrates," or "(see Figure 3 for an example)."
- **Reference visuals in your text.** If you are using only one photograph on a page, you might say something like "(see photo)" or "As the photo above demonstrates."
- **Pay attention to formatting.** When formatting your paper for publication, be sure the visual aid falls on the same page as the reference.

Captions

Use the following guidelines to write effective captions.

- **Write complete sentences in your captions, not sentence fragments.** Labeling is an exception. For example, if you were providing three photos showing three different members of the shrew family in a biology paper, simply labeling each photo with the shrew's biological name may be enough.

- **Keep captions short and to the point.** Ideally, a caption should be no longer than two or three sentences. In many cases, one sentence is enough.
- **Use the caption to reinforce a key point from your writing** or to introduce related information that will interest readers.
- When appropriate, provide source information at the end of your caption.

→ TRY IT OUT!

Directions: The following paragraph originally appeared in a biology textbook. Locate at least one visual aid to accompany the paragraph. Then adapt the paragraph to make reference to the visual aid. Also write a caption to accompany the visual aid.

Life in the Greenhouse

New Orleans. New York. Miami. Amsterdam. Alexandria. Mumbai. Ho Chi Minh City. Bangkok. Hong Kong. Shanghai. Tokyo. According to predictions of the effects of global warming, some of the great cities of the world may share a common future—portions of each may experience catastrophic flooding and become essentially uninhabitable. New Orleans provides a stark example. In August 2005, when Hurricane Katrina came onshore along the Gulf Coast of the United States, 80% of the city was inundated. A massive evacuation and relief effort could not prevent the deaths of over 1500 residents or adequately attend to the needs of those impacted by the storm and flooding. Even today, significant portions of New Orleans—a major metropolis in one of the richest countries on Earth—remain essentially abandoned. Imagine the impact of such a disaster on cities and communities that lack the resources of the United States.

—Belk and Maier, *Biology: Science for Life with Physiology,* p. 93.

15 Revising Paragraphs

Learning Goals

In this chapter, you will learn how to

GOAL 1 Identify topic sentences that lack a point of view

GOAL 2 Identify topic sentences that are too broad

GOAL 3 Identify topic sentences that are too narrow

GOAL 4 Identify when you have strayed off topic

GOAL 5 Revise underdeveloped paragraphs

GOAL 6 Identify and eliminate irrelevant details

GOAL 7 Revise to ensure that details are logically arranged and developed

GOAL 8 Revise to ensure your paragraph is balanced

GOAL 9 Identify and eliminate unnecessary repetition

WRITE ABOUT IT!

How many shots do you suppose it takes to get the perfect photograph? Write a list of the factors a photographer might consider in choosing the right photograph.

Photographers take many shots to get just the right one. As a writer, you need to take many "shots" at a paragraph or essay to get it right. That is, you need to write several drafts before the paragraph or essay says what you want it to say.

Some students find revision a troublesome step because it is difficult for them to see what is wrong with their own work. After working hard on a first draft, it is tempting to say to yourself that you've done a great job and to think, "This is fine." Other times, you may think you have explained and supported an idea clearly when actually you have not. In other words, you may be blind to your own paper's weaknesses. Almost all writing, however, needs and benefits from revision. An idea map can help you spot weaknesses and discover what you may not have done as well as you thought.

In this chapter, idea maps are used to show how to identify some of the problems you may encounter in your writing. An idea map will show how each of your ideas fits with and relates to all of the other ideas in a paragraph or essay. When you draw an idea map, you reduce your ideas to a skeleton form that allows you to see and analyze them more easily.

This chapter will discuss nine questions to ask that will help you identify weaknesses in your writing, and it will suggest ways to revise your paragraphs to correct each weakness.

1. **Does the topic sentence express a point of view?**
2. **Is the topic sentence too broad?**
3. **Is the topic sentence too narrow?**
4. **Does the paragraph stray from the topic?**
5. **Are there enough supporting details?**
6. **Does every detail belong?**
7. **Are the details arranged and developed logically?**
8. **Is the paragraph balanced?**
9. **Is the paragraph repetitious?**

WRITING

DOES THE TOPIC SENTENCE EXPRESS A POINT OF VIEW?

GOAL 1 Identify topic sentences that lack a point of view

A topic sentence should identify your topic *and* express an attitude or viewpoint. It must make a point about the topic.

If your topic is the old roller coaster at Starland Park, it is not enough to make a general statement of fact in your topic sentence.

LACKS POINT OF VIEW   There is an old roller coaster at Starland Park.

Your reader would rightly ask in this case, "So what?" A topic sentence needs to tell the reader what is important or interesting about your topic. It should state the point you are going to make in the rest of the paragraph. For every topic, you can find many points to make in a topic sentence. For example:

EXPRESSES POINT OF VIEW   The old roller coaster at Starland Park is unsafe and should be torn down.

The old roller coaster at Starland Park no longer seems as frightening as it did when I was young.

Three types of people go on the old roller coaster at Starland Park: the brave, the scared, and the stupid.

If you write a topic sentence that does not express a viewpoint, you will find you have very little or nothing to write about in the remainder of the paragraph. Look at these topic sentences:

| LACKS POINT OF VIEW | Pete works at the YMCA. |
| EXPRESSES POINT OF VIEW | Pete got over his shyness by working at the YMCA. |

If you used the first topic sentence, "Pete works at the YMCA," what else could you include in your paragraph? If you instead used the second topic sentence, you would have something to write about. You could describe Pete before and after he began working at the YMCA, discuss positive aspects of the job, or give examples of friends Pete has made through his work.

Notice how the following topic sentences have been revised to express a point of view.

| LACKS POINT OF VIEW | Mark plays soccer. |
| REVISED | Mark's true personality comes out when he plays soccer. [Details can explain Mark's personality as revealed by his soccer game.] |

| LACKS POINT OF VIEW | Professor Cooke teaches accounting. |
| REVISED | Professor Cooke makes accounting practical. [Details can describe how Professor Cooke makes accounting skills relevant to everyday life.] |

| LACKS POINT OF VIEW | I read newspapers. |
| REVISED | I recommend reading newspapers from back to front. [Details can give reasons why this method is best.] |

The following suggestions will help you revise your topic sentence if you discover that it lacks a point of view:

1. **Use brainstorming, freewriting, or branching.** Try to generate more ideas about your topic. Study your results to discover a way to approach your topic.

2. **Ask yourself questions about your topic sentence.** Specifically, ask "Why?" "How?" "So what?" or "Why is this important?" Answering your own questions will give you ideas for revising your topic sentence.

EXERCISE 15-1   Revising Topic Sentences

Working Together

Directions: The following topic sentences lack a point of view. Working with a classmate, revise each one to express an interesting view on the topic.

| SENTENCE | I took a biology exam today. |
| REVISED | The biology exam that I took today contained a number of surprises. |

1. I am taking a math course this semester.

    REVISED   _____

    _____

2. I purchased a video camera last week.

   REVISED _____

   _____

3. Soft rock was playing in the dentist's office.

   REVISED _____

   _____

4. Sam has three televisions and four radios in his household.

   REVISED _____

   _____

5. There is one tree on the street where I live.

   REVISED _____

   _____

6. Many people wear headphones on their way to work.

   REVISED _____

   _____

7. Our sociology professor will give us three exams.

   REVISED _____

   _____

8. The first hurricane of the season is predicted to strike land tomorrow.

   REVISED _____

   _____

9. My four-year-old son has learned the alphabet.

   REVISED _____

   _____

10. Juanita enrolled her son in a day-care center.

    REVISED _____

    _____

    ■

IS THE TOPIC SENTENCE TOO BROAD?

| GOAL 2 Identify topic sentences that are too broad |

Some topic sentences express a point of view, but they are too broad in scope.

TOO BROAD   The death penalty is a crime against humanity.

This statement cannot be supported in a single paragraph. Lengthy essays, even entire books, have been written to argue this opinion.

A broad topic sentence promises more than you can reasonably deliver in a single paragraph. It leads to writing that is vague and rambling. With a broad topic sentence, you will end up with too many facts and ideas to cover or too many generalities (general statements) that do not sufficiently explain your topic sentence. In the following example, note the broad topic sentence and its effects on paragraph development.

Sample Paragraph

All kinds of violent crimes in the world today seem to be getting worse. Sometimes I wonder how people could possibly bring themselves to do such horrible things. One problem may be the violent acts shown on television programs. Some people think crime has a lot to do with horror movies and television programs. We have no heroes to identify with other than criminals. News reporting of crimes is too "real"; it shows too much. Kids watch these programs without their parents and don't know what to make of them. Parents should spend time with their children and supervise their play.

The topic sentence above promises more than a good paragraph can reasonably deliver: to discuss all violent crimes in the world today and their worsening nature. If you reread the paragraph, you will see that in the supporting sentences the author wanders from topic to topic. She first mentions violence on television, then moves to lack of heroes. Next she discusses news reporting that is too graphic, then switches to children watching programs alone. Finally, she ends with parental supervision of children. Each point about possible causes of violence or ways to prevent it seems underdeveloped.

An effective topic sentence needs to be more focused. For example, the topic sentence for a paragraph about crime might focus on one type of crime in one city and one reason for its increase.

> **FOCUSED**   Home burglaries are increasing in Owensville because of increased drug usage.

Another effective topic sentence for a paragraph on crime could focus on one possible cause of rising violence in the workplace.

> **FOCUSED**   The mass layoffs in the past few years have led to more criminal acts by desperate, unemployed workers.

The topic sentence of the following paragraph is also too broad.

Sample Paragraph

People often forget the spirit and value of life and concentrate on worldly goods. These people buy things for show—nice cars, nice clothes, nice houses. These people are scraping their pennies together just to live well. They do not realize that things not from the store are just as nice. Their health, their families, and the people they care about are far more important than money. You can be rich and poor at the same time.

Because the topic was too broad, the writer continued to use general statements throughout the paragraph and to repeat the same or similar ideas. A more effective approach might be to select one worldly good and show how it affects one person.

FOCUSED   My sister is so concerned with dressing stylishly that she ignores everyone around her.

Now the writer can explain how an emphasis on clothing detracts from her sister's relationship with others.

Another effective topic sentence might focus the paragraph on not taking good health for granted:

FOCUSED   I used to think I could buy my way to happiness, but that was before I lost my good health.

The following suggestions will help you revise your topic sentence if you discover that it is too broad:

1. **Narrow your topic.** A topic that is too broad often produces a topic sentence that is too broad. Narrow your topic by subdividing it into smaller topics. Continue subdividing until you produce a topic that is manageable in a single paragraph.

2. **Rewrite your topic sentence to focus on one aspect or part of your topic.** Ask yourself, "What is the part of this topic that really interests me or that I care most about? What do I know most about the topic and have the most to say about?" Then focus on *that* aspect of the topic.

3. **Apply your topic sentence to a specific time and place.** Ask yourself, "How does this broad topic that I'd like to write about relate to some particular time and place that I know about? How can I make the general topic come alive by using a well-defined example?"

4. **Consider using one of your supporting sentences as a topic sentence.** Reread your paragraph; look for a detail that could be developed or expanded.

EXERCISE 15-2   Revising Topic Sentences
Writing in Progress

Directions: Turn each of the following broad topic sentences into a well-focused topic sentence that could lead to an effective paragraph. Remember that your topic sentence must also include a point of view. Then compare your answers with your classmates' answers to see the variety of effective topic sentences that can come from a broad one.

TOO BROAD   Hunting is a worthwhile and beneficial sport.

REVISED   Hunting deer in overpopulated areas is beneficial to the herd.

1. I would like to become more creative.

    REVISED   _____

    _____

2. Brazil is a beautiful country.

    REVISED   _____

    _____

3. Pollution is a big problem.

    REVISED   _____

    _____

4. The space program is amazing.

    REVISED _____

    _____

5. It is very important to learn Japanese.

    REVISED _____

    _____

6. We must protect the environment.

    REVISED _____

    _____

7. Lani is a good mother.

    REVISED _____

    _____

8. The book was interesting.

    REVISED _____

    _____

9. Lots of magazines are published.

    REVISED _____

    _____

10. Honesty is important.

    REVISED _____

    _____

■

IS THE TOPIC SENTENCE TOO NARROW?

GOAL 3 Identify topic sentences that are too narrow

If your topic sentence is too narrow, you will realize it right away because you won't have enough to write about to complete your paragraph. Topic sentences that are too narrow also frequently lack a point of view.

TOO NARROW	My birdfeeder attracts yellow songbirds.
REVISED	Watching the different birds at our feeder is a pleasant diversion enjoyed by our entire family, including our cat.
TOO NARROW	My math instructor looks at his watch frequently.
REVISED	My math instructor has a number of nervous habits that detract from his lecture presentations.

The following suggestions will help you revise your topic sentence when it is too narrow:

1. **Broaden your topic to include a wider group or range of items or ideas.** For example, do not write about one nervous habit; write about several. Look for patterns and trends that could form the basis of a new, broader topic sentence.

2. **Broaden your topic so that it takes in both causes and effects or makes comparisons or contrasts.** For example, do not write only about how fast an instructor lectures. Also write about the effect of his lecture speed on students trying to take notes, or contrast that instructor with others who have different lecture styles.

3. **Brainstorm and research; try to develop a more general point from your narrower one.** Ask yourself, "What does this narrow point mean? What are its larger implications?" Suppose you've written the following topic sentence:

I wanted to buy a CD this week, but it was not in my budget.

You could expand this idea to discuss the importance or value of making and following a weekly budget.

NEED TO KNOW
Topic Sentences

Ineffective paragraphs may frustrate, confuse, or bore your reader.

A weak topic sentence may

- lack a point of view or attitude toward the topic.
- be too broad.
- be too narrow.

To revise a topic sentence that lacks a point of view

- use brainstorming, freewriting, or branching.
- ask yourself questions about your topic sentence to focus on a particular viewpoint.

To narrow a topic sentence that is too broad, consider

- narrowing your topic.
- rewriting your topic sentence to focus on one aspect of your topic.
- applying your topic sentence to a specific time and place.
- using one of your supporting sentences as a topic sentence.

To broaden a topic sentence that is too narrow, consider

- broadening your topic to make it more inclusive.
- broadening your topic to consider causes and effects or to make comparisons or contrasts.
- brainstorming and researching to develop a more general point.

EXERCISE 15-3   Broadening Topic Sentences

Directions: Turn each of the following narrow topic sentences into a broader, well-focused topic sentence that could lead to an effective paragraph. Remember that your topic sentence must also include a point of view. Then compare your answers with your classmates' answers to see the variety of effective topic sentences that can come from a narrow one.

TOO NARROW   Football players wear protective helmets.

REVISED   Football players wear several types of protective equipment to guard against injuries.

1. I planted a tomato plant in my garden.

   REVISED _____

   _____

2. The cafeteria served hot dogs and beans for lunch.

   REVISED _____

   _____

3. Orlando sings in a low key.

   REVISED _____

   _____

4. Suzanne bought a stapler for her desk.

   REVISED _____

   _____

5. Koala bears are really marsupials, not bears.

   REVISED _____

   _____

6. On our vacation, we stopped at a small town called Boothbay Harbor.

   REVISED _____

   _____

7. Homemade bread contains no preservatives.

   REVISED _____

   _____

8. At Halloween, the girl dressed as a witch.

   REVISED _____

   _____

9. The comedian told a joke about dental floss.

   REVISED _____

   _____

10. We had a family portrait taken for Christmas.

REVISED _____

_____

■

DOES THE PARAGRAPH STRAY FROM THE TOPIC?

GOAL 4   Identify when you have strayed off topic

When you are writing a first draft of a paragraph, it is easy to drift away from the topic. As you write, one idea triggers another, and that idea another, and eventually you end up with ideas that have little or nothing to do with your original topic, as in the following first-draft student paragraph.

Sample Student Paragraph

One Example of Toxic Waste
The disposal of toxic waste has caused serious health hazards. Love Canal is one of the many toxic dump sites that have caused serious health problems. This dump site in particular was used by a large number of nearby industries. The canal was named after a man named Love. Love Canal, in my opinion, was an eye-opener on the subject of toxic dump sites. It took about ten years to clean the dump site up to a livable condition. Many people living near Love Canal developed cancers. There were many miscarriages and birth defects. This dump site might have caused irreversible damage to our environment, so I am glad it has been cleaned up.

The following idea map shows the topic sentence of the paragraph and, underneath it, the supporting details that directly relate to the topic sentence. All the unrelated details are in a list to the right of the map. Note that the concluding sentence is also included in the map, since it is an important part of the paragraph.

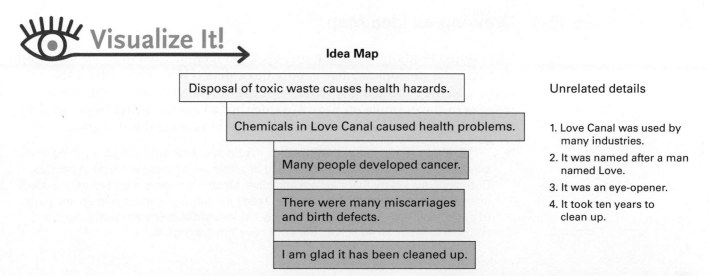

In this paragraph the author began by supporting her topic sentence with the example of Love Canal. However, she began to drift when she explained how Love Canal was named. To revise this paragraph, the author could include more detailed information about Love Canal health hazards or examples of other disposal sites and their health hazards.

You can use an idea map to spot where you begin to drift away from your topic. To do this, take the last idea in the map and compare it with your topic sentence.

Does the last idea directly support your topic sentence? If not, you may have drifted from your topic. Check the second-to-last detail, going through the same comparison process. Working backward, you'll see where you started to drift. This is the point at which to begin revising.

What to Do If You Stray Off Topic

Use the following suggestions to revise your paragraph if it strays from your topic:

1. **Locate the last sentence that does relate to your topic, and begin your revision there.** What could you say next that *would* relate to the topic?

2. **Consider expanding your existing ideas.** If, after two or three details, you have strayed from your topic, consider expanding the details you have, rather than searching for additional details.

3. **Reread your brainstorming, freewriting, or branching to find more details.** Look for additional ideas that support your topic. Do more brainstorming, if necessary.

4. **Consider changing your topic.** Drifting from your topic is not always a loss. Sometimes by drifting you discover a more interesting topic than your original one. If you decide to change topics, revise your entire paragraph. Begin by rewriting your topic sentence.

EXERCISE 15-4   **Drawing an Idea Map**

Directions: Read the following first-draft paragraph. Then draw an idea map that includes the topic sentence, only those details that support the topic sentence, and the concluding sentence. List the unrelated details to the side of the map, as in the example on page 413. Identify where the writer began to stray from the topic, and make specific suggestions for revising this paragraph.

> Junk food lacks nutrition and is high in calories. Junk food can be anything from candy and potato chips to ice cream and desserts. All of these are high in calories. But they are so tasty that they are addictive. Once a person is addicted to junk food, it is very hard to break the addiction. To break the habit, one must give up any form of sugar. And I have not gone back to my old lifestyle in over two weeks. So it is possible to break an addiction, but I still have the craving. ■

EXERCISE 15-5   **Writing a Paragraph**

Writing in Progress

Directions: Write a paragraph on one of the following topics. Then draw an idea map of it. Use the same procedure you used in Exercise 15-4. If you have strayed from your topic, revise your paragraph using the suggestions given above.

1. A memorable sight, sound, or meal
2. City language or country language
3. Trends in TV ads
4. A crowd you have watched or been a part of
5. The way that a certain friendship developed ■

ARE THERE ENOUGH SUPPORTING DETAILS?

GOAL 5 Revise underdeveloped paragraphs

The details in a paragraph should give your reader sufficient information to make your topic sentence believable. Paragraphs that lack necessary detail are called **underdeveloped paragraphs**. Underdeveloped paragraphs lack supporting sentences to prove or explain the point made in the topic sentence. As you read the following student paragraph, keep the topic sentence in mind and consider whether the rest of the sentences support it.

Sample Student Paragraph

I am a very impatient person, and my impatience interferes with how easily I can get through a day. If I ask for something, I want it immediately. If I'm going somewhere and I'm ready and somebody else isn't, I get very upset. I hate driving behind someone who drives slowly when I cannot pass. I think that annoys me the most, and it never happens unless I am in a hurry. If I were less impatient, I would probably feel more relaxed and less pressured.

This paragraph begins with a topic sentence that is focused (it is neither too broad nor too narrow) and that includes a point of view. It promises to explain how the writer's impatience makes it difficult for him to get through a day. However, the rest of the paragraph does not fulfill this promise. Instead, the writer gives two very general examples of his impatience: (1) wanting something and (2) waiting for someone. The third example, driving behind a slow driver, is a little more specific, but it is not developed well. The last sentence suggests, but does not explain, that the writer's impatience makes him feel tense and pressured.

Taking into account the need for more supporting detail, the author revised his paragraph as follows:

Revised Paragraph

I am a very impatient person, and my impatience interferes with how easily I can get through a day. For example, when I decide to buy something, such as a new CD, I *have* to have it right away—that day. I usually drop everything and run to the store. Of course, I shortchange myself on studying, and that hurts my grades. My impatience hurts me, too, when I'm waiting for someone, which I hate to do. If my friend Alex and I agree to meet at noon to work on his car, I get annoyed if he's even five minutes late. Then I usually end up saying something nasty or sarcastic like "Well, where *were* you?" which I regret later. Perhaps I am most impatient when I'm behind the steering wheel. If I get behind a slow driver, I get annoyed and start honking and beeping my horn. I know this might fluster the other driver, and afterwards I feel guilty. I've tried talking to myself to calm down; sometimes it works, so I hope I'm overcoming this bad trait.

Did you notice that the writer became much more specific in the revised version? He gave an example of something he wanted—a CD—and he described his actions and their consequences. The example of waiting for someone was provided by the incident involving his friend Alex. Finally, the writer explained the driving example in more detail and stated its consequences. With the extra details and supporting examples, the paragraph is more interesting and effective.

The following suggestions will help you revise an underdeveloped paragraph:

1. **Analyze your paragraph sentence by sentence.** If a sentence does not add new, specific information to your paragraph, delete it or add to it so that it becomes relevant.

2. **Think of specific situations, facts, or examples that illustrate or support your topic.** Often you can make a general sentence more specific.

3. **Brainstorm, freewrite, or branch.** To come up with additional details or examples to use in your paragraph, try some prewriting techniques. If necessary, start fresh with a new approach and new set of ideas.

4. **Reexamine your topic sentence.** If you are having trouble generating details, your topic sentence may be the problem. Consider changing the approach.

   EXAMPLE   Rainy days make me feel depressed.

   REVISED   Rainy days, although depressing, give me a chance to catch up on household chores.

5. **Consider changing your topic.** If a paragraph remains troublesome, look for a new topic and start over.

EXERCISE 15-6   Revising a Paragraph

Directions: The following paragraph is poorly developed. What suggestions would you make to the writer to improve the paragraph? Write them in the space provided. Be specific. Which sentences are weak? How could each be improved?

> I am attending college to improve myself. By attending college, I am getting an education to improve the skills that I'll need for a good career in broadcasting. Then, after a successful career, I'll be able to get the things that I need to be happy in my life. People will also respect me more.

_____

_____

_____

_____

EXERCISE 15-7   Evaluating a Paragraph

Directions: Evaluate the following paragraph by answering the questions that follow it.

One of the best ways to keep people happy and occupied is to entertain them. Every day people are being entertained, whether it is by a friend for a split second or by a Broadway play for a few hours. Entertainment is probably one of the nation's biggest businesses. Entertainment has come a long way from the past; it has gone from plays in the park to films in eight-screen movie theaters.

1. Evaluate the topic sentence. What is wrong with it? How could it be revised?

   _____

   _____

2. Write a more effective topic sentence on the topic of entertainment.

   _____

   _____

3. Evaluate the supporting details. What is wrong with them?

   _____

   _____

4. What should the writer do to develop her paragraph?

   _____

   _____

5. Use the topic sentence you wrote in question 2 above to develop a paragraph about entertainment.

   _____

   _____

   _____

   _____

   _____

   _____

   _____

   _____

EXERCISE 15-8   Writing a Paragraph
Writing in Progress

Directions: Develop one of the topic sentences you wrote in Exercise 15-2 into a paragraph that uses good supporting details. Then draw an idea map of your paragraph, and revise your paragraph as needed. ▪

NEED TO KNOW

Adding Supporting Details

To revise an underdeveloped paragraph,

- analyze your paragraph sentence by sentence.

- think of specific situations, facts, or examples that illustrate or support your main point.

- use brainstorming, freewriting, or branching.

- reexamine your topic sentence.

- consider changing your topic.

 Analyze It!

Directions: The topic sentence on the left is ineffective because it is too broad. On the right, rewrite the topic sentence to be more specific. Then rewrite the paragraph so that it contains concrete details that support the topic sentence.

There are a wide variety of books available for leisure reading. Many people find that thrillers—novels that have an exciting plot—make great "escape" literature. Thrillers are usually easy to read. Thrillers sometimes overlap with mysteries, another popular genre. Then there are science fiction and romances, too. When choosing a book for leisure reading, a person should consider the difficulty level of the book. Some people find it relaxing to read nineteenth-century novels, but other readers are frustrated by the unfamiliar language and slow action. It is not always easy to find the perfect book, but the library offers helpful resources for the determined leisure reader.

Topic Sentence: _____

_____

_____

_____

_____

_____

_____

_____

DOES EVERY DETAIL BELONG?

GOAL 6 Identify and eliminate irrelevant details

Every detail in a paragraph must directly support the topic sentence or one of the other details. Unrelated information should not be included, a mistake one student made in the following first-draft paragraph.

Sample Student Paragraph

In a world where stress is an everyday occurrence, many people relieve stress through entertainment. There are many ways to entertain ourselves and relieve stress. Many people watch movies to take their minds off day-to-day problems. However, going to the movies costs a lot of money. Due to the cost, some people rent movies at video stores. Playing sports is another stress reliever. Exercise always helps to give people a positive attitude and keeps them in shape. Racquetball really keeps you in shape because it is such a fast game. A third form of entertainment is going out with friends. With friends, people can talk about their problems and feel better about them. But some friends always talk and never listen, and such conversation creates stress instead of relieving it. So if you are under stress, be sure to reserve some time for entertainment.

The following idea map shows that this writer included four unrelated details:

Visualize It!

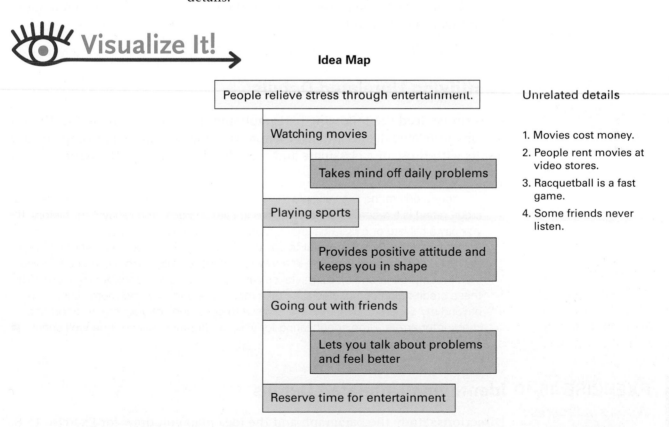

Idea Map

People relieve stress through entertainment.

- Watching movies
  - Takes mind off daily problems
- Playing sports
  - Provides positive attitude and keeps you in shape
- Going out with friends
  - Lets you talk about problems and feel better
- Reserve time for entertainment

Unrelated details

1. Movies cost money.
2. People rent movies at video stores.
3. Racquetball is a fast game.
4. Some friends never listen.

To spot unrelated details, draw an idea map. To decide whether a detail is unrelated, ask, "Does this detail directly explain the topic sentence or one of the other details?" If you are not sure, ask, "What happens if I take this out?"

If meaning is lost or if confusion occurs, the detail is important. Include it in your map. If you can make your point just as well without the detail, mark it "unrelated."

In the sample student paragraph on page 419, the high cost of movies and the low-cost alternative of renting videos do not directly explain how or why movies are entertaining. The racquetball detail does not explain how exercise relieves stress. The detail about friends not listening does not explain how talking to friends is helpful in reducing stress.

Making Sure Every Detail Belongs

The following suggestions will help you use supporting details more effectively:

1. **Add explanations to make the connections between your ideas clearer.** Often a detail may not seem to relate to the topic because you have not explained *how* it relates. For example, health-care insurance may seem to have little to do with the prevention of breast cancer deaths until you explain that mammograms, which are paid for by some health-care plans, can prevent deaths.

2. **Add transitions.** Transitions make it clearer to your reader how one detail relates to another.

3. **Add new details.** If you've deleted several nonessential details, your paragraph may be too sketchy. Return to the prewriting step to generate more details you can include.

EXERCISE 15-9   Identifying Unrelated Details
Working Together

Directions: Read the following paragraph and draw an idea map of it. Underline any unrelated details and list them to the side of your map. Compare your results with those of a classmate and then decide what steps the writer should take to revise this paragraph.

Your credit rating is a valuable thing that you should protect and watch over. A credit rating is a record of your loans, credit card charges, and repayment history. If you pay a bill late or miss a payment, that information becomes part of your credit rating. It is, therefore, important to pay bills promptly. Some people just don't keep track of dates; some don't even know what date it is today. Errors can occur in your credit rating. Someone else's mistakes can be put on your record, for example. Why these credit-rating companies can't take more time and become more accurate is beyond my understanding. It is worthwhile to get a copy of your credit report and check it for errors. Time spent caring for your credit rating will be time well spent. ■

EXERCISE 15-10 Identifying Unrelated Details
Writing in Progress

Directions: Study the paragraph and the idea map you drew for Exercise 15-8. Check for unrelated details. If you find any, revise your paragraph using the suggestions given above. ■

ARE THE DETAILS ARRANGED AND DEVELOPED LOGICALLY?

GOAL 7 Revise to ensure that details are logically arranged and developed

Details in a paragraph should follow some logical order. As you write a first draft, you are often more concerned with expressing your ideas than with presenting them in the correct order. As you revise, however, you should make sure you have followed a logical arrangement. Chapter 13 discusses various methods of arranging and developing details. The following "Need to Know" box reviews these arrangements:

NEED TO KNOW

Methods of Arranging and Developing Details

METHOD	DESCRIPTION
1. Time sequence	Arranges details in the order in which they happen.
2. Spatial	Arranges details according to their physical location.
3. Least/most	Arranges details from least to most or from most to least, according to some quality or characteristic.

Chapter 14 discusses several methods of organizing and presenting material. The "Need to Know" box below reviews these arrangements.

NEED TO KNOW

Methods of Organizing and Presenting Material

METHOD	DESCRIPTION
1. Narration	Arranges events in the order in which they occurred.
2. Description	Arranges descriptive details spatially or uses the least/most arrangement.
3. Example	Explains by giving situations that illustrate a general idea or statement.
4. Definition	Explains by giving a subject's category or distinguishing characteristics.
5. Comparison and contrast	Explains an idea by comparing or contrasting it with another, usually more familiar, idea.
6. Classification	Explains by identifying types or categories.
7. Process	Arranges steps in the order in which they are to be completed.
8. Cause and effect	Explains why something happened or what happened as a result of a particular action.
9. Argument	Takes a position on an issue.

Your ideas need a logical arrangement to make them easy to follow. Poor organization creates misunderstanding and confusion. After drafting the following paragraph, a student drew an idea map that showed her organization was haphazard.

Sample Student Paragraph

When I was pregnant with my son, I wondered if life would ever be normal again. There were the nights I couldn't sleep because of all the kicking and the baby moving up to my lungs so I couldn't breathe. That was when I really had it! Each month I got bigger and bigger, and after a while I was so big I couldn't bend over or see my feet. Then there was the morning sickness. I don't know why they call it that because you're sick all the time for the first two months. Then there were all those doctor visits during which she told me, "Not for another week or two." Of course, when I realized my clothes didn't fit, I broke down and cried. But all of a sudden everything started up, and I was at the hospital delivering the baby two weeks early, and it's like it happened so fast and it was all over, and I had the most beautiful baby in my arms and I knew it was worth all that pain and suffering.

Idea Map

> When I was pregnant, I wondered if life would ever be normal.

> Couldn't sleep—baby kicking, breathing difficult

> Got bigger and bigger

> Morning sickness

> Doctor: "Not for another week"

> Clothes didn't fit

> Birth

An idea map lets you see quickly when a paragraph has no organization or when an idea is out of order. This student's map showed that her paragraph did not present the events of her pregnancy in the most logical arrangement: time sequence. She therefore reorganized the events in the order in which they happened and revised her paragraph as follows:

Revised Paragraph

When I was pregnant with my son, I wondered if life would ever be normal again. First there was the morning sickness. I don't know why they call it that because I was sick all the time for the first two months. Of course, when I realized my clothes didn't fit, I broke down and cried. Each month I got bigger and bigger, and finally I was so big I couldn't bend over or see my feet. Then there were the nights I couldn't sleep because of all the kicking and the baby moving up to my lungs so I couldn't breathe. That was when I really had it. Finally, there were all those doctor visits during which she told me, "Not for another week or two." But all of a sudden everything started to happen, and I was at the hospital delivering the baby two weeks early. Everything happened so fast. It was all over, and I had the most beautiful baby in my arms. Then I knew it was worth all that pain and suffering.

Arranging and Developing Details Logically

The following suggestions will help you revise your paragraph if it lacks organization:

1. **Review the methods of arranging and developing details and of organizing and presenting material** (see the "Need to Know" boxes on page 421). Will one of those arrangements work? If so, number the ideas in your idea map according to the arrangement you choose. Then begin revising your paragraph.

   If you find one or more details out of logical order in your paragraph, do the following:

   - **Number the details in your idea map to indicate the correct order, and revise your paragraph accordingly.**
   - **Reread your revised paragraph and draw another idea map.**
   - **Look to see if you've omitted necessary details.** After you have placed your details in a logical order, you are more likely to recognize gaps.

2. **Look at your topic sentence again.** If you are working with a revised arrangement of supporting details, you may need to revise your topic sentence to reflect that arrangement.

3. **Check whether additional details are needed.** Suppose, for example, you are writing about an exciting experience and you decide to use the time-sequence arrangement. Once you make that decision, you may need to add details to enable your reader to understand exactly how the experience happened.

4. **Add transitions.** Transitions help make your organization obvious and easy to follow.

■ **EXERCISE 15-11 Evaluating Arrangement of Ideas**

Directions: Read the following student paragraph, and draw an idea map of it. Evaluate the arrangement of ideas. What revisions would you suggest?

> The minimum wage is not an easily resolved problem; it has both advantages and disadvantages. Its primary advantage is that it does guarantee workers a minimum wage. It prevents the economic abuse of workers. Employers cannot take advantage of workers by paying them less than the minimum. Its primary disadvantage is that the minimum wage is not sufficient for older workers with families to support. For younger workers, such as teenagers, however, this minimum is fine. It provides them with spending money and some economic freedom from their parents. Another disadvantage is that as long as people, such as a teenagers, are willing to work for the minimum, employers don't need to pay a higher wage. Thus, the minimum wage prevents experienced workers from getting more money. But the minimum wage does help our economy by requiring a certain level of income per worker. ■

■ **EXERCISE 15-12 Evaluating Arrangement of Ideas**

Writing in Progress

Directions: Review the paragraph and idea map you produced for Exercise 15-8. Evaluate the logical arrangement of your points and details, and revise if needed. ■

IS THE PARAGRAPH BALANCED?

GOAL 8 Revise to ensure your paragraph is balanced

An effective paragraph achieves a balance among its points. That is, each idea receives an appropriate amount of supporting detail and emphasis. The following student paragraph lacks balance, as its idea map on the following page shows.

Sample Student Paragraph

Waiting

Waiting is very annoying, exhausting, and time-consuming. Waiting to buy books at the college store is an example of a very long and tiresome task. I need to buy books, and so does everyone else. This causes the lines to be very long. Most of the time I find myself leaning against the wall daydreaming. Sometimes I will even leave the line and hope to come back when the store isn't extremely busy. But that never works because everyone else seems to get the same idea. So I finally realize that I just have to wait. Another experience is waiting for a ride home from school or work. My ride always seems to be the last car to pull up in the parking lot. When I am waiting for my ride, I often wonder what it would be like to own a car or if I will ever make it home. Waiting in line at a fast-food restaurant is also annoying because, if it is fast, I shouldn't have to wait. Waiting for an elevator is also no fun. Waiting just seems to be a part of life, so I might as well accept it.

Idea Map

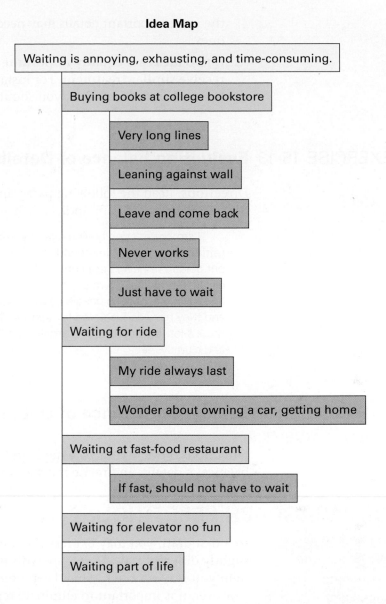

As the idea map above shows, a major portion of the paragraph is devoted to waiting in line to buy books. The second example, waiting for a ride, is not as thoroughly explained. The third example, waiting at a fast-food restaurant, is treated in even less detail, and the fourth, waiting for an elevator, has the least detail. To revise, the writer should expand the treatment of waiting for rides, fast food, and elevators, and perhaps decrease the treatment of the bookstore experience. An alternative solution would be for the writer to expand the bookstore experience and eliminate the other examples. In this case, a new topic sentence would be needed.

Making Sure Your Paragraph Is Balanced

The following suggestions will help you revise your paragraph for balance:

1. **Not every point or example must have the *same* amount of explanation.** For example, more complicated ideas require more explanation than simpler, more obvious ones. When you are using a least/most arrangement,

the more important details may need more coverage than the less important ones.

2. **If two ideas are equally important and equally complicated, they should receive similar treatment.** For instance, if you include an example or statistic in support of one idea, you should do so for the other.

EXERCISE 15-13 Evaluating Balance of Details

Directions: Read the following paragraph, and draw an idea map of it. Evaluate the balance of details and indicate where more details are needed.

> I am considering buying a puppy. There are four breeds I am looking at: golden retrievers, beagles, Newfoundlands, and cocker spaniels. Cocker spaniels are cute, but golden retrievers are cute *and* intelligent. Golden retrievers are very gentle with children, and I have two sons. They are also very loyal. But they have a lot of fur, and they shed, unlike beagles, which have short fur. Newfoundlands are very large, and they have dark-colored fur that would show up on my rug. Newfoundlands also drool a lot. My apartment is small, so a Newfoundland is probably just too big, furry, and clumsy. ■

EXERCISE 15-14 Evaluating Balance of Details
Writing in Progress

Directions: Review your paragraph and idea map for Exercise 15-8. Evaluate the balance of details, and revise if necessary. ■

IS THE PARAGRAPH REPETITIOUS?

GOAL 9 Identify and eliminate unnecessary repetition

In a first draft, you may express the same idea more than once, each time in a slightly different way. As you are writing a first draft, repetitive statements may help you stay on track. They keep you writing and help generate new ideas. However, it is important to eliminate repetition at the revision stage. Repetitive statements add nothing to your paragraph. They detract from its clarity. An idea map will bring repetition to your attention quickly because it makes it easy to spot two or more very similar items.

As you read the following first-draft student paragraph, see if you can spot the repetitive statements. Then notice how the idea map on the next page clearly identifies the repetition.

Sample Student Paragraph

Chemical waste dumping is an environmental concern that must be dealt with, not ignored. The big companies care nothing about the environment. They would just as soon dump waste in our backyards as not. This has finally become a big issue and is being dealt with by forcing the companies to clean up their own messes. It is incredible that large companies have the nerve to dump just about anywhere. The penalty should be steep. When the companies are caught, they should be forced to clean up their messes.

 **Visualize It!**

Idea Map

Chemical waste dumping must be dealt with.

Big companies care nothing about environment

Just as soon dump in our backyards

Dumping has become big issue—companies forced to clean up own mess

Companies have nerve to dump just about anywhere

Penalty should be steep

When caught, clean up should be required

The idea map shows that points 1, 2, and 4 say nearly the same thing—that big companies don't care about the environment and dump waste nearly anywhere. Because there is so much repetition, the paragraph lacks development. To revise, the writer first needs to eliminate the repetitious statements. Then she needs to generate more ideas that support her topic sentence and explain why or how chemical waste dumping must be dealt with.

How to Avoid Repetition

The following suggestions will help you revise a paragraph with repetitive ideas:

1. **Try to combine ideas.** Select the best elements and wording of each idea and use them to produce a revised sentence. Add more detail if needed.

2. **Review places where you make deletions.** When you delete a repetitious statement, check to see whether the sentence before and the sentence after the deletion connect. Often a transition will be needed to help the paragraph flow easily.

3. **Decide whether additional details are needed.** Often we write repetitious statements when we don't know what else to say. Thus, repetition often signals lack of development.

4. **Watch for statements that are only slightly more general or specific than one another.** For example, although the first sentence below is general and the second is more specific, they repeat the same idea.

> Ringing telephones can be distracting. The telephone that rang constantly throughout the evening distracted me.

To make the second sentence a specific example of the idea in the first sentence, rather than just a repetition of it, the writer would need to add specific details about how the telephone ringing throughout the evening was a distraction.

EXERCISE 15-15 **Identifying and Revising Repetitive Statements**

Directions: Read the following paragraph and delete all repetitive statements. Make suggestions for revision.

Children misbehaving is an annoying problem in our society. I used to work as a waiter at Denny's, and I have seen many incidences in which parents allow their children to misbehave. I have seen many situations that you would just not believe. Once I served a table at which the parents allowed their four-year-old to make his toy spider crawl up and down my pants as I tried to serve the food. The parents just laughed. Children have grown up being rewarded for their actions, regardless of whether they are good or bad. Whether the child does something the parents approve of or whether it is something they disapprove of, they react in similar ways. This is why a lot of toddlers and children continue to misbehave. Being rewarded will cause the child to act in the same way to get the same reward. ■

NEED TO KNOW
Using Idea Maps

An idea map is a visual display of the ideas in your paragraph. It allows you to see how ideas relate to one another and to identify weaknesses in your writing. You can use idea maps to answer the following five questions that will help you revise your paragraphs:

- Does the paragraph stray from the topic?
- Does every detail belong?
- Are the details arranged and developed logically?
- Is the paragraph balanced?
- Is the paragraph repetitious?

EXERCISE 15-16 **Identifying and Revising Repetitive Statements**
Writing in Progress

Directions: Review your paragraph and idea map for Exercise 15-8. Identify and revise any repetitive statements. ■

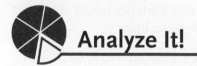 Analyze It!

Directions: The following paragraph strays from its topic and includes details that do not belong. Revise the paragraph by deleting all sentences that do not directly support the thesis.

Do you have trouble getting out of the house on time in the morning? If you are not a naturally well-organized person, you may need to overcompensate by being super organized in the morning. A detailed checklist can help you accomplish the seemingly impossible goal of leaving home exactly when you are supposed to. It is especially difficult to leave on time if you are tired or feeling lazy. When making such a checklist, most people find it helpful to backtrack to the previous evening. Do you have clean clothes for the next day, or do you need to do a load of laundry? Are your materials for school or work neatly assembled, or is there a landslide of papers covering your desk? Do you need to pack a lunch? You get the picture. In your checklist, include tasks to complete the night before as well as a precise sequence of morning tasks with realistic estimates of the time required for each task. If you have children, help them make checklists to keep track of homework assignments. Child development experts stress the importance of predictable structure in children's lives. If you live with a friend or spouse, make sure to divide all chores in an equitable way. Often one person tends to be neater than the other, so you may need to make compromises, but having an explicit agreement about household responsibilities can help prevent resentment and conflict at home.

A STUDENT ESSAY

The Writing Task

Chase Beauclair wrote this essay for a college writing class. As you read, pay special attention to the use of description and the development of the paragraphs.

Title suggests the thesis

Balancing the Extremes: Finding an Adult Diet Through Trial and Error
Chase Beauclair

1   The first few years of true independence in the lives of young adults are sure to be a very complicated and stressful time as they are forced to learn how to successfully manage their own lives away from the watchful eye of their parents. Although eating is one of the most basic human functions, developing healthy habits around food can be one of the most difficult tasks for young adults to fully master. Surrounding almost every college campus in the United States is a bevy of fast food restaurants and cheap diners that cater to crowds demanding quantity over quality, remain open all night, and, in many cases, deliver. College dining halls also offer an endless buffet of questionable choices where students can eat until they are sick. Both of these factors contribute to the process of trial and error during each young adult's

Thesis statement

Topic sentence

Beauclair inserts details describing the first stage of eating

Topic sentence

Details about stage 2

Topic sentence

Details about stage 3

college career in the transition from an unsupervised child at a smorgasbord to a responsible adult making healthy, reasonable food choices. There are four phases that students typically move between: the initial stage of careless abandon, the period of reigned in spending and frugal choices, the health conscious connoisseur phase, and the final balance of a diet of moderation. While some people's habits may not vary too widely, almost every college student does fall into one of these four stages at one point, and eventually, to varying degrees of success, finds a balance between the extremes.

2   The first stage of every college student's transition into adulthood is the result of the newfound freedom of living away from the rules and regulations of their parents and the predictability of three well-balanced meals a day. The two priorities of every student are adjusting to the increased workload of a college schedule and the dramatic increase in social activity that comes with living with hundreds, if not thousands, of people their age. At this point in time the only rules are eat when hungry and give in to cravings. Along with the considerable number of other mistakes college students eventually learn from, the overindulgence in greasy, late-night deliveries, early morning energy drinks, and fast food runs rank high amongst the things college freshmen love to do away from the judgmental eye of mom and dad. At some point, the food debauchery catches up to students, usually when they can no longer afford the bills or their clothes stop fitting like they used to, and they realize that their current habits are unsustainable.

3   Once the panic sets in and people see that endless food spending is not the most economic use of their resources, college students typically rush to the other extreme and refuse to spend their money on food that they could be getting with their pre-paid meal plans. The individual who refuses to go out to dinner with friends epitomizes the frugal dining stage and most typically has a dorm room stuffed full of fruit, cereal, and to-go boxes smuggled out of the dining hall. It is easy to identify the students who have overspent and are now eating on a budget because they always have a dining tray overflowing with a wide assortment of dishes and can often be seen returning to the food line for seconds, or sometimes thirds. The total lack of balance and constant overloading of one or two daily meals eventually grows tiresome, as does the unending indigestion, and students slowly become willing to, once again, spend their money on food.

4   The trial and error from the last two dining phases usually forces students to re-prioritize their lives, and, as a result, they often start going back to the gym, eating healthier, and refining their palette on higher quality meals. Students rediscover fruits and vegetables and start to eat breakfast again for the first time since they stopped living with their parents. At this point, quality and not quantity is driving most of the students' food choices, so that they may be spending just as much money as before but there is no guilt or health complications accompanying their decisions. While past experiences are a big part of the shift, students also become more aware of where they eat because they feel that they can use their choices in restaurants and food preferences to define their sensibilities and appear more adult. College students feel that the ritual of dining out is an important component of socializing, and they want to prove to their peers that they are part of the latest trends in the local food culture. Choices of restaurants are now all about finding the latest food truck, the newest fusion

of dissimilar cuisines, or finding the place that is the most organic. Dining is no longer only about abating hunger, but it is also about social identity.

Topic sentence

5   Towards the end of their college careers, students start to grow more independent, and through the process of trial and error, and countless transitions between several different dietary phases, they have more or less discovered the habits that best suit their needs. They realize that there is room for all of their preferences to coexist in moderation. Occasionally it is okay to order a pizza late at night and it is also okay to take advantage of cheap student meals when the opportunity presents itself. After all of the fads and subsequent mistakes, students learn that balance and moderation are essential to their eating habits as they move forward.

Details about the final stage

Conclusion reemphasizes the thesis statement

6   Some people are more successful at finding balance in their diets than others, but for the most part, the eating habits of college students eventually settle into a sustainable and relatively health conscious combination and coexist as something resembling an adult's diet. Obviously there is variation, and people will emphasize certain dietary phases more than others. Also, people never really settle into a singular set of eating habits and continually change as they get older, but the foundation is definitely set during the college years of young adulthood.

Examining Student Writing

1. What is Beauclair's purpose for writing the essay?
2. How is the essay organized?
3. Highlight the transitions that move the reader from one topic to another.
4. Evaluate the title. Could Beauclair have chosen a more descriptive title?

Paragraph Writing Scenarios

Friends and Family

1. Write a paragraph that begins "The most important thing I learned from my mother is . . ."
2. Write about an event that stands out in the history of your family.

Classes and Campus Life

1. Which of the "Three R's" (Reading, Writing, and Arithmetic) is the most difficult for you? What are you doing to make it easier?
2. Do you think race should be considered in awarding financial aid? Why or why not?

Working Students

1. Write a paragraph that begins "When I go to bed at night, I worry about . . ."
2. Write an imaginary job description that fits you perfectly.

Communities and Cultures

1. What is a typical weekend activity you enjoy doing with a group?
2. Write a paragraph about what you would miss most about your present community if you had to move away.

WRITING ABOUT A READING

The following reading, "You Can't Be Thin Enough: Body Images and the Mass Media," is from the book *Sociology: A Down-to-Earth Approach to Core Concepts*, by James M. Henslin.

Step 1: Preview the reading.

Step 2: Connect the reading to your own experience: How would you describe the ideal body type? Are most people content or dissatisfied with their body type? Why?

Step 3: Read and respond to the questions in the margin.

THINK AS YOU READ

Based on your preview, what is the author's attitude toward his subject?

The author begins by asking questions. How do these questions introduce the subject and suggest the thesis?

Express the thesis in your own words.

Why did the author include a picture of these particular women?

You Can't Be Thin Enough: Body Images and the Mass Media
James M. Henslin

1   When you stand before a mirror, do you like what you see? To make your body more attractive, do you watch your weight or work out? You have ideas about what you should look like. Where did you get them?

2   TV and magazine ads keep pounding home the message that our bodies aren't good enough, that we've got to improve them. The way to improve them, of course, is to buy the advertised products: hair extensions for women, hairpieces for men, hair transplants, padded bras, diet programs, anti-aging products, and exercise equipment. Muscular hulks show off machines that magically produce "six-pack abs" and incredible biceps—in just a few minutes a day. Female movie stars effortlessly go through their own tough workouts without even breaking into a sweat. Women and men get the feeling that attractive members of the opposite sex will flock to them if they purchase that wonder-working workout machine.

3   Although we try to shrug off such messages, knowing that they are designed to sell products, the messages still get our attention. They penetrate our thinking and feelings, helping to shape ideal images of how we "ought" to look. Those models so attractively clothed and coiffed as they walk down the runway, could they be any thinner? For women, the message is clear: You can't be thin enough. The men's message is also clear: You can't be muscular enough.

All of us contrast the reality we see when we look in the mirror with our culture's ideal body types. The thinness craze encourages some people to extremes, as with Paris Hilton. It also makes it difficult for larger people to have positive self-images. Overcoming this difficulty, Queen Latifah is in the forefront of promoting an alternative image.

How are the messages
different for men and women?

4   Woman or man, your body isn't good enough. It sags where it should be firm. It bulges where it should be smooth. It sticks out where it shouldn't, and it doesn't stick out enough where it should.

Does the author mean what
he is saying here?

5   And—no matter what your weight is—it's too much. You've got to be thinner. Exercise takes time, and getting in shape is painful. Once you do get in shape, if you slack off it seems to take only a few days for your body to sag into its previous slothful, drab appearance. You can't let up, you can't exercise enough, and you can't diet enough.

Is the author recommending
these procedures? Describe
his tone.

6   But who can continue at such a torrid pace, striving for what are unrealistic cultural ideals? A few people, of course, but not many. So liposuction is appealing. Just lie there, put up with a little discomfort, and the doctor will vacuum the fat right out of your body. Surgeons can transform flat breasts into super breasts overnight. They can lower receding hairlines and smooth furrowed brows. They remove lumps with their magical tummy tucks, and can take off a decade with their rejuvenating skin peels, face lifts, and Botox injections.

7   With impossibly shaped models at *Victoria's Secret* and skinny models showing off the latest fashions in *Vogue* and *Seventeen*, half of U.S. adolescent girls feel fat and count calories. Some teens even call the plastic surgeon. Anxious lest their child violate peer ideals and trail behind in her race for popularity, parents foot the bill. Some parents pay $25,000 just to give their daughters a flatter tummy.

What do you think the
author's opinion of these
surgeons is?

8   With peer pressure to alter the body already intense, surgeons keep stoking the fire. A sample ad: "No Ifs, Ands or Butts. You Can Change Your Bottom Line in Hours!" Some surgeons even offer gift certificates—so you can give your loved ones liposuction or Botox injections along with their greeting card.

What other countries besides
the United States have an obsession with thinness?

9   The thinness craze has moved to the East. Glossy magazines in Japan and China are filled with skinny models and crammed with ads touting diet pills and diet teas. In China, where famine used to abound, a little extra padding was valued as a sign of good health. Today, the obsession is thinness. Not-so-subtle ads scream that fat is bad. Some teas come with a package of diet pills. Weight-loss machines, with electrodes attached to acupuncture pressure points, not only reduce fat but also build breasts—or so the advertisers claim.

Why does the author use the
word "supposedly"?

10   Not limited by our rules, advertisers in Japan and China push a soap that supposedly "sucks up fat through the skin's pores." What a dream product! After all, even though our TV models smile as they go through their paces, those exercise machines do look like a lot of hard work.

11   Then there is the other bottom line: Attractiveness does pay off. U.S. economists studied physical attractiveness and earnings. The result? "Good-looking" men and women earn the most, "average-looking" men and women earn more than "plain" people, and the "ugly" earn the least. In Europe, too, the more attractive workers earn more. Then there is that potent cash advantage that "attractive" women have: They attract and marry higher-earning men.

Highlight two financial
advantages of attractiveness.

12   More popularity *and* more money? Maybe you can't be thin enough after all. Maybe those exercise machines are a good investment. If only we could catch up with the Japanese and develop a soap that would suck the fat right out of our pores. You can practically hear the **jingle**[1] now.

Describe the author's attitude
or tone in this paragraph.
Has this tone been consistent
throughout the reading?

---

[1] **jingle** a catchy song used in advertising

Examining the Reading Using an Idea Map MyWritingLab

Review the reading by completing the missing parts of the idea map shown below.

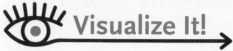 Visualize It! →

Title	**You Can't Be Thin Enough: Body Images and the Mass Media**
Thesis	TV and magazine ads send the message that our bodies aren't good enough and we've got to improve them.

_____
_____

The messages penetrate our thinking and feelings, shaping ideal images of how we "ought" to look.

Women should be thinner; men should be more muscular.

_____
_____

Unrealistic cultural ideals make liposuction, cosmetic surgery, and other procedures appealing.

_____

Attractiveness pays off financially.

_____
_____

_____
_____
_____

Conclusion	Concluding reference to the title and to the Japanese fat-sucking soap.

Strengthening Your Vocabulary   MyWritingLab

Using the word's context, word parts, or a dictionary, write a brief definition of each of the following words as it is used in the reading.

1. penetrate (paragraph 3) _____
2. coiffed (paragraph 3) _____
3. slothful (paragraph 5) _____
4. torrid (paragraph 6) _____
5. receding (paragraph 6) _____
6. furrowed (paragraph 6) _____
7. rejuvenating (paragraph 6) _____
8. violate (paragraph 7) _____
9. potent (paragraph 11) _____

Reacting to Ideas: Discussion and Journal Writing   MyWritingLab

Get ready to write about the reading by discussing the following:

1. Discuss Western culture's ideal body types. How do these "ideal" bodies affect your own body image?
2. What is the purpose of the photograph included with the selection?
3. Would you consider cosmetic surgery or any of the other procedures described in the article? Why or why not?
4. Discuss the last paragraph of the reading. What do you think the author is revealing about his attitude toward the subject? ∎

Paragraph Options   MyWritingLab

1. Write a paragraph answering the first question posed in paragraph 1: "When you stand before a mirror, do you like what you see?"
2. Who or what shapes or influences your ideas about what you should look like? Write a paragraph explaining your answer.
3. What is your opinion of teenagers having cosmetic surgery as described in the reading? Write a paragraph explaining your answer.

Essay Options   MyWritingLab

4. Look through a popular magazine and study the ads it contains. Identify several that send the message that "our bodies aren't good enough," and choose two to write about in an essay. Describe the product being marketed and the ideal body type featured in the ad. Be sure to evaluate the effectiveness of each ad.
5. Choose a TV program to analyze. What body images are portrayed on the show? How realistic are these images? Is there evidence of cultural stereotypes on the show? Pay particular attention to the commercials that air during the show. What products are being advertised? What body images are featured in the commercials? Write an essay describing your observations.

∎ ∎ ∎ ∎

Revision Checklist

Paragraph Development

1. Is the topic manageable (neither too broad nor too narrow)?
2. Is the paragraph written with the reader in mind?
3. Does the topic sentence identify the topic?
4. Does the topic sentence make a point about the topic?
5. Does each sentence support the topic sentence?
6. Is there sufficient detail?
7. Is there a sentence at the end that brings the paragraph to a close?

Sentence Development

8. Are there any sentence fragments, run-on sentences, or comma splices?
9. Are ideas combined to produce more effective sentences?
10. Are adjectives and adverbs used to make the sentences vivid and interesting?
11. Are relative clauses and prepositional phrases like *-ing* phrases used to add detail?
12. Are pronouns used correctly and consistently? ■

SELF-TEST SUMMARY

To test yourself, cover the Answer column with a sheet of paper and answer each question in the left column. Evaluate each of your answers as you work by sliding the paper down and comparing your answer with what is printed in the Answer column.

	QUESTION	ANSWER
GOAL 1 Identify topic sentences that lack a point of view	How do you revise a topic sentence that lacks a point of view?	Revise a topic sentence that lacks a point of view by • using brainstorming, freewriting, or branching to generate ideas. • asking yourself questions about your topic sentence.
GOAL 2 Identify topic sentences that are too broad	How do you revise a topic sentence that is too broad?	Revise a topic sentence that is too broad by • narrowing your topic. • rewriting your topic sentence to focus on one aspect of your topic. • applying your topic sentence to a specific time and place. • using one of your supporting sentences as a topic sentence.

	QUESTION	ANSWER
GOAL 3 Identify topic sentences that are too narrow	How do you revise a topic sentence that is too narrow?	Revise a topic sentence that is too narrow by • broadening your topic to include a wider range of items or ideas. • broadening your topic to consider causes and effects or to make comparisons or contrasts. • brainstorming and research to develop a more general point.
GOAL 4 Identify when you have strayed off topic	How do you identify when you have strayed off topic?	Use an idea map to spot where you begin to stray off topic. Starting with the last idea in the map, compare it with your topic sentence; work backward to check whether each detail directly supports your topic sentence.
GOAL 5 Revise underdeveloped paragraphs	How do you revise an underdeveloped paragraph?	Revise an underdeveloped paragraph by • analyzing the paragraph sentence by sentence. • thinking of specific situations, facts, or examples that illustrate or support the topic. • brainstorming, freewriting, or branching to come up with additional details.
GOAL 6 Identify and eliminate irrelevant details	How do you identify and eliminate unrelated details? How can you use supporting details more effectively?	Use an idea map to identify and eliminate details that do not explain the topic sentence or one of the other details. Use details more effectively by adding explanations, transitions, and new details.
GOAL 7 Revise to ensure that details are logically arranged and developed	How do you revise a paragraph that lacks organization?	Revise a paragraph that lacks organization by • reviewing the methods of arranging details and organizing material. • looking at your topic sentence again and revising if necessary. • deciding whether additional details are needed. • adding transitions.
GOAL 8 Revise to ensure your paragraph is balanced	What is a balanced paragraph?	In a balanced paragraph, each idea receives an appropriate amount of supporting detail and emphasis. Not every point must have the same amount of explanation, but two ideas that are equally important should receive similar treatment.
GOAL 9 Identify and eliminate unnecessary repetition	How do you revise a paragraph with repetitive ideas?	Revise a paragraph with repetitive ideas by • combining ideas. • reviewing places where you make deletions. • deciding whether additional details are needed. • checking for statements that are only slightly different from one another.

MyWritingLab *Visit Ch. 15 Revising Paragraphs in MyWritingLab to test your understanding of the chapter objectives.*

16 Essay Basics and Development

Learning Goals

In this chapter, you will learn how to

GOAL 1 Structure an effective essay

GOAL 2 Select a topic and plan an essay

GOAL 3 Write an effective thesis statement

GOAL 4 Locate specific, relevant evidence to support your thesis

GOAL 5 Use transitions to clearly relate ideas

GOAL 6 Write effective titles, introductions, and conclusions

GOAL 7 Analyze essay questions and plan answers

WRITE ABOUT IT!

The photograph above shows a building under construction. Write a sentence explaining how constructing a building is similar to the task of writing.

Your sentence probably included the idea that writing is a work in progress; it is a series of steps. In this chapter you will learn how to write essays. You will learn how to structure an essay, write an effective thesis statement, support your thesis with evidence, and write effective introductions, conclusions, and titles.

WRITING

AN OVERVIEW OF THE ESSAY

If you can write a paragraph, you can write an essay. The structure is similar, and they have similar parts. A paragraph expresses one main idea, called the **topic**, and is made up of several sentences that support that idea. The main idea is expressed in a sentence called the **topic sentence**. An essay also expresses one key idea called the **thesis**. This is expressed in a sentence called the **thesis statement**. The chart below shows how the parts of the paragraph are very much like the parts of an essay.

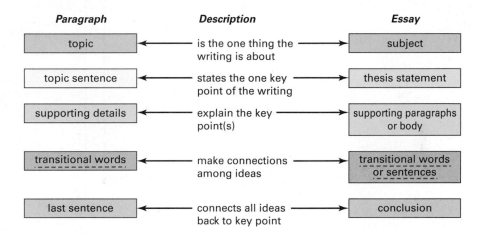

Paragraph	Description	Essay
topic	is the one thing the writing is about	subject
topic sentence	states the one key point of the writing	thesis statement
supporting details	explain the key point(s)	supporting paragraphs or body
transitional words	make connections among ideas	transitional words or sentences
last sentence	connects all ideas back to key point	conclusion

THE STRUCTURE OF AN ESSAY

GOAL 1 Structure an effective essay

Think of the organization of an essay as modeling the organization of a paragraph, with one idea being explained by supporting details. Because an essay is usually at least three paragraphs long, and often more, it needs an opening paragraph, called the **introduction**, that focuses the reader and provides necessary background information before the thesis is presented. The paragraphs that support the thesis are called the **body** of the essay. Due to length and complexity, an essay also needs a final paragraph, called the **conclusion**, to draw the ideas discussed together and bring it to an end. You can visualize the organization of an essay as shown on the following page.

PLANNING YOUR ESSAY

GOAL 2 Select a topic and plan an essay

An essay requires more time spent in planning and organization than does a single paragraph, although the process is the same. It involves selecting an appropriate topic and generating ideas. The topic for an essay should be broader than for a single paragraph. For more information on broadening or narrowing topics, see Chapter 17, pages 464–466. To generate ideas for an essay, use the techniques you learned in Chapter 11 for generating ideas for paragraphs.

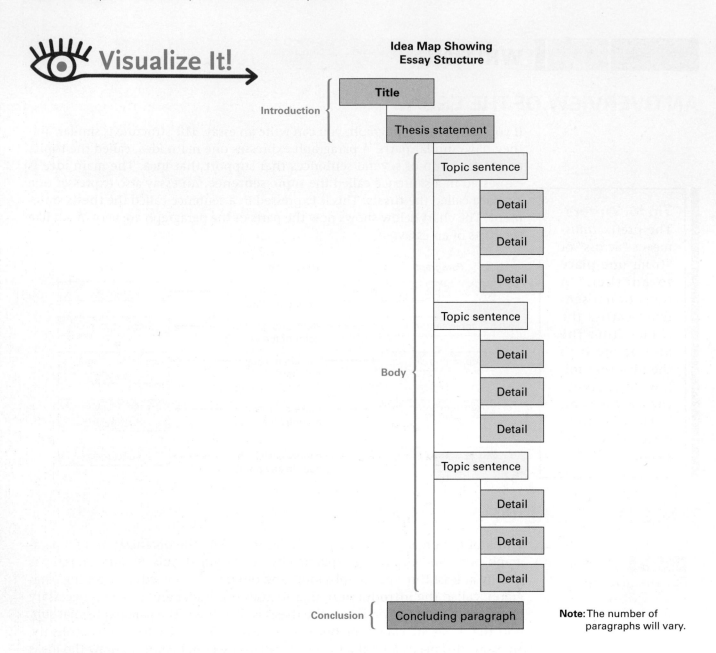

Visualize It!

Idea Map Showing Essay Structure

Introduction
- Title
- Thesis statement

Body
- Topic sentence
  - Detail
  - Detail
  - Detail
- Topic sentence
  - Detail
  - Detail
  - Detail
- Topic sentence
  - Detail
  - Detail
  - Detail

Conclusion
- Concluding paragraph

Note: The number of paragraphs will vary.

EXERCISE 16-1
Working Together

Narrowing a Topic and Generating Ideas

Directions: Choose one of the following topics, narrow it down, and generate ideas for a two-page essay. Exchange your work with a classmate and evaluate each other's work.

1. Organic or health foods
2. Natural disasters
3. Predictable or unpredictable behaviors
4. Teenage fads or fashions
5. Controlling stress
6. Valued possessions
7. An unfortunate accident or circumstance
8. A technological advance ▪

WRITING STRONG THESIS STATEMENTS

To develop a sound essay, you must begin with a well-focused thesis statement. A **thesis statement** tells your reader what your essay is about and gives clues to how the essay will unfold. The thesis statement should not only identify your topic but also express the main point about your topic that you will explain or prove in your essay.

Some students think they should be able to just sit down and write a thesis statement. But a thesis statement rarely springs fully formed into a writer's mind: it evolves and, in fact, may change significantly during the process of prewriting, grouping ideas, drafting, and revising. The next section will show you how to draft a thesis statement and how to polish it into a focused statement.

GOAL 3 Write an effective thesis statement

Grouping Your Ideas to Discover a Thesis Statement

The first step in developing a thesis statement is to generate ideas to write about. Use one of the three prewriting methods you have studied: (1) freewriting, (2) brainstorming, and (3) branching. Refer to page 272 Chapter 11, "Planning and Organizing," for a review of these strategies. Once you have ideas to work with, the next step is to group or connect your ideas to form a thesis. Let's see how one student produced a thesis following these steps.

The instructor in Catherine Lee's writing course assigned a two- to three-page essay on food choices or trends. After brainstorming a list of various food options including fast foods, oversized meals, raw foodism and organic foods, she decided to write about veganism. She then did a second brainstorming about the benefits and drawbacks of veganism. She came up with the following list:

Animal rights

Friends don't understand

Carbon footprint

Stereotype of undernourishment

Problems with travel

Growing vegan community

Companies producing vegan food

Self-satisfaction

Questioning by friends and family

Limited menu options in restaurants

Some people unable to give up meat/dairy

Health benefits

Cravings for goodies

Food lists

Avoid cholesterol and fats

Lee's next step in writing her essay was to select usable ideas and try to group or organize them logically. In the brainstorming list above, Lee saw two main groups of ideas: benefits for choosing veganism and obstacles of a vegan lifestyle.

Benefits: improve one's health, reduce unhealthy food consumption, environmental impact, animal rights, self-satisfaction

Obstacles: lack of understanding, questioning, limited food choices, travel issues

Once Lee had grouped her ideas together into these categories, she wrote a tentative thesis statement:

> Veganism offers numerous benefits, including good health, a chance to make positive change through promoting environmental health and animal rights, and endless self-assurance; a vegan will run into some difficulties along the way, but in the end the personal benefits and supportive vegan community offer an enjoyable lifestyle.

This thesis statement identifies her topic—veganism—and suggests that she will present both benefits and obstacles. You can see how this thesis statement grew out of her idea groupings. Furthermore, this thesis statement gives her readers clues as to how she will organize the essay. A reader knows from this preview which benefits and obstacles she will discuss and in what order.

How to Group Ideas

How do you know which ideas to group? Look for connections and relationships among ideas that you generate during prewriting. Here are some suggestions:

1. **Look for categories.** Try to discover how you can classify and subdivide your ideas. Think of categories as titles or slots in which you can place ideas. Look for a general term that is broad enough to cover several of your ideas. For example, Lee broke down the many aspects of veganism into benefits and obstacles. Suppose you were writing a paper on favoritism. You could break down the topic by a category, such as place.

   SAMPLE THESIS STATEMENT   Whether it's practiced in the workplace, in a classroom, or on Capitol Hill, favoritism is unfair.

2. **Try organizing your ideas chronologically.** Group your ideas according to the clock or calendar.

   SAMPLE THESIS STATEMENT   From the ancient Mayans to King Henry VIII's court to present-day Congress, personal relationships have always played a role in professional achievement.

3. **Look for similarities and differences.** When working with two or more topics, see if you can approach them by looking at how similar or different they are.

   SAMPLE THESIS STATEMENT   The two great pioneers of psychotherapy, Freud and Jung, agreed on the concept of the libido but completely disagreed on other issues.

4. **Separate your ideas into causes and effects or problems and solutions.** You can often analyze events and issues in this way.

   SAMPLE THESIS STATEMENT   The phrase "it takes a village to raise a child" means that birth parents alone do not determine what an individual will grow up to be.

5. **Divide your ideas into advantages and disadvantages, or pros and cons.** When you are evaluating a proposal, product, or service, this approach may work.

> **SAMPLE THESIS STATEMENT**   Deciding on a major before starting college can either help a student stay focused and on track or keep him or her from discovering new interests.

6. **Consider several different ways to approach your topic or organize and develop your ideas.** As you consider what your thesis statement is going to be, push yourself to see your topic from a number of different angles or from a fresh perspective.

For example, Lee could have examined her brainstorming list and decided to focus only on restaurant menu options for vegans, describing in detail how to locate acceptable items, question servers, and build one's own meal from available choices. In other words, within every topic lie many possible thesis statements.

Guidelines for Writing Thesis Statements

A thesis statement should explain what your essay is about, and it should also give your readers clues to its organization. Think of your thesis statement as a promise; it promises your reader what your paper will deliver. Here are some guidelines to follow for writing an effective thesis statement:

1. **It should state the main point of your essay.** It should not focus on details; it should give an overview of your approach to your topic.

> **TOO DETAILED**   Because babies don't know anything about the world around them, parents should allow them to touch toys and other objects.
>
> **REVISED**   Because babies don't know anything about the world around them when they are born, they need to spend lots of time touching, holding, and exploring the everyday things we take for granted.

2. **It should assert an idea about your topic.** Your thesis should express a viewpoint or state an approach to the topic.

> **LACKS AN ASSERTION**   Advertisers promote beer during football games.
>
> **REVISED**   One of the reasons you see so many beer ads during ball games is that men buy more beer than women.

3. **It should be as specific and detailed as possible.** For this reason, it is important to review and rework your thesis *after* you have written and revised drafts.

> **TOO GENERAL**   You need to take a lot of clothes with you when you go camping.
>
> **REVISED**   Because the weather can change so quickly in the Adirondacks, it is important to pack clothing that will protect you from both sun and rain.

4. **It may suggest the organization of your essay.** Mentioning key points that will be discussed in the essay is one way to do this. The order in which you mention them should be the same as the order in which you discuss them in your essay.

DOES NOT SUGGEST ORGANIZATION	Learning to read is important for your whole life.
REVISED	Literacy is a necessary tool for academic, professional, and personal success.

5. **It should not be a direct announcement.** Do not begin with phrases such as "In this paper I will . . ." or "My assignment was to discuss . . ."

DIRECT ANNOUNCEMENT	What I am going to write about is how working out can make you better at your job.
REVISED	Exercise can dramatically improve the performance of everyone, from front office to assembly-line workers.

6. **It should offer a fresh, interesting, and original perspective on the topic.** A thesis statement can follow the guidelines discussed above, but, if it seems dull or predictable, it needs more work.

PREDICTABLE	Complex carbohydrates are good for you.
REVISED	Diets that call for cutting out carbohydrates completely are overlooking the tremendous health benefits of whole grains.

EXERCISE 16-2   Writing a Thesis Statement
Writing in Progress

Directions: Using the topic you chose and the ideas you generated about it in Exercise 16-1, develop a thesis statement. ■

SUPPORTING YOUR THESIS WITH SUBSTANTIAL EVIDENCE

GOAL 4 Locate specific, relevant evidence to support your thesis

Every essay you write should offer substantial evidence in support of your thesis statement. This evidence makes up the body of your essay. **Evidence** can consist of personal experience, anecdotes (stories that illustrate a point), examples, reasons, descriptions, facts, statistics, and quotations (taken from sources).

Many students have trouble locating concrete, specific evidence to support their theses. Though prewriting yields plenty of good ideas and helps you focus your thesis, prewriting ideas may not always provide sufficient evidence. Often you need to brainstorm again for additional ideas. At other times, you may need to consult one or more sources to obtain further information on your topic.

The table on the next page lists ways to support a thesis statement and gives an example of how Lee could use each one in her essay on the benefits and drawbacks of veganism.

TABLE 16-1   WAYS TO ADD EVIDENCE

Topic: Veganism

Support Your Thesis By	Example
Telling a story (narration)	Relate a story of someone who decided to become a vegan
Adding descriptive detail (description)	Describe options on a vegan restaurant menu
Giving an example	Give examples of questions that friends ask
Giving a definition	Define the term "carbon footprint"
Making comparisons	Compare two companies that produce vegan food
Making distinctions (contrast)	Show the difference between veganism and vegetarianism
Discussing types or kinds (classification)	Classify types of foods vegans consume (protein, vegetables, grains)
Explaining how something works (process)	Explain how to find acceptable foods on a restaurant menu
Giving reasons (causes)	Explain why dairy is not consumed
Analyzing effects	Explain how practicing veganism reduces one's carbon footprint

The table offers a variety of ways Lee could add evidence to her essay, but she would not need to use all of them. Instead, she should choose the one that is the most appropriate for her audience and purpose. Lee could also use different types of evidence in combination. For example, she could *describe* a vegan meal and *contrast* it to a vegetarian meal.

Use the following guidelines in selecting evidence to support your thesis:

1. **Be sure your evidence is relevant.** hat is, it must directly support or explain your thesis.

2. **Make your evidence as specific as possible.** Help your readers see the point you are making by offering detailed, concrete information. For example, if you are explaining the dangers of driving while intoxicated, include details that make that danger seem immediate: victims' names and injuries, types of vehicle damage, statistics on the loss of life, and so on.

3. **Be sure your information is accurate.** It may be necessary to check facts, verify stories you have heard, and ask questions of individuals who may have provided information.

4. **Locate sources that provide evidence.** Because you may not know enough about your topic and lack personal experience, you may be unable to provide strong evidence. When this happens, locate several sources on your topic.

5. **Be sure to document any information that you borrow from other sources.** See Chapter 12, page 297, "Avoiding Plagiarism and Citing Sources" for more information.

EXERCISE 16-3   Writing a First Draft

Writing in Progress

Directions: Write a first draft of an essay for the thesis statement you wrote in Exercise 16-2. Support your thesis statement with at least three types of evidence. ■

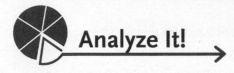

Analyze It!

Directions: On the left is the brainstorming one student did on the topic of space exploration. Study the brainstorming and use the key on the right to identify and group the ideas into three sets of related ideas that could be used in an essay. Choose one of the topics, create a topic sentence, and list the ideas you would use in the order in which you would use them.

Space Exploration

what if Columbus and other explorers hadn't taken the risk to explore new worlds?

space travel inspires younger generation

space travel a luxury when poverty, famine, and war on Earth

recent Gallup poll shows 71% of Americans support the space program

why not just use robots—why risk human lives?

achievements of Hubble telescope, International Space Station, humans on moon

national trauma from shuttle disasters

space shuttle Challenger and Columbia deaths

basic scientific research often leads to unexpected practical applications

exploring space could involve discoveries that solve energy crisis and other problems

natural resources on other planets

NASA-developed technologies (led to laptop computers, solar power cells)

no matter how advanced the technology, human error will always cause problems

satellite enabled telephone and TV communications, global navigation, weather forecast

adverse health effects of weightlessness (bone loss, muscle damage, loss of red blood cells)

is it worth it to go to the moon?

travel to other planets takes too long

astronauts vulnerable to cosmic radiation

V = value of space program
R = risks of space program
D = disadvantages of space program

A STUDENT ESSAY

The Writing Task

As you read Catherine Lee's essay below, consider how she developed her essay on veganism. While reading, notice in particular the types of reasons she uses, the obstacles she presents, and how her thesis statement promises what her essay delivers.

A Lifestyle of Commitment:
The perks and obstacles of veganism
Catherine Lee

1   Though most people in the world are meat-eaters, the majority of these people know about vegetarianism: a way of life centered on eliminating meat from one's diet. However, not nearly as many people have heard of veganism, and even fewer would be able to give its definition. Veganism is a new concept compared to vegetarianism, and it describes an extension of the vegetarian abstinence from meat into an abstinence from all animal products. Such animal products include dairy, eggs, any food products that have traces of dairy as ingredients, and, for the strictest vegans, honey, candies made with gelatin, and some kinds of sugar. Clearly, going vegan is a big commitment that requires willpower, dedication, and attention to detail. **A vegan lifestyle offers good health, a chance to make positive change through promoting environmental health and animal rights, and endless self-assurance; a vegan will run into some difficulties along the way, including questions from curious peers and restrictive menu options when eating out and travelling, but in the end the personal benefits and supportive vegan community offer an enjoyable lifestyle that is difficult to refuse.**

Thesis statement

Topic sentence

Explanation of how veganism improves one's health

2   The widely adopted reason for going vegan is to improve one's health. Being vegan cuts out intake of cholesterol and fat from meat and dairy products and increases reliance on the three foundations of the food pyramid: vegetables, fruits, and grains. There is a common stereotype that vegans are undernourished, and some people will claim that they tried going vegan but felt weak. It is likely that these people did not adopt a proper, balanced vegan diet. Going vegan is an adjustment for a body that has depended on meat and dairy since birth, but extensive research and informed choices will ease this transition. There are several ways to replace the nutrients from meat and dairy. Many people worry that they may not get enough protein, but the truth is that green vegetables, hearty grains, beans, and soy products add more than enough protein to a daily diet. Admittedly, being vegan does not cut all goodies out of the equation: there is an abundant selection of vegan chocolates, cookies, and pastries to enjoy. Regardless of whether or not one indulges in these goodies, a vegan diet will undoubtedly make anyone more aware of her diet and daily food choices.

Topic sentence

Details about how veganism contributes to positive changes in the world

3   Not only is veganism a great way to improve health, but it also contributes to making positive change in the world. As much as veganism may be a health fad, there are also environmental and animal-rights-based reasons to stop eating meat and dairy. As well-known filmmakers and authors like Michael Moore and Michael Pollan have demonstrated, animals are treated horrifically on many meat and dairy production farms. They are often boosted with hormones, stuck in cages with no room to move, force-fed, separated from their parents or offspring, and brutally slaughtered. Eliminating meat and dairy from one's diet also helps the environment. A tremendous amount of energy is used and pollution created in the manufacture of meat products. Being vegan drastically reduces one's carbon footprint.

Topic sentence

Details about emotional benefits of going vegan

4   To be frank, going vegan will make any person feel great about herself. When people learn about a friend's veganism, they usually gush about how much they admire that person for her bravery and good health. They may even take on an apologetic tone and tell the vegan about how they tried going vegan for one week but could not kick their love for cheese. Furthermore, explaining one's reasons for being vegan is a positive reinforcement of one's good morals and health, environmental consciousness, and social responsibility. As a vegan, one also has the opportunity to inspire others to follow the same path.

Topic sentence

Explanation of obstacle #1: questions from curious friends

5   Despite these perks, there are some obstacles that a vegan must navigate. Firstly, every vegan must be ready to answer a lot of questions. A vegan must be educated about her veganism and well-versed in what she can and cannot eat. People will incessantly ask a vegan to explain her reasons for being vegan and come up with extensive lists of food items to ask which items are permitted. Common points of confusion are: eggs (they are not meat or dairy, so why can't vegans eat them?), honey (some vegans refuse to eat honey, and some are more lenient about it), bread, and pasta. Some people may even be argumentative about veganism, especially if they are avid meat-lovers. A vegan must be prepared to defend her choice, and to put up with any jokes aimed at her by her meat- and dairy-loving friends.

Topic sentence

Details about obstacle #2: eating out

6   A vegan must also be prepared to face restrictive food options when eating out. Unless she has carefully picked a group of all vegetarian and vegan friends, the chances are that a vegan's friends will not always want to go out to vegan restaurants or cook vegan meals. So, a vegan must be prepared to be accommodating, especially at Italian and American restaurants whose dishes are predominantly meaty or slathered in dairy products. Eventually, a vegan will develop a keen eye for picking out the only salad without cheese or identifying a combination of veggie-friendly side dishes that will constitute a meal. A vegan must always remember to ask the waiter if there are any animal products in a dish before ordering.

Topic sentence

Details about obstacle #3: travelling

7   This dining flexibility must also apply when travelling, especially when visiting a foreign country. A vegan should, if possible, scope out vegetarian and vegan-friendly grocery stores and restaurants online ahead of time, and always pay attention to the customer reviews. When travelling, CLIF bars are a vegan's best friend. A vegan should always bring at least one CLIF or other

nutrition bar for every day of travel. These bars will supplement any measly salads or insufficient snacks that a vegan might resort to while travelling.

Conclusion: Lee recaps the benefits and challenges of going vegan and encourages the reader to give it a try.

8   This may all sound like a bit of a hassle, and one might wonder, "do I really want to go through the trouble of changing my entire diet, having to explain myself to those around me, and constantly worrying about whether the food outside my home is okay to eat?" The answer to this question is "Yes." Though peers will ask questions, ordering at non-vegan restaurants might be difficult, and travelling may necessitate nutrition bars as a dietary supplement, the benefits of good health, environmental and social consciousness, and self-assurance far outweigh these difficulties. Beyond these personal benefits, one will find a vegan community that enthusiastically supports this lifestyle. In the past ten years or so, veganism has skyrocketed and the vegan community seems to be growing exponentially. In nearly every city in the United States, there is at least one vegan restaurant, and in every major city in the US there is a plethora of vegan restaurants, cafes, bakeries, groceries, and even retail stores. Companies such as Tofurkey, Field Roast, and Silk make imitation meats and dairy products that can make even the meatiest meat-lover's mouth melt. Vegans are always excited to meet other vegans, share restaurant recommendations, discuss great recipes, and even give general lifestyle advice. So, to any reader curious about exploring the vegan side of life: Give it a try! If nothing else, it will be a good experience.

EXAMINING STUDENT WRITING

1. How effectively is Lee's thesis statement expressed?
2. Evaluate Lee's support for her thesis. Is it relevant, specific, and detailed? What other types of evidence might she have used to strengthen her essay?
3. Evaluate the essay's title. Is it interesting and engaging? Suggest other titles that might be effective.
4. What plan of organization has Lee used? Is the essay logically organized? How could the organization be improved?

MAKING CONNECTIONS AMONG YOUR IDEAS CLEAR

GOAL 5 Use transitions to clearly relate ideas

To produce a well-written essay, be sure to make it clear how your ideas relate to one another. There are several ways to do this:

1. **Use transitional words and phrases.** The transitional words and phrases that you learned in Chapter 14 for connecting ideas are helpful for making your essay flow smoothly and communicate clearly. Table 16-2 on the next page lists useful transitions for each method of organization. Notice the use of these transitional words and phrases in Lee's essay: *however, firstly, also.*

2. **Write a transitional sentence.** This sentence is usually the first sentence in the paragraph. It might come before the topic sentence or it might *be* the topic sentence. Its purpose is to link the paragraph in which it appears with the paragraph before it. Sometimes it comes at the end of the paragraph and links the paragraph to the following one.

TABLE 16-2 USEFUL TRANSITIONAL WORDS AND PHRASES

Method of Development	Transitional Words and Phrases
Least/Most or Most/Least	most important, above all, especially, particularly important, less important
Spatial	above, below, behind, beside, next to, inside, outside, to the west (north, etc.), beneath, near, nearby, next to
Time Sequence	first, next, now, before, during, after, eventually, finally, at last, later, meanwhile, soon, then, suddenly, currently, after, afterward, after a while, as soon as, until
Narration/Process	first, second, then, later, in the beginning, when, after, following, next, during, again, after that, at last, finally
Description	see Spatial and Least/Most or Most/Least above
Example	for example, for instance, to illustrate, in one case
Definition	means, can be defined as, refers to, is
Classification	one, another, second, third
Comparison	likewise, similarly, in the same way, too, also
Contrast	however, on the contrary, unlike, on the other hand, although, even though, but, in contrast, yet
Cause and Effect	because, consequently, since, as a result, for this reason, therefore, thus

3. **Repeat key words.** Repeating key words from either the thesis statement or the preceding paragraph helps your reader see connections among ideas. In Lee's essay, notice the repetition of key words and phrases such as *diet* and *health*.

EXERCISE 16-4 Analyzing Your Draft
Writing in Progress

Directions: Review the draft you wrote for Exercise 16-3. Analyze how effectively you have connected your ideas. Add key words or transitional words, phrases, or sentences, as needed. ■

WRITING THE INTRODUCTION, CONCLUSION, AND TITLE

GOAL 6 Write effective titles, introductions, and conclusions

The introduction, conclusion, and title each serve a specific function. Each one strengthens your essay and helps your reader better understand your ideas.

Writing the Introduction

An introductory paragraph has three main purposes.

1. **It presents your thesis statement.**
2. **It interests your reader in your topic.**
3. **It provides any necessary background information.**

Although your introductory paragraph appears first in your essay, it does *not* need to be written first. In fact, it is sometimes best to write it last, after you have developed your ideas, written your thesis statement, and drafted your essay.

We have already discussed writing thesis statements earlier in the chapter (see p. 441). Here are some suggestions on how to interest your reader in your topic:

TABLE 16-3 WAYS TO INTEREST YOUR READER	
Technique	**Example**
Ask a provocative or controversial question	How would you feel if the job you had counted on suddenly fell through?
State a startling fact or statistic	Last year, the U.S. government spent a whopping billion dollars a day on interest on the national debt.
Begin with a story or an anecdote	The day Liam Blake left his parka on the bus was the first day of what would become the worst snowstorm the city had ever seen.
Use a quotation	Robert Frost wrote "Two roads diverged in a wood, and I—/I took the one less traveled by,/And that has made all the difference."
State a little-known fact, a myth, or a misconception	What was Harry S. Truman's middle name? Stephen? Samuel? Simpson? Actually, it's just plain "S." There was a family dispute over whether to name him for his paternal or maternal grandfather, an argument that was settled by simply using the common initial "S."

A straightforward, dramatic thesis statement can also capture your reader's interest, as in the following example:

> The first day I walked into Mr. Albierto's advanced calculus class, I knew I had made a huge mistake.

An introduction should also provide the reader with any necessary background information. Consider what information your reader needs to understand your essay. You may, for example, need to define the term *genetic engineering* for a paper on that topic. At other times, you might need to provide a brief history or give an overview of a controversial issue.

Now reread the introduction to Lee's essay on page 447. How does she introduce her topic?

EXERCISE 16-5   Revising Your Introduction

Writing in Progress

Directions: Revise the introduction to the essay you wrote for Exercise 16-3. ∎

Writing the Conclusion

The final paragraph of your essay has two functions: It should reemphasize your thesis statement and draw the essay to a close. It should not be a direct announcement, such as "This essay has been about . . ." or "In this paper I hoped to show that . . ."

It's usually best to revise your essay at least once *before* working on the conclusion. During your first or second revision, you often make numerous changes in both content and organization, which may, in turn, affect your conclusion.

Here are a few effective ways to write a conclusion. Choose one that will work for your essay.

1. **Look ahead.** Project into the future and consider outcomes or effects.

2. **Return to your thesis.** If your essay is written to prove a point or convince your reader of the need for action, it may be effective to end with a sentence that recalls your main point or calls for action. If you choose this way to conclude, be sure not to merely repeat your first paragraph. Be sure to reflect on the thoughts you developed in the body of your essay.

3. **Summarize key points.** Especially for longer essays, briefly review your key supporting ideas. Notice how Lee's concluding paragraph touches upon her two main points: the benefits and challenges of veganism.

If you have trouble writing your conclusion, it's probably a tip-off that you need to work further on your thesis or organization.

EXERCISE 16-6   Revising Your Conclusion
Writing in Progress

Directions: Write or revise a conclusion for the essay you wrote for Exercise 16-3. ■

Selecting a Title

Although the title appears first in your essay, it is often the last thing you should write. The title should identify the topic in an interesting way, and it may also suggest the focus. To select a title, reread your final draft, paying particular attention to your thesis statement and your overall method of development. Here are a few examples of effective titles:

"Which Way Is Up?" (for an essay on mountain climbing)

"A Hare Raising Tale" (for an essay on taking care of rabbits)

"Topping Your Bottom Line" (for an essay on how to increase profitability)

To write accurate and interesting titles, try the following tips:

1. **Write a question that your essay answers.** For example: "What Are the Signs That It's Safe to Approach a Strange Dog?"

2. **Use key words that appear in your thesis statement.** If your thesis statement is "Diets rich in lean beef can help teenagers maintain higher levels of useable iron," your title could be "Lean Beef Is Good for Teens."

3. **Use brainstorming techniques to generate options.** Don't necessarily go with the first title that pops into your mind. If in doubt, try out some options on friends to see which is most effective.

| **EXERCISE 16-7** | **Choosing a Title** |

Writing in Progress

Directions: Come up with a good title for the essay you wrote for Exercise 16-3. ■

WRITING ESSAY-EXAM ANSWERS

GOAL 7 Analyze essay questions and plan answers

You can master the art of writing good essay-exam answers. The following suggestions and strategies will help:

1. **Read the directions carefully.** They may, for example, tell you to answer only two out of four questions.

2. **Plan your time.** For example, if you have to answer two essay questions in a 50-minute class session, give yourself 20 to 25 minutes for each one.

3. **Answer the easiest question first.** Doing so may take you less time than you budgeted, and consequently, you can spend additional time on harder questions.

4. **Analyze each question.** Look for words that tell you what to write about and how to organize your answer. If an exam question says, "Trace the history of advertising in the United States," the word *trace* tells you to organize your essay using a time-sequence arrangement. The question also identifies and focuses the topic—the history of advertising.

5. **Plan your answer.** On the back of the exam or on a separate sheet of paper that you will not turn in, jot down ideas you will include in your essay. Arrange your ideas to follow the method of development suggested in the question.

6. **Write your thesis statement.** A thesis statement is like a topic sentence. It announces what your essay will be about. Thesis statements in essay-exam answers should be simple and straightforward. Start by rewording the question.

SAMPLE ESSAY QUESTION	SAMPLE THESIS STATEMENT
Describe the psychological factors that may affect a person's decision to change jobs.	There are five psychological factors that may affect a person's decision to change jobs.
Define and give an example of age discrimination.	Age discrimination takes place whenever people are mistreated or unfairly judged simply because of how old they are.

7. **Present adequate supporting details.** Write a separate paragraph for each major supporting detail. Begin each paragraph with a topic sentence that introduces each new point. Each paragraph should provide relevant and sufficient support for the topic sentence.

8. **Proofread your answer.** Be sure to leave enough time to proofread your answer. Check for errors in spelling, punctuation, and grammar.

9. **If you run out of time . . .** If you run out of time before you have finished answering the last question, don't panic. Take the last minute or two to make a list or outline of the other points you planned to cover. Some instructors will give you partial credit for this outline.

Essay Writing Scenarios

Friends and Family

1. Describe a family item you would save in the event of a natural disaster. Whose was it, and why is it special to you?
2. Write an essay that begins "The best vacation my family ever took together was . . ."

Classes and Campus Life

1. Mark Twain wrote, "The person who *does* not read good books has no advantage over the person who *can't* read them." Write a short essay explaining what you think he meant.
2. Where do you do your best work, in class discussions or alone on a computer? Why?

Working Students

1. Explain which you'd prefer, a job in which you deal with people or with things.
2. Describe something you do in your daily life that you would never do at work.

Communities and Cultures

1. Community leaders can be elected officials or ordinary citizens. Write an essay about one person who makes (or has made) a difference in your community.
2. Describe one thing you did as a teenager to fit in with a particular group.

WRITING ABOUT A READING

In this article from *The Atlantic*, the author explores what happens to us physically and mentally when we choose not to tell the truth.

Step 1: Preview the reading.

Step 2: Connect the reading to your own experience: How important is honesty to you? In what situations is lying acceptable?

Step 3: Read and respond to the questions in the margin.

THINK AS YOU READ

Based on your preview, predict the author's answer to the question posed in the article's title.

What does this subtitle tell you about the content and organization of the reading? Does it suggest the thesis? Highlight the thesis when you encounter it.

The author asks questions. Predict how he will answer them.

What is the difference between liars and bullshitters?

Why is this example included?

IS LYING BAD FOR US?

Richard Gunderman, MD, PhD

There are mental and physical consequences, but we should strive to live more truthfully, regardless, to best understand reality.

1   It has been estimated that the average American tells 11 lies per week. Is this bad for us? Suppose we knew that a lie would never be detected, nor would we be punished. Suppose we had some means of ensuring that the lie would never cause us any physical or psychological harm through loss of sleep or the like. Suppose even that telling the lie would actually redound to our benefit, at least in the sense that it would secure us the pleasure, status, wealth, or power that those fudging the truth commonly seek. Under these circumstances, would it still make sense to tell the truth? Or would lying become the prudent course of action?

2   In his 2005 runaway philosophy best seller, *On Bullshit*, Princeton University's Harry Frankfurt distinguishes between lying and what he called "bullshit." Though liars do not tell the truth, they care about it, while the bullshitter does not even care about the truth and seeks merely to impress. Liars tell deliberate untruths, while bullshitters merely do not admit when they do not know something. This is a particularly pervasive form of untruth in my own orbits, medicine and academia, where people wish others to believe that we know more than we do. So instead of saying, "I don't know," we make things up, merely giving the appearance of knowledge while actually saying nothing.

3   We live in a culture where it is increasingly common to encourage lying, and even to suppose that there is nothing problematic about doing so. In his new book, *Heads in Beds*, former hospitality industry employee Jacob Tomsky encourages hotel guests to bend the truth to their own advantage. For example, he states that guests need never pay for in-room movies. Here is how: "Watch and enjoy any movie. Call down and say you accidentally clicked on it. Or it froze near the end. Or it never even started. If the desk attendant offers to restart the movie, say you are about to go to bed or leave, and ask them instead just to remove the charges." Voila!

4   This bit of advice has been presented under the rubric, "Things every guest must know." It is only one of many points at which Tomsky shows guests how, by saying things that are not true, it is possible to avoid all manner

of hotel charges. Ever pay for using items in a minibar? "These are the most often disputed charges on any hotel bill." After enjoying your snack or beverage, just say, "I never used these items." Worried about a same-day cancellation penalty? Call the property and tell the front desk you've had a personal emergency and won't arrive till next week. They will change the reservation. Then call back later and cancel next week's reservation at no penalty.

What other implicit messages does this advice suggest?

5   The implicit message? Honesty is for the unsophisticated.

6   One recent study laid the groundwork of a case for honesty by suggesting that liars are less healthy. Researchers at the University of Notre Dame followed 110 people over a period of ten weeks. Half of the participants were asked to stop lying over this period of time, and the other half were not. Both groups took weekly polygraph tests to determine how many times they had lied in the previous week. Those who were able to reduce by three the number of lies they told had four fewer mental health complaints (such as feeling tense) and three fewer physical health complaints (such as headaches) than those who did not.

7   Why might this be? A number of explanations might be invoked. One would be that it takes more work to lie, because liars need to think through everything they say to a much greater degree in order to avoid detection. Another might be that it is more stressful to lie. This is likely to be particularly true when lies are exposed, resulting in shame, embarrassment, and other unpleasantries. But even if the lying is never detected, the piling up of lies tends to make relationships with colleagues, friends, and family members shallower and less meaningful. And it could be that living with the guilt of lying is toxic in itself, especially in extreme cases where we are "living a lie." Could we lower our blood pressure, narrow our waistline, reduce our dependence on antidepressants, and perhaps even prolong our lives merely by exaggerating less about our accomplishments and making up fewer excuses when we are late or fail to complete tasks? Suppose the answer to this question is yes. Suppose that those who reduce their weekly lies by one-half lose on average ten pounds, report feeling more confident and content, and end up living on average an additional three years, compared to those who continue lying at the same rate. Would this reduce the level of mendacity in America?

Summarize the reasons that explain why lying is not healthy.

8   I suspect the answer is a resounding yes. Many of us would tell fewer lies if we thought doing so would make us healthier. Of course, it would not be good news for some sectors of the health care industry, which have a vested interest in collecting revenue from efforts to improve health. What if the sales of antidepressants, the number psychologist and psychiatrist office visits, and the number of heart surgeries all declined? On the other hand, perhaps pharmaceuticals could be developed that would reduce the impulse to tell falsehoods, and mental health professionals and hospitals could offer tuition-generating courses on how to stop lying.

For whom is lying beneficial?

9   Whether the health care industry can monetize honesty or not, however, a more fundamental problem remains. Do we want to live in families, communities, or societies where truth telling needs to be incentivized? Do we want our spouses and children, our friends and neighbors, and our colleagues and

associates to be asking themselves on a regular basis, "Really, why shouldn't I lie?" Surely most of us wish to live in a community where people can be relied on to tell the truth, regardless its effects on waistlines, pocketbooks, social standing, career prospects, and even our general level of happiness. Isn't there something inherently wrong with lying?

Explain the meaning of "bad faith." What are its effects?

10   Perhaps the most powerful moral argument for honesty has to do with what the French philosopher Jean-Paul Sartre called "bad faith." Liars deceive others, but in a sense, liars also deceive themselves. When we lie we tend to distort our own view of reality, and the more often we lie, the more habitual this distortion becomes. Over time, the habit of lying divorces us further and further from reality, so we see less and less clearly the choices before us and what is at stake in them. Eventually, we may find ourselves unable to see what we are really doing and how it is affecting others and ourselves. We end up leading inauthentic and irresponsible lives.

Why is this photograph included? What does it add to the author's message?

Express the author's conclusion in your own words. Has the author provided enough evidence to support this conclusion?

11   To tell the truth is to live authentically and responsibly, to really live. At times we may make honest mistakes, misperceiving what is really happening, failing to see things in appropriate context, or even operating unknowingly on deliberate untruths. Whenever possible, however, we should be honest with others and ourselves. When we are honest, we ground ourselves most completely in the world we actually inhabit, being as real as we can with others, and reducing as much as possible the distance between the way things seem to be and the way they really are. In the final analysis, honesty means avoiding illusion and unreality, instead keeping life as real as we possibly can.

WRITING IN RESPONSE TO READING

Examining the Reading Using an Idea Map   MyWritingLab

Review the reading by completing the missing parts of the idea map shown below.

 Visualize It! →

Title   **Is Lying Bad for Us?**

Thesis   Lying has _____ and _____ consequences.

Harry Frankfurt distinguishes between _____ and _____.

Liars care about the truth and tell deliberate untruths.

Bullshitters _____, seek only to _____, and _____

It is increasingly common in our culture to _____.

Jacob Tomsky encourages hotel guests to _____ _____.

Liars may be less _____.

Study participants who told fewer lies had _____.

Explanations include:

_____

_____

_____

_____ may be toxic.

Most powerful moral argument for honesty has to do with _____.

Lying distorts our _____.

_____

To tell the truth means to live _____.

Conclusion   _____

Strengthening Your Vocabulary   `MyWritingLab`

Using the word's context, word parts, or a dictionary, write a brief definition of each of the following words as it is used in the reading.

1. redound (paragraph 1) _____

2. prudent (paragraph 1) _____

3. pervasive (paragraph 2) _____

4. rubric (paragraph 4) _____

5. mendacity (paragraph 7) _____

6. monetize (paragraph 9) _____

7. incentivized (paragraph 9) _____

Reacting to Ideas: Discussion and Journal Writing   `MyWritingLab`

Get ready to write about the reading by discussing the following:

1. What was the author's purpose in writing this article?

2. Evaluate the kinds of supporting evidence the author uses in this article. In your opinion, which types of evidence—opinions, statistics, facts, examples—were most persuasive?

3. Do you agree that in our culture it is increasingly common to encourage lying? In what ways does our culture support the idea that honesty is for the unsophisticated?

4. What do you consider to be the most important or fundamental reason(s) to be truthful?

5. What details do you notice about the photograph that correspond to the reading?

Paragraph Options   `MyWritingLab`

1. Is it ever OK to lie? In what situations do you think lying is preferable to telling the truth? Write a paragraph explaining your answers.

2. Have you ever experienced "toxic" effects, either physical or emotional, from telling a lie? Write a paragraph describing the lie and its effects.

3. Can you think of an example from your own life that illustrates the difference between lying and "bullshit," as described in paragraph 2? Write a paragraph telling about it.

Essay Options   `MyWritingLab`

4. What can you tell from this reading about the author's attitude toward lying and truthfulness? Write an essay examining the ways the author reveals his attitude.

5. Write an essay answering the author's question in paragraph 9: "Isn't there something inherently wrong with lying?"

6. The author concludes that honesty is essential to living an authentic life. Write an essay explaining whether you agree or disagree with the author's conclusion.

■ ■ ■ ■

Revision Checklist

Paragraph Development

1. Is the topic manageable (neither too broad nor too narrow)?
2. Is the paragraph written with the reader in mind?
3. Does the topic sentence identify the topic?
4. Does the topic sentence make a point about the topic?
5. Does each sentence support the topic sentence?
6. Is there sufficient detail?
7. Is there a sentence at the end that brings the paragraph to a close?

Sentence Development

8. Are there any sentence fragments, run-on sentences, or comma splices?
9. Are ideas combined to produce more effective sentences?
10. Are adjectives and adverbs used to make the sentences vivid and interesting?
11. Are relative clauses and prepositional phrases like -*ing* phrases used to add detail?
12. Are pronouns used correctly and consistently?

Essay Development

13. Does the essay accomplish its purpose?
14. Is the essay appropriate for the audience?
15. Is the thesis statement clearly expressed?
16. Does each paragraph support the thesis?
17. Is the essay logically organized?
18. Are transitions used to connect your ideas?
19. Are the introduction, conclusion, and title effective?

SELF-TEST SUMMARY

To test yourself, cover the Answer column with a sheet of paper and answer each question in the left column. Evaluate each of your answers as you work by sliding the paper down and comparing your answer with what is printed in the Answer column.

	QUESTION	ANSWER
Goal 1 Structure an effective essay	How do you structure or organize an essay?	An essay needs an opening paragraph (introduction) that focuses the reader and provides background information before presenting the thesis, paragraphs that support the thesis (the body), and a final paragraph (conclusion) to draw ideas together and bring the essay to an end.
Goal 2 Select a topic and plan an essay	What is involved in selecting a topic and planning an essay?	For an essay, you must select an appropriate topic and generate ideas. The topic for an essay should be broader than for a single paragraph.
Goal 3 Write an effective thesis statement	What does a thesis statement do? What are guidelines for writing thesis statements?	A thesis statement tells your reader what your essay is about and gives clues to how the essay will unfold. A thesis statement should • state the main point of your essay. • assert an idea about your topic. • be specific and detailed. • suggest the organization of your essay. • not make a direct announcement. • offer a fresh, interesting, original perspective.
Goal 4 Locate specific, relevant evidence to support your thesis	How do you select evidence to support your thesis?	Support your thesis by • making sure your evidence directly supports or explains your thesis. • offering detailed, concrete, and accurate information. • locating sources on your topic and documenting information from those sources.
Goal 5 Use transitions to clearly relate ideas	How do you show how your ideas relate to one another?	Show how your ideas relate to one another by using transitional words and phrases, writing a transitional sentence, and repeating key words.
Goal 6 Write effective titles, introductions, and conclusions	What are the three main purposes of an introductory paragraph? How do you write an effective conclusion? How do you write an effective title?	An introductory paragraph presents your thesis statement, interests your reader in your topic, and provides necessary background information. Write a conclusion by looking ahead, returning to your thesis, or summarizing key points. Write a title by asking a question, using key words from your thesis statement, or brainstorming to generate options.

SELF-TEST SUMMARY *(continued)*

	QUESTION	ANSWER
Goal 7 Analyze essay questions and plan answers	How do you write essay-exam answers?	Strategies for writing essay-exam answers include reading the directions carefully, planning your time, answering the easiest question first, analyzing each question, planning your answer, writing a thesis statement, presenting adequate supporting details, and proofreading your answer.

MyWritingLab *Visit Ch. 16 ESSAY BASICS AND DEVELOPMENT in MyWritingLab to test your understanding of the chapter objectives.*

EDITING PRACTICE

The following paragraph lacks transitions to connect its details. Revise it by adding transitional words or phrases where useful.

Anyone who has been to a professional hockey game has a right to be disgusted. It is especially true if you have attended one in the past five years. Players are permitted to bash each other on the ice. They are allowed to get away with it. Sometimes players are encouraged to do this. Often they are encouraged by their coaches or other players. People are starting to object to paying good money to attend a game. This is especially true when most of what you get to see is a street fight. Hockey is a contact sport. It is understandable that arguments will break out among players. This causes tempers to flare. It is unfair to subject fans to a dramatic show of violence. Most of the fans have paid good money to watch the game, not the fights. The National Hockey League should fine and suspend players. They should do this each time they get into a fight. If they did this, soon the players would be playing hockey with appropriate sportsmanlike conduct instead of fighting.

17 Avoiding Common Problems in Essays

Learning Goals

In this chapter, you will learn how to

GOAL 1 Choose a topic that is not too broad

GOAL 2 Choose a topic that is not too narrow

GOAL 3 Revise your thesis statement so it clearly states your purpose

GOAL 4 Add evidence to underdeveloped essays

GOAL 5 Restructure disorganized essays and add transitions

GOAL 6 Use idea maps as revision tools

GOAL 7 Seek help from classmates, your instructors, and a writing lab

SKATING RINK OPENING POSTPONED DUE TO ICE! Please ask for details

WRITE ABOUT IT!

The skating rink sign shown above humorously demonstrates writing that is unclear and ineffective. Revise the sign to express what you think the writer probably meant. In your own writing, be sure to watch for errors and search for ways to make your sentences and paragraphs more effective. Once you know what to look for, it is also easy to spot errors and areas that need improvement in your essays. Even the best writers run into problems; it is not uncommon for writers to make several starts and numerous revisions before they are satisfied with what they have written. Sometimes they even scrap what they have written and start afresh. In this chapter you will learn how to identify and fix five key problems you may encounter in writing essays. Specifically, you will learn to identify and fix topics that are too broad or too narrow, ineffective thesis statements, underdeveloped essays, and disorganized essays. You will also learn to use revision maps to evaluate your essays.

WRITING

PROBLEM #1: THE TOPIC IS TOO BROAD

GOAL 1 Choose a topic that is not too broad

One common mistake in writing an essay is choosing a topic that is too broad. No matter how hard you work, if you begin with a topic that is too broad, you will not be able to produce a successful essay. If your topic is too broad, there will be too much information to include, and you will not be able to cover all the important points with the right amount of detail.

Suppose you are taking a sociology class and have been asked to write a two-page paper on your impression of campus life so far. If you just wrote down the title "Campus Life" and started writing, you would find that you had too much to say and probably would not know where to start. Should you write about your classes, meeting new friends, adjusting to differences between high school and college, or managing living arrangements? Here are a few more examples of topics that are too broad:

- Pollution (Choose one type and focus on causes or effects.)
- Vacations (Choose one trip and focus on one aspect of the trip, such as meeting new people.)
- Movies (Choose one movie and concentrate on one feature, such as character development, plot, or humor.)

How to Identify the Problem

Here are the symptoms of a topic that is too broad:

1. **You have too much to say.** If it seems as if you could go on and on about the topic, it is probably too broad.
2. **You feel overwhelmed.** If you feel the topic is too difficult or the task of writing about it is unmanageable, you may have too much to write about. Another possibility is that you have chosen a topic about which you do not know enough.
3. **You are not making progress.** If you feel stuck, your topic may be too broad. It also may be too narrow (see Problem #2 on page 466).
4. **You are writing general statements and not explaining them.** Having too much to cover forces you to make broad, sweeping statements that you cannot explain in sufficient depth.

How to Narrow a Broad Topic

One way to narrow a topic that is too broad is to divide it into subtopics using the topic-narrowing techniques shown in Chapter 11, page 269. Then choose one subtopic and use it to develop new ideas for your essay.

Another way to limit a broad topic is to answer questions that will limit it. Here are six questions that are useful in limiting your topic to a particular place, time, kind, or type:

1. **Who?**
2. **What?**
3. **When?**
4. **Where?**
5. **Why?**
6. **How?**

Suppose your topic is job hunting. You realize it is too broad and apply the questions below.

TOPIC: JOB HUNTING	
QUESTIONS	**EXAMPLES**
Who?	Who can help me with job hunting? (This question limits the topic to people and agencies that offer assistance.)
What?	What type of job am I seeking? (This question limits the topic to a specific occupation.)
When?	When is the best time to job hunt? (This question limits the topic to a particular time frame, such as right after graduation.)
Where?	Where is the best place to find job listings? (This question limits the topic to one source of job listings, such as the Internet.)
Why?	Why is it important to network with friends and family? (This question limits the topic to one way to search for jobs.)
How?	How should I prepare my résumé? (This question limits the topic to one aspect of job hunting.)

EXERCISE 17-1   Narrowing a Topic
Working Together

Directions: Working with a classmate, narrow three of the following topics to one aspect that is manageable in a two-page essay.

1. Athletics
2. Public education
3. The military
4. The change of seasons
5. Television programming
6. Crime
7. Principles to live by
8. Children's toys ■

PROBLEM #2: THE TOPIC IS TOO NARROW

GOAL 2 Choose a topic that is not too narrow

Another common mistake is to choose a topic that is too narrow. If you decide to write about the effects of the failure of Canada geese to migrate from western New York during the winter, you will probably run out of ideas, unless you are prepared to do extensive library or Internet research. Instead, broaden your topic to the migration patterns of Canada geese. Here are a few more examples of topics that are too narrow:

- The history of corn mazes in the Ohio River valley
- Shopping on eBay for designer handbags
- The attitude of a nasty receptionist at the veterinarian's office

How to Identify the Problem

Here are the symptoms of a topic that is too narrow:

1. **After a paragraph or two, you have nothing left to say.** If you run out of ideas and keep repeating yourself, your topic is probably too narrow.

2. **Your topic does not seem important.** If your topic seems insignificant, it probably is. One reason it may be insignificant is that it focuses on facts rather than ideas.

3. **You are making little or no progress.** A lack of progress may signal a lack of information.

4. **Your essay is too factual.** If you find you are focusing on small details, your topic may be too narrow.

How to Broaden a Narrow Topic

To broaden a topic that is too narrow, try to extend it to cover more situations or circumstances. If your topic is the price advantage of shopping for your chemistry textbook on the Internet, broaden it to include various other benefits of Internet shopping for textbooks. Discuss price, but also consider convenience and free shipping. Do not limit yourself to one type of textbook. Specifically, to broaden a topic that is too narrow:

1. **Think of other situations, events, or circumstances that illustrate the same idea.**

2. **Think of a larger concept that includes your topic.**

EXERCISE 17-2   Broadening a Topic

Directions: Broaden three of the following topics to ones that are manageable in a two-page essay.

1. A groom who wore sneakers to his formal wedding
2. Materials needed for _____ (a craft or hobby)
3. Your parents' attitude toward crime
4. Your local high school's dress code that prohibits short skirts
5. An annoying advertisement

6. A friend's pet peeve
7. A child's first word
8. Missing a deadline for a college psychology paper ■

PROBLEM #3: THE THESIS STATEMENT NEEDS REVISION

GOAL 3 Revise your thesis statement so it clearly states your purpose

The best time to evaluate and, if necessary, revise your thesis statement is after you have written a first draft. At that time you can see if your essay delivers what your thesis promises. If it does not, it needs revision, or you need to refocus your essay.

How to Identify the Problem

Here are the characteristics of a weak thesis statement:

1. The essay does not explain and support the thesis.
2. The thesis statement does not cover all the topics included in the essay.
3. The thesis statement is vague or unclear.
4. The thesis statement makes a direct announcement.

How to Revise Your Thesis Statement

When evaluating your thesis statement, ask the following questions:

1. **Does my essay develop and explain my thesis statement?** As you write an essay, its focus and direction may change. Revise your thesis statement to reflect any changes. If you discover that you drifted away from your original thesis and you want to maintain it, work on revising so that your paper delivers what your thesis statement promises.

2. **Is my thesis statement broad enough to cover all the points I made in the essay?** As you develop your first draft, you may find that one idea leads naturally to another. Both must be covered by the thesis statement. For example, suppose your thesis statement is "Because of the number of patients our clinic sees in a day, the need for nurse practitioners has increased dramatically." If, in your essay, you discuss lab technicians and interns as well as nurses, then you need to broaden your thesis statement.

3. **Does my thesis statement use vague or unclear words that do not clearly focus the topic?** For example, in the thesis statement "Physical therapy can help bursitis," the word *help* is vague and does not suggest how your essay will approach the topic. Instead, if your paper discusses the effectiveness of physical therapy, this approach should be reflected in your thesis: "When it comes to chronic bursitis, deep tissue massage by a trained physical therapist can be very effective."

EXERCISE 17-3   Evaluating and Revising Thesis Statements

Directions: Identify what is wrong with each of the following thesis statements, and revise each one to make it more effective.

1. Most people like to dance.
2. Call the doctor when you're sick.

3. Everyone should read the newspaper.

4. It's important to keep your receipts.

5. Driving in snow is dangerous. ■

EXERCISE 17-4
Writing in Progress

Writing a Thesis Statement

Directions: Choose one of the topics you worked with in Exercise 17-1 or 17-2. Generate ideas about the topic and write a tentative thesis statement. ■

PROBLEM #4: THE ESSAY IS UNDERDEVELOPED

GOAL 4 Add evidence to underdeveloped essays

An underdeveloped essay is one that lacks sufficient information and evidence to support the thesis.

How to Identify the Problem

Here are the characteristics of an underdeveloped essay:

1. The essay seems to ramble or is unfocused.

2. The essay repeats information or says the same thing in slightly different ways.

3. The essay makes general statements but does not support them.

4. The essay lacks facts, examples, comparisons, or reasons.

How to Revise an Underdeveloped Essay

Tip for Writers

Ramble means "talk or write a lot without staying on one point or making your main idea clear." *Unfocused* suggests the same problem.

Use the following suggestions to revise an underdeveloped essay:

1. **Delete sentences that are repetitious and add nothing to the essay.** If you find you have little or nothing left, do additional brainstorming, free-writing, or branching to discover new ideas. If this technique does not work, consider changing your topic to one about which you have more to say.

2. **Make sure your topic is not too broad or too narrow.** If it is, use the suggestions for topic revision given earlier in the chapter on page 464 and page 466.

3. **Go through your essay sentence by sentence and highlight any ideas that you could further develop and explain.** Develop these ideas into separate paragraphs.

4. **Make sure each topic sentence is clear and specific.** Then add details to each paragraph that make it sharp and convincing.

EXERCISE 17-5   **Writing an Essay**
Writing in Progress

Directions: Using the thesis statement you wrote in Exercise 17-4, write an essay. Then evaluate and revise it, if necessary, using the suggestions given on the previous page. ■

PROBLEM #5: THE ESSAY IS DISORGANIZED

GOAL 5 Restructure disorganized essays and add transitions

A disorganized essay is one that does not follow a logical method of development. A disorganized essay makes it difficult for your readers to follow your train of thought. If readers must struggle to follow your ideas, they may stop reading or lose their concentration. In fact, as they struggle to follow your thinking, they may miss important information or misinterpret what you are saying.

How to Identify the Problem

Use the following questions to help you evaluate the organization of your essay:

1. Does every paragraph in the essay support or explain your thesis statement?
2. Do you avoid straying from your topic?
3. Does each detail in each paragraph explain the topic sentence?
4. Do you make it clear how one idea relates to another by using transitions?

How to Revise Disorganized Essays

To improve the organization of your essay, use one of the methods of organization discussed in Chapter 14. Here is a brief review:

METHOD OF ORGANIZATION	PURPOSE
Narration	Presents events in the order in which they happened
Description	Gives descriptive, sensory details
Example	Explains a situation or idea by giving circumstances that illustrate it
Definition	Explains the meaning of a term by giving its class and distinguishing characteristics
Comparison and Contrast	Focuses on similarities and differences
Classification	Explains by organizing a topic into groups or categories
Process	Describes the order in which things are done
Cause and Effect	Explains why things happen or what happens as a result of something else
Argument	Gives reasons to support a claim

Once you have chosen and used a method of development, be sure to use appropriate transitions to connect your ideas.

Another way to spot and correct organizational problems is to draw an idea or revision map as discussed on the next page. Using a map will help you visualize the progression of your ideas graphically and see which ideas fit and which do not.

EXERCISE 17-6 *Writing in Progress*	**Evaluating Organization**

Directions: Evaluate the organization of the essay you wrote in Exercise 17-5. Revise it using the suggestions given on the previous page. ■

USING MAPS TO GUIDE YOUR REVISION

GOAL 6 Use idea maps as revision tools

In Chapter 15, "Revising Paragraphs," you learned to draw revision maps to evaluate paragraphs. The same strategy works well for essays, too. A revision map will help you evaluate the overall flow of your ideas as well as the effectiveness of individual paragraphs.

To draw an essay revision map, begin by listing your title at the top of the page. Write your thesis statement underneath it, and then list the topic of each paragraph. Next, work through each paragraph, recording your ideas in abbreviated form. Then write the key words of your conclusion. If you find details that do not support the topic sentence, record those details to the right of the map. Use the model on page 471 as a guide.

When you've completed your revision map, conduct the following tests:

1. **Read your thesis statement along with your first topic sentence.** Does the topic sentence clearly support your thesis? If not, revise it to make the relationship clearer. Repeat this step for each topic sentence.

2. **Read your topic sentences, one after the other, without reading the corresponding details.** Is there a logical connection between them? Have you arranged them in the most effective way? If not, revise to make the connection clearer or to improve your organization.

3. **Examine each individual paragraph.** Are there enough relevant, specific details to support the topic sentence?

4. **Read your introduction and then look at your topic sentences.** Does the essay deliver what the introduction promises?

5. **Read your thesis statement and then your conclusion.** Are they compatible and consistent? Does the conclusion agree with and support the thesis statement?

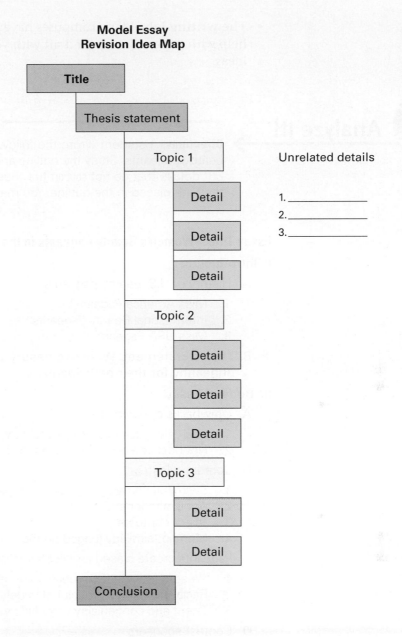

**Model Essay
Revision Idea Map**

EXERCISE 17-7   **Drawing a Revision Map**

Writing In Progress

Directions: Draw a revision map of the essay you wrote and revised in Exercises 17-5 and 17-6. Make further revisions as needed. ■

SEEKING FURTHER HELP

GOAL 7 Seek help from classmates, your instructors, and a writing lab

If the suggestions offered in this chapter do not help you solve a problem with a particular essay, be sure to use the following resources:

* **Your classmates.** Ask a classmate to read your essay and make comments and suggestions.

* **Your instructor.** Visit your instructor during office hours. Take a draft of your paper with you and have specific questions in mind.

- **The writing lab.** Many campuses have a writing lab where students can get help with papers. Take your draft with you and ask for feedback and revision ideas.

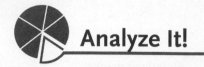 **Analyze It!**

Directions: A student wrote the following outline for an essay on American beauty pageants. Study the outline and identify what is wrong with it. Cross out details that do not support the thesis statement or do not belong where they are placed in the outline. You may add new details, if needed.

Essay Title: "Women's Beauty Pageants in the United States"

I. Introduction
   A. History of U.S. beauty pageants
      1. Miss America Pageant
      2. International Beauty Pageants
      3. Miss USA Pageant
   B. Thesis statement: Woman's beauty pageants are unfair to women and unhealthy for their participants.

II. Body of Essay
   A. Drawbacks outweigh benefits
      1. Such entertainment is harmful to women
      2. Not best way to support charities and worthy causes
   B. Content rules
      1. Swimsuit and evening gown competition
      2. Age limitations
      3. Talent contests
      4. Men not similarly judged on their looks
   C. Pageants create biased, unfair standards of beauty
      1. Western standards of beauty are used
      2. Racial and ethnic groups not widely represented
      3. Talent and congeniality carry little weight in judging
   D. Contest sponsors
      1. Commercial advertisers
      2. Other types of promoters
   E. Pageants are degrading for women
      1. Create "cattle show" mentality
      3. Undermine the goals and progress of women's rights
   F. Pageants promote physically unhealthy practices
      1. Pressure to become thin creates health problems
         a. Anorexia
         b. Other eating disorders
         c. Liposuction
      2. Little emphasis on women's intelligence, talent, character, skills

III. Conclusion
   A. Surprising that beauty pageants are still so popular worldwide
   B. Women should not support these pageants

A STUDENT ESSAY

The Writing Task

Amanda Keithley wrote this essay as an assignment in her writing class. As you read, take note of how she used stories to help the reader dismiss stereotypes and see the "real" faces of homelessness. In order to protect the privacy of the individuals, Keithley has used fictitious names.

Title suggests thesis

Breaking Down Barriers with Stories
Amanda Keithley

Introduction: Keithley describes several engaging scenes to capture the interest of her readers

1   In this moment there is a man standing at a stop light with a cardboard sign that reads "ANYTHING HELPS" in the dark, thick letters of a Sharpie. In this same moment there is a woman entering a shelter with her two children—a single mother unable to pay the rent. There is a man who gets a job at a restaurant and leaves the streets for good. There is

a woman who dies—she spent too many cold nights sleeping with her face pressed to concrete. There are homeless individuals in every community, city, village, town, and corner of this world. Homelessness, in its most basic definition, is to be without a home; however, the term "homeless" has come to be associated with many stereotypes such as poverty, destitution, drug addiction, alcohol addiction, violence, apathy, and criminality, among others. These stereotypes are destructive to the humanity and dignity of homeless people and restrict their true identity as neighbor and friend from being visible. These stereotypes are grossly incorrect in many cases and are used to dehumanize, distance, and disguise those who should be most visible in society as they are those with the most need. Thankfully there is a way to break through the stereotypes and see

Thesis statement

the face of a homeless man or woman and call him or her friend. Barriers are commonly broken down by stories, and it is through hearing another's story and not social justice, advocacy, or charity that a human life is made visible.

Topic sentence

2   Meet Jerry. Jerry sells Real Change newspapers for $2 outside of a local grocery store every morning and afternoon five days a week. It is important for

The author introduces her readers to Jerry

his story to be heard and his person made visible. When Jerry speaks, he often laughs and the lines around his eyes crinkle so that he looks like he's laughing even when he's not. His jovial look is at odds with his story though because it is dark and filled with hardship. Jerry used to drive trucks until the day he crashed and lost everything—his house, car, money, and most of his relationships with family and friends. Being homeless alienated him from his loved ones and society.

A common phrase Jerry repeats when telling his story is "thank you for listening." Jerry's thankfulness exposes his great need for being heard and making his story known. Look at Jerry, speak with Jerry, and see that he is genuine and kind, full of life and desiring to love and be loved. Jerry's story contains brokenness and darkness that many cannot begin to fathom, but his longing for reconciliation and love is what all search for in life and what binds human lives together.

Topic sentence

3   Meet Greg. Greg sits outside of QFC in a thin green sweatshirt all seasons of the year. He sometimes holds a sign that says something like "Homeless Please Help" and other times he just sits there and smiles as people pass him by. It is evident when interacting with him that not many people speak with him each day, or look him in the eye. Like Jerry, he is keen to share his story with anyone who will listen. Greg goes by the street name "Wolf," but he answers to both. Being homeless for most of his life, Wolf has found it difficult to live without sufficient food and shelter, but even more so he has found it difficult to keep relationships while on the streets. He is now in his fifties, but he has dreams of owning his own craft store and making it a space for homeless people to create and be in community with one another. Wolf has good days and days when the weight of his situation is too much for him to carry on his own. A fellow homeless man, John, is his only friend, but Wolf would have many friends if people stopped to talk with him once in a while. Every smile, he says, gives him hope that one day his story will be different; he will triumph over his adversity.

The author introduces her readers to Greg

Topic sentence

4   Meet Mary. Mary is a young girl who prostitutes herself and lives in the homes of unknown men and occasionally on the streets. She is looking for ways to learn to love herself. Mary writes beautiful poems that startle and shake what is deepest and most human in others. In white stiletto heels and lime green hair, she stands and reads her poems in her deep and even voice. The rhythm of her voice alone tears small rips in the hearts of her listeners. Mary's poems are about abuse, rape, eating disorders, prostitution, abandonment, poverty, loneliness, suicide, and drugs. Poetry is the avenue by which she tells her story to those who will listen. When Mary writes a poem, she performs the act of creating something beautiful out of great pain and suffering, and this gives her great joy. Poetry is deeply healing for Mary, and when she is able to share her poems with others, it is a powerful experience for her and her audience. Both are changed by the understanding that passes between poet and audience as Mary's story is told and heard.

The author introduces her readers to Mary

Topic sentence

5   Meet Isabella. Isabella is a single mother of three who was forced to leave her job at a jewelry store when her husband left her. She now lives at Hope Place women's shelter with her three children and is going through a counseling program to help prepare her for future employment. Isabella wants to give her daughters the best life that she can, and she desires to provide for them in a way her own parents did not. Hope Place has provided Isabella with more than just shelter and food. Her children are able to go to school, and she is able to learn job skills in one of the shelter's various programs of empowerment. Isabella hopes to find a good job that pays enough for her to move out of the shelter and pay for a babysitter to watch the kids after they get out of school. There are times when Isabella can't see a way out of the poverty that has overwhelmed her, but the community of women in the shelter are supportive and hopeful that she will find a job and be able to care for her family.

The author introduces her readers to Isabella

Conclusion: Keithley reflects on the faces of homelessness and reemphasizes her thesis.

6   The stories of Jerry, Wolf, Mary, and Isabella render the identity of homelessness as varied and multilayered. There is great diversity found in the homeless population and great diversity makes for many different stories. Not all who are homeless are alcoholics, and not all who are homeless are jobless. There are many stereotypes that prevent real relationships from being formed between the homeless and the community that they live in, but these stereotypes can be overturned by listening to someone's story and making visible his or her life, dignity, and humanity. To truly "see" someone past the stereotypes society has placed upon them by looking them in the eyes is to make visible the invisible and call them friend.

Examining Student Writing

1. How does the visual that accompanies this reading relate to Keithley's thesis? What other types of visuals might have helped to communicate the thesis?

2. How did Keithley organize her essay?

3. The topic sentences are unconventional. How do they help the author communicate her thesis? What alternative, more informational topic sentences could have been used?

4. Evaluate Keithley's introduction. What other ways could she have introduced her topic while building interest?

5. Highlight three places where Keithley uses descriptive details effectively.

Essay Writing Scenarios

Friends and Family

1. Compare the jobs your grandparents held with those your parents hold. How has the level and type of job changed over time? What does this change suggest about family growth and change?

2. Write an essay about where you preferred to play as a child; at a park or playground, in a backyard, on a street, at a friend's house, etc.

Classes and Campus Life

1. What kind of person is attracted to your major? Describe the qualities someone should have if he or she is interested in this field.

2. Write an essay about something you did really well in high school.

Working Students

1. Many students work and attend college at the same time. What skills does it take to balance school and work?

2. Write an essay about what you will look for in your next job. How will it be different from the job you have currently?

Communities and Cultures

1. Traditionally, men and women have had very different roles in different cultures. Write an essay about one thing that only women used to do in your culture that men now also do, or vice versa.

2. People do many things to show off their status in a community. Describe one thing that people buy, drive, or wear to show that they are important.

WRITING ABOUT A READING

Humorist Brian Doyle wrote this piece, "Irreconcilable Dissonance: The Threat of Divorce as the Glue of Marriage," about marriage and divorce.

Step 1: Preview the reading.

Step 2: Connect the reading to your own experience: Are you or anyone you know divorced? What were the reasons for the divorce?

Step 3: Read and respond to the questions in the margin.

THINK AS YOU READ

Based on your preview, how does the author feel about marriage and divorce?

Why does the author begin by explaining his marital status this way? Highlight the thesis statement when you come to it, or express it in your own words.

Throughout the essay, underline the reasons the author cites for why people get divorced.

Why does he choose these particular examples?

IRRECONCILABLE DISSONANCE: THE THREAT OF DIVORCE AS THE GLUE OF MARRIAGE

Brian Doyle

1   I have been married once to the woman to whom I am still married, so far, and one thing I have noticed about being married is that it makes you a lot more attentive to divorce, which used to seem like something that happened to other people, but doesn't anymore, because of course every marriage is pregnant with divorce, and also now I know a lot of people who are divorced, or are about to be, or are somewhere in between those poles, for which shadowy status there should be words like mivorced or darried or sleeperated or schleperated, but there aren't, so far.

2   People seem to get divorced for all sorts of reasons, and I find myself taking notes, probably defensively, but also out of sheer amazement at the chaotic wilderness of human nature. For example, I read recently about one man who got divorced so he could watch all sixty episodes of *The Wire* in chronological order. Another man got divorced after thirty years so he could, he said, fart in peace. Another man got divorced in part because he told his wife he had an affair, but he didn't have an affair, he just couldn't think of any other good excuse to get divorced, and he didn't want to have an affair, or be with anyone else other than his wife, because he liked his wife, and rather enjoyed her company as a rule, he said, but he just didn't want to be married to her every day anymore, he preferred to be married to her every second or third day, but she did not find that a workable arrangement, and so they parted company, confused.

3   Another man I read about didn't want to get divorced, he said, but when his wife kept insisting that they get divorced because she had fallen in love with another guy, he, the husband, finally agreed to get divorced, and soon after he found himself dating the other guy's first wife; as the first guy said, who could invent such a story?

4   I read about a woman who divorced her husband because he picked his nose. I read about a woman who got divorced because her husband never remembered to pay their property taxes and finally, she said, it was just too

much. Is it so very much to ask, she asked, that the person who shares responsibility for your life remembers to pay your joint taxes? Does this have to be a crisis every year? She seemed sort of embarrassed to say what she said, but she said it.

Why is a cartoon appropriate for this selection?

...honestly I just feel like we don't communicate like we used to!

5   It seems to me that the reasons people divorce are hardly ever for the dramatic reasons that we assume are the reasons people get divorced, like snorting cocaine for breakfast or discovering that the minister named Bernard who you married ten years ago is actually a former convict named Ezzard with a wife in Wisconsin, according to the young detective who sat down in your office at the accounting firm one morning and sounded embarrassed about some things he had come to tell you that you should know.

Do you agree that people hardly ever divorce for dramatic reasons?

6   I read about a couple who got divorced because of "irresolute differences," a phrase that addled me for weeks. Another couple filed for divorce on the grounds of irreconcilable dissonance, which seemed like one of those few times in life when the exact right words are applied to the exact right reason for those words. I read about another woman who divorced her husband because one time they were walking down the street, the husband on the curb side in accordance with the ancient courteous male custom of being on that side so as to receive the splatter of mud or worse from the street and keep such splatter from the pristine acreage of his beloved, and as they approached a fire hydrant he lifted his leg, puppylike, as a joke, and she marched right to their lawyer's office and instituted divorce proceedings. That particular woman refused to speak to reporters about the reasons for divorce, but you wonder what the iceberg was under that surface, you know?

Why does the phrase "irresolute differences" addle or confuse the author?

What does the author mean by his reference to an iceberg under the surface?

7   The first divorce I saw up close, like the first car crash you see up close, is imprinted on the inside of my eyelids, and I still think about it, not because it happened, but because years after it happened it seems so fated to have happened. How could it be that two people who really liked each other, and who took a brave crazy leap on not just living together, which lots of mammals do, but swearing fealty and respect in front of a huge crowd, and filing taxes as a joint entity, and spawning a child, and cosigning mortgages and car loans, how could they end up signing settlement papers on the dining room table and then wandering out into the muddy garden to cry? How could that be?

To what does the author compare divorce? What do you notice about the length of the author's sentences in this paragraph and others? Does his style suit the subject matter?

8   The saddest word I've heard wrapped around divorce like a tattered blanket is tired, as in "We were both just tired," because being tired seems so utterly normal to me, so much the rug always bunching in that one spot no

What is the author's response to the idea that people get divorced because they are tired?

What does the author mean by "the shagginess of things?"

What does the author say makes marriage work?

What is the author's final point?

matter what you do, the slightly worn dish rack, the belt with extra holes punched with an ice pick that you borrowed from your cousin for exactly this purpose, the flashlight in the pantry that has never had batteries and never will, that the thought of tired being both your daily bread and also grounds for divorce gives me the willies. The shagginess of things, the way they never quite work out as planned and break down every other Tuesday, necessitating wine and foul language and duct tape and the wrong-size screw quietly hammered into place with the bottom of the garden gnome, seems to me the very essence of marriage; so if what makes a marriage work (the constant shifting of expectations and eternal parade of small surprises) is also what causes marriages to dissolve, where is it safe to stand?

9   Nowhere, of course. Every marriage is pregnant with divorce, every day, every hour, every minute. The second you finish reading this essay, your spouse could close the refrigerator, after miraculously finding a way to wedge the juice carton behind the milk jug, and call it quits, and the odd truth of the matter is that because she might end your marriage in a moment, and you might end hers, you're still married. The instant there is no chance of death is the moment of death.

WRITING IN RESPONSE TO READING

Examining the Reading Using an Idea Map   MyWritingLab

Review the reading by filling in the missing parts of the idea map below.

Title
Irreconcilable Dissonance: The Threat of Divorce as the Glue of Marriage

Thesis
_____
_____

Doyle says people divorce for strange reasons and gives examples.

_____
_____

The first divorce Doyle had experience with has stayed with him and he doesn't really understand why they divorced.

_____
_____
_____

Conclusion
Doyle states that every marriage is pregnant with divorce and it could happen at any moment, and because of this, you stay married to each other.

Strengthening Your Vocabulary   MyWritingLab

Using the word's context, word parts, or a dictionary, write a brief definition of each of the following words as it is used in the reading.

1. irresolute (paragraph 6) _____

2. irreconcilable (paragraph 6) _____

3. dissonance (paragraph 6) _____

4. pristine (paragraph 6) _____

5. fealty (paragraph 7) _____

6. spawning (paragraph 7) _____

7. willies (paragraph 8) _____

Reacting to Ideas: Discussion and Journal Writing   MyWritingLab

Get ready to write about the reading by discussing the following:

1. Consider what we expect divorce to be. Must it always be chaotic and angry?

2. Discuss Doyle's writing. Do you think he's funny? Do you think divorce is a topic appropriate for humor?

3. Write about the reasons that caused you to suddenly not like a friend or family member at one point. Were those reasons enough to end your relationship with each other?

4. Discuss how the cartoon relates to and adds to the article.

Paragraph Options   MyWritingLab

1. Write a paragraph describing a divorce you know about. What were the reasons? Do you think they were justified? How do they compare to the reasons Doyle offers?

2. Doyle compares marriage and divorce with life and death. How are they alike? How does the prospect of divorce or death make marriage or life better? Write a paragraph discussing this.

Essay Options   MyWritingLab

3. Do you believe that any marriage could just suddenly end without warning? Do you think people who are married think about divorce as often as Doyle suggests? Write an essay discussing this.

4. Why do you think the divorce rate is so high? Write an essay discussing the reasons.

■ ■ ■ ■

Revision Checklist

Paragraph Development

1. Is the topic manageable (neither too broad nor too narrow)?
2. Is the paragraph written with the reader in mind?
3. Does the topic sentence identify the topic?
4. Does the topic sentence make a point about the topic?
5. Does each sentence support the topic sentence?
6. Is there sufficient detail?
7. Is there a sentence at the end that brings the paragraph to a close?

Sentence Development

8. Are there any sentence fragments, run-on sentences, or comma splices?
9. Are ideas combined to produce more effective sentences?
10. Are adjectives and adverbs used to make the sentences vivid and interesting?
11. Are relative clauses and prepositional phrases like -*ing* phrases used to add detail?
12. Are pronouns used correctly and consistently?

Essay Development

13. Does the essay accomplish its purpose?
14. Is the essay appropriate for the audience?
15. Is the thesis statement clearly expressed?
16. Does each paragraph support the thesis?
17. Is the essay logically organized?
18. Are transitions used to connect the ideas?
19. Are the introduction, conclusion, and title effective?

SELF-TEST SUMMARY

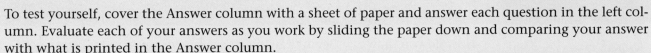

To test yourself, cover the Answer column with a sheet of paper and answer each question in the left column. Evaluate each of your answers as you work by sliding the paper down and comparing your answer with what is printed in the Answer column.

	QUESTION	ANSWER
Goal 1 Choose a topic that is not too broad	How do you identify a topic that is too broad? How do you narrow a topic?	A topic may be too broad if you have too much to say, you feel overwhelmed, you are not making progress, or you are writing general statements and not explaining them. Narrow a topic by dividing it into subtopics or by answering questions that limit the topic to a particular place, time, kind, or type.
Goal 2 Choose a topic that is not too narrow	How do you identify a topic that is too narrow? How do you broaden a topic?	A topic may be too narrow if you run out of ideas after a few paragraphs, your topic does not seem important, you are not making progress, or your essay is too factual. Broaden a topic by thinking of other situations that illustrate the same idea or by thinking of a larger concept that includes your topic.
Goal 3 Revise your thesis statement so it clearly states your purpose	What are the characteristics of a weak thesis statement?	A thesis statement is weak if • the essay does not support the thesis. • the thesis statement does not cover all the topics included in the essay. • the thesis statement is unclear. • the thesis statement makes a direct announcement.
Goal 4 Add evidence to underdeveloped essays	How do you revise an underdeveloped essay?	Revise an underdeveloped essay by • deleting repetitious sentences. • making sure your topic is not too broad or too narrow. • examining each sentence and highlighting ideas that could be further developed. • making sure each topic sentence is clear and specific.
Goal 5 Restructure disorganized essays and add transitions	How do you evaluate the organization of your essay?	Evaluate the organization of your essay by asking: • Does every paragraph support your thesis statement? • Do you avoid straying from your topic? • Does each detail in each paragraph explain the topic sentence? • Do you use transitions to make it clear how one idea relates to another?

SELF-TEST SUMMARY *(continued)*

	QUESTION	ANSWER
Goal 6 Use idea maps as revision tools	How do you draw an essay revision map?	Begin drawing an essay revision map by listing your title at the top of the page. Write your thesis statement underneath it, then list the topic of each paragraph. Work through each paragraph, and then write the key words of your conclusion. Record any details that do not support the topic sentence to the right of the map.
Goal 7 Seek help from classmates, your instructors, and a writing lab	What resources can help you solve a problem with an essay?	Helpful resources include your classmates, your instructor, and the writing lab on campus.

MyWritingLab *Visit Ch. 17 AVOIDING COMMON PROBLEMS IN ESSAYS in MyWritingLab to test your understanding of the chapter objectives.*

PART VI

A Thematic Reader

Thinking Before Reading

The article below was originally published in *Maclean's*, a Canadian weekly news magazine. The magazine is considered a serious news publication that reports on national and international affairs, including news events, social issues, business, and culture. In "Love Is a Four-Number Word," the author asks: Should romantic partners share their online passwords? Before you read:

Step 1: Preview the reading.

Step 2: Connect the reading to your own experience:

    a. If you are in a romantic relationship, do you and your romantic partner know each other's e-mail, phone, and social media passwords?

    b. What is the difference (if any) between two spouses asking for each other's passwords and parents asking for their teenaged children's passwords?

Step 3: As you read, ask yourself questions such as those that appeared in the marginal annotations for the other professional readings throughout the book. Mark and annotate to record your answers.

READING

LOVE IS A FOUR-NUMBER WORD

Rebecca Eckler

That magical password that unlocks your phone could seal a romance—or ruin it

1   "We're over," an acquaintance said recently of her boyfriend of four months. "He gave me his password on our third date and then changed it and refused to give me the new one. Passwords and secrets do not belong in loving relationships. Transparency does."

2   That old question, debated in certain circles, of how soon you go "all the way" has been replaced by a new one: when to share the password to your phone. Handing over those prized digits so your partner can see your texts, emails, photos and recent phone calls—in other words, your entire social existence at a glance—is either romantic or creepy, depending on whom you ask.

3   Real estate lawyer Warren Fireman and his wife of 13 years share passwords. Often they lie in bed at the end of the day reading each other's phones. "I just look to see what was going on in her day and she does the same. She has a huge family and so do I, so there is always something going on. We like to be kept in the loop." Singer Carrie Underwood once said in an interview that she does the same with her hockey-player husband's phone after she's been on the road. As Fireman puts it, "We're happily married. We have nothing to hide."

4   But many women, hurt in past relationships, may want the password sooner rather than later, says Sara Fawkes, a counselor based in Toronto. It's often an ongoing negotiation, she says. "Some people are just very secretive. You need to figure out what the motivation is for asking."

5   More transparency is not always better. A Calgary-based art dealer says she's no longer allowed to look at her husband's phone after having his passwords for a decade. "We were getting into too many fights. I would read something I didn't like, and he'd argue that I didn't know the context, and that caused fights." She still has qualms. "When you share a house and a family but not your password, it seems like you have something to hide," she says. But she admits she is much happier now. "I can't see stuff I may not like. We don't fight nearly as much." Another woman got her partner's password after a month of dating—"because I was always snooping anyway. I'd see him signing off with an 'xo' to someone and I'd get freaked out. I was questioning everything. I learned that he signed off 'xo' to everyone. That was just him. I do sometimes wish I didn't have [the password]," she confesses.

6   Michael, a 42-year-old accountant, has been dating a woman for a month. He says he'd never give her his password. "If she asked me on our third or fourth or even 10th date, I would find it aggressive. You need some boundaries." Once, he let her look at his phone and she saw he had looked at a dating site. "I didn't join or anything. But the questions came fast and furiously."

7   Password sharing can be about a kind of affectionate voyeurism more than suspicion. Many women say that if they see their partner's or date's phone and know the password, they'll look, mostly because they are bored. Allan Cameron, a clinical social worker and therapist, is interested in the symbolism of password sharing. "Perhaps it's an example of oversharing. The idea that our partner's every thought, thread or Google search is of value and something we need access to, is disconcerting," he says. "This privileging of the mundane yields little to the real task of developing a full and authentic relationship." But he also sees password sharing as an attempt to speed up the formation of trust, which used to be painstakingly earned.

8   As with most things, once it's given, it's hard to take back. "A person may go with the demand to share their password but feel they are too exposed or have moved too quickly. They may rescind their password offer," he suggests—which creates other tensions.

9   Toronto-based therapist Tammy Laber says one of the things she does with couples when there has been an affair is to suggest that they share passwords so the "wronged" spouse can regain trust. While the debate rages, Fireman has another thought. "Maybe instead of us lying in bed and looking at each other's phones," he jokes, "we should just talk more."

WRITING IN RESPONSE TO READING

Reviewing the Reading   MyWritingLab

Answer each of the following questions using complete sentences.

1. According to the woman quoted in the first paragraph, what does the word *transparency* mean with respect to relationships?

2. What does Allan Cameron mean when he says that password sharing is an example of "oversharing" (paragraph 7)?

3. Why does therapist Tammy Laber recommend that couples who are recovering from an affair share their passwords?

4. According to the article, what motivations may cause people to ask for their romantic partners' passwords?

5. What may happen if one romantic partner changes his or her passwords and refuses to share the new passwords?

Examining the Reading Using an Idea Map   `MyWritingLab`

Draw an idea map of the reading, using the guidelines on page 31.

Strengthening Your Vocabulary   `MyWritingLab`

Using the word's context, word parts, or a dictionary, write a brief definition of each of the following words as it is used in the reading.

1. qualms (paragraph 5) _____

2. voyeurism (paragraph 7) _____

3. disconcerting (paragraph 7) _____

4. mundane (paragraph 7) _____

5. painstakingly (paragraph 7) _____

6. rescind (paragraph 8) _____

Reacting to Ideas: Discussion and Journal Writing   `MyWritingLab`

Get ready to write about the reading by discussing the following:

1. How does the author hint at her own opinion on the topic in the last paragraph of the article?

2. When does a romantic relationship go from "casual" to "serious"? In addition to password sharing, what are some other signs of a "serious" relationship?

3. How does the old saying "Ignorance is bliss" relate to the content of this article?

4. Is there a difference between "reading your romantic partner's text messages" and "snooping"? If so, how would you define the difference? If you think they are the same, explain why.

5. In paragraph 7, Allan Cameron states, "This privileging of the mundane yields little to the real task of developing a full and authentic relationship." Explain what he means.

 Thinking Visually   6. How does the photo accompanying this article add to or detract from it? Write a caption to accompany the photo.

Paragraph Options   `MyWritingLab`

1. Michael, the accountant quoted in paragraph 6, says "you need some boundaries [in a relationship]." Write a paragraph in which you explore some boundaries that need to be respected in the early stages of a relationship.

2. The therapist mentioned in paragraph 9 suggests that password sharing is one way to help couples regain trust after an affair. Write a paragraph in which you offer some other suggestions for regaining trust after an affair.

3. Write a paragraph in which you agree or disagree with the following statement from paragraph 1: "Passwords and secrets do not belong in loving relationships. Transparency does."

Essay Options   MyWritingLab

4. The author of "Love Is a Four-Number Word" suggests that password sharing may be one component of a successful relationship. Write an essay in which you explore at least three areas that are necessary to a successful romantic relationship.

5. Write an essay in which you argue that someone who demands to know all your passwords would not be a good romantic or life partner. Alternatively, write an essay in which you explain to a romantic partner why you do not want to share all of your passwords.

6. This article explores the pros and cons of just one element of romantic relationships: password sharing. Write an essay in which you explore the pros and cons of another element of romantic relationships. For example, you might write about living together, working for the same company, relocating to be closer to a romantic partner, or any other topic you find interesting.

■ ■ ■ ■

THEME 1   DATING AND RELATIONSHIPS - SELECTION 2

Thinking Before Reading

The following article originally appeared in *Human Communication: The Basic Course* and *The Interpersonal Communication Book,* both Pearson textbooks by Joseph DeVito. As you read, note that the author shares some statistics on Internet romance and presents information on the advantages and disadvantages of online relationships. How does knowing the sources of the article help you predict the author's approach to the topic?

Step 1: Preview the reading.

Step 2: Connect the reading to your own experience:

   a. Have you ever visited an online dating site? If so, how often do you visit one? If not, why not?

   b. Have you (or someone you know) been successful in establishing a relationship with someone you met online? How long did the relationship last? Would you consider pursuing another online relationship? Why or why not?

Step 3: As you read, ask yourself questions such as those that appeared in the marginal annotations for the other professional readings throughout the book. Mark and annotate to record your answers.

READING

TECHNOLOGY AND LOVE

Joseph DeVito

1   A 2006 report from the Pew Internet Research Center notes that 11 percent of all Internet users (and 37 percent of single Internet users) have visited Internet dating sites. And 17 percent report that they've begun long-term relationships with people they met online (Madden  & Lenhart, 2006). According to another report, between 2007 and 2009, 21 percent of heterosexual couples and 61 percent of same-sex couples met online (Rosenbloom, 2011). And *Time* magazine reports that 23 million Americans log on to one of the 4,000 online dating sites each month (Steinmetz, 2013). Match.com, in its 2013 advertisements, reports that one out of five relationships begin online. Clearly, the Internet is growing in importance in the development, maintenance, and even the deterioration of romantic relationships. And, according to the 2013 FBI website, dating and romantic relationship scams are likewise becoming more common (and more sophisticated).

2   In face-to-face relationships, you perceive the other person through nonverbal cues—you see the person's eyes, face, body—and you form impressions immediately. In online relationships of just a few years ago, physical attractiveness was signaled exclusively through words and self-descriptions (Levine. 2000). Under those circumstances, as you can appreciate, the face-to-face encounter strongly favored those who were physically attractive, whereas the online encounter favored those who were verbally adept at self-presentation and did not disadvantage less attractive individuals. Now, with photos, videos, and voice a part of many online dating and social networking sites, this distinction is fading—though it is probably not entirely erased. Certainly the face-to-face encounter still provides more nonverbal cues about the physical person.

Advantages of Online Relationships

3   There are many advantages to establishing relationships online. For example, online relationships are safe in terms of avoiding the potential for physical violence or sexually transmitted diseases. Unlike relationships established

in face-to-face encounters, in which physical appearance tends to outweigh personality. Internet communication reveals people's inner qualities first. Rapport and mutual self-disclosure become more important than physical attractiveness in promoting intimacy (Cooper & Sportolari, 1997). And, contrary to some popular opinion, online relationships rely just as heavily on the ideals of trust, honesty, and commitment as do face-to-face relationships (Whitty & Gavin, 2001).

4   Friendship and romantic interaction on the Internet are a natural boon to shut-ins and extremely shy people, for whom traditional ways of meeting others are often difficult. Computer talk is empowering for those with "physical disabilities or disfigurements," for whom face-to-face interactions are often superficial and often end with withdrawal (Bull & Rumsey, 1988; Lea & Spears, 1995). By eliminating the physical cues, computer talk equalizes the interaction and doesn't put the disfigured person, for example, at an immediate disadvantage in a society where physical attractiveness is so highly valued. On the Internet you're free to reveal as much or as little about your physical self as you wish, when you wish.

5   Another obvious advantage is that the number of people you can reach is so vast that it's relatively easy to find someone who matches what you're looking for. The situation is like finding a book that covers just what you need from a library of millions of volumes rather than from a collection holding only several thousand.

Disadvantages of Online Relationships

6   Of course, there are also disadvantages: For one thing, and depending on the technology you're using you may not be able to see the other person in an online encounter. And even if you exchange photos, how certain can you be that the photos are of the person or that they were taken recently? In addition, you may not be able to hear the person's voice, and this too hinders you as you seek to develop a total picture of the other person.

7   Online, people can present a false self with little chance of detection; minors may present themselves as adults, and adults may present themselves as children in order to conduct illicit sexual communications and perhaps meetings. Similarly, people can present themselves as poor when they're rich, as mature when they're immature, as serious and committed when they're just enjoying the online experience. Although people can also misrepresent themselves in face-to-face relationships, the fact that it's easier to do online probably accounts for the greater frequency of misrepresentation in computer relationships (Cornwell & Lundgren, 2001).

8   Another potential disadvantage is that computer interactions may become all-consuming and may take the place of face-to-face interpersonal relationships.

WRITING IN RESPONSE TO READING

Reviewing the Reading   MyWritingLab

Answer each of the following questions using complete sentences.

1. According to a Pew Internet Research Center report, what percentage of single Internet users have visited online dating sites?

2. Of those people who met online, how do heterosexual couples compare with same-sex couples?

3. According to the article, how has the presentation of physical attractiveness changed in online relationships?

4. List three advantages of establishing online romantic relationships.

5. According to the author, what are some ways that people misrepresent themselves in online relationships?

Examining the Reading Using an Idea Map   MyWritingLab

Draw an idea map of the reading, *Technology and Love*, using the guidelines on page 31

Strengthening Your Vocabulary   MyWritingLab

Using the word's context, word parts, or a dictionary, write a brief definition of each of the following words as it is used in the reading.

1. deterioration (paragraph 1) _____

2. perceive (paragraph 2) _____

3. adept (paragraph 2) _____

4. rapport (paragraph 3) _____

5. boon (paragraph 4) _____

6. hinders (paragraph 6) _____

7. illicit (paragraph 7) _____

Reacting to Ideas: Discussion and Journal Writing   MyWritingLab

Get ready to write about the reading by discussing the following:

1. Suppose you decided to subscribe to the services of an online dating site. How would you describe yourself to a potential partner? Would you focus more on inner or outer beauty? Why?

2. In paragraph 3, the author states that "online relationships rely just as heavily on the ideals of trust, honesty, and commitment as do face-to-face relationships." Do you agree or disagree with this statement, and why?

3. Do you have a preferred method for meeting new people? For example, do you like to meet people through mutual friends on Facebook, or by joining campus organizations, or some other method?

4. Suppose all of your friends were involved in long-term relationships and you were not? Would you consider looking for love on the Internet? Why or why not?

5. How would you describe the author's approach to the topic of technology and love? Does this article exhibit any bias?

Thinking Visually
6. How does the photo accompanying this article add to or detract from the article's main points? Write a caption to accompany the photo.

Paragraph Options   `MyWritingLab`

1. In a paragraph, describe your ideal mate.

2. Write a paragraph in which you suggest some ways you can use technology to be romantic.

3. In paragraph 7, the author lists some dangers involved with using the Internet to find possible romantic partners. Write a paragraph in which you list and explain at least two additional dangers.

Essay Options   `MyWritingLab`

4. In an essay, describe three characteristics of an ideal relationship.

5. In paragraph 4, the author states that "friendship and romantic interaction on the Internet are a boon to shut-ins and extremely shy people." Write an essay in which you discuss several other groups of people whose relationships with others can benefit from the Internet.

6. Write an essay in which you discuss ways to maintain a quality Internet relationship.

CRITICAL READING AND WRITING

Integrating Ideas   `MyWritingLab`

After completing Reading #1 ("Love Is a Four-Number Word") and Reading #2 ("Technology and Love"), choose one of the following questions to answer.

1. Both readings focus on technology in human relationships. Which reading takes a strongly positive approach to the topic, and which provides more of a "pro and con" approach? Write a paragraph explaining your answer. To which approach do you respond better, and why?

2. Both readings touch on the topic of transparency. What exactly is transparency, and why is it important in an online and a face-to-face relationship? Write a paragraph or essay in which you answer these questions.

3. In a paragraph or essay, compare the tone of each reading and the authors' differences in style. Which article did you enjoy reading more, and why? Which reading is more critical in its analysis, and which one is more biased?

4. Thinking about the content of both readings, write an essay in which you provide a list of "do's" and "don'ts" for dating on the Internet.

■ ■ ■ ■

THEME 2   SURVEILLANCE AND THE RIGHT TO PRIVACY—SELECTION 1

Thinking Before Reading

This reading selection from a textbook titled *Society in Focus* describes the increasing use of surveillance monitoring systems in public places. Read the selection to discover the benefits and risks of high-tech surveillance.

Step 1: Preview the reading.

Step 2: Connect the reading to your own experience:

   a. Have you noticed surveillance cameras monitoring you anywhere? How did it make you feel?

   b. Consider a world in which everything everyone does is recorded. How do you feel about that?

Step 3: As you read, ask yourself questions such as those that appeared in the marginal annotations for the other professional readings throughout the book. Mark and annotate to record your answers.

READING

A SURVEILLANCE SOCIETY

William E. Thompson and Joseph V. Hickey

1   The cameras are familiar to most people, perhaps even comforting to some. They are perched high atop almost every lamppost, rooftop, and street light. Elsewhere, they are undetectable, except to the authorities. Video cameras are never turned off. They pan up and down, left and right, surveying traffic, pedestrians, and everything else in public view, day and night.

Growing Trends

Big Brother

a fictional character from George Orwell's futuristic novel *1984* who is the dictator of a totalitarian state

dystopian

nightmarish worst case scenario

2   You might be thinking that this scene offers a glimpse of the future. Perhaps it is a dark, futuristic vision, much like George Orwell's nightmare of **Big Brother** monitoring and controlling people's lives down to the smallest details. But by now you are aware that *things are not necessarily what they seem*.

3   This is not some grim, **dystopian** vision of the future, but a growing trend almost everywhere in the world—including most shopping malls and stores, almost all government and corporate offices, and many other social arenas. In the name of public security, the British have been most active of all nations in installing surveillance monitoring systems. In the beginning, they were tried in a handful of "trouble spots." Now more than 4.2 million cameras have been installed throughout Britain, and the average Londoner can expect his or her picture to be taken hundreds of times each day. Alarmed at the amount of surveillance and the astonishing amount of personal data that is hoarded by the state and by commercial organizations, Ross Clark asks whom should we fear most: the government agencies that are spying on us or the criminals who seem to prosper in the swirling fog of excessive data collection?

4   Since the 9/11 terrorist attacks, the United States has been trying to catch up. Times Square in New York and the nation's capital have seen a proliferation of surveillance cameras installed in public places. Experiments in face-recognition technology have been expanded, and "photo radar" that uses cameras and computers to photograph license plates, identify traffic violators, and issue citations is catching on as well. And in all cases, the technology has also grown more sophisticated. The USA PATRIOT Act, passed after 9/11 and renewed in 2006, expanded the government's authority to "spy" on private citizens.

5   In the private sector, cameras and computers are abundant and socially accepted. Today, there are millions of tiny private security cameras at hotels, malls, parking lots—everywhere businesses and shoppers can be found. The new digital surveillance systems are more sophisticated than those

from just a few years ago. Today's technology not only can scan businesses and malls, but also analyze what it is watching and recording and, if something is unusual, alert security. Likewise, digital security systems can now record, store, and index images, making it possible for security personnel to "instantly retrieve images of every person who passed through a door on any given day."

Surveillance Technologies

6   High-tech surveillance devices are becoming more common across the urban landscape. Although many people may be wary of these devices, few are aware that they are but a small part of surveillance technologies that now routinely monitor all of our personal histories, daily routines, and tastes. And 9/11 and global terrorist threats have increased public willingness for added security and new surveillance technologies.

7   Police and military surveillance is impressive—with video scanners, electronic ankle monitors, night-vision goggles, and pilotless airborne spy vehicles, to name just a few. But high-tech surveillance has expanded well beyond the police and military to thousands of corporations, government agencies, and even individuals who routinely monitor the workplace, marketplace, and almost all other social arenas. As one sociologist noted, "Being able to hide and remain anonymous has become more difficult . . . we are moving toward a glass village in which everyone is available for view online."

Information Sharing

8   Today, corporations and government agencies routinely share databases. In "computer matching," organizations swap back and forth personal information on different kinds of populations and combine them to suit their own needs. The Pentagon's "Total Information Awareness Program" is one of the most ambitious plans to combine computer databases. The Pentagon maintains that it relies mainly on information from government, law enforcement, and intelligence databases to "forestall terrorism," but its use of other kinds of data—like personal financial and health records—remains unresolved. Critics argue that because such a system could (and some say already has) tap into e-mail, culling records, and credit card and banking transactions as well as travel documents, it poses a direct threat to civil liberties.

9   Similar arguments were made after the Passage of the USA PATRIOT Act in 2001, which gave the government the right to "search suspected terrorists'

library records—and add them to government databases—without the patron ever knowing." By early 2002, one study found that over 85 libraries had already been asked for information on patrons in connection with the 9/11 investigation.

10   Post-9/11 surveillance surfaced as a controversial political issue in 2006 when it was discovered that after the 9/11 attacks the government gave approval to the highly secretive National Security Agency (NSA) to solicit phone records of private citizens from the nation's largest phone companies. Only weeks later it was revealed that the government also had begun monitoring the banking habits of private citizens in an effort to thwart terrorist activities. Open debates developed over how much personal privacy Americans were willing to relinquish for the promise of safety from terrorism. Nevertheless, the act was renewed in 2006.

11   The government is not the only one in the spying business. Some of the most sophisticated surveillance devices are available to the public and can be ordered from retail catalogues. For example, night-vision goggles can be had for the price of a good video camera. High-tech scanners are available that can trace ink patterns and read the content of letters "without ever breaking the seal" (Brin, 1996: 308). Brin believes that there is a good possibility that as cameras get smaller and more mobile we should expect "mosquito-scale drones" that fly in and out of office and home windows, making privacy difficult or impossible. Of course, cell phones and other mobile devices with digital cameras have proliferated, as have pinhole cameras, microvideo systems, and wireless video that potentially could make everyone part of the security apparatus.

The Impact of Surveillance

12   Journalists have largely focused their attention on how surveillance relates to political citizenship and "privacy" issues, but much more is involved. According to sociologist David Lyon, new surveillance systems have expanded to the point at which they have become a major social institution that affects all social relationships, as well as people's very identities, personal space, freedom, and dignity. Increasingly, data images—computer-integrated profiles of each individual's finances, health, consumer preferences, ethnicity, neighborhood, education, criminal record, and other "significant" characteristics—are the "looking-glass" that provide social judgments about "who we are" and our life changes. Using the old South Africa as his guide, Lyon asks, will the new "non-persons," segregated by surveillance systems, be bankrupt individuals or perhaps nonconsumers?

13   Many people see the benefits of new surveillance as far outweighing the risks and argue that only criminals and terrorists should be concerned about the intensification of surveillance. They assert, "Why should I worry about privacy? I have nothing to hide." Lyon himself makes the point that dark visions about corporate and government Big Brothers may be counterproductive in that they may produce nothing more than paranoia, **fatalism**, and inaction. New surveillance, in fact, both constrains and enables. Although it is unequally distributed, with large organizations controlling most information technologies, these same technologies have given ordinary people access to many new channels of participation and protest, not only nationally but globally. Today's increases in identity theft, spying, selling of personal information, and other

fatalism

the belief that events are determined by fate and cannot be changed by human actions

technological invasions of privacy prompted one sociologist to conclude that "public access to private information has taken on even more ominous tones."

WRITING IN RESPONSE TO READING

Reviewing the Reading   MyWritingLab

Answer each of the following questions using complete sentences.

1. What kinds of information do corporations and governments share?
2. What does the Pentagon's Total Information Awareness Program plan to do?
3. What impact did 9/11 have on libraries?
4. What kinds of monitoring did the government institute after 9/11?
5. What types of surveillance devices are available to the public?

Examining the Reading Using an Idea Map   MyWritingLab

Draw an idea map of the reading, using the guidelines on page 31.

Strengthening Your Vocabulary   MyWritingLab

Using the word's context, word parts, or a dictionary, write a brief definition of each of the following words as it is used in the reading.

1. wary (paragraph 6) _____
2. culling (paragraph 8) _____
3. thwart (paragraph 10) _____
4. apparatus (paragraph 11) _____
5. paranoia (paragraph 13) _____

Reacting to Ideas: Discussion and Journal Writing   MyWritingLab

Get ready to write about the reading by discussing the following:

1. How might information from surveillance cameras be misused? How can this be prevented?
2. How do we balance the government's need to gather information with our need for privacy?
3. What other threats to privacy occur in today's society?

 Thinking Visually   4. What point in the reading does the photo reinforce?

Paragraph Options   MyWritingLab

1. Write a paragraph explaining your views on whether or not private citizens should have access to surveillance equipment for their own personal use.
2. Do you agree that corporations and government agencies should be permitted to share surveillance information with each other? Write a paragraph exploring this.

Essay Options   MyWritingLab

3. Write an essay explaining how you feel about the government being able to access information about you from health, financial, and even library records. Do you believe this is a violation of your privacy?

4. Do you agree with those who say only criminals and terrorists should be worried about government surveillance? Write an essay expressing your views.

■ ■ ■ ■

| THEME 2 | SURVEILLANCE AND THE RIGHT TO PRIVACY—SELECTION 2 |

Thinking Before Reading

The following article originally appeared in *The Huffington Post*, an Internet newspaper and blog. It covers many areas of society, from politics and government through business, entertainment, and culture. As you read, note the author's tone. How does the title of the article help you predict the author's approach to the topic?

Step 1: Preview the reading.

Step 2: Connect the reading to your own experience:

a. Have you ever had your fingerprints taken, your retina scanned, or a sample of your DNA extracted? If you have not, would you consent to these methods in order to get a job you want?

b. Do you feel safer as a result of the post-9/11 War on Terror? How much do you know about U.S. government surveillance of its citizens? When was the last time you felt your picture was being taken without your permission?

Step 3: As you read, ask yourself questions such as those that appeared in the marginal annotations for the other professional readings throughout the book. Mark and annotate to record your answers.

READING

SMILE, THE GOVERNMENT IS WATCHING: NEXT GENERATION IDENTIFICATION

*"You had to live—did live, from habit that became instinct—in the assumption that every sound you made was overheard, and, except in darkness, every movement was **scrutinized**."* —George Orwell, *1984*

scrutinized
carefully examined

1   Brace yourselves for the next wave in the surveillance state's steady incursions into our lives. It's coming at us with a lethal one-two punch.

biometric
biologically based

2   To start with, there's the government's integration of facial recognition software and other **biometric** markers into its identification data programs. The FBI's Next Generation Identification (NGI) system is a $1 billion boondoggle that is aimed at dramatically expanding the government's current ID database from a fingerprint system to a facial recognition system. NGI will use a variety of biometric data, cross-referenced against the nation's growing network of surveillance cameras to not only track your every move but create a permanent "recognition" file on you within the government's massive databases.

3   By the time it's fully operational in 2014, NGI will serve as a vast data storehouse of "iris scans, photos searchable with face recognition technology, palm prints, and measures of gait and voice recordings alongside records of fingerprints, scars, and tattoos." One component of NGI, the Universal Face Workstation, already contains some 13 million facial images, gleaned from "criminal mug shot photos" taken during the booking process. However, with major search engines having "accumulated face image databases that in their size dwarf the Earth's population," it's only a matter of time before the government taps into the trove of images stored on social media and photo sharing websites such as Facebook.

4   Also aiding and abetting police in their efforts to track our every movement in real time is Trapwire, which allows for quick analysis of live feeds from **CCTV** surveillance cameras. Some of Trapwire's confirmed users are the DC police, and police and casinos in Las Vegas. Police in New York, Los Angeles, Canada, and London are also thought to be using Trapwire.

5   Using Trapwire in conjunction with NGI, police and other government agents will be able to pinpoint anyone by checking the personal characteristics stored in the database against images on social media websites, feeds from the thousands of CCTV surveillance cameras installed throughout American cities (there are 3,700 CCTV cameras tracking the public in the New York subway system alone), as well as data being beamed down from the more than 30,000 surveillance drones taking to the skies within the next eight years. Given that the drones' powerful facial recognition cameras will be capable of capturing minute details, including every mundane action performed by every person in an entire city simultaneously, soon there really will be nowhere to run and nowhere to hide, short of living in a cave, far removed from technology.

6   NGI will not only increase sharing between federal agencies, opening up the floodgates between the Department of Homeland Security, the State Department, the Department of Justice, and the Department of Defense, but states can also get in on the action. The system was rolled out in Michigan in February 2012, with Hawaii, Maryland, South Carolina, Ohio, New Mexico, Kansas, Arizona, Tennessee, Nebraska, and Missouri on the shortlist for implementation, followed by Washington, North Carolina, and Florida in the near future.

7   Going far beyond the scope of those with criminal backgrounds, the NGI data includes criminals and non-criminals alike—in other words, innocent American citizens. The information is being **amassed** through a variety of routine procedures, with the police leading the way as prime collectors of biometrics for something as non-threatening as a simple moving violation. For example, the New York Police Department began photographing **irises** of suspects and arrestees in 2010, routinely telling suspects that the scans were

CCTV
closed-circuit TV

amassed
gathered

iris
the color part of the eye

mandatory, despite there being no law requiring defendants to have their irises scanned. Police departments across the country are now being equipped with the Mobile Offender Recognition and Information System, or MORIS, a physical iPhone add-on that allows officers patrolling the streets to scan the irises and faces of individuals and match them against government databases.

8   The nation's courts are also doing their part to "build" the database, requiring biometric information as a precursor to more lenient sentences. In March 2012, New York Governor Andrew Cuomo signed a law allowing DNA evidence to be collected from anyone convicted of a crime, even if it's a non-violent misdemeanor. New York judges have also begun demanding mandatory iris scans before putting defendants on trial. Some **Occupy Wall Street** protesters who were arrested for trespassing and disorderly conduct were actually assigned bail based upon whether or not they consented to an iris scan during their booking. In one case, a judge demanded that an Occupy protestor, who was an unlikely flight risk, pay $1,000 bail because she refused to have her iris scanned.

9   Then there are the nation's public schools, where young people are being conditioned to mindlessly march in lockstep to the pervasive authoritarian dictates of the surveillance state. It was here that surveillance cameras and metal detectors became the norm. It was here, too, that schools began reviewing social media websites in order to police student activity. With the advent of biometrics, school officials have gone to ever more creative lengths to monitor and track students' activities and whereabouts, even for the most mundane things. For example, students in Pinellas County, Fla., are actually subjected to vein recognition scans when purchasing lunch at school.

10   Of course, the government is not the only looming threat to our privacy and bodily integrity. As with most invasive technologies, the groundwork to accustom the American people to the so-called benefits or conveniences of facial recognition is being laid quite effectively by corporations. For example, a new Facebook application, Facedeals, is being tested in Nashville, Tenn., which enables businesses to target potential customers with specialized offers. Yet another page borrowed from Stephen Spielberg's 2002 *Minority Report*, the app works like this: Businesses install cameras at their front doors which, using facial recognition technology, identify the faces of Facebook users and then send coupons to their smartphones based upon things they've "liked" in the past.

11   Making this noxious mix even more troubling is the significant margin for error and abuse that goes hand in hand with just about every government-instigated program, only more so when it comes to biometrics and identification databases. Take, for example, the Secure Communities initiative. Touted by the Department of Homeland Security as a way to crack down on illegal immigration, the program attempted to match the inmates in local jails against the federal immigration database. Unfortunately, it resulted in Americans being arrested for reporting domestic abuse and occasionally flagged U.S. citizens for deportation. More recently, in July 2012, security researcher Javier Galbally demonstrated that iris scans can be spoofed, allowing a hacker to use synthetic images of an iris to trick an iris-scanning device into thinking it had received a positive match for a real iris over 50 percent of the time.

Occupy Wall Street
a movement that protests income inequality (rich vs. poor)

juggernaut
a powerful force

12   The writing is on the wall. With technology moving so fast and assaults on our freedoms, privacy and otherwise, occurring with increasing frequency, there is little hope of turning back this technological, corporate and governmental **juggernaut**. Even trying to avoid inclusion in the government's massive identification database will be difficult. The hacktivist group Anonymous suggests wearing a transparent plastic mask, tilting one's head at a 15-degree angle, wearing obscuring makeup, and wearing a hat outfitted with Infra-red LED lights as methods for confounding the cameras' facial recognition technology.

13   Consider this, however: While the general public, largely law-abiding, continues to be pried on, spied on and treated like suspects by a government that spends an exorbitant amount of money on the security-intelligence complex (which takes in a sizeable chunk of the $80 billion yearly intelligence budget), the government's attention and resources are effectively being diverted from the true threats that remain at large—namely, those terrorists abroad who seek, through overt action and implied threat, to continue the reign of terror in America begun in the wake of the 9/11 attacks.

WRITING IN RESPONSE TO READING

Reviewing the Reading   `MyWritingLab`

Answer each of the following questions using complete sentences.

1. What does NGI stand for and what is its goal?
2. Approximately how many closed-circuit cameras are used in the New York City subway system?
3. Which was the first U.S. state to implement the NGI system?
4. What does the MORIS application allow police officers to do?
5. According to the author, in which social institution did surveillance cameras and metal detectors become "the norm"?
6. What methods can the average person use to outsmart cameras' facial-recognition technology?

Examining the Reading Using an Idea Map   `MyWritingLab`

Draw an idea map of the reading, using the guidelines on page 31.

Strengthening Your Vocabulary   `MyWritingLab`

Using the word's context, word parts, or a dictionary, write a brief definition of each of the following words as it is used in the reading.

1. incursions (paragraph 1) _____
2. boondoggle (paragraph 2) _____
3. gait (paragraph 3) _____
4. trove (paragraph 3) _____
5. minute (paragraph 5) _____
6. precursor (paragraph 8) _____

7. mundane (paragraph 9) _____

8. noxious (paragraph 11) _____

9. instigated (paragraph 11) _____

10. exorbitant (paragraph 13) _____

Reacting to Ideas: Discussion and Journal Writing   [MyWritingLab]

Get ready to write about the reading by discussing the following:

1. Have you ever felt "targeted" by ads as a result of your presence on Facebook or other social media? Explain the types of ads you have received and why you think you received them.

2. What are some of the possible benefits of Trapwire? What are some possible drawbacks?

3. Do you think that non-serious crimes (like minor traffic violations) warrant iris scans? Why or why not?

4. Is the government justified in using NGI and other biometric systems to manage immigration issues? Why or why not?

 Thinking Visually

5. How does the photo accompanying this article add to or detract from it? Write a caption to accompany the photo.

Paragraph Options   [MyWritingLab]

1. The quote that begins the article comes from the novel *1984* by George Orwell, originally published in 1949. Conduct a Web search to learn more about the novel. Then write a paragraph explaining how the themes of *1984* are related to the topics in this article.

2. What is the author's attitude toward NGI, the government, and government surveillance? Summarize the author's approach to the topics, referring to specific sentence or phrases that support your answer.

3. Would you be open to receiving the types of deals offered by Facedeals (as discussed in paragraph 10)? Why or why not? Write a paragraph explaining your answer.

Essay Options   [MyWritingLab]

4. Write an essay in which you argue in favor of NGI, MORIS, and the other technologies discussed in this article. In other words, if you think of this article as discussing the "con" side of surveillance technology, write an essay exploring the "pro" side.

5. Why do you think grammar and high schools have begun to track students' online activities? Do you think this type of surveillance is warranted? Why or why not? Write an essay in which you express your opinions.

6. Although the word is not used explicitly, this article is concerned with the idea of *privacy*. Do you think that today's college students (as well as younger students) have different expectations of privacy than older generations? Among your group of friends or classmates, what is considered "private" and what is considered "public" and therefore postable on Facebook or other social media? Write an essay in which you explore some ideas related to privacy in an online world.

CRITICAL READING AND WRITING

Integrating Ideas   MyWritingLab

After completing Reading #3 ("A Surveillance Society") and Reading #4 ("Smile, the Government Is Watching: Next Generation Identification"), choose one of the following questions to answer.

1. Compare and contrast the authors' approaches to technological surveillance. Which article is more balanced? Which is more biased? What words would you use to describe each author's tone?

2. Both articles make it clear that the increase in surveillance is a direct result of the events of 9/11. How do you think the world has changed since that day? Overall, do you think an increase in public surveillance helps make society safer from terrorist attacks? Or do you think the money spent on surveillance technology could be used in better ways?

3. Advocates of surveillance technology often say, "If you're not doing anything wrong, you have nothing to worry about." Do you agree with this statement? Do you think it justifies covert surveillance and the collection of people's personal data (including techniques like iris scans and facial recognition software)?

4. Both articles touch on the ways that businesses can use new surveillance techniques to target consumers. Do you think the government should share its data with businesses that are looking to market their products? What are the potential benefits and drawbacks to doing so?

■ ■ ■ ■

THEME 3   BULLYING—SELECTION 1

Thinking Before Reading

The following article originally appeared in *Teaching Tolerance*, a magazine sponsored and published by the Southern Poverty Law Center. According to its Web site, the magazine's mission is to "reduce prejudice, improve intergroup relations, and support equitable school experiences for our nation's children."

Step 1: Preview the reading.

Step 2: Connect the reading to your own experience:

a. Have you ever been bullied at school, or have you ever witnessed another student being bullied? If so, what happened?

b. How much do you know about cyberbullying? What does the term mean to you?

Step 3: As you read, ask yourself questions such as those that appeared in the marginal annotations for the other professional readings throughout the book. Mark and annotate to record your answers.

READING

THERE ARE NO BULLIES: JUST CHILDREN WHO BULLY—AND YOU CAN HELP THEM

Adrienne van der Valk

1   Bullying is a hot-button issue. High-profile lawsuits and suicides have thrust bullying into the spotlight. More schools are implementing policies designed to protect victims and crack down on perpetrators. In some schools, however, these efforts are outpacing education about bullying and the conditions that compel youth to engage in it. For the sake of all students, the time has come to look closely at two questions: Why do kids bully? How can we help them stop?

Why Do Kids Bully?

2   Bullying is a behavior, not an identity. For behavior to qualify as bullying, two conditions must exist:

- The aggressor must intend to hurt or intimidate someone less powerful.
- The behavior must be repeated.

3   A young person's behavior may meet these conditions in some situations but not others, which leaves schools, parents, and researchers searching for underlying motives.

4   Jaana Juvonen, a professor of developmental psychology at the University of California, Los Angeles, explores the motives of power and control in her research on bullying. "We're talking about strategic behavior that is there for a particular purpose . . . to fill a need. And the need is being able to control others," says Juvonen. "These are kids who are very deliberately, intentionally trying to hurt another kid. They want to dominate and feel powerful . . . Then the question in terms of how to help [a child who] bullies is to ask, 'Why do they have this need for control and power?'"

5   While attempting to answer this question, Juvonen has noticed that bullying behavior spikes during transition years, particularly the transition from elementary to middle school.

6   "It is during these times of social uncertainty where some kids resort to . . . primitive means to establish a social **hierarchy**," she says. "When you get into a new social environment you really don't have a sense of where you fit in, where you rank, who are your friends versus foes. It is helpful to have this dominance hierarchy."

hierarchy
ranking

7   Why some kids take this path and others don't isn't well established. What is clear is that aggressive kids often perceive ambiguous interactions— and even facial expressions—as negative or threatening. Kara Penniman, a school-based social worker in Columbus, OH, notes that students who bully often think their behavior is justified because others are "out to get them," and this belief touches off a cycle of negative interactions.

8   "Many kids who exhibit bullying behavior ... don't see themselves often as being particularly powerful," Penniman explains. "Sometimes they themselves are experiencing intimidation, threats, power, and control problems with other people, so it can be really common for them to see themselves as the victim."

9   Ultimately, though, all youth who exhibit bullying behavior—victims of aggression or not—are using bullying as a tool to meet a strong need, says Juvonen.

10   "[There are] these incredibly powerful cyclical pathways," she says. "Kids learn that there's this unmet need to feel powerful, to be able to control others, then you act in certain ways and you get rewarded for it." These rewards, however, exist in the short term only.

11   According to bullying experts Dan Olweus, Sue Limber, and Sharon F. Mahalie, 60% of boys who bullied others in middle school had at least one criminal conviction by the age of 24; 40% had three or more convictions. A recent study published in the *Journal of the American Medical Association* reported that youth who bully are at increased risk for depression, conduct disorders, substance abuse, and suicide.

How Can We Help?

12   The painful effects of bullying lead many educators to focus on justice and safety for students who are targeted and to feel contempt for those responsible for the pain—an approach that often results in harsh disciplinary measures, such as suspensions and expulsions from school.

13   These zero-tolerance measures may appear responsive, but Juvonen and most experts who study school discipline warn against policies that make school a threatening, uncertain place. Juvonen notes that in addition to not addressing the root causes of bullying, such harsh tactics fuel the perception that youth have no choice but to fight for themselves.

14   The most effective bullying interventions don't focus on only one category of kids, but rather acknowledge that all students benefit when schools empower youth and teach them about healthy relationships.

15   **Support students at risk**. Adopting comprehensive programming designed to promote social and emotional competencies is a great way to support students at risk of bullying. Judy Kerner, a special education teacher and behavioral support specialist, teaches one such class and works closely with youth who bully. She teaches skills that shift her students' thinking patterns—not only about others, but also about themselves.

16   Penniman, like Kerner, finds that individual conversations between skilled teachers or counselors and youth can be effective. She asks kids what behavioral role models they're emulating when they act out aggressively and if the strategies they use are working. This approach opens up a conversation in which the youth's perspective is central to the dialogue.

17   "I also do psychoeducation about some of the long-term consequences of bullying," Penniman says. "So, providing information . . . on what the impact is for bullies, what some long-term consequences are for them occupationally

and educationally." She doesn't deliver this information as a threat, but as a tool to empower students to take control of their choices and future.

18   **Target transition years**. For students predisposed to aggression, changing schools can be the catalyst that leads them to bullying.

19   Mentorship or buddy programs can help transitioning students feel less fearful. First-year bridge or tutorial programs provide an excellent opportunity for students to develop relationships and talk about school culture within a small home-team group that promotes student input. For youth at particular risk, educators can implement a formal or informal transition plan. This might include regular check-ins or school-based visits with siblings, coaches, clergy, former teachers, or anyone the youth identifies as a positive source of support.

20   **Change the language of bullying**. Many educators think that the term bully has become an ill-defined buzzword that contributes to binary thinking (bullies are evil, victims are innocent) and feeds zero-tolerance approaches. Penniman says that she rarely, if ever, uses the word with her clients.

21   "It's kind of inflammatory for most kids because oftentimes schools have a zero-tolerance policy toward bullying," she explains. "So if kids acknowledge that as a common cultural behavior within their peer group ... they are kind of admitting something that is completely not tolerated in schools, so there is not very much room for them to talk about change or growth or doing something different."

22   Experts recommend talking instead about healthy relationships, behavior, rights and choices. Ideally, schools should train the entire staff to align the way they talk about these expectations so students hear consistent messages. Talking about **empathy** and relationship choices also dismantles the perception that being a "bully" is a fixed identity.

empathy
ability to understand and share another person's feelings

23   **Look to the future**. Empathy is key, not just for addressing bullying behavior, but for educators as well. It's important to remember that these tough kids are still young people—and the window of opportunity to work with them is small.

24   School is a social arena in which students try on roles, says cultural studies expert Alissa Sklar. Without guidance and alternatives, aggressive students may find that the role of "bully" becomes increasingly rigid, an outcome with potentially devastating consequences for them and others.

25   "A lot of the rhetoric of bullying ... paints the kids who are bullies as ogres or monsters," Sklar says. "But by doing this, we're really doing everyone a great disservice. We're missing a golden opportunity to teach them. We need to remember that kids and teens who [bully] ... are still growing up. When we help them, we're also helping those they target—and those who might have been bullied by them in the future."

Cyberbullying

26   Bullying and technology overlap to such a degree that addressing one necessitates addressing the other. Schools are increasingly being asked to

respond to cyberbullying incidents that don't occur on school property, but bleed into the culture.

proactive
taking charge

27   Youth and media expert Alissa Sklar recommends that educators take a **proactive** leadership role in educating students—especially students who exhibit aggressive behaviors—about digital citizenship and the unique dynamics of technology-based bullying.

The Basics

28 • Phone and computer screens lead many people to behave in ways they would not in person. Screens do not, however, decrease the painful impact of insulting or hurtful language and images.

   • Targeting another person online can magnify hurtful consequences for the victim because of the public nature of the aggression. Bullying others online can also potentially magnify the consequences for perpetrators.

replicable
able to be copied

proliferation
rapid increase

   • Anything communicated digitally is infinitely **replicable** and impossible to delete. No one can truly "take back" anything posted to the Internet.

   • The **proliferation** of technology (particularly smartphones) means that students targeted by bullying can no longer find safety at home, among friends, or even by changing schools.

WRITING IN RESPONSE TO READING

Reviewing the Reading   `MyWritingLab`

Answer each of the following questions using complete sentences.

1. According to Jaana Juvonen, which specific need does bullying fulfill?
2. At which grade levels does bullying behavior show a marked increase?
3. Why is it common for schoolyard bullies to see themselves as victims, not bullies?
4. What are the links among bullying behavior, criminal behavior, and mental health?
5. What is a possible drawback to a zero-tolerance approach to bullying in schools?
6. List at least three approaches that can be taken to support students who are at risk of becoming bullies.
7. Why do some experts prefer not to use the word *bully*?

Examining the Reading Using an Idea Map   `MyWritingLab`

Draw an idea map of the reading, using the guidelines on page 31.

Strengthening Your Vocabulary   `MyWritingLab`

Using the word's context, word parts, or a dictionary, write a brief definition of each of the following words as it is used in the reading.

1. intimidate (paragraph 2) _____

2. transition (paragraph 5) _____

3. foes (paragraph 6) _____

4. ambiguous (paragraph 7) _____

5. contempt (paragraph 12) _____

6. comprehensive (paragraph 15) _____

7. emulating (paragraph 16) _____

8. catalyst (paragraph 18) _____

9. siblings (paragraph 19) _____

10. binary (paragraph 20) _____

11. inflammatory (paragraph 21) _____

12. rhetoric (paragraph 25) _____

Reacting to Ideas: Discussion and Journal Writing   `MyWritingLab`

Get ready to write about the reading by discussing the following:

1. What does the author mean when she says, "Bullying is a behavior, not an identity" (paragraph 2)?

2. Why might bullies feel the need to control a situation?

3. This article focuses on the steps taken to manage bullying. What steps might be taken to help the victims of bullying?

4. Suppose a particular school district sends its students to grammar school for grades K–5 and then to middle school for grades 6–8. At which grades might mentorship or buddy programs be most useful? Why?

5. The author refers to a "social hierarchy" in paragraph 6. What exactly does this term mean, and how does it relate to the term "dominance hierarchy" (also in paragraph 6)?

Paragraph Options   `MyWritingLab`

1. Write a paragraph in which you define two terms: *bullying* and *cyberbullying*.

2. Suppose you are a teacher. A student comes to you complaining that he is being bullied by a classmate. Write a paragraph explaining some of the actions you would take to correct the problem.

3. In a paragraph, explain why cyberbullying can be so much more damaging and pervasive than traditional schoolyard bullying.

Essay Options   `MyWritingLab`

4. According to the author, bullying is a "hot-button issue" in schools. What are some other hot-button issues in schooling today? Write an essay in which you explore another controversial topic in schooling.

5. Olweus, Limber, and Mahalic studied male bullies (paragraph 11). Do you think females can engage in bullying behavior, too? How might female bullies differ from male bullies? How might they be similar? Write an essay exploring these questions.

6. Do you think bullies should be expelled from school? Why or why not? Write an essay in which you state and support your opinion.

■ ■ ■ ■

THEME 3   BULLYING—SELECTION 2

Thinking Before Reading

The following article originally appeared in *Psychology Today*, a magazine devoted to helping a general audience understand the many facets of psychology. The magazine considers itself a serious one that makes sophisticated psychological research accessible to readers. As you read the article, note the author's tone and approach to the subject.

Step 1: Preview the reading.

Step 2: Connect the reading to your own experience:

    a. Have you ever been bullied in the workplace? If so, what happened and how did you feel? How would you define a "workplace bully"?

    b. Have you ever witnessed an employee (perhaps at a retail store, on a construction site, or in a hotel or motel) being bullied in the workplace? If so, what happened?

Step 3: As you read, ask yourself questions such as those that appeared in the marginal annotations for the other professional readings throughout the book. Mark and annotate to record your answers.

READING

THE SILENT EPIDEMIC: WORKPLACE BULLYING

Ray Williams

1   Workplace bullying has become a silent epidemic in North America, one that has huge hidden costs in terms of employee well being and productivity. Also known as psychological harassment or emotional abuse, bullying involves the conscious repeated effort to wound and seriously harm another person not with violence, but with words and actions. Bullying damages the physical, emotional, and mental health of the person who is targeted.

2   The workplace bully abuses power, brings misery to his/her target and endeavors to steal the target's self-confidence. Bullies often involve others using many tactics such as blaming for errors, unreasonable work demands, insults, putdowns, stealing credit, threatening job loss, and discounting accomplishments.

How serious is the bullying problem in the workplace?

3   In two surveys by the Workplace Bullying Institute (WBI) and Zogby International, where bullying was defined as "repeated mistreatment: sabotage by others that prevented work from getting done, verbal abuse, threatening conduct, intimidation and humiliation," 35% of workers experienced bullying first hand, and 62% of the bullies were men. A Harris Interactive poll conducted in 2011 revealed that 34% of women reported being bullied in the workplace.

4   Who are these bullies? The WBI concluded that while perpetrators can be found in all ranks within organizations, the vast majority are bosses— managers, supervisors, and executives.

What's the impact of bullying behavior?

attrition
the rate at which employees
leave a company

5   Bullies create a terrible toll within an organization. Their behavior leads to increased levels of stress among employees, higher rates of absenteeism, and higher than normal **attrition**. Because bullies often get results by getting more short-term production out of employees, they are tolerated. One study by John Medina showed that workers stressed by bullying performed 50% worse on cognitive tests. Other studies estimate the financial costs of bullying at more than $200 billion per year.

6   A study by Dr. Noreen Tehrani, who counseled victims of violence in Northern Ireland, and soldiers returning from overseas combat and victims of workplace bullying, concluded that bullying exhibited similar psychological and physical symptoms—nightmares and extreme anxiety, and a variety of physical ailments.

7   Swedish researchers, led by Anna Nyberg at the Stress Institute in Stockholm, have published a study in the *Journal of Occupational and Environmental Medicine* on the issue of leaders' behavior and employee health. They studied more than 3,100 men over a 10-year period in typical work settings. They found that employees who had managers who were incompetent, inconsiderate, secretive and uncommunicative were 60% more likely to suffer a heart attack or other life-threatening **cardiac** condition. By contrast, employees who worked with "good" leaders were 40% less likely to suffer heart problems. Nyberg said, "for all those who work under managers who they perceive behave strangely, or in any way they don't understand, and they feel stressed, the study confirms this develops into a health risk."

cardiac
related to the heart

8   A study of 6,000 British office workers found employees who felt that their supervisors treated them fairly had a 30% lower risk of heart disease. A 2008 meta-analysis of the connection between health and leadership by Jana Kuoppala and associates concluded that good leadership was associated with a 27% reduction in sick leave and a 46% reduction in disability pensions. The same study concluded that employees with good leaders were 40% more likely to report the highest levels of psychological well being, including lower levels of anxiety and depression.

9   In an article by Richard Williams, Wallace Higgins, and Harvey Greenberg, published in the *Boston Globe*, the authors cited numerous research studies regarding leadership style and the health of employees. They concluded "your boss can cause you stress, induce depression and anxiety or even trigger the onset of serious illnesses. It is not just bad managers who can negatively affect employee health, but it is also the halfhearted and mediocre who put employees on the sick list." And the cost is huge in terms of lost productivity, healthcare costs and employee turnover. The authors argue that a whole new field of litigation in the United States is developing—"lawsuits against 'bad bosses' and the organizations that negligently allow them to supervise."

10   According to the WBI, 40% of the targets of bulling never told their employers, and of those that did, 62% reported that they were ignored. According to Dr. Gary Namie, Research Director at WBI, and author of *The Bully at Work: What You Can Do to Stop the Hurt and Reclaim Your Dignity on the*

Job, 81% of employers are either doing nothing to address bullying or actually resisting action when requested to do something.

What are the reasons for this bullying behavior?

11   Dr. Robert Sutton of Stanford University, and author of *The No A—h—Rule: Building a Civilized Workplace and Surviving One That Isn't*, argues that in business and sports it is assumed that if you are a big winner, you can get away with being a jerk. And overwhelmingly, these "jerks" [his word is stronger] are bosses. Sutton claims this behavior affects the bottom line through increased turnover, absenteeism, and decreased commitment and performance. He says the time spent counseling or **appeasing** these people, consoling victimized employees, reorganizing departments of teams, and arranging transfers produce significant hidden costs for the company.

appeasing
placating

12   As John Baldoni, author of nine books on leadership, including *Lead By Example* and *Lead Your Boss*, says bullies may "get employees to comply, but not to commit. Compliance is okay for day-to-day operations, but when an organization is faced with a challenge or even a crisis, you need employees who are willing to go the extra mile. People who work for a bully are biding their time looking for a way out, or a time when the bully will be replaced."

What kind of people are bullies in the workplace?

13   Lisa M. S. Barrow, author of *In Darkness Light Dawns: Exposing Workplace Bullying*, says "Bullies typically possess a Type A personality; they are competitive and appear driven, operating as they do from a sense of urgency. This has its advantages in the workplace but the shadow side of Type A is the tendency to become frustrated and verbally abusive when things don't go according to plan. Impatience and temper tantrums are common for Type A individuals who haven't engaged in the personal growth required to gain self-awareness, maintain emotional stability, and consider situations from multiple points of view. Because of the bully's 'two-faced nature'—considerate if things are going well and abusive if not—his/her presence in an organization can cause the work environment to become tense. People feel as if they are walking on eggshells around the bully. They feel he/she is a sleeping giant, who could, upon waking, explode with rage. Above all, bullies crave power and control, and this craving underlies much of what they do, say, and fail to do and say. Bullies use charm and deceit to further their own ends and seem oblivious to the trail of damage they leave behind, as long as their appetites for power and control are fulfilled."

14   Lynn Taylor, author of *Tame Your Terrible Office Tyrant*, writes in an article in *Psychology Today* that a 5-year national study of bullying from 2004 to 2009 of psychological traits of bosses, showed that "self-oriented" spiked by 50% to claim the top spot over other characteristics. Taylor reported that 70% of Americans in her survey said "bosses and toddlers with too much power, act alike."

15   Contrary to conventional wisdom, the targets of office bullies are not the new, inexperienced and less confident employees. The targets, according to research, are the highly competent, accomplished, experienced, and popular

employees. And making them targets makes it harder for them to get notice or reprieve. Independent, experienced workers pose the greatest threat to the bullies. And when bullies find targets that refuse to be controlled and intimidated, they escalate their behavior.

16   It's possible, as well, that bullying is part of a larger issue of a growing culture of incivility. Researchers at the University of California, Berkeley and University of Southern California shows that bosses who are in over their heads are more likely to bully subordinates. That's because feelings of inadequacy trigger them to lash out at others. The researchers found a direct link among supervisors and upper management between self-perceived incompetence and aggression. The findings were gleaned from four separate studies, published in the journal *Psychological Science*.

17   Is there a relationship between bosses' bullying behavior and narcissism? The incidents of narcissistic bosses such as Bernard Madoff or Ken Lay seem to be on the increase. According to Jim Moral, Professor of Management at Florida State, 31% of employees surveyed reported that their boss was prone to exaggerate his or her accomplishments and downplay the contributions of others. The study concluded that the narcissistic bosses created toxic environments resulting in declining productivity.

18   The recent economic downturn, with layoffs and financial pressures on managers to perform, may have exacerbated the bullying problem. Research conducted by Wayne Hochwarter and Samantha Englehardt at Florida State University concluded that "employer-employee relations are at one of the lowest points in history," with a significant decline in basic civility.

19   Is bullying a reflection of a general decline in civility? In poll after poll, Americans have voiced concern over the erosion of civility. According to a poll by Weber Shandwick, 65% of Americans say the lack of civility is a major problem in the country and feel the negative **tenor** has worsened during the financial crisis and recession.

tenor
tone

20   Pier M. Forni, author of *The Civility Solution: What To Do When People Are Rude* and director of The Civility Initiative at Johns Hopkins University says, "In today's America, incivility is on prominent display: in the schools, where bullying is pervasive; in the workplace, where an increasing number are more stressed out by coworkers than their jobs; on the roads, where road rage **maims** and kills; in politics, where **strident** intolerance takes the place of earnest dialogue; and on the Web, where many check their inhibitions at the digital door."

maims
causes significant harm

strident
harsh

21   According to a 2008 study published in the *Canadian Journal of Cultural Studies*, allegiance to many old public virtues such as the Bill of Rights, the Geneva Convention, and the rule of domestic and international law is now commonly mocked or dismissed as **quaint** by significant people in power and persuasion.

quaint
old-fashioned

22   Some also suggest that there is a "blame the victim" mentality developing in the nation that somehow contends that the victims of crime, domestic violence, poverty, workplace conflict, and foreign civilian populations "had it coming," rationalized by the artificial justification of "toughness" or "responsibility."

So what's being done about workplace bullying?

23   Sutton encourages organizations to do something about it. Among the companies that keep the jerks out are Google's "no jerk" policy and business software company Success Factors, instituting a similar rule, which includes lengthy job interviews and probing questions designed to uncover brow-beating tendencies.

24   Robert Mueller, author of *Bullying Bosses*, and Marilyn E. Veincentotzs, author of *How Organizations Empower the Bully Boss*, contend that both organizations and employees need to confront bully bosses and refuse to accept their bullying behavior.

25   In the United States, 20 states are now exploring legislation that would put bullying on the legal radar screen. In Canada, the provinces of Ontario, Saskatchewan, and Quebec have passed legislation that addresses workplace bullying, although both countries are far behind countries in Europe and New Zealand.

26   One thing is for sure; the problem of workplace bullying will not go away anytime soon and may never be fully remedied until enough people call for a return to a culture of civility, and demand that governments and organizations take action.

WRITING IN RESPONSE TO READING

Reviewing the Reading   MyWritingLab

Answer each of the following questions using complete sentences.

1. Briefly define "workplace bullying." What are two synonyms for "workplace bullying"?
2. Who is more likely to be a bully, a man or a woman? Who is more likely to be bullied, men or women?
3. Are workplace bullies typically found in the low, middle, or high ranks of a company?
4. According to the study by Dr. Noreen Tehrani, what are the psychological and physical effects of being bullied in the workplace?
5. What are some of the positive effects of having a good manager in the workplace?
6. What is a Type A personality?
7. According to Lisa Barrow, what do workplace bullies crave?
8. Which of the world's countries have made the greatest strides in addressing the issue of workplace bullying?

Examining the Reading Using an Idea Map   MyWritingLab

Draw an idea map of the reading, using the guidelines on page 31.

Strengthening Your Vocabulary [MyWritingLab]

Using the word's context, word parts, or a dictionary, write a brief definition of each of the following words or phrases as it is used in the reading.

1. endeavors (paragraph 2) _____
2. discounting (paragraph 2) _____
3. toll (paragraph 5) _____
4. cognitive (paragraph 5) _____
5. mediocre (paragraph 9) _____
6. the bottom line (paragraph 11) _____
7. oblivious (paragraph 13) _____
8. reprieve (paragraph 15) _____
9. narcissism (paragraph 17) _____
10. exacerbated (paragraph 18) _____

Reacting to Ideas: Discussion and Journal Writing [MyWritingLab]

Get ready to write about the reading by discussing the following:

1. Paragraph 2 lists several tactics used by workplace bullies. Can you add any others to this list?

2. Why do you think that bosses and managers are more likely to be bullies than rank-and-file employees?

3. Who was the best boss you ever had? The worst? Why? Did your bad boss exhibit any bullying behaviors to anyone in the workplace?

4. John Baldoni, quoted in paragraph 12, says that bullies may "get employees to comply, but not to commit." What exactly does he mean?

5. Would you consider yourself a Type A personality? Why or why not? What do you think are the benefits and drawbacks to having a Type A personality?

6. Why do you think successful, well-liked people are more likely to be the target of bullying?

 Thinking Visually 7. How does the photo accompanying this article add to or detract from it? Write a caption to accompany the photo.

Paragraph Options [MyWritingLab]

1. Paragraph 23 makes reference to Google's "no jerk" policy. Write a paragraph in which you explain the "no jerk" policy you would institute in your own workplace.

2. Suppose you are a boss or manager. An employee comes to you complaining that he is being bullied by a co-worker. Write a paragraph explaining the actions you would take to correct the problem.

3. In a paragraph, summarize (a) the negative effects of bullying in the workplace, and (b) the positive effects of good leadership.

Essay Options   MyWritingLab

4. Paragraph 16 talks about the "culture of incivility." Write an essay in which you explore various examples of rudeness or incivility that you have encountered. Provide suggestions for ways to make society more civil or polite.

5. Write an essay in which you recount an episode of workplace bullying you experienced or witnessed. What exactly happened? How did each party behave and respond?

6. The article outlines the many positive effects of positive management. Write an essay in which you explain what exactly a good boss is and does. (You might also discuss what a good boss is *not* or does *not* do.)

CRITICAL READING AND WRITING

Integrating Ideas   MyWritingLab

After completing Reading #5 ("There Are No Bullies: Just Children Who Bully—And You Can Help Them") and Reading #6 ("The Silent Epidemic: Workplace Bullying"), choose one of the following questions to answer.

1. Which types of content (topics, themes, and so on) are common to both readings?

2. The article about workplace bullying does not make any reference to "cyberbullying" in the workplace. Do you think cyberbullying is common in the workplace? Why or why not?

3. How do you think the motives of cyberbullies are similar to those of workplace bullies? How, if at all, are they different?

4. What are some key differences between cyberbullying and workplace bullying?

■ ■ ■ ■

PART VII

Reviewing the Basics

GUIDE TO REVIEWING THE BASICS

OVERVIEW

Most of us know how to communicate in our own language. When we talk or write, we put our thoughts into words and, by and large, we make ourselves understood. But many of us do not know the specific terms and rules of grammar. Grammar is a system that describes how language is put together. Grammar must be learned, almost as if it were a foreign language.

Why is it important to study grammar, to understand grammatical terms like *verb, participle,* and *gerund* and concepts like *agreement* and *subordination?* There are several good reasons. Knowing grammar will allow you to

- **recognize an error in your writing and correct it.** Your papers will read more smoothly and communicate more effectively when they are error free.

- **understand the comments of your teachers and peers.** People who read and critique your writing may point out a "fragment" or a "dangling modifier." You will be able to revise and correct the problems.

- **write with more impact.** Grammatically correct sentences are signs of clear thinking. Your readers will get your message without distraction or confusion.

As you will see in this section, "Reviewing the Basics," the different areas of grammatical study are highly interconnected. The sections on parts of speech, sentences, punctuation, mechanics, and spelling fit together into a logical whole. To recognize and correct a run-on sentence, for example, you need to know both sentence structure *and* punctuation. To avoid errors in capitalization, you need to know parts of speech *and* mechanics. If grammar is to do you any good, your knowledge of it must be thorough. As you review the following "basics," be alert to the interconnections that make language study so interesting.

Grammatical terms and rules demand your serious attention. Mastering them will pay handsome dividends: error-free papers, clear thinking, and effective writing.

A Understanding the Parts of Speech

The eight parts of speech are **nouns**, **pronouns**, **verbs**, **adjectives**, **adverbs**, **conjunctions**, **prepositions**, and **interjections**. Each word in a sentence functions as one of these parts of speech. Being able to identify the parts of speech in sentences allows you to analyze and improve your writing and to understand grammatical principles discussed later in this section.

It is important to keep in mind that *how* a word functions in a sentence determines *what* part of speech it is. Thus, the same word can be a noun, a verb, or an adjective, depending on how it is used.

NOUN

He needed some blue wallpaper.

VERB

He will wallpaper the hall.

ADJECTIVE

He went to a wallpaper store.

A.1 NOUNS

A **noun** names a person, place, thing, or idea.

People	*woman, winner, Maria Alvarez*
Places	*mall, hill, Indiana*
Things	*lamp, ship, air*
Ideas	*goodness, perfection, harmony*

The form of many nouns changes to express **number** (**singular** for one, **plural** for more than one): *one bird, two birds; one child, five children.* Most nouns can also be made **possessive** to show ownership by the addition of *-'s: city's, Norma's.*

Sometimes a noun is used to modify another noun:

NOUN MODIFYING DIPLOMA

Her goal had always been to earn a college diploma.

517

Nouns are classified as **proper**, **common**, **collective**, **concrete**, **abstract**, **count**, and **noncount**.

1. **Proper nouns** name specific people, places, or things and are always capitalized: *Martin Luther King, Jr.; East Lansing; Ford Taurus*. Days of the week and months are considered proper nouns and are capitalized.

   PROPER NOUN PROPER NOUN   PROPER NOUN
   In September Allen will attend Loyola University.

2. **Common nouns** name one or more of a general class or type of person, place, thing, or idea and are not capitalized: *president, city, car, wisdom*.

   COMMON NOUN COMMON NOUN   COMMON NOUN   COMMON NOUN
   Next fall the students will enter college to receive an education.

3. **Collective nouns** name a whole group or collection of people, places, or things: *committee, team, jury*. They are usually singular in form.

   COLLECTIVE NOUN   COLLECTIVE NOUN
   The flock of mallards is flying over the herd of bison.

4. **Concrete nouns** name tangible things that can be tasted, seen, touched, smelled, or heard: *sandwich, radio, pen*.

   CONCRETE NOUN   CONCRETE NOUN
   The frozen pizza was stuck in the freezer.

5. **Abstract nouns** name ideas, qualities, beliefs, and conditions: *honesty, goodness, poverty*. Use a singular verb with an abstract noun.

   ABSTRACT NOUNS ABSTRACT NOUN
   Their marriage was based on love, honor, and trust.

   ABSTRACT NOUN
   Poverty is a major problem in the United States.
   SINGULAR VERB

6. **Count nouns** name items that can be counted. Count nouns can be made plural, usually by adding -*s* or -*es*: *one river, three rivers; one box, ten boxes*. Some count nouns form their plural in an irregular way: *man, men; goose, geese*.

   COUNT NOUN   COUNT NOUN   COUNT NOUN
   The salespeople put the invoices in their files.

7. **Noncount nouns** name ideas or qualities that cannot be counted. Noncount nouns almost always have no plural form: *air, knowledge, unhappiness*.

   NONCOUNT NOUN   NONCOUNT NOUN
   As the rain pounded on the windows, she tried to find the courage to walk home from work.

A.2 PRONOUNS

A **pronoun** is a word that substitutes for or refers to a noun or another pronoun. The noun or pronoun to which a pronoun refers is called the pronoun's **antecedent**. A pronoun must agree with its antecedent in person, number, and gender (these terms are discussed later in this section).

> After the campers discovered the cave, they mapped it for the next group, which was arriving next week. [The pronoun *they* refers to its antecedent, *campers*; the pronoun *it* refers to its antecedent, *cave*; the pronoun *which* refers to its antecedent, *group*.]

The eight kinds of pronouns are **personal, demonstrative, reflexive, intensive, interrogative, relative, indefinite,** and **reciprocal.**

1. **Personal pronouns** take the place of nouns or pronouns that name people or things. A personal pronoun changes form to indicate **person, gender, number,** and **case.**

    Person is the grammatical term used to distinguish the speaker (**first person:** *I, we*); the person spoken to (**second person:** *you*); and the person or thing spoken about (**third person:** *he, she, it, they*). **Gender** is the term used to classify pronouns as **masculine** (*he, him*); **feminine** (*she, her*); or **neuter** (*it*). **Number** classifies pronouns as **singular** (one) or **plural** (more than one). Some personal pronouns also function as adjectives modifying nouns (*our house*).

PERSON	SINGULAR	PLURAL
First person	I, me, my, mine	we, us, our, ours
Second person	you, your, yours	you, your, yours
Third person		
Masculine	he, him, his	
Feminine	she, her, hers	they, them, their, theirs
Neuter	it, its	

    I called my manager about my new clients. She wanted to know as soon as they placed their first orders. "Your new clients are important to us," she said.

    *[1ST-PERSON SINGULAR] I
    [1ST-PERSON SINGULAR (PRONOUN/ADJECTIVE)] my
    [1ST-PERSON SINGULAR (PRONOUN/ADJECTIVE)] my
    [3RD-PERSON SINGULAR] She
    [3RD-PERSON PLURAL] they
    [3RD-PERSON PLURAL (PRONOUN/ADJECTIVE)] their
    [2ND-PERSON SINGULAR (PRONOUN/ADJECTIVE)] Your
    [1ST-PERSON PLURAL] us
    [3RD-PERSON SINGULAR] she*

    A pronoun's **case** is determined by its function as a subject (**subjective** or **nominative case**) or an object (**objective case**) in a sentence. A pronoun that shows ownership is in the **possessive case.**

2. **Demonstrative pronouns** refer to particular people or things. The demonstrative pronouns are *this* and *that* (singular) and *these* and *those* (plural). (*This, that, these,* and *those* can also be demonstrative adjectives when they modify a noun.)

This is more thorough than that.

The red shuttle buses stop here. These go to the airport every hour.

3. **Reflexive pronouns** indicate that the subject performs actions to, for, or upon itself. Reflexive pronouns end in *-self* or *-selves*.

We excused ourselves from the table and left.

PERSON	SINGULAR	PLURAL
First person	myself	ourselves
Second person	yourself	yourselves
Third person	himself	
	herself	themselves
	itself	

4. An **intensive pronoun** emphasizes the word that comes before it in a sentence. Like reflexive pronouns, intensive pronouns end in *-self* or *-selves*.

The filmmaker herself could not explain the ending.

They themselves repaired the copy machine.

Note: A reflexive or intensive pronoun should not be used as a subject of a sentence. An antecedent for the reflexive pronoun must appear in the same sentence.

INCORRECT	Myself create colorful sculpture.
CORRECT	I myself create colorful sculpture.

5. **Interrogative pronouns** are used to introduce questions: *who, whom, whoever, whomever, what, which, whose.* The correct use of *who* and *whom* depends on the role the interrogative pronoun plays in a sentence or clause. When the pronoun functions as the subject of the sentence or clause, use *who.* When the pronoun functions as an object in the sentence or clause, use *whom.*

What happened?

Which is your street?

Who wrote *Ragtime?* [*Who* is the subject of the sentence.]

Whom should I notify? [*Whom* is the object of the verb *notify: I should notify whom?*]

6. **Relative pronouns** relate groups of words to nouns or other pronouns and often introduce adjective clauses or noun clauses (see p. 552). The relative pronouns are *who, whom, whoever, whomever,* and *whose* (referring to people) and *that, what, whatever,* and *which* (referring to things).

In 1836 Charles Dickens met John Forster, who became his friend and biographer.

We read some articles that were written by former astronauts.

7. **Indefinite pronouns** are pronouns without specific antecedents. They refer to people, places, or things in general.

<u>Someone</u> has been rearranging my papers.

<u>Many</u> knew the woman, but <u>few</u> could say they knew her well.

Here are some frequently used indefinite pronouns:

SINGULAR		PLURAL
another	nobody	all
anybody	none	both
anyone	no one	few
anything	nothing	many
each	one	more
either	other	most
everybody	somebody	others
everyone	someone	several
everything	something	some
neither		

8. The **reciprocal pronouns** *each other* and *one another* indicate a mutual relationship between two or more parts of a plural antecedent.

   Dión and Sharon congratulated <u>each other</u> on their high grades.

EXERCISE 1   Identifying Nouns and Pronouns

Directions: In each of the following sentences (a) circle each noun and (b) underline each pronoun.

EXAMPLE   When <u>we</u> finished the (project), <u>our</u> (manager) celebrated by ordering (pizza) for <u>everyone</u> in the (office).

1. I know the course will be challenging, but I will do whatever it takes to succeed.

2. The blue whale can weigh up to 150 tons; its heart alone weighs as much as a car.

3. Victor and his co-workers collaborated on the report, but he wrote the final version himself.

4. Whoever calls to identify the song playing on the radio will win a free ticket to a concert.

5. My son and daughter both love sports: his favorite sport is basketball, and hers is baseball.

6. Anybody who owns a car can save a small fortune on repairs by taking a basic course in automotive mechanics.

7. Whose leftover food is making the refrigerator smell bad?

8. Kayla is president of a club that promotes environmental awareness and encourages students to use their bikes instead of cars.

9. During the horror movie, my friend and I kept screaming and grabbing each other.

10. This is a busy time of year, but that is no excuse for skipping your workout.

■

A.3 VERBS

Verbs express action or state of being. A grammatically complete sentence has at least one verb in it.

There are three kinds of verbs: **action verbs**, **linking verbs**, and **helping verbs** (also known as **auxiliary verbs**).

1. **Action verbs** express physical and mental activities.

> Mr. Ramirez <u>dashed</u> for the bus.
>
> The incinerator <u>burns</u> garbage at high temperatures.
>
> I <u>think</u> that seat is taken.
>
> The programmer <u>worked</u> until 3:00 A.M.

Action verbs are either **transitive** or **intransitive**. The action of a **transitive verb** is directed toward someone or something, called the **direct object** of the verb. Direct objects receive the action of the verb. Transitive verbs require direct objects to complete the meaning of the sentence.

	TRANSITIVE	DIRECT
SUBJECT	VERB	OBJECT
Amalia	<u>made</u>	clocks.

An **intransitive verb** does not need a direct object to complete the meaning of the sentence.

		INTRANSITIVE
	SUBJECT	VERB
The	traffic	<u>stopped</u>.

Some verbs can be both transitive and intransitive, depending on their meaning and use in a sentence.

INTRANSITIVE   The traffic <u>stopped</u>. [no direct object]

> DIRECT OBJECT

TRANSITIVE   The driver <u>stopped</u> the <u>bus</u> at the corner.

2. A **linking verb** expresses a state of being or a condition. A linking verb connects a noun or pronoun to words that describe the noun or pronoun. Common linking verbs are forms of the verb *be* (*is, are, was, were, being, been*), *become, feel, grow, look, remain, seem, smell, sound, stay*, and *taste*.

> Their child <u>grew</u> tall.
>
> The office <u>looks</u> messy.
>
> Mr. Davenport <u>is</u> our accountant.

3. A **helping (auxiliary) verb** helps another verb, called the **main verb**, to convey when the action occurred (through verb tense) and to form questions. One or more helping verbs and the main verb together form a **verb phrase**. Some helping verbs, called **modals**, are always helping verbs:

can, could	shall, should
may, might	will, would
must, ought to	

The other helping verbs can sometimes function as main verbs as well:

am, are, be, been, being, did, do, does

had, has, have

is, was, were

The verb *be* is a very irregular verb, with eight forms instead of the usual five: *am, is, are, be, being, been, was, were.*

> HELPING MAIN
> VERB   VERB

The store <u>will</u> <u>close</u> early on holidays.

> HELPING   MAIN
> VERB   VERB

<u>Will</u> the store <u>close</u> early on New Year's Eve?

Forms of the Verb

All verbs except *be* have five forms: the **base form** (or dictionary form), the **past tense**, the **past participle**, the **present participle**, and the **-s form**. The first three forms are called the verb's **principal parts**. The **infinitive** consists of *to* plus a base form: *to go, to study, to talk.* For **regular verbs**, the past tense and past participle are formed by adding *-d* or *-ed* to the base form. **Irregular verbs** follow no set pattern to form their past tense and past participle.

TENSE	REGULAR	IRREGULAR
Base form	work	eat
Past tense	worked	ate
Past participle	worked	eaten
Present participle	working	eating
-s form	works	eats

Verbs change form to agree with their subjects in person and number (see p. 246); to express the time of their action (**tense**); to express whether the action is a fact, command, or wish (**mood**); and to indicate whether the subject is the doer or the receiver of the action (**voice**).

A. Parts of Speech

Principal Parts of Irregular Verbs

Consult the following list and your dictionary for the principal parts of irregular verbs.

BASE FORM	PAST TENSE	PAST PARTICIPLE
be	was, were	been
become	became	become
begin	began	begun
bite	bit	bitten
blow	blew	blown
burst	burst	burst
catch	caught	caught
choose	chose	chosen
come	came	come
dive	dived, dove	dived
do	did	done
draw	drew	drawn
drive	drove	driven
eat	ate	eaten
fall	fell	fallen
find	found	found
fling	flung	flung
fly	flew	flown
get	got	gotten
give	gave	given
go	went	gone
grow	grew	grown
have	had	had
know	knew	known
lay	laid	laid
lead	led	led
leave	left	left
lie	lay	lain
lose	lost	lost
ride	rode	ridden
ring	rang	rung
rise	rose	risen
say	said	said
set	set	set
sit	sat	sat
speak	spoke	spoken
swear	swore	sworn
swim	swam	swum
tear	tore	torn
tell	told	told
throw	threw	thrown
wear	wore	worn
write	wrote	written

Tense

The **tenses** of a verb express time. They convey whether an action, process, or event takes place in the present, past, or future.

The three **simple tenses** are **present**, **past**, and **future**. The **simple present** tense is the base form of the verb (and the *-s* form of third-person singular subjects; see p. 236); the **simple past** tense is the past-tense form; and the **simple future** tense consists of the helping verb *will* plus the base form.

The **perfect tenses**, which indicate completed action, are **present perfect**, **past perfect**, and **future perfect**. They are formed by adding the helping verbs *have* (or *has*), *had*, or *will have* to the past participle.

In addition to the simple and perfect tenses, there are six progressive tenses. The **simple progressive tenses** are the **present progressive**, the **past progressive**, and the **future progressive**. The progressive tenses are used for continuing actions or actions in progress. These progressive tenses are formed by adding the present, past, and future forms of the verb *be* to the present participle. The **perfect progressive tenses** are the **present perfect progressive**, the **past perfect progressive**, and the **future perfect progressive**. They are formed by adding the present perfect, past perfect, and future perfect forms of the verb *be* to the present participle.

The following chart shows all the tenses for a regular verb and an irregular verb in the first person. (For more on tenses, see p. 236.)

TENSE	REGULAR	IRREGULAR
Simple present	I talk	I go
Simple past	I talked	I went
Simple future	I will talk	I will go
Present perfect	I have talked	I have gone
Past perfect	I had talked	I had gone
Future perfect	I will have talked	I will have gone
Present progressive	I am talking	I am going
Past progressive	I was talking	I was going
Future progressive	I will be talking	I will be going
Present perfect progressive	I have been talking	I have been going
Past perfect progressive	I had been talking	I had been going
Future perfect progressive	I will have been talking	I will have been going

Mood

The **mood** of a verb indicates the writer's attitude toward the action. There are three moods in English: **indicative**, **imperative**, and **subjunctive**.

The **indicative mood** is used for ordinary statements of fact or questions.

The light <u>flashed</u> on and off all night.

<u>Did</u> you <u>check</u> the batteries?

The **imperative mood** is used for commands, suggestions, or directions. The subject of a verb in the imperative mood is *you*, though it is not always included.

<u>Stop</u> shouting!

<u>Come</u> to New York for a visit.

<u>Turn</u> right at the next corner.

The **subjunctive mood** is used for wishes, requirements, recommendations, and statements contrary to fact. For statements contrary to fact or for wishes, the past tense of the verb is used. For the verb *be,* only the past-tense form *were* is used.

If I <u>had</u> a million dollars, I'd take a trip around the world.

If my supervisor <u>were</u> promoted, I would be eligible for her job.

To express suggestions, recommendations, or requirements, the base form is often used.

I recommend that the houses <u>be</u> sold after the landscaping is done.

The registrar required that Maureen <u>pay</u> her bill before attending class.

Voice

Transitive verbs (those that take objects) may be in either the active voice or the passive voice (see p. 249). In an **active-voice** sentence, the subject performs the action described by the verb; that is, the subject is the actor. In a **passive-voice** sentence, the subject is the receiver of the action. The passive voice of a verb is formed by using an appropriate form of the helping verb *be* and the past participle of the main verb.

SUBJECT IS   ACTIVE
ACTOR   VOICE

Dr. Hillel <u>delivered</u> the report on global warming.

SUBJECT
IS RECEIVER   PASSIVE VOICE

The report on global warming <u>was delivered</u> by Dr. Hillel.

EXERCISE 2   Changing Verb Tense

Directions: Revise the following sentences, changing each verb from the present tense to the tense indicated.

    EXAMPLE   I <u>check</u> the inventory of office supplies.

    PAST TENSE   *I checked the inventory of office supplies.*

1. They <u>explain</u> the problem to the computer technician.

    SIMPLE FUTURE _____

2. Kwan <u>reads</u> fairy tales to his daughter.

    PRESENT PROGRESSIVE _____

3. I <u>sell</u> the most product replacement plans.

PAST PERFECT _____

4. The carefree days of summer <u>come</u> to an end.

FUTURE PROGRESSIVE _____

5. Scientists <u>detect</u> evidence of liquid water on one of Saturn's moons.

PRESENT PERFECT _____

_____

6. Robert <u>laughs</u> at his cat's attempt to catch a fly.

PAST PROGRESSIVE _____

7. I <u>complete</u> my degree requirements in May.

FUTURE PERFECT _____

8. Darren <u>prepares</u> his final presentation for the course.

PAST PERFECT PROGRESSIVE _____

_____

9. The campus singing groups <u>rehearse</u> for two months.

FUTURE PERFECT PROGRESSIVE _____

_____

10. Emily and Teresa <u>play</u> soccer on the weekends.

PRESENT PERFECT PROGRESSIVE _____

_____

■

A.4 ADJECTIVES

Adjectives modify nouns and pronouns. That is, they describe, identify, qualify, or limit the meaning of nouns and pronouns. An adjective answers the question *Which one?*, *What kind?*, or *How many?* about the word it modifies.

WHICH ONE?	The <u>twisted</u>, <u>torn</u> umbrella was of no use to its owner.
WHAT KIND?	The <u>spotted</u> owl has caused <u>heated</u> arguments in the Northwest.
HOW MANY?	<u>Many</u> customers waited for <u>four</u> days for Internet service to be restored.

In form, adjectives can be **positive** (implying no comparison), **comparative** (comparing two items), or **superlative** (comparing three or more items). (See p. 164 for more on the forms of adjectives.)

POSITIVE
The computer is <u>fast</u>.

COMPARATIVE
Your computer is <u>faster</u> than mine.

SUPERLATIVE
This is the <u>fastest</u> computer I have ever used.

A. Parts of Speech

There are two general categories of adjectives. **Descriptive adjectives** name a quality of the person, place, thing, or idea they describe: *mysterious* man, *green pond*, *healthy* complexion. **Limiting adjectives** narrow the scope of the person, place, or thing they describe: *my computer*, *this tool*, *second try*.

Descriptive Adjectives

A **regular** (or **attributive**) adjective appears next to (usually before) the word it modifies. Several adjectives can modify the same word.

> The enthusiastic new hairstylist gave short, lopsided haircuts.
>
> The wealthy dealer bought an immense blue vase.

Sometimes nouns function as adjectives modifying other nouns: *tree house*, *hamburger bun*.

A **predicate adjective** follows a linking verb and modifies or describes the subject of the sentence or clause (see p. 541; see p. 549 on clauses).

> PREDICATE ADJECTIVE
>
> The meeting was long. [modifies the subject, *meeting*]

Limiting Adjectives

1. The **definite article**, *the*, and the **indefinite articles**, *a* and *an*, are classified as adjectives. *A* and *an* are used when it is not important to specify a particular noun or when the object named is not known to the reader (*A radish adds color to a salad*). *The* is used when it is important to specify one or more of a particular noun or when the object named is known to the reader or has already been mentioned (*The radishes from the garden are on the table*).

   A squirrel visited the feeder that I just built. The squirrel tried to eat some bird food.

2. When the possessive pronouns *my, your, his, her, its, our,* and *their* are used as modifiers before nouns, they are considered **possessive adjectives**.

   Your friend borrowed my laptop for his trip.

3. When the demonstrative pronouns *this, that, these,* and *those* are used as modifiers before nouns, they are called **demonstrative adjectives**. *This* and *these* modify nouns close to the writer; *that* and *those* modify nouns more distant from the writer.

   Buy these wireless headsets, not those wired ones.

   This freshman course is a prerequisite for those advanced courses.

4. **Cardinal adjectives** are words used in counting: *one, two, twenty,* and so on.

   I read four biographies of Jack Kerouac and seven articles about his work.

5. **Ordinal adjectives** note position in a series.

   The first biography was too sketchy, whereas the second one was too detailed.

6. **Indefinite adjectives** provide nonspecific, general information about the quantities and amounts of the nouns they modify. Some common indefinite adjectives are *another, any, enough, few, less, little, many, more, much, several,* and *some.*

   <u>Several</u> people asked me if I had <u>enough</u> blankets or if I wanted the thermostat turned up a <u>few</u> degrees.

7. The **interrogative adjectives** *what, which,* and *whose* modify nouns and pronouns used in questions.

   <u>Which</u> radio station do you like? <u>Whose</u> music do you prefer?

8. The words *which* and *what,* along with *whichever* and *whatever,* are **relative adjectives** when they modify nouns and introduce subordinate clauses.

   She couldn't decide <u>which</u> job she wanted to take.

9. **Proper adjectives** are adjectives derived from proper nouns: *Spain* (noun), *Spanish* (adjective); *Freud* (noun), *Freudian* (adjective). Most proper adjectives are capitalized.

   Shakespeare lived in <u>Elizabethan</u> England.
   The speaker used many <u>French</u> expressions.

EXERCISE 3   Revising by Adding Adjectives

Directions: Revise each of the following sentences by adding at least three adjectives.

> EXAMPLE   My jacket provided little protection from the wind.
>
> REVISED   *My flimsy jacket provided little protection from the bitter, gusting wind.*

1. The aroma of freshly baked bread greeted us as we entered the farmhouse.

   _____

2. Amalie's goal is to establish a preschool program that will meet the needs of children.

   _____

3. The barking of my neighbor's dog kept me awake for most of the night.

   _____

4. In the lab, students must follow rules about the use of equipment and materials.

   _____

5. I could hear my friend's laugh rising above the voices of other people at the reception.

_____

_____

6. A customer service representative must have communication skills and a patient personality.

_____

_____

7. My daughter constructs buildings out of blocks to house her collection of toy animals.

_____

_____

8. The painting that Akiko exhibited at the student art show was a success.

_____

_____

9. The lights of the aurora borealis created a display in the night sky.

_____

_____

10. As a volunteer at the local animal shelter, Susan solicits donations and helps find owners for the pets.

_____

_____

■

A.5 ADVERBS

Adverbs modify verbs, adjectives, other adverbs, or entire sentences or clauses (see p. 549 on clauses). Like adjectives, adverbs describe, qualify, or limit the meaning of the words they modify.

An adverb answers the question *How?, When?, Where?, How often?,* or *To what extent?* about the word it modifies.

HOW?	Cheryl moved <u>awkwardly</u> because of her stiff neck.
WHEN?	I arrived <u>yesterday</u>.
WHERE?	They searched <u>everywhere</u>.
HOW OFTEN?	He telephoned <u>repeatedly</u>.
TO WHAT EXTENT?	Simon was <u>rather</u> slow to answer his e-mail.

Many adverbs end in *-ly* (*lazily, happily*), but some adverbs do not (*fast, here, much, well, rather, everywhere, never, so*), and some words that end in *-ly* are not adverbs (*lively, friendly, lonely*). Like all other parts of speech, an adverb may best be identified by examining its function within a sentence.

I quickly skimmed the book. [modifies the verb *skimmed*]

Very angry customers crowded the service desk. [modifies the adjective *angry*]

He was injured quite seriously. [modifies the adverb *seriously*]

Apparently, the job was bungled. [modifies the whole sentence]

Like adjectives, adverbs have three forms: **positive** (does not suggest any comparison), **comparative** (compares two actions or conditions), and **superlative** (compares three or more actions or conditions; see also p. 164).

POSITIVE   POSITIVE

Noah rose early and crept downstairs quietly.

COMPARATIVE   COMPARATIVE

Levi rose earlier than Noah and crept downstairs more quietly.

SUPERLATIVE

Bill rose the earliest of anyone in the house and crept downstairs most quietly.

SUPERLATIVE

Some adverbs, called **conjunctive adverbs** (or **adverbial conjunctions**)—such as *however, therefore,* and *besides*—connect the ideas of one sentence or clause to those of a previous sentence or clause. They can appear anywhere in a sentence. (See p. 137 for how to punctuate sentences containing conjunctive adverbs.)

CONJUNCTIVE ADVERB

James did not want to go to the library on Saturday; however, he knew the books were overdue.

The sporting-goods store was crowded because of the sale. Leila, therefore, was asked to work extra hours.

CONJUNCTIVE ADVERB

Some common conjunctive adverbs are listed below, including several phrases that function as conjunctive adverbs.

CONJUNCTIVE ADVERBS			
accordingly	for example	meanwhile	otherwise
also	further	moreover	similarly
anyway	furthermore	namely	still
as a result	hence	nevertheless	then
at the same time	however	next	thereafter
besides	incidentally	nonetheless	therefore
certainly	indeed	now	thus
consequently	instead	on the contrary	undoubtedly
finally	likewise	on the other hand	

A. Parts of Speech

| EXERCISE 4 | Using Adverbs |

Directions: Write a sentence using each of the following comparative or superlative adverbs.

EXAMPLE   earlier: The library is open until 5:00 on weekdays, but it closes earlier on weekends.

1. fastest: _____

_____

2. less carefully: _____

_____

3. most cheaply: _____

_____

4. higher: _____

_____

5. best: _____

_____

6. more generously: _____

_____

7. hardest: _____

_____

8. closer: _____

_____

9. least efficiently: _____

_____

10. better: _____

_____
■

A.6 CONJUNCTIONS

Conjunctions connect words, phrases, and clauses. There are three kinds of conjunctions: **coordinating**, **correlative**, and **subordinating**. **Coordinating** and **correlative conjunctions** connect words, phrases, or clauses of equal grammatical rank. (A **phrase** is a group of related words lacking a subject, a predicate, or both. A **clause** is a group of words containing a subject and a predicate; see pp. 538 and 539.)

1. The **coordinating conjunctions** are *and, but, nor, or, for, so,* and *yet.* These words must connect words or word groups of the same kind. Therefore, two

nouns may be connected by *and,* but a noun and a clause cannot be. *For* and *so* can connect only independent clauses.

COORDINATING
NOUN   CONJUNCTION   NOUN

We studied the novels of Toni Morrison and Alice Walker.

COORDINATING
CONJUNCTION
VERB   VERB

The copilot successfully flew and landed the disabled plane.

COORDINATING   INDEPENDENT
INDEPENDENT CLAUSE   CONJUNCTION   CLAUSE

The carpentry course sounded interesting, so Meg enrolled.

COORDINATING   SUBORDINATE
INDEPENDENT CLAUSE   CONJUNCTION   CLAUSE

We hoped that the mail would come soon and that it would contain our bonus check.

2. **Correlative conjunctions** are pairs of words that link and relate grammatically equivalent parts of a sentence. Some common correlative conjunctions are *either/or, neither/nor, both/and, not/but, not only/but also,* and *whether/or.* Correlative conjunctions are always used in pairs.

CORRELATIVE CONJUNCTIONS

Either the electricity was off, or the bulb had burned out.

3. **Subordinating conjunctions** connect dependent, or subordinate, clauses to independent clauses (see p. 93). Some common subordinating conjunctions are *although, because, if, since, until, when, where,* and *while.*

SUBORDINATING CONJUNCTION

Although the movie got bad reviews, it drew big crowds.

SUBORDINATING CONJUNCTION

She received a lot of mail because she was a reliable correspondent.

A.7 PREPOSITIONS

A **preposition** links and relates its **object** (a noun or a pronoun) to the rest of the sentence. Prepositions often show relationships of time, place, direction, and manner.

PREPOSITION   OBJECT OF PREPOSITION

I walked around the block.

PREPOSITION   OBJECT OF PREPOSITION

She called during our meeting.

A. Parts of Speech

COMMON PREPOSITIONS				
along	besides	from	past	up
among	between	in	since	upon
around	beyond	near	through	with
at	by	off	till	within
before	despite	on	to	without
behind	down	onto	toward	
below	during	out	under	
beneath	except	outside	underneath	
beside	for	over	until	

Some prepositions consist of more than one word; they are called **phrasal prepositions** or **compound prepositions**.

PHRASAL PREPOSITION   OBJECT OF PREPOSITION

According to our records, you have enough credits to graduate.

PHRASAL PREPOSITION   OBJECT OF PREPOSITION

We decided to make the trip in spite of the snowstorm.

COMMON PHRASAL PREPOSITIONS		
according to	in addition to	on account of
aside from	in front of	out of
as of	in place of	prior to
as well as	in regard to	with regard to
because of	in spite of	with respect to
by means of	instead of	

The object of the preposition often has modifiers.

OBJ. OF   OBJ. OF
PREP.   MODIFIER PREP.   PREP.   MODIFIER PREP.

Not a sound came from the child's room except a gentle snoring.

Sometimes a preposition has more than one object (a **compound object**).

COMPOUND OBJECT OF PREPOSITION

PREPOSITION

The Laundromat was between campus and home.

Usually the preposition comes before its object. In interrogative sentences, however, the preposition sometimes follows its object.

OBJECT OF PREPOSITION   PREPOSITION

What did your supervisor ask you about?

The preposition, object or objects of the preposition, and the object's modifiers all form a **prepositional phrase**.

PREPOSITIONAL PHRASE

The scientist conducted her experiment throughout the afternoon and early evening.

There may be many prepositional phrases in a sentence.

PREPOSITIONAL PHRASE   PREPOSITIONAL PHRASE

The water from the open hydrant flowed into the street.

The noisy kennel was underneath the beauty salon, despite the complaints of customers.

Alongside the weedy railroad tracks, an old hotel with faded grandeur stood near the abandoned brick station on the edge of town.

Prepositional phrases frequently function as adjectives or adverbs. If a prepositional phrase modifies a noun or pronoun, it functions as an adjective. If it modifies a verb, adjective, or adverb, it functions as an adverb.

The auditorium inside the conference center has a special sound system. [adjective modifying the noun *auditorium*]

The doctor looked cheerfully at the patient and handed the lab results across the desk. [adverbs modifying the verbs *looked* and *handed*]

EXERCISE 5   Using Prepositional Phrases

Directions: Expand each of the following sentences by adding a prepositional phrase in the blank.

EXAMPLE   Hummingbirds sip nectar *from flowers*.

1. The meteorologist predicts that the heat wave will continue

   _____.

2. _____, Kate sat in the front row and took careful notes.

3. I cautiously stepped _____ to keep my new shoes dry.

4. The batter hit the ball so hard that it flew _____.

5. If you misplace your house key, use the extra key located

   _____.

6. The orchestra conductor walked _____ and raised his baton.

7. My daughter always hides _____ when we play hide and seek.

8. When Sofia walks _____, she often picks up seashells.

9. Our manager said the report must be completed _____.

10. When Jamal opened the door, the cat ran _____ and escaped outside.

A.8 INTERJECTIONS

Interjections are words that express emotion or surprise. They are followed by an exclamation point, comma, or period, depending on whether they stand alone or serve as part or all of a sentence. Interjections are used in speech more than in writing.

Wow! What an announcement!

So, was that lost letter ever found?

Well, I'd better be going.

MyWritingLab *Visit Part A Understanding the Parts of Speech to test your understanding of the Part objectives.*

A **sentence** is a group of words that expresses a complete thought about something or someone. A sentence must contain a **subject** and a **predicate**.

Subject	*Predicate*
Telephones	ring.
Cecilia	laughed.
Time	will tell.

Depending on their purpose and punctuation, sentences are **declarative**, **interrogative**, **exclamatory**, or **imperative**.

A **declarative sentence** makes a statement. It ends with a period.

SUBJECT PREDICATE

The snow fell steadily.

An **interrogative sentence** asks a question. It ends with a question mark (?).

SUBJECT PREDICATE

Who called?

An **exclamatory sentence** conveys strong emotion. It ends with an exclamation point (!).

SUBJECT   PREDICATE

Your photograph is in the company newsletter!

An **imperative sentence** gives an order or makes a request. It ends with either a period or an exclamation point, depending on how mild or strong the command or request is. In an imperative sentence, the subject is *you,* but this often is not included.

PREDICATE

Get me a fire extinguisher now! [The subject *you* is understood: (*You*) get me a fire extinguisher now!]

B.1 SUBJECTS

The **subject** of a sentence is whom or what the sentence is about. It is who or what performs or receives the action expressed in the predicate. The subject is often a **noun**, a word that names a person, place, thing, or idea.

> Julia worked on her math homework.
> The rose bushes must be watered.
> Honesty is the best policy.

The subject of a sentence can also be a **pronoun**, a word that refers to or substitutes for a noun.

> She revised the memo three times.
> I will attend the sales meeting.
> Although the ink spilled, it did not get on my shirt.

The subject of a sentence can also be a group of words used as a noun.

> Reading e-mail from friends is my idea of a good time.

Simple Versus Complete Subjects

The **simple subject** is the noun or pronoun that names what the sentence is about. It does not include any **modifiers**—that is, words that describe, identify, qualify, or limit the meaning of the noun or pronoun.

> SIMPLE SUBJECT
> The bright red concert poster caught everyone's eye.

> SIMPLE SUBJECT
> Online banking has revolutionized the banking industry.

When the subject of a sentence is a proper noun (the name of a particular person, place, or thing), the entire name is considered the simple subject.

> SIMPLE SUBJECT
> Martin Luther King, Jr., was a famous leader.

The **simple subject** of an imperative sentence is *you.*

> SIMPLE SUBJECT
> [You] Remember to bring the sales brochures.

The **complete subject** is the simple subject plus its modifiers.

> COMPLETE SUBJECT
> SIMPLE SUBJECT
> The sleek, black limousine waited outside the church.

Tip for Writers

A *sentence* is a group of words containing both a subject and a predicate. The subject is the part of the sentence that tells you whom or what the sentence is about.

The predicate is the part of the sentence that contains the main verb. It is also the part of the sentence that tells you what the subject is doing or that describes the subject.

COMPLETE SUBJECT

Fondly remembered as a gifted songwriter, fiddle player, and storyteller, Quintin Lotus Dickey lived in a cabin in Paoli, Indiana.

SIMPLE SUBJECT

Compound Subjects

Some sentences contain two or more subjects joined with a coordinating conjunction (*and, but, nor, or, for, so, yet*). Those subjects together form a **compound subject**.

COMPOUND SUBJECT

Maria and I completed the marathon.

COMPOUND SUBJECT

The computer, the printer, and the cable box were unusable during the blackout.

B.2 PREDICATES

The **predicate** indicates what the subject does, what happened to the subject, or what is being said about the subject. The predicate must include a **verb**, a word or group of words that expresses an action or a state of being (for example, *run, invent, build, know, will decide, become*).

Joy swam sixty laps.

The thunderstorm replenished the reservoir.

Sometimes the verb consists of only one word, as in the previous examples. Often, however, the main verb is accompanied by a helping verb (see p. 523).

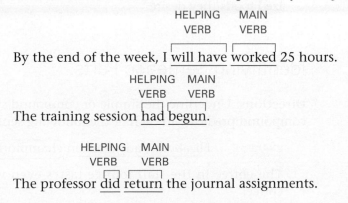

HELPING   MAIN
VERB   VERB

By the end of the week, I will have worked 25 hours.

HELPING   MAIN
VERB   VERB

The training session had begun.

HELPING   MAIN
VERB   VERB

The professor did return the journal assignments.

Simple Versus Complete Predicates

The **simple predicate** is the main verb plus its helping verbs (together known as the **verb phrase**). The simple predicate does not include any modifiers.

SIMPLE PREDICATE

The proctor hastily collected the blue books.

SIMPLE PREDICATE

The moderator had introduced the next speaker.

The **complete predicate** consists of the simple predicate, its modifiers, and any complements (words that complete the meaning of the verb; see p. 541). In general, the complete predicate includes everything in the sentence except the complete subject.

COMPLETE PREDICATE

SIMPLE PREDICATE

The music sounds better from the back of the room.

COMPLETE PREDICATE

SIMPLE PREDICATE

Hannah decided to change the name of her company to something less controversial and confusing.

Compound Predicates

Some sentences have two or more predicates joined by a coordinating conjunction (*and, but, nor*). These predicates together form a **compound predicate**.

COMPOUND PREDICATE

Marcia unlocked her bicycle and rode away.

COMPOUND PREDICATE

The supermarket owner will survey his customers and order the specialized foods they desire.

EXERCISE 6   Identifying Sentence Parts

Directions: Underline the simple or compound subject and circle the simple or compound predicate in each of the following sentences.

EXAMPLE   Elizabeth Cady Stanton championed women's rights.

1. The coffee in the staff lounge tastes even worse than vending-machine coffee!

2. Of all the pediatricians in the clinic, Dr. Alvarez has the gentlest beside manner.

3. Students in the nursing program and staff of the local hospital are organizing a community health fair.

4. In their reviews of the new Italian restaurant, food critics praised the linguini with clam sauce and raved about the lobster ravioli.

5. By the end of next year, I will have repaid most of my student loans.

6. For many film stars of the 1940s, singing and dancing were essential job skills.

7. Kenji and his friend jog for 30 minutes most mornings and lift weights at least twice a week.

8. Last spring my sister took a criminal justice course and audited a sociology course.

9. Many well-known actors and other media celebrities made appearances at the political fund-raiser.

10. The art of modern sculptor Claes Oldenburg includes giant replicas of small, mundane objects such as a button or a lipstick. ■

B.3 COMPLEMENTS

A **complement** is a word or group of words used to complete the meaning of a subject or object. There are four kinds of complements: **subject complements**, which follow linking verbs; **direct objects** and **indirect objects**, which follow transitive verbs (verbs that take an object); and **object complements**, which follow direct objects.

Linking Verbs and Subject Complements

A linking verb (such as *be, become, seem, feel, taste*) links the subject to a **subject complement**, a noun or adjective that renames or describes the subject. (See p. 522 for more about linking verbs.) Nouns that function as complements are called **predicate nominatives** or **predicate nouns**. Adjectives that function as complements are called **predicate adjectives**.

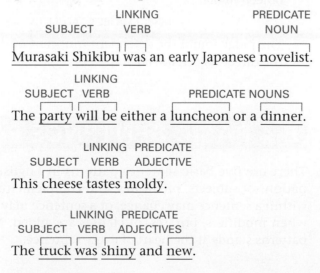

(See p. 522 for more about linking verbs.)

Direct Objects

A **direct object** is a noun or pronoun that receives the action of a transitive verb (see p. 522). A direct object answers the question *What?* or *Whom?*

TRANSITIVE VERB   DIRECT OBJECT

The pharmacist helped us. [The pharmacist helped *whom?*]

TRANSITIVE VERB   DIRECT OBJECTS

Jillian borrowed a bicycle and a visor. [Jillian borrowed *what?*]

Indirect Objects

An **indirect object** is a noun or pronoun that receives the action of the verb indirectly. Indirect objects name the person or thing *to whom* or *for whom* something is done.

TRANSITIVE   INDIRECT   DIRECT
VERB   OBJECT   OBJECT

The computer technician gave me the bill. [He gave the bill *to whom?*]

TRANSITIVE VERB   INDIRECT OBJECTS   DIRECT OBJECTS

Eric bought his wife and son some sandwiches and milk. [He bought food *for whom?*]

Object Complements

An **object complement** is a noun or adjective that modifies (describes) or renames the direct object. Object complements appear with verbs like *name, find, think, elect, appoint, choose,* and *consider.*

DIRECT OBJECT   NOUN AS OBJECT COMPLEMENT

We appointed Joshua our representative. [*Representative* renames the direct object, *Joshua.*]

DIRECT OBJECT   ADJECTIVE AS OBJECT COMPLEMENT

The judge found the defendant innocent of the charges. [*Innocent* modifies the direct object, *defendant.*]

B.4 BASIC SENTENCE PATTERNS

There are five basic sentence patterns in English. They are built with combinations of subjects, predicates, and complements. The order of these elements within a sentence may change, or a sentence may become long and complicated when modifiers, phrases, or clauses are added. Nonetheless, one of five basic patterns stands at the heart of every sentence.

PATTERN 1		
Subject +	***Predicate***	
I	shivered.	
Brittany	swam.	

PATTERN 2		
Subject +	***Predicate*** +	***Direct Object***
Anthony	ordered	a new desk.
We	wanted	freedom.

PATTERN 3		
Subject +	***Predicate*** +	***Subject Complement***
The woman	was	a welder.
Our course	is	interesting.

PATTERN 4			
Subject +	***Predicate*** +	***Indirect Object*** +	***Direct Object***
My friend	loaned	me	a laptop.
The company	sent	employees	a questionnaire.

PATTERN 5			
Subject +	***Predicate*** +	***Direct Object*** +	***Object Complement***
I	consider	her singing	exceptional.
Lampwick	called	Jiminy Cricket	a beetle.

B. Parts of Sentences

EXERCISE 7   Using Complements

Directions: Complete each sentence with a word or words that will function as the type of complement indicated.

EXAMPLE   The students elected Liang __president of the Student Senate__.
object complement

1. These gardenias smell so _____ that they are making me sneeze.
predicate adjective

2. Matt checked the _____ of the previous meeting to verify that the
direct object
committee had reached agreement on the issue.

3. When my kids were young, I always sang _____ lullabies at bedtime.
indirect object

4. Some fans were not impressed by the band's latest releases, but I found the
new songs _____ and _____.
object complements

5. My grandparents have been _____ for 50 years, and they are still
in love.   predicate adjective

6. Caitlin e-mailed her _____ a map showing the location of her new
apartment.   indirect object

7. As I spend more time with my co-worker, we are becoming
closer _____.
predicate noun

8. When Damian walked across the stage to receive his diploma, he seemed very _____ and _____ .
   <u>predicate adjectives</u>

9. Latoya and her business partner are planning to open a new

   _____ .
   <u>direct object</u>

10. The professor warned students that keeping up with the assigned reading in this course could be a _____ . ■
    <u>predicate noun</u>

B.5 EXPANDING THE SENTENCE WITH ADJECTIVES AND ADVERBS

A sentence may consist of just a subject and a verb.

> Lei studied.
>
> Rumors circulated.

Most sentences, however, contain additional information about the subject and the verb. Information is commonly added in three ways:

- **by using adjectives and adverbs**
- **by using phrases** (groups of words that lack either a subject or a predicate or both)
- **by using clauses** (groups of words that contain both a subject and a predicate)

Using Adjectives and Adverbs to Expand Your Sentences

Adjectives are words used to modify or describe nouns and pronouns (see p. 527). Adjectives answer questions about nouns and pronouns such as *Which one?, What kind?, How many?* Using adjectives is one way to add detail and information to sentences.

WITHOUT ADJECTIVES	Dogs barked at cats.
WITH ADJECTIVES	Our three large, brown dogs barked at the two terrified spotted cats.

Note: Sometimes nouns and participles are used as adjectives (see p. 545 on participles).

NOUN USED AS ADJECTIVE

People are rediscovering the milk bottle.

PRESENT PARTICIPLE   PAST PARTICIPLE
USED AS ADJECTIVE   USED AS ADJECTIVE

Mrs. Simon had a swimming pool with a broken drain.

Adverbs add information to sentences by modifying or describing verbs, adjectives, or other adverbs (see p. 530). An adverb usually answers the question *How?, When?, Where?, How often?,* or *To what extent?*

WITHOUT ADVERBS	I will clean.
	The audience applauded.
WITH ADVERBS	I will clean <u>very</u> <u>thoroughly</u> <u>tomorrow</u>.
	The audience applauded <u>loudly</u> and <u>enthusiastically</u>.

B.6 EXPANDING THE SENTENCE WITH PHRASES

A **phrase** is a group of related words that lacks a subject, a predicate, or both. A phrase cannot stand alone as a sentence. Phrases can appear at the beginning, middle, or end of a sentence.

WITHOUT PHRASES	I noticed the stain.
	Sal researched the topic.
	Manuela arose.
WITH PHRASES	<u>Upon entering the room</u>, I noticed the stain <u>on the expensive carpet</u>.
	<u>At the local aquarium</u>, Sal researched the topic <u>of shark attacks</u>.
	<u>An amateur astronomer</u>, Manuela arose <u>in the middle of the night</u> to observe the lunar eclipse but, <u>after waiting ten minutes in the cold</u>, gave up.

There are eight kinds of phrases: **noun**; **verb**; **prepositional**; three kinds of **verbal phrases** (**participial**, **gerund**, and **infinitive**); **appositive**; and **absolute**.

Noun and Verb Phrases

A noun plus its modifiers is a **noun phrase** (*red shoes, the quiet house*). A main verb plus its helping verb is a **verb phrase** (*had been exploring, is sleeping;* see p. 523 on helping verbs.)

Prepositional Phrases

A **prepositional phrase** consists of a preposition (for example, *in, above, with, at, behind*), an object of the preposition (a noun or pronoun), and any modifiers of the object. (See p. 534 for a list of common prepositions.) A prepositional phrase functions like an adjective (modifying a noun or pronoun) or an adverb (modifying a verb, adjective, or adverb). You can use prepositional phrases to tell more about people, places, objects, or actions. A prepositional phrase usually adds information about time, place, direction, manner, or degree.

As Adjectives

The woman <u>with the briefcase</u> is giving a presentation <u>on meditation techniques</u>.

Both <u>of the telephones behind the partition</u> were ringing.

As Adverbs

The fire drill occurred <u>in the morning</u>.

I was curious <u>about the new human resources director</u>.

The conference speaker came <u>from Australia</u>.

<u>With horror</u>, the crowd watched the rhinoceros's tether stretch <u>to the breaking point</u>.

A prepositional phrase can function as part of the complete subject or as part of the complete predicate but should not be confused with the simple subject or simple predicate.

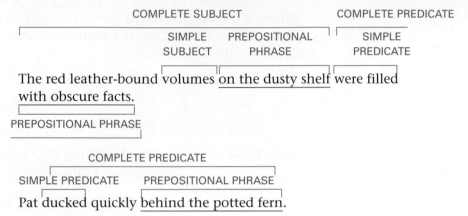

Verbal Phrases

A **verbal** is a verb form that cannot function as the main verb of a sentence. The three kinds of verbals are **participles**, **gerunds**, and **infinitives**. A **verbal phrase** consists of a verbal and its modifiers.

Participles and Participial Phrases

All verbs have two participles: present and past. The **present participle** is formed by adding *-ing* to the base form (*walking, riding, being*). The **past participle** of regular verbs is formed by adding *-d* or *-ed* to the base form (*walked, baked*). The past participle of irregular verbs has no set pattern (*ridden, been*). (See p. 524 for a list of common irregular verbs and their past participles.) Both the present participle and the past participle can function as adjectives modifying nouns and pronouns.

PAST PARTICIPLE   PRESENT PARTICIPLE
AS ADJECTIVE   AS ADJECTIVE

<u>Irritated</u>, Natalia circled the <u>confusing</u> traffic rotary once again.

A **participial phrase** consists of a participle and any of its modifiers.

PARTICIPIAL PHRASE

PARTICIPLE

We listened for Isabella <u>climbing the rickety stairs</u>.

PARTICIPIAL PHRASE

PARTICIPLE

Disillusioned with the whole system, Kay sat down to think.

PARTICIPIAL PHRASE

PARTICIPLE

The singer, having caught a bad cold, canceled his performance.

Gerunds and Gerund Phrases

A **gerund** is the present participle (the *-ing* form) of the verb used as a noun.

Shoveling is good exercise.

Rex enjoyed gardening.

A **gerund phrase** consists of a gerund and its modifiers. A gerund phrase, like a gerund, is used as a noun and can therefore function in a sentence as a subject, a direct or indirect object, an object of a preposition, a subject complement, or an appositive.

GERUND PHRASE

Photocopying the report took longer than Alice anticipated. [subject]

GERUND PHRASE

The director considered making another monster movie. [direct object]

GERUND PHRASE

She gave running three miles daily credit for her health. [indirect object]

GERUND PHRASE

Before learning Greek, Omar spoke only English. [object of the preposition]

GERUND PHRASE

Her business is designing collapsible furniture. [subject complement]

GERUND PHRASE

Gabriel's trick, memorizing license plates, has come in handy. [appositive]

Infinitives and Infinitive Phrases

The **infinitive** is the base form of the verb as it appears in the dictionary preceded by the word *to*. An infinitive phrase consists of the infinitive and any modifiers. An **infinitive phrase** can function as a noun, an adjective, or an adverb. When it is used as a noun, an infinitive phrase can be a subject, object, complement, or appositive.

INFINITIVE PHRASE

To love one's enemies is a noble goal. [noun used as subject]

INFINITIVE PHRASE

The season to sell bulbs is the fall. [adjective modifying *season*]

INFINITIVE PHRASE

The chess club met to practice for the state championship. [adverb modifying *met*]

Sometimes the *to* in an infinitive phrase is not used.

Tyler helped us learn the new accounting procedure. [The *to* before *learn* is understood.]

Note: Do not confuse infinitive phrases with prepositional phrases beginning with the preposition *to*. In an infinitive phrase, *to* is followed by a verb; in a prepositional phrase, *to* is followed by a noun or pronoun, or an adjective and a noun.

Appositive Phrases

An **appositive** is a noun that explains, restates, or adds new information about another noun. An **appositive phrase** consists of an appositive and its modifiers. (See p. 559 for punctuation of appositive phrases.)

APPOSITIVE

Claude Monet completed the painting *Water Lilies* around 1903.
[adds information about the noun *painting*]

APPOSITIVE PHRASE
APPOSITIVE

Francis, my neighbor with a large workshop, lent me a wrench. [adds information about the noun *Francis*]

Absolute Phrases

An **absolute phrase** consists of a noun or pronoun and any modifiers followed by a participle or a participial phrase. An absolute phrase modifies an entire sentence, not any particular word within the sentence. It can appear anywhere in a sentence and is set off from the rest of the sentence with a comma or commas. There may be more than one absolute phrase in a sentence.

ABSOLUTE PHRASE

The winter being over, the geese returned.

ABSOLUTE PHRASE

Senator Arden began his speech, his voice rising to be heard over the loud applause.

ABSOLUTE PHRASE

A vacancy having occurred, the hotel manager called the first name on the reservations waiting list.

EXERCISE 8   Expanding Sentences

Directions: Expand each of the following sentences by adding adjectives, adverbs, and/or phrases (prepositional, verbal, appositive, or absolute).

EXAMPLE   Mike and Chen studied.

EXPANDED   *The day before the exam, Mike and Chen studied together for three hours*
            without a single break.

1. I hung a poster. _____

_____

2. The squirrel snatched a seed. _____

_____

3. Thomas invited Monica. _____

_____

4. Midori demonstrated. _____

_____

5. I am working. _____

_____

6. Tyrell included graphs. _____

_____

7. Canoeing was an experience. _____

_____

8. The leader scheduled a meeting. _____

_____

9. Angelina helped her grandfather. _____

_____

10. I walked. _____

_____ ∎

B.7 EXPANDING THE SENTENCE WITH CLAUSES

A **clause** is a group of words that contains a subject and a predicate. A clause is either **independent** (also called **main**) or **dependent** (also called **subordinate**).

An **independent clause** can stand alone as a grammatically complete sentence.

INDEPENDENT CLAUSE   INDEPENDENT CLAUSE

SUBJECT PREDICATE SUBJECT PREDICATE

The alarm sounded, and I awoke.

INDEPENDENT CLAUSE   INDEPENDENT CLAUSE

SUBJECT   PREDICATE   SUBJECT   PREDICATE

The scientist worried. The experiment might fail.

B. Parts of Sentences

INDEPENDENT CLAUSE   INDEPENDENT CLAUSE

SUBJECT PREDICATE   SUBJECT PREDICATE

He bandaged his ankle. It had been sprained.

A **dependent clause** has a subject and a predicate, but it cannot stand alone as a grammatically complete sentence because it does not express a complete thought. Most dependent clauses begin with either a **subordinating conjunction** or a **relative pronoun**. These words connect the dependent clause to an independent clause.

SUBORDINATING

CONJUNCTION SUBJECT PREDICATE

because the alarm sounded

SUBORDINATING

CONJUNCTION SUBJECT   PREDICATE

that the experiment might fail

RELATIVE PRONOUN

(SUBJECT)   PREDICATE

which had been sprained

These clauses do not express complete thoughts and therefore cannot stand alone as sentences. When joined to independent clauses, however, dependent clauses function as adjectives, adverbs, and nouns and are known as **adjective** (or **relative**) **clauses**, **adverb clauses**, and **noun clauses**. Noun clauses can function as subjects, objects, or complements.

COMMON SUBORDINATING CONJUNCTIONS		
after	inasmuch as	that
although	in case	though
as	in order that	unless
as far as	insofar as	until
as if	in that	when
as soon as	now that	whenever
as though	once	where
because	provided that	wherever
before	rather than	whether
even if	since	while
even though	so that	why
how	supposing that	
if	than	
RELATIVE PRONOUNS		
that	which	
what	who (whose, whom)	
whatever	whoever (whomever)	

Adjective Clause

DEPENDENT CLAUSE

He bandaged his ankle, which had been sprained. [modifies *ankle*]

Adverb Clause

DEPENDENT CLAUSE

Because the alarm sounded, I awoke. [modifies *awoke*]

Noun Clause

DEPENDENT CLAUSE

The scientist worried that the experiment might fail. [direct object of *worried*]

Sometimes the relative pronoun or subordinating conjunction is implied or understood rather than stated. Also, a dependent clause may contain an implied predicate. When a dependent clause is missing an element that can clearly be supplied from the context of the sentence, it is called an **elliptical clause**.

ELLIPTICAL CLAUSE

Reality TV is more entertaining than dramas [are]. [*Are* is the understood predicate in the elliptical dependent clause.]

ELLIPTICAL CLAUSE

Canadian history is among the subjects [that] the book discusses. [*That* is the understood relative pronoun in the elliptical dependent clause.]

Relative pronouns are generally the subject or object in their clauses. *Who* and *whoever* change to *whom* and *whomever* when they function as objects.

B.8 BASIC SENTENCE CLASSIFICATIONS

Depending on its structure, a sentence can be classified as one of four basic types: **simple**, **compound**, **complex**, or **compound-complex**.

Simple Sentences

A **simple sentence** has one independent (main) clause and no dependent (subordinate) clauses (see p. 93). A simple sentence contains at least one subject and one predicate. It may have a compound subject, a compound predicate, and various phrases, but it has only one clause.

SUBJECT PREDICATE

Sap rises.

COMPOUND PREDICATE

SUBJECT

In the spring the sap rises in the maple trees and is boiled to make a thick, delicious syrup.

B. Parts of Sentences

Compound Sentences

A **compound sentence** has at least two independent clauses and no dependent clauses (see p. 132). The two independent clauses are usually joined with a comma and a coordinating conjunction (*and, but, for, nor, or, so, yet*). Sometimes the two clauses are joined with a semicolon and no coordinating conjunction or with a semicolon and a conjunctive adverb like *nonetheless* or *still* followed by a comma. (See p. 531 on conjunctive adverbs and p. 137 on punctuation.)

INDEPENDENT CLAUSE

Reading a novel by Henry James is not like reading a thriller, but with patience the rewards are greater.

INDEPENDENT CLAUSE

INDEPENDENT CLAUSE   INDEPENDENT CLAUSE

I set out to explore the North River near home; I ended up at Charlie's Clam Bar.

Complex Sentences

A **complex sentence** has one independent clause and one or more dependent clauses (see p. 134). The clauses are joined by subordinating conjunctions or relative pronouns (see p. 99).

INDEPENDENT CLAUSE   DEPENDENT CLAUSE

We tried to find topics to talk about while we waited for the bus.

INDEPENDENT CLAUSE   DEPENDENT CLAUSE

The receptionist greeted me warmly as I entered the office because I hadn't seen her in a long time.

DEPENDENT CLAUSE

Compound-Complex Sentences

A **compound-complex sentence** contains two or more independent clauses and one or more dependent clauses (see p. 132).

DEPENDENT CLAUSE   INDEPENDENT CLAUSE

If students work part-time, they must plan their studies carefully, and they must limit their social lives.

INDEPENDENT CLAUSE

INDEPENDENT CLAUSE   INDEPENDENT CLAUSE   INDEPENDENT CLAUSE

It was mid-March, and the pond had begun to melt; I walked toward it expectantly as I wondered if I could go skating one last time.

DEPENDENT CLAUSE   DEPENDENT CLAUSE

EXERCISE 9   Combining Sentences

Directions: Combine each of the following pairs of sentences into a single sentence by forming independent and/or dependent clauses. You may need to add, change, or delete words.

> **EXAMPLE**   **a.** The flip-flops were not selling well.
>
> **b.** The store marked down the price of the flip-flops.
>
> **COMBINED**   *The flip-flops were not selling well, so the store marked down the price.*

1. **a.** Alicia is good at making minor plumbing repairs.
   b. Alicia does not attempt to fix electrical problems.

   _____

   _____

2. **a.** My brother, an excellent gourmet cook, tried a new dessert recipe.
   b. The new dessert recipe was a total disaster.

   _____

   _____

3. **a.** Yuan previewed the course syllabus online.
   b. Yuan decided to take a different course instead.

   _____

   _____

4. **a.** First the clay tiles must be thoroughly dried in the sun.
   b. Then the clay tiles are fired in the kiln.

   _____

5. **a.** Only a few people signed up for the summer course.
   b. The summer course has been canceled.

   _____

6. **a.** Ezra, the host of the potluck barbecue, will grill hamburgers and veggie dogs.
   b. Each guest will bring soda or a side dish.

   _____

   _____

7. **a.** Rachel is enrolled in the local community college.
   b. Rachel is studying to become an emergency medical technician.

   _____

   _____

8. **a.** Keisha will babysit her sister's kids on Saturday.
   b. Keisha will take the kids to the park.

   _____

9. **a.** The Meals On Wheels program is looking for volunteers to deliver meals.

   b. The volunteers must use their own cars to deliver the meals.

   _____

   _____

10. **a.** Some students study best late at night.

    b. Other students do their best studying in the morning.

    _____

    _____ ■

MyWritingLab *Visit Part B Understanding the Parts of Sentences to test your understanding of the Part objectives.*

B. Parts of Sentences

C Using Punctuation Correctly

C.1 END PUNCTUATION

When to Use Periods

Use a period in the following situations:

1. To end a sentence unless it is a question or an exclamation.

We washed the car even though we knew a thunderstorm was imminent.
Note: Use a period to end a sentence that states an indirect question or indirectly quotes someone's words or thoughts.

> INCORRECT   Courtney wondered if she would be on time?
>
> CORRECT   Courtney wondered if she would be on time.

2. To punctuate many abbreviations.

> M.D.   B.A.   P.M.   B.C.   Mr.   Ms.

Do not use periods in acronyms, such as *NATO* and *AIDS,* or in abbreviations for most organizations, such as *NBC* and *NAACP.*
Note: If a sentence ends with an abbreviation, the sentence has only one period, not two.

> The train was due to arrive at 7:00 P.M.

When to Use Question Marks

Use question marks after direct questions.

> How long can a coral snake grow?

If a quotation ends in a question mark, place the question mark within the closing quotation marks.

> She asked the barista, "Do you have white mocha?"

If a quotation is included in a sentence that asks a question, the question mark goes after the closing quotation mark.

Did you say Amber said, "I will not come"?

Note: Use a period, not a question mark, after an indirect question.

She asked the barista if they had white mocha.

When to Use Exclamation Points

Use an exclamation point at the end of a sentence that expresses particular emphasis, excitement, or urgency. Use exclamation points sparingly, however, especially in academic writing.

What a beautiful day it is!   Dial 911 right now!

Tip for Writers

PUNCTUATION

Practice recognizing punctuation marks, and make sure you know what they mean and how to use them. Using punctuation incorrectly can sometimes change the meaning of your sentences. Here are two examples:

1. When your friends help, you stop working.
    When your friends help you, stop working.

2. Did she finally marry Roger?
    Did she finally marry, Roger?

C.2 COMMAS

The comma is used to separate parts of a sentence from one another. If you omit a comma when it is needed, you risk making a clear and direct sentence confusing.

When to Use Commas

Use a comma in the following situations:

1. **Before a coordinating conjunction that joins two independent clauses** (see p. 112).

    Terry had planned to leave work early, but he was delayed.

2. **To separate a dependent (subordinate) clause from an independent clause when the dependent clause comes first in the sentence** (see p. 141).

    After I left the library, I went to the computer lab.

3. **To separate introductory words and phrases from the rest of the sentence.**

   Unfortunately, I forgot my umbrella.

   To pass the baton, I will need to locate my teammate.

   Exuberant over their victory, the football-team members carried the quarterback on their shoulders.

4. **To separate a nonrestrictive phrase or clause from the rest of a sentence.** A **nonrestrictive** phrase or clause is added to a sentence but does not change the sentence's basic meaning.

   To determine whether an element is nonrestrictive, read the sentence without the element. If the meaning of the sentence does not essentially change, then the commas are *necessary*.

   My sister, who is a mail carrier, is afraid of dogs. [The essential meaning of this sentence does not change if we read the sentence without the subordinate clause: My sister is afraid of dogs. Therefore, commas are needed.]

   Mail carriers who have been bitten by dogs are afraid of them. [If we read this sentence without the subordinate clause, its meaning changes considerably: Mail carriers are afraid of dogs. It seems to say that all mail carriers are afraid of dogs. In this case, adding commas is incorrect.]

5. **To separate three or more items in a series.**

   Note: A comma is *not* used *after* the last item in the series.

   I plan to take math, psychology, and writing next semester.

6. **To separate coordinate adjectives: two or more adjectives that are not joined by a coordinating conjunction and that equally modify the same noun or pronoun.**

   The thirsty, hungry children returned from a day at the beach.

   To determine if a comma is needed between two adjectives, use the following test. Insert the word *and* between the two adjectives. Also try reversing the order of the two adjectives. If the phrase makes sense in either case, a comma is needed. If the phrase does not make sense, do not use a comma.

   The tired, angry child fell asleep. [*The tired and angry child* makes sense; so does *The angry, tired child*. Consequently, the comma is needed.]

   Sarah is an excellent psychology student. [*Sarah is an excellent and psychology student* does not make sense, nor does *Sarah is a psychology, excellent student*. A comma is therefore not needed.]

7. **To separate parenthetical expressions from the clauses they modify.** Parenthetical expressions are added pieces of information that are not essential to the meaning of the sentence.
   Most students, I imagine, can get jobs on campus.

8. **To separate a transition from the clause it modifies.**
   In addition, I will revise the bylaws.

9. **To separate a quotation from the words that introduce or explain it.**
   Note: The comma goes *inside* the closing quotation marks.
   "Shopping," Jade explained, "is a form of relaxation for me."
   Jade explained, "Shopping is a form of relaxation for me."

10. **To separate dates, place names, and long numbers.**

October 10, 1994, is my birthday.

Dayton, Ohio, was the first stop on the tour.

Participants numbered 1,777,716.

11. **To separate phrases expressing contrast.**

Sam's good nature, not his wealth, explains his popularity.

EXERCISE 10   Adding Commas

Directions: Revise each of the following sentences by adding commas where needed.

EXAMPLE   If you feel like seeing a movie tonight, give me a call.

1. According to the American Red Cross Hurricane Katrina and Hurricane Rita destroyed more than 350,000 homes.
2. Many fans who attended the rock concert thought the band sounded great but some were disappointed that the concert was so short.
3. "If you're feeling brave" said Lin "we could ski down the black-diamond trail."
4. Diego met with his academic advisor who is the chair of the computer science department to discuss career options.
5. When I switched to a vegan diet I quit eating meat fish eggs and milk.
6. During Ben's performance review the manager commended him for his positive respectful interactions with patrons.
7. Tonight as you may recall is your night to do the dishes.
8. Volunteering for Habitat for Humanity has been a pleasure not a burden.
9. I don't have time to go swimming right now; besides it looks like it's going to rain.
10. Shauna is planning to visit her friend in Washington D.C. when the cherry trees bloom.

C.3 UNNECESSARY COMMAS

It is as important to know where *not* to place commas as it is to know where to place them. The following rules explain where it is incorrect to place them:

1. **Do not place a comma between a subject and its verb, between a verb and its complement, or between an adjective and the word it modifies.**

INCORRECT   The stunning, imaginative, and intriguing, painting, became the hit of the show.

CORRECT   The stunning, imaginative, and intriguing painting became the hit of the show.

2. **Do not place a comma between two verbs, subjects, or complements used as compounds.**

COMPOUND VERB

INCORRECT   Kaitlin called, and asked me to come by her office.

CORRECT   Kaitlin called and asked me to come by her office.

3. **Do not place a comma before a coordinating conjunction joining two dependent clauses.**

DEPENDENT CLAUSE

INCORRECT   The city planner examined blueprints that the park designer had submitted, and that the budget officer had approved.

DEPENDENT CLAUSE

CORRECT   The city planner examined blueprints that the park designer had submitted and that the budget officer had approved.

4. **Do not place commas around restrictive clauses, phrases, or appositives.** Restrictive clauses, phrases, and appositives are modifiers that are essential to the meaning of the sentence.

INCORRECT   The girl, who grew up down the block, became my lifelong friend.

CORRECT   The girl who grew up down the block became my lifelong friend.

5. **Do not place a comma before the word *than* in a comparison or after the words *like* and *such* as in an introduction to a list.**

INCORRECT   Some snails, such as, the Oahu tree snail, have more colorful shells, than other snails.

CORRECT   Some snails, such as the Oahu tree snail, have more colorful shells than other snails.

6. **Do not place a comma next to a period, a question mark, an exclamation point, a dash, or an opening parenthesis.**

INCORRECT   "When will you come back ?," Dillon's son asked him.

CORRECT   "When will you come back ?" Dillon's son asked him.

INCORRECT   The bachelor button, (also known as the cornflower) grows well in ordinary garden soil.

CORRECT   The bachelor button (also known as the cornflower) grows well in ordinary garden soil.

7. **Do not place a comma between cumulative adjectives.** Cumulative adjectives, unlike coordinate adjectives (see p. 557), cannot be joined by *and* or rearranged.

INCORRECT   The light, yellow, rose blossom was a pleasant birthday surprise. [The light and yellow and rose blossom does not make sense, so the commas are incorrect.]

CORRECT   The light yellow rose blossom was a pleasant birthday surprise.

C.4 COLONS AND SEMICOLONS

When to Use a Colon

A colon follows an independent clause and usually signals that the clause is to be explained or elaborated on. Use a colon in the following situations:

1. **To introduce items in a series after an independent clause.** The series can consist of words, phrases, or clauses.

   I am wearing three popular colors: gray, black, and white.

2. **To signal a list or a statement introduced by an independent clause** ending with the *following* or *as follows.*

   The directions are as follows: take Main Street to Oak Avenue and then turn left.

3. **To introduce a quotation that follows an introductory independent clause.**

   My brother made his point quite clear: "Never borrow my car without asking me first!"

4. **To introduce an explanation.**

   Mathematics is enjoyable: it requires a high degree of accuracy and peak concentration.

5. **To separate titles and subtitles of books.**

   Biology: A Study of Life

Note: A colon must always follow an independent clause. It should not be used in the middle of a clause.

> **INCORRECT**   My favorite colors are: red, pink, and green.
>
> **CORRECT**   My favorite colors are red, pink, and green.

When to Use a Semicolon

Use a semicolon in the following situations:

1. **To separate two closely related independent clauses not connected by a coordinating conjunction** (see p. 115).

   Sam had a 99 average in math; he earned an A in the course.

2. **To separate two independent clauses joined by a conjunctive adverb** (see p. 137).

   Margaret earned an A on her term paper; consequently, she was exempt from the final exam.

3. **To separate independent clauses joined with a coordinating conjunction if the clauses are very long or if they contain numerous commas.**

   By late afternoon, having tried on every pair of black checked pants in the mall, Maribel was tired and cranky; but she still had not found what she needed to complete her outfit for the play.

4. **To separate items in a series if the items are lengthy or contain commas.**

   The soap opera characters include Marianne Loundsberry, the heroine; Maya and Sarah, her children; Barry, her ex-husband; and Louise, her best friend.

5. **To correct a comma splice or run-on sentence** (see pp. 115 and 121).

EXERCISE 11   Adding Colons and Semicolons

Directions: Correct each of the following sentences by placing colons and semi-colons where necessary. Delete any incorrect punctuation.

> EXAMPLE   Even when I'm busy, I try to make time for my three favorite hobbies: reading, gardening, and biking.

1. When Kyoko plans a hike, she makes sure her backpack contains the following items; water, power bars, sunscreen, bug repellent, a windbreaker, and a cell phone.

2. Mark Twain said it best, "The difference between the almost right word and the right word . . . 'tis the difference between the lightning-bug and the lightning."

3. Consider this amazing fact, the superheated air, that surrounds a bolt of lightning, is about four times hotter than the surface of the sun.

4. I couldn't have made it through college without coffee; in fact, if I were writing a memoir about that period, the title would probably be "College, The Coffee Years."

5. The classic movie, *Casablanca*, had a stellar cast; Humphrey Bogart, who played the role of Rick, Ingrid Bergman, who played Ilsa, and Claude Rains, who played Louis.

6. It is certainly reassuring when a pediatrician tells you not to worry about your sick child, however, you also need to trust your own instincts and advocate for your child.

7. Any decent job should provide: a fair salary, reasonable working hours, and a safe work environment, these elements are nonnegotiable.

8. When I was a child, my grandfather gave me clear instructions for picking strawberries, pick the berries that are bright red, but leave the light, red berries.

9. The last thing Jasper needed was responsibility for another pet, nevertheless, the large, dark, pleading, eyes of the abandoned puppy, proved irresistible.

10. For my son's birthday, his two cousins, and several children from the neighborhood joined us for a picnic in the park, everyone had a great time. ■

C.5 DASHES, PARENTHESES, HYPHENS, APOSTROPHES, QUOTATION MARKS

Dashes (—)

The dash is used to (1) separate nonessential elements from the main part of the sentence, (2) create a stronger separation, or interruption, than commas or parentheses, and (3) emphasize an idea, create a dramatic effect, or indicate a sudden change in thought.

My sister—the friendliest person I know—will visit me this weekend.

My brother's most striking quality is his ability to make money—or so I thought until I heard of his bankruptcy.

Do not leave spaces between the dash and the words it separates.

Parentheses ( )

Parentheses are used in pairs to separate extra or nonessential information that often amplifies, clarifies, or acts as an aside to the main point. Unlike dashes, parentheses de-emphasize information.

Some large breeds of dogs (golden retrievers and Newfoundlands) are susceptible to hip deformities.

The prize was dinner for two (maximum value, $50.00) at a restaurant of one's choice.

Hyphens (-)

Hyphens have the following primary uses:

1. **To split a word when dividing it between two lines of writing or typing** (see p. 568).

2. **To join two or more words that function as a unit, either as a noun or as a noun modifier.**

   mother-in-law   single-parent families
   twenty-year-old   school-age children
   state-of-the-art sound system

Apostrophes (')

Use apostrophes in the following situations:

1. **To show ownership or possession.** When the person, place, or thing doing the possessing is a singular noun, add -'s to the end of it, regardless of what its final letter is.

   The man's DVD player   John Keats's poetry
   Aretha's best friend

- With plural nouns that end in -s, add only an apostrophe to the end of the word.

   the twins' bedroom   postal workers' hours
   teachers' salaries

   With plural nouns that do not end in -s, add -'s.

   children's books   men's slacks

- Do not use an apostrophe with the possessive adjective *its.*

   INCORRECT   It's frame is damaged.

   CORRECT   Its frame is damaged.

2. **To indicate omission of one or more letters in a word or number.** Contractions are used in informal writing but usually not in formal academic writing.

it's [it is]	hasn't [has not]
doesn't [does not]	'57 Ford [1957 Ford]
you're [you are]	class of '12 [class of 2012]

Quotation Marks (" ")

Quotation marks separate a direct quotation from the sentence that contains it. Here are some rules to follow in using quotation marks.

1. **Quotation marks are always used in pairs.**

   Note: A comma or period goes at the end of the quotation, inside the quotation marks.

   Shana declared, "I never expected D'Andre to give me a watch for Christmas."

   "I never expected D'Andre to give me a watch for Christmas," Shana declared.

2. **Use single quotation marks for a quotation within a quotation.**

   My literature professor said, "Byron's line 'She walks in beauty like the night' is one of his most sensual."

   Note: When quoting long prose passages of more than four typed lines, do not use quotation marks. Instead, set off the quotation from the rest of the text by indenting each line one inch from the left margin. This format is called a **block quotation.**

   The opening lines of the Declaration of Independence establish the purpose of the document:

   > When in the Course of human events it becomes necessary for one people to dissolve the political bonds which have connected them with another, and to assume among the powers of the earth, the separate and equal station to which the Laws of Nature and of Nature's God entitle them, a decent respect to the opinions of mankind requires that they should declare the causes which impel them to the separation.

3. **Use quotation marks to indicate titles of songs, short stories, poems, reports, articles, and essays.** Books, movies, plays, operas, paintings, statues, and the names of television series are italicized.

   "Rappaccini's Daughter" (short story)

   American Idol (television series)

   "The Road Not Taken" (poem)

   Huckleberry Finn (book)

4. **Colons, semicolons, exclamation points, and question marks, when not part of the quoted material, go outside of the quotation marks.**

   What did George mean when he said, "People in glass houses shouldn't throw stones"?

EXERCISE 12   Adding Punctuation

Directions: To the following sentences, add dashes, apostrophes, parentheses, hyphens, and quotation marks where necessary.

> EXAMPLE   All faculty members' e-mail addresses are listed in the college directory.

1. Whenever my friend has a personal problem, he just buys another self help book.

2. What famous play includes the line, I have always relied on the kindness of strangers?

3. If a movie is rated PG parental guidance suggested, I preview it myself to make sure that its appropriate for my eight year old son.

4. When asked to identify the greatest rock song of all time, the music critic replied, That's easy the song Stairway to Heaven by the band Led Zeppelin.

5. Answering customers questions about computer products is Aarons responsibility.

6. One of Maya Angelous most beloved poems is I Know Why the Caged Bird Sings; equally inspirational is her poem I Rise.

7. Be careful if you see the horses ears flattened against its head, as this may mean that the horse is about to kick.

8. If you can wait a minute, said Serena, Id be happy to check that price for you.

9. Alfred Hitchcocks film *Psycho* possibly the greatest horror movie of all time has terrified generations of viewers since its release in 1960.

10. The professor assigned two more Hemingway stories, in addition to My Old Man: Hills Like White Elephants and A Clean Well-Lighted Place. ■

MyWritingLab *Visit Part C Using Punctuation Correctly to test your understanding of the Part objectives.*

D Managing Mechanics and Spelling

D.1 CAPITALIZATION

In general, capital letters are used to mark the beginning of a sentence, to mark the beginning of a quotation, and to identify proper nouns. Here are some guidelines on capitalization:

What to Capitalize	*Example*
1. First word in every sentence	Prewriting is useful.
2. First word in a direct quotation	Sarah commented, "That exam was difficult!"
3. Names of people and animals, including the pronoun *I*	Aladdin Michelle Obama Spot
4. Names of specific places, cities, states, nations, geographic areas, or regions	New Orleans the Southwest Lake Erie
5. Government and public offices, departments, buildings	Williamsville Library House of Representatives
6. Names of social, political, business, sporting, cultural organizations	Boy Scouts Buffalo Bills
7. Names of months, days of the week, holidays	August Tuesday Halloween
8. In titles of works: the first word following a colon, the first and last words, and all other words except articles, prepositions, and conjunctions	*Biology: A Study of Life* "Once More to the Lake"
9. Races, nationalities, languages	African-American, Italian, English
10. Religions, religious figures, sacred books	Hindu, Hinduism, God, Allah, the Bible
11. Names of products	Tide, Buick

What to Capitalize	**Example**
12. Personal titles when they come right before a name	Professor Rodriguez Senator Hatch
13. Major historic events	World War I
14. Specific course titles	History 201 Introduction to Psychology

EXERCISE 13   Capitalizing Words

Directions: Circle any letters that need capitalization.

EXAMPLE   Henry Thoreau said, "ⓣo regret deeply is to live afresh."

1. Artist Georgia O'Keeffe lived for many years in new mexico, painting images that captured the stark beauty of the american southwest.

2. I haven't completed my paper for professor Stern yet, so I will have to finish writing it over the thanksgiving break.

3. On april 9, 1865, the american civil war drew to a close when confederate general Robert E. Lee surrendered at appomattox court house.

4. The springfield city library now offers free access to wireless internet service.

5. The first five books of the old testament of the bible form the sacred jewish text of the pentateuch.

6. Science is not my strongest subject, so I took the course physics for poets to fulfill my science requirement.

7. Baseball legend Jackie Robinson, who played for the brooklyn dodgers, told the story of his life in the book *I never had it made: an autobiography of Jackie Robinson.*

8. The great salt lake, located in northern utah, is much saltier than the pacific ocean; the salty water makes swimmers unusually buoyant, so they float very easily.

9. The novel *all quiet on the western front* tells the story of a young soldier's experience during world war I.

10. My daughter refuses to eat anything but kellogg's frosted flakes for breakfast; while she eats, she studies the picture of tony the tiger on the cereal box. ■

D.2 ABBREVIATIONS

An abbreviation is a shortened form of a word or phrase that is used to represent the whole word or phrase. The following is a list of common acceptable abbreviations:

What to Abbreviate	**Example**
1. Some titles before or after people's names	Mr. Ling Samuel Rosen, M.D. *but* Professor Ashe
2. Names of familiar organizations, corporations, countries	CIA, IBM, VISTA, USA

3. Time references preceded or followed by a number

7:00 A.M.
3:00 P.M.
A.D. 1973

4. Latin terms when used in footnotes, references, or parentheses

i.e. [*id est*, "that is"]
et al. [*et alii*, "and others"]

Here is a list of things that are usually *not* abbreviated in a paragraph or essay:

What Not to Abbreviate	*Example*	
	Incorrect	*Correct*
1. Units of measurement	thirty in.	thirty inches
2. Geographic or other place names when used in sentences	N.Y. Elm St.	New York Elm Street
3. Parts of written works when used in sentences	Ch. 3	Chapter 3
4. Names of days, months, holidays	Tues.	Tuesday
5. Names of subject areas	psych.	psychology

EXERCISE 14   Revising Abbreviations

Directions: Correct the inappropriate use of abbreviations in the following sentences. If a sentence contains no errors, write *C* beside it.

EXAMPLE   The tiny lizard is only about four ~~cm~~ long.
centimeters

_____ 1. Homer Hickam, a boy known for building homemade rockets during the 1950s, became a NASA engineer as an adult.

_____ 2. A great sprinter, Susan is expected to win the fifty-yd. dash.

_____ 3. Spicy foods—e.g., hot peppers—sometimes disagree with me.

_____ 4. My English lit. class meets Tues. and Th. at 2:00.

_____ 5. Some convicted criminals have been freed from prison after DNA testing proved they were innocent.

_____ 6. The co. I work for is located on Walnut St. in Phila.

_____ 7. I stayed up until 3:00 a.m. to finish reading the final chap. of this exciting novel.

_____ 8. The *Aeneid,* Virgil's epic poem about the founding of Rome, was written about 30 B.C.E.

_____

_____ 9. During Aug., the heat in TX can be brutal.

_____

_____ 10. Prof. Jenkins has a very engaging lecture style.

_____ ■

D.3 HYPHENATION AND WORD DIVISION

On occasion you may want to divide and hyphenate a word on one line and continue it on the next. Here are some guidelines for dividing words.

1. **Divide words only when necessary.** Frequent word divisions make a paper difficult to read.

2. **Divide words between syllables.** Consult a dictionary if you are unsure how to break a word into syllables.

   di-vi-sion   pro-tect

3. **Do not divide one-syllable words.**

4. **Do not divide a word so that a single letter is left at the end of a line.**

   INCORRECT   a-typical

   CORRECT   atyp-ical

5. **Do not divide a word so that fewer than three letters begin the new line.**

   INCORRECT   visu-al

   CORRECT   vi-sual

   INCORRECT   caus-al [This word cannot be divided at all.]

6. **Divide compound words only between the words.**

   some-thing   any-one

7. **Divide words that are already hyphenated only at the hyphen.**
   ex-policeman

EXERCISE 15   Dividing Words

Directions: Insert a diagonal (/) mark where each word should be divided. Write *N* in the margin if the word should not be divided.

   EXAMPLE   fic/tion

_____ 1. crashing   _____ 4. amorphous

_____ 2. splurge   _____ 5. glory

_____ 3. cross-reference   _____ 6. elite

_____ 7. unsteady   _____ 9. x-ray

_____ 8. sandpaper   _____ 10. property ■

D.4 NUMBERS

Numbers can be written as numerals (600) or words (six hundred). Here are some guidelines for when to use numerals and when to use words:

When to Use Numerals	Example
1. Numbers that are spelled with more than two words	375 students
2. Days and years	August 10, 1993
3. Decimals, percentages, fractions	56.7 59 percent 1¾ cups
4. Exact times	9:27 A.M.
5. Pages, chapters, volumes; acts and lines from plays	chapter 12 volume 4
6. Addresses	122 Peach Street
7. Exact amounts of money	$5.60
8. Scores and statistics	23–6 5 of every 12

When to Use Words	Example
1. Numbers that begin sentences	Two hundred ten students attended the lecture.
2. Numbers of one or two words	sixty students two hundred women

D. Mechanics and Spelling

■ EXERCISE 16   Revising Misused Numbers

Directions: Correct the misuse of numbers in the following sentences. If a sentence contains no errors, write *C* next to it.

EXAMPLE   I planned to read fifty pages last night, but I only made it to page ~~forty-two~~. 42

_____ 1. When we rehearse Act 6 of the play, I keep messing up line sixteen.

_____ 2. Beat one and three-quarters cups of sugar into the softened butter.

_____ 3. In 2011 a Gallup survey showed that roughly 7 out of 10 Americans own a dog or a cat.

_____ 4. Lola ran the race in fourteen point three seconds.

_____ **5.** 46 percent of Americans have used the Internet, e-mail, or text messaging to participate in the political process.

_____ **6.** The world's population is expected to reach almost nine billion by the year 2042.

_____ **7.** According to the syllabus, we need to read chapters seven and eight by next week.

_____ **8.** Jian's daughter proudly reported that she had saved two dollars and twenty-seven cents in her piggy bank.

_____ **9.** On weekdays, I always set my alarm for 7:10 a.m., but I generally hit the snooze bar and sleep for another 15 or 20 minutes.

_____ **10.** When I was ten years old, my goal was to read every volume of the encyclopedia, but I only finished part of volume 1. ■

D.5 SUGGESTIONS FOR IMPROVING SPELLING

Correct spelling is important in a well-written paragraph or essay. The following suggestions will help you submit papers without misspellings:

1. **Do not worry about spelling as you write your first draft.** Checking a word in a dictionary at this point will interrupt your flow of ideas. If you do not know how a word is spelled, spell it the way it sounds. Circle or underline the word so you remember to check it later.

2. **Keep a list of words you commonly misspell.** This list can be part of your error log.

3. **Every time you catch an error or find a misspelled word on a paper returned by your instructor, add it to your list.**

4. **Study your list.** Ask a friend to quiz you on the words. Eliminate words from the list after you have passed several quizzes on them.

5. **Develop a spelling awareness.** You'll find that your spelling will improve just by your being aware that spelling is important. When you encounter a new word, notice how it is spelled and practice writing it.

6. **Pronounce words you are having difficulty spelling.** Pronounce each syllable distinctly.

7. **Review basic spelling rules.** Your college library or learning lab may have manuals, workbooks, or computer programs that cover basic rules and provide guided practice.

8. **Be sure to have a dictionary readily available when you write.**

9. **Read your final draft through once, checking only for spelling errors.** Look at each word carefully, and check the spelling of those words of which you are uncertain.

D.6 SIX USEFUL SPELLING RULES

The following six rules focus on common spelling trouble spots:

1. **Is it *ei* or *ie*?**

   Rule: Use *i* before *e,* except after *c* or when the syllable is pronounced *ay* as in the word *weigh.*

   > EXAMPLE *i* before *e:* bel<u>ie</u>ve, n<u>ie</u>ce
   >
   > except after *c:* rec<u>ei</u>ve, conc<u>ei</u>ve
   >
   > or when pronounced *ay:* n<u>ei</u>ghbor, sl<u>ei</u>gh

   Exceptions: either   neither   foreign   forfeit
   height   leisure   seize   weird

2. **When adding an ending, do you keep or drop the final *e*?**

   Rules: **a.** Keep the final *e* when adding an ending that begins with a consonant. (Vowels are *a, e, i, o, u,* and sometimes *y;* all other letters are consonants.)

   hope → hope<u>ful</u>   aware → awar<u>eness</u>

   live → live<u>ly</u>   force → forc<u>eful</u>

   b. Drop the final *e* when adding an ending that begins with a vowel.

   hope → hop<u>ing</u>   file → fil<u>ing</u>

   note → not<u>able</u>   write → writ<u>ing</u>

   Exceptions: argument   truly   changeable
   awful   manageable   courageous
   judgment   noticeable   outrageous
   acknowledgment

3. **When adding an ending, do you keep the final *y*, change it to *i*, or drop it?**

   Rules: **a.** Keep the *y* if the letter before the *y* is a vowel.

   del<u>ay</u> → dela<u>ying</u>   b<u>uy</u> → b<u>uy</u>ing   pr<u>ey</u> → pr<u>ey</u>ed

   b. Change the *y* to *i* if the letter before the *y* is a consonant, but keep the *y* for the *-ing* ending.

   def<u>y</u> → def<u>i</u>ance   marr<u>y</u> → marr<u>i</u>ed

4. **When adding an ending to a one-syllable word, when do you double the final letter if it is a consonant?**

   Rules: **a.** In one-syllable words, double the final consonant when a single vowel comes before it.

   dr<u>op</u> → dr<u>opp</u>ed   sh<u>op</u> → sh<u>opp</u>ed   p<u>it</u> → p<u>itt</u>ed

   b. In one-syllable words, *don't* double the final consonant when two vowels or a consonant comes before it.

   f<u>ix</u> → f<u>ix</u>able   s<u>ound</u> → s<u>ound</u>ed

   r<u>eal</u> → r<u>eal</u>ize

5. **When adding an ending to a word with more than one syllable, when do you double the final letter if it is a consonant?**

   Rules: a. In multisyllable words, double the final consonant when a single vowel comes before it and the stress falls on the last syllable. (Vowels are *a, e, i, o, u,* and sometimes *y*. All other letters are consonants.)

   be<u>gin</u>´ → begi<u>nn</u>ing   trans<u>mit</u>´ → transmi<u>tt</u>ed

   re<u>pel</u>´ → repe<u>ll</u>ing

   b. In multisyllable words, do *not* double the final consonant when (a) a vowel comes before it *and* (b) the stress is not on the last syllable once the new ending is added.

   refer → reference

   admit → admittance

6. **To form a plural, do you add -*s* or -*es*?**

   Rules: a. For most nouns, add -*s*.

   cat → cat<u>s</u>   house → house<u>s</u>

   b. Add -*es* to words that end in -*o* if the -*o* is preceded by a consonant.

   her<u>o</u> → her<u>oes</u>   potat<u>o</u> → potat<u>oes</u>

   Exceptions: zoos, radios, ratios, and other words ending with two vowels.

   c. Add -*es* to words ending in -*ch, -sh, -ss, -x,* or -*z*.

   chur<u>ch</u> → chur<u>ches</u>   fo<u>x</u> → fo<u>xes</u>   di<u>sh</u> → di<u>shes</u>

MyWritingLab *Visit Part D Managing Mechanics and Spelling to test your understanding of the Part objectives.*

Commonly Misused Words and Phrases

This list is intended as a guide to words and phrases that often are confusing. If the word or phrase you seek is not here, check in a good dictionary.

a, an   Use *an* before words that begin with a vowel sound (the vowels are *a, e, i, o,* and *u*) or a silent *h: an airplane, an honor.* Use *a* before words that begin with a consonant sound: *a book, a house.*

a while, awhile   *A while* is a phrase containing an article and a noun; *awhile* is an adverb meaning "for some time." *A while* can be used following a preposition, such as *for: Wait here for a while. Awhile* is used to modify a verb: *We need to rest awhile.*

accept, except   *Accept* is a verb that means "receive"; *She accepted the gift gratefully. Except* is usually a preposition meaning "other than," "but," or "excluding": *Everyone has left except me.*

advice, advise   *Advice* is a noun: *He gave me his best advice about health insurance. Advise* is a verb: *I can only advise you about it.*

affect, effect   *Affect* is almost always a verb meaning "influence": *Smoking affects one's health. Effect* can be either a verb or a noun. In its usual use, as a noun, it means "result": *The drug has several side effects.* When *effect* is used as a verb, it means "cause" or "bring about": *The committee was able to effect a change in the law.*

all ready, already   *All ready* means "completely prepared." *Already* means "by this time" or "previously."

all right, alright   Although the form *alright* is often used, most authorities regard it as a misspelling of *all right.*

all together, altogether   *All together* means "as a group" or "in unison": *The workers presented their grievance all together to the supervisor. Altogether* is an adverb that means "completely" or "entirely": *His answer was not altogether acceptable.*

allusion, illusion   An *allusion* is an indirect reference or a hint: *Her allusions about his weight embarrassed him.* An *illusion* is a false idea or appearance: *Cosmetic surgery is intended to create the illusion of youth.*

almost, most   See *most, almost.*

alot, lots, lots of   *Alot* should be written only as two words: *a lot*. It is an informal substitute for *many* or *much*, as are *lots* and *lots of*. You should avoid all three in formal writing.

among, between   See *between, among*.

amount of, number of   Use *amount of* to refer to quantities that cannot be counted: *A large amount of milk had been left in the refrigerator.* Use *number of* with quantities that can be counted: *A large number of eggs had been left in the carton.*

and/or   Avoid using *and/or* unless your writing is of a technical, business, or legal nature. Remember that in these types of writing *and/or* indicates *three* options: one *or* the other *or* both.

anybody, any body; anyone, any one   *Anybody* and *anyone* are indefinite pronouns that mean "any person at all": *Does anybody (anyone) have change for a dollar? Any body* consists of a noun modified by the adjective *any*: *Is any body of government responsible for this injustice? Any one*, the pronoun *one* modified by *any*, refers to a certain person or thing in a group: *You may choose any one of the desserts with your entree.*

anyone, any body   See *anybody, any body; anyone, any one*.

anyplace, anywhere   *Anyplace* is informal for *anywhere* and should be avoided in formal writing.

anyways, anywheres, nowheres; anyway, anywhere, nowhere   Use *anyway, anywhere,* and *nowhere* rather than the forms ending in *-s*.

as   Using *as* instead of *because, since,* or *while* can lead to confusion: *The ball game was canceled as it started raining.* Here, *as* could mean either "because" or "when." Avoid using *as* rather than *whether* or *who*:

> whether
> We are not sure ~~as~~ we can be there.

> who
> She is the person ~~as~~ interrupted my lunch hour.

as, as if, as though, like   See *like, as, as if, as though*.

bad, badly   *Bad* is an adjective; *badly* is an adverb. *Badly* should be used to modify verbs: *They sang quite badly. Bad* can be used to modify nouns or pronouns: *The bad behavior irritated the child's hostess.* In addition, *bad* should be used after linking verbs, such as *am, is, become, feel,* or *seem: She felt bad last night.*

being as, being that   Use *because* or *since* rather than these expressions. Besides being informal, they can make sentences awkward.

between, among   Use *between* when referring to two things or people: *My wife and I divide the household chores between us.* Use *among* for three or more things or people: *The vote was evenly divided among the four candidates.*

bring, take   Use *bring* to describe the movement of an object toward you: *Bring me the newspaper, please.* Use *take* when the movement is away from you: *Will you take these letters to the mailbox?*

can, may   In formal writing you should make a distinction between *can* and *may. Can* refers to the ability to do something: *He can run a mile in less than five minutes. May* indicates permission: *You may choose whichever DVD you want.*

censor, censure   *Censor* as a verb means "edit or ban from the public for moral or political reasons": *The school board voted not to* censor *the high school reading lists but to recommend novels with literary merit.* The verb *censure* means "criticize or condemn publicly": *The member of Congress was* censured *because of questionable fund-raising practices.*

complement, compliment   *Complement* is a verb meaning "complete, add to, or go with": *They make a good couple; their personalities* complement *each other. Compliment* as a verb means "praise or flatter": *I must* compliment *you on your quick wit.* As a noun it means "flattering remark": *You should not regard his* compliments *as sincere.*

conscience, conscious   *Conscience* is a noun meaning "sense of moral right or wrong": *His* conscience *required him to return the lost wallet. Conscious* is an adjective meaning "alert, aware, awake": *Were you* conscious *of the change in temperature?*

continual, continuous   *Continual* means "happening regularly": Continual *calls by telemarketers are a nuisance. Continuous* means "happening for a long period of time without interruption": *The car alarm made a* continuous, *high-pitched noise.*

could have, could of   See *of, have.*

data   *Data,* the plural form of the Latin noun *datum,* means "facts or information." *Data* is often accepted as either a plural or a singular noun: *These data* are *conclusive. This data* is *conclusive.* Though technically correct, the singular form *datum* is rarely used.

different from, different than   *Different from* is the preferred expression: *Today is* different from *yesterday.* However, when *different from* leads to an awkward construction, *different than* is becoming acceptable: *Today Cheryl is* different than *she was last month* (avoids *from what she was last month*).

disinterested, uninterested   *Disinterested* means "objective or impartial": *The dispute was mediated by a* disinterested *party. Uninterested* means "not interested": *She was so* uninterested *in the football game that she nearly fell asleep.*

doesn't, don't   *Don't* is the contraction for *do not,* not for *does not: We* don't *want it.*

         doesn't
She ~~don't~~ have any.

due to   The phrase *due to* should be used only when it functions as a predicate adjective after a linking verb (usually a form of *be*): *His ill health was* due to *his poor diet.* It should not be used as a preposition meaning "because of" or "on account of":

        because of
The ball game was canceled ~~due to~~ bad weather.

effect, affect   See *affect, effect.*

elicit, illicit   *Elicit* is a verb meaning "draw out" or "bring to light": *The police were unable to* elicit *any information from the accomplice. Illicit* is an adjective meaning "illegal": *The suspect had* illicit *drugs on his person.*

emigrate, immigrate   See *immigrate, emigrate.*

etc.   This is the abbreviation for the Latin *et cetera,* meaning "and so on." Ending a list with *etc.* is acceptable in informal writing and in some technical writing and business reporting. However, in formal writing it is preferable to end a list with an example or with *and so on.*

everyday, every day   *Everyday* is an adjective that means "ordinary" or "usual": *They decided to use their <u>everyday</u> dishes for the party. Every day,* an adjective and a noun, means "occurring on a daily basis": *<u>Every day</u>, he walks the dog in the morning.*

explicit, implicit   *Explicit* is an adjective that means "clearly stated": *I left <u>explicit</u> instructions for the worker. Implicit* means "indirectly stated or implied": *The fact that he didn't object indicated his <u>implicit</u> approval of the arrangement.*

farther, further   When referring to distance, use *farther: He lives <u>farther</u> from work than she does.* When you mean "additional," use *further: Upon <u>further</u> consideration, I accept the position.*

fewer, less   *Fewer* refers to items that can be counted: *There are <u>fewer</u> people here today than yesterday. Less* refers to a general amount that cannot be counted: *We have <u>less</u> orange juice than I thought.*

firstly, secondly, thirdly   Use *first, second, third* instead to avoid sounding pretentious and needing to add *-ly* to remaining numbers in a list.

further, farther   See *farther, further.*

get   *Get* is a verb used in many slang and colloquial expressions. Avoid the following uses:

That really ~~got to~~ me.   (annoyed (moved))

We've ~~got to~~ go now.   (must)

I ~~got back at~~ her.   (took revenge on)

Don't ~~get~~ sick.   (become)

~~Get moving on~~ that.   (Start doing)

We ~~got to~~ the party late.   (arrived at)

We ~~got done~~ early.   (finished)

good, well   *Good* is an adjective: *I enjoy a <u>good</u> workout.* It should not be used as an adverb. *Well* should be used instead:

We ate ~~good~~ on our vacation.   (well)

Well can also be an adjective when used with verbs expressing feeling or state of being: *She feels <u>well</u> today.*

got to   See *get.*

hanged, hung   *Hanged* is the past tense and past participle form of the verb *hang,* meaning "execute": *He was <u>hanged</u> as a traitor. Hung* is the past tense and past participle form of the verb *hang* in all its other meanings: *We <u>hung</u> the picture above the fireplace.*

have, of   See *of, have.*

have got to   See *get.*

he/she, his/her; he or she, his or her   At one time, it was permissible to use *he* to mean *he or she.* Now, this is seldom appropriate. Use *he or she* and *his or her,* rather than *he/she, his/her,* when referring to a person whose gender is unknown: *Everyone must learn to walk before <u>he or she</u> runs.* If using these or other "double" pronouns becomes awkward, revise your sentence by using the plural pronoun or by refocusing the sentence.

When you meet ~~each guest~~ ᵍᵘᵉˢᵗˢ, ask ~~him or her~~ ᵗʰᵉᵐ to show ~~his or her~~ ᵗʰᵉⁱʳ ID ~~card~~ ᶜᵃʳᵈˢ.

When you meet guests, ask them to show their ID cards.

When you meet each guest, *ask to see* an ID card.

hisself   *Hisself* is nonstandard. Use *himself.*

hung, hanged   See *hanged, hung.*

if, whether   Use *if* when expressing a condition: *If I leave early, I can beat the rush hour traffic.* Use *whether* when expressing an alternative: *I don't know whether to stay or to leave.*

illicit, elicit   See *elicit, illicit.*

illusion, allusion   See *allusion, illusion.*

immigrate, emigrate   *Immigrate (to)* means "come to a country": *They recently immigrated to the United States. Emigrate (from)* means "leave a country": *They emigrated from Mexico for economic reasons.*

implicit, explicit   See *explicit, implicit.*

imply, infer   Speakers or writers *imply.* They suggest or hint at something: *He implied that he was unhappy with my work.* Listeners or readers *infer* by drawing conclusions from what they have read, heard, or seen: *I inferred that I need to become more conscientious.*

in, into, in to   Use *in* to indicate position or location: *Your book is in the drawer.* Use *into* to show movement: *They were led into a winding corridor.* Sometimes *in* and *to* are used close together as separate words: *They gave in to our requests.*

in regard to, in regards to   *In regards to* confuses two other phrases—*in regard to* and *as regards.* Use either of the last two or use *regarding: In regard to (as regards; regarding) your last phone call, I will arrive in time for the 2:30 meeting.*

infer, imply   See *imply, infer.*

irregardless, regardless   *Irregardless* is nonstandard. Use *regardless* instead.

is when, is where   *When* and *where* are often used incorrectly in sentences that define. Using just *is* or rewording your sentence can correct this faulty construction:

A touchdown ~~is when~~ ⁱˢ ˢᶜᵒʳᵉᵈ ʷʰᵉⁿ you cross your opponent's goal line with

the ball in your possession.

A touchdown ~~is when you cross~~ ⁱˢ ᶜʳᵒˢˢⁱⁿᵍ your opponent's goal line with

the ball in your possession.

Art history ~~is where you study~~ ⁱˢ ᵗʰᵉ ˢᵗᵘᵈʸ ᵒᶠ the world's great art treasures.

its, it's   *Its* is the possessive case form of the pronoun *it;* no apostrophes are used to show possession with personal pronouns (*his, hers, its, theirs*). *The poodle scratched its ear. It's* is the contraction for *it is: It's time for a change.*

kind, sort, type   These words are singular and should be used with singular modifiers and verbs: *This kind of book is expensive.* They should be used in their plural forms with plural modifiers and verbs: *These types of pens work best.* Using *a* following *type of, kind of,* or *sort of* is incorrect:

What type of ~~a~~ dog is that?

Also, omitting *of* is nonstandard:

I can't guess what type_{of} car that is.

kind of, sort of   Avoid using *kind of* or *sort of* in formal speech or writing to mean "somewhat" or "rather":

The movie was ~~kind of~~ scary. *[rather]*

The traffic was ~~sort of~~ slow this morning. *[somewhat]*

lay, lie   *Lay* is a transitive verb meaning "put or place." Its principal parts are *lay, laid, laid*: *Lay your bag here. She laid her bag here. She has laid her bag here every day. Lie* is an intransitive verb meaning "recline or be situated." Its principal parts are *lie, lay, lain*: *Lie down for a while. He lay down for a while. He has lain down every few hours.*

leave, let   *Leave* is a verb that means "depart," "exit," or "let be": *We will leave the room, so that you can be left alone. Let* means "permit or allow": *They would not let me go.*

less, fewer   See *fewer, less*.

like, as, as if, as though   *Like* is a preposition and should be used only with a noun or a noun phrase: *You look like your mother.* Do not use *like* as a conjunction to introduce subordinate clauses. Use *as, as if,* or *as though.*

Do ~~like~~ I tell you. *[as]*

She looks ~~like~~ she is ready to fall asleep. *[as if (as though)]*

loose, lose   *Loose* is an adjective meaning "not tight" or "not attached securely": *A loose brick fell into the fireplace. Lose* is a verb that means "misplace" or "not win": *Don't lose your way in the woods. They will lose the game unless they score soon.*

lots, lots of   See *alot, lots, lots of.*

may, can   See *can, may.*

may be, maybe   *May be* is a verb phrase: *The train may be late this morning. Maybe* is an adverb meaning "perhaps" or "possibly": *Maybe we can have lunch together tomorrow.*

may have, may of   See *of, have.*

media, medium   *Media* is the plural form of *medium*: *Of all the broadcast media, television is the medium that reaches most households.*

might have, might of   See *of, have.*

most, almost   *Most* should not be used in place of *almost.* When you mean "nearly," use *almost*; when you mean "the greatest number or quantity" use *most*: *She gets most of her exercise by walking to work almost every day.*

nowhere, nowheres   See *anyways, anywheres, nowheres.*

number of, amount of   See *amount of, number of.*

of, have   *Of* is spelled the way the contraction *'ve,* for *have,* sounds. Always write *could have, may have, might have, should have,* and *would have.*

off, off of   Use *off* or *from* instead of *off of:*

The poodle jumped off ~~of~~ the bed as I entered the room.

OK, O.K., okay   All three of these spellings are acceptable in informal writing, but they should be avoided in formal writing or speech.

percent (per cent), percentage   *Percent* should be used with a specific number: *Less than 40 percent of the class passed the exam. Percentage* is used when no number is referred to: *A large percentage of adults cannot program a VCR.*

plus   *Plus* is used as a preposition meaning "in addition to." *His skill plus his compassion made him a fine surgeon.* It should not be used as a conjunction in place of *and.*

He is very skillful, ~~plus~~ *and* he is compassionate.

principal, principle   The noun *principal* can mean "sum of money (excluding interest)" or "important person in an organization": *At any time, you can pay the principal on this loan. The high school principal distributed the awards.* As an adjective, *principal* means "most important": *His principal concern was their safety. Principle* is a noun meaning "rule or standard": *The principles stated in the Constitution guide our democracy.*

raise, rise   *Raise* is a transitive verb meaning "lift." Its principal parts are *raise, raised,* and *raised: Raise the flag at sunrise. He raised the flag at sunrise. They have raised the flag at sunrise for years. Rise* is an intransitive verb meaning "go higher" or "get to one's feet." Its principal parts are *rise, rose,* and *risen: I rise early on weekends. The sun gradually rose in the sky. The bread dough has already risen.*

real, really   *Real* is an adjective meaning "genuine" or "actual": *He found a real gold coin. Really* is an adverb meaning "very or extremely": *He is really proud of his discovery.*

reason is because, reason is that   Use *that* rather than *because* in formal speech and writing:

The reason I am late is ~~because~~ *that* my car broke down.

regardless, irregardless   See *irregardless, regardless.*

set, sit   *Set* is a transitive verb meaning "put or place." Its principal parts are *set, set, set: Please set the pitcher on the table. I set it on the counter, instead. I will set it on the table later. Sit* is an intransitive verb meaning "be seated." Its principal parts are *sit, sat,* and *sat: I sit in the front row. He sat behind me. They have sat for too long.*

shall, will   *Shall* was once preferred for use with *I* or *we* and for expressing determination. Today, *will* and *shall* are practically interchangeable for these instances, so *will* is acceptable for expressing future time with *be,* in all uses. *Shall* is now used primarily in polite questions: *Shall we dance?*

should have, should of   See *of, have.*

sometime, some time, sometimes   *Sometime* is an adverb meaning "at an unspecified point in the future": *We'll see that movie sometime. Some time* is an adjective (*some*) and a noun (*time*), and as a phrase it means "a period of time": *We'll find some time for that later.* *Sometimes* is an adverb meaning "now and then": *Sometimes recreation must be viewed as important.*

sort   See *kind, sort, type.*

sort of   See *kind of, sort of.*

stationary, stationery   *Stationary* is an adjective meaning "not moving": *Attach the birdhouse to a stationary object, such as a tree.* *Stationery* is a noun meaning "writing paper": *She sent a note on her personal stationery.*

suppose to, use to, supposed to, used to   *Suppose to* and *use to* are nonstandard and unacceptable substitutes for *supposed to* and *used to.*

sure, surely   *Sure* is an adjective: *She was sure she was correct.* *Surely* is an adverb: *She is surely correct.*

sure and, try and, sure to, try to   *Sure to* and *try to* are the correct forms.

take, bring   See *bring, take.*

than, then   *Than* is a conjunction that is used to make a comparison: *That is larger than I thought.* *Then* is an adverb used to indicate time: *Let's finish this first and then have dinner.*

that, which, who   Frequently, there is confusion about these relative pronouns. *That* refers to persons, animals, and things; *which* refers to animals and things; and *who* (and *whom*) refer to persons. To keep the distinctions clear, follow these guidelines.

1. Use *who* (*whom*) when referring to persons: *He is the one who won the contest.*
2. Use *which* for animals and things when it introduces nonrestrictive clauses: *My iPod, which I bought at Walmart, works perfectly.*
3. Use *that* for animals and things when introducing restrictive relative clauses: *Everything that I did was misunderstood.*

their, there, they're   *Their* is a possessive pronoun: *They gave their tickets to the usher.* *There* is an adverb indicating place: *Put the chair over there, please.* *They're* is the contraction of *they are*: *They're going to be disappointed.*

theirself, theirselves, themself, themselves   *Theirself, theirselves,* and *themself* are nonstandard substitutes for *themselves*: *They built the boat by themselves.*

these kind(s), these sort(s), these type(s)   See *kind, sort, type.*

to, too, two   *To* is either a preposition indicating direction or part of an infinitive: *I'm going to the store to buy groceries.* *Too* is an adverb meaning "also" or "more than enough": *She is too thin to be healthy. Can I come too?* *Two* is a number: *I'll be home in two hours.*

toward, towards   These words are interchangeable, but *toward* is preferred in American English. Use consistently whichever form you choose.

try and, try to   See *sure and, try and, sure to, try to.*

type   See *kind, sort, type.*

use to, used to   See *suppose to, use to, supposed to, used to.*

wait for, wait on   *Wait for* means "await" or "pause in expectation": *Wait for me at the bus stop.* *Wait on* means "serve" or "act as a waiter": *The restaurant owner waited on us.*

way, ways   *Ways* is a colloquial substitute for *way*. In formal writing and speech, use *way*:

> We have a long ~~ways~~ *way* to go.

well, good   See *good, well.*

whether, if   See *if, whether.*

which, who, that   See *that, which, who.*

who's, whose   *Who's* is the contraction of *who is: Who's knocking on the door? Whose* is the possessive form of *who: Whose car is that? Naomi is the one whose mother is the famous writer.*

will, shall   See *shall, will.*

would have, would of   See *of, have.*

your, you're   *Your* is a possessive pronoun: *Your apology is accepted. You're* is the contraction of *you are: You're welcome to join us for dinner.*

MyWritingLab *Visit Part E Commonly Misused Words and Phrases to test your understanding of the Part objectives.*

Credits

Photo Credits

Chapter 1

p. 1: Micheala Brandi/Fotolia.

Chapter 2

p. 17, **left to right:** Nyul/Fotolia, Fotolia.

p. 20; p. 35: AP Photo/Alden Pellett, File.

p. 39: Pan Xunbin/Shutterstock.

Chapter 3

p. 70: West Wild West/Fotolia.

p. 76: Stock Snapper/Fotolia.

p. 77: Bigemrg/Fotolia.

p. 78: Brent Hofacker/Fotolia.

p. 79: Frances Roberts/Alamy.

p. 80: Mehmet Dilsiz/Shutterstock.

p. 81: Big Stock Media/Fotolia.

Chapter 4

p. 82: 2008 World Wildlife Fun Public Service Announcement.

p. 104: Zuma Wire/Newscom.

Chapter 5

p. 110: Blue Sky Images/Fotolia.

p. 125: Cristovao/Shutterstock.

Chapter 6

p. 131: Dale Mitchell/Fotolia.

p. 147: Photographee.eu/Fotolia.

Chapter 7

p. 153: NfrPictures/Fotolia.

p. 155: Jack Ziegler/The New Yorker Collection/The Cartoon Bank.

p. 171: Laufer/Fotolia.

Chapter 8

p. 176, **left to right:** Alexandra Sitnikova/Fotolia.

p. 176: Get4net/Fotolia.

p. 192: AP Photo/Rafiq Maqbool.

p. 194: XNA Photos/Newscom.

p. 200: Danny Hooks.

p. 201: Irochka/Fotolia.

p. 202: Effe45/Fotolia.

p. 203: Geo Martinez/Shutterstock.

p. 205: Iofoto/Fotolia.

p. 206: Milissenta/Fotolila.

Chapter 9

p. 207: Tony Lilley/Alamy.

p. 230: Peter Essick/Aurora Photos/Corbis.

Chapter 10

p. 235: Igor Mojzes/Fotolia.

p. 254: WaterFrame/Alamy.

p. 260: Monkey Business/Fotolia.

p. 261: Claudio Divizia.

p. 264: iQoncept/Fotolia.

Chapter 11

p. 266: Christian Delbert/Fotolia.

p. 268: George Booth/The New Yorker Collection/The Cartoon Bank.

p. 282: Hurst Photo/Shutterstock.

Chapter 12

p. 288: Advertising Archives.

p. 293: Bloomberg/Getty.

p. 311: CartoonStock, www.CartoonStock.com.

Chapter 13

p. 317: Fotola70/Fotolia.

Chapter 14

p. 336: Dave King/DK Images.

p. 387: Vlad Teodor/Shutterstock.

p. 395, **top to bottom:** Diwector/Fotolia, Andrewgenn, Samarets1984/Fotolia.

p. 396, **top to bottom:** Diwector/Fotolia, Kibsri/Fotolia, Raw Pixel/Fotolia, Diwector/Fotolia.

p. 397: Mmmg/Fotolia.

p. 399, **top to bottom:** Kati Molin/Fotolia, Arkady Chubykin/Fotolia.

p. 400: Giuseppe Porzani/Fotolia.

p. 401: Rebekka Ivacson/Fotolia

p. 402: Eric Isselée/Fotolia.

Chapter 15

p. 404: Niall McDiarmid/Alamy.

p. 432: SPN Photos/Newscom.

Chapter 16

p. 438: Ghost/Fotolia.

p. 457: Digitex/Fotolia.

Chapter 17

p. 463: Alex Hinds/Alamy.

p. 473: Nikki Zalewski/Fotolia.

p. 477: CartoonStock, www.CartoonStock.com.

Chapter PVI

p. 484: Mast3r/Fotolia.

p. 488: Reich/Fotolia.

p. 493: Smuki/Fotolia.

p. 497: Igor/Fotolia.

p. 507: Radoslaw Korga/Fotolia.

Text Credits

Chapter 1

p. 10: Claire Stroupe, "The Allure of Reality TV." Reprinted by permission of the author.

Chapter 2

p. 29: Byer and Shainberg, Living Well: Health in Your Hands, Jones & Bartlett. Reprinted by permission of Curtis O. Byer.

p. 30: Byer and Shainberg, Living Well: Health in Your Hands, Jones & Bartlett. Reprinted by permission of Curtis O. Byer.

p. 39: Michael D. Johnson, Human Biology: Concepts and Current Issues, 7th Ed., (c) 2014, p. 354. Reprinted and Electronically reproduced by permission of Pearson Education, Inc., Upper Saddle River, New Jersey.

Chapter 3

p. 45: Gerald Audesir, Teresa Audesir, Bruce E. Byers, Biology: Life on Earth, 8th Ed., (c) 2008, p. 381. Reprinted and Electronically reproduced by permission of Pearson Education, Inc., Upper Saddle River, New Jersey.

p. 46: Copyright © 2011 by Houghton Mifflin Harcourt Publishing Company. Reproduced by permission from The American Heritage Dictionary of the English Language, Fifth Edition.

p. 49: Copyright © 2011 by Houghton Mifflin Harcourt Publishing Company. Reproduced by permission from The American Heritage Dictionary of the English Language, Fifth Edition.

p. 51: Copyright © 2013 by Houghton Mifflin Harcourt Publishing Company. Reproduced by permission from The American Heritage Roget's Thesaurus.

p. 67: Byer and Shainberg, Living Well: Health in Your Hands, Jones & Bartlett. Reprinted by permission of Curtis O. Byer.

p. 89: Kevin Sieff, "Afghan Women Caught Between Modernity, Tradition," The Washington Post, November 28 © 2012 Washington Post Company. All rights reserved. Used by permission and protected by the Copyright Laws of the United States. The printing, copying, redistribution, or retransmission of this Content without express written permission is prohibited.

Chapter 4

p. 103: Denise Flaim, "Tails in Jail." Reprinted with permission of the author.

Chapter 5

p. 125: Timothy Kudo, "I Killed People in Afghanistan, Was I Right or Wrong," The Washington Post, Jan 25, 2013. Reprinted by permission of the author.

Chapter 6

p. 147: Robin W. Simon, "The Joys of Parenthood, Reconsidered," Contexts, May 2008, vol 7. Copyright © 2008, American Sociological Association. Reprinted by permission of Sage Publications.

Chapter 7

p. 172: The 2012 Racial and Gender Report Card: Major League Baseball. Reprinted with permission of Richard Lapchick.

Chapter 8

p. 194: Reprinted by permission. Walk Like You Have Somewhere to Go, Lucille O'Neal, 2010. Thomas Nelson, Inc., Nashville, Tennessee. All rights reserved.

Chapter 9

p. 229: From Current Health, January 2, 2010. Copyright © 2010 by The Weekly Reader Corporation. Reprinted by permission of Scholastic, Inc.

Chapter 10

p. 254: Virginia Sole-Smith, Sweatshops at Sea, UTNE Reader, Sept/Oct 2010. Reprinted with permission of the author.

Chapter 11

p. 280: Jessica Nantka, "I Don't Want a Promotion." Reprinted by permission of the author.

p. 282: Used with permission of Bloomberg L.P. Copyright © 2014. All rights reserved.

Chapter 12

p. 303: Jacob Frey, "Writing in Progress: Three versions of "Professional Athletes as Role Models." Reprinted by permission of the author.

p. 308: Jessica Beebe, "Pinterest: Social Media with a Twist." Reprinted by permission of the author.

Chapter 13

p. 331: Brent Staples, "A Brother's Murder," The New York Times, March 30 © 1986 The New York Times. All rights reserved. Used by permission and protected by the Copyright Laws of the United States. The printing, copying, redistribution, or retransmission of this Content without express written permission is prohibited.

p. 328: Sarah Frey, "Leadership: Moving Others Forward." Reprinted by permission of the author.

Chapter 14

p. 341: Excerpts from "Foxy" and "Earth" from the book A Yellow Raft in Blue Water by Michael Dorris. Copyright © 1987 by Michael Dorris. Reprinted by permission of Henry Hold and Company, LLC.

p. 346: Excerpts from "Foxy" and "Earth" from the book A Yellow Raft in Blue Water by Michael Dorris. Copyright © 1987 by Michael Dorris. Reprinted by permission of Henry Hold and Company, LLC.

p. 364: Ted Sawchuck. Reprinted by permission of the author.

p. 376: Donald W. Tuff, "Animals Should Be Used in Medical Research," Animals and Research, NEA Higher Education Advocate, National Education Association. Reprinted with permission.

p. 378: Angela Molina, "Animals Should Not Be Used in Medical Research," Animals and Research, NEA Higher Education Advocate, National Education Association. Reprinted with permission.

p. 384: Aurora Gilbert, "Employment: Not Just a Post-Graduation Agenda." Reprinted by permission of the author.

p. 387: Aaron Marks, "In a Sea of Smartphones, Going Off the Grid," NYULocal. Reprinted by permission.

p. 341: Ted Sawchuck. Reprinted by permission of the author.

p. 351: Ted Sawchuck. Reprinted by permission of the author.

p. 355: Ted Sawchuck. Reprinted by permission of the author.

p. 368: Ted Sawchuck. Reprinted by permission of the author.

Chapter 15

p. 429: Chase Beauclair, "Balancing the Extremes." Reprinted by permission of the author.

Chapter 16

p. 447: Catherine Lee, "A Lifestyle of Commitment: The Perks and Obstacles of Veganism." Reprinte by permission of the author.

p. 455: Richard Gunderman, "Is Lying Bad for Us?" © 2013 The Atlantic Media Co., as first published in The Atlantic Magazine. All rights reserved. Distributed by Tribune Content Agency, LLC.

Chapter 17

p. 473: Amanda Keithley, "Breaking Down Barriers with Stories." Reprinted by permission of the author.

p. 476: Brian Doyle, "Irreconcilable Dissonance: The Threat of Divorce as the Glue of Marriage," Originally published in Oregon Humanities, Fall/Winter 2009. Reprinted with permission.

Part VI

p. 492: William Thompson, Joseph V. Hickey, Society in Focus: An Introduction to Sociology, 7th Ed., © 2011, pp. 573–574, 580–581. Reprinted and Electronically reproduced by permission of Pearson Education, Inc., Upper Saddle River, New Jersey.

p. 484: Rebecca Eckler, jounalist, blogger and author of Knocked Up, The Mommy Mob and How to Raise a Boyfriend. "Love is a Four Number Word," Macleans. Reprinted by permission of the author.

p. 488: Joseph DeVito, "Technology and Love" (Lindsay - Natalie should have the rest of the source info for this reading in Part VI).

p. 496: John Whitehead, "Smile, the Government is Watching: Next Generation Identification," The Huffington Post, Sep. 18, 2012. Reprinted with permission.

Index

W

Y